Literary Journalism

Literary Journalism

A NEW COLLECTION
OF THE BEST
AMERICAN
NONFICTION

EDITED AND WITH INTRODUCTIONS BY

Norman Sims and
Mark Kramer

BALLANTINE BOOKS | NEW YORK

A Ballantine Book
Published by The Random House Publishing Group

Compilation copyright © 1995 by Norman Sims and Mark Kramer

Published in the United States by Ballantine Books, an imprint of The Random House Publishing Group, a division of Random House, Inc., New York, and simultaneously in Canada by Random House of Canada Limited, Toronto.

Acknowledgments

Norman Sims wishes to thank Barrett Robbins for research assistance; Mark Bryant, editor of *Outside* magazine, and Bob Thompson, editor of *The Washington Post Magazine*, for their assistance; Deborah Rubin; and his colleagues in the Five College Writers' Group in Amherst, Massachusetts, especially Madeleine Blais, Michael Lesy, and Kim Townsend, and all the writers who have participated in discussions at The Art of Nonfiction Writers' Conferences in Amherst since 1989.

Mark Kramer wishes to thank his wife, Susan Eaton, and Yvonne Abraham, Tony Bell, Steven Biel, Lisa Birk, Susan Blau, Olga Genkina, Harry George, William Green, Fred Hapgood, Craig Infanger, Vladimir Klimenko, Vitaly Korotich, Sidney and Esther Kramer, Mark Kuchment, Cameron Laird, Samuel McCracken, Beth Marshall, Allan Mustard, Noel Perrin, Sean Ploen, Sergei Sossinsky, Richard Todd, Don Van Atta, Robert Weiss, and Sarah Wernick.

Both editors thank Joëlle Delbourgo and Lesley Malin Helm at Ballantine.

Contents

Literary Journalism

The Art of Literary Journalism

Norman Sims

The true state of every nation is the state of common life.
— Samuel Johnson, *A Journey to the Western Islands* (1775)

Since the first volume of this anthology, *The Literary Journalists*, was published a decade ago, literary journalism has become widely discussed among writers and general readers, and has been taught in ever-increasing numbers of college and high school classes. Its appeal has grown from the solid foundations of the form—immersion reporting, narrative techniques that free the voice of the writer, and high standards of accuracy.

An exciting and creative genre, it is now regularly employed in areas previously avoided by writers with literary ambitions, such as business, and in complicated scientific and technical writing. The boundaries of literary journalism have been expanded in turn by travel writing and memoir, forms that traditionally allow writers more voice. Standard reporting hides the voice of the writer, but literary journalism gives that voice an opportunity to enter the story, sometimes with dramatic irony.

At a time when journalism seems crowded with celebrities, literary journalism pays respect to ordinary lives. Literary journalists write narratives focused on everyday events that bring out the hidden patterns of community life as tellingly as the spectacular stories that make newspaper headlines. In 1775, for instance, Dr. Samuel Johnson mentioned a small detail, the "incommodiousness" of Scottish windows, which "keeps them very closely shut," that he thought symbolized the national character. Stories about wandering, work, and family—about the things that happen all the time—can reveal the structures and strains of real life. They say more about most citizens' lives than do stories of singular disasters or quirky celebrities.

Literary journalists do, of course, sometimes tell stories about dignitaries and celebrities. But the genre's classics deal with the feelings and experiences of commoners. James Agee's *Let Us Now Praise Famous Men* (1941) was an account of sharecroppers' experiences during the Depression. Lillian Ross's "The Yellow Bus" (1960) dared to report on something as mundane as a high school field trip to New York City. Although the A-bomb attack that began his book was a spectacular news event, even John Hersey's *Hiroshima* (1946) chronicled ordinary lives in the moments and weeks following the explosion. Professor Tom Connery of the University of St. Thomas remarked recently that literary journalism delivers "this felt sense of the quality of life at a particular time and place," and that it addresses a question cultural historians pose: "How did it feel to live and act in a particular period of human history?"

This collection samples recently published work by several generations of literary journalists who are still shaping the genre. Joseph Mitchell began writing in the 1930s and was a colleague of A. J. Liebling, John Hersey, and Lillian Ross at *The New Yorker*. In the 1960s Calvin Trillin, John McPhee, and Jane Kramer began writing literary journalism when flashier personalities dominated the movement then known as New Journalism. Tracy Kidder, Mark Singer, Mark Kramer, Walt Harrington, and Joseph Nocera followed in the 1970s and '80s, having learned from the New Journalism and contributing a breadth of talents and practices to the genre that moved it into the mainstream. The most recent arrivals here, including Ted Conover, Susan Orlean, Richard Preston, Brent Staples, David Quammen, and Adrian Nicole LeBlanc, continue to develop a form of writing that reaches back not just four or five generations, but all the way to Daniel Defoe's writings in the early 1700s. They join a tradition established by Mark Twain, Stephen Crane, Abraham Cahan, George Ade, W.E.B. Du Bois, John Reed, John Dos Passos, Ernest Hemingway, James Agee, George Orwell, A. J. Liebling, Janet Flanner, E. B. White, and Mary McCarthy.

These days, writers such as Tracy Kidder spend their time and literary talents exploring the meanings in the lives of engineers, carpenters, and schoolteachers. It seems strange that national-caliber writers are forsaking the corridors of power and electing instead to chronicle what Susan Orlean calls "the dignity of ordinariness." It's the same work fiction writers have taken on, Mark Kramer commented to me, "but mainstream fiction has been liberated from writing about society's nobility for far longer than nonfiction." Although access is part of the reason, these writers find ordinary people and the drama, emotion, and complexity in their lives a worthy focus.

Writers approach literary journalism with different perspectives, voices, and experiences, but their work shares several elements. Mark Kramer's introduction details literary journalism's common characteristics. Kramer, who taught for a decade at Smith College, now teaches at Boston University. I asked him to share some of what he tells the graduate students in his seminar, and his essay here is the result.

Since the first volume of this anthology was published, I have asked several writers how they practice their craft, and how they feel about it. The outward characteristics of literary journalism—immersion reporting, accuracy, symbolic representation, complicated structures, and voice—don't reveal the authors' inner processes of creativity. I've included here some of their comments on access, the symbolism of facts, research strategies, and techniques shared with both fiction and ethnography. Their insights are important because these writers are shaping a major genre that has grown in both complexity and popularity during the last decade.

Hanging Around Access

Joe Nocera wanted to talk about characterization. It is an important item in any literary toolbox. Although he often writes about business celebrities, he is most interested in the routine culture of business life and its reach into the wider world.

While writing *A Piece of the Action* (1994), the book that grew out of his article "The Ga-Ga Years," Nocera had pinned a long strip of paper to the walls of his third-floor office in Northampton, Massachusetts. It began near the door with "1955," followed by consecutive dates and handwritten notes, stretching around the room until it reached the present day at the far wall. Along this time line he had sketched the rise of the money culture—the penetration into middle-class life of the credit card, the mutual fund, the certificate of deposit, and the stockbroker. Nocera explained that the structure of the book was a series of interlocking character studies; one person invents the Visa card, another the mutual fund, and these later allow someone else to shift the strategies of Citibank. The transformation in American life that he writes about seemed embodied in the well-dressed, well-educated, and often prosperous people streaming past in the street outside his window.

In the 1980s Nocera and several other writers discovered that business is a legitimate subject for literary journalism. Business writing at most American newspapers was then one step above obituaries on the career status ladder. Nocera says those attitudes changed after publication of David McClintick's book *Indecent Exposure* (1982), about a financial scandal in Hollywood, and Steve Brill's work at *The American Lawyer*, which pried open previously closed fields. Their efforts "woke people up to the idea of drama and the understanding of the essential human element of business. To me, that's what this movement is all about: realizing that these stories do not revolve around numbers but around people with all the same motivations as anyone," Nocera said.

His own apprenticeship had been served as a political reporter. In 1982, *Texas Monthly*'s executive editor, Nick Lemann, suggested Nocera write about a relatively unknown Amarillo oilman named T. Boone Pickens, Jr., and his relations with Wall Street. Industry analysts told Nocera, "He's about to do a deal. He's about to do a takeover. That's the word on the street." Pickens wouldn't say anything. One day, Cities Service Co. launched a preemptive strike to take over Pickens's company, and the financial battle was joined. Nocera got on the next plane to New York and spent the month of June in the Waldorf-Astoria watching ten of Pickens's men try to take over a company.

"This was like any other form of good storytelling," Nocera said, "revolving around conflicts and personalities and drama and all the human dimensions. Being in a takeover requires enormous psychological skills. Whatever ingredients it takes to write good nonfiction were there in spades in this takeover deal." Few writers since have gotten such close access to a dramatic major business maneuver.

Today, perhaps cautioned by Nocera's success, lawyers herd reporters far from the action during takeovers. Unfortunately, reconstructing events through interviews doesn't provide readers the same realism. Mark Singer, who wrote about a bank failure in Oklahoma in *Funny Money* (1985), wasn't there when deals happened. "I met these characters afterward and reported the dialogue I had with them firsthand. I never re-created a scene. You just can't," Singer said. Boone Pickens had given Nocera access, but today, business leaders want to negotiate for quote approval. They won't let reporters hang out in the office, and they use press agents as shields. The most industrious business writers react by doing more intensive investigative reporting. Nocera would prefer "hanging around access," which is simply permission to watch the conduct of ordinary life. While that approach may not deliver the big event, it immerses readers, along with the writer, in the culture of business.

"In any kind of literary journalism," Nocera said, "you have to build a bond of trust. You have to get people to let their hair down when you're around, to be willing to forget about you as a reporter, and to say things. They may end up hating you afterwards. In the last five or six years in business journalism, the reporting has gotten more sophisticated. As reporters have become less and less willing to be pawns to a PR department, there is less and less trust out there. It's become increasingly difficult to get the access and be able to get a sense of the person you're writing about." He said if reporters could gain access the way

Tracy Kidder had for his Pulitzer Prize–winning book, *The Soul of a New Machine* (1981), in which he watched a design team build a computer, then the need to do investigative reporting would diminish.

However good a writer's access, the main actors may not reveal themselves, or may not tell the good stories that reveal the human lives behind the action. Like any thorough reporter, Nocera makes a practice of going to other parties—the associate fired five years ago, the competitor, the critic—for anecdotes. "I would say investigative reporting of the sort I do is not necessarily adversarial," Nocera said. "But the mere fact you're going outside the company to get information is seen as an adversarial act. It means you're trying to find out things they don't want you to know. I see it as getting the stuff that will make this article or book come to life." Nocera punctuates his sentences with emphatic expressions. "I want business people to be *three dimensional*. I want to show that they have these good qualities but that not all of their qualities are great. I want to bring them to life. They don't see how it's in their best interest. They just *don't get it*."

An Idea Disguised as a Fact

Mark Singer's office in the headquarters of *The New Yorker* looked as if he had been spending entirely too much time there. Piles of notebooks and old copies of the *New York Times* cluttered the carpet and desk. On the nearly empty, disorganized bookshelf were Sanford Bennett's *Exercising in Bed*, Tobias Wolff's *This Boy's Life*, and Dave Barry's *Greatest Hit$*. The disarray gave the new, fashionably white offices of the magazine some of the scruffy character of the old. But the powerful computer on the desk contradicted the mood. On it, Singer was organizing 45,000 words of notes for one article that was distilled to 14,000 words by the time it ran. He had dozens of similar projects stored.

During his twenty years at *The New Yorker*, Singer has seen a lot of excellent nonfiction, which has in turn shaped his own work. From the day he first arrived, he looked to Joe Liebling, Joseph Mitchell, Calvin Trillin, and John McPhee as "the authors of my style book." He has since added Ian Frazier, author of *Great Plains* and *Family*, and Jane Kramer to that list.

"You can't take an idea and write about an idea," Singer said. We were talking about Errol Morris, an eclectic filmmaker whom Singer had profiled in *The New Yorker*, and our discussion had turned to the symbolic and creative aspects of nonfiction writing. "I can only work with facts. Errol Morris was an interesting person—fact. It's not like I had this idea: Let's go find an ironic filmmaker. There was very specific, tangible stuff. The story then goes in the direction the facts lead.

"It's the kind of thing that makes literary journalism or lengthy discursive nonfiction so interesting. You don't know where the story is going to go, and you don't know what you're going to say. It's no different from writing fiction in that respect. You don't know what's going to come out of your typewriter when you sit down to do the piece, or how you're going to say it. There's still the pleasure of discovering what's on your own mind, the way a poet or essayist or fiction writer does."

A few months later the same topic came up in a conversation with *Outside* magazine columnist David Quammen, who lives in Montana. Quammen had been saying that symbolism plays a central role in his work. "I always called it synecdoche," he said, "which is an idea disguised as a fact. It has to be a fact first and appreciated as a fact. Then the aftertaste has symbolism." Quammen said he was struck by a line in William Howarth's introduction to *The John McPhee Reader* that suggested McPhee "buffs and polishes a fact until it reflects a greater reality." The small, symbolic things—such as the Scottish windows Dr. Johnson mentioned—when cast in a dramatic narrative, can grow and wrap themselves in meaning.

At an earlier interview, I asked John McPhee what he tried to *avoid* in his writing. He replied precisely, as if he dealt with the question often: "The expression of concepts and ideas without illustration, without narrative and exemplification, a form of thematic directness instead of the indirectness that comes with sketching characters and letting the abstract or conceptual values be implied. I've never been comfortable trying to address those things head-on. I avoid it because I think the writing is more artistic without it."

Mark Singer's article about Errol Morris—one ironist writing about another—took Singer into an unexpected realm of fact. Morris uses unconventional techniques in his filmmaking, such as setting a woman in front of the camera and recording her conversation—but not asking her any questions. "I learned something very important from Morris," Singer said. "I really have to shut up and let the subject talk. That's what Morris did so well on film. Of course, he gets to edit and do whatever he likes with that. I learned something about reporting there, too: Don't be as intrusive, literally as intrusive, in an interview. Just let the subjects talk and they will reveal things to you.

"The way I do it is to tell the story with a lot of dialogue. You break up the exposition with scenery. There is something happening where people are interacting with each other. I would be lost without dialogue. That's a conscious awareness on my part. People want to read factual narrative. *Tell me a story.* Tell me a story. That's what this still comes down to."

It was as if two *New Yorker* writers were echoing each other. McPhee had once told me, "Through dialogue, words, the presentation of the scene, you can turn over the material to the reader. The reader is ninety-some percent of what's creative in creative writing. A writer simply gets things started. You dole out material, but if you give too much, you spoil it." How writers handle the material determines what readers can do with it.

In the 1970s Tom Wolfe suggested that the New Journalism required scene-by-scene construction, saturation reporting, third-person point of view, and a detailing of the status lives of the subjects. In 1984 *The Literary Journalists* broadened the set of characteristics to include immersion reporting, accuracy, voice, structure, responsibility, and symbolic representation. Writers I've spoken with more recently have wanted to add to the list a personal involvement with their materials, and an artistic creativity not often associated with nonfiction. An innovative genre that is still developing, literary journalism resists narrow definitions.

Writer Nick Lemann has argued that narrative technique can be an empty vessel if it lacks a solid intellectual content. If the defining moments of twentieth-century journalism have been the arrival of narrative technique in New Journalism and investigative technique during Watergate, Lemann says, then the next challenge is achieving the explanatory power of, say, political scientists. "If the issues of narrative technique that dominated the consciousness of nonfiction writers for most of this century now seem to have been largely worked out and therefore to have become less compelling," he said, "the issues of intellectual content, style, and voice (and of their marriage to the narrative form) have only just begun to be explored."

Richard Todd, former executive editor of *The Atlantic* and of *New England Monthly*, who heads his own imprint at Houghton Mifflin (and whose authors include Tracy Kidder, Adrian Nicole LeBlanc, and Mark Kramer), put the art of literary journalism in simpler terms that fall into agreement with Mark Singer's attitude: "Voice and story are the only tools." *Story* includes all the narrative techniques, as well as the intellectual substance of a tale. *Voice*, a distinguishing literary mark, advances the feeling of something created, sculpted, authored by a particular spirit. The ways in which literary journalists handle research strategy, structure, voice, characterization, and symbolic representation reflect their creativity. More critics agree with that now, but twenty-five years ago, when Tom Wolfe raised the debate, literary journalism was not yet on anyone's list of artistic prose forms.

"I used to be very afraid of the idea that this was *art*," Mark Singer said. "I'm not afraid of that word anymore because it's O.K. to try to write something beautiful and to think of yourself as something more than a carpenter with a box of tools. Instead of making a table, you're making a *beautiful* table. That's part of the process of growing into a medium and listening."

The Revealing Things

It took a good pace to keep up with Joseph Mitchell as he approached Sloppy Louie's restaurant in the Fulton Fish Market at the southern tip of Manhattan. Mitchell was then eighty-one years old. Impeccably dressed, healthy, vigorous, courteous to everyone, he looked a dozen years younger. He has been a staff writer of *The New Yorker* since 1938. The host at Sloppy Louie's welcomed Mitchell warmly and led us to a table in a side room.

Sloppy Louie's played the central role in the title piece of his collected works, *Up in the Old Hotel* (1992). Mitchell located much of his nonfiction in the Fulton Fish Market, and he joined the city commissions that preserved the area as a historic district. After a lunch of fresh bluefish with lots of lemon, Mitchell discussed the nonfiction articles that have made him a cult figure to at least two generations of writers.

Mitchell forewarned me—as he later did readers in the introduction to his collected works—that he is given to what he describes as "graveyard humor." He's the kind of guy who says things like "It's a funny thing about a cemetery, how cheerful it'll make you. Maybe it's only me." Mitchell collects woodcuts by the Mexican folk artist José Guadalupe Posada, macabre prints of everyday life with the characters portrayed as skeletons. "He greatly influenced this idea I had of trying to put death against a background. I had a feeling that a lot of people suffer from the idea of death, in their minds, and that a humorous aspect of it is a relief," Mitchell said. "It was Old Testament humor, if I make any sense: the humor of Ecclesiastes—vanity, vanity, all is vanity. Gogolian humor. Brueghelian humor. I'm thinking of that painting by Brueghel showing the halt leading the blind, which, as I see it, is graveyard humor."

Mitchell looked around Sloppy Louie's, which was busy with Wall Street–types, and mentioned a Dutch Master's print of a miser locked in his room counting his money, with Death standing just outside the door. It reminded him of the fish market and the turnover of firms. "Whatever quality is in my newspaper or magazine writing," he said, "has come from the desire to put in a background, which is constantly changing, people who are constantly changing, but an *attitude* toward life and death that doesn't change. It makes the people who are aware of it more eager to enjoy whatever's going on."

We strolled through the market, Mitchell commenting on the history and architecture of the buildings, and took a cab back to his office at *The New Yorker*. This was before *The New Yorker* moved. The office had ancient linoleum flooring and wooden chairs.

Mitchell said the most important element in his writing is "the revealing remark." If you talk to someone long enough, he said, they will reveal their pain and their experiences. "To tell you the truth, after a while I got an idea that if I had any skill, it grew out of this fact that I'm not easily bored. I can talk to anybody. What you try to do is select the revealing things of this life. If I talk to them long enough, the most amazing things come out." He recalled talking to the woman in the Edgewater Cemetery in "The Rivermen." "She was so proud, and she was almost ghoulish about how wonderfully the roses grew. She said, 'Look, they put their roots right down in the coffins.' Now, why would that be funny? I don't know, but there you are."

Mitchell felt a connection to the river and to the people who earned their livelihoods from it. He tried to capture the view of the shad fishermen, to convey their lives to the reader. Generation after generation of shad came up the Hudson River to meet generation after generation of fishermen, dating from the Native Americans. Now the shad still come up through the Lower Bay and the Narrows into the Hudson, he said, but during the journey they begin to taste of kerosene. "If you don't have an interest, if you're not involved, to write a piece like that takes *so* much energy. You don't have the energy unless there's something inside you to begin with. Fact writing doesn't demand that energy." Something in the story of Edgewater symbolized the essence of life for Mitchell, and his creativity led him to let his story spiral in that direction.

"You want to take the reader to the last sentence," Mitchell said, sitting in the old swivel chair in his office. "That's the whole point of the story. I don't want to take him there just by *fact*. I want to take the reader there by going through an experience that I had that was revealing. I've been after telling a story perhaps with the same structure the fiction writer uses."

Mitchell, Kidder, and others in this collection acknowledge using the same techniques as fiction writers—excepting, of course, invention. Whether they are working in fiction or nonfiction, writers share similar problems in portraying characters and revealing inner experiences. Admitting that there are overlapping characteristics between the two forms has been perhaps the biggest controversy of literary journalism. Other equally important connections have attracted less attention. The shared methods of history writing and literary journalism can be seen in the Pulitzer Prize–winning books *The Making of the Atomic Bomb* (1986) by Richard Rhodes and *Common Ground* (1985) by J. Anthony Lukas. The overlap between memoir and literary journalism can be seen in Sue Hubbell's *A Book of Bees* (1988), Annie Dillard's *An American Life* (1987) about growing up in Pittsburgh, and Peter Matthiessen's *The Snow Leopard* (1978). In *Literary Journalism*, David Quammen, Walt Harrington, and Brent Staples use memoir; Joe Mitchell writes a nonfiction piece that has parallels in the novel; Quammen, John McPhee, and Richard Preston overlap science writing; Mark Singer, Calvin Trillin, Adrian Nicole LeBlanc, and Tracy Kidder overlap biography, or "the end of biography" in Kidder's case; Ted Conover, Mark Kramer, Susan Orlean, and Jane Kramer share ethnographic research techniques; Conover's and Mark Kramer's pieces border on travel writing. As Mark Kramer once put it while discussing these border-crossing tendencies, "The point of literary journalism is to cross fields, to marry, to rejoin our compartmentalized modern experience."

Bear Witness to Them

Ted Conover dropped out of Amherst College for a year to ride the rails with hoboes. His adventure turned into his senior thesis, and a year after he graduated, into his first book, *Rolling Nowhere* (1984). "After I finished writing my anthropology thesis, an ethnography of railroad tramp life, I felt I had left out one of the most interesting things," Conover said, "which is what it was like for a person from a relatively sheltered middle-class background like me to live this way.

"That personal reaction is as powerful a storyteller as the best ethnographic research. It adds to the ethnographic research to say what it was like when that guy said he was going to kill you or what it was like to fall off a train. When people hear you've lived with hoboes, that's the kind of question they're most interested in having answered. What was it like? Then my job becomes to describe what it was like for the hobo and what it was like for me. The story is about us both."

Conover helps the reader see how membership in a subculture shapes a person's reactions. His second book, *Coyotes* (1987), brought the reader into a group of illegal Mexican immigrants picking oranges in Arizona. His third book, *Whiteout* (1991), took Conover away from hoboes and agricultural workers into the status-conscious culture of Aspen, Colorado.

"I'm a good part anthropologist," Conover said. "Participant observation, which is the anthropological method, is the way I prefer to pursue journalism. It means a reliance not on the interview so much as on the shared experience with somebody. The idea to me that journalism and anthropology go together, which sort of dawned on me while I was writing *Rolling Nowhere*, was a great enabling idea for my life—the idea that I could learn about different people and different aspects of the world by placing myself in situations, and thereby see more than you ever could just by doing an interview."

Conover said the participant/observer gains a privileged knowledge available to neither the participant nor the observer. "A hobo riding on the freights is not going to understand what's interesting about his life in the way you do. At the same time, you could go down to the freight yard every weekend for a year and not begin to understand the desolate feeling you have when your partners steal your stuff, when the police look at you as one of *them*, when your friends don't recognize you on the street. That comes only through a commitment to putting yourself on the line in that very immediate way."

His research strategy leads to rich material, but the risks are real. In Africa, Conover hid in the American embassy for a while to avoid the police. In *Coyotes*, he accompanied a group of Mexican workers as they navigated across the U.S. border. The Mexican police harassed them, took their possessions, and beat them. "I'm not insane," Conover commented. "I don't seek out the overloaded ferry that's going to sink on its next crossing. But at the same time I'm not traveling for my amusement so much as to see things that interest me and to bear witness to them in some way."

John McPhee agrees. "Participation is a way of finding a narrative," McPhee told me, "a way to find something more interesting to report than a *Playboy* interview."

Professor Doug Birkhead of the University of Utah has argued that journalism, while it has become increasingly focused on political affairs, still "reflects an impulse to bring events into a forum so that they may be publicly accounted for. The press traditionally has sought to make itself—and us—bear the responsibility of being witnesses rather than merely onlookers." In that respect, he says, journalism hasn't changed much since it began.

Literary journalists share a goal of bearing witness, and a certainty that there is more to common life than just politics. The twentieth century has given us a wealth of political writing by literary journalists— John Reed on the Mexican and Russian revolutions, George Orwell on the Spanish Civil War, James Agee on the Depression, Edgar Snow on the Chinese Revolution, Michael Herr on Vietnam. Like Ted Conover, those writers placed themselves as participants or witnesses, rather than as distanced onlookers. While not exclusively focused on ordinary life, their works relied on the everyday experiences of soldiers and peasants to convey the feeling of the times. Because personal experience illuminates political issues, literary journalists are likely to write about politics by letting individuals represent larger groups. George Orwell's *Down and Out in Paris and London* (1933) is an example, and Jane Kramer's "Fernande Pelletier" uses a similar representative strategy in this collection. Conover's works on hoboes, Mexican immigrants, and AIDS all imply political issues, but he bears witness to the common life and lets the audience's reaction inform the politics.

A native of Denver, Conover speaks with an excitement that suggests he has something to say and no particular reason to hesitate. His first Brooklyn apartment was across from a place where Walt Whitman's old lodgings once stood and a block from Norman Mailer's house. Walking along the Brooklyn Heights promenade, Conover saw a landscape as stirring as any in Colorado: the Brooklyn Bridge, the Statue of Liberty, southern Manhattan, and the Fulton Fish Market.

Travel writing became second nature to Conover and some other literary journalists because it invites narrative, everyday interactions, and the voice of a guide. Conover's narrator serves as a measure of cultural difference, bridging the distance between the subjects' world and the readers'. He tries to avoid weighing down his narrator with preformed conclusions. "On the other hand," he added, "I'm really interested, and I think readers are interested, in knowing my personal opinion. A temptation for a lot of first-person nonfiction writers is to hector the reader or browbeat him and make too clear their own biases and not let the story tell itself. The quality of the first-person voice— what you say, and how you say it—is really important. I want to be a likable narrator. I want people who wouldn't read a book about Mexican immigrants to read my book because they see me as a tour guide they can trust or believe. Actually, I think they will *only* read it if they see me that way."

The journey itself resonates in the writer's life. Without some resonance, the research would be an energy drain, as Joseph Mitchell said. The use of travel writing, with its first-person narration, is a strategy for dealing with a particular kind of story. "It has to be something that matters, or else it will be flat," Conover said. Conover didn't go to Africa to see the landscape and meet new people. "The piece is about AIDS and the role these men play in spreading it, and how they get it, and how their behavior is changing and how it isn't. There are all sorts of parallels with our own behavior, I think. It sheds light on both them and us."

Conover exercises creativity in the decisions he makes getting the story: "I try to experiment with different perspectives. If it's an upstairs-downstairs place like Aspen, go upstairs and then go downstairs. Look at a party from the point of view of a caterer, then look at it from the point of view of a party-goer. To me, the creativity begins not when I sit down to write, but back when I'm envisioning the book and what kinds of situations I can insinuate myself into. That's what you begin with. Then, if you let your mind be changed, you discover things both about your subject and yourself that you didn't imagine. For example, Aspen, besides being a place of disgusting debauchery and excessive wealth, is a place with some decent people in it, a place where even a socially responsible type might end up having a really great time. Regretting it, mind you.

"If you're honest, a story unfolds in all kinds of directions. Aspen was a much more complicated project than I ever guessed it would be, just because my reactions to it were complicated. It wasn't easy to dismiss. It appealed to me much more than I ever wanted to admit until I had to sit down and write about it. That was all a part of growing as a writer, to deal with ever greater complexities."

The Materials Start Shaping You

Now in his sixties, John McPhee has silky brown hair, thinning in back, and a grizzled beard. He wears dark-rimmed glasses and, typically, outdoorsy clothes. After decades in the sunshine, crow's-feet have appeared at the corners of his eyes. Otherwise, his appearance hasn't changed much in the last dozen years. Sitting in his living room in Princeton, New Jersey, where he has lived since 1962, he twists around restlessly. He had dislocated his right shoulder cross-country skiing in the Sierras. The sling prevents his normal hand gestures—punching a pillow with his finger or waving a hand distractedly and exclaiming "Woooo!" as he describes his disappointment when, say, an editor turned down one of his early articles.

McPhee is as unpretentious in person as he seems on the page. He has written twenty-three books in thirty years, all of them still in print. Surprisingly, he sometimes lacks confidence.

"When I collect material, in terms of confidence, I blow hot and cold, but generally it's a pleasant time," McPhee said. "When I've got all my material together and I face it, when I'm making the structure, I'm quite excited by that, and I don't feel despair. I feel in charge of myself and my materials. It entrances me. It may take weeks to form this structure, to know where it's going to end, to know why it's going to end there, to know how it's going to get there. I get all that done, and then when I turn to doing the piece of writing and all I have is that blank screen and a knowledge of what I want to do, then I sink way down. My confidence in my craft goes to zero. That continues throughout the first draft. During the second total go-through, this may be eight months later, I recover somewhat."

McPhee borrowed the term "globally unstable" that architects use for the time when a building is framed and the girders are rising toward the sky but the structure has not yet firmed up. He had a globally unstable feeling about *Rising from the Plains* (1986), his third book about geology, until long after it was finished. Before writing *The Pine Barrens* (1968), McPhee collected his notes of miscellaneous scenes and sketches of people, then returned home. "I spent two weeks on a picnic table right outside the window here," McPhee said, pointing out into the yard, "lying on my back in agony and despair, staring up at the trees. I had no idea how I was going to tell the story."

McPhee loves to talk about how he crafts the structures of his writing. On this day, however, the conversation turned from structure to the ambitions of his students at Princeton and of other young writers.

McPhee himself knew early in life what he wanted to do, and feels lucky. Such single-minded concentration on a career is uncharacteristic of writers, McPhee said. They usually "wiggle around from one thing to another and finally fetch up" as writers. "When a person is twenty-one or twenty-two years old and facing that great enigma about what to do, envying the law students or medical students who can get on a set of rails and run on it and know where they're going, the writer doesn't know. But a writer should also bear in mind there are numerous paths to this goal and they're all O.K. It's like a huge river with a lot of islands in it. You can go around an island to the left or right. You can go to this or that island. You might get into an eddy. But you're still in the river. You're going to get there. If the person expects the big answer at twenty-one, that's ridiculous. Everyone's in the dark."

A few islands interrupted McPhee's journey. He experimented with fiction, television script writing, and newswriting at *Time* magazine. "I knew a lot of people when I was young who thought they knew, when they were nineteen years old, just what sort of writers they wanted to be. Whatever it was, poet, novelist. They picked their suit of clothing before they tried it on to see if it fits. A writer ought to write in every genre. Try poetry. Find out how bad you can be at it, or good, but probably bad." McPhee eventually grasped his goal as a *New Yorker* writer. He recognized the power and the possibilities in nonfiction for narrative, dialogue, character sketching, metaphor. He learned to take trips with his subjects, rather than interviewing them, while seeking the matrix of a narrative.

McPhee has written about geology, nuclear physics, medicine, nature's quirks, and about people at work—a canoe maker, a doctor, a game warden, a sailor, and a ship's captain. As a narrator, McPhee guides readers through thickets of technical information. "Real people in real places," that's how he describes his work. "I go off and look at people who are not making news and find in their stories something a great deal more interesting to me than the fact that somebody was murdered on the street."

McPhee's narratives blend the experiences of people with science and fact. He's grown ever more deft during thirty years of practice. One key technique is the digression, or "meander," as Mary Paumier Jones described it in the first edition of the journal *Creative Nonfiction*. Literary journalists meander around driving narratives so much that some have called it extended digressive narrative nonfiction.

"You're on a lake in Maine," McPhee explained. "The narrative has brought you to a place where you're camped next to the lake and there's a loon on the water. You're entranced with loons and you always have been, so you take this opportunity to discuss loons before we come back to the narrative. That's a 'set piece' on loons." When he was writing *The Deltoid Pumpkin Seed* (1973), a book about an experimental airplane designer, McPhee put a sign on the wall above his desk: HAVE THE COURAGE TO DIGRESS. He didn't mean that every piece of writing should wander away from the central narrative in a uniform chaos. But by skipping away from the narrative, a careful writer can provide background information or build the emotional foundation for a story.

Nonfiction writers cannot alter the raw material as a novelist might; the pressure in literary journalism is exerted in the opposite direction—the material alters the writer's initial conceptions. "You have a general idea but the materials start shaping you. If they don't, God help you," McPhee said.

Looking from his living room couch toward the kitchen, McPhee compared a nonfiction writer to a cook. "A cook goes out to the market and starts reacting. Go to a good market because you want to react. You start collecting material. When my friend Alan Lieb, a chef, sees a scallop that's four inches in diameter, he buys it. When he went in the market that morning, he did not know he was going to see that. He wasn't even thinking scallops, but for the next two days that's all he dealt with because the great big scallops were so interesting to him. A nonfiction writer is like that. You go to this market and you don't know what's going to happen.

"When you get home you've got this pile of stuff and you have to make something out of it. You have no idea what's going to happen. If you bring back the material and then start dealing with it, the structure rises organically out of the mass of raw material as collected. It makes sense for that body of material.

"The ideal would be to go out and come back with the biggest variety of material you could find: sketches of characters—how many people can be developed as characters so they are really standing free, in the round?—places, the scenery, the science involved, the history, the landscape. You're not inventing it. You're making something of what you collect and lay in a great big pile on a table in front of you. A potpourri of raw material."

Creativity and innovation, for nonfiction writers, grow in decisions made at every level of the process—how to research the material, as Conover mentioned; which characters to bring in rounded form to the page; finding the proper voice; discovering how to tell the story and when to digress.

They Belong to Storytelling

Reading literary journalism, we are tempted to ask if this is *really* nonfiction or if the author has invented some of the dialogue and details that make ordinary characters seem more noble or real. Those who have attempted to capture whole conversations or to portray scenes with fidelity know the problems. Literary journalism requires a difficult and tedious method of reporting. Tracy Kidder spent a year in a nursing home, day after day, taking notes, listening to conversations. "I just wanted to be there when something was happening," Kidder said. "I've done this enough to be patient. I can spend five hundred hours taking notes and use none of them, and then in ten minutes everything happens."

The duration and depth of reporting give literary journalists the raw materials they need, but that's not enough. The details have to be right. As Singer, Quammen, and McPhee mentioned to me, the ideas of literary journalism grow from facts. Mark Kramer warns that the readers of literary journalism are experienced and intelligent; they know about the world and how it works. A writer who makes mistakes, who doesn't convey a realistic world, will lose the most knowing readers.

A skilled writer who plans to devote a year to reporting in a nursing home, or studying the Mississippi River, or deciphering Russian bureaucrats will also spend the same time examining his own involvement in the story. Personal engagement with the subject may not be there at first, but the job will be dreary and the result drab if something doesn't develop.

The liveliness of literary journalism, which critics compare to fiction, comes from combining this personal engagement with perspectives from sociology and anthropology, memoir writing, fiction, history, and standard reporting. In an essay on "Blurred Genres," the anthropologist Clifford Geertz argues that a similar blending of perspectives altered the sociological imagination and left social scientists "free to shape their work in terms of its necessities rather then according to received ideas." Literary journalists are boundary crossers in search of a deeper perspective on our lives and times.

John McPhee dislikes the idea of a blurred line between fiction and nonfiction. Nevertheless, his personal approach to topics has been energized by drawing on scientific inquiries, social science techniques, and perspectives from literary theory.

Other writers are more at ease with the blurring, as long as readers understand that the writers don't make things up. "My writing is more and more like fiction," Tracy Kidder admitted candidly. "Some people criticize nonfiction writers for 'appropriating' the techniques and devices of fiction writing. Those techniques, except for invention of character and detail, never belonged to fiction. They belong to storytelling. In nonfiction you can create a tone and a point of view. Point of view affects everything that follows. It's like a turn in the road. Once you make that turn, everything follows. If you want to change something, you have to go all the way back to that decision. The point is to write as well as George Eliot in *Middlemarch* and to find ways to do that in nonfiction."

Breakable Rules for Literary Journalists

Mark Kramer

When writers, readers, English teachers, librarians, bookstore people, editors, and reviewers discuss extended digressive narrative nonfiction these days, they're fairly likely to call it literary journalism. The previous term in circulation was Tom Wolfe's contentious "New Journalism." Coined in the rebellious mid-sixties, it was often uttered with a quizzical tone and has fallen out of use because the genre wasn't really alternative to some *old* journalism, and wasn't really new.

Literary journalism is a duller term. Its virtue may be its innocuousness. As a practitioner, I find the "literary" part self-congratulating and the "journalism" part masking the form's inventiveness. But "literary journalism" is roughly accurate. The paired words cancel each other's vices and describe the sort of nonfiction in which arts of style and narrative construction long associated with fiction help pierce to the quick of what's happening—the essence of journalism.

This journalism in fact has a proper pedigree. Daniel Defoe, writing just after 1700, is the earliest cited by Norman Sims, one of the few historians of the form. The roster also includes Mark Twain in the nineteenth century and Stephen Crane at the start of the twentieth. Before and just after the Second World War, James Agee, Ernest Hemingway, A. J. Leibling, Joseph Mitchell, Lillian Ross, and John Steinbeck tried out narrative essay forms. Norman Mailer, Truman Capote, Tom Wolfe, and Joan Didion followed, and somewhere in there, the genre came into its own—that is, its writers began to identify themselves as part of a movement, and the movement began to take on conventions and to attract writers. Public consciousness of a distinct genre has risen, slowly.

In the 1970s John McPhee, Edward Hoagland, and Richard Rhodes—among others now in their fifties and sixties—broadened the form, joined in the 1980s by several dozen (then) youthful counterparts, including Tracy Kidder and Mark Singer. Richard Preston and Adrian Nicole LeBlanc, the youth of this collection, began publishing in their twenties, and both had studied literary journalism in seminars—a sure sign a new genre has arrived. Another sign is a change in its treatment by book review editors. They used to assign area experts routinely—geologists to review McPhee's *Basin and Range* (1981), computer programmers to review Kidder's *The Soul of a New Machine*—with neither brand of scientist generically qualified to assay the subtle narrative techniques and deft wordsmithing. Now editors are likelier to assign such reviewing to other writers and to critics.

New forms of the written word that catch on are infrequent literary occurrences. Still, writers will forever seek ways beyond the constraints of any form. Literary journalism has established an encampment ringed by overlapping cousin-genres—travel writing, memoir, ethnographic and historical essays, some fiction and even ambiguous semifiction stemming from real events—all tempting fields just beyond rickety fences.

Literary journalism has been growing up, and readers by the million seek it out. But it has been a you-know-it-when-you-see-it form. The following annotated list of defining traits derives from the work in this anthology and works by other authors I've cited. It reflects authors' common practices, as the "rules" of harmony taught in composition classes mirror composers' habits. Like those rules, these suggest methods that have worked well. But however accurately represented, rules for making art will surely be stretched and reinvented again and again.

---

1. Literary journalists immerse themselves in subjects' worlds and in background research. Speaking at a relaxed meeting of the Nieman Fellows at Harvard University, shortly after he'd won the Pulitzer Prize for *The Soul of a New Machine*, Tracy Kidder enraged several young journalists with an offhand comment—that literary journalists are, overall, more accurate than daily journalists. He recalls telling them, "It has to be true; our reporting takes months, and you're sent to get a story and write it up in three hours, and do two more before leaving work. A privileged journalist might get a few weeks for a feature."

Literary journalists hang out with their sources for months and even years. It's a reward—and risk—of the trade, as I've discovered on many projects. I spent one glorious June with a baseball team; I wandered intermittently in backwoods Russia through six years of *perestroika* and the ensuing confused transition. I spent a year in hospital operating rooms, and years in the fields and corporate offices of America's farms. Every writer in this anthology has had similar experiences. The reporting part of the work is engrossing and tedious. It is not social time. One stays alert for meaningful twists of narrative and character, all the while thinking about how to portray them and about how to sustain one's welcome.

The point of literary journalists' long immersions is to comprehend subjects at a level Henry James termed "felt life"—the frank, unidealized level that includes individual difference, frailty, tenderness, nastiness, vanity, generosity, pomposity, humility, all in proper proportion. It shoulders right on past official or bureaucratic explanations for things. It leaves quirks and self-deceptions, hypocrisies and graces intact and exposed; in fact, it uses them to deepen understanding.

This is the level at which we think about our own everyday lives, when we're not fooling ourselves. It's surely a hard level to achieve with other people. It takes trust, tact, firmness, and endurance on the parts of both writer and subject. It most often also takes weeks or months, including time spent reading up on related economics, psychology, politics, history, and science. Literary journalists take elaborate notes retaining wording of quotes, sequences of events, details that show personality, atmosphere, and sensory and emotional content. We have more time than daily journalists are granted, time to second-guess and rethink first reactions. Even so, making sense of what's happening—writing with humanity, poise, and relevance—is a beguiling, approachable, unreachable goal.

2. *Literary journalists work out implicit covenants about accuracy and candor with readers and with sources.* No Un-Literary-Journalistic-Activities Committee subpoenas the craft's corner cutters. Literary journalists, unlike newspaper reporters, are solo operatives. You can see the writers here, in their first few paragraphs, establishing their veracity with readers by displays of forthrightness and street savvy. These are important moments. They imply the rules the author elects to follow. Readers are the ultimate judges of which authors don't play fairly. They have had the last word in several publicized cases. Two areas of ethical concern often jumble together in discussions of the scrupulousness of literary journalism: (a) the writer's relationship to readers and (b) the writer's relationships to sources.

(a) The Writer's Relationship to Readers
A few distinguished essayists we retrospectively link to literary journalism did indeed commit acts that, if done by writers today, would be considered downright sinful: They combined or improved upon scenes, aggregated characters, refurbished quotations, and otherwise altered what they knew to be the nature of their material.

What distinguished them from fiction writers may have been merely intention—presumably to convey to readers the "sense" of an actuality. In fact, one of the genre's grand old men, Joseph Mitchell, whose work is in this collection, has written about and spoken to interviewers about using composite characters and scenes in his 1948 classic *Old Mr. Flood*. John Hersey, author of *Hiroshima*, did the same thing with the main character of his 1944 article "Joe Is Home Now" (however, he later complained about the practice among New Journalists). Mitchell never complained, and neither writer did it again.

I have no trouble comprehending the liberty of either of these artists trying things out. Other pioneers, including George Orwell (in "Shooting an Elephant") and Truman Capote (in *In Cold Blood* (1966)) apparently also recast some events, and my private verdict is to find them similarly exculpated by virtue of the earliness (and elegance) of their experimentation, and by the presumed lack of intention to deceive. None violated readers' expectations for the genre, because there weren't yet strong expectations—or much of a genre, for that matter—to violate.

Still, if you reread those essays having learned they portray constructed events, you may find yourself second-guessing what was real. One wouldn't bother doing this with a novel. The ambiguity is distracting. Today, literary journalism is a genre readers recognize and read expecting civil treatment. The power of the prose depends on the readers' accepting the ground rules the works implicitly proclaim.

There is a category of exceptions, and I'd argue it describes material that falls outside the modern understanding of what literary journalism is. By the time he published *The Executioner's Song*, in 1979, about a triple murderer named Gary Gilmore, Norman Mailer elected to specify his liberation from restrictive factuality. The dust jacket bore the odd description "A True Life Novel." Although such truth-in-labeling doesn't explicitly demarcate what parts are actual, it's a good-faith proclamation to readers that they've entered a zone in which a nonfiction writer's covenant with readers may be a tease, a device, but doesn't quite apply. It would take a naive audience to misconstrue clearly self-proclaiming "docudramas" such as Errol Morris's *The Thin Blue Line* (which Mark Singer writes about in this collection) or Mailer's sort of "docufiction." Most readers will instead savor, whether as art or entertainment, the deliberate byplay of reality against fancy, in this often wholesome, but always special category of film and prose that straddles the line.

However, chats with writer friends and panel discussions at writing conferences have me convinced that literary journalists have come to share a stodgier tacit understanding with readers, one so strong that it amounts to a contract: that the writers do what they appear to do, which is to get reality as straight as they can manage, and not make it up. Some, of course, admit in private to moments of temptation, moments when they've realized that tweaking reality could sharpen the meaning or flow of a scene. If any writers have gone ahead and actually tweaked, however, they're no longer chatting about it to friends, nor talking about it on panels. In recent years, a few literary journalists have drawn heavy fire for breaking trust with readers. It is not a subject about which readers are neutral.

Conventions literary journalists nowadays talk about following to keep things square with readers include: no composite scenes, no misstated chronology, no falsification of the discernible drift or proportion of events, no invention of quotes, no attribution of thoughts to sources unless the sources have said they'd had those very thoughts, and no unacknowledged deals with subjects involving payment or editorial control. Writers do occasionally pledge away use of actual names and identifying details in return for ongoing frank access, and notify readers they've done so. These conventions all add up to keeping faith. The genre makes less sense otherwise. Sticking to these conventions turns out to be straightforward.

Writers discover how to adhere to them and still structure essays creatively. There's no reason a writer can't place a Tuesday scene prior to a Monday scene, if the writer thinks readers should know how a situation turned out before knowing how it developed. It is easy to keep readers unconfused and undeceived, just by letting them know what you're doing. While narrating a scene, a literary journalist may wish to quote comments made elsewhere, or embed secondary scenes or personal memories; it is possible to do all these things faithfully, without blurring or misrepresenting what happened where and when, simply by explaining as you go along. Like other literary journalists, I've found that, in fact, annoying, inconsistent details that threaten to wreck a scene I'm writing are often signals that my working theories about events need more work, and don't quite explain what's happened yet.

Not tweaking deepens understanding. And getting a slice of life down authentically takes flexibility and hard labor. Readers appreciate writing that does the job. It is not accidental that the rise of literary journalism has been accompanied by authors' nearly universal adherence to these conventions, which produce trustworthy, in-the-know texts and reliable company for readers.

(b) Writer's Relationships to Sources

The writer's reliable companionship with sources can cause difficulty. An inescapable ethical problem arises from writers' necessarily intense ongoing relationships with subjects. Gaining satisfactory continuing access is always a tough problem; most potential subjects are doing quite well at life with no writers anywhere in the neighborhood, and their lives are tangles of organizational and personal affiliations. Yet, in order to write authentically at the level of "felt life," literary journalists will seek from subjects the sustained candor usually accorded only spouses, business partners, and dearest friends. Strong social and legal strictures bind husbands, wives, partners, and pals to only the most tactful public disclosure of private knowledge. Literary journalists' own honorable purposes, on the other hand, require as much public disclosure as possible.

During the months a writer stays around subjects, even a forthright relationship (that has commenced with full discussion of intentions, signing of releases, and display of past articles and books) is likely to develop into something that feels to both parties a lot like partnership or friendship, if not quite like marriage. The ticklish questions the writer comes up against are these: Does the subject see himself revealing information to a friend, at the same moment the writer sees himself hearing information from a source? And, how responsible is the writer for the consequences of such perceptions?

Writers, in good faith, try all sorts of ways to get and keep good access without falsifying their intentions. The most obvious has been to write about people who either don't mind or else actually like the prospect of being written about. Anthropologists say "access downward" is easier than "access upward." Literary journalists (including me) have had cordial continuing access to people far from the world of books, who just like the company of the writer and the sound of the project—including hoboes riding the rails, migrant workers sneaking across the border, merchant seamen, teen prostitutes, high school football players, plain dirt farmers.

Another category, exemplary subjects—a dynamic schoolteacher, a deft surgeon, a crew of tip-top carpenters, a dexterous canoemaker, a hard-bargaining corporate farm executive—also welcome attention, sometimes because they have causes they hope to represent, such as bigger school budgets, lessened malpractice liability, or fairer crop subsidies.

My own rule has been to show past articles, to make clear the public exposure involved, to explain my publisher's and my commitments of time and money, to stipulate that subjects won't get to edit manuscript or check quotes. Then I go ahead—if I'm still welcome after all that, and sometimes I'm not. In a few cases, I have doubted that subjects understood my intentions or their consequences well enough to consent, or I've felt consent hadn't been freely given but was influenced by boss's orders (for example, the nurses in an operating room where my subject worked). Then, I've made it my business to do no harm. By luck, I've been able to write what I wished, without having these occasional moments alter essential content. Every genre, whether daily or literary journalism, poetry, or fiction, ultimately depends on the integrity of the writer.

3. *Literary journalists write mostly about routine events.* The ecology of convenient access impels literary journalists toward routine events, not extraordinary ones. The need to gain long-term, frank access has forced writers to seek material in places that can be visited, and to avoid, in spite of longings to the contrary, places that can't. The level of access required is so high that it has largely determined the direction of literary journalists' efforts.

The goal during "reporting" or "fieldwork" is not to become socialized as an insider, as an intern at a firm might en route to a job. It is to know what insiders think about, to comprehend subjects' experiences and perspectives and understand what is routine to them. Insiders who eventually read a literary journalist's account should find it accurate and relevant, but not from an inside perspective. At first, when I spent time with surgeons, blood alarmed me—an unsurgeonlike attitude. By the end of a year witnessing controlled mayhem, my attention had shifted. I knew when the surgeon found bleeding routine, and recognized the rare moments when it alarmed him. My rookie reaction wasn't relevant to a surgeon's world; my later reaction served me better in comprehending his perspective.

Routine needn't mean humdrum. Most anyone's life, discovered in depth and from a compassionate perspective, is interesting. Some very routine subjects, however, haven't been breached, and seem unbreachable except by insiders. Oddly, one major constraint is legal. Commission from a national magazine in hand, I once approached an attorney well known for effectively defending many suspected murderers. He was tempted by the prospect of an article about his daily work. I sketched out the access I'd need—including entrée to his office discussions with and about a current client. The attorney backed away. I'd be out beyond the umbrella of attorney-client privilege, he said, and could be challenged, and perhaps subpoenaed, for questioning on what I'd heard. His client could then sue him for malpractice.

Uncontaminated access to top levels of big business during a major deal has also proved nearly beyond reach, mostly because corporate sources perceive that allowing a journalist to roam might exceed prudent fiduciary responsibility, and might subject them to suit. Also, businesspeople work repeatedly within a circle of associates, and whoever let in a writer unbound by the circle's prospect of mutual advantage could be seen as breaking trust. Writers occasionally do make it through these barriers. A few kiss-and-tell versions of business deals have also been written by former players. And writerly *post-factum* reconstructions sometimes re-create dramas of complex deals.

A cousin, true-crime reporting, also reconstructs events *post-factum*. Murderers usually try not to do their work in front of writers. But criminal cases subsequently open access to the most secret places, starting the moment the deed is revealed. Cooperative culprits looking for redemption, variety, or forgiveness, vengeful family members, and elaborate court records have taken writers far into hidden inner worlds— after the fact.

Nonfiction writers are fated to arrive late. Something that a literary journalist can only do in the first person, with hindsight, after chance has subjected him to bad or good fortune, is to write about a person about to be mugged, slip on a banana peel, or find a pot of gold. Once in a while, something untoward happens to a writer, and readers may profit from the author's misfortune—Francis Steegmuller's "The Incident at Naples" (which ran in *The New Yorker* in 1986) comes to mind. Steegmuller describes being robbed and injured while on holiday. Perhaps it is to push this limit that writers go adventuring—sailing into nasty seas and living to tell, hunting in the green hills of Africa and bagging the limit in close calls. Before disaster destroyed the lives of Christa MacAuliff and the *Challenger* astronauts, NASA had signed up writers wishing to go space traveling. Among the applicants was Tracy Kidder, who has gone on instead to write about aging.

4. *Literary journalists write in "intimate voice," informal, frank, human, and ironic.* In literary journalism, the narrator is neither the impersonal, dutiful explainer and qualifier of academic writing, who presents research material carefully but without special consideration of readers, nor the seemingly objective and factual, judgment-suspending, orthodox informant of newswriting. The narrator of literary journalism has a personality, is a whole person, intimate, frank, ironic, wry, puzzled, judgmental, even self-mocking—qualities academics and daily news reporters dutifully avoid as unprofessional and unobjective. They're taught to discount their personal reactions about other people and to advance no private opinions. From the perspective of the institutions or

intellectual traditions sponsoring such prose, there are sound civic, commercial, scientific, and discipline-abetting reasons for curtailing the appearance of private judgment. The effect of both academic and news styles is to present readers with what appear to be *the facts*, delivered in unemotional, nonindividuated, conventionalized, and therefore presumably fair and neutral voice. Obviously, they leave lots out.

The defining mark of literary journalism is the personality of the writer, the individual and intimate voice of a whole, candid person not representing, defending, or speaking on behalf of any institution, not a newspaper, corporation, government, ideology, field of study, chamber of commerce, or travel destination. It is the voice of someone naked, without bureaucratic shelter, speaking simply in his or her own right, someone who has illuminated experience with private reflection, but who has not transcended crankiness, wryness, doubtfulness, and who doesn't blank out emotional realities of sadness, glee, excitement, fury, love. The genre's power is the strength of this voice. It is an unaffiliated social force—although its practice has been mostly benign. It is one of the few places in media where mass audiences may consume unmoderated individual assertion, spoken on behalf of no one but the adventurous author.

The voice is rarely no-holds-barred, accusatory, or confessional, however, even though some writers—Tom Wolfe comes to mind—are adept at making it look that way. In most literary journalism, an informal, competent, reflective voice emerges, a voice speaking with knowledgeable assurance about topics, issues, personal subjects, a voice that reflects—often only indirectly, as subtext—the writer's self-knowledge, self-respect, and conscience. I suggest to my Boston University writing workshop that members find their voices by imagining they're telling fairly close friends whose wit they respect about an incident they'd observed and taken seriously, linked to fields they'd studied. What emerges is a sociable, humorously self-aware, but authoritative voice—I hear it at dinner parties when people tell anecdotes. Reading it feels companionable.

This voice is a handy invention for essay writers, not a quirky preference, nor merely a way of getting into the act. It is an effective tool for a difficult modern job. It enables an author to step around acculturated views of relationships and issues that are usually guarded by walls of formal language and invisible institutional alliances. The powers of the candid, intimate voice are many, and they bother people who insist on idealized versions of reality. Formality of language protects pieties, faiths, taboos, appearances, official truths. The intimate voice sidesteps such prohibitions, says things in the mode that professionals-in-the-know use when they leave work feeling pensive and confide to friends or lovers. It is the voice in which we disclose how people and institutions *really* are. It is a key characteristic of literary journalism, and is indeed something new to journalism.

A former newspaper reporter told me she'd interviewed a city traffic department official and found him stentorian and self-promoting, not sharp on issues, but a charming good-old-boy at local politics. She liked him, but she had his number. Nevertheless, her newspaper article, she recalled, had started something like, "The long-awaited design plans for a new highway exit were released today by the Office of Traffic Management." Her observations about the man and the jokes her knowing colleagues made about him in the bar near the newsroom afterwards are sorts of material a literary journalist might bring into a narrative about, say, the complex actuality of planning and building a highway exit—along with, perhaps, material on traffic management, bureaucratic structures, urban finance, executive psychology, the politics of urban renewal, and on the meanings of driving and self-promotion and good-old-boyhood in the writer's own life.

The audience is invited, when reading literary journalism, to adopt complex and relaxed expectations about meaning, and to share something excluded from academic and news articles—the author's ironic vision. Irony—the device of leading readers to consider a scene in more knowing terms than some of its actors do—is virtually taboo in other forms of nonfiction. Two exceptions come to mind, and in both places, literary journalism turns up. The *Wall Street Journal* is the one major American paper that regularly runs ironic features on its front page. This may be because management there defines its audience as well-heeled, powerful, and in-the-know—in short, as "not everyone," but an elite sector of the whole community, those on top, sharing some views of the world below. And Sunday newspaper magazines often feature a wholesome type of ironic voice, in articles whose narrators relate personal experiences with some sensitive aspect of communal morality—prejudice, costly sickness, the burdens of aging and of mental illness. Walt Harrington's piece, essentially on the growth of interracial tolerance, both his own and our nation's, is in that spirit. As the piece illustrates, the power of irony need not emerge from sarcasm or meanness. It can bind a community, simply by expanding contexts of events beyond what the actors usually consider.

5. *Style counts, and tends to be plain and spare.* A mark of literary journalism that shows right from the start of a piece is efficient, individual, informal language. The writers here have worked their language until it is spare, stylish, and controlled. Ear may be the least teachable skill of

writing. Elegant, simple expression is the goal, what many poets and novelists reach toward, too. People discern character in part by divining who'd make those word choices. Impersonal or obdurate speakers get found out. Clean, lucid, personal language draws readers toward experiencing the immediacy of scenes, and the force of ideas.

"If you want to see the invisible world, look at the visible one," Howard Nemerov said in his enchanted essay "On Metaphor." The best language of literary journalists is also evocative, playful, sharpened by active verbs, sparing of abstract verbs, adjectives, adverbs, and the many indolent forms of "to be," taut in its grammatical linkages. Such uncluttered style is gracious—clear and pleasant in its own right, and suited for leading readers not merely to picture, but to feel events. Readers resist clumsy writing, often without thinking much about what's wrong, but engage with good prose, often as heedlessly. Feeling transports readers as mere logic cannot.

6. *Literary journalists write from a disengaged and mobile stance, from which they tell stories and also turn and address readers directly.* David Quammen, like the other authors here, occupies a strategic stance in relation to his material in "Strawberries Under Ice." He is the host. He entertains by telling you a good winter camping tale, immersing you in it so you feel the immediacy of it, its past, its impending future, and the ongoing "now" of it. He also guides you, his presumptive social intimate, through his evaluation of it, exiting from story to informative digressions about glaciers and his psychology, then reentering action.

Readers experience this well-spoken, worldly, witty, cagey storytelling buddy warmly, in good measure because Quammen the writer isn't trapped within the events he portrays. He describes events (that happened to Quammen the subject) from a "retrospective platform," recollecting action and considering its shape, meanings, and metaphoric echoes.

This mobile stance of the writer is another key element in literary journalism. Each author in this anthology, while telling tales, repeatedly looks directly at the reader, comments, digresses, brings in associative material, background, previous events—not necessarily personal ones—then reengages the story. When the author drops you back at the spot where the tale's been left off, the place feels familiar. "Oh, good," says the well-hosted reader, realizing the story is back on screen, "now I find out what happens next." The reader rejoins with enhanced perspective on the events, gained from the digressive material. The forward-moving leading edge of the narrative, from which such digressions and returns happen, may be called "the moving now"—it's a term useful for discerning essay structure. Good storytellers often digress at moments when especially interesting action is pending, and not at the completion of action. Lucid storytelling, skillful selection of moments for pertinent digression, returning to the "moving now," are among the essential elements out of which literary journalists construct essays.

The literary journalist's mobile stance is not quite borrowed property of novelists—in fiction, the reader can never be sure the author has stepped away from the story, and can't quite shake the presumption that even an author's most out-of-story asides might turn out to be another layer of story. When the literary journalist digresses and then returns to narrative, the author's real-world knowledge juxtaposes with story. This mobile stance is an amazing device, full of power.

The authors in this anthology have varied approaches to this mobile stance. Jane Kramer mostly tells *about* scenes, conversing with readers, but at several refined moments fully sets scenes, drawing readers into experiencing them. Her erudition and grasp of the larger meanings of her subject infuse these moments. We see her scenes with a pleasant knowingness; we are newly sophisticated by her erudition. Tracy Kidder, on the other hand, does almost nothing but tell tales, suspending action for digressive comments to readers only occasionally. Both authors' stances aid their control of the reader's developing experience.

7. *Structure counts, mixing primary narrative with tales and digressions to amplify and reframe events.* Most literary journalism is primarily narrative, telling stories, building scenes. Each piece here carries readers along one, and often a second and third, story line. Walt Harrington's "A Family Portrait in Black & White" achronologically braids several discrete narratives that explore his relationship to racism, starting nearly currently and flashing back. He relates the events of his own interracial courtship and marriage, and also plaits in the stories of several of his wife's relatives, and the story of the relaxing of American racial attitudes.

The sequence of scenes and digressions—some brushed past, some dwelled upon—along with the narrator's mobile stance relative to these tales and asides, comprise narrative structure. Literary journalists have developed a genre that permits them to sculpt stories and digression as complexly as novelists do. At any moment the reader will probably be located somewhere along the time line of at least one unfolding tale and a few developing ideas. Quammen's "Strawberries Under Ice," at first glance an example of unusually charming science writing on glaciers, is in fact a coyly constructed narrative of the purgation of his soul, and once that's well along, of his courtship and marriage, of the miracle of love and its metaphorical expression in the warming effect of ice, of paradoxical and intimate metaphors, finally of rebirth from the warmth of a snow cave. Because of Quammen's crafty structuring of these elements, the piece creeps up on you. When authors make decisions about structure—order of scenes, points of digression, how intensively to develop which elements of stories and digressions—they consider the effects of the order and intensities chosen on readers' experience.

8. *Literary journalists develop meaning by building upon the readers' sequential reactions.* Readers are likely to care about how a situation came about and what happens next when they are experiencing it with the characters. Successful literary journalists never forget to be entertaining. The graver the writer's intentions, and the more earnest and crucial the message or analysis behind the story, the more readers ought to be kept engaged. Style and structure knit story and idea alluringly.

If the author does all this storytelling and digressing and industrious structure-building adroitly, readers come to feel they are heading somewhere with purpose, that the job of reading has a worthy destination. The sorts of somewheres that literary journalists reach tend to marry eternal meanings and everyday scenes. Richard Preston's "The Mountains of Pi," for instance, links the awkward daily lives of two shy Russian émigré mathematicians to their obscure intergalactic search for hints of underlying order in a chaotic universe.

Readers take journeys designed by authors to tease out the ineluctable within the everyday; the trip will go nowhere without their imaginative participation. Ultimately, what an author creates aren't sequential well-groomed paragraphs on paper, but sequential emotional, intellectual, and even moral experiences that readers undertake. These are engaging, patterned experiences, akin to the sensations of filmgoing, not textbook reading. What these pieces mean isn't on paper at all.

The writer paints sensory scenes, confides on a level of intimacy that stirs readers' own experiences and sensations, and sets up alchemical interplay between constructed text and readers' psyches. The readers' realizations are what the author and readers have made together.

Why has this union of detailed fact, narratives, and intimate voice risen so remarkably in this century?

Many traditions that defined behaviors and beliefs at the start of the century have fragmented or vaporized. In 1900 a few hundred categories described the routines of labor, and a handful of patterns defined propriety. These days, there are ten thousand sorts of job and of propriety. In the same period, science, which had promised answers, order, and ease, has yielded convolution, danger, and vast domains of knowl-

edge that seem crucial to everyone but comprehensible only by specialists. And in a culture that once called upon experts, and leaders with
creeds, for piloting, august authority has run aground. Presidents, priests,
generals on horseback, professors in ivory towers—none can command
collective faith these days.

Yet somehow this has not resulted in universal despair. A formidable crowd of citizens wants, I'm sure with more urgency than ever, to
read books and essays that comprehend what's happening in its complexity. They demand not just information, but visions of how things fit
together now that the center cannot hold. A public that rarely encountered the personal imaginations of others at the turn of the century, now
devours topical bestsellers, films and TV shows that cast issues narra-
tively, and literary journalism.

Literary journalism helps sort out the new complexity. If it is not an
antidote to bewilderment, at least it unites daily experiences—including
emotional ones—with the wild plenitude of information that can be applied to experience. Literary journalism couples cold fact and personal
event, in the author's humane company. And that broadens readers'
scans, allows them to behold others' lives, often set within far clearer
contexts than we can bring to our own. The process moves readers,
and writers, toward realization, compassion, and in the best of cases,
wisdom.

I'll even claim that there is something intrinsically political—and
strongly democratic—about literary journalism, something pluralistic,
pro-individual, anti-cant, and anti-elite. That seems inherent in the
common practices of the form. Informal style cuts through the obfus-
cating generalities of creeds, countries, companies, bureaucracies, and
experts. And narratives of the felt lives of everyday people test idealiza-
tions against actualities. Truth is in the details of real lives.

Joseph Mitchell

Anne Hall

One of the great literary journalists, Joseph Mitchell started working for editors Harold Ross and William Shawn at *The New Yorker* in 1938, after a career as a feature writer for the *New York World-Telegram* and the *New York Herald Tribune*. Mitchell and A. J. Liebling, another great feature writer from the New York newspapers, brought literary journalism to the magazine with their profiles of boxers, con-men, and characters from the Bowery and the Fulton Fish Market.

Mitchell's books include *My Ears Are Bent* (1938), *McSorley's Wonderful Saloon* (1943), *Old Mr. Flood* (1948), *The Bottom of the Harbor* (1959), and *Joe*

Gould's Secret (1965). He wrote "The Mohawks in High Steel" in 1949, which appeared in Edmund Wilson's *Apologies to the Iroquois* (1960). In 1992, Pantheon published *Up in the Old Hotel*, a collected edition of Mitchell's work except his newspaper features. *Up in the Old Hotel* made the *New York Times* bestseller list of 1992. In its end-of-the-year review, *Time* magazine referred to it as "among the best books of any year." In 1994 Modern Library reissued *The Bottom of the Harbor*, which contains "The Rivermen."

During the period between his last publication in 1965 and the reissue of his works, Mitchell's reputation remained strong among nonfiction writers. A private man, he kept his office at *The New Yorker*, refused interviews, and was rumored to be at work on a new book. Stories about Mitchell's writing circulated among a virtual cult of fans. Critics called him the best reporter in America and analyzed his work for its symbolism.

Mitchell specialized in writing about the characters in the Fulton Fish Market in Manhattan. He was drawn to the community of rivermen in Edgewater, New Jersey, who had survived for generations by working on tugboats and excursion boats on the river, by fishing for shad during the annual run, and before that by cutting paving blocks for New York City from a local quarry. He was trying to preserve that past in his story, perhaps as a seed of resurrection.

Mitchell, now eighty-six years old, is currently working on an autobiography for Pantheon.

The Rivermen

I often feel drawn to the Hudson River, and I have spent a lot of time through the years poking around the part of it that flows past the city. I never get tired of looking at it; it hypnotizes me. I like to look at it in midsummer, when it is warm and dirty and drowsy, and I like to look at it in January, when it is carrying ice. I like to look at it when it is stirred up, when a northeast wind is blowing and a strong tide is running—a new-moon tide or a full-moon tide—and I like to look at it when it is slack. It is exciting to me on weekdays, when it is crowded with ocean craft, harbor craft, and river craft, but it is the river itself that draws me, and not the shipping, and I guess I like it best on Sundays, when there are lulls that sometimes last as long as half an hour, during which, all the way from the Battery to the George Washington Bridge, nothing moves upon it, not even a ferry, not even a tug, and it becomes as hushed and dark and secret and remote and unreal as a river in a dream. Once, in the course of such a lull, on a Sunday morning in April, 1950, I saw a sea sturgeon rise out of the water. I was on the New Jersey side of the river that morning, sitting in the sun on an Erie Railroad coal dock. I knew that every spring a few sturgeon still come in from the sea and go up the river to spawn, as hundreds of thousands of them once did, and I had heard tugboatmen talk about them, but this was the first one I had ever seen. It was six or seven feet long, a big, full-grown sturgeon. It rose twice, and cleared the water both times, and I plainly saw its bristly snout and its shiny little eyes and its white belly and its glistening, greenish-yellow, bony-plated, crocodilian back and sides, and it was a spooky sight.

I prefer to look at the river from the New Jersey side; it is hard to get close to it on the New York side, because of the wall of pier sheds. The best points of vantage are in the riverfront railroad yards in Jersey City, Hoboken, and Weehawken. I used to disregard the "DANGER" and "RAILROAD PROPERTY" and "NO TRESPASSING" signs and walk into these yards and wander around at will. I would go out to the end of one of the railroad piers and sit on the stringpiece and stare at the river for hours, and nobody ever bothered me. In recent years, however, the railroad police and pier watchmen have become more and more inquisitive. Judging from the questions they ask, they suspect every stranger hanging around the river of spying for Russia. They make me uneasy. Several years ago, I began going farther up the river, up to Edgewater, New Jersey, and I am glad I did, for I found a new world up there, a world I never knew existed, the world of the rivermen.

Edgewater is across the river from the upper West Side of Manhattan; it starts opposite Ninety-fourth Street and ends opposite 164th Street. It is an unusually narrow town. It occupies a strip of stony land between the river and the Palisades, and it is three and a half miles long and less than half a mile wide at its widest part. The Palisades tower over it, and overshadow it. One street, River Road, runs the entire length of it, keeping close to the river, and is the main street. The crosstown streets climb steeply from the bank of the river to the base of the Palisades, and are quite short. Most of them are only two blocks long, and most of them are not called streets but avenues or terraces or places or lanes. From these streets, there is a panoramic view of the river and the Manhattan skyline. It is a changeable view, and it is often spectacular. Every now and then—at daybreak, at sunset, during storms, on starry summer nights, on hazy Indian-summer afternoons, on blue, clear-cut, stereoscopic winter afternoons—it is astonishing.

The upper part of Edgewater is largely residential. This is the oldest part of town, and the narrowest, but it still isn't entirely built up. There are several stretches of trees and underbrush, and several bushy ravines running down to the river, and a number of vacant lots. The lots are grown up in weeds and vines, and some of them are divided by remnants of stone walls that once divided fields or pastures. The streets are lined with old trees, mostly sweet gums and sycamores and tulip trees. There are some wooden tenements and some small apartment houses and some big old blighted mansions that have been split up into apartments, but one-family houses predominate. The majority are two-story houses, many of them set back in good-sized yards. Families try to outdo each other in landscaping and ornamenting their yards, and bring home all sorts of odds and ends for the purpose; in yard after yard conventional garden ornaments such as sundials and birdbaths and wagon wheels painted white stand side by side with objects picked up around the riverfront or rescued during the demolition of old buildings. The metal deckhouse of an old Socony tanker barge is in the front yard of one house on River Road; it is now a garden shed. In the same yard are a pair of mooring bitts, a cracked stone eagle that must have once been on the façade of a public building or a bank, and five of those cast-iron stars that are set in the walls of old buildings to cap the ends of strengthening rods. In the center of a flower bed in one yard is a coal-hole cover and in the center of a flower bed in an adjoining yard is a manhole cover. In other yards are old anchors and worm wheels and buoys and bollards and propellers. Edgewater used to be linked to Manhattan by a ferry, the Edgewater-125th Street ferry. Most of the captains, wheelsmen, and deckhands on the ferryboats were Edgewater men, and had been for generations, and the ferry was the pride of the town. It stopped running in 1950; it was ruined by the George Washington Bridge and the Lincoln Tunnel. There are relics of it in a dozen yards. In former Mayor Henry Wissel's yard, on Hilliard Avenue, there is a chain post that came off the vehicle gangway of the ferryboat *Shadyside*, and the *Shadyside*'s fog bell hangs beside his door. In former Fire Chief George Lasher's yard, on Undercliff Avenue, there is a hookup wheel that came off the landing stage of the old ferryhouse. It resembles a ship's wheel. Chief Lasher has painted it white, and has trained a climbing rose on it.

In the middle of Edgewater, around and about River Road and the foot of Dempsey Avenue, where the ferryhouse used to stand, there is a small business district. In addition, a few stores and a few neighborhood saloons of the type known in New Jersey as taverns are scattered along River Road in the upper and lower parts of town.

The lower part of Edgewater is called Shadyside; the ferryboat was named for it. It is a mixed residential and factory district. The majority of the factories are down close to the river, in a network of railroad sidings, and piers jut out from them. Among them are an Aluminum Company of America factory, a coffee-roasting plant, a factory that makes roofing materials, a factory that makes sulphuric acid, and a factory that makes a shortening named Spry. On the roof of the Spry factory is an enormous electric sign; the sign looms over the river, and on rainy, foggy nights its pulsating, endlessly repeated message, "SPRY FOR BAKING," "SPRY FOR BAKING," "SPRY FOR BAKING," seems to be a cryptic warning of some kind that New Jersey is desperately trying to get across to New York.

There are six or seven large factories in Shadyside and six or seven small ones. The Aluminum Company factory is by far the largest, and there is something odd about it. It is made up of a group of connecting buildings arranged in a U, with the prongs of the U pointed toward the river, and inside the U, covering a couple of acres, is an old cemetery. This is the Edgewater Cemetery. Most of the old families in Edgewater have plots in it, and some still have room in their plots and continue to bury there. The land on which Edgewater is situated and the land for some distance along the river above and below it was settled in the seventeenth century by Dutch and Huguenot farmers. Their names are on the older gravestones in the cemetery—Bourdettes and Vreelands and Bogerts and Van Zandts and Wandells and Dyckmans and Westervelts and Demarests. According to tradition, the Bourdette family came in the sixteen-thirties—1638 is the date that is usually specified—and was the first one there; the name is now spelled Burdette or Burdett. Some of the families came over from Manhattan and some from down around Hoboken. They grew grain on the slopes, and planted orchards in the shelter of the Palisades. In the spring, during the shad and sturgeon runs, they fished, and took a large part of their catch to the city. The section was hard to get to, except by water, and it was rural and secluded for a long time. In the early eighteen-hundreds, some bluestone quarries were opened, and new people, most of whom were English, began to come in and settle down and intermarry with the old farming and fishing families. They were followed by Germans, and then by Irish straight from Ireland. Building stones and paving blocks and curbing for New York City were cut in the quarries and carried to the city on barges—paving blocks from Edgewater are still in place, under layers of asphalt, on many downtown streets. Some of the new people worked in the quarries, some worked on the barges, some opened blacksmith shops and made and repaired gear for the quarries and the barges, some opened boatyards, and some opened stores. The names of dozens of families who were connected with these enterprises in one way or another are on gravestones in the newer part of the cemetery; Allison, Annett, Carlock, Cox, Egg, Forsyth, Gaul, Goetchius, Hawes, Hewitt, Jenkins, Stevens, Truax, and Winterburn are a few. Some of these families died out, some moved away, and some are still flourishing. The enterprises themselves disappeared during the first two decades of this century; they were succeeded by the Shadyside factories.

The land surrounding the Edgewater Cemetery was once part of a farm owned by the Vreeland family, and the Aluminum Company bought this land from descendants of a Winterburn who married a Vreeland. As a condition of the sale, the company had to agree to provide perpetual access to the cemetery. To reach it, funerals go through the truck gate of the factory and across a freight yard and up a cement ramp. It is a lush old cemetery, and peaceful, even though the throb of machinery can be felt in every corner of it. A part-time caretaker does a good deal of gardening in it, and he likes bright colors. For borders, he uses the same gay plants that are used in flower beds at race tracks and seaside hotels—cannas, blue hydrangeas, scarlet sage, and cockscomb.

Old men and old women come in the spring, with hoes and rakes, and clean off their family plots and plant old-fashioned flowers on them. Hollyhocks are widespread. Asparagus has been planted here and there, for its feathery ferny sprays. One woman plants sunflowers. Coarse, knotty, densely tangled rosebushes grow on several plots, hiding graves and gravestones. The roses that they produce are small and fragile and extraordinarily fragrant, and have waxy red hips almost as big as crab apples. Once, walking through the cemetery, I stopped and talked with an old woman who was down on her knees in her family plot, setting out some bulbs at the foot of a grave, and she remarked on the age of the rosebushes. "I believe some of the ones in here now were in here when I was a young woman, and I am past eighty," she said. "My mother—this is her grave—used to say there were rosebushes just like these all over this section when she was a girl. Along the riverbank, beside the roads, in people's yards, on fences, in waste places. And she said *her* mother—that's her grave over there—told her she had heard from *her* mother that all of them were descended from one bush that some poor uprooted woman who came to this country back in the Dutch times potted up and brought along with her. There used to be a great many more in the cemetery than there are now—they overran everything—and every time my mother visited the cemetery she would stand and look at them and kind of laugh. She thought they were a nuisance. All the same, for some reason of her own, she admired them, and enjoyed looking at them. 'I know why they do so well in here,' she'd say. 'They've got good strong roots that go right down into the graves.' "

The water beside several of the factory piers in Shadyside has been deepened by dredging to depths ranging between twenty and thirty feet. Everywhere else along Edgewater the inshore water is shallow. Off the upper part of town are expanses of shoals that are called the Edgewater Flats. They are mucky, miry, silty, and oily. Stretches of them are exposed at low tide, or have only a foot or two of water over them. In some places, they go out two hundred yards before they reach a depth of six feet. For generations, the Edgewater Flats have been a dumping ground for wrecks. Out in them, lying every which way, as if strewn about long ago by a storm, are the ruins of scores of river vessels. Some of these vessels were replaced by newer vessels and laid up in the flats against a time that they might possibly be used again, and that time never came. Some got out of commission and weren't worth repairing, and were towed into the flats and stripped of their metal and abandoned. Some had leaks, some had fires, and some had collisions. At least once a day, usually when the tide is at or around dead ebb, flocks of harbor gulls suddenly appear and light on the wrecks and scavenge the refuse that has collected on them during the rise and fall of the tide, and for a little while they crawl with gulls, they become white and ghostly with gulls, and then the gulls leave as suddenly as they came. The hulks of three ferryboats are out in the flats—the *Shadyside*, the *George Washington*, and the old *Fort Lee*. Nothing is left of the *Shadyside* but a few of her ribs and part of her keel. There are old tugboats out there, and old dump scows, and old derrick lighters, and old car floats. There are sand-and-gravel barges, and brick barges, and stone barges, and coal barges, and slaughterhouse barges. There are five ice barges out there, the last of a fleet that used to bring natural ice down to New York City from the old icehouse section along the west shore of the river, between Saugerties and Coxsackie. They have been in the flats since 1910, they are waterlogged, and they sit like hippopotamuses in the silt.

Close to shore are some barges that are still being used. They are drawn up in a straggly row, facing the shore, and narrow, zigzaggy footwalks built on piles made of drift lumber go out to them. These are second-hand railroad barges. They were once owned by the Pennsylvania, the Erie, the New York Central, the Jersey Central, and other railroads that operate barge fleets in the harbor. Their bottoms are sound and their roofs are tight, but they got too old to be jerked this way and that by tugs in a hurry and bumped about and banged into (most of them are over forty years old, and several are over sixty), so they were discarded and sold. Some are owned by shadfishermen, who move them up or down the river at the start of the shad season and tie them up along the bank, each fisherman placing his barge as close as possible to his row of nets. The fishermen eat and sleep aboard them and use them as bases while the shad are running, and then return them to the flats and keep them there the rest of the year and store their equipment in them. Others are owned by boat clubs. There are seven boat clubs on the Edgewater riverfront, and four are quartered in secondhand railroad barges. One club, the Undercliff Motor Boat Club, owns two, but uses both for the winter storage of its boats, and has its quarters in an old queen of an oyster barge named the *G. M. Still*. The wholesale oyster companies in New York City used to carry on their businesses in specially built barges that were docked the year round at piers on the East River, just north of Fulton Fish Market. These barges had two or three decks, and could hold huge stocks of oysters. They were top-heavy but beautifully made. Some had balconies with banisters shaped like tenpins on their upper decks, and the offices in several had mahogany paneling; the reputation of an oyster company partly depended on the splendor of its barge. There were over a dozen oyster barges on the East River at one time, and all were painted a variety of colors and all had ostentatious black-and-gold nameboards across their fronts and all flew swallowtail pennants; people visited the waterfront just to see them. The *G. M. Still* was the last to go. It was owned by George M. Still, Inc., the planters of Diamond Point oysters, and its final East River location was at a pier at the foot of Pike Street, under the Manhattan Bridge; it was there for a generation. In 1949, the city took over this pier, and the Still company was unable to find another, so it moved ashore, and sold the barge to a dealer in old boats, who sold it to the boat club. The *G. M. Still* is almost eighty years old—it was built in 1880—and the recent years have been hard on it. Even so, not all the teardrops, icicles, scallops, and other scroll-saw curlicues that once ornamented it have disappeared, and its last coat of paint under the Still ownership—black, yellow, white, orange, and green—has not entirely faded, and the balcony on the bow end of its upper deck looks as regal as ever.

Although Edgewater is only a short ride by subway and bus from the heart of New York City, it has some of the characteristics of an isolated and ingrown old town in New England or the South. The population is approximately four thousand, and a large proportion of the people are natives and know each other, at least to speak to. A surprising number of them are related, some so distantly that they aren't at all sure just how. The elderly people take a deep interest in local history, a good deal of which has been handed down from generation to generation by word of mouth, and nearly all of them who are natives consider themselves authorities on the subject. When these elderly people were young, quite a few men and women bearing the names of the original Dutch and Huguenot families were still living in old family mansions along River Road—one old man or one old woman living alone, as often as not, or, in some cases, two old bachelor brothers or two old spinster sisters living together, or an old woman living with a bachelor son or a spinster daughter—and they remember them. They know in a general way how the present-day old families are interrelated, and how several of these families are related to the original families. They can fish around in their memories and bring up vital statistics and stray facts and rumors and old jokes and sayings concerning a multitude of people who have been dead and gone for a generation, and can point out where buildings stood that have been torn down for fifty years. Sometimes, in the manner of old people in old towns, unable to tell only a little when they know so much, they respond to a simple question with a labyrinthine answer. One day, shortly after I began going up to Edgewater, I became acquainted with an elderly native named Henry R. Gaul, and went for a walk with him. Mr. Gaul is a retired oil-company executive. For many years, the Valvoline Oil Company operated a refinery on the riverbank in Shadyside, and Mr. Gaul was chief clerk there. He is secretary of the Undercliff Motor Boat Club and, to have something to do, he looks after the club's winter-storage barges and its headquarters barge, the old *G. M. Still.* His friends call him Henny. Walking on River Road, Mr. Gaul and I came to an automobile that had broken down. It was alongside the curb, and two men in greasy overalls were working on it. One had the hood up, and was bent over the engine. The other was underneath the automobile, flat on his back. As we were passing by, the man underneath thrust his head out, to say something to the man working on the engine. As he did so, he caught sight of Mr. Gaul. "Hello, Henny," he said.

Mr. Gaul was startled. He paused and turned and peered down at the man's face, and then said, "Oh, hello, Bill." "That was Bill Ingold," he said as we resumed our walk. "He runs the Edgewater Garage."

I was curious about the name; Mr. Gaul had referred to several names as old Edgewater names, and I asked him if Ingold was another one of them.

"Ingold?" he said. "Well, I should hope to think it is. It isn't one of the old Dutch names, but it's old enough, and Bill's got some of the old Dutch blood in him anyhow, through his mother's people. Knickerbocker Dutch. Not that he'd ever mention it. That's the way it is in Edgewater. There's a number of people over here who have old, old families back behind them—much older, I dare say, than the families back behind a high percentage of the people in the *Social Register* in New York—but you'd never find it out from them. Bill's mother was a Bishop, and *her* mother was a Carlock. The old Dutch blood came down to him through the Carlocks. The Carlocks were big people over here once, but they had a preponderance of daughters and the name died out. They owned land, and one branch of them ran a boatyard. The boatyard was torn down years and years ago, but I can tell you where it stood. Did you ever notice an ancient old clapboard building on the upper part of River Road with a saloon in it named Sulyma's Bar & Grill? Well, in the old days that building was a hotel named the Buena Vista Hotel, only we called it Walsch's, after the family that ran it. And just before you got to Walsch's, on the right, in between River Road and the river, was Carlock's Boatyard. Bill Ingold's father was also named Bill—William, that is, William F. He was in the Edgewater Fire Department. In fact, he was Fire Chief. He was a highly respected man, and I'll tell you a little story to illustrate that. There used to be an old gentleman in Edgewater named Frederick W. Winterburn. Mr. Winterburn was rich. He had inherited money, and he had married money, and he had made money. His wife was a Vreeland, and she was related to the Dyckmans *and* the Westervelts. Among other things, he owned practically the whole of Shadyside, and he lived down there. He lived in a big house overlooking the river, and he had a rose garden in front and an orchard in back. On warm summer nights, walking along River Road, you could smell the roses in his garden. And you could smell the peaches in his orchard, all soft and ripe and still warm from the sun and a little breeze blowing across them. And you could smell the grapes hanging on a fence between the garden and the orchard. They were fox grapes, and they had a musky smell. I'd give anything to smell those grapes again. The garden had marble statues in it. Statues of women. Naked women. Naked marble women. Goddesses, I guess you'd call them. In the moonlight, they looked real. It's all gone now, and there's a factory there. One piece of Mr. Winterburn's property surrounded the Edgewater Cemetery. His parents were buried in this cemetery, and his wife's people all the way back to the seventeenth century were buried in there, and he knew he was going to be buried in there, and he took a personal interest in it. In 1909 or 1910 or thereabouts—it might've been a few years earlier or a few years later—Mr. Winterburn was beginning to have a feeling that time was running out on him, he wouldn't be here much longer, although to tell you the truth he lived quite a few years more, and one day he asked five men to come to his house. All of them were from old Edgewater families and had people buried in the cemetery, and one of them was Bill Ingold's father, Fire Chief Ingold. 'Sit down, boys,' Mr. Winterburn said, 'I want to talk to you. Boys,' he said, 'my family owns much more space in the cemetery than it'll ever need or make use of, and I'm going to set aside a section of it for a poor plot. Any bona fide resident of Edgewater who dies a pauper can be buried in this plot, free of charge. And suicides that are turned away by other cemeteries can be buried in there, provided they're residents. And non-residents that drown in the river and wash up on the Edgewater riverfront and don't have any identification on them, the way it sometimes happens, it doesn't make any difference if it looks accidental or looks as if they threw themselves in, they can be buried in there. Furthermore, I'm going to set up a trust fund, and I'm going to fix it so the principal can't ever be touched, whereas the interest can be used in perpetuity to keep up the cemetery. And I want you boys to form a cemetery association and elect a president and a secretary and a treasurer, and the duties of these officers shall be to keep an eye on the cemetery and visit it every now and then and make a tour of inspection through it and hire a caretaker and see that he keeps the weeds cut and the leaves raked and whenever the occasion arises rule on who can be buried in the poor plot and who can't be.' So they put it to a vote, and

Fire Chief Ingold was elected president without any discussion whatsoever. It was taken for granted. That's how respected he was. And after
he died, Bill was elected president, and he's held the office ever since. Did I
mention Bill's mother was a Bishop? Well, she was. The Bishops were . . ."

Some of the people in Edgewater commute to jobs in New York
City, and some work in the river towns south of Edgewater, which are,
in order, going south, North Bergen, Guttenberg, West New York,
Weehawken, Hoboken, and Jersey City, but the majority work in the
factories in Shadyside. A score or so of men are spoken of around town
as rivermen. This word has a special shade of meaning in Edgewater: a
riverman not only works on the river or kills a lot of time on it or near
it, he is also emotionally attached to it—he can't stay away from it.
Charles Allison is an example. Mr. Allison lives in Edgewater and works
in North Bergen. He is a partner in the Baldwin & Allison Dry Dock
Co., a firm that operates a drydock and calks and repairs barges and
drives piles and builds docks and does marine surveying and supplies
pumps for salvage work, but that is only one of the reasons he is looked
upon as a riverman. The main reason is that the river has a hold on him.
Most days he is on or around it from early in the morning until sunset. Nevertheless, he often goes down to it at night and walks beside it.
Even on Sundays and holidays, he often goes down to it. The offices of
the drydock company are in a superstructure built on the deck of an old
railroad barge that is permanently docked at a pier in North Bergen,
and Mr. Allison has had big wide windows put in three of the walls of
his private office, so that he can sit at his desk and see up, down, and
across the river. Every spring, he takes a leave of absence from the drydock, and spends from six weeks to two months living aboard a shad
barge on the river and fishing two rows of shad nets with a crew of
hired fishermen.

Some men work full time on the river—on ferries, tugs, or barges—
and are not considered rivermen; they are simply men who work on the
river. Other men work only a part of the year on the river and make
only a part of their living there but *are* considered rivermen. Mr. Ingold,
the garage proprietor, is one of these. His garage is on River Road, facing the river. It is a typical small, drafty, one-story garage, except that
hanging on its walls, in among the fan belts and the brake linings and
the dented chromium hubcaps and the calendars with naked girls on
them, are anchors and oars and hanks of netting and dozens of rusty old
eelpots. Also, standing in a shallow box of sand in the middle of the
floor is a stove of a kind that would be recognizable only to people who
are familiar with harbor shipping; it is shaped like an oil drum and
burns coke and is a kind that is used in barges and lighters to keep per-

ishable freight from freezing. Mr. Ingold took it out of an old Erie Railroad fruit-and-vegetable barge. In the winter, a group of elderly Edgewater men, most of whom are retired, sit around it and gossip and
argue; in the summer, they move their chairs up front to the door,
where they can look out on the river and the Manhattan skyline. Mr.
Ingold owns two shad barges and several shad boats, and keeps them at
a landing a short walk up the river from the garage. Off and on during
the winter, he and another riverman, Eustus R. Smith, stretch shad nets
across the floor of the garage and put them in shape. They rig new nets,
and mend and splice old ones. They are helped occasionally by Mr. Ingold's son, Willy, and by Mr. Smith's son, Charlie. In the spring, Mr.
Ingold leaves the garage in the hands of two mechanics, and he and his
son and Mr. Smith and his son go out on the river and become shadfishermen for a couple of months. In the late fall and early winter, when the
eels in the river are at their best and bring the highest prices, Mr. Ingold
and Willy set eelpots. They set sixty, and their favorite grounds are up
around Spuyten Duyvil, where the Harlem River runs into the Hudson. Some nights during the eel season, after knocking off work in the
garage, Mr. Ingold gets in an outboard and goes up to Spuyten Duyvil
and attends to the pots, drawing them up hand over hand from the bottom and taking out the trapped eels and putting in fresh bait, and some
nights Willy goes up. On dark nights, they wear miner's caps that have
head lamps on them. Mr. Ingold has been dividing his time between
the garage and the river for thirty-five years. Invariably, at the end of the
shad season he is so tired he has to hole up in bed for a few days, and he
always resolves to stay put in the garage from then on—no man can
serve two masters—but when the eel season comes around he always
finds himself back on the river again.

The riverman I know best is an old-timer named Harry Lyons. Harry
is seventy-four, and has been around the river all his life. He lives with
his wife, Mrs. Juel Lyons, in a two-story frame-and-fieldstone house
backed up against the base of the Palisades, on Undercliff Avenue, in
the upper part of Edgewater. He owns a shad barge and an assortment
of boats, and keeps them anchored just off the riverbank, a few minutes' walk from his house. Harry is five feet six, and weighs a hundred
and fifty. He is one of those short, hearty, robust men who hold themselves erect and swagger a little and are more imposing than many
taller, larger men. He has an old-Roman face. It is strong-jawed and
prominent-nosed and bushy-eyebrowed and friendly and reasonable
and sagacious and elusively piratical. Ordinarily, down on the riverfront,
he looks like a beachcomber: he wears old pants and a windbreaker and

old shoes with slashes cut in them, and he goes bareheaded and his hair sticks straight up. One day, however, by chance, I ran into him on a River Road bus, and he was on his way to a funeral down in Weehawken, and he was wearing his Sunday clothes and his hair was brushed and his face was solemn, and I was surprised at how distinguished he looked; he looked worldly and cultivated and illustrious.

Harry spends a large part of his time wandering up and down the riverfront looking at the river, or sitting on his barge looking at the river, but he isn't lazy. He believes in first things first; if there is anything at home or on the barge that should be attended to, he goes ahead and attends to it, and then sits down. He is handy with tools, and has a variety of skills. He is a good fisherman, a good netmaker, a fairly good carpenter, a fairly good all-round mechanic, and an excellent fish cook. He is especially good at cooking shad, and is one of the few men left who know how to run an old-fashioned Hudson River shad bake. Shad bakes are gluttonous springtime blowouts that are held in the middle or latter part of the shad season, generally under the trees on the riverbank, near a shad barge. They are given by lodges and labor unions, and by business, social, political, and religious organizations, and by individuals. Former Mayor Wissel—he was Mayor of Edgewater for thirty years—used to give one every year for the public officials in Edgewater and nearby towns.

When Harry is engaged to run a bake, he selects a sufficient number of roe shad from his own nets and dresses them himself and takes the roes out of them. He has a shad boner come up from Fulton Fish Market and bone them. Then, using zinc roofing nails, he nails them spread-eagle fashion to white-oak planks, one fish to a plank; the planks are two feet long, a foot and a half wide, and an inch thick, and have adjustable props fixed to their sides so that it is possible to stand them upright or tilt them backward. He nails two or three strips of bacon across each fish. When it is time to cook the fish—they aren't baked, they are broiled—he props the planks up, fish-side foremost, in a ring around a bed of charcoal that has been burning on the ground for hours and is red-hot and radiant. He places the planks only six inches or so from the coals, but he gradually moves them farther back, so that the fish will broil slowly and pick up the flavors of the bacon and the oak; they broil for almost an hour. Every so often, he takes a turn around the ring and thoroughly mops each fish with a cotton mop, which he keeps dipping into a pot of melted butter. While Harry looks after the shad, Mrs. Lyons looks after the roes, cooking them in butter in huge frying pans. Pickled beets and new potatoes boiled in their skins are usually served with the shad and the roe. Paper plates are used. The people eat on tables made of boards laid across sawhorses, and are encouraged to have several helpings. Cooked shad-bake style by an expert, shad is crusty on the outside and tender and rich and juicy on the inside (but not too rich, since a good deal of the oil has been broiled out of it), and fully justifies its scientific name, *Alosa sapidissima*, the *"Alosa"* of which means "shad" and the *"sapidissima"* of which means "good to eat to a superlative degree." Shad bakes require a lot of work, and most of them are small affairs. Some years, the New Jersey Police Chiefs' Association gives a big one. Some years, a group of boss fishmongers in Fulton Market gives a big one. Some years, the Palisades Interstate Park Commission gives a big one. The biggest on the river is one that Harry and Mrs. Lyons have been giving for over twenty years for the benefit of the building fund of Mrs. Lyons' church. This bake is held on the riverbank a short distance above the George Washington Bridge, usually on the Sunday following Mother's Day Sunday, and every year around two hundred and fifty people come to it.

Mrs. Lyons is a handsome, soft-spoken blond woman, quite a few years younger than Harry. She is a native of Fort Lee, the next town on the river north of Edgewater. Her maiden name was Kotze, her parents were Swiss-German, and she was brought up a Roman Catholic. When she was a young woman, out of curiosity, while visiting a friend in Brooklyn, she attended a meeting of a congregation of the Reorganized Church of Jesus Christ of Latter Day Saints, which is the oldest and most widespread of several schismatic branches of the Mormon religion. A number of prophecies and warnings from the Book of Mormon, an apocalyptic Mormon scripture, were read at the meeting, and she was deeply impressed by them. She borrowed a copy of the Book and studied it for some weeks, whereupon she left the Catholic Church and joined the Reorganized Church. The congregation with which she is affiliated holds its services in a hall in the Masonic Temple in Lyndhurst, New Jersey. Harry was brought up an Episcopalian, but he doesn't feel strongly about denominations—one is as good as another to him—and since his marriage he has gone regularly to the Reorganized Church services. Harry and his wife have one daughter, Audrey. She is a member of the Reorganized Church, and went to Graceland College, a junior college sponsored by the church, in Lamoni, Iowa. She is married to John Maxcy, who is a Buick salesman in Englewood, New Jersey, and they have two children—Michele, who is sixteen, and Brian, who is eleven.

Harry is generally supposed to know more about the river than any of the other rivermen, and a great deal of what he knows was handed down to him; his family has lived beside the river for a long time, and many of his ancestors on both sides were rivermen. He has old Dutch blood and old English blood, and gravestones of ancestors of his are all over the Edgewater Cemetery. He is related to several of the oldest families in New York and New Jersey. Through his mother, who was a Truax, he is a descendant of Philippe du Trieux, one of the first settlers of New York City. Du Trieux was a Walloon who lived in Amsterdam and who came to New Amsterdam in 1624 and built a house either on a lane that is now Beaver Street or on a lane that is now Pearl Street—the historians aren't sure which. A scholarly study of his descendants—the name has been spelled Truex or Truax for generations—was published in installments in *The New York Genealogical and Biographical Record* in 1926, 1927, and 1928. In this study, Harry is listed in the tenth generation of descent from du Trieux.

Harry was born in the upper part of Edgewater, in May, 1884. The house in which he was born is still standing; it is just up the street from the house he lives in now. He went to school in what people of his generation in Edgewater refer to as "the old schoolhouse." This was a wooden building on River Road, on a bluff above the river. It had only two rooms—one for the lower grades and one for the upper grades—and was torn down many years ago. I once heard several old-timers sitting around the barge stove in Ingold's garage get on the subject of the old schoolhouse. One of them, former Fire Chief Lasher, said that he had gone to it, and mentioned a number of men around town who had gone to it at the same time, among them Bill Ingold and Charlie Allison and Harry Lyons, and I asked him what kind of student Harry Lyons had been. "Oh, Harry was bright enough, but he was like the rest of us—he didn't apply himself," Chief Lasher said. "All he studied was the river. At recess, he'd race down to the river and fool around in the mud and attend to some old eelpot he had down there, or crab trap, or bait car, or whatever it was, and I've never in my life seen anybody get so muddy. He was famous for it. He'd get that sticky river mud all over him, and he wouldn't even try to get it off. Some days, when recess was over, he'd be so muddy the teacher wouldn't let him come back in— she'd send him home. I've been watching rivermen a long time, and they're all like that; they love the mud. Harry's nickname was Hotch. People in Edgewater used to have an expression, if they wanted to say that somebody or something was unusually muddy, they'd say that he or she or it was as muddy as Hotch Lyons. Once in a long while, you still hear somebody come out with that expression. I was standing in line at the A. & P. one day last summer and just ahead of me were two ladies my age. I went to school with them, and I remember them when they were little girls, and I remember them when they were young women, and I remember them when they were middle-aged women in the prime of life, and I imagine the same thought that crosses my mind when I look at them nowadays must also cross their minds when they look at me—How fast time flew! So we were standing there, and one of them turned to the other and said, 'The rain this morning beat down my tomato bushes, and I went out and tried to straighten them up, and I got as muddy as Hotch Lyons,' and all three of us burst out laughing. It brought back the old times."

Harry's father, William Masters Lyons, was an engineer on the Edgewater ferry. Harry was never as close to him as he was to his maternal grandfather, Isaac Truax, who was a riverman. "My father had a good disposition, but he was serious," Harry says. "My grandfather Truax would say things that were funny—at least, to me. He would mimic people and say awful things about them. When I was just a little tiny boy, I began to eat most of my meals at his house and follow him around. He was a great one for going out on the river in the wind and the rain and all kinds of weather, and I'd go along. And then, on a nice sunshiny day, when he should've been out on the river, he'd sit on the porch and read. He didn't have much education, and he didn't even think much of schools, but he had three books that he liked—two books of Shakespeare's writings that had come down to him from his father, and a big Bible with pictures in it that would lift the hair on your head— and he'd sometimes read things to me and explain them, or try to."

Mr. Truax shadfished, and set fykes. A fyke is a long, tunnel-like net that is set on or close to the bottom. It is held open by a series of wooden hoops; a pair of wings flaring out from its mouth guide fish into it; and it catches a little of everything. The spring when Harry was fifteen, Mr. Truax made an unusually large fyke and set it in an inshore channel of the river, off Fort Lee, and Harry quit school to help him operate it. "I decided it was about time for me to graduate from school," Harry says, "so I graduated out the back door." Once or twice a week, if fish prices were good in the city, Mr. Truax and Harry would empty the fyke and row or sail their catch down to one of the riverfront markets in lower Manhattan. Sometimes they would go to Gansevoort Market or Washington Market, on the Hudson, and sometimes they would keep on and go around the Battery to Fulton Market, on the East River. Mr. Truax owned a horse and wagon. If prices were poor, he and Harry would drive out in the country and sell their fish at farmhouses. "My grandfather knew all the fish-eating country people in this part of Bergen County," Harry says, "and they liked to see him coming down the road. If they didn't have any money to spend he'd swap them fish for anything they had, and we'd go home with a wide variety of country

produce in the wagon—sausage meat and headcheese and blood pud-
ding and hard cider and buttermilk and duck eggs and those good old
heavy yellow-fleshed strong turnipy-tasting turnips that they call ruta-
bagas, and stuff like that. One day, we drove up in a man's yard, and he
had just cut down a bee tree in the woods in back of his house, and we
swapped him a bucket of live eels for a quart of wild honey."

When Harry was nineteen, Mr. Truax gave up fishing with fykes
and began to depend entirely on what he made from shadfishing. For
ten years or so, Harry helped him fish a couple of rows of shad nets in
the spring, and worked the rest of the year at jobs he picked up on or
around the river. He worked mostly as a deckhand on tugboats. He
worked on two of the Valvoline Oil Company's tugs, the *Magnet* and
the *Magic Safety*, and on several of the tugs in the New York, New
Haven & Hartford's fleet. Mr. Truax died in 1913, aged eighty-four.
For three years thereafter, Harry fished a row of shad nets of his own
and set a fyke of his own. In 1915, he got married, and began to worry
about money for the first time in his life. In 1916, a fireman's job became
open in the Edgewater Fire Department, and he took it. Edgewater has
three firehouses. Firehouse No. 1, in which Harry was stationed, is on
River Road, a few yards north of the site of the old schoolhouse. It faces
the river, and it has a wooden bench in front of it. "Before I joined the
Fire Department," Harry once said, "my main occupation was sitting
down looking at the river. After I joined the department, that continued to be my main occupation, only I got paid for it." He was a fireman
for twenty-six years, and was allowed to take a leave of absence every
spring and fish a row of shad nets. He became eligible for a pension in
1942. On April 1st of that year, at the start of the shad season, he retired,
and resumed his life as a full-time riverman.

In the spring, Harry sets shad nets. In the fall, he sets eelpots. Some
days, he goes crabbing. Now and then, in every season, not for money
but for fun and for the table, he fishes with a hand line or a bamboo pole
or a rod and reel. He is an accomplished bait-caster, and it is a pleasure
to watch him stand on the bank and cast a knot of bloodworms to the
outer edge of the flats, out past the wrecks, and bring in a striped bass.
He isn't a striped-bass snob, however, and he often joins the old men
and women who come down to the river on sunny afternoons and pole-
fish from the bank for anything at all that will bite. Many of the old
men and women are opinionated and idiosyncratic, and he enjoys listening to them, and observing the odd rigs that they devise and the
imaginative baits that they use. Around Edgewater, catfish and tomcod
and lafayettes and eels are about the only fish that can be caught close to
the bank, but that is all right with Harry; he doesn't look down on any

of these fish. In common with most of the rivermen, he has a great liking for catfish; he likes to catch them and he likes to eat them. In the
spring and early summer, large numbers of catfish show up in the lower
Hudson; the spring freshets bring them down from fresh water. Some
are enormous. In 1953, one was caught near the George Washington
Bridge that weighed over thirty pounds, and every year a few are
caught around Edgewater that weigh between ten and twenty pounds.
One Saturday afternoon last spring, an old Negro woman fishing a
short distance up the bank from Harry caught two big ones, one right
after the other. Harry and several other fishermen went over to look at
them, and one of the fishermen, who had a hand scale, weighed them; the
first weighed seventeen pounds and the second weighed twelve. Harry
asked the old woman what kind of bait she had been using. "Chicken
guts," she said. Harry also has a great liking for tomcod. The tomcod is
a greedy little inshore fish that belongs to the cod family and resembles
the deep-sea codfish in every respect but size—it seldom gets much
longer that seven inches or weighs more than half a pound, and it gives
the appearance of being a midget codfish. It comes into the waters
around the city to feed and to spawn, and it is almost as ubiquitous as
the eel. There are a few tomcod in every part of the harbor every month
of the year. In the late fall and early winter, during their spawning runs,
they are abundant, and some days thousands upon thousands of them
are caught from piers and sea walls and bulkheads and jetties all the
way from Rockaway Point to the Battery, and from the banks of the
Hudson and the East River and the Harlem River and the Arthur Kill
and the Kill van Kull. They are eaten mainly in the homes of the people
who catch them; I have rarely seen them in fish stores, and have never
seen them on a menu. Harry thinks the tomcod is greatly undervalued;
it is what he calls a sweet-meated fish, and he considers it the best fish,
next to shad and snapper bluefish, that enters the river. "There's only
one thing wrong with tommycods," he once said. "It takes seventeen of
them to make a dozen." On sunny, crystal-clear mornings in the fall,
when it is possible to see into the water, he gets in one of his boats and
rows out into the flats and catches some river shrimp. River shrimp—
they are also called harbor shrimp and mud shrimp, and are really
prawns—are tiny; they are only about an inch and a quarter long, including the head. There are sometimes dense swarms of them in the
slues between the barges. Harry catches them with a dip net and emp-
ties them into a bucket. When he has a supply, he rows farther out into
the flats and ties up to one of the old wrecks and sits there and fishes for
tomcod, using a hand line and baiting the hook with the shrimp. Occasionally, he pops some of the shrimp into his mouth—he eats them raw

and spits out the shells. By noon, as a rule, he has all the tomcod he can use; he has often caught a hundred and fifty in a morning.

Every so often during January, February, and March, Harry gets up early and puts some sandwiches in his pockets and goes down to his barge and starts a fire in one of the stoves in it and spends the day working on his shadfishing gear. While the river wind hisses and purrs and pipes and whistles through cracks and knotholes in the sides of the barge, he paints an anchor, or overhauls an outboard motor, or makes one net out of the strongest parts of two or three old ones. He works in a leisurely fashion, and keeps a pot of coffee on the stove. Sometimes he goes over and sits beside a window and watches the traffic on the river for an hour or so. Quite often, in the afternoon, one of the other rivermen comes in and helps himself to a cup of coffee and sits down and gossips for a while. Harry's barge is a big one. It is a hundred and ten feet long and thirty-two feet wide. Except for narrow little decks at its bow and stern, it is covered with a superstructure made of heart-pine posts and white-pine clapboards. The superstructure is patched here and there with tar paper, and has a tar-paper roof. It is an old Delaware, Lackawanna & Western barge; on its sides are faded signs that say, "D L & W #530." It is forty-two years old. When it was thirty years old, a fire that broke out in some cargo damaged parts of its interior; the Lackawanna repaired it and used it for two more years, and then sold it to Harry. Harry has partitioned off two rooms in the bow end of it— one for a galley and one for a bunkroom. In the middle of the bunkroom is a statuesque old claw-footed Sam Oak stove. Around the stove are seven rickety chairs, no two of which are mates. One is a swivel chair whose spring has collapsed. Built against one of the partitions, in three tiers, are twelve bunks. Harry usually makes a fire in the Sam Oak stove and works in the bunkroom; there is a stove in the galley that burns bottled gas and is much easier to manage, but he feels more at home with the Sam Oak, which burns coal or wood. He sometimes uses driftwood that he picks up on the riverbank. The galley and the bunkroom take up less than a third of the space in the barge. The rest of the space is used for storage, and scattered about in it are oars and sweeps and hawsers and kerosene lanterns and shad-bake planks and tin tubs and blocks and tackles and cans of boat paint and sets of scales and stacks of fish boxes. Hanging in festoons from the rafters are dozens of nets, some of which are far too old and ripped and rotten ever to be put in the water again.

One day in late February, the weather was surprisingly sunny and warm. It was one of those balmy days that sometimes turn up in the winter, like a strange bird blown off its course. Walking back to my office after lunch, I began to dawdle. Suddenly the idea occurred to me, why not take the afternoon off and go over to Edgewater and go for a walk along the river and breathe a little clean air for a change. I fought a brief fight with my conscience, and then I entered the Independent subway at Forty-second Street and rode up to the 168th Street station and went upstairs to the Public Service bus terminal and got a No. 8 bus. This bus goes across the George Washington Bridge and heads south and runs through a succession of riverfront towns, the second of which is Edgewater. It is a pleasant trip in itself. At the town limits of Edgewater, there is a sign that says, "WELCOME TO EDGEWATER. WHERE HOMES AND INDUSTRY BLEND. EDGEWATER CHAMBER OF COMMERCE." A couple of bus stops past this sign, I got out, as I usually do, and began to walk along River Road. I looked at my watch; I had made good connections, and the trip from Forty-second Street had taken only thirty-six minutes. The sunshine was so warm that my overcoat felt burdensome. All along the west side of River Road, women had come out into their front yards and were slowly walking around, looking at the dead stalks and vines in their flower beds. I saw a woman squat sideways beside what must have been a bulb border and rake away some leaves with her fingers. She peered at the ground for a few moments, and then swept the leaves back with one sweep of her hand. In the upper part of Edgewater, River Road is high above the river, and a steep, wooded slope lies between the east side of it and the riverbank. Just past the George Washington School, a public school on the site of the old schoolhouse, there is a bend in the road from which it is possible to look down almost on the tops of the shad barges drawn up close to the riverbank along there. I looked the barges over, and picked out Harry's. Smoke was coming from its stovepipe, and I decided to stop by and have a cup of coffee with Harry. Several paths descend from the road to the riverbank. Children like to slide on them and play on them, and they are deeply rutted. As I started down one of them, Harry came out on the bow deck of his barge and looked up and saw me and waved. A few minutes later, I crossed the riverbank and went out on the ramshackle footwalk that extends from the riverbank to his barge and climbed the ladder that is fixed to the bow and stepped on deck, and he and I shook hands. "Go inside and get yourself a cup of coffee and bring it out here, why don't you," he said, "and let's sit in the sun a little while."

When I returned to the deck, Harry motioned toward the riverbank with his head and said, "Look who's coming." Two men had just started up the footwalk. One was a stranger to me. The other was an old friend and contemporary of Harry's named Joe Hewitt. I have run into him a number of times, and have got to know him fairly well. Mr.

Hewitt is six feet two and portly and red-faced. He lives in Fort Lee, but he is a native of Edgewater and belongs to one of the old Edgewater families. He went to school in the old schoolhouse at the same time as Harry, and fished and worked around the river for a few years, and then went to a business school on Park Row, in Manhattan, called the City Hall Academy. Through an uncle, who was in the trucking business and often trucked shad from Edgewater and other riverfront towns to Fulton Market during the shad season, he got a job as a clerk in the old Fulton Market firm of John Feeney, Inc. He became head bookkeeper in Feeney's, and subsequently worked for several other firms in the fish market. He retired over ten years ago. He spends a lot of time in Edgewater, and often hangs out in Ingold's garage. Years ago, Mr. Hewitt bought three tracts of cheap land along the Hackensack River, one in Hudson County and two in Bergen county; he speaks of them as "those mosquito bogs of mine." In recent years, two of these tracts have increased in value enormously, and he has sold sections of them for housing developments and shopping centers, and has become well-to-do. He is a generous man, and often goes out of his way to help people. Once in a while, a riverman gets in a bad jam of some kind and is broke to begin with and other rivermen take up a collection for him, and Mr. Hewitt almost always gives more than anyone else. However, despite his generosity and kindness, he has a bleak outlook on life, and doesn't try to hide it. "Things have worked out very well for you, Joe," I once heard another retired man remark to him one day in Ingold's garage, "and you ought to look at things a little more cheerful than you do." "I'm not so sure I have anything to be cheerful about," Mr. Hewitt replied. "I'm not so sure you have, either. I'm not so sure anybody has."

"Who is the man with Mr. Hewitt?" I asked Harry.

"I never saw him before," Harry said.

Mr. Hewitt came up the ladder first, and stepped on deck, puffing and blowing.

"The sun was so nice we decided to walk down from Fort Lee," he said, "and what a mistake that was! The traffic is getting worse and worse on River Road. Oh, it scares me! Those big heavy trucks flying past, it's worth your life to step off the curb. Slam on their brakes, they couldn't stop; you'd be in the hospital before they even slowed down. You'd be lying on the operating table with an arm off, an arm and a leg, an arm and a leg and one side of your head, and they'd still be rolling. And the noise they make! The shot and shell on the battlefield wouldn't be much worse. What was that old poem? How'd it go, how'd it go? I used to know it. 'In Flanders fields the poppies blow, between the crosses, row on row . . .' And good God, gentlemen, the Cadillacs! While we were standing there, wait-

ing and waiting for a chance to cross, six big black Cadillacs shot by, practically one right after the other, and it wasn't any funeral, either."

"Times are good, Joe," said Harry. "Times are good."

"Thieves," said Mr. Hewitt.

His companion reached the top of the ladder and awkwardly stepped
on deck. "Gentlemen," said Mr. Hewitt, "this is my brother-in-law Frank
Townsend." He turned to Harry. "Harry," he said, "you've heard me
speak of Frank. He's Blanche's younger brother, the one who's in the
sprinkler-system business. Or was. He's retired now." He turned to me.
"Blanche is my wife," he said. Then he turned to Mr. Townsend. "Sit
down, Frank," he said, "and get your breath." Mr. Townsend sat down on
a capstan. "Frank lives in Syracuse," continued Mr. Hewitt. "He's been
down in Florida, and he's driving back, and he's spending a few days with
us. Since he retired, he's got interested in fishing. I told him the shadfishermen all along the Hudson are getting ready for shad season, and he's never
seen a shad barge, and I thought I'd bring him down here and show him
one, and explain shadfishing to him."

Harry's eyebrows rose. "Shadfishing hasn't changed much through
the years, Joe," he said, "but it's been a long, long time since you lifted a
net. Maybe you better let me do the explaining."

"I wish you would," said Mr. Hewitt. "I was hoping you would."

"I'll make it as brief as possible," said Harry, walking over to the edge
of the deck. "Step over here, Mr. Townsend, and look over the side. Do
you see those poles lying down there in the mud? They're shagbark-
hickory poles, and they're fifty to seventy feet long, and they're the
foundation of shadfishing; everything else depends on them. During shad
season, we stick them up in the river in rows at right angles to the shore,
and hitch our nets to them. When the season's finished, we pull them up
and bring them in here in the flats and bed them in the mud on both sides
of our barges until we're ready to use them again. They turn green down
there, from the green slime, but that's all right—the slime preserves them.
As long as we keep them damp, they stay strong and supple and sound. If
we let them dry out, they lose their strength and their give and start to rot."

Mr. Townsend interrupted Harry. "How much do they cost you?"
he asked.

"Shad is an expensive fish, Mr. Townsend, not to speak of shad
roe," Harry said, "and one of the reasons is it's expensive to fish for. You
can't just pick up the phone and order a shad pole from a lumberyard.
You have to hunt all over everywhere and find a farmer who has some
full-grown hickory trees in his woods and is willing to sell some, and
even then he might not have any that are tall enough and straight
enough and strong enough and limber enough. I get mine from a

farmer who owns some deep woods in Pennsylvania. When I need some new ones, I go out there—in the dead of winter, usually, a couple of months before shad season starts—and spend the whole day tramping around in his woods looking at his hickories. And I don't just look at a tree—I study it from all sides and try to imagine how it would take the strain if it was one of a row of poles staked in the Hudson River holding up a shad net and the net was already heavy with fish and a full-moon tide was pushing against the net and bellying it out and adding more fish to it all the time. I study hundreds of them. Then I pick out the likeliest-looking ones and blaze them with an axe. The farmer cuts them down, and sends them up here on a trailer truck. Then I and a couple of men around the river go to work on them and peel their bark off and trim their knots off and smooth them down with adzes and drawknives and planes until there's no splinters or rough spots on them anywhere that the net could catch on. Then we sharpen their butt ends, to make it easier to drive them into the river bottom. I pay the farmer eighteen to twenty dollars apiece for them. After the trucking charges are added to that, and the wages of the men who help me trim them, I figure they cost me between thirty-five and forty dollars apiece. You need at least forty of them for every row you fish. Tugboats are always blundering into them at night and passing right over them and bending them down until they crack in two, so you also have to have a supply of spares set aside. In other words, the damned things run into money."

Some young girls—there were perhaps a dozen of them, and they were eight or nine or maybe ten years old—had come down one of the paths from River Road, and now they were chasing each other around on the riverbank. They were as overexcited as blue jays, and their fierce, jubilant, fresh young voices filled the air.

"School's out," said Harry.

Several of the girls took up a position near the shore end of the footwalk to Harry's barge. Two of them started turning a rope and singing a rope-jumping song, a third ran in and started jumping the rope, and the others got in line. The song began:

> "*Mama, Mama,*
> *I am ill.*
> *Send for the doctor*
> *To give me a pill.*
> *Doctor, Doctor,*
> *Will I die?*
> *Yes, my child,*
> *And so will I—*"

Mr. Hewitt looked at them gloomily. "They get louder every year," he said.

"I like to hear them," said Harry. "It's been sixty years since I was in school, but I know exactly how they feel. Now, Mr. Townsend, to get back to shadfishing," he continued, "the first thing a man starting out as a shadfisherman has to have is a supply of poles, and the next thing he has to have is a row—that is, a place in the river where he can stake his poles year after year. In the old days, a man could pretty much decide for himself where his row should be, just so he didn't get too close to another man's row or get out in a ship channel or interfere with access to a pier. However, the shipping interests and the tugboat interests were always complaining that the shadfishermen acted as if they owned the river, and vice versa, so the Army Engineers finally stepped in. The Engineers have jurisdiction over all the navigable rivers in the country, insofar as the protection of navigation is concerned. About twenty years ago, just before World War Two, they went out and made a study of the Hudson from the standpoint of shadfishing versus navigation, and the outcome was they abolished some of the rows and left some right where they were and moved some and laid out a few new ones. Every year, they re-survey the rows, and some years they move or abolish one or two more. The best rows are in what's called the lower river—the section from the mouth of the river, down at the Battery, to the east-and-west boundary line between New Jersey and New York, which is about twenty miles up. Now, all the way up to this point the north-and-south boundary line between the two states is the middle of the river, and it so happens that all this distance all the shad rows are in the half of the river that belongs to New Jersey—there can't be any over in the New York half, because the main ship channel is in it. At present, there are fifty-five of these rows. The first row is off the big New York Central grain elevator in the railroad yards in Weehawken, about on a level with Sixtieth Street in Manhattan. It's a short row, only five hundred feet across, and it's entirely too near the ocean-liner traffic to suit me. Now and then, a big Cunarder or a Furness Line boat or a Swedish American Line boat will back out of one of the piers in the Fifties, and when she gets out in the river she'll keep on backing to get in position to go down the channel, and her backwash will hit the first row and churn the net up and down and whip it against the poles and empty the fish out of it. Some days, the backwash of those boats can be felt practically all the way to Albany. The fifty-fifth row is off the village of Alpine, which is about on a level with Yonkers and just below the east-and-west boundary line. Up above this line, the whole river belongs to New York, and the New York shadfishermen take over. Some of them fish the same as we do, in rows, with nets hitched to poles, but most of them fish with nets that they drift from boats. Their rows aren't as good as ours. One reason is, you're bound to catch more fish if you have the first crack at them. And another reason is, the sooner shad are caught after they leave the sea—or, a plainer way of putting it, the less time they spend in the river water—the better they taste and the more they're worth. The Engineers have the say-so as to where a row can be placed, but the Conservation Department of the state in whose waters the row is located has the say-so as to who can fish it. The New Jersey rows don't change hands very often; once a man gets one, he can renew his rights to it every year, and he generally holds on to it until he dies, and then it goes to whoever's next on the waiting list. You don't rent a row—what you do is, every year you take out a license for each row you fish, and a license costs twenty-five dollars. Most of the rows off Edgewater and Weehawken are very old. One of the Edgewater rows has been fished for at least a hundred and fifty years, and maybe a good while longer. A man named Bill Ingold fishes it now, but it's still called the Truax row, after my grandfather, Isaac Truax, who fished it for many years. When my grandfather had it, it was called the Scott row, after the man who had it ahead of him. I've heard the name of the man who had it ahead of Scott and the name of the man who had it ahead of him, but they've faded out of my mind. I've got two rows in my name. They're the first two rows north of the George Washington Bridge. They're both twelve-hundred-foot rows, which is the length of most of the rows. The last few years, I've been fishing only one of them the whole season through. It's the lower one. If you ever drive over the bridge on the westbound roadway during shad season, look up the river a little ways and you'll see my poles."

Mr. Townsend had grown tired of standing, and he sat back down on the capstan.

"Sometime in the latter half of March," continued Harry, "I and three or four men that I swap labor with get together and move this barge up the river. They help me move mine, I help them move theirs; they help me stake my poles, I help them stakes theirs. We tie the barge to a launch owned by one of the men and tow her up on the tide, and take her to a point beside the riverbank half a mile or so above the bridge, where she'll be convenient to both my rows. We run a hawser from that capstan you're sitting on to a tree on the bank and draw her up close to the bank, with the bow facing the bank, and then we anchor her with three anchors—port, starboard, and stern. She stays there for the duration of shad season. Then we get out on the bank and put up a rack to mend nets on and a gallows to hang a set of scales on. The land

along there is owned by the Palisades Interstate Park, and a shadfisherman pays rent for the space he uses on the riverbank on the basis of how
many rows he fishes—the rate is two hundred dollars a row for the season. Then we go back to the flats and start snaking my poles out of the
mud and loading them on a peculiar-looking kind of craft called a double boat. A double boat consists of two forty-foot scows connected together side by side but with a narrow space left in between them. It
resembles a raft, as much as it resembles anything. When we get it loaded,
we tow it up the river on the tide, the same as we towed the barge, and
then we start staking the poles. Until a few years ago, this was a job
shadfishermen dreaded. We'd anchor the double boat over the place we
wanted the pole to go, and we'd stand the pole up in the narrow in-
between space I mentioned, to keep it steady. Then we'd lash a crosspiece on the pole, and two men, the heavier the better, would climb up
and stand on the crosspiece and hold on to the pole and bend their
knees and make a kind of jumping motion, keeping time with each
other, until they drove the butt end of the pole into the river bottom.
Sometimes they'd have to jump for hours to get a pole down far
enough. Sometimes more weight would be needed and two more men
would get up on the crosspiece. The two on the inside would hold on to
the pole and the two on the outside would hold on to the two on the inside, and they'd jump and grunt and jump and grunt, and it was a
strange sight to watch, particularly to people watching it from shore
who didn't have the slightest idea what was going on out there. Shad
poles are spaced from twenty-five to thirty feet apart, and you have to
put down from forty-one to forty-nine poles on a twelve-hundred-foot
row, counting the outside poles, so you can just imagine the jumping we
used to have to do. Nowadays, it's much simpler. We have a winch sitting on a platform in the middle of the double boat, and we simply
stand the pole in place and put a short length of chain around it up toward its upper end and hook a cable from the winch onto the chain, and
the winch exerts a powerful downward pull on the chain and forces the
butt end of the pole into the bottom.

"By the last week in March, the shad barges are in place all along
the Hudson and the shad poles are up. There's a number of old retired
or half-retired sea cooks and tugboat cooks in Edgewater and Weehawken, and they come out of retirement around this time and take
jobs as cooks on shad barges. They work on the same barges year after
year. As soon as the cooks get situated in the galleys, the shadfishermen
start living aboard. Around the same time, men start showing up in
Edgewater who haven't been seen in town since last shad season. You
need highly skilled fishermen to handle shad nets, and for many years

there hasn't been enough local help to go around, so every spring fisher-men from other places come and take the jobs. A shadfisherman gener-ally hires from two to five of them for each row he fishes, and pays them a hundred or so a week and bunk and board. Most of them are Norwe-gians or Swedes. Some come from little ports down in South Jersey, such as Atlantic Highlands, Port Monmouth, Keyport, Point Pleasant, and Wildwood. In other seasons, they do lobstering or pound-fishing, or go out on draggers or scallopers. Some come from a small dragger fleet that works out of Mill Basin, in Brooklyn. Some come from Fulton Mar-ket—old fishermen who work as fillet cutters and go back to fishing only during shad season. Some don't come from any particular place, but roam all over. One man didn't show up in Edgewater year before last, the best man with a shad net I ever saw, and last year he did show up, and I asked him where he'd been. 'I worked my way home on a tanker to see my sis-ter,' he said, and by 'home' he meant some port in Norway, 'and then I worked on a Norwegian sealer that hunted harp seals along the coast of Labrador, and then I worked my way back here on a tanker, and then I worked awhile in the shrimp fleet in Galveston, Texas, and the last few months I worked on a bait-clam dredge in Sheepshead Bay.' They know how to do almost any kind of commercial fishing—and if they don't they can pick it up between breakfast and lunch and do it better by supper than the ones who taught them. When they come aboard a barge, all they ever have with them is an old suitcase in one hand and an old sea bag slung over one shoulder that they carry their boots and oilskins in, and they seldom say much about themselves. In times past, there were quite a few rummies among them, real old thirty-second-degree rummies, but the rummies seem to have dropped by the wayside. Oh, there's a few left.

"Every year, on one of the last days in March or one of the first days in April, the shad start coming in from the sea. They enter the mouth of the harbor, at Sandy Hook, and straggle around awhile in the Lower Bay, and then they go through the Narrows and cross the Upper Bay and enter the mouth of the Hudson and head for their spawning grounds. There are several of these grounds. The main one begins eighty miles up the river, up around Kingston, and extends to Coxsackie—a distance of twenty-five miles. This stretch of the river has a great many sandbars in it, and creek mouths and shallow coves and bays. As a rule, shad are four years old when they make their first trip in, and they keep on coming in once every year until their number is up. You can take a scale off a shad and look at the scars on it and tell how many times the shad has spawned, and every season we see quite a few who managed to escape our nets as many as five or six times and go up and spawn before

they finally got caught, not to speak of the fact that they managed to
keep from being eaten by some other fish all those years. Roe shad average around three and a half to four pounds, and bucks average around two
and a half to three. The roes are always heavier. Once in a while, we see a
seven-pound roe, or an eight-pounder, or a nine-pounder. I caught one
once that weighed thirteen and a half pounds."

"Just think how many fish she must've spawned in her time," said
Mr. Townsend. "If it had been me that caught her, I'd've patted her on
the back and put her back in."

"A commercial fisherman is supposed to catch fish, Mr. Townsend,
not put them back in," Harry said. "Anyway, as a matter of fact, I killed
her getting her loose from the net. The shad won't come into the river
until the temperature of the river water reaches forty degrees or thereabouts, and that's what we watch for. Day after day, when the water
starts approaching this temperature, we go out just before every flood
tide and hang a short net called a jitney in the spaces between several
poles toward the far end of the row. This is a trial net. The shad may
start trickling in, only three or four showing up on each tide, and continue that way for days, or avalanches of them may start coming in all at
once, but as soon as we find the first ones in the trial net, however many
there are, even if there's only one, we go to work in earnest. Just before
the next flood tide begins, I and two or three of the hired fishermen take
a regular-sized net out to the row in a shad boat. A shad boat is fifteen
to twenty feet long and high and sharp in the bow and low and square
and roomy in the stern. It has a well in its bottom, up forward, in which
to sit an outboard motor—although you can row it if you want to—and
it's unusually maneuverable. We have the net piled up in the stern, and
we work our way across the downriver side of the row, and go from
pole to pole, feeding the net out and letting the bottom of it sink and tying the top of it to the poles. It's like putting up a fence, only it's an underwater fence. Where my row is, the water ranges in depth from
twenty to thirty feet, and I use a net that's twenty feet deep. The net has
iron rings sewed every few feet along the bottom of it to weight it down
and hold it down. In addition, on each end of it, to anchor it, we tie a
stone called a dropstone. Several blocks north of here, there's a ravine
running down from River Road to the riverbank. In the middle of the
ravine is a brook, and beside the brook is an old abandoned wagon road
all grown over with willow trees and sumac and sassafras and honey-
suckle and poison ivy. Years ago, the main business of Edgewater was
cutting paving blocks for New York City, and wagons carrying loads of
these blocks to a dock on the riverbank used to come down this road. It

was a rocky road, and you can still see ruts that the wheel rims wore in the rocks. Through the years, a good many paving blocks bounced off the wagons and fell in the brook, and the drivers were too lazy to pick them up, and that's where we get our dropstones. If we lose one in the river, we go up with a crowbar and root around in the mud and tree roots and rusty tin cans in the bed of the brook and dig out another one. Some of us have a notion the blocks are lucky. I wouldn't think of using any other kind of dropstone.

"By the time we have the net hung all the way across, the flood tide is in full flow, pushing and pressing against the net and bellying it out in the spaces between the poles. We go on back to the barge and leave the net to take care of itself for the duration of the tide. If enough shad to amount to anything come up the river in the tide, some of them are bound to hit it. They'll either hit it head on and stick their heads in the meshes and gill themselves or they'll hit it sideways and tangle themselves in it and the tide will hold them against it the way the wind holds a scrap of paper against a fence. In this part of the river, the tide runs from three and a half to six hours, according to the time of the month and the strength and direction of the wind, and it runs faster on the bottom than it does on the top, and it'll trick you. When we judge it's getting on toward the time it should start slowing down, we go back out to the row in the shad boat and get ready to lift the net. Quite often, we're way too early, and have to stop at the first pole and sit there in the boat with our hands in our laps and bide our time. We might sit there an hour. If it's during the day, we sit and look up at the face of the Palisades, or we look at the New York Central freight trains that seem to be fifteen miles long streaking by on the New York side, or we look downriver at the tops of the skyscrapers in the distance. I've never been able to make up my mind about the New York skyline. Sometimes I think it's beautiful, and sometimes I think it's a gaudy damned unnatural sight. If it's in the nighttime, we look at that queer glare over midtown Manhattan that comes from the lights in Times Square. On cold, clear nights in April, sitting out on the river in the dark, that glare in the sky looks like the Last Judgment is on the way, or the Second Coming, or the end of the world. Every little while, we stick an oar straight into the water and try to hold it there, to test the strength of the tide. We have to time things very carefully. We want the net to stay down and catch fish as long as possible, but if we wait too long to get started the tide will begin to ebb before we get across the row, and belly the net in the opposite direction, and dump the fish out. I sit beside the outboard motor and handle the boat, and I usually have three fishermen aboard. When I give the signal to let's get going, two of the fishermen stand up side by side in the stern, and one unties the net at the first pole. Then, while one holds on to the top of the net, the other pulls the bottom of it up to the top—that's called pursing it. Then they start drawing it into the boat, a little at a time. The third man stands a few feet farther back, and helps wherever he's needed most. We proceed from pole to pole, untying the net and drawing it in. As it comes aboard, the men shake it and jerk it and twitch it and seesaw it and yank it this way and that, and the fish spill out of it and fall to the bottom of the boat. The men tear a lot of holes in the net that way, but it can't be helped. As the net piles up in the stern, the fish pile up amidships. When we get to the end of the row, if we've had a good lift, we'll have over a thousand shad piled up amidships, bucks and roes all jumbled together, flipping and flopping and beating the air with their tails, each and every one of them fit to be cooked by some great chef at the Waldorf-Astoria and served on the finest china, and the boat'll almost be awash. I must've seen a million shad in my time, and I still think they're beautiful—their thick bodies, their green backs, their silver sides, their sawedged bellies, the deep forks in their tails. The moment we draw in the end of the net, we turn about and head for the riverbank. We beach the boat, and all four of us grab hold of the net—it's dripping wet and heavy as lead—and heave it onto a kind of low-sided box with four handles on it called a net box. We carry this up on the bank, and spread the net on the net rack. Then, while one man starts picking river trash out of the net and mending it and getting it ready for the next flood tide, I and the two other men unload the fish and sort them and weigh them and pack them in wooden boxes, a hundred or so pounds to a box. The roes bring a much higher price than the bucks, and we pack them separately. I write my name on each box with a black crayon, and below it I write 'A. & S.' That stands for Ackerly & Sandiford, the wholesale firm in Fulton Market that I ship to. There's always some trucker over here who understands shadfishing and makes a business every spring of trucking shad to market. Joe's uncle, old Mr. John Hewitt, used to do it years ago, first with a dray, then with a truck. In recent years, a man named George Indahl has been doing it. Usually, about the time we get through boxing a lift, one of his trucks comes down the little one-lane dirt road that runs along the riverbank up where I anchor my barge, and the driver stops and picks up my boxes. Then he goes on down the line and stops at the next shadfisherman's place, and keeps on making stops until he has a load, and then he high-tails it for South Street."

"South Street is the main street in Fulton Market, Frank," Mr. Hewitt said to Mr. Townsend. "Most of the fishmongers have their stands on it. There's an old saying in the market, 'When the shad are running in the Hudson, South Street is bloody.' "

"My place on the riverbank is kind of hard to get to, although you can see it from the bridge," Harry continued, "but the first few days of shad season, every time we come in with a lift, we find a little crowd standing there. They're mostly old men. They stand around and watch us bring the fish ashore and sort them and box them, and the sight of the shad seems to do them good. Some are old men from Edgewater and Fort Lee. Others are old men I never see any other time. They show up year after year, and I say hello to them and shake hands, but I don't know their names, let alone where they come from. I don't even know if they come from New Jersey or New York. Several have been coming for so many years that I tell them to wait until the others have gone, and I give them a shad, a roe shad. They're well-to-do-looking men, some of them, and could probably buy me and sell me, but they bring a newspaper to wrap their fish in and a paper bag to carry it in, and the way they thank me, you'd think I was giving them something really valuable. One of them, who'd been showing up every spring for years and years with his paper bag all neatly folded in his overcoat pocket, didn't show up last spring. 'The poor old boy, whoever he was,' I said to myself, when I happened to think of him, 'he didn't last the winter.' Day by day, the little crowd gets smaller and smaller, and after the first week or so only an occasional person shows up, and things settle down to a routine. Not that they get dull. Lifting a shad net is like shooting dice—you never get tired of seeing what comes up. One lift, we may get only two or three fish all the way across; next lift, we may get a thousand. One lift, we may get mostly bucks; next lift, roes may outnumber bucks three to one. And shad aren't the only fish that turn up in a shad net. We may find a dozen big catfish lying in the belly of the net, or a couple of walleyed pike, or some other kind of fresh-water fish. A freshet brought them down, and they were making their way back up the river, and they hit the net. Or we may find some fish that strayed in from the ocean on a strong tide—bluefish or blackfish or fluke or mossbunkers or goosefish, or a dozen other kinds. Or we may find some ocean fish that run up the river to spawn the same as shad, such as sea sturgeon or alewives or summer herring. Sea sturgeon are the kind of sturgeon whose roe is made into caviar. Some of them get to be very old and big. Going up the river, they keep leaping out of the water, and suddenly, at least once every season, one of them leaps out of the water right beside my boat, and it's so big and long and ugly and covered all over with warts that it scares me—it might be eight, nine, ten, or eleven feet long and weigh a couple of hundred pounds. We get quite a few of the young ones in our nets, and now and then, especially during the latter part of the season, we lift the net and there's a gaping big hole in it, and we know that a full-grown one came up the river sometime during the tide, an old-timer, and hit the net and went right through it. Several years ago, an eighty-one-pounder hit the net sideways while we were lifting it, and began to plunge around in it, and it was as strong as a young bull, but the men braced themselves and took a firm grip on the net and held on until it wore itself out, and then they pulled it aboard.

"The bulk of the shad go up the river between the middle of April and the middle of May. Around the middle of May, we begin to see large numbers of what we call back-runners coming down the river—shad that've finished spawning and are on their way back to sea. We don't bother them. They eat little or nothing while they're on their spawning runs, and by this time they're so feeble and emaciated they can just barely make it. If we find them in our nets, we shake them back into the water. Shad keep right on coming into the river until around the end of June, but during May the price goes lower and lower, and finally they aren't worth fishing for. In the last week in May or the first week in June, we pull up our poles and move our barges back to the flats.

"The young shad stay up on the spawning grounds through the summer. In October and the early part of November, when the water starts getting cold, they come down the river in huge schools and go out to sea. Way up in November, last year, they were still coming down. One morning, a week or so before Thanksgiving, I was out in the flats, tied up to an old wreck, fishing for tomcod, and all of a sudden the water around my boat became alive with little shad—pretty little silver-sided things, three to five inches in length, flipping right along. I dropped a bucket over the side and brought up half a dozen of them, and they were so lively they made the water in the bucket bubble like seltzer water. I looked at them a few minutes, and then I poured them back in the river. 'Go on out to sea,' I said to them, 'and grow up and get some flesh on your bones, and watch yourselves and don't get eaten by other fish, and four years from now, a short distance above the George Washington Bridge,' I said, 'maybe our paths will cross again.' "

Mr. Townsend and Mr. Hewitt and I had been listening closely to Harry, and none of us had paid any further attention to the young girls jumping rope on the riverbank. Shortly after Harry stopped talking, all of us became aware at the same moment that the girls turning the rope were singing a new song. Just then, the girl jumping missed a jump, and another girl ran in to take her place, whereupon the girls turning the rope started the new song all over again. Their voices were rollicking, and they laughed as they sang. The song began:

> *"The worms crawl in,*
> *The worms crawl out.*
> *They eat your guts*
> *And spit them out.*
> *They bring their friends*
> *And their friends' friends, too.*
> *And there's nothing left*
> *When they get through . . ."*

Harry laughed. "They've changed it a little," he said. "That line used to go, 'And you look like hell when they get through.' "

" 'The worms crawl in, the worms crawl out. They play pinochle on your snout,' " said Mr. Townsend. "That's the way I remember it. 'One little worm who's not so shy crawls up your nose and out your eye.' That's another line I remember."

"Let's go inside," said Mr. Hewitt. "It's getting cold out here. We'll all catch pneumonia."

"You know what they used to say about pneumonia, Joe," Harry said. " 'Pneumonia is the old man's friend.' "

"A lot of what they used to say," said Mr. Hewitt, "could just as well've been left unsaid."

Stopping, he stepped from the deck into the passageway of the barge and walked past the galley and into the bunkroom, and the rest of us followed. There is a bulletin board on the partition that separates the bunkroom from the storage quarters beyond. Tacked on it are mimeographed notices dating back ten years concerning new shadfishing regulations or changes in old ones—some from the Corps of Engineers, United States Army, and some from the Division of Fish and Game, Department of Conservation and Economic Development, State of New Jersey. Also tacked on the bulletin board is a flattened-out pasteboard box on which someone has lettered with boat paint: "OLD FISHERMEN NEVER DIE—THEY JUST SMELL THAT WAY." Tacked on the partition to the right of the bulletin board are several Coast and Geodetic charts of the river and the harbor. Tacked to the left of it are a number of group photographs taken at shad bakes run by Harry. One photograph shows a group of fishmongers from Fulton Market lined up in two rows at a shad bake on the riverbank, and Mr. Hewitt himself is in the second row. The fishmongers are looking straight at the camera. Several are holding up glasses of beer. All have big smiles on their faces. Mr. Hewitt went over to this photograph and began to study it. Mr. Townsend and I sat down in chairs beside the stove. Harry opened the stove door and punched up the fire with a crowbar. Then he sat down.

"Oh, God, Harry," said Mr. Hewitt after he had studied the photograph awhile, "it was only just a few short years ago this picture was made, and a shocking number of the fellows in it are dead already. Here's poor Jimmy McBarron. Jimmy was only forty-five when he died, and he was getting along so well. He was president of Wallace, Keeney, Lynch, one of the biggest firms in the market, and he had an interest in a shrimp company in Florida. And here's Mr. John Matthews, who was secretary-treasurer of Chesebro Brothers, Robbins & Graham. He was a nice man. A little stiff and formal for the fish market. 'How do you do, Mr. Hewitt?' he used to say to me, when everybody else in the market called me Joe, even the lumpers on the piers. And here's Matt Graham, who was one of the partners in the same firm. A nicer man never lived than Matt Graham. He went to work in the market when he was fifteen years of age, and all he ever knew was fish, and all he ever wanted to know was fish."

"I used to ship to him," said Harry. "I shipped to him when he was with Booth Fisheries, long before he went with Chesebro. I shipped him many a box of shad, and he always treated me fair and square."

Mr. Hewitt continued to stare at the photograph.

"This one's alive," he said. "This one's dead. This one's alive. At least, I haven't heard he's dead. Here's Drew Radel, who was president of the Andrew Radel Oyster Company, planters and distributors of Robbins Island oysters. He died only last year. Sixty-five, the paper said. I had no idea he was that far along. I ran into him the summer before he died, and he looked around fifty. He's one man I can honestly say I never heard a bad word spoken about him. Here's a man who kept books for companies all over the market, the same as I did. He worked for Frank Wilkisson and Eastern Commission and George M. Still and Middleton, Carman and Lockwood & Winant and Caleb Haley and Lester & Toner and Blue Ribbon, and I don't know how many others— a real old-fashioned floating bookkeeper. I ate lunch across from him at the front table in Sloppy Louie's two or three times a week year in and year out, and now I can't even think of his name. Eddie Something-or-Other. He's still alive, last I heard. Retired. Lives in Florida. His wife had money; he never saved a cent. Grows grapefruit, somebody said. If I felt I had to grow something, by God, it wouldn't be grapefruit. This man's alive. So's this man. Dead. Dead. Dead. Three in a row. Alive. Alive. Alive. Dead. Alive. And here's a man, I won't mention his name and I shouldn't tell about this, but a couple of years ago, when I saw in the *New York Times* that he was dead, the thought flashed into my mind, 'I do hope they bury him in Evergreen Cemetery.' "

He turned away from the photograph, and came over and sat down.

"And I'll tell you the reason that particular thought flashed into my mind," he said. "This fellow was the biggest woman chaser in the market, and one of the biggest talkers on the subject I ever heard. When he and I were young men in the market together, he used to tell me about certain of his experiences along that line out in Brooklyn, where he lived. Tell *me*—hell! he told everybody that would listen. At that time, Trommer's Brewery was the finest brewery in Brooklyn. It was at the corner of Bushwick Avenue and Conway Street, and out in front of it was a beer garden. The brewery maintained the beer garden, and it was a show place. They had tables in the open, and a large restaurant indoors with at least a dozen big potted palms stood up in it. During the summer, they had a German orchestra that played waltz music. And directly across the street from the beer garden was the main gate of Evergreen Cemetery. After a burial, it was customary for the mourners to stop in Trommer's beer garden and drown their sorrow in Trommer's White Label and rejoice in the fact that it was the man or the woman they'd left out in the cemetery's turn to go, and not theirs. On Sundays, people would take the streetcar out to the cemetery and visit the graves of relatives and friends, and then they'd go over to Trommer's beer garden for sandwiches and beer. Now this fellow I'm talking about, he used to dress up on Sundays and go out to the cemetery and walk up and down the cemetery paths until he found some young widow out there by herself visiting her husband's grave, and she didn't have to be too damned young, and he'd go over and get acquainted with her and sympathize with her, and she'd cry and he'd cry, and then he'd invite her over to Trommer's beer garden, and they'd sit there and have some beers and listen to the music and talk, and one thing would lead to another."

Mr. Hewitt leaned over and opened the stove door and spat on the red-hot coals. "To hear him tell it," he said, "he was hell on widows. He knew just what to say to them."

"Did this gentleman ever get married himself?" asked Mr. Townsend. He sounded indignant.

"He was married twice," said Mr. Hewitt. "A year or two before he died, he divorced his first wife and married a woman half his age."

"I hope some man came up to her in the cemetery when she was visiting his grave and got acquainted with her and sympathized with her," Mr. Townsend said, "and one thing led to another."

Mr. Hewitt had lost interest in this turn of the conversation. "It's highly unlikely she ever visited his grave," he said.

Mr. Townsend shrugged his shoulders. "Ah, well," he said. "In that case."

Mr. Hewitt got up and went over and scrutinized the photograph again. "I look a lot older now than I did when this picture was made," he said, "and there's no denying that." He continued to scrutinize the photograph for a few more minutes, and then returned to his chair.

"When I was young," he said, "I had the idea death was for other people. It would happen to other people but not to me. That is, I couldn't really visualize it happening to me. And if I did allow myself to think that it would happen to me, it was very easy to put the thought out of my mind—if it had to take place, it would take place so far in the distant future it wasn't worth thinking about, let alone worrying about, and then the years flew by, and now it's right on top of me. Any time now, as the fellow said, the train will pull into the station and the trip will be over."

"Ah, well," said Mr. Townsend.

"It seems to me it was only just a few short years ago I was a young man going back and forth to work," said Mr. Hewitt, "and the years flew by, they really flew by, and now I'm an old man, and what I want to know is, what was the purpose of it? I know what's going to take place one of these days, and I can visualize some of the details of it very clearly. There'll be one twenty-five-dollar wreath, or floral design, or whatever they call them now, and there'll be three or maybe four costing between twelve dollars and a half and fifteen dollars, and there'll be maybe a dozen running from five to ten dollars, and I know more or less what the preacher will say, and then they'll take me out to the Edgewater Cemetery and lay me beside my parents and my brothers and sisters and two of my grandparents and one of my great-grandparents, and I'll lie there through all eternity while the Aluminum Company factory goes put-put-put."

Harry laughed. "You make the Aluminum Company factory sound like a motorboat," he said.

"I don't go to funerals any more," said Mr. Townsend. "Funerals breed funerals."

"My grandfather used to like the word 'mitigate,'" Harry said. "He liked the sound of it, and he used it whenever he could. When he was a very old man, he often got on the subject of dying. 'You can't talk your way out,' he'd say, 'and you can't buy your way out, and you can't shoot your way out, and the only thing that mitigates the matter in the slightest is the fact that nobody else is going to escape. Nobody—no, not one.'"

"I know, I know," said Mr. Hewitt, "but what's the purpose of it?"

"You supported your wife, didn't you?" asked Harry. "You raised a family, didn't you? That's the purpose of it."

"That's no purpose," said Mr. Hewitt. "The same thing that's going to happen to me is going to happen to them."

"The generations have to keep coming along," said Harry. "That's all I know."

"You're put here," said Mr. Hewitt, "and you're allowed to eat and draw breath and go back and forth a few short years, and about the time you get things in shape where you can sit down and enjoy them you wind up in a box in a hole in the ground, and as far as I can see, there's no purpose to it whatsoever. I try to keep from thinking such thoughts, but the last few years almost everything I see reminds me of death and dying, and time passing, and how fast it passes. I drove through Shadyside the other day, and I noticed that some of those factories down there are getting real smoky-looking and patched up and dilapidated, and the thought immediately occurred to me, 'I'm older than most of those factories. I remember most of them when they were brand-new, and, good God, look at them now.' And to tell the truth, I'm pretty well patched up myself. I've maybe not had as many operations as some people, but I've had my share. Tonsils, adenoids, appendix, gall bladder, prostate. I wear false teeth, and I've worn them for years—'your dentures,' my dentist calls them; 'Oh, for God's sake,' I said to him, '*I* know what they are, and *you* know what they are.' And the last time I went to the eye doctor he prescribed two pairs of glasses, one for ordinary use and one for reading, and I can't really see worth a damn out of either one of them. I've got varicose veins from walking around on wet cement floors in Fulton Market all those years, and I have to wear elastic stockings that are hell to get on and hell to get off and don't do a damned bit of good, and I've got fallen arches and I have to wear some kind of patented arch supports that always make me feel as if I'm about to jump, and I've never known the time I didn't have corns—corns and bunions and calluses."

"Oh, come on, Joe," said Harry. "Don't you ever get tired talking about yourself?"

A shocked look appeared on Mr. Hewitt's face. "I wasn't talking about myself, Harry," he said, and his voice sounded surprised and hurt. "I was talking about the purpose of life."

Harry started to say something, and then got up and went out to the galley. It had become too warm, and I went over and opened the window. I put my head out of the window and listened for a few moments to the lapping of the water against the side of the barge. Two of Harry's shad boats moored to stakes in the flats were slowly shifting their positions, and I could see that the tide was beginning to change. I heard the click of the refrigerator door in the galley, and then Harry returned to the bunkroom, bringing four cans of beer. He paused for a moment in front of Mr. Hewitt. "I'm sorry I said that, Joe," he said. "I was just trying to get your mind on something else." Then he stood the cans on the bunkroom table and started opening them. "As far as I'm concerned," he said, "the purpose of life is to stay alive and to keep on staying alive as long as you possibly can."

Calvin Trillin

Writing for *The New Yorker* must be fun. Look at some of the topics Calvin Trillin has taken up: booking acts for a performing arts series; a camp for children with cancer and serious blood disorders; how the royalties get distributed from the song "Why Do Fools Fall in Love?"; food; travel; murder; politics; humor; and cultural analysis. Trillin began working for *The New Yorker* in 1963. Since then he has written dozens of articles for *The New Yorker* and *The Nation* and has published thirteen books.

 Many writers and readers consider Trillin one of the best reporters in print. Even his food articles are cultural portraits—all four volumes of them. His articles on barbecue alone would constitute a popular book.

His major pieces of literary journalism are collected in *U.S. Journal* (1971), *Killings* (1984), and *American Stories* (1991). Trillin dedicated *Killings* to Joseph Mitchell, "the *New Yorker* reporter who set the standard." Trillin's most recent book, *Remembering Denny* (1993), explores the question: Whatever happened to the most popular kid in class? In Trillin's own class at Yale it was Denny Hansen, the star athlete and most-likely-to, who committed suicide thirty-five years after graduation.

Since 1967 Trillin has been traveling around the country, writing the pieces now collected in his books. Once, while working in the South, Trillin met some local newspaper reporters who couldn't imagine why a writer from *The New Yorker* had come all that way. "Only one person had died, and she had not been an important person," Trillin wrote. "Her family was not particularly important, and neither was the person accused of causing her death. The way she had died did not reflect any national trends. Her death had been the central event in what struck me as a remarkable family drama, but it seemed trivialized by the old newspaper phrase used to describe such dramas—a human-interest story. The best I could manage was 'It sounded interesting.' "

First Family
of Astoria

You can't really talk about Astoria without talking about the Flavels. It isn't that Astoria's history is so thin that it can be dominated by one family. As visitors are informed at the city limits, Astoria is the "Oldest Settlement West of the Rockies," dating from a post that John Jacob Astor's Pacific Fur Company established a dozen miles from the mouth of the Columbia River in 1811. As early as 1836, Washington Irving wrote an entire book about Astoria, although his inspiration was apparently not the history Astoria had seen but the fee Astor was willing to pay. By then, the fur-trading post had withered and died—not through any fault of John Jacob Astor's, readers were assured by Irving, who wrote, "It is painful, at all times, to see a grand and beneficial stroke of genius fail of its aim." By the later part of the nineteenth century, though, Astoria was thriving, thanks to its proximity to the mouth of the Columbia and to a supply of lumber and salmon that appeared to be inexhaustible.

Finnish and Swedish and Norwegian gill-netters worked the river by boat; horses that were kept in barns built on pilings in the river were brought out on the islands exposed at low tide, to haul in seines. Astoria's waterfront was lined with canneries, where the salmon was processed by a contract-labor force so uniformly Chinese that when an automatic fish-skinner was finally invented it was known as an Iron Chink. Astoria's port was busy sending the product of its lumber mills across the Pacific, and there was also work for its mariners close to home, on the Columbia bar—the shallow passage where a local pilot is taken aboard to deal with the tricky combination of tides and currents and winds brought together by the meeting of the ocean and the river. Throughout all this, Astoria, like any number of small towns in the Pacific Northwest, nurtured grandiose dreams of its destiny. A promotional poster published in 1926 says, under a drawing of the skyscrapers envisioned on the banks of the Columbia, "The Future New York of the Pacific—God's Highway to the Sea."

In the decades beginning around the time of the Civil War, God did not control the Highway to the Sea. The Columbia bar belonged to Captain George Flavel. One of the earliest bar pilots licensed by the State of Oregon, Flavel managed to put together what amounted to a bar-pilotage cartel. A ship going into or out of the Columbia River had to deal with him, and his rates reflected a keen awareness that options to his services were not readily available. In those days, talk about the Flavels included a lot of talk about the Captain's stranglehold on the bar; an editorial of the times refers to him as "this bloodsucker at the mouth of the river." Still, by the time Captain Flavel died, in 1893, after a business career that had expanded from bar pilotage and shipping to include timber and banking and real estate, one newspaper said, "The death of Captain George Flavel removes from our midst Astoria's most prominent citizen."

A decade before his death, George Flavel had erected an elaborate Victorian mansion, in a style described as Queen Anne or Italianate or Carpenter Gothic, and from there his widow, who had been only fourteen when she married the Captain, presided over Astoria society for thirty years the way Mrs. Astor was said to have presided over society in the New York of the Atlantic. (According to one rather rarefied theory, the Flavels lorded it over the other "pioneer families" of Astoria not simply because of their wealth and prominence but because most of the other families had come overland by wagon instead of arriving by ship.) The Captain's spinster daughters—Miss Nellie, a coloratura soprano, and Miss Katie, an accomplished pianist—lived out their lives in the mansion, although they were often mentioned in the newspapers for having returned from music studies in Europe or having departed to spend the winter season in New York. The Captain's son—also a captain, also named George—assumed his father's place among the most prominent citizens of Astoria.

The mansion eventually passed into the hands of the Clatsop County Historical Society, which began guided tours and published a booklet devoted to the history of the family. Long before that, the Flavel line had shifted to another mansion: in 1901, the second Captain George Flavel built a less grandiose but extraordinarily handsome frame house of his own several blocks away from where his sisters were holding their musicales. His son—Harry M. Flavel, the grandson of the founder— inherited that house, as well as his father's position as president of the Flavels' bank. The daughters born to Harry M. and his first wife settled in California, but he and his second wife, a schoolteacher named Florence Sherman, started another family, which remained in Astoria. Harry M. Flavel died in 1951. His widow, Florence, is now in her nineties. Their children, Mary Louise and Harry Sherman, neither of whom has ever

married, are in their sixties. In other words, the current Flavels are presumably the last Flavels that Astoria will have available to talk about,
and, it has to be said, Astoria has made the most of the opportunity.

Astoria did not become the New York of the Pacific. It reached its high
point, of about twenty-five thousand inhabitants, during the Second
World War, partly because of the wartime level of activity at a local
naval base. The naval base closed, though, and improved dredging of
the Columbia pulled a lot of port business upriver, toward Portland.
Astoria also began to suffer from the fact that neither salmon nor lumber turned out to have been in limitless supply after all. In Astoria these
days, it's still possible to see a gigantic freighter being loaded with hemlock trunks on their way to Japan, but almost all the mills have closed.
The waterfront, which once had twenty-two canneries and at least that
many saloons, is quiet. The headquarters of Bumble Bee, which had
provided the town with what one resident calls "the sort of people who
serve on school boards," packed up and moved to San Diego a dozen
years ago. The great ethnic neighborhoods—the Finns in Uniontown,
the Swedes and Norwegians in Uppertown—have largely broken up,
through intermarriage and the departure of the young to follow the job
market.

   People who still live in Astoria tend to look back with some longing
to the days when there was work for any able-bodied young man who
wasn't afraid of it, but they also tend to accept the hand they've been
dealt. They are often described as stoic, a characteristic associated with the
dark countries in the northernmost part of Europe and with people who
work hard in industries based on elements that seem beyond anyone's
control—the number of fish in the river, say, or the amount of lumber
needed by some faraway country nobody has ever been to. Astoria remains a place strongly marked by its history. It has a working waterfront,
even if there hasn't been much work lately, and streets full of splendid
Victorian houses that rise from downtown in a way that is likely to reward a casual glance out the kitchen window with a magnificent view
of the river and a couple of freighters and the hills of Washington state
on the northern bank. In recent years, a sprinkling of outsiders, some of
them drawn by the Victorian houses and the history, have settled in
Astoria. Still, it remains less than half the size it once was—that rare
example of an Oregon coastal town that has lost population.

   There is agreement in Astoria that the Flavel family has also been
in decline. Some say that it was in Harry M.'s time that the family's performance began to fall behind its prominence. Although Harry M.
Flavel is remembered as a charming man, he was not the civic heavy-

weight that his father and grandfather had been. ("What he had to give was different than what they gave to this community," an Astoria editor said at the time of his death. "He gave cheerful self-effacement, a warm and gentle honesty that the world needs much of these days.") He apparently did not overwork after the family bank was acquired by a larger bank. Even before Harry M. Flavel died, there was talk about erratic and angry behavior by his son, Harry S. One summer evening in 1947, when the younger Harry was only twenty, a man named Fred Fulton, who lived next door to the Flavels in a nearby beach community, heard Florence Flavel shouting for help. Fulton rushed into the Flavel house, broke through an upstairs hall door to free Mrs. Flavel, and then, trying to break into the bedroom to which young Harry had fled, was cut on the arm with a hatchet. At Harry's trial for assault with a dangerous weapon, the Flavels agreed, according to the local paper, that Mrs. Flavel had been in no danger, her son having locked her into her room simply so she could concentrate on finding a key that was important to him. ("The son considered the evening of June 5, 1947, as good a time as any for having her look for it, the youth's testimony established.") Harry Flavel, arguing that he had used the hatchet in self-defense, said that he had been frightened by a strange look on Fulton's face; Florence and Mary Louise Flavel said that Fulton was surely drunk. Young Flavel was found not guilty, but for a while he was known to some as Hatchet Harry.

He turned out to have an aptitude for matters scientific and mechanical, which came in handy for maintaining the commercial property the family still owned in downtown Astoria—basically, two buildings, on Ninth and Commercial, with eight or nine storefronts that were rented for years to such substantial enterprises as a bank and the local power-company office. No one doubted Harry's intelligence—he seemed to soak up knowledge, not just from books but also from unlikely sources, like tool catalogues or the sides of shipping cartons—but he had an intensity that often made people uneasy. "Harry would go along all right for a while," a lifelong Astoria resident has said, "and then something would set him off."

Mary Louise Flavel, who was more sociable than her brother, and always made a fine first impression, seemed to have inherited the family interest in music. She was active in the local concert series, which would have made her Great-Aunt Nellie and her Great-Aunt Katie proud, except that the best-known stories about the family participation became stories about how the Flavels had promised to underwrite one of the concerts and then reneged or stories about the night that the police came to haul Mary Louise Flavel off to jail because she refused to leave a Community Concert reception she had not been invited to. For some years in the sixties, she spent most of her time in New York; according to the talk in Astoria, she had become friendly with Jerome Hines, the Metropolitan basso, and, maybe with his help, had become a manager of opera singers. But she returned in the early seventies, full of stories about the New York opera world, which some people in town said they'd take with a grain of salt, and she moved back with her mother and her brother in the imposing house her grandfather had built.

From then on, it was common to see at least two of the three surviving Flavels together. Florence Flavel and her daughter were regular worshippers at the Presbyterian church, which had been built largely through the beneficence of the Flavel family. Mary Louise and Harry would usually appear together when there was business to go over with their downtown tenants. A tenant who had just had a visit of an hour or two with Harry and Mary Louise would sometimes discover that their mother had been waiting outside in the car the entire time. As the years passed, the Flavels seemed close to the exclusion of other people. Florence and Mary Louise might call on a neighbor for tea, but the neighbor did not return the visit. Although strangers were shown daily through the ornate mansion built by the original Captain, it became unusual for anybody at all to enter the house in which Flavels were living.

The absence of eyewitness reports about the imposing Flavel residence, of course, only increased curiosity about what might be found inside. In Astoria, winters are long and dark; because it isn't exactly on the way to any place, it has an atmosphere of isolation that enriches local legends. A lot of people who live in Astoria have been there a long time—long enough to respond to a Finnish name, for instance, with stories of how the Finns of Uniontown were considered clannish and dangerously left-wing, long enough to have traded legends about how ships owned by old Captain Flavel's competitors seemed to experience bad luck, if that's what it was. One prominent citizen believes that, in the way some places are called City of Churches, and Portland, a couple of hours to the southeast, is called the Rose City, Astoria could be called City of Rumors. A place the size of Astoria is likely to have at least one rather reclusive family living in a large house, but it isn't normally the first family of the town. Since before the Civil War, the Flavels had been the subject of a lot of talk in Astoria—talk about the old Captain's scheme to establish a town called Flavel, say, or about his son's purchase of Astoria's first motorcar, or about his grandson's divorce—and the talk didn't stop simply because there was no longer a Flavel at the bank.

There were some known facts. It was clear, for instance, that the Flavels adopted stray dogs. It was clear that Harry's angry shouting could sometimes be heard by neighbors and passersby. But a lot of stories about the Flavels tended to have more than one version. Maybe Harry used the bannister in the Flavels' house for firewood and maybe he chopped it up with his hatchet just to irritate his mother or sister and maybe it wasn't a hatchet but a chain saw and maybe the bannister was removed for some perfectly sensible reason that nobody happens to know. Maybe Mary Louise returned from New York because she ran out of her share of the Flavel estate and maybe because her only client was stolen by another agency and maybe because her father (who died fifteen years or so before this version could have taken place) went to New York and found her starving herself to death in a luxurious Park Avenue apartment. Maybe when Florence and Mary Louise Flavel wanted to go on a trip around the world that Harry was said to oppose they left secretly by cab after Harry dropped them off at church and maybe they secretly borrowed a car and left it in the Park 'n' Fly at the Portland airport.

There was consistent talk in Astoria about Harry and Mary Louise Flavel showing up in the dark of night in the premises of businesses that rented space in their buildings on Commercial Street. Some people thought they had extra keys; some people preferred to think that they appeared, as burglars sometimes appear in Astoria, through abandoned streets that became basement-level tunnels when the old downtown burned in the twenties and the new downtown was built right on top of it. What people agree on was that the Flavels were, for some of their tenants and other Astorians they came in contact with, difficult to deal with. "Difficult?" a local businessman said not long ago. "Impossible!" A woman who once had to negotiate with the Flavels in a meeting having to do with a historical-society matter—a meeting that seemed dominated by Mary Louise Flavel's concern that the family was not being given its due—has said, "It was the longest three hours of my life, and I count major surgery and childbirth."

Some businesspeople in Astoria gave the Flavels a wide berth because they had a reputation for being litigious. One retailer, a woman who came to Astoria from a different part of the country, recalls being impressed by Mary Louise Flavel while looking for a suitable space for her store ("She talked about being an impresario in New York. I thought she was smart, interesting"), and then, after choosing another space, being told she would be hearing from the Flavels' lawyer about breach of a verbal contract. As it turned out, the retailer was not sued, but there are businesspeople in Astoria who would swear that she's the only one. The Flavels were not always the plaintiffs. At one point, the hotel at the Portland airport got a judgment against Mary Louise Flavel—the contention was that she and her mother had maintained a room there for some months and had not paid for it—and when lawyers tried to attach Flavel property in Astoria there was a flurry of countersuits. Merchants traded stories about goods delivered on approval or loan that were hard to get back. Nobody knew whether the Flavels had a shortage of money or a disinclination to spend it, but it was known that they were not easy people to collect a bill from. For one thing, the collectors couldn't get in the door. Kandy Renninger, the only private process-server in Astoria, says that the first time she successfully served Harry Flavel, a lawyer who had no involvement in the dispute stopped her on the street half an hour later to congratulate her.

All this might have been made more irritating to the residents of Astoria by the fact that the Flavels—particularly Mary Louise Flavel— seemed to have an air appropriate for people who still controlled the bar pilotage and the bank and a good part of downtown. Even after the huge house seemed somewhat neglected and Mary Louise Flavel's wardrobe seemed to have narrowed, she retained a rather grand manner. "Mary Louise seems almost aristocratic," a man who has dealt with her in Astoria said recently. "Once, I had a long conversation with her, and only at the very end did I notice that the lining of her coat was hanging loose. It was not apparent at first, because of her bearing." Some residents of Astoria didn't mind her manner—she was not really arrogant—but some residents felt that they were being condescended to by someone whose house needed painting.

Mary Louise Flavel has always had her defenders in Astoria. There are people who believe, for instance, that she should have been invited to that Community Concert reception—she had been an effective member of the society—and that the fault lay not with her but with a highhanded chairman. An older resident who has known her all her life said not long ago, "Mary Louise is a nice girl, just as normal as she could be—well, a little eccentric with her renters." One of the theories about the eccentricity of the Flavel family is that Florence and Mary Louise grew strange trying to cope with Harry, or that they were in thrall to Harry, either because he was physically menacing to them or because he may have somehow ended up with the Flavel money. But there are also people in Astoria who believe that Mary Louise is the most difficult member of the family, particularly when it comes to business.

What seemed to bother a lot of people in Astoria about the Flavels was that their way of doing business—never settling for the hand they were dealt—often worked. According to the stories, a merchant might take back a somewhat used item rather than cause an argument or a lawsuit. Although people who are difficult to collect from may have trouble getting credit, they may also end up paying less. "They seemed to get a thrill out of getting the better of people," one resident of Astoria said not long ago. "They had a miraculous way of coming out on top." As the years passed and the Flavels got a bit more reclusive and, in the minds of some Astorians, quite a bit more irritating, a lot of the talk about Astoria's first family was not about how much they had done for the town but how much they seemed to get away with. Then, in 1983, Harry Flavel got involved in an incident that it seemed unlikely he was going to be able to come out of on top. It involved a young man named Alec Josephson.

Alec Josephson's forebears were Northern Europeans who made their living from salmon. His maternal grandparents spoke Finnish at home. His father's father was a Swedish gill-netter. In February of 1983, when the encounter with Harry Flavel took place, Alec Josephson was twenty-two years old and had recently married; a former captain of the high-school basketball team, he was taking some community-college courses and hoping, as he put it, to "go into the Army and jump out of air-planes." On the evening in question, he had watched a Portland Trail Blazers game on television with some friends and shared a pitcher or two of beer with them at the Workers Tavern, in Uniontown; at around ten-thirty, he was on his way home when he was startled by a noise that made him think his car had been hit by a rock. Enraged, Josephson stopped his car—this was on Irving Street, a residential street about ten blocks above the river—and went looking for what he assumed would prove to be kids up to no good.

He found Harry Flavel—in a dark walkway next to the gymnasium of the Roman Catholic school, Star of the Sea. Flavel had been out walking two dogs and had thought that Josephson was travelling too fast. Apparently, the noise Josephson had heard was Flavel's chain dog leash being swung at the car. There were some angry words. Hearing an argument from his room in the rectory nearby, Father Arthur Dernbach called the police. A couple of minutes later, after going down to see for himself what was happening, Father Dernbach phoned again, to say that an ambulance would be needed: the one man who remained there, next to the gym, had been stabbed. From what the emergency-room surgeon said later, Father Dernbach's intervention saved Alec Josephson's life. Josephson had lost a lot of blood. A blade had come within half an inch of passing completely through his body—entering at the stomach and nicking the nerves near his spine at the back.

The police showed up at the Flavels' pretty quickly. Josephson had been able to say that the man who stabbed him was an older man who had been walking two dogs, and a neighbor knew who routinely walked his dogs on that stretch of Irving Street every night. But talking to Harry Flavel about the events of the evening turned out to be a problem. Nobody had ever had an easy time getting into the Flavels' house, and the police who showed up to ask him about the stabbing of Alec Josephson were no exception. As the police and the District Attorney, Steven Gerttula, stood on the front porch, the Flavels talked to the city manager on the telephone. (They had phoned the city manager, Harry Flavel later testified, because they knew that the police chief was out of town, leaving in charge an officer who had not long before refused Flavel's request to help him make a citizen's arrest of a tenant, and had done what Flavel called "nasty little things to me and my family.") Flavel turned himself in a couple of days later, and the police eventually got a warrant to search the Flavel house for a weapon. But there was muttering in Astoria that Harry Flavel had once again been allowed to get away with something.

Flavel was charged with attempted murder and first-degree assault, which in Oregon is assault that involves using a deadly weapon with an intent to do serious injury. He pleaded not guilty, insisting that he had acted completely in self-defense against someone he referred to as a "madman." In a pre-trial hearing, Flavel's attorney, a well-known Portland criminal lawyer named Des Connall, managed to get a ruling that would have admitted a lie-detector test that he considered supportive of Flavel's version of events. By the time that ruling was reversed and a few more postponements were granted, more than two years had passed. Alec Josephson was just about fully recovered—the nick in the nerves near his spine having caused a slight weakness that lingered in one leg. In the spring of 1985, Harry Flavel finally came to trial, in St. Helens, the seat of the adjoining county. A change of venue had been granted after a hearing in which an assistant of Connall's who had taken a telephone survey among potential jurors in Clatsop County testified that she had not received a single positive response to a question about Harry Flavel's general reputation, and that many of the times she had recorded a "no opinion" it was because "when I would ask the question I would get a lot of laughs."

It was a particularly contentious trial. It lasted more than two weeks, and it wasn't difficult for those attending to get the impression that Des Connall was reluctant to let a day pass without a motion for a mistrial. Connall and Glenn Faber, the deputy district attorney who tried the

case, were constantly embroiled in bitterly contested matters of procedure and admissibility of evidence. The defense spent an extraordinary
amount of time trying to prove that Josephson had consumed more
than the half-dozen beers he acknowledged having had during that
long evening, and the prosecution, in addition to presenting evidence to
contradict that contention, argued that the effort to portray Josephson
as drunk was simply an attempt to find some way of making Harry
Flavel's story believable. Flavel testified, more or less as he had testified
forty years before in his trial for assaulting his next-door neighbor with
a hatchet, that he had acted completely in self-defense, trying to calm
down a young man who seemed drunk or "drug-crazed" or somehow
deranged. According to Flavel's testimony, Josephson, constantly
threatening to kill him, had come at him perhaps a dozen times, swaying before him between attacks with a strange look on his face. Flavel
said that even after he took out his pocketknife and waved it threaten-
ingly Josephson tried to choke him, and would have surely killed him if
the knife hadn't been used.

The prosecution argued that it was absurd to believe that the tiny
Boy Scout knife Flavel carried had inflicted the wound that the attending surgeon described as having reminded him of a bayonet wound.
Josephson, acknowledging that he had shouted at Flavel angrily and
called him a "fucking jerk," testified that the only time he had touched
Flavel was when he grabbed him in order to keep him from leaving before he had given his name and address. The prosecution presented
some circumstantial evidence that argued against Flavel's version of
events—the angle and size of the wound, for instance, and Flavel's behavior after the stabbing—but basically the jury had to decide whether
to believe Harry Flavel or Alec Josephson, the only two people who
knew for certain what had happened behind the Star of the Sea gym
that night. The jury found Harry Flavel not guilty of attempted murder but guilty of first-degree assault.

In Oregon at the time, a trial judge automatically handed down the
statutory sentence for a crime—up to twenty years for first-degree assault—and then turned the defendant over to a state board, which would
decide the actual time to be served. Under the guidelines then in place,
Flavel would probably have done two or three years. But the judge, after
imposing the customary sentence, suspended it, and gave Flavel five years'
probation, on the condition that he pay restitution to Josephson for medical expenses and serve a year in the county jail. Flavel was certainly going
to appeal the guilty verdict—even before the sentencing, his lawyers had
moved for a new trial—and Des Connall told the judge, in open court,
that the trial had contained so many errors of law that the verdict would

obviously be overturned on appeal. The judge agreed that the year in jail
would not have to be served until the appeals process had been exhausted.
There are those in Astoria who believe that he did not understand what
"exhausting the appeals process" would mean to the Flavels.

Harry Flavel's strongest ground for appeal had been discovered by
a defense lawyer among the medical bills handed in for restitution:
when Josephson's recovery seemed to be going more slowly than it
should, he had undergone nearly a dozen sessions of "hypnotherapy,"
administered by a mental-health counsellor whose only degree, it
turned out, was a certificate in mortuary science. Because of the delay in
starting the trial, this had been well before Josephson took the stand,
and the defense pointed out that it had not been carried out according
to state rules designed to prevent the enhancing of a witness's memory
through hypnosis—rules that in Oregon include the videotaping of all
sessions. That argument was rejected without comment by the Oregon
Supreme Court, and so were a number of others. The defense turned to
the federal system, and managed to take the case all the way up to the
Supreme Court of the United States twice, also without success. The
way people in Astoria tended to see it, the Flavels were using their
money—which seemed to be there when they needed it, despite their
reputation for thriftiness—to try to get away with something yet again.
As the appeals worked their way through the courts in the years following Harry Flavel's conviction, it was often said in Astoria that Harry
Flavel would never see the inside of a jail.

During the appeals process, Mary Louise Flavel tried some more
direct approaches: she would show up, unannounced, at the door of an
appeals-court judge or an influential public official, making her usual
excellent first impression, and stay the evening, presenting her argument that the entire case was simply a malicious witch-hunt. That didn't
work, either. Apparently, there was some hope among defense lawyers
that, even if the appeals did not succeed, the passing of time and the
cooling down of community concern about the incident might induce
the judge to drop the condition of probation which called for Harry
Flavel, a reclusive man in his sixties, to spend a year in jail. But that didn't
happen. Finally, in August of 1990, the court accepted Glenn Faber's
argument that all appeals had been exhausted. The lead paragraph of
the account in the *Daily Astorian* summed up the judge's order in four
words: "Go directly to jail."

By that point, though, the defense had a new argument. Five years
had passed since the sentence was handed down. During that period,
Harry Flavel had reported to his probation officer regularly; he had just
turned over to the court the final payment for restitutions. Defense

lawyers argued that, the assigned probationary term having been served, the judge no longer had any jurisdiction over Harry Flavel. The judge responded by extending the probation for a year to make time for the jail term; the defense appealed his right to make that extension; and, just before Harry Flavel was due to turn himself over to the sheriff, a higher court stayed the jailing so that it could consider the appeal. But there were two new problems. One was that Mary Louise Flavel had stopped payment on the final restitution check. The other was that Harry Flavel was nowhere to be found. Neither was his sister. Neither was their mother. Neither were their two dogs. The Flavels, people in Astoria said, were on the lam.

For two months, there was no word of the Flavels. Then, toward the end of October of 1990, Harry Flavel turned up in jail in Montgomery County, Pennsylvania. Apparently, there had been a question about whether the Flavels had removed some towels from their room at a motel in Willow Grove, outside Philadelphia, and a check of their license plate turned up the information that Harry Flavel was wanted in Oregon. An extradition order was granted, but Flavel, to the surprise of no one in Astoria, contested it. On New Year's Eve of 1990, with the argument over extradition still in progress, he was released from jail on payment of a fifty-thousand-dollar cash bond. After some delays having to do with which lawyer would represent him, a hearing was set for March 5, 1991, at the Montgomery County Courthouse. Harry Flavel did not appear. The Flavels were off again. Some people in Astoria wondered whether going from motel room to motel room in a gang that included a ninety-two-year-old woman and two dogs was really preferable to going to jail for a year in Astoria. In the words of one resident, "It couldn't have been much like '*Thelma & Louise.*'"

In November of 1991, fifteen months or so after the Flavels had left Astoria, a maintenance man at the Residence Inn in Tewksbury, Massachusetts, not far from Boston, became suspicious about a family that had been in residence a long time. It isn't unusual for people to stay awhile at the Residence Inn, which is designed more like an apartment complex than a motel; it's sometimes used by people in training programs for nearby high-tech industries and by executives who have been transferred to the area and are still house-hunting. The family in question, though, didn't fit either of those profiles, and they paid their bills in cash. The maintenance man, who was a former police officer, checked their license plate, and not long after that a couple of F.B.I. agents showed up at the door to arrest Harry Flavel. Three months later, after a number of delays and appeals, a Boston judge ruled that Flavel had to return to Oregon. Three months after that, on June 8, 1992, Harry Flavel was finally in the Clatsop County jail, awaiting a hearing at which the court would decide whether to revoke his probation. The *Daily Astorian* began its story, "Harry Flavel is back in town."

By that time, some people in Astoria—particularly the sort of people who are interested in the history and the Victorian houses—had begun to look on Harry Flavel's case with a certain amount of amusement. At the Ricciardi Gallery, where customers can order espresso and latte, in the Pacific Northwest manner, and linger over copies of the *New York Times*, in the New York manner, a steady stream of citizens came by to have a look at a painting of a younger man standing in the window of a house that looks just like the house that Harry and Mary Louise and Florence Flavel lived in. Its title is "Harry at Home." Among the coffee drinkers, there was a certain amount of speculation about what being on the lam with the Flavels might have been like and how long the saga of Harry Flavel's criminal case could last. "I love the Hitchcock element," one resident said not long ago. "I love the story that their house seemed so haunted that when the police did the search for the weapon policemen with loaded guns were afraid to go down to the basement. It's like having a caricature of a first family."

Shortly after her son's arrest, Florence Flavel fell seriously ill, and she is on a respirator in a hospital not far from Tewksbury. There has been talk in Astoria that Mary Louise Flavel was living in sordid conditions in some tiny motel room, but in fact she is living in the same neat two-bedroom unit at the Residence Inn that the family was in when her brother was picked up. She remains well spoken and courteous—a rather handsome gray-haired woman, gracious in the way someone in the leading family of a town might be gracious; so that in recounting a story, say, she might remark with approval that someone had a strong handshake or seemed to have been properly brought up. She still likes to talk about her days as a manager of opera singers; among the keepsakes she has with her is a copy of a full-page ad in *Musical America* with a portrait of the tenor Flavanio Labo and a notation that exclusive management is by Mary Louise Flavel. In those days, she says, Rudolf Bing had such faith in her judgment of young singers that when she recommended a young baritone to the Metropolitan Bing offered him a contract without troubling to hear him sing.

James Sardos, who has been Jerome Hines' manager for thirty years, rolls his eyes at the story about Bing, but he says that Mary Louise Flavel did manage Flavanio Labo, a small but mighty Italian tenor, and "through a kind of innocent persistence" got him back into the Metropolitan after his contract had been dropped. Sardos remembers her as a fan—an opera fan and, particularly, a fan of Jerome Hines—who eventually got into the business, and didn't do badly at it for a few years, handling Labo and perhaps a few other singers. Jerome Hines, who, at seventy-one, is still giving concerts, agrees. He says that she had indeed grown close to him and his family at one time—in 1955, she became godmother to his first son—but that contact with her grew faint after she moved back to Astoria. The last time the Hineses saw her, he says, was when she showed up at their place in New Jersey in December of 1990. Among the topics she wanted to discuss was whether Hines could be of some help in raising fifty thousand dollars to bail her brother out of jail in Pennsylvania. He couldn't.

Mary Louise Flavel says that, whatever people in Astoria may believe about her reasons for giving up her career as a manager of opera singers, she returned to Astoria simply because her mother needed help with the management of the downtown property, her brother's interest being in the maintenance end rather than the business end. Without becoming angry or defensive, she can dismiss all the Astoria versions of the stories about the Flavel family—even versions supported by a number of eyewitnesses—and replace them with versions that show the family to be at least innocent and probably put upon. A lot of her stories involve someone who seemed nice at first but turned out not to be—that next-door neighbor who got cut with a hatchet in 1947, for instance, who, she says, chose to believe that Florence Flavel was crying out for help when she was actually having an allergic reaction to some medicine. Mary Louise Flavel does not accept the proposition that the Flavels were ever on the lam. They had been forced to remain in Astoria for the five years of her brother's probation, she says, and when that ended they took a trip. She speaks of it the way her Aunt Nellie or her Aunt Katie might have spoken of a motor tour of the West or a visit to New York during the winter season.

They first went to Denver, she says, because "my former next-door neighbor, a young actress, was living in Denver and she had wanted me to come visit her." But Florence Flavel, her daughter says, suffered from the altitude in Denver, so the family headed south, and proceeded to the East Coast along a route that was close to sea level. In Mary Louise Flavel's telling of the tale, the three-thousand-mile journey across the country is much more slowly paced than *Thelma &Louise*: quiet mornings when Florence Flavel preferred to rest instead of moving to the next destination; rather leisurely days in the car, with regular stops to walk their two dogs, Odin II and Dugan; a week's stay in Virginia when Florence Flavel got pneumonia.

And where were they headed? To Philadelphia, she says, where Dr. Martin T. Orne, an expert on the effects of hypnosis on court testimony, happens to live. Apparently, they never actually saw Dr. Orne, although Mary Louise Flavel says that she paid a visit to his house and had a nice conversation with his wife. Then, after a stop in New York— she had been hoping to ask the advice of a lawyer she knew when she lived in the city, she says, but he turned out to have died—they came to the Residence Inn, which they chose because of its proximity to the Boston area and its welcoming attitude toward their dogs.

Why the Boston area? Dershowitz. According to Miss Flavel, her brother had read the books of Alan Dershowitz, the Harvard Law School professor who has handled a number of high-profile appeals, and believed that Dershowitz had the experience and the intelligence to get the original conviction overturned. She says that they attended some of Dershowitz's lectures ("fascinating, very interesting") and tried to pin him down for an appointment, to no avail. "We had at least three appointments," she says. "But something more important always came up—I mean from his point of view." On the day her brother was taken to jail in Boston, Mary Louise Flavel says, "I immediately went to Professor Dershowitz's house to tell him that it was an emergency. He lives in Cambridge, just a block from the governor. Beautiful residential area." She says that Dershowitz, about to leave for California, suggested another lawyer, but that the recommended lawyer had a secretary who turned out to be "haughty." In fighting her brother's extradition to Oregon, she also tried the direct approach that she had used in Oregon: apparently, she knows how close Dershowitz lives to the governor because she approached the governor, both at a ceremony in downtown Boston and at home. But her stories of such efforts tend to begin with the person in question giving the impression of being a trustworthy and open person but sooner or later "turning cold."

Mary Louise Flavel sees the prosecution of her brother as a miscarriage of justice that has been aided by "untrue, inflammatory, prejudicial" press coverage. One of the letters she sent Dershowitz was written on a copy of an article from the Portland *Oregonian* that she had color-coded, so that yellow highlighting indicated material she believes is contradicted by the trial transcripts and pink highlighting indicated material—a story, for instance, about Harry's locking her and her mother out on the balcony that wraps around part of the second story of their house and spraying them with a garden hose—that she categorizes as "maliciously fabricated and false." She often quotes third parties—a woman who quietly approached her at the supermarket in Astoria to say that Harry was being railroaded; a veterinarian who said that one of the Flavels' dogs might have been poisoned—to bolster her contention that her family has been persecuted. She has at times accused Steven Gerttula, the District Attorney, of being a cousin of Alec Josephson, on the Finnish side of the Josephson family, and both she and her brother sometimes see his prosecution as a vendetta that can be traced to some of the run-ins the Flavels have had with the city and the county and the police. But she also talks about a less specific animus in Astoria against the Flavel family. "Sometimes, we meet people and they like us because one of their ancestors worked for Captain Flavel and was well treated," she has said. "But sometimes we meet people and they hate us. They don't know why and we don't know why. Something having to do with their grandfather and grandmother—things we know nothing about."

It would be difficult to find anybody in Astoria who believes that what has happened to Harry Flavel is the result of any sort of vendetta. "For Harry, the whole world's out of step and he's in step," someone who has known the Flavels for years said recently, expressing a sentiment that is often heard in Astoria. "He's above the law. Everything's unfair. He could have taken his medicine and saved himself a couple of hundred thousand." Still, as one resident put it not long after Flavel's return, "The District Attorney's office is obviously not unhappy about seeing Harry Flavel get his comeuppance. These people have just been so *irritating*."

Steven Gerttula, who says he is not related to Alec Josephson, believes that the problem is that Harry Flavel has been treated not too harshly but too leniently, beginning with the original sentence of probation rather than prison and the judge's willingness to postpone the jail term even then. People who worked on the prosecution side tend to think that the trial judge was overimpressed by the self-assurance of a big-shot Portland defense lawyer. (Since Flavel says that his counsel absolutely assured him that he would be acquitted, and then absolutely assured him that the conviction would be overturned, he might have been overimpressed by the self-assurance of a big-shot Portland defense lawyer himself.) The unfortunate impression given by the Flavel case, Gerttula believes, is that someone with enough money—and Flavel's willingness to walk away from a fifty-thousand-dollar bond in Pennsylvania convinced a lot of people in Astoria that he had enough money—can subvert the legal system.

In recent months, both Gerttula and Glenn Faber have left the Clatsop County District Attorney's office for private practice. The position of the county is still that Flavel's probation should be revoked—meaning that he would serve a penitentiary term, presumably minus the time that he has already spent in jail—but, eight months after Harry Flavel got back to town, the hearing to decide that has not been held. The judge recently recused himself. Flavel, not for the first time, has been between lawyers. At this point, the case of Oregon v. Harry Sherman Flavel seems becalmed, but that is not to say that the Flavels have exhausted the appeals process. Reminded not long ago that no appeals court has ever ruled on Flavel's contention that the judge lost jurisdiction over him after the five years of probation were over—a contention some lawyers think of as perhaps audacious but not necessarily without merit—Gerttula just smiled and nodded.

Harry Flavel is sixty-five now—an intense man, with longish gray hair and a jailhouse pallor. He still seems to be the sort of man who might be described, as he has been described by a longtime acquaintance, as "always on the edge." He still seems to be the sort of man who might be described, as he is often described in Astoria, as terrifically smart—practically a genius, some say, in matters mechanical. (According to one story in Astoria, Flavel completely took apart the boiler of his house, but the story then splits into the customary two versions on the question of whether he managed to get it back together.) When he meets with a visitor, he takes copious notes on yellow legal pads, even if the visitor is an old friend just trying to buck up his spirits, and he's alert to anything he considers a misstatement. A visitor who begins a sentence by saying "If you believe you are innocent" will be interrupted instantly and almost angrily: "I don't *believe* I am innocent. I *know* I am innocent."

These days, Flavel is not easily diverted from the subject of his case. He is conversant not only with the events of that night—he still insists that Josephson was drunk or high on drugs or disoriented by steroids or badly affected by the movie "The Warriors," which had come on just after the Trail Blazers game, or in a "self-induced psychosis"—but also with areas of law having to do with, say, special conditions of probation and the effect of hypnosis on testimony. Flipping furiously through the pages of his legal pad, he'll cite an Oregon regulation or a case out of North Carolina. He says that the jury consisted of "unsophisticated people from a semi-rural area who didn't understand the concept of self-defense and didn't reach a just verdict." Far from believing that he has subverted the legal system, he insists that it is his right—his duty, really—to appeal an unjust verdict. ("I believed that the system had self-correcting factors built in. I fully expected to have it correct its errors.")

He sees himself as the true victim: "I went to trial and I told the truth and this is what happened to me."

The complaints that Harry Flavel is getting away with something are not quite as pointed now that he will have to file his appeals from the Clatsop County jail. Counting the time in Pennsylvania and Massachusetts, he has already served much more than a year. He has, according to his sister, exhausted his inheritance on legal fees. He has spent months as a fugitive—although he wouldn't acknowledge that he was a fugitive. ("When I left the state of Oregon, I was a free man. The judge acted illegally. He had no jurisdiction.") The rest of his family—and the Flavels, of course, have always been a close family—are at the other end of the continent. An outsider might expect to find in Astoria a body of sentiment for calling a halt to the whole business and letting Harry Flavel go home.

Steven Gerttula says that he has not heard those feelings expressed— quite the opposite—and other people who circulate widely in the community agree that Astoria simply doesn't have much sympathy for Harry Flavel. Asked why, both of the Flavels are likely to mention a saying about Russians that in their view works equally well for Finns: nothing makes them happier than the misfortune of their neighbor. The Flavels, of course, have no capital of good will to draw on. In the words of one businessman, "They haven't exactly been lovable over the years." In addition to everything else, downtown people often mention the family's neglect of its commercial real estate, which now consists of facing lines of nearly empty storefronts. Lately, there has been some discussion about whether the tourism industry, properly developed, might be an answer to Astoria's economic problems: the area already has, among other attractions, a fine maritime museum and a monument to Lewis and Clark, and a tour through the mansion that was built by Captain George Flavel. The last thing the town boosters want is the appearance of near-abandonment on an important downtown corner.

Harry Flavel may have been slowed down some by the events of the past several years, but he hasn't lost his capacity to irritate. "When they brought him back here and he came into court, he looked so much older and tireder," one of the people who had worked on the prosecution said recently. "I really felt some sympathy for him. I thought, This thing has really cost him. Then he started haranguing the judge. I thought, Now I remember this guy. It all came back."

Not long ago, one resident said that, however much Astorians complain about the Flavels, they feed on the family's story, and would hate to see it end. If Astoria is to be the City of Rumors, he points out, it has to have prominent people to spread rumors about, and in recent years the cast has been thinning. Even if the Flavels are a caricature of a first family, they are the only first family that Astoria has. Mary Louise Flavel would not put it that way, but her interpretation of the events of the last several years sometimes seems close to that. "If our name were not Flavel, in Astoria," she said, "this would not be happening to us."

Susan Orlean

Gasper Tringale

Susan Orlean grew up in a suburb of Cleveland and majored in American literature at the University of Michigan. After school, she moved to Oregon, where she worked for a small magazine and then for a weekly newspaper in Portland. She was supposed to be covering the county, but she thwarted the assignment so thoroughly that the editor finally told her to go ahead and write what she wanted. "I wrote a profile of the old highway in Portland that was made obsolete by the Interstate. It was a ghost town. I like writing about streets," she said.

Later she worked for the *Boston Phoenix*, a weekly alternative newspaper, and wrote a *Boston Globe* column in the Sunday magazine about the defining qualities of New England. Her columns are collected in *Red Sox and Bluefish* (1987). She followed with a book called *Saturday Night* (1990), about her travels around the country learning what people do with the premier night of the weekend—polka dancing in Jessup, Maryland; car-cruising in Elkhart, Indiana; parading fashions in Los Angeles. While researching *Saturday Night*, she also wrote for *Rolling Stone*, the *New York Times Magazine*, *Spy*, and *Vogue*.

"The American Man at Age Ten" began as an assignment from *Esquire*. The editors wanted a celebrity profile of Macaulay Culkin, star of the movie *Home Alone*, but Orlean didn't want anything to do with it. She agreed to write about a ten-year-old of her choosing. At first Colin, her subject, wasn't particularly interested in her cover story for *Esquire*. "The first few days he would hardly look at me," Orlean said. "Then one day at the end of school he said, 'Do you want to see my bedroom and meet my dog?' And I thought, 'We've done it!' There was a threshold we crossed when he started treating me as one of his ten-year-old friends. I was no longer a foreign object."

Since 1992 Orlean has been a staff writer for *The New Yorker*. Her "Talk of the Town" pieces typically are taken from things seen on the streets. "I'd rather walk home from work and dawdle. I dawdle with enthusiasm. You cannot manufacture that feeling. These stories are so particular in tone and spirit. If I didn't have an emotional connection, I would find it difficult. I actually believe deeply in the dignity of ordinariness," Orlean said, "in a ten-year-old kid who takes very seriously his mixed-up notion of the name of the college he will attend. I find myself drawn to that. That moves me about subjects." She approaches lengthy projects cautiously. "It's like getting married when I think of a long idea. Am I ready for the commitment?"

Along with several "Popular Chronicles" projects for *The New Yorker*, her longer commitment at the moment is to a book she calls *The House in My Head*, which will be "an exploration of my living room." As she discovered while researching *Saturday Night*, many Americans stay home on the weekend. Her new book, instead of being about going out on Saturday night, will be about staying in.

The American Man
at Age Ten

If Colin Duffy and I were to get married, we would have matching superhero notebooks. We would wear shorts, big sneakers, and long, baggy T-shirts depicting famous athletes every single day, even in the winter. We would sleep in our clothes. We would both be good at Nintendo Street Fighter II, but Colin would be better than me. We would have some homework, but it would never be too hard and we would always have just finished it. We would eat pizza and candy for all of our meals. We wouldn't have sex, but we would have crushes on each other and, magically, babies would appear in our home. We would win the lottery and then buy land in Wyoming, where we would have one of every kind of cute animal. All the while, Colin would be working in law enforcement—probably the FBI. Our favorite movie star, Morgan Freeman, would visit us occasionally. We would listen to the same Eurythmics song ("Here Comes the Rain Again") over and over again and watch two hours of television every Friday night. We would both be good at football, have best friends, and know how to drive; we would cure AIDS and the garbage problem and everything that hurts animals. We would hang out a lot with Colin's dad. For fun, we would load a slingshot with dog food and shoot it at my butt. We would have a very good life.

Here are the particulars about Colin Duffy: He is ten years old, on the nose. He is four feet eight inches high, weighs seventy-five pounds, and appears to be mostly leg and shoulder blade. He is a handsome kid. He has a broad forehead, dark eyes with dense lashes, and a sharp, dimply smile. I have rarely ever seen him without a baseball cap. He owns several, but favors a University of Michigan Wolverines model, on account of its pleasing colors. The hat styles his hair into wild disarray. If you ever managed to get the hat off his head, you would see a boy with a nimbus of golden-brown hair, dented in the back, where the hat hits him.

Colin lives with his mother, Elaine; his father, Jim; his older sister, Megan; and his little brother, Chris, in a pretty pale-blue Victorian house on a bosky street in Glen Ridge, New Jersey. Glen Ridge is a serene and civilized old town twenty miles west of New York City. It does not have much of a commercial district, but it is a town of amazing lawns. Most of the houses were built around the turn of the century and are set back a gracious, green distance from the street. The rest of the town seems to consist of parks and playing fields and sidewalks and backyards—in other words, it is a far cry from South-Central Los Angeles and from Bedford-Stuyvesant and other, grimmer parts of the country where a very different ten-year-old American man is growing up today.

There is a fine school system in Glen Ridge, but Elaine and Jim, who are both schoolteachers, choose to send their children to a parents' cooperative elementary school in Montclair, a neighboring suburb. Currently, Colin is in fifth grade. He is a good student. He plans to go to college, to a place he says is called Oklahoma City State College University. OCSCU satisfies his desire to live out west, to attend a small college, and to study law enforcement, which OCSCU apparently offers as a major. After four years at Oklahoma City State College University, he plans to work for the FBI. He says that getting to be a police officer involves tons of hard work, but working for the FBI will be a cinch, because all you have to do is fill out one form, which he has already gotten from the head FBI office. Colin is quiet in class but loud on the playground. He has a great throwing arm, significant foot speed, and a lot of physical confidence. He is also brave. Huge wild cats with rabies and gross stuff dripping from their teeth, which he says run rampant throughout his neighborhood, do not scare him. Otherwise, he is slightly bashful. This combination of athletic grace and valor and personal reserve accounts for considerable popularity. He has a fluid relationship to many social groups, including the superbright nerds, the ultrajocks, the flashy kids who will someday become extremely popular and socially successful juvenile delinquents, and the kids who will be elected president of the student body. In his opinion, the most popular boy in his class is Christian, who happens to be black, and Colin's favorite television character is Steve Urkel on *Family Matters*, who is black, too, but otherwise he seems uninterested in or oblivious to race. Until this year, he was a Boy Scout. Now he is planning to begin karate lessons. His favorite schoolyard game is football, followed closely by prison dodge ball, blob tag, and bombardo. He's crazy about athletes, although sometimes it isn't clear if he is absolutely sure of the difference between human athletes and Marvel Comics action figures. His current athletic hero is Dave Meggett. His current best friend is named Japeth. He used to have another best friend named Ozzie. According to Colin, Ozzie was found on a doorstep, then changed his name to Michael and moved to Massachusetts, and then Colin never saw him or heard from him again.

He has had other losses in his life. He is old enough to know people who have died and to know things about the world that are worrisome. When he dreams, he dreams about moving to Wyoming, which he has visited with his family. His plan is to buy land there and have some sort of ranch that would definitely include horses. Sometimes when he talks about this, it sounds as ordinary and hard-boiled as a real estate appraisal; other times it can sound fantastical and wifty and achingly naive, informed by the last inklings of childhood—the musings of a balmy real estate appraiser assaying a wonderful and magical landscape that erodes from memory a little bit every day. The collision in his mind of what he understands, what he hears, what he figures out, what popular culture pours into him, what he knows, what he pretends to know, and what he imagines, makes an interesting mess. The mess often has the form of what he will probably think like when he is a grown man, but the content of what he is like as a little boy.

He is old enough to begin imagining that he will someday get married, but at ten he is still convinced that the best thing about being married will be that he will be allowed to sleep in his clothes. His father once observed that living with Colin was like living with a Martian who had done some reading on American culture. As it happens, Colin is not especially sad or worried about the prospect of growing up, although he sometimes frets over whether he should be called a kid or a grown-up; he has settled on the word *kid-up*. Once, I asked him what the biggest advantage to adulthood will be, and he said, "The best thing is that grown-ups can go wherever they want." I asked him what he meant, exactly, and he said, "Well, if you're grown-up, you'd have a car, and whenever you felt like it, you could get into your car and drive somewhere and get candy."

Colin loves recycling. He loves it even more than, say, playing with little birds. That ten-year-olds feel the weight of the world and consider it their mission to shoulder it came as a surprise to me. I had gone with Colin one Monday to his classroom at Montclair Cooperative School. The Coop is in a steep, old, sharp-angled brick building that had served for many years as a public school until a group of parents in the area took it over and made it into a private, progressive elementary school. The fifth-grade classroom is on the top floor, under the dormers, which gives the room the eccentric shape and closeness of an attic. It is a rather informal environment. There are computers lined up in an adjoining room and instructions spelled out on the chalkboard—BRING IN: 1) A

CUBBY WITH YOUR NAME ON IT, 2) A TRAPPER WITH A 5-POCKET ENVE-
LOPE LABELED SCIENCE, SOCIAL STUDIES, READING/LANGUAGE ARTS,
MATH, MATH LAB/COMPUTER; WHITE LINED PAPER; A PLASTIC PENCIL
BAG; A SMALL HOMEWORK PAD, 3) LARGE BROWN GROCERY BAGS—but
there is also a couch in the center of the classroom, which the kids take
turns occupying, a rocking chair, and three canaries in cages near the door.

It happened to be Colin's first day in fifth grade. Before class began,
there was a lot of horsing around, but there were also a lot of conversations about whether Magic Johnson had AIDS or just HIV and whether
someone falling in a pool of blood from a cut of his would get the disease. These jolts of sobriety in the midst of rank goofiness are a ten-
year-old's specialty. Each one comes as a fresh, hard surprise, like finding
a razor blade in a candy apple. One day, Colin and I had been discussing horses or dogs or something, and out of the blue he said, "What
do you think is better, to dump garbage in the ocean, to dump it on
land, or to burn it?" Another time, he asked me if I planned to have
children. I had just spent an evening with him and his friend Japeth,
during which they put every small, movable object in the house into
Japeth's slingshot and fired it at me, so I told him that I wanted children
but that I hoped they would all be girls, and he said, "Will you have an
abortion if you find out you have a boy?"

At school, after discussing summer vacation, the kids began choosing the jobs they would do to help out around the classroom. Most of
the jobs are humdrum—putting the chairs up on the tables, washing
the chalkboard, turning the computers off or on. Five of the most humdrum tasks are recycling chores—for example, taking bottles or stacks
of paper down to the basement, where they would be sorted and prepared for pickup. Two children would be assigned to feed the birds and
cover their cages at the end of the day.

I expected the bird jobs to be the first to go. Everyone loved the
birds; they'd spent an hour that morning voting on names for them
(Tweetie, Montgomery, and Rose narrowly beating out Axl Rose, Bugs,
Ol' Yeller, Fido, Slim, Lucy, and Chirpie). Instead, they all wanted to
recycle. The recycling jobs were claimed by the first five kids called by
Suzanne Nakamura, the fifth-grade teacher; each kid called after that
responded by groaning, "Suzanne, aren't there any more recycling jobs?"
Colin ended up with the job of taking down the chairs each morning.
He accepted the task with a sort of resignation—this was just going to
be a job rather than a mission.

On the way home that day, I was quizzing Colin about his world views.
"Who's the coolest person in the world?"
"Morgan Freeman."

"What's the best sport?"

"Football."

"Who's the coolest woman?"

"None. I don't know."

"What's the most important thing in the world?"

"Game Boy." Pause. "No, the world. The world is the most important thing in the world."

Danny's pizzeria is a dark little shop next door to the Montclair Cooperative School. It is not much to look at. Outside, the brick facing is painted muddy brown. Inside, there are some saggy counters, a splintered bench, and enough room for either six teenagers or about a dozen ten-year-olds who happen to be getting along well. The light is low. The air is oily. At Danny's, you will find pizza, candy, Nintendo, and very few girls. To a ten-year-old boy, it is the most beautiful place in the world.

One afternoon, after class was dismissed, we went to Danny's with Colin's friend Japeth to play Nintendo. Danny's has only one game, Street Fighter II Champion Edition. Some teenage boys from a nearby middle school had gotten there first and were standing in a tall, impenetrable thicket around the machine.

"Next game," Colin said. The teenagers ignored him.

"Hey, we get next game," Japeth said. He is smaller than Colin, scrappy, and, as he explained to me once, famous for wearing his hat backward all the time and having a huge wristwatch and a huge bedroom. He stamped his foot and announced again, "Hey, we get next game."

One of the teenagers turned around and said, "Fuck you, *next game*," and then turned back to the machine.

"Whoa," Japeth said.

He and Colin went outside, where they felt bigger.

"Which street fighter are you going to be?" Colin asked Japeth.

"Blanka," Japeth said. "I know how to do his head-butt."

"I hate that! I hate the head-butt," Colin said. He dropped his voice a little and growled, "I'm going to be Ken, and I will kill you with my dragon punch."

"Yeah, right, and monkeys will fly out of my butt," Japeth said.

Street Fighter II is a video game in which two characters have an explosive brawl in a scenic international setting. It is currently the most popular video-arcade game in America. This is not an insignificant amount of popularity. Most arcade versions of video games, which end up in pizza parlors, malls, and arcades, sell about two thousand units. So far, some fifty thousand Street Fighter II and Street Fighter II Championship Edition arcade games have been sold. Not since Pac-Man, which was released the year before Colin was born, has there been a video game as popular as Street Fighter. The home version of Street Fighter is the most popular home video game in the country, and that, too, is not an insignificant thing. Thirty-two million Nintendo home systems have been sold since 1986, when it was introduced in this country. There is a Nintendo system in seven of every ten homes in America in which a child between the ages of eight and twelve resides. By the time a boy in America turns ten, he will almost certainly have been exposed to Nintendo home games, Nintendo arcade games, and Game Boy, the hand-held version. He will probably own a system and dozens of games. By ten, according to Nintendo studies, teachers, and psychologists, game prowess becomes a fundamental, essential male social marker and a schoolyard boast.

The Street Fighter characters are Dhalsim, Ken, Guile, Blanka, E. Honda, Ryu, Zangief, and Chun Li. Each represents a different country, and they each have their own special weapon. Chun Li, for instance, is from China and possesses a devastating whirlwind kick that is triggered if you push the control pad down for two seconds and then up for two seconds, and then you hit the kick button. Chun Li's kick is money in the bank, because most of the other fighters do not have a good defense against it. By the way, Chun Li happens to be a girl—the only female Street Fighter character.

I asked Colin if he was interested in being Chun Li. There was a long pause. "I would rather be Ken," he said.

The girls in Colin's class at school are named Cortnerd, Terror, Spacey, Lizard, Maggot, and Diarrhea. "They do have other names, but that's what we call them," Colin told me. "The girls aren't very popular."

"They are about as popular as a piece of dirt," Japeth said. "Or, you know that couch in the classroom? That couch is more popular than any girl. A thousand times more." They talked for a minute about one of the girls in their class, a tall blonde with cheerleader genetic material, who they allowed was not quite as gross as some of the other girls. Japeth said that a chubby, awkward boy in their class was boasting that this girl liked him.

"No way," Colin said. "She would never like him. I mean, not that he's so . . . I don't know. I don't hate him because he's fat, anyway. I hate him because he's nasty."

"Well, she doesn't like him," Japeth said. "She's been really mean to me lately, so I'm pretty sure she likes me."

"Girls are different," Colin said. He hopped up and down on the balls of his feet, wrinkling his nose. "Girls are stupid and weird."

"I have a lot of girlfriends, about six or so," Japeth said, turning contemplative. "I don't exactly remember their names, though."

The teenagers came crashing out of Danny's and jostled past us, so we went inside. The man who runs Danny's, whose name is Tom, was leaning across the counter on his elbows, looking exhausted. Two little boys, holding Slush Puppies, shuffled toward the Nintendo, but Colin and Japeth elbowed them aside and slammed their quarters down on the machine. The little boys shuffled back toward the counter and stood gawking at them, sucking on their drinks.

"You want to know how to tell if a girl likes you?" Japeth said. "She'll act really mean to you. That's a sure sign. I don't know why they do it, but it's always a sure sign. It gets your attention. You know how I show a girl I like her? I steal something from her and then run away. I do it to get their attention, and it works."

They planned four quarters' worth of games. During the last one, a teenager with a quilted leather jacket and a fade haircut came in, pushed his arm between them, and put a quarter down on the deck of the machine.

Japeth said, "Hey, what's that?"

The teenager said, "I get next game. I've marked it now. Everyone knows this secret sign for next game. It's a universal thing."

"So now we know," Japeth said. "Colin, let's get out of here and go bother Maggie. I mean Maggot. Okay?" They picked up their backpacks and headed out the door.

Psychologists identify ten as roughly the age at which many boys experience the gender-linked normative developmental trauma that leaves them, as adult men, at risk for specific psychological sequelae often manifest as deficits in the arenas of intimacy, empathy, and struggles with commitment in relationships. In other words, this is around the age when guys get screwed up about girls. Elaine and Jim Duffy, and probably most of the parents who send their kids to Montclair Cooperative School, have done a lot of stuff to try to avoid this. They gave Colin dolls as well as guns. (He preferred guns.) Japeth's father has three motorcycles and two dirt bikes but does most of the cooking and cleaning in their home. Suzanne, Colin's teacher, is careful to avoid sexist references in her presentations. After school, the yard at Montclair Cooperative is filled with as many fathers as mothers—fathers who hug their kids when they come prancing out of the building and are dismayed when their sons clamor for Supersoaker water guns and war toys or take pleasure in beating up girls.

In a study of adolescents conducted by the Gesell Institute of Human Development, nearly half the ten-year-old boys questioned said they thought they had adequate information about sex. Nevertheless, most ten-year-old boys across the country are subjected to a few months of sex education in school. Colin and his class will get their dose next spring. It is yet another installment in a plan to make them into new, improved men with reconstructed notions of sex and male-female relationships. One afternoon I asked Philip, a schoolmate of Colin's, whether he was looking forward to sex education, and he said, "No, because I think it'll probably make me really, really hyper. I have a feeling it's going to be just like what it was like when some television reporters came to school last year and filmed us in class and I got really hyper. They stood around with all these cameras and asked us questions. I think that's what sex education is probably like."

At a class meeting earlier in the day:

Suzanne: "Today was our first day of swimming class, and I have one observation to make. The girls went into their locker room, got dressed without a lot of fuss, and came into the pool area. The boys, on the other hand, the *boys* had some sort of problem doing that rather simple task. Can someone tell me what exactly went on in the locker room?"

Keith: "There was a lot of shouting."

Suzanne: "Okay, I hear you saying that people were being noisy and shouting. Anything else?"

Christian: "Some people were screaming so much that my ears were killing me. It gave me, like, a huge headache. Also, some of the boys were taking their towels, I mean, after they had taken their clothes off, they had their towels around their waists and then they would drop them really fast and then pull them back up, really fast."

Suzanne: "Okay, you're saying some people were being silly about their bodies."

Christian: "Well, yeah, but it was more like they were being silly about their pants."

Colin's bedroom is decorated simply. He has a cage with his pet parakeet, Dude, on his dresser, a lot of recently worn clothing piled haphazardly on the floor, and a husky brown teddy bear sitting upright in a chair near the foot of his bed. The walls are mostly bare, except for a Spiderman poster and a few ads torn out of magazines he has thumbtacked up. One of the ads is for a cologne, illustrated with several small photographs of cowboy hats; another, a feverish portrait of a woman on a horse, is an ad for blue jeans. These inspire him sometimes when he lies in bed and makes plans for the move to Wyoming. Also, he happens to like ads. He also likes television commercials. Generally speaking, he likes consumer products and popular culture. He partakes avidly but not indiscriminately. In fact, during the time we spent together, he provided a running commentary on merchandise, media, and entertainment:

"The only shoes anyone will wear are Reebok Pumps. Big T-shirts are cool, not the kind that are sticky and close to you, but big and baggy and long, not the kind that stop at your stomach."

"The best food is Chicken McNuggets and Life cereal and Frosted Flakes."

"Don't go to Blimpie's. They have the worst service."

"I'm not into Teenage Mutant Ninja Turtles anymore. I grew out of that. I like Donatello, but I'm not a fan. I don't buy the figures anymore."

"The best television shows are on Friday night on ABC. It's called TGIF, and it's *Family Matters*, *Step by Step*, *Dinosaurs*, and *Perfect Strangers*, where the guy has a funny accent."

"The best candy is Skittles and Symphony bars and Crybabies and Warheads. Crybabies are great because if you eat a lot of them at once you feel so sour."

"Hyundais are Korean cars. It's the only Korean car. They're not that good because Koreans don't have a lot of experience building cars."

"The best movie is *City Slickers*, and the best part was when he saved his little cow in the river."

"The Giants really need to get rid of Ray Handley. They have to get somebody who has real coaching experience. He's just no good."

"My dog, Sally, costs seventy-two dollars. That sounds like a lot of money but it's a really good price because you get a flea bath with your dog."

"The best magazines are *Nintendo Power*, because they tell you how to do the secret moves in the video games, and also *Mad* magazine and *Money Guide*—I really like that one."

"The best artist in the world is Jim Davis."

"The most beautiful woman in the world is not Madonna! Only Wayne and Garth think that! She looks like maybe a . . . a . . . slut or something. Cindy Crawford looks like she would look good, but if you see her on an awards program on TV she doesn't look that good. I think the most beautiful woman in the world probably is my mom."

Colin thinks a lot about money. This started when he was about nine and a half, which is when a lot of other things started—a new way of walking that has a little macho hitch and swagger, a decision about the Teenage Mutant Ninja Turtles (con) and Eurythmics (pro), and a persistent curiosity about a certain girl whose name he will not reveal. He knows the price of everything he encounters. He knows how much college costs and what someone might earn performing different jobs. Once, he asked me what my husband did; when I answered that he was a lawyer, he snapped, "You must be a rich family. Lawyers make $400,000 a year." His preoccupation with money baffles his family. They are not struggling, so this is not the anxiety of deprivation; they are not rich, so he is not responding to an elegant, advantaged world. His allowance is five dollars a week. It seems sufficient for his needs, which consist chiefly of quarters for Nintendo and candy money. The remainder is put into his Wyoming fund. His fascination is not just specific to needing money or having plans for money: It is as if money itself, and the way it makes the world work, and the realization that almost everything in the world can be assigned a price, has possessed him. "I just pay attention to things like that," Colin says. "It's really very interesting."

He is looking for a windfall. He tells me his mother has been notified that she is in the fourth and final round of the Publisher's Clearinghouse Sweepstakes. This is not an ironic observation. He plays the New Jersey lottery every Thursday night. He knows the weekly jackpot; he knows the number to call to find out if he has won. I do not think this presages a future for Colin as a high-stakes gambler; I think it says more about the powerful grasp that money has on imagination and what a large percentage of a ten-year-old's mind is made up of imaginings. One Friday, we were at school together, and one of his friends was asking him about the lottery, and he said, "This week it was $4 million. That would be I forget how much every year for the rest of your life. It's a lot, I think. You should play. All it takes is a dollar and a dream."

Until the lottery comes through and he starts putting together the Wyoming land deal, Colin can be found most of the time in the backyard. Often, he will have friends come over. Regularly, children from the neighborhood will gravitate to the backyard, too. As a technical matter of real-property law, title to the house and yard belongs to Jim and Elaine Duffy, but Colin adversely possesses the backyard, at least from 4:00 each afternoon until it gets dark. As yet, the fixtures of teenage life—malls, video arcades, friends' basements, automobiles—either hold little interest for him or are not his to have.

He is, at the moment, very content with his backyard. For most intents and purposes, it is as big as Wyoming. One day, certainly, he will grow and it will shrink, and it will become simply a suburban backyard and it won't be big enough for him anymore. This will happen so fast that one night he will be in the backyard, believing it a perfect place, and by the next night he will have changed and the yard as he imagined it will be gone, and this era of his life will be behind him forever.

Most days, he spends his hours in the backyard building an Evil Spider-Web Trap. This entails running a spool of Jim's fishing line from every surface in the yard until it forms a huge web. Once a garbageman picking up the Duffys' trash got caught in the trap. Otherwise, the Evil Spider-Web Trap mostly has a deterrent effect, because the kids in the neighborhood who might roam over know that Colin builds it back there. "I do it all the time," he says. "First I plan who I'd like to catch in it, and then we get started. Trespassers have to beware."

One afternoon when I came over after a few rounds of Street Fighter at Danny's, Colin started building a trap. He selected a victim for inspiration—a boy in his class who had been pestering him—and began wrapping. He was entirely absorbed. He moved from tree to tree, wrapping; he laced fishing line through the railing of the deck and then back to the shed; he circled an old jungle gym, something he'd outgrown and abandoned a few years ago, and then crossed over to a bush at the back of the yard. Briefly, he contemplated making his dog, Sally, part of the web. Dusk fell. He kept wrapping, paying out fishing line an inch at a time. We could hear mothers up and down the block hooting for their kids; two tiny children from next door stood transfixed at the edge of the yard, uncertain whether they would end up inside or outside the web. After a while, the spool spun around in Colin's hands one more time and then stopped; he was out of line.

It was almost too dark to see much of anything, although now and again the light from the deck would glance off a length of line, and it would glint and sparkle. "That's the point," he said. "You could do it with thread, but the fishing line is invisible. Now I have this perfect thing and the only one who knows about it is me." With that, he dropped the spool, skipped up the stairs of the deck, threw open the screen door, and then bounded into the house, leaving me and Sally the dog trapped in his web.

Richard Preston

Michelle Preston

Richard Preston earned a doctorate at Princeton University in 1983, studying with John McPhee and William Howarth. Since then, he has written three books and several articles for *The New Yorker*, all on scientific topics.

McPhee's writing students, Preston said, are called McPhinos, and an astonishing 60 percent of them become professional writers. "A neutrino is a small, massless particle emitted in a nuclear reaction," Preston said. "Neutrinos can penetrate through the earth without reacting with it. A McPhino will get hung up."

Preston's first book, *First Light* (1987), reports on the worlds of amateur astronomers watching for comets, and of "deep sky" astronomers trying to see the primeval light just now reaching earth from the edge of the universe.

His second book, *American Steel* (1991), tells how the creator of an innovative recycling plant brought steel making back to the Midwest. The drama of hot steel on a factory floor still carries a dramatic punch.

Preston calls his latest book, the bestselling *The Hot Zone* (1994), "an interesting exercise in nonfiction horror." It's about scientific control of emerging viruses many times more deadly than AIDS. A human being in contact with these viruses dies in "a full blown biological meltdown."

"The Mountains of Pi" began as an idea for a "Talk of the Town" article in *The New Yorker*. Preston had seen a note in *Science News* about mathematicians at Columbia University calculating the digits of pi. He met the Chudnovsky brothers in their overheated, cluttered apartment and learned they were building a supercomputer out of mail-order parts. He quickly decided they'd require a longer article, and he told them so. After calculating pi to a billion digits, Preston recalls, the idea of 18,000 words horrified them. "They said, 'You mustn't do it. We aren't interesting people.' I told them that when I hear someone say, 'I'm not an interesting person,' it sets off all my alert buttons as a reporter. People who say they aren't interesting are often the *most* interesting people. They looked at each other and said, 'We can agree this is a theorem, but we are an exception to the theorem.' " Preston and his wife, Michelle, have become good friends with the Chudnovskys—who claim to have never read the article.

The Mountains of Pi

Gregory Volfovich Chudnovsky recently built a supercomputer in his apartment from mail-order parts. Gregory Chudnovsky is a number theorist. His apartment is situated near the top floor of a run-down building on the West Side of Manhattan, in a neighborhood near Columbia University. Not long ago, a human corpse was found dumped at the end of the block. The world's most powerful supercomputers include the Cray Y-MP C90, the Thinking Machines CM-5, the Hitachi S-820/80, the nCube, the Fujitsu parallel machine, the Kendall Square Research parallel machine, the NEC SX-3, the Touchstone Delta, and Gregory Chudnovsky's apartment. The apartment seems to be a kind of container for the supercomputer at least as much as it is a container for people.

Gregory Chudnovsky's partner in the design and construction of the supercomputer was his older brother, David Volfovich Chudnovsky, who is also a mathematician, and who lives five blocks away from Gregory. The Chudnovsky brothers call their machine m zero. It occupies the former living room of Gregory's apartment, and its tentacles reach into other rooms. The brothers claim that m zero is a "true, general-purpose supercomputer," and that it is as fast and powerful as a somewhat older Cray Y-MP, but it is not as fast as the latest of the Y-MP machines, the C90, an advanced supercomputer made by Cray Research. A Cray Y-MP C90 costs more than thirty million dollars. It is a black monolith, seven feet tall and eight feet across, in the shape of a squat cylinder, and is cooled by liquid freon. So far, the brothers have spent around seventy thousand dollars on parts for their supercomputer, and much of the money has come out of their wives' pockets.

Gregory Chudnovsky is thirty-nine years old, and he has a spare frame and a bony, handsome face. He has a long beard, streaked with gray, and dark, unruly hair, a wide forehead, and wide-spaced brown eyes. He walks in a slow, dragging shuffle, leaning on a bentwood cane, while his brother, David, typically holds him under one arm, to prevent him from toppling over. He has severe myasthenia gravis, an auto-immune disorder of the muscles. The symptoms, in his case, are muscular weakness and difficulty in breathing. "I have to lie in bed most of the time," Gregory once told me. His condition doesn't seem to be getting better, and doesn't seem to be getting worse. He developed the disease when he was twelve years old, in the city of Kiev, Ukraine, where he and David grew up. He spends his days sitting or lying on a bed heaped with pillows, in a bedroom down the hall from the room that houses the supercomputer. Gregory's bedroom is filled with paper; it contains at least a ton of paper. He calls the place his junk yard. The room faces east, and would be full of sunlight in the morning if he ever raised the shades, but he keeps them lowered, because light hurts his eyes.

You almost never meet one of the Chudnovsky brothers without the other. You often find the brothers conjoined, like Siamese twins, David holding Gregory by the arm or under the armpits. They complete each other's sentences and interrupt each other, but they don't look alike. While Gregory is thin and bearded, David has a stout body and a plump, clean-shaven face. He is in his early forties. Black-and-gray curly hair grows thickly on top of David's head, and he has heavy-lidded deep-blue eyes. He always wears a starched white shirt and, usually, a gray silk necktie in a foulard print. His tie rests on a bulging stomach.

The Chudnovskian supercomputer, m zero, burns two thousand watts of power, and it runs day and night. The brothers don't dare shut it down; if they did, it might die. At least twenty-five fans blow air through the machine to keep it cool; otherwise something might melt. Waste heat permeates Gregory's apartment, and the room that contains m zero climbs to a hundred degrees Fahrenheit in summer. The brothers keep the apartment's lights turned off as much as possible. If they switched on too many lights while m zero was running, they might blow the apartment's wiring. Gregory can't breathe city air without developing lung trouble, so he keeps the apartment's windows closed all the time, with air-conditioners running in them during the summer, but that doesn't seem to reduce the heat, and as the temperature rises inside the apartment the place can smell of cooking circuit boards, a sign that m zero is not well. A steady stream of boxes arrives by Federal Express, and an opposing stream of boxes flows back to mail-order houses, containing parts that have bombed, along with letters from the brothers demanding an exchange or their money back. The building superintendent doesn't know that the Chudnovsky brothers have been using a supercomputer in Gregory's apartment, and the brothers haven't expressed an eagerness to tell him.

The Chudnovskys, between them, have published a hundred and fifty-four papers and twelve books, mostly in collaboration with each other, and mostly on the subject of number theory or mathematical physics. They work together so closely that it is possible to argue that they are a single mathematician—anyway, it's what they claim. The brothers lived in Kiev until 1977, when they left the Soviet Union and, accompanied by their parents, went to France. The family lived there for six months, then emigrated to the United States and settled in New York; they have become American citizens.

The brothers enjoy an official relationship with Columbia University: Columbia calls them senior research scientists in the Department of Mathematics, but they don't have tenure and they don't teach students. They are really lone inventors, operating out of Gregory's apartment in what you might call the old-fashioned Russo-Yankee style. Their wives are doing well. Gregory's wife, Christine Pardo Chudnovsky, is an attorney with a midtown law firm. David's wife, Nicole Lannegrace, is a political-affairs officer at the United Nations. It is their salaries that help cover the funding needs of the brothers' supercomputing complex in Gregory and Christine's apartment. Malka Benjaminovna Chudnovsky, a retired engineer, who is Gregory and David's mother, lives in Gregory's apartment. David spends his days in Gregory's apartment, taking care of his brother, their mother, and m zero.

When the Chudnovskys applied to leave the Soviet Union, the fact that they are Jewish and mathematical attracted at least a dozen K.G.B. agents to their case. The brothers' father, Volf Grigorevich Chudnovsky, who was severely beaten by the K.G.B. in 1977, died of heart failure in 1985. Volf Chudnovsky was a professor of civil engineering at the Kiev Architectural Institute, and he specialized in the structural stability of buildings, towers, and bridges. He died in America, and not long before he died he constructed in Gregory's apartment a maze of bookshelves, his last work of civil engineering. The bookshelves extend into every corner of the apartment, and today they are packed with literature and computer books and books and papers on the subject of numbers. Since almost all numbers run to infinity (in digits) and are totally unexplored, an apartmentful of thoughts about numbers holds hardly any thoughts at all, even with a supercomputer on the premises to advance the work.

The brothers say that the "m" in "m zero" stands for "machine," and that they use a small letter to imply that the machine is a work in progress. They represent the name typographically as "m0." The "zero" stands for success. It implies a dark history of failure—three duds (in Gregory's apartment) that the brothers now refer to as negative three, negative two, and negative one. The brothers broke up the negative machines for scrap, got on the telephone, and waited for Federal Express to bring more parts.

M zero is a parallel supercomputer, a type of machine that has lately come to dominate the avant-garde in supercomputer architecture, because the design offers succulent possibilities for speed in solving problems. In a parallel machine, anywhere from half a dozen to thousands of processors work simultaneously on a problem, whereas in a so-called serial machine—a normal computer—the problem is solved one step at a time. "A serial machine is bound to be very slow, because the speed of the machine will be limited by the slowest part of it," Gregory said. "In a parallel machine, many circuits take on many parts of the problem at the same time." As of last week, m zero contained sixteen parallel processors, which ruminate around the clock on the Chudnovskys' problems.

The brothers' mail-order supercomputer makes their lives more convenient: m zero performs inhumanly difficult algebra, finding roots of gigantic systems of equations, and it has constructed colored images of the interior of Gregory Chudnovsky's body. According to the Chudnovskys, it could model the weather or make pictures of air flowing over a wing, if the brothers cared about weather or wings. What they care about is numbers. To them, numbers are more beautiful, more nearly perfect, possibly more complicated, and arguably more real than anything in the world of physical matter.

The brothers have lately been using m zero to explore the number pi. Pi, which is denoted by the Greek letter π, is the most famous ratio in mathematics, and is one of the most ancient numbers known to humanity. Pi is approximately 3.14—the number of times that a circle's diameter will fit around the circle. Here is a circle, with its diameter:

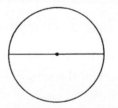

Pi goes on forever, and can't be calculated to perfect precision: 3.14159265358979323846264338327950288419716939993751.... This is known as the decimal expansion of pi. It is a bloody mess. No apparent pattern emerges in the succession of digits. The digits of pi march to infinity in a predestined yet unfathomable code: they do not repeat periodically, seeming to pop up by blind chance, lacking any perceivable order, rule, reason, or design—"random" integers, ad infinitum. If a deep and beautiful design hides in the digits of pi, no one knows what it is, and no one has ever been able to see it by staring at the digits. Among mathematicians, there is a nearly universal feeling that it will never be possible, in principle, for an inhabitant of our finite universe to discover the system in the digits of pi. But for the present, if you want to attempt it, you need a supercomputer to probe the endless scrap of leftover pi.

Before the Chudnovsky brothers built m zero, Gregory had to derive pi over the telephone network while lying in bed. It was inconvenient. Tapping at a small keyboard, which he sets on the blankets of his bed, he stares at a computer display screen on one of the bookshelves beside his bed. The keyboard and the screen are connected to Internet, a network that leads Gregory through cyberspace into the heart of a Cray some-where else in the United States. He calls up a Cray through Internet and programs the machine to make an approximation of pi. The job begins to run, the Cray trying to estimate the number of times that the diameter of a circle goes around the periphery, and Gregory sits back on his pillows and waits, watching messages from the Cray flow across his display screen. He eats dinner with his wife and his mother and then, back in bed, he takes up a legal pad and a red felt-tip pen and plays with number theory, trying to discover hidden properties of numbers. Meanwhile, the Cray is reaching toward pi at a rate of a hundred million operations per second. Gregory dozes beside his computer screen. Once in a while, he asks the Cray how things are going, and the Cray replies that the job is still active. Night passes, the Cray running deep toward pi. Unfortu-nately, since the exact ratio of the circle's circumference to its diameter dwells at infinity, the Cray has not even begun to pinpoint pi. Abruptly, a message appears on Gregory's screen: LINE IS DISCONNECTED.

"What the hell is going on?" Gregory exclaims. It seems that the Cray has hung up the phone, and may have crashed. Once again, pi has demonstrated its ability to give a supercomputer a heart attack.

"Myasthenia gravis is a funny thing," Gregory Chudnovsky said one day from his bed in the junk yard. "In a sense, I'm very lucky, because I'm alive, and I'm alive after so many years." He has a resonant voice and a Russian accent. "There is no standard prognosis. It sometimes strikes young women and older women. I wonder if it is some kind of sluggish virus."

It was a cold afternoon, and rain pelted the windows; the shades were drawn, as always. He lay against a heap of pillows, with his legs folded under him. He wore a tattered gray lamb's-wool sweater that had multiple patches on the elbows, and a starched white shirt, and baggy blue sweatpants, and a pair of handmade socks. I had never seen socks like Gregory's. They were two-tone socks, wrinkled and floppy, hand-sewn from pieces of dark-blue and pale-blue cloth, and they looked comfortable. They were the work of Malka Benjaminovna, his mother. Lines of computer code flickered on the screen beside his bed.

This was an apartment built for long voyages. The paper in the room was jammed into the bookshelves, from floor to ceiling. The brothers had wedged the paper, sheet by sheet, into manila folders, until the folders had grown as fat as melons. The paper also flooded two free-standing bookshelves (placed strategically around Gregory's bed), five chairs (three of them in a row beside his bed), two steamer trunks, and a folding cocktail table. I moved carefully around the room, fearful of triggering a paperslide, and sat on the room's one empty chair, facing the foot of Gregory's bed, my knees touching the blanket. The paper was piled in three-foot stacks on the chairs. It guarded his bed like the flanking towers of a fortress, and his bed sat at the center of the keep. I sensed a profound happiness in Gregory Chudnovsky's bedroom. His happiness, it occurred to me later, sprang from the delicious melancholy of a life chained to a bed in a disordered world that breaks open through the portals of mathematics into vistas beyond time or decay.

"The system of this paper is archeological," he said. "By looking at a slice, I know the year. This slice is 1986. Over here is some 1985. What you see in this room is our working papers, as well as the papers we used as references for them. Some of the references we pull out once in a while to look at, and then we leave them somewhere else, in another pile. Once, we had to make a Xerox copy of a book three times, and we put it in three different places in the piles, so we would be sure to find it when we needed it. Unfortunately, once we put a book into one of these piles we almost never go back to look for it. There are books in there by Kipling and Macaulay. Actually, when we want to find a book it's easier to go back to the library. Eh, this place is a mess. Eventually, these papers or my wife will turn me out of the house."

Much of the paper consists of legal pads covered with Gregory's handwriting. His holograph is dense and careful, a flawless minuscule written with a red felt-tip pen—a mixture of theorems, calculations, proofs, and conjectures concerning numbers. He uses a felt-tip pen because he doesn't have enough strength in his hand to press a pencil on paper. Mathematicians who have visited Gregory Chudnovsky's bedroom have come away dizzy, wondering what secrets the scriptorium may hold. Some say he has published most of his work, while others wonder if his bedroom holds unpublished discoveries. He cautiously refers to his steamer trunks as valises. They are filled to the lids with compressed paper. When Gregory and David used to fly to Europe to speak at conferences, they took both "valises" with them, in case they needed to refer to a theorem, and the baggage particularly annoyed the Belgians. "The Belgians were always fining us for being overweight," Gregory said.

Pi is by no means the only unexplored number in the Chudnovskys' inventory, but it is one that interests them very much. They wonder whether the digits contain a hidden rule, an as yet unseen architecture, close to the mind of God. A subtle and fantastic order may appear in the digits of pi way out there somewhere; no one knows. No one has ever proved, for example, that pi does not turn into nothing but nines and zeros, spattered to infinity in some peculiar arrangement. If we were to explore the digits of pi far enough, they might resolve into a breathtaking numerical pattern, as knotty as "The Book of Kells," and it might mean something. It might be a small but interesting message from God, hidden in the crypt of the circle, awaiting notice by a mathematician. On the other hand, the digits of pi may ramble forever in a hideous cacophony, which is a kind of absolute perfection to a mathematician like Gregory Chudnovsky. Pi looks "monstrous" to him. "We know absolutely *nothing* about pi," he declared from his bed. "What the hell does it mean? The definition of pi is really very simple—it's just the ratio of the circumference to the diameter—but the complexity of the sequence it spits out in digits is really unbelievable. We have a sequence of digits that looks like gibberish."

"Maybe in the eyes of God pi looks perfect," David said, standing in a corner of the room, his head and shoulders visible above towers of paper.

Pi, or π, has had various names through the ages, and all of them are either words or abstract symbols, since pi is a number that can't be shown completely and exactly in any finite form of representation. Pi is a transcendental number. A transcendental number is a number that exists but can't be expressed in any finite series of either arithmetical or algebraic operations. For example, if you try to express pi as the solution to an equation you will find that the equation goes on forever. Expressed in digits, pi extends into the distance as far as the eye can see, and the digits never repeat periodically, as do the digits of a rational number. Pi slips away from all rational methods used to locate it. Pi is a transcendental number because it transcends the power of algebra to display it in its totality. Ferdinand Lindemann, a German mathematician, proved the transcendence of pi in 1882; he proved, in effect, that pi can't be written on a piece of paper, not even on a piece of paper as big as the universe. In a manner of speaking, pi is indescribable and can't be found.

Pi possibly first entered human consciousness in Egypt. The earliest known reference to pi occurs in a Middle Kingdom papyrus scroll,

written around 1650 B.C. by a scribe named Ahmes. Showing a re-
strained appreciation for his own work that is not uncommon in a
mathematician, Ahmes began his scroll with the words "The Entrance
Into the Knowledge of All Existing Things." He remarked in passing
that he composed the scroll "in likeness to writings made of old," and
then he led his readers through various mathematical problems and
their solutions, along several feet of papyrus, and toward the end of the
scroll he found the area of a circle, using a rough sort of pi.

Around 200 B.C., Archimedes of Syracuse found that pi is some-
where between $3^{10}/_{71}$ and $3^{1}/_{7}$—that's about 3.14. (The Greeks didn't use
decimals.) Archimedes had no special term for pi, calling it "the
perimeter to the diameter." By in effect approximating pi to two places
after the decimal point, Archimedes narrowed the known value of pi to
one part in a hundred. There knowledge of pi bogged down until the
seventeenth century, when new formulas for approximating pi were
discovered. Pi then came to be called the Ludolphian number, after Ludolph van Ceulen, a German mathematician who approximated it to
thirty-five decimal places, or one part in a hundred million billion billion billion—a calculation that took Ludolph most of his life to accomplish, and gave him such satisfaction that he had the digits engraved on
his tombstone, at the Ladies' Church in Leiden, in the Netherlands. Ludolph and his tombstone were later moved to Peter's Church in Leiden,
to be installed in a special graveyard for professors, and from there the
stone vanished, possibly to be turned into a sidewalk slab. Somewhere
in Leiden, people may be walking over Ludolph's digits. The Germans
still call pi the Ludolphian number. In the eighteenth century, Leon-
hard Euler, mathematician to Catherine the Great, called it p or c. The
first person to use the Greek letter π for the number was William Jones,
an English mathematician, who coined it in 1706 for his book "A New
Introduction to the Mathematics." Euler read the book and switched to
using the symbol π, and the number has remained π ever since. Jones
probably meant π to stand for the English word "periphery."

Physicists have noted the ubiquity of pi in nature. Pi is obvious in
the disks of the moon and the sun. The double helix of DNA revolves
around pi. Pi hides in the rainbow, and sits in the pupil of the eye, and
when a raindrop falls into water pi emerges in the spreading rings. Pi
can be found in waves and ripples and spectra of all kinds, and therefore pi occurs in colors and music. Pi has lately turned up in super-
strings, the hypothetical loops of energy vibrating inside subatomic
particles. Pi occurs naturally in tables of death, in what is known as a
Gaussian distribution of deaths in a population; that is, when a person
dies, the event "feels" the Ludolphian number.

It is one of the great mysteries why nature seems to know mathematics. No one can suggest why this necessarily has to be so. Eugene Wigner, the physicist, once said, "The miracle of the appropriateness of the language of mathematics for the formulation of the laws of physics is a wonderful gift which we neither understand nor deserve." We may not understand pi or deserve it, but nature at least seems to be aware of it, as Captain O. C. Fox learned while he was recovering in a hospital from a wound sustained in the American Civil War. Having nothing better to do with his time than lie in bed and derive pi, Captain Fox spent a few weeks tossing pieces of fine steel wire onto a wooden board ruled with parallel lines. The wires fell randomly across the lines in such a way that pi emerged in the statistics. After throwing his wires eleven hundred times, Captain Fox was able to derive pi to two places after the decimal point, to 3.14. If he had had a thousand years to recover from his wound, he might have derived pi to perhaps another decimal place. To go deeper into pi, you need a powerful machine.

The race toward pi happens in cyberspace, inside supercomputers. In 1949, George Reitwiesner, at the Ballistic Research Laboratory, in Maryland, derived pi to two thousand and thirty-seven decimal places with the ENIAC, the first general-purpose electronic digital computer. Working at the same laboratory, John von Neumann (one of the inventors of the ENIAC) searched those digits for signs of order, but found nothing he could put his finger on. A decade later, Daniel Shanks and John W. Wrench, Jr., approximated pi to a hundred thousand decimal places with an I.B.M. 7090 mainframe computer, and saw nothing. The race continued desultorily, through hundreds of thousands of digits, until 1981, when Yasumasa Kanada, the head of a team of computer scientists at Tokyo University, used a NEC supercomputer, a Japanese machine, to compute two million digits of pi. People were astonished that anyone would bother to do it, but that was only the beginning of the affair. In 1984, Kanada and his team got sixteen million digits of pi, noticing nothing remarkable. A year later, William Gosper, a mathematician and distinguished hacker employed at Symbolics, Inc., in Sunnyvale, California, computed pi to seventeen and a half million decimal places with a Symbolics workstation, beating Kanada's team by a million digits. Gosper saw nothing of interest.

The next year, David H. Bailey, at the National Aeronautics and Space Administration, used a Cray 2 supercomputer and a formula discovered by two brothers, Jonathan and Peter Borwein, to scoop twenty-nine million digits of pi. Bailey found nothing unusual. A year after that, in 1987, Yasumasa Kanada and his team got a hundred and thirty-four million digits of pi, using an NEC SX-2 supercomputer. They saw nothing of interest. In 1988, Kanada kept going, past two hundred million digits, and saw further amounts of nothing. Then, in the spring of 1989, the Chudnovsky brothers (who had not previously been known to have any interest in calculating pi) suddenly announced that they had obtained four hundred and eighty million digits of pi—a world record—using supercomputers at two sites in the United States, and had seen nothing. Kanada and his team were a little surprised to learn of unknown competition operating in American cyberspace, and they got on a Hitachi supercomputer and ripped through five hundred and thirty-six million digits, beating the Chudnovskys, setting a new world record, and seeing nothing. The brothers kept calculating and soon cracked a billion digits, but Kanada's restless boys and their Hitachi then nosed into a little *more* than a billion digits. The Chudnovskys pressed onward, too, and by the fall of 1989 they had squeaked past Kanada again, having computed pi to one billion one hundred and thirty million one hundred and sixty thousand six hundred and sixty-four decimal places, without finding anything special. It was another world record. At that point, the brothers gave up, out of boredom.

If a billion decimals of pi were printed in ordinary type, they would stretch from New York City to the middle of Kansas. This notion raises the question: What is the point of computing pi from New York to Kansas? The question has indeed been asked among mathematicians, since an expansion of pi to only forty-seven decimal places would be sufficiently precise to inscribe a circle around the visible universe that doesn't deviate from perfect circularity by more than the distance across a single proton. A billion decimals of pi go so far beyond that kind of precision, into such a lunacy of exactitude, that physicists will never need to use the quantity in any experiment—at least, not for any physics we know of today—and the thought of a billion decimals of pi oppresses even some mathematicians, who declare the Chudnovskys' effort trivial. I once asked Gregory if a certain impression I had of mathematicians was true, that they spent immoderate amounts of time declaring each other's work trivial. "It is true," he admitted. "There is actually a reason for this. Because once you know the solution to a problem it usually is trivial."

Gregory did the calculation from his bed in New York, working through cyberspace on a Cray 2 at the Minnesota Supercomputer Center, in Minneapolis, and on an I.B.M. 3090-VF supercomputer at the I.B.M. Thomas J. Watson Research Center, in Yorktown Heights, New York. The calculation triggered some dramatic crashes, and took half a year, because the brothers could get time on the supercomputers only in bits and pieces, usually during holidays and in the dead of night. It was also quite expensive—the use of the Cray cost them seven hundred and fifty dollars an hour, and the money came from the National Science Foundation. By the time of this agony, the brothers had concluded that it would be cheaper and more convenient to build a supercomputer in Gregory's apartment. Then they could crash their own machine all they wanted, while they opened doors in the house of numbers. The brothers planned to compute *two* billion digits of pi on their new machine—to try to double their old world record. They thought it would be a good way to test their supercomputer: a maiden voyage into pi would put a terrible strain on their machine, might blow it up. Presuming that their machine wouldn't overheat or strangle on digits, they planned to search the huge resulting string of pi for signs of hidden order. If what the Chudnovsky brothers have seen in the Ludolphian number is a message from God, the brothers aren't sure what God is trying to say.

On a cold winter day, when the Chudnovskys were about to begin their two-billion-digit expedition into pi, I rang the bell of Gregory Chudnovsky's apartment, and David answered the door. He pulled the door open a few inches, and then it stopped, jammed against an empty cardboard box and a wad of hanging coats. He nudged the box out of the way with his foot. "Look, don't worry," he said. "Nothing *unpleasant* will happen to you. We will not turn *you* into digits." A Mini Mag-Lite flashlight protruded from his shirt pocket.

We were standing in a long, dark hallway. The lights were off, and it was hard to see anything. To try to find something in Gregory's apartment is like spelunking; that was the reason for David's flashlight. The hall is lined on both sides with bookshelves, and they hold a mixture of paper and books. The shelves leave a passage about two feet wide down the length of the hallway. At the end of the hallway is a French door, its mullioned glass covered with translucent paper, and it glowed.

The apartment's rooms are strung out along the hallway. We passed a bathroom and a bedroom. The bedroom belonged to Malka Benjaminovna Chudnovsky. We passed a cave of paper, Gregory's junk yard. We passed a small kitchen, our feet rolling on computer cables. David opened the French door, and we entered the room of the supercomputer. A bare light bulb burned in a ceiling fixture. The room contained seven display screens: two of them were filled with numbers; the others were turned off. The windows were closed and the shades were drawn. Gregory Chudnovsky sat on a chair facing the screens. He wore the usual outfit—a tattered and patched lamb's-wool sweater, a starched white shirt, blue sweatpants, and the hand-stitched two-tone socks. From his toes trailed a pair of heelless leather slippers. His cane was hooked over his shoulder, hung there for convenience. I shook his hand. "Our first goal is to compute pi," he said. "For that we have to build our own computer."

"We are a full-service company," David said. "Of course, you know what 'full-service' means in New York. It means 'You want it? You do it yourself.' "

A steel frame stood in the center of the room, screwed together with bolts. It held split shells of mail-order personal computers—cheap P.C. clones, knocked wide open, like cracked walnuts, their meat spilling all over the place. The brothers had crammed special logic boards inside the personal computers. Red lights on the boards blinked. The floor was a quagmire of cables.

The brothers had also managed to fit into the room masses of empty cardboard boxes, and lots of books (Russian classics, with Cyrillic lettering on their spines), and screwdrivers, and data-storage tapes, and software manuals by the cubic yard, and stalagmites of obscure trade magazines, and a twenty-thousand-dollar computer workstation that the brothers no longer used. ("We use it as a place to stack paper," Gregory said.) From an oval photograph on the wall, the face of their late father—a robust man, squinting thoughtfully—looked down on the scene. The walls and the French door were covered with sheets of drafting paper showing circuit diagrams. They resembled cities seen from the air: the brothers had big plans for m zero. Computer disk drives stood around the room. The drives hummed, and there was a continuous whirr of fans, and a strong warmth emanated from the equipment, as if a steam radiator were going in the room. The brothers heat their apartment largely with chips.

Gregory said, "Our knowledge of pi was barely in the millions of digits—"

"We need many billions of digits," David said. "Even a billion digits is a drop in the bucket. Would you like a Coca-Cola?" He went into the kitchen, and there was a horrible crash. "Never mind, I broke a glass," he called. "Look, it's not a problem." He came out of the kitchen carrying a glass of Coca-Cola on a tray, with a paper napkin under the glass, and as he handed it to me he urged me to hold it tightly, because a Coca-Cola spilled into—He didn't want to think about it; it would set back the project by months. He said, "Galileo had to build his telescope—"

"Because he couldn't afford the Dutch model," Gregory said.

"And we have to build our machine, because we have—"

"No money," Gregory said. "When people let us use their computer, it's always done as a kindness." He grinned and pinched his finger and thumb together. "They say, 'You can use it as long as nobody *complains*.' "

I asked the brothers when they planned to build their supercomputer. They burst out laughing. "You are sitting inside it!" David roared.

"Tell us how a supercomputer should look," Gregory said.

I started to describe a Cray to the brothers.

David turned to his brother and said, "The interviewer answers our questions. It's Pirandello! The interviewer becomes a person in the story." David turned to me and said, "The problem is, you should change your thinking. If I were to put inside this Cray a chopped-meat machine, you wouldn't know it was a meat chopper."

"Unless you saw chopped meat coming out of it. Then you'd suspect it wasn't a Cray," Gregory said, and the brothers cackled.

"In ten years, a Cray will fit in your pocket," David said.

Supercomputers are evolving incredibly fast. The notion of what a supercomputer is and what it can do changes from year to year, if not from month to month, as new machines arise. The definition of a supercomputer is simply this: one of the fastest and most powerful scientific computers in the world, for its time. The power of a supercomputer is revealed, generally speaking, in its ability to solve tough problems. A Cray Y-MP8, running at its peak working speed, can perform more than two billion floating-point operations per second. Floating-point operations—or flops, as they are called—are a standard measure of speed. Since a Cray Y-MP8 can hit two and a half billion flops, it is considered to be a gigaflop supercomputer. Giga (from the Greek for "giant") means a billion. Like all supercomputers, a Cray often cruises along significantly below its peak working speed. (There is a heated controversy in the supercomputer industry over how to measure the typical working performance of any given supercomputer, and there are many claims and counterclaims.) A Cray is a so-called vector-processing machine, but that design is going out of fashion. Cray Research has announced that next year it will begin selling an even more powerful parallel machine.

"Our machine is a gigaflop supercomputer," David Chudnovsky told me. "The working speed of our machine is from two hundred million flops to two gigaflops—roughly in the range of a Cray Y-MP8. We can probably go faster than a Y-MP8, but we don't want to get too specific about it."

M zero is not the only ultrapowerful silicon engine to gleam in the Chudnovskian œuvre. The brothers recently fielded a supercomputer named Little Fermat, which they designed with Monty Denneau, an I.B.M. supercomputer architect, and Saed Younis, a graduate student at the Massachusetts Institute of Technology. Younis did the grunt work:

he mapped out circuits containing more than fifteen thousand connections and personally plugged in some five thousand chips. Little Fermat is seven feet tall, and sits inside a steel frame in a laboratory at M.I.T., where it considers numbers.

What m zero consists of is a group of high-speed processors linked by cables (which cover the floor of the room). The cables form a network of connections among the processors—a web. Gregory sketched on a piece of paper the layout of the machine. He drew a box and put an "X" through it, to show the web, or network, and he attached some processors to the web:

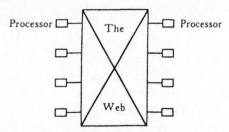

"Each processor is connected to a high-speed switching network that connects it to all the others," he said. "It's like a telephone network—everybody is talking to everybody else. As far as I know, no one except us has built a machine that has this type of web. In other parallel machines, the processors are connected only to near neighbors, while they have to talk to more distant processors through intervening processors. Think of a phone system: it wouldn't be very pleasant if you had to talk to distant people by sending them messages through your neighbors. But the truth is that nobody really knows how the hell parallel machines should perform, or the best design for them. Right now we have eight processors. We plan to have two hundred and fifty-six processors. We will be able to fit them into the apartment."

He said that each processor had its own memory attached to it, so that each processor was in fact a separate computer. After a processor was fed some data and had got a result, it could send the result through the web to another processor. The brothers wrote the machine's application software in FORTRAN, a programming language that is "a dinosaur from the late fifties," Gregory said, adding, "There is always new life in this dinosaur." The software can break a problem into pieces, sending the pieces to the machine's different processors. "It's the principle of divide and conquer," Gregory said. He said that it was very hard to know what exactly was happening in the web when the machine was running—that the web seemed to have a life of its own.

"Our machine is mostly made of connections," David said. "About ninety per cent of its volume is cables. Your brain is the same way. It is mostly made of connections. If I may say so, your brain is a liquid-cooled parallel supercomputer." He pointed to his nose. "This is the fan."

The design of the web is the key element in the Chudnovskian architecture. Behind the web hide several new findings in number theory, which the Chudnovskys have not yet published. The brothers would not disclose to me the exact shape of the web, or the discoveries behind it, claiming that they needed to protect their competitive edge in a worldwide race to develop faster supercomputers. "Anyone with a hundred million dollars and brains could be our competitor," David said dryly.

The Chudnovskys have formidable competitors. Thinking Machines Corporation, in Cambridge, Massachusetts, sells massively parallel supercomputers. The price of the latest model, the CM-5, starts at one million four hundred thousand dollars and goes up from there. If you had a hundred million dollars, you could order a CM-5 that would be an array of black monoliths the size of a Burger King, and it would burn enough electricity to light up a neighborhood. Seymour Cray is another competitor of the brothers, as it were. He invented the original Cray series of supercomputers, and is now the head of the Cray Computer Corporation, a spinoff from Cray Research. Seymour Cray has been working to develop his Cray 3 for several years. His company's effort has recently been troubled by engineering delays and defections of potential customers, but if the machine ever is released to customers it may be an octagon about four feet tall and four feet across, and it will burn more than two hundred thousand watts. It would melt instantly if its cooling system were to fail.

Then, there's the Intel Corporation. Intel, together with a consortium of federal agencies, has invested more than twenty-seven million dollars in the Touchstone Delta, a five-foot-high, fifteen-foot-long parallel supercomputer that sits in a computer room at Caltech. The machine consumes twenty-five thousand watts of power, and is kept from overheating by chilled air flowing through its core. One day, I called Paul Messina, a Caltech research scientist, who is the head of the Touchstone Delta project, to get his opinion of the Chudnovsky brothers. It turned out that Messina hadn't heard of them. As for their claim to have built a pi-computing gigaflop supercomputer out of mail-order parts for around seventy thousand dollars, he flatly believed it. "It can be done, definitely," Messina said. "Of course, seventy thousand dollars is just the cost of the components. The Chudnovskys are counting very little of their human time."

Yasumasa Kanada, the brothers' pi rival at Tokyo University, uses a Hitachi S-820/80 supercomputer that is believed to be considerably faster than a Cray Y-MP8, and it burns close to half a million watts— half a megawatt, practically enough power to melt steel. The Chudnovsky brothers particularly hoped to leave Kanada and his Hitachi in the dust with their mail-order funny car.

"We want to test our hardware," Gregory said.

"Pi is the best stress test for a supercomputer," David said.

"We also want to find out what makes pi different from other numbers. It's a business."

"Galileo saw the moons of Jupiter through his telescope, and he tried to figure out the laws of gravity by looking at the moons, but he couldn't," David said. "With pi, we are at the stage of looking at the moons of Jupiter." He pulled his Mini Mag-Lite flashlight out of his pocket and shone it into a bookshelf, rooted through some file folders, and handed me a color photograph of pi. "This is a piscape," he said. The photograph showed a mountain range in cyberspace: bony peaks and ridges cut by valleys. The mountains and valleys were splashed with colors—yellow, green, orange, violet, and blue. It was the first eight million digits of pi, mapped as a fractal landscape by an I.B.M. GF-11 supercomputer at Yorktown Heights, which Gregory had programmed from his bed. Apart from its vivid colors, pi looks like the Himalayas.

Gregory thought that the mountains of pi seemed to contain structure. "I see something systematic in this landscape, but it may be just an attempt by the brain to translate some random visual pattern into order," he said. As he gazed into the nature beyond nature, he wondered if he stood close to a revelation about the circle and its diameter. "Any very high hill in this picture, or any flat plateau, or deep valley, would be a sign of *something* in pi," he said. "There are slight variations from randomness in this landscape. There are fewer peaks and valleys than you would expect if pi were truly random, and the peaks and valleys tend to stay high or low a little longer than you'd expect." In a manner of speaking, the mountains of pi looked to him as if they'd been molded by the hand of the Nameless One, *Deus absconditus* (the hidden God), but he couldn't really express in words what he thought he saw and, to his great frustration, he couldn't express it in the language of mathematics, either.

"Exploring pi is like exploring the universe," David remarked.

"It's more like exploring underwater," Gregory said. "You are in the mud, and everything looks the same. You need a flashlight. Our computer is the flashlight."

David said, "Gregory—I think, really—you are getting tired."

A fax machine in a corner beeped and emitted paper. It was a message from a hardware dealer in Atlanta. David tore off the paper and stared at it. "They didn't ship it! I'm going to kill them! This is a service economy. Of course, you know what that means—the service is terrible."

"We collect price quotes by fax," Gregory said.

"It's a horrible thing. Window-shopping in supercomputerland. We can't buy everything—"

"Because everything won't *exist*," Gregory said.

"We only want to build a machine to compute a few transcendental numbers—"

"Because we are not licensed for transcendental meditation," Gregory said.

"Look, we are getting nutty," David said.

"We are not the only ones," Gregory said. "We are getting an average of one letter a month from someone or other who is trying to prove Fermat's Last Theorem."

I asked the brothers if they had published any of their digits of pi in a book.

Gregory said that he didn't know how many trees you would have to grind up in order to publish a billion digits of pi in a book. The brothers' pi had been published on fifteen hundred microfiche cards stored somewhere in Gregory's apartment. The cards held three hundred thousand pages of data, a slug of information much bigger than the Encyclopædia Britannica, and containing but one entry, "Pi." David offered to find the cards for me; they had to be around here somewhere. He switched on the lights in the hallway and began to shift boxes. Gregory rifled bookshelves.

"Please sit down, Gregory," David said. Finally, the brothers confessed that they had temporarily lost their pi. "Look, it's not a problem," David said. "We keep it in different places." He reached inside m zero and pulled out a metal box. It was a naked hard-disk drive, studded with chips. He handed me the object. "There's pi stored on this drive." It hummed gently. "You are holding some pi in your hand. It weighs six pounds."

Months passed before I visited the Chudnovskys again. The brothers had been tinkering with their machine and getting it ready to go for two billion digits of pi, when Gregory developed an abnormality related to one of his kidneys. He went to the hospital and had some CAT scans made of his torso, to see what things looked like, but the brothers were disappointed in the pictures, and persuaded the doctors to give them the

CAT data on a magnetic tape. They took the tape home, processed it in m zero, and got spectacular color images of Gregory's torso. The images showed cross-sectional slices of his body, viewed through different angles, and they were far more detailed than any image from a CAT scanner. Gregory wrote the imaging software. It took him a few weeks. "There's a lot of interesting mathematics in the problem of imaging a body," he remarked. For the moment, it was more interesting than pi, and it delayed the brothers' probe into the Ludolphian number.

Spring came, and Federal Express was active at the Chudnovskys' building. Then the brothers began to calculate pi, slowly at first, more intensely as they gained confidence in their machine, but in May the weather warmed up and Con Edison betrayed the brothers. A heat wave caused a brownout in New York City, and as it struck, m zero automatically shut itself down, to protect its circuits, and died. Afterward, the brothers couldn't get electricity running properly through the machine. They spent two weeks restarting it, piece by piece.

Then, on Memorial Day weekend, as the calculation was beginning to progress, Malka Benjaminovna suffered a heart attack. Gregory was alone with his mother in the apartment. He gave her chest compressions and breathed air into her lungs, although David later couldn't understand how his brother didn't kill himself saving her. An ambulance rushed her to St. Luke's Hospital. The brothers were terrified that they would lose her, and the strain almost killed David. One day, he fainted in his mother's hospital room and threw up blood. He had developed a bleeding ulcer. "Look, it's not a problem," he said later. After Malka Benjaminovna had been moved out of intensive care, Gregory rented a laptop computer, plugged it into the telephone line in her hospital room, and talked to m zero at night through cyberspace, driving the supercomputer toward pi and watching his mother's blood pressure at the same time.

Malka Benjaminovna improved slowly. When St. Luke's released her, the brothers settled her in her room in Gregory's apartment and hired a nurse to look after her. I visited them shortly after that, on a hot day in early summer. David answered the door. There were blue half circles under his eyes, and he had lost weight. He smiled weakly and greeted me by saying, "I believe it was Oliver Heaviside, the English physicist, who once said, 'In order to know soup, it is not necessary to climb into a pot and be boiled.' But, look, if you want to be boiled you are welcome to come inside." He led me down the dark hallway. Malka Benjaminovna was asleep in her bedroom, and the nurse was sitting beside her. Her room was lined with bookshelves, packed with paper—it was an overflow repository.

"Theoretically, the best way to cool a supercomputer is to submerge it in water," Gregory said, from his bed in the junk yard.

"Then we could add goldfish," David said.

"That would solve all our problems."

"We are not good plumbers, Gregory. As long as I am alive, we will not cool a machine with water."

"What is the temperature in there?" Gregory asked, nodding toward m zero's room.

"It grows to thirty-four degrees Celsius. Above ninety Fahrenheit. This is not good. Things begin to fry."

David took Gregory under the arm, and we passed through the French door into gloom and pestilential heat. The shades were drawn, the lights were off, and an air-conditioner in a window ran in vain. Sweat immediately began to pour down my body. "I don't like to go into this room," Gregory said. The steel frame in the center of the room—the heart of m zero—had acquired more logic boards, and more red lights blinked inside the machine. I could hear disk drives murmuring. The drives were copying and recopying segments of transcendental numbers, to check the digits for perfect accuracy. Gregory knelt on the floor, facing the steel frame.

David opened a cardboard box and removed an electronic board. He began to fit it into m zero. I noticed that his hands were marked with small cuts, which he had got from reaching into the machine.

"David, could you give me the flashlight?" Gregory said.

David pulled the Mini Mag-Lite from his shirt pocket and handed it to Gregory. The brothers knelt beside each other, Gregory shining the flashlight into the supercomputer. David reached inside with his fingers and palpated a logic board.

"Don't!" Gregory said. "O.K., look. No! No!" They muttered to each other in Russian. "It's too small," Gregory said.

David adjusted an electric fan. "We bought it at a hardware store down the street," he said to me. "We buy our fans in the winter. It saves money." He pointed to a gauge that had a dial on it. "Here we have a meat thermometer."

The brothers had thrust the thermometer between two circuit boards in order to look for hot spots inside m zero. "Beef Rare— Ham—Beef Med—Pork."

"You want to keep the machine below 'Pork,' " Gregory remarked. He lifted a keyboard out of the steel frame and typed something on it, staring at a display screen. Numbers filled the screen. "The machine is checking its memory," he said. A buzzer sounded. "It shut down!" he said. "It's a disk-drive controller. The stupid thing obviously has problems."

"It's mentally deficient," David commented. He went over to a bookshelf and picked up a hunting knife. I thought he was going to plunge it into the supercomputer, but he used it to rip open a cardboard box. "We're going to ship the part back to the manufacturer," he said to me. "You had better send it in the original box or you may not get your money back. Now you know the reason this apartment is full of empty boxes. We have to save them. Gregory, I wonder if you are tired."

"If I stand up now, I will fall down," Gregory said, from the floor. "Therefore, I will sit in my center of gravity. I will maintain my center of gravity. Let me see, meanwhile, what is happening with this machine." He typed something on his keyboard. "You won't believe it, Dave, but the controller now seems to work."

"We need to buy a new one," David said.

"Try Nevada."

David dialled a mail-order house in Nevada that here will be called Searchlight Computers. He said loudly, in a thick Russian accent, "Hi, Searchlight. I need a fifteen-forty controller.... No! No! No! I don't need anything else! Just the controller! Just a naked unit! Naked! How much you charge? ... Two hundred and fifty-seven dollars?"

Gregory glanced at his brother and shrugged. "Eh."

"Look, Searchlight, can you ship it to me Federal Express? For tomorrow morning. How much? ... *Thirty-nine dollars* for Fed Ex? Come on! What about afternoon delivery? ... *Twenty*-nine dollars before 3 P.M.? *Relax*. What is your name? ... Bob. Fine. O.K. So it's two hundred and fifty-seven dollars plus twenty-nine dollars for Federal Express?"

"Twenty-nine dollars for Fed Ex!" Gregory burst out. "It should be fifteen." He pulled a second keyboard out of the steel frame and tapped the keys. Another display screen came alive and filled with numbers.

"Tell me this," David said to Bob in Nevada. "Do you have thirty-day money-back guarantee? ... No? Come on! Look, any device might not work."

"Of course, a part *might* work," Gregory muttered to his brother. "But it usually doesn't."

"Question Number Two: The Fed Ex should not cost twenty-nine bucks," David said to Bob. "No, nothing! I'm just asking." David hung up the phone. "I'm going to call A.K.," he said. "Hi, A.K., this is David Chudnovsky, calling from New York. A.K., I need another controller, like the one you sent. Can you send it today Fed Ex? ... How much you charge? ... Naked! I want a naked unit! Not in a shoebox, nothing!"

A rhythmic clicking sound came from one of the disk drives. Gregory remarked to me, "We are calculating pi right now."

"Do you want my MasterCard? Look, it's really imperative that I get my unit tomorrow. A.K., please, I really need my unit bad." David hung up the telephone and sighed. "This is what has happened to a pure mathematician."

"Gregory and David are both extremely childlike, but I don't mean childish at all," Gregory's wife, Christine Pardo Chudnovsky, said one muggy summer day, at the dining-room table. "There is a certain amount of play in everything they do, a certain amount of fooling around between two brothers." She is six years younger than Gregory; she was an undergraduate at Barnard College when she first met him. "I fell in love with Gregory immediately. His illness came with the package." She is still in love with him, even if at times they fight over his heaps of paper. ("I don't have room to put my things down," she says to him.) As we talked, though, pyramids of boxes and stacks of paper leaned against the dining-room windows, pressing against the glass and blocking daylight, and a smell of hot electrical gear crept through the room. "This house is an example of mathematics in family life," she said. At night, she dreams that she is dancing from room to room through an empty apartment that has parquet floors.

David brought his mother out of her bedroom, settled her at the table, and kissed her on the cheek. Malka Benjaminovna seemed frail but alert. She is a small, white-haired woman with a fresh face and clear blue eyes, who speaks limited English. A mathematician once described Malka Benjaminovna as the glue that holds the Chudnovsky family together. She was an engineer during the Second World War, when she designed buildings, laboratories, and proving grounds in the Urals for testing the Katyusha rocket; later, she taught engineering at schools around Kiev. She handed me plates of roast chicken, kasha, pickles, cream cheese, brown bread, and little wedges of The Laughing Cow cheese in foil. "Mother thinks you aren't getting enough to eat," Christine said. Malka Benjaminovna slid a jug of Gatorade across the table at me.

After lunch, and fortified with Gatorade, the brothers and I went into the chamber of m zero, into a pool of thick heat. The room enveloped us like noon on the Amazon, and it teemed with hidden activity. The disk drives clicked, the red lights flashed, the air-conditioner hummed, and you could hear dozens of whispering fans. Gregory leaned on his cane and contemplated the machine. "It's doing many jobs at the moment," he said. "Frankly, I don't know what it's doing. It's doing some algebra, and I think it's also backing up some pieces of pi."

"Sit down, Gregory, or you will fall," David said.

"What is it doing now, Dave?"

"It's blinking."

"It will die soon."

"Gregory, I heard a funny noise."

"You really heard it? Oh, God, it's going to be like the last time—"

"That's it!"

"We are dead! It crashed!"

"Sit down, Gregory, for God's sake!"

Gregory sat on a stool and tugged at his beard. "What was I doing before the system crashed? With God's help, I will remember." He jotted a few notes in a laboratory notebook. David slashed open a cardboard box with his hunting knife and lifted out a board studded with chips, for making color images on a display screen, and plugged it into m zero. Gregory crawled under a table. "Oh, shit," he said, from beneath the table.

"Gregory, you killed the system again!"

"Dave, Dave, can you get me a flashlight?"

David handed his Mini Mag-Lite under the table. Gregory joined some cables together and stood up. "Whoo! Very uncomfortable. David, boot it up."

"Sit down for a moment."

Gregory slumped into a chair.

"This monster is going on the blink," David said, tapping a keyboard.

"It will be all right."

On a screen, m zero declared, "The system is ready."

"Ah," David said.

The drives began to click, and the parallel processors silently multiplied and conjoined huge numbers. Gregory headed for bed, David holding him by the arm.

In the junk yard, his nest, his paper-lined oubliette, Gregory kicked off his gentleman's slippers, lay down on the bed, and predicted the future. He said, "The gigaflop supercomputers of today are almost useless. What is needed is a teraflop machine. That's a machine that can run at a trillion flops, a trillion floating-point operations per second, or roughly a thousand times as fast as a Cray Y-MP8. One such design for a teraflop machine, by Monty Denneau, at I.B.M., will be a parallel supercomputer in the form of a twelve-foot-wide box. You want to have at least sixty-four thousand processors in the machine, each of which has the power of a Cray. And the processors will be joined by a network that has the total switching capacity of the entire telephone network in the United States. I think a teraflop machine will exist by 1993. Now, a better machine is a petaflop machine. A petaflop is a quadrillion flops, a quadrillion floating-point operations per second, so a petaflop machine is a thousand times as fast as a teraflop machine, or a million times as fast as a Cray Y-MP8. The petaflop machine will exist by the year 2000, or soon afterward. It will fit into a sphere less than a hundred feet in diameter. It will use light and mirrors—the machine's network will consist of optical cables rather than copper wires. By that time, a gigaflop 'supercomputer' will be a single chip. I think that the petaflop machine will be used mainly to simulate machines like itself, so that we can begin to design some *real* machines."

In the nineteenth century, mathematicians attacked pi with the help of human computers. The most powerful of these was Johann Martin Zacharias Dase, a prodigy from Hamburg. Dase could multiply large numbers in his head, and he made a living exhibiting himself to crowds in Germany, Denmark, and England, and hiring himself out to mathematicians. A mathematician once asked Dase to multiply 79,532,853 by 93,758,479, and Dase gave the right answer in fifty-four seconds. Dase extracted the square root of a hundred-digit number in fifty-two minutes, and he was able to multiply a couple of hundred-digit numbers in his head during a period of eight and three-quarters hours. Dase could do this kind of thing for weeks on end, running as an unattended supercomputer. He would break off a calculation at bedtime, store everything in his memory for the night, and resume calculation in the morning. Occasionally, Dase had a system crash. In 1845, he bombed while trying to demonstrate his powers to a mathematician and astronomer named Heinrich Christian Schumacher, reckoning wrongly every multiplication that he attempted. He explained to Schumacher that he had a headache. Schumacher also noted that Dase did not in the least understand theoretical mathematics. A mathematician named Julius Petersen once tried in vain for six weeks to teach Dase the rudiments of Euclidean geometry, but they absolutely baffled Dase. Large numbers Dase could handle, and in 1844 L. K. Schulz von Strassnitsky hired him to compute pi. Dase ran the job for almost two months in his brain, and at the end of the time he wrote down pi correctly to the first two hundred decimal places—then a world record.

To many mathematicians, mathematical objects such as the number pi seem to exist in an external, objective reality. Numbers seem to exist apart from time or the world; numbers seem to transcend the universe; numbers might exist even if the universe did not. I suspect that in their hearts most working mathematicians are Platonists, in that they take it as a matter of unassailable if unprovable fact that mathematical reality stands apart from the world, and is at least as real as the world, and possibly gives shape to the world, as Plato suggested. Most mathematicians would probably agree that the ratio of the circle to its diameter exists brilliantly in the nature beyond nature, and would exist even if the human mind was not aware of it, and might exist even if God had not bothered to create it. One could imagine that pi existed before the universe came into being and will exist after the universe is gone. Pi may even exist apart from God, in the opinion of some mathematicians, for while there is reason to doubt the existence of God, by their way of thinking there is no good reason to doubt the existence of the circle.

"To an extent, pi is more real than the machine that is computing it," Gregory remarked to me one day. "Plato was right. I am a Platonist. Of course pi is a natural object. Since pi is there, it exists. What we are doing is really close to experimental physics—we are 'observing pi.' Since we can observe pi, I prefer to think of pi as a natural object. Observing pi is easier than studying physical phenomena, because you can prove things in mathematics, whereas you can't prove anything in physics. And, unfortunately, the laws of physics change once every generation."

"Is mathematics a form of art?" I asked.

"Mathematics is partially an art, even though it is a natural science," he said. "Everything in mathematics does exist now. It's a matter of *naming* it. The thing doesn't arrive from God in a fixed form; it's a matter of representing it with symbols. You put it through your mind in order to make sense of it."

Mathematicians have sorted numbers into classes in order to make sense of them. One class of numbers is that of the rational numbers. A rational number is a fraction composed of integers (whole numbers): $\frac{1}{1}$, $\frac{1}{3}$, $\frac{3}{5}$, $\frac{10}{71}$, and so on. Every rational number, when it is expressed in decimal form, repeats periodically: $\frac{1}{3}$, for example, becomes .333.... Next, we come to the irrational numbers. An irrational number can't be expressed as a fraction composed of whole numbers, and, furthermore, its digits go to infinity without repeating periodically.

The square root of two ($\sqrt{2}$) is an irrational number. There is simply no way to represent any irrational number as the ratio of two whole numbers; it can't be done. Hippasus of Metapontum supposedly made this discovery in the fifth century B.C., while travelling in a boat with some mathematicians who were followers of Pythagoras. The Pythagoreans believed that everything in nature could be reduced to a ratio of two whole numbers, and they threw Hippasus overboard for his discovery, since he had wrecked their universe. Expanded as a decimal, the square root of two begins 1.41421 ... and runs in "random" digits forever. It looks exactly like pi in its decimal expansion; it is a hopeless jumble, showing no obvious system or design. The square root of two is not a transcendental number, because it can be found with an equation. It is the solution (root) of an equation. The equation is $x^2 = 2$, and a solution is the square root of two. Such numbers are called algebraic.

While pi is indeed an irrational number—it can't be expressed as a fraction made of whole numbers—more important, it can't be expressed with finite algebra. Pi is therefore said to be a transcendental number, because it transcends algebra. Simply and generally speaking, a transcendental number can't be pinpointed through an equation built from a finite number of integers. There is no finite algebraic equation built from whole numbers that will give an exact value for pi. The statement can be turned around this way: pi is not the solution to any equation built from a less than infinite series of whole numbers. If equations are trains threading the landscape of numbers, then no train stops at pi.

Pi is elusive, and can be approached only through rational approximations. The approximations hover around the number, closing in on it, but do not touch it. Any formula that heads toward pi will consist of a chain of operations that never ends. It is an infinite series. In 1674, Gottfried Wilhelm Leibniz (the co-inventor of the calculus, along with Isaac Newton) noticed an extraordinary pattern of numbers buried in the circle. The Leibniz series for pi has been called one of the most beautiful mathematical discoveries of the seventeenth century:

$$\frac{\pi}{4} = \frac{1}{1} - \frac{1}{3} + \frac{1}{5} - \frac{1}{7} + \frac{1}{9} - \ldots$$

In English: pi over four equals one minus a third plus a fifth minus a seventh plus a ninth—and so on. You follow the odd numbers out to infinity, and when you arrive there and sum the terms, you get pi. But since you never arrive at infinity you never get pi. Mathematicians find it deeply mysterious that a chain of discrete rational numbers can connect so easily to geometry, to the smooth and continuous circle.

As an experiment in "observing pi," as Gregory Chudnovsky puts it, I computed the Leibniz series on a pocket calculator. It was easy, and I got results that did seem to wander slowly toward pi. As the series progresses, the answers touch on 2.66, 3.46, 2.89, and 3.34, in that order. The answers land higher than pi and lower than pi, skipping back and forth across pi, and gradually closing in on pi. A mathematician would say that the series "converges on pi." It converges on pi forever, playing hopscotch over pi but never landing on pi.

You can take the Leibniz series out a long distance—you can even dramatically speed up its movements toward pi by adding a few corrections to it—but no matter how far you take the Leibniz series, and no matter how many corrections you hammer into it, when you stop the operation and sum the terms, you will get a *rational* number that is somewhere around pi but is not pi, and you will be damned if you can put your hands on pi.

Transcendental numbers continue forever, as an endless non-repeating string, in whatever rational form you choose to display them, whether as digits or as an equation. The Leibniz series is a beautiful way to represent pi, and it is finally mysterious, because it doesn't tell us much about pi. Looking at the Leibniz series, you feel the independence of mathematics from human culture. Surely, on any world that knows pi the Leibniz series will also be known. Leibniz wasn't the first mathematician to discover the Leibniz series. Nilakantha, an astronomer, grammarian, and mathematician who lived on the Kerala coast of India, described the formula in Sanskrit poetry around the year 1500.

It is worth thinking about what a decimal place means. Each decimal place of pi is a range that shows the *approximate* location of pi to an accuracy ten times as great as the previous range. But as you compute the next decimal place you have no idea where pi will appear in the range. It could pop up in 3, or just as easily in 9, or in 2. The apparent movement of pi as you narrow the range is known as the random walk of pi.

Pi does not move; pi is a fixed point. The algebra wobbles around pi. There is no such thing as a formula that is steady enough or sharp enough to stick a pin into pi. Mathematicians have discovered formulas that converge on pi very fast (that is, they skip around pi with rapidly increasing accuracy), but they do not and cannot hit pi. The Chudnovsky brothers discovered their own formula in 1984, and it attacks pi with great ferocity and elegance. The Chudnovsky formula is the fastest series for pi ever found which uses rational numbers. Various other series for pi, which use irrational numbers, have also been found, and they converge on pi faster than the Chudnovsky formula, but in practice they run more slowly on a computer, because irrational numbers are harder to compute. The Chudnovsky formula for pi is thought to be "extremely beautiful" by persons who have a good feel for numbers, and it is based on a torus (a doughnut), rather than on a circle. It uses large assemblages of whole numbers to hunt for pi, and it owes much to an earlier formula for pi worked out in 1914 by Srinivasa Ramanujan, a mathematician from Madras, who was a number theorist of unsurpassed genius. Gregory says that the Chudnovsky formula "is in the style of Ramanujan," and that it "is really very simple, and can be programmed into a computer with a few lines of code."

In 1873, Georg Cantor, a Russian-born mathematician who was one of the towering intellectual figures of the nineteenth century, proved that the set of transcendental numbers is infinity more extensive than the set of algebraic numbers. That is, finite algebra can't find or describe most numbers. To put it another way, most numbers are infinitely long and non-repeating in any rational form of representation. In this respect, most numbers are like pi.

Cantor's proof was a disturbing piece of news, for at that time very few transcendental numbers were actually known. (Not until nearly a decade later did Ferdinand Lindemann finally prove the transcendence of pi; before that, mathematicians had only conjectured that pi was transcendental.) Perhaps even more disturbing, Cantor offered no clue, in his proof, to what a transcendental number might look like, or how to construct such a beast. Cantor's celebrated proof of the existence of uncountable multitudes of transcendental numbers resembled a proof that the world is packed with microscopic angels—a proof, however, that does not tell us what the angels look like or where they can be found; it merely proves that they *exist* in uncountable multitudes. While Cantor's proof lacked any specific description of a transcendental number, it showed that algebraic numbers (such as the square root of two) are few and far between: they poke up like marker buoys through the sea of transcendental numbers.

Cantor's proof disturbed some mathematicians because, in the first place, it suggested that they had not yet discovered *most* numbers, which were transcendentals, and in the second place that they lacked any tools or methods that would determine whether a given number was transcendental or not. Leopold Kronecker, an influential older mathematician, rejected Cantor's proof, and resisted the whole notion of "discovering" a number. (He once said, in a famous remark, "God made the integers, all else is the work of man.") Cantor's proof has withstood such attacks, and today the debate over whether transcendental numbers are a work of God or man has subsided, mathematicians having decided to work with transcendental numbers no matter who made them.

The Chudnovsky brothers claim that the digits of pi form the most nearly perfect random sequence of digits that has ever been discovered. They say that nothing known to humanity appears to be more deeply unpredictable than the succession of digits in pi, except, perhaps, the haphazard clicks of a Geiger counter as it detects the decay of radioactive nuclei. But pi is not random. The fact that pi can be produced by a relatively simple formula means that pi is orderly. Pi looks random only because the pattern in the digits is fantastically complex. The Ludolphian number is fixed in eternity—not a digit out of place, all characters in their proper order, an endless sentence written to the end of the world by the division of the circle's diameter into its circumference. Various simple methods of approximation will always yield the same succession of digits in the same order. If a single digit in pi were to be changed anywhere between here and infinity, the resulting number would no longer be pi; it would be "garbage," in David's word, because to change a single digit in pi is to throw all the following digits out of whack and miles from pi.

"Pi is a damned good fake of a random number," Gregory said. "I just wish it were not as good a fake. It would make our lives a lot easier."

Around the three-hundred-millionth decimal place of pi, the digits go 88888888—eight eights pop up in a row. Does this mean anything? It appears to be random noise. Later, ten sixes erupt: 6666666666. What does this mean? Apparently nothing, only more noise. Somewhere past the half-billion mark appears the string 123456789. It's an accident, as it were. "We do not have a good, clear crystallized idea of randomness," Gregory said. "It cannot be that pi is truly random. Actually, a truly random sequence of numbers has not yet been discovered."

No one knows what happens to the digits of pi in the deeper regions, as the number is resolved toward infinity. Do the digits turn into nothing but eights and fives, say? Do they show a predominance of sevens? Similarly, no one knows if a digit stops appearing in pi. This conjecture says that after a certain point in the sequence a digit drops out completely. For example, no more fives appear in pi—something like that. Almost certainly, pi does not do such things, Gregory Chudnovsky thinks, because it would be stupid, and nature isn't stupid. Nevertheless, no one has ever been able to prove or disprove a certain basic conjecture about pi: that every digit has an equal chance of appearing in pi. This is known as the normality conjecture for pi. The normality conjecture says that, on average, there is no more or less of any digit in pi: for example, there is no excess of sevens in pi. If all digits do appear with the same average frequency in pi, then pi is a "normal" number—"normal" by the narrow mathematical definition of the word. "This is the simplest possible conjecture about pi," Gregory said. "There is absolutely no doubt that pi is a 'normal' number. Yet we can't prove it. We don't even know how to *try* to prove it. We know very little about transcendental numbers, and, what is worse, the number of conjectures about them isn't growing." No one knows even how to tell the difference between the square root of two and pi merely by looking at long strings of their digits, though the two numbers have completely distinct mathematical properties, one being algebraic and the other transcendental.

Even if the brothers couldn't prove anything about the digits of pi, they felt that by looking at them through the window of their machine they might at least see something that could lead to an important conjecture about pi or about transcendental numbers as a class. You can learn a lot about all cats by looking closely at one of them. So if you wanted to look

closely at pi how much of it could you see with a very large supercomputer? What if you turned the universe into a supercomputer? What
then? How much pi could you see? Naturally, the brothers had considered
this project. They had imagined a computer built from the universe.
Here's how they estimated the machine's size. It has been calculated
that there are about 10^{79} electrons and protons in the observable universe;
this is the so-called Eddington number of the universe. (Sir Arthur
Stanley Eddington, the astrophysicist, first came up with the number.)
The Eddington number is the digit 1 followed by seventy-nine zeros:
10,000,000,000,000,000,000,000,000,000,000,000,000,000,000,000,000,
000,000,000,000,000,000,000,000,000. Ten vigintsextillion. The Eddington
number. It declares the power of the Eddington machine.

The Eddington machine would be the universal supercomputer. It
would be made of all the atoms in the universe. The Eddington machine would contain ten vigintsextillion parts, and if the Chudnovsky
brothers could figure out how to program it with FORTRAN they
might make it churn toward pi. "In order to study the sequence of pi,
you have to store it in the Eddington machine's memory," Gregory said.
To be realistic, the brothers thought that a practical Eddington machine
wouldn't be able to store pi much beyond 10^{77} digits—a number that is
only a hundredth of the Eddington number. Now, what if the digits of
pi only begin to show regularity beyond 10^{77} digits? Suppose, for example, that pi manifests a regularity starting at 10^{100} decimal places? That
number is known as a googol. If the design in pi appears only after a
googol of digits, then not even the Eddington machine will see any system in pi; pi will look totally disordered to the universe, even if pi contains a slow, vast, delicate structure. A mere googol of pi might be only
the first knot at the corner of a kind of limitless Persian rug, which is
woven into increasingly elaborate diamonds, cross-stars, gardens, and
cosmogonies. It may never be possible, in principle, to see the order in
the digits of pi. Not even nature itself may know the nature of pi.

"If pi doesn't show systematic behavior until more than ten to the
seventy-seven decimal places, it would really be a disaster," Gregory
said. "It would be actually horrifying,"

"I wouldn't give up," David said. "There might be some other way
of leaping over the barrier—"

"And of attacking the son of a bitch," Gregory said.

The brothers first came in contact with the membrane that divides the
dreamlike earth from mathematical reality when they were boys, growing up in Kiev, and their father gave David a book entitled "What is
Mathematics?," by two mathematicians named Richard Courant and

Herbert Robbins. The book is a classic—millions of copies of it have been printed in unauthorized Russian and Chinese editions alone—and after the brothers finished reading "Robbins," as the book is called in Russia, David decided to become a mathematician, and Gregory soon followed his brother's footsteps into the nature beyond nature. Gregory's first publication, in the journal *Soviet Mathematics—Doklady*, came when he was sixteen years old: "Some Results in the Theory of Infinitely Long Expressions." Already you can see where he was headed. David, sensing his younger brother's power, encouraged him to grapple with central problems in mathematics. Gregory made his first major discovery at the age of seventeen, when he solved Hilbert's Tenth Problem. (It was one of twenty-three great problems posed by David Hilbert in 1900.) To solve a Hilbert problem would be an achievement for a lifetime; Gregory was a high-school student who had read a few books on mathematics. Strangely, a young Russian mathematician named Yuri Matyasevich had just solved Hilbert's Tenth Problem, and the brothers hadn't heard the news. Matyasevich has recently said that the Chudnovsky method is the preferred way to solve Hilbert's Tenth Problem.

The brothers enrolled at Kiev State University, and both graduated summa cum laude. They took their Ph.D.s at the Institute of Mathematics at the Ukrainian Academy of Sciences. At first, they published their papers separately, but by the mid-nineteen-seventies they were collaborating on much of their work. They lived with their parents in Kiev until the family decided to try to take Gregory abroad for treatment, and in 1976 Volf and Malka Chudnovsky applied to the government to emigrate. Volf was immediately fired from his job.

The K.G.B. began tailing the brothers. "Gregory would not believe me until it became totally obvious," David said. "I had twelve K.G.B. agents on my tail. No, look, I'm not kidding! They shadowed me around the clock in two cars, six agents in each car. Three in the front seat and three in the back seat. That was how the K.G.B. operated." One day, in 1976, David was walking down the street when K.G.B. officers attacked him, breaking his skull. He went home and nearly died, but didn't go to the hospital. "If I had gone to the hospital, I would have died for sure," he told me. "The hospital is run by the state. I would forget to breathe."

On July 22, 1977, plainclothesmen from the K.G.B. accosted Volf and Malka on a street in Kiev and beat them up. They broke Malka's arm and fractured her skull. David took his mother to the hospital. "The doctor in the emergency room said there was no fracture," David said.

Gregory, at home in bed, was not so vulnerable. Also, he was conspicuous in the West. Edwin Hewitt, a mathematician at the University of Washington, in Seattle, had visited Kiev in 1976 and collaborated with Gregory on a paper, and later, when Hewitt learned that the Chudnovsky family was in trouble, he persuaded Senator Henry M. Jackson, the powerful member of the Senate Armed Services Committee, to take up the Chudnovskys' case. Jackson put pressure on the Soviets to let the family leave the country. Just before the K.G.B. attacked the parents, two members of a French parliamentary delegation that was in Kiev made an unofficial visit to the Chudnovskys to see what was going on. One of the visitors, a staff member of the delegation, was Nicole Lannegrace, who married David in 1983. Andrei Sakharov also helped to draw attention to the Chudnovskys' increasingly desperate situation. Two months after the parents were attacked, the Soviet government unexpectedly let the family go. "That summer when I was getting killed by the K.G.B., I could never have imagined that the next year I would be in Paris or that I would wind up in New York, married to a beautiful Frenchwoman," David said. The Chudnovsky family settled in New York, near Columbia University.

If pi is truly random, then at times pi will appear to be ordered. Therefore, if pi is random it contains accidental order. For example, somewhere in pi a sequence may run 07070707070707 for as many decimal places as there are, say, hydrogen atoms in the sun. It's just an accident. Somewhere else the same sequence of zeros and sevens may appear, only this time interrupted by a single occurrence of the digit 3. Another accident. Those and all other "accidental" arrangements of digits almost certainly erupt in pi, but their presence has never been proved. "Even if pi is not truly random, you can still assume that you get *every* string of digits in pi," Gregory said.

If you were to assign letters of the alphabet to combinations of digits, and were to do this for all human alphabets, syllabaries, and ideograms, then you could fit any written character in any language to a combination of digits in pi. According to this system, pi could be turned into literature. Then, if you could look far enough into pi, you would probably find the expression "See the U.S.A. in a Chevrolet!" a billion times in a row. Elsewhere, you would find Christ's Sermon on the Mount in His native Aramaic tongue, and you would find versions of the Sermon on the Mount that are pure blasphemy. Also, you would find a dictionary of Yanomamo curses. A guide to the pawnshops of Lubbock. The book about the sea which James Joyce supposedly declared he would write after he finished "Finnegans Wake." The collected transcripts of "The Tonight Show" rendered into Etruscan. "Knowledge of All Existing Things," by Ahmes the Egyptian scribe.

Each occurrence of an apparently ordered string in pi, such as the words "Ruin hath taught me thus to ruminate/That Time will come and take my love away," is followed by unimaginable deserts of babble. No book and none but the shortest poems will ever be seen in pi, since it is infinitesimally unlikely that even as brief a text as an English sonnet will appear in the first 10^{77} digits of pi, which is the longest piece of pi that can be calculated in this universe.

Anything that can be produced by a simple method is by definition orderly. Pi can be produced by various simple methods of rational approximation, and those methods yield the same digits in a fixed order forever. Therefore, pi is orderly in the extreme. Pi may also be a powerful random-number generator, spinning out any and all possible combinations of digits. We see that the distinction between chance and fixity dissolves in pi. The deep connection between disorder and order, between cacophony and harmony, in the most famous ratio in mathematics fascinated Gregory and David Chudnovsky. They wondered if the digits of pi had a personality.

"We are looking for the appearance of some rules that will distinguish the digits of pi from other numbers," Gregory explained. "It's like studying writers by studying their use of words, their grammar. If you see a Russian sentence that extends for a whole page, with hardly a comma, it is definitely Tolstoy. If someone were to give you a million digits from somewhere in pi, could you tell it was from pi? We don't really look for patterns; we look for rules. Think of games for children. If I give you the sequence one, two, three, four, five, can you tell me what the next digit is? Even a child can do it; the next digit is six. How about this game? Three, one, four, one, five, nine. Just by looking at that sequence, can you tell me the next digit? What if I gave you a sequence of a million digits from pi? Could you tell me the next digit just by looking at the sequence? Why does pi look like a totally unpredictable sequence with the highest complexity? We need to find out the rules that govern this game. For all we know, we may never find a rule in pi."

Herbert Robbins, the co-author of "What Is Mathematics?," is an emeritus professor of mathematical statistics at Columbia University. For the past six years, he has been teaching at Rutgers. The Chudnovskys call him once in a while to get his advice on how to use statistical tools to search for signs of order in pi. Robbins lives in a rectilinear house that has a lot of glass in it, in the woods on the outskirts of Princeton. Some of the twentieth century's most creative and powerful discoveries in statistics and probability theory happened inside his head. Robbins is a tall, restless man in his seventies, with a loud voice, furrowed cheeks, and penetrating eyes. One recent day, he stretched himself out on a daybed in a garden room in his house and played with a rubber band, making a harp across his fingertips.

"It is a very difficult philosophical question, the question of what 'random' is," he said. He plucked the rubber band with his thumb, *boink, boink*. "Everyone knows the famous remark of Albert Einstein, that God does not throw dice. Einstein just would not believe that there is an element of randomness in the construction of the world. The question of whether the universe is a random process or is determined in some way is a basic philosophical question that has nothing to do with mathematics. The question is important. People consider it when they decide what to do with their lives. It concerns religion. It is the question of whether our fate will be revealed or whether we live by blind chance. My God, how many people have been murdered over an answer to that question! Mathematics is a lesser activity than religion in the sense that we've agreed not to kill each other but to discuss things."

Robbins got up from the daybed and sat in an armchair. Then he stood up and paced the room, and sat at a table in the room, and sat on a couch, and went back to the table, and finally returned to the daybed. The man was in constant motion. It looked random to me, but it may have been systematic. It was the random walk of Herbert Robbins.

"Mathematics is broken into tiny specialties today, but Gregory Chudnovsky is a generalist who knows the whole of mathematics as well as anyone," he said as he moved around. "You have to go back a hundred years, to David Hilbert, to find a mathematician as broadly knowledgeable as Gregory Chudnovsky. He's like Mozart: he's the last of his breed. I happen to think the brothers' pi project is a will-o'-the-wisp, and is one of the least interesting things they've ever done. But what do I know? Gregory seems to be asking questions that can't be answered. To ask for the system in pi is like asking 'Is there life after death?' When you die, you'll find out. Most mathematicians are not interested in the digits of pi, because the question is of no practical importance. In order for a mathematician to become interested in a problem, there has to be a possibility of solving it. If you are an athlete, you ask yourself if you can jump thirty feet. Gregory likes to ask if he can jump around the world. He likes to do things that are impossible."

At some point after the brothers settled in New York, it became obvious that Columbia University was not going to be able to invite them to become full-fledged members of the faculty. Since then, the brothers have always enjoyed cordial personal relationships with various members of the faculty, but as an institution the Mathematics Department has been unable to create permanent faculty positions for them. Robbins and a couple of fellow-mathematicians—Lipman Bers and the late Mark Kac—once tried to raise money from private sources for an endowed chair at Columbia to be shared by the brothers, but the effort failed. Then the John D. and Catherine T. MacArthur Foundation awarded Gregory Chudnovsky a "genius" fellowship; that happened in 1981, the first year the awards were given, as if to suggest that Gregory is a person for whom the MacArthur prize was invented. The brothers can exhibit other fashionable paper—a Prix Peccot-Vimont, a couple of Guggenheims, a Doctor of Science *honoris causa* from Bard College, the Moscow Mathematical Society Prize—but there is one defect in their résumé, which is the fact that Gregory has to lie in bed most of the day. The ugly truth is that Gregory Chudnovsky can't get a permanent job at any American institution of higher learning because he is physically disabled. But there are other, more perplexing reasons that have led the Chudnovsky brothers to pursue their work in solitude, outside the normal academic hierarchy, since the day they arrived in the United States.

Columbia University has awarded each brother the title of senior research scientist in the Department of Mathematics. Their position at Columbia is ambiguous. The university officially considers them to be members of the faculty, but they don't have tenure, and Columbia doesn't spend its own funds to pay their salaries or to support their research. However, Columbia does give them health-insurance benefits and a housing subsidy.

The brothers have been living on modest grants from the National Science Foundation and various other research agencies, which are funnelled through Columbia and have to be applied for regularly. Nicole Lannegrace and Christine Chudnovsky financed m zero out of their paychecks. Christine's father, Gonzalo Pardo, who is a professor of dentistry at the State University of New York at Stony Brook, built the steel frame for m zero in his basement during a few weekends, using a wrench and a hacksaw.

The brothers' mode of existence has come to be known among mathematicians as the Chudnovsky Problem. Herbert Robbins eventually decided that it was time to ask the entire American mathematics profession why it could not solve the Chudnovsky Problem. Robbins is a member of the National Academy of Sciences, and in 1986 he sent a letter to all of the mathematicians in the academy:

> I fear that unless a decent and honorable position in the American educational and research system is found for the brothers soon, a personal and scientific tragedy will take place for which all American mathematicians will share responsibility. . . .

I have asked many of my colleagues why this situation exists, and what can be done to put an end to what I regard as a national disgrace. I have never received an answer that satisfies me. . . . I am asking you, then, as one of the leaders of American mathematics, to tell me what you are prepared to do to acquaint yourselves with their present circumstances, and if you are convinced of the merits of their case, to find a suitable position somewhere in the country for them as a pair.

There wasn't much of a response. Robbins says that he received three written replies to his letter. One, from a faculty member at a well-known East Coast university, complained about David Chudnovsky's personality. He remarked that "when David learns to be less overbearing" the brothers might have better luck. He also did not fully understand the tone of Robbins' letter: while he agreed that some resolution to the Chudnovsky Problem must be found, he thought that Herb Robbins ought to approach the subject realistically and with more candor. ("More candor? How could I have been more candid?" Robbins asked.) Another letter came from a faculty member at Princeton University, who offered to put in a good word with the National Science Foundation to help the brothers get their grants, but did not mention a job at Princeton or anywhere else. The most thoughtful response came from a faculty member at M.I.T., who remarked, "It does seem odd that they have not been more sought after." He wondered if in some part this might be a consequence of their breadth. "A specialist appears as a safer investment to a cautious academic administrator. I'm sorry I have nothing more effective to propose."

An emotional reaction to Robbins' campaign on behalf of the Chudnovskys came a bit later from Edwin Hewitt, the mathematician who had helped get the family out of the Soviet Union, and one of the few Americans who has ever worked with Gregory Chudnovsky. Hewitt wrote to colleagues, "I have collaborated with many excellent mathematicians . . . but with no one else have I witnessed an outpouring of mathematics like that from Gregory. He simply KNOWS what is true and what is not." In another letter, Hewitt wrote:

The Chudnovsky situation is a national disgrace. Everyone says, "Oh, what a crying shame" & then suggests that they be placed at *somebody else's institution*. No one seems to want the admittedly burdensome task of caring for the Chudnovsky family. I imagine it would be a full-time, if not an impossible, job. We may remember that both Mozart and Beethoven were disagreeable people, to say nothing of Gauss.

The brothers would have to be hired as a pair. Gregory won't take any job unless David gets one, and vice versa. Physically and intellectually commingled, like two trees that have grown together at the root and bole, the brothers claim that they can't be separated without becoming deadfalls and crashing to the ground. To hire the Chudnovsky pair, a department would have to create a joint opening for them. Gregory can't teach classes in the normal way, because he is more or less confined to bed. It would require a small degree of flexibility in a department to allow Gregory to concentrate on research, while David handled the teaching. The problem is that Gregory might still have the pleasure of working with a few brilliant graduate students—a privilege that might not go down well in an American academic department.

"They are prototypical Russians," Robbins said. "They combine a rather grandiose vision of themselves with an ability to live on scraps rather than compromise their principles. These are people the world is not able to cope with, and they are not making it any easier for the world. I don't see that the world is particularly trying to keep Gregory Chudnovsky alive. The tragedy—the *disgrace*, so to speak—is that the American scientific and educational establishment is not benefitting from the Chudnovskys' assistance. Thirteen years have gone by since the Chudnovskys arrived here, and where are all the graduate students who would have worked with the brothers? How many truly great mathematicians have you ever heard of who couldn't get a job? I think the Chudnovskys are the only example in history. This vast educational system of ours has poured the Chudnovskys out on the sand, to waste. Yet Gregory is one of the remarkable personalities of our time. When I go up to that apartment and sit by his bed, I think, My God, when I was a student at Harvard I was in contact with people far less interesting than this. What happens to me in Gregory's room is like that line in the Gerard Manley Hopkins poem: 'Margaret, are you grieving/Over Goldengrove unleaving?' I'm grieving, and I guess it's me I'm grieving for."

"Two billion digits of pi? Where do they keep them?" Samuel Eilenberg said to me. Eilenberg is a gifted and distinguished topologist, and an emeritus professor of mathematics at Columbia University. He was the chairman of the department when the question of hiring the brothers first became troublesome to Columbia. "There is an element of fatigue in the Chudnovsky Problem," he said. "In the academic world, we have to be careful who our colleagues are. David is a pain in the neck. He interrupts people, and he is not interested in anything except what concerns him and his brother. He is a nudnick! Gregory is certainly unusual, but he is not great. You can spend all your life computing digits.

What for? You know in advance that you can't see any regularity in pi. It's about as interesting as going to the beach and counting sand. I wouldn't be caught dead doing that kind of work! Most mathematicians probably feel this way. An important ingredient in mathematics is taste. Mathematics is mostly about giving pleasure. The ultimate criterion of mathematics is aesthetic, and to calculate the two-billionth digit of pi is to me abhorrent."

"Abhorrent—yes, most mathematicians would probably agree with that," said Dale Brownawell, a respected number theorist at Penn State. "Tastes change, though. If something were to begin to show up in the digits of pi, it would boggle everyone's mind." Brownawell met the Chudnovskys at the Vienna airport when they escaped from the Soviet Union. "They didn't bring much with them, just a pile of bags and boxes. David would walk through a wall to do what is right for his brother. In the situation they are in, how else can they survive? To see the Chudnovskys carrying on science at such a high level with such meagre support is awe-inspiring."

Richard Askey, a prominent mathematician at the University of Wisconsin at Madison, occasionally flies to New York to sit at the foot of Gregory Chudnovsky's bed and learn about mathematics. "David Chudnovsky is a very good mathematician," Askey said to me. "Gregory is one of the few great mathematicians of our time. Gregory is so much better than I am that it is impossible for me to say how good he really is. Is he the best in the world, or one of the three best? I feel uncomfortable evaluating people at that level. The brothers' pi stuff is just a small part of their work. They are really trying to find out what the word 'random' means. I've heard some people say that the brothers are wasting their time with that machine, but Gregory Chudnovsky is a very intelligent man, who has his head screwed on straight, and I wouldn't begin to question his priorities. The tragedy is that Gregory has had hardly any students. If he dies without having passed on not only his knowledge but his whole way of thinking, then it will be a great tragedy. Rather than blame Columbia University, I would prefer to say that the blame lies with all American mathematicians. Gregory Chudnovsky is a national problem."

"It looks like kvetching," Gregory said from his bed. "It looks cheap, and it is cheap. We are here in the United States by our own choice. I don't think we were somehow wronged. I really can't teach. So what does one want to do about it? Attempts to change the system are very expensive and time-consuming and largely a waste of time. We barely have time to do the things we want to do."

"To reform the system?" David said, playing his flashlight across the ceiling. "In this country? Look. Come on. It's much easier to reform a totalitarian system."

"Yes, you just make a decree," Gregory said. "Anyway, this sort of talk moves into philosophical questions. What is life, and where does the money come from?" He shrugged.

Toward the end of the summer of 1991, the brothers halted their probe into pi. They had surveyed pi to two billion two hundred and sixty million three hundred and twenty-one thousand three hundred and thirty-six digits. It was a world record, doubling the record that the Chudnovskys had set in 1989. If the digits were printed in ordinary type, they would stretch from New York to Southern California. The brothers had temporarily ditched their chief competitor, Yasumasa Kanada—a pleasing development when the brothers considered that Kanada had access to a half-megawatt Hitachi monster that was supposed to be faster than a Cray. Kanada reacted gracefully to the Chudnovskys' achievement, and he told *Science News* that he might be able to get at least a billion and a half digits of pi if he could obtain enough time on a Japanese supercomputer.

"You see the advantage to being truly poor. We had to build our machine, but now we get to use it, too," Gregory said.

The Chudnovskys' machine had spent its time both calculating pi and checking the result. The job had taken about two hundred and fifty hours on m zero. The machine had spent most of its time checking the answer, to make sure each digit was correct, rather than doing the fundamental computation of pi.

"We have done our tests for patterns, and there is nothing," Gregory said. "It would be rather stupid if there were something in a few billion digits. There are the usual things. The digit three is repeated nine times in a row, and we didn't see that before. Unfortunately, we still don't have enough computer power to see anything in pi."

Such was their scientific conclusion, and yet the brothers felt that they may have noticed something in pi. It hovered out of reach, but it seemed a little closer now. It was a slight sign of order—a possible sign—and it had to do with the running average of the digits. You can take an average of any string of digits in pi. It is like getting a batting average, an average height, an average weight. The average of the digits in pi should be 4.5. That's the average of the decimal digits zero through nine. The brothers noticed that the average seems to be slightly skewed. It stays a little high through most of the first billion digits, and then it stays a little low through the next billion digits. The running average of pi looks like a tide that rises and retreats through two billion digits, as if a distant moon were passing over a sea of digits, pulling them up and down. It may or may not be a hint of a rule in pi. "It's unfortunately not statistically significant yet," Gregory said. "It's close to the edge of significance." The brothers may have glimpsed only their desire for order. The tide that seems to flow through pi may be nothing but aimless gabble, but what if it is a wave rippling through pi? What if the wave begins to show a weird and complicated pulsation as you go deeper in pi? You could become obsessive thinking about things like this. You might have to build more machines. "We need a trillion digits," David said. A trillion digits printed in ordinary type would stretch from here to the moon and back, twice. The brothers thought that if they didn't get bored with pi and move on to other problems they would easily collect a trillion digits in a few years, with the help of increasingly powerful supercomputing equipment. They would orbit the moon in digits, and head for Alpha Centauri, and if they lived and their machines held, perhaps someday they would begin to see the true nature of pi.

Gregory is lying in bed in the junk yard, a keyboard on his lap. He offers to show me a few digits of pi, and taps at the keys.

On the screen beside his bed, m zero responds: "Please, give the beginning of the decimal digit to look."

Gregory types a command, and suddenly the whole screen fills with the raw Ludolphian number, moving like Niagara Falls. We observe pi in silence for quite a while, until it ends with:

... 18820 54573 01261 27678 17413 87779 66981 15311 24707 34258 41235 99801 92693 52561 92393 53870 24377 10069 16106 22971 02523 30027 49528 06378 64067 12852 77857 42344 28836 88521 72435 85924 57786 36741 32845 66266 96498 68308 59920 06168 63376 85976 35341 52906 04621 44710 52106 99079 33563 54625 71001 37490 77872 43403 57690 01699 82447 20059 93533 82919 46119 87044 02125 12329 11964 10087 41341 42633 88249 48948 31198 27787 03802 08989 05316 75375 43242 20100 43326 74069 33751 86349 40467 52687 79749 68922 29914 46047 47109 31678 05219 48702 00877 32383 87446 91871 49136 90837 88525 51575 35790 83982 20710 59298 41193 81740 92975 31.

"It showed the last digits we've found," Gregory says. "The last shall be first."

"Thanks for asking," m zero remarks, on the screen.

Walt Harrington

Molly Roberts

Walt Harrington's family portrait originally appeared in *The Washington Post Magazine*, where he is a staff writer. It later became a chapter in his book *Crossings: A White Man's Journey Into Black America* (1992).

His work for *The Washington Post Magazine* has been collected in *American Profiles* (1992). Harrington's articles portrayed how a family was changed by the suicide of a child, the way in which a father dealt with the kidnapping of his infant son, and the everyday lives of an elderly woman, a homicide detective, a fundamentalist family, a retarded man, and an amateur stock car racer.

"At age forty-two," Harrington said, "I am still an outsider, more curious about the routine than the aberrant, more interested in understanding people than in criticizing them." The son of a milkman, he grew up outside Chicago, went to a small college in rural Illinois because it offered a full scholarship, then went to graduate school in sociology at the University of Missouri. While there, he read James Agee's *Let Us Now Praise Famous Men*, the essays of Wendell Berry, the nature writing of Aldo Leopold and Edward Abbey, and New Journalism by Tom Wolfe and Gay Talese. He finished a master's degree in sociology and then earned another in journalism.

During an apprenticeship at small magazines and at newspapers, he read John McPhee and E. B. White, "who so seamlessly blend detail and meaning," and the fiction of Tolstoy, Faulkner, Willa Cather, and Robert Penn Warren. He arrived at *The Washington Post Magazine* and took up what he calls "intimate journalism." His goal was to understand people as they understand themselves. He has taken one of Mark Twain's lines as a motto: "What a wee little part of a person's life are his acts and words! His real life is led in his head, and is known to none but himself. All day long, and every day, the mill of his brain is grinding, and his thoughts, not those other things, are his history."

"The Journalism of Everyday Life is infinite:" he wrote in *American Profiles*, "a farmer as winter comes to the farm, a country priest, three men who have for years met every Saturday morning to play basketball, a week in the life of a suburban housewife, the annual deer-hunting expedition, a high-school football quarterback, a welfare mother, a pool shark, an aspiring jazz musician, an old man and an old woman who fall in love in a nursing home."

He added a note of caution on writing about everyday life. "If you aren't learning intimate details about your ordinary subjects that you believe are too personal for print, you're probably doing a poor job of reporting. If you don't often struggle with the ethics of what you will include in your profiles of ordinary people, you're either a schmuck or not really facing the ethical dilemmas."

A Family Portrait in Black & White

My journey begins in the dentist's chair. The nurse's fingers are pressing dental dough into my lower incisors, and she and the doctor are playing dueling banjos with funny stories about their kids, when in walks another dentist, dropping by to say hello. "I've got a good one," he says cheerfully, and then he tells a racist joke. I can't recall the joke, only that it ends with a black man who is stupid. Dead silence. It's just us white folks here in the room, but my dentist and his nurse know my wife, who is black, and they know my son and my daughter, who are, as they describe themselves, tan and bright tan. How many racist jokes have I heard in my life? Five, maybe ten thousand, at least. But today— for the first time, for who knows exactly why—I am struck with a deep, sharp pain. I look at this man, with his pasty face, pale hair and weak lips, and I think: *This idiot's talking about my son!*

I want to shake him, shove him against the wall. I say nothing. Quickly, my dentist grabs a tool, the nurse extracts the dough, and the idiot leaves. But I remain behind in suspended animation. It isn't the joke. It isn't the tension in the air. It isn't even the idiot. It is my recognition: I've crossed a line, and I know I have, and I know that for an instant I've traveled to a place where white Americans don't go. I feel revulsion and anger at this man. I feel fear and anguish for my children. I feel helpless. Am I, I wonder, feeling like a black man?

A memory: A long time ago, when I was 8, maybe 9, I sat with my grandmother on the steps of her house in the country outside Chicago, snapping fresh beans. My grandmother was a large, stern woman with a baritone voice, round wire glasses and gray hair swept up in that old Gibson Girl fashion. I called her Big Grandma with fear and respect. That day, she told me she'd been to "the city"—Chicago Heights, Ill., which in the 1950s was an industrial town of about 35,000. Big Grandma said she'd seen "coloreds" everywhere. Then she said this: While standing in line at the Walgreen drugstore, she'd heard one colored lady tell another colored lady, "I *always* carries a razor in *my* purse." Big Grandma said this with a dramatic inflection, a shiver and a kind of rage, but I missed her complex meanings.

Coloreds, I thought, what in the world are *coloreds*?

I had no idea. But from her tone, I knew not to ask. Instead, I decided that *coloreds* were people whose skin, for mysterious reasons, resembled a concoction of melted crayons stirred into a weird, beautiful swirl. I remember this thought so clearly because of my later amazement when I went to Chicago Heights with Big Grandma and she pointed out a "colored." I was disappointed. They weren't *colored* after all.

Three decades later, sitting in the dentist's chair, I'm struck by how much I am still like that little boy who believed he understood what he absolutely did not. Ten years of marriage to a black woman, two children, years of visiting my wife's family in rural Kentucky, years of births and deaths, years of hunting with my father-in-law, Alex, his brother Bobby and their friend Carl, years of shared bottles of Old Forester, shared jokes, lies and hunting knives—years of what I believed was a life lived across the color line . . . Yet only today, for the first time, have I felt, *felt*, the intimate intrigues and confusions of race in America.

Only today, for the first time, have I crossed the line.

My wife's father, Alex, slips the rubber band off the large, tightly rolled paper, uncurls it, smooths it on the coffee table and then begins tracing the antecedents of his life. He starts in the upper left-hand corner, touching each name with the fingertips of his left hand: Tyler, Otha, Lou Emma, Annie, Beulah, Effie, Pratt, Samuel, Dollie and Shed, who was his father. He then follows the branches of the handwritten family tree to his mother, Stella, through the names of his four brothers, to his own name, to those of his two sons, to that of his only daughter, Keran, who is my wife, and beyond to my name and those of our children, Matthew and Kyle. For this genealogical tour, for a tour of another world, I have come to my in-laws' farm outside Glasgow, Ky., where Alex grew up.

Thank the idiot in the dentist's office: His callousness has made me realize that what I know—about my wife and my children, about this thing called *race*—is really nothing at all. I'm here for a simple and complicated reason: My children share a heritage that I may understand historically and intellectually but for which I have no intuitive, no emotional, grasp. I hope, somehow, to change that.

I think of Alex as a friend. He's a soft-spoken man who cannot, to my mother-in-law's constant consternation, be hurried no matter what the occasion. At 58, he's still handsome, lean and youthful. His sideburns and sparse mustache are sprinkled with gray. My children describe his complexion as brown-tan. He wears low-hanging Rustler jeans and a red-plaid flannel shirt over a crew-neck T-shirt, and he gently pads around the house in white socks. He's—how shall I say it?—something of an eccentric: He fries bull gonads for breakfast. (Served with well-seasoned brown gravy, they taste like tender chicken gizzards.) He maintains an antique Model A Ford, an antique Coke machine and an antique Seeburg jukebox. He drives a hundred miles for a bottle of moonshine whiskey to share with his friends. Posted at his driveway is a classic jockey-boy statue—except that Alex has painted him bright white and named him Joe Zeller, after an old white friend. Alex is a country boy who left the country at 15, lying to the Air Force recruiter about his age. He had pure motivation to lie—he was just a hot-step ahead of the law for having sold a few illegally garnered gasoline stamps during World War II. He laughs: It's hard to believe more than four decades have passed. A few years ago—after serving in the Air Force in West Germany, England, France, California, Washington and Illinois—Alex and his wife, Celeste, retired to Glasgow.

"I gotta die somewhere," he says, smiling.

This morning, Alex and I are up at 6:30 and on the road, a twisting, two-lane stretch of blacktop called Kentucky 90. We are driving to Alex's beginnings, on the only road that runs the 40 miles from Glasgow, a town of 12,646 people in southwest Kentucky, to Burkesville, a drab little burg set down in lavish forest along the Cumberland River. It's cold this morning, 35 degrees, but the Burkesville sky after dawn is so blue that it seems to disappear into itself, and the air is as clean as freshly washed glass. A hundred years ago, Burkesville—or rather a place called Lawson Bottom 11 miles northeast of Burkesville—was home to Alex's mother's family. Lawson Bottom was even named after her family, quite an accomplishment and quite an anomaly in the South of those days.

Alex didn't grow up in Lawson Bottom. His mother had migrated to Glasgow as a young woman, and Alex visited the farm only sporadically as a boy. Yet he has always seemed to have Lawson Bottom in him, carried its memory proudly, in a way that my wife and her brothers do not. As we make the final turn onto Lawson Bottom Road, Alex—for at least the hundredth time—tells me the story of taking his fiancee, Celeste, who was a college girl from a nice family of schoolteachers, to visit the farm in 1951. When they arrived at Lawson Bottom that first time, folks were so happy to see them that one of Alex's aunts called for a feast: "*Paee*-tehr," she yelled to her son, as Alex recalls with an exaggerated *Cain*-tucky accent, "go out and kill a *chai*-kin." Peter did—shooting its head off with a single rifle shot. From somewhere deep inside, Alex laughs so hard that his car swerves briefly to the left. He loves that story. It inevitably makes city folks cringe, and it inevitably reminds Alex of how far he and his family and his race have come.

These days, the Lawsons are long gone from Lawson Bottom—except for Alex's cousin Reid, a 66-year-old man who has lived away from the "holler" only six months of his life. When Alex and I pull into the drive, Reid is outside hefting the wooden top off the well. The pump has stopped, but he's unconcerned. Lawson Branch, a tiny mountain-fed stream, runs only 20 feet away, and it is an "everlasting" stream, as they call it, meaning that it never runs dry. If Reid must, he'll simply dip water from the branch for washing clothes or even for drinking, as the Cherokee Indians might have done 200 years ago. But that won't be necessary. Alex was a master sergeant and an airplane mechanic in the Air Force—at least he was once they stopped dumping blacks into kitchen, janitorial and paper-shuffling jobs in the '50s—and for the cost of a $4.50 electrical switch, he'll have Reid's pump whirring in a couple of hours.

While Alex works, Reid leads me toward the house, walking deliberately with his hands stuffed deep into the pockets of his old green coat. He's a tall man, only slightly stooped with the years. He has been lean all his life, and only recently has he put on a little weight around the middle. He wears jeans, leather boots and a tan work shirt. On his head rests an orange hunting cap: "Burkesville Fertilizer." The hat sits back, angled to the right atop a full shock of chalk-white hair. "Let me put a dry stick in the stove," Reid says, heading back out the front door for five huge pieces of split cedar. I sit in a creaking chair, one of only three, and survey the single room in which Reid lives. It's as if I'm inside an old, sepia-toned photograph: the "Warm Morning" wood stove in the center of the room, the bare light bulb hanging overhead, the long on-off string running from the light and tied to the bedpost, the dog-eared Bible, the brown cross painted on the unpainted drywall, the strong and—to my own weak, city-dweller nostrils—nauseating smell of dead mice in the walls, a cold-weather condition that can't be avoided on the farm. Reid is like a movie frame halted in time, the living embodiment of where Alex's family began a century ago.

Through the clouded window next to his bed, Reid points to a tuft of young trees, mostly elm, just across the drive on this side of Lawson Branch. There stood the family homeplace, the house of patriarch Berry Lawson—born 1865, died 1915. The legend of Berry Lawson has been handed down in the family for generations, and I have heard it not only from Reid but from my wife's grandmother, Stella, before she died and from my wife's great-aunt Minnie, a short, 81-year-old wisp of woman with light, soft skin and wavy gray hair. She's known to everyone as Aunt G, after her middle name, Glatha.

There are no pictures of my wife's great-great-grandfather Berry, only the memories of his children, who say Berry Lawson was small and strong—and nearly white, with muted African features and straight, jet-black hair. "Good hair," as Aunt G still calls it. Berry's parentage, like that of so many in the simultaneously Jim Crow and miscegenational Old South, was fuzzy. He was raised by a white bachelor farmer named Billy Mayes and his spinster sister, Sally. Everyone assumed Berry was Billy's son by a neighboring black woman, a Lawson, who died when Berry was 5. When Billy Mayes and Sally died, they left Berry the 250-acre farm. Reid says blacks and whites always got along in Lawson Bottom, but a black man—even a half-black man—owning so much land didn't sit well with everybody, particularly one rich white farmer who complained that no colored man should be allowed to own such fertile land.

But Berry did, and he set about raising his family with his wife, Ada. Their log cabin was magnificent against the shacks and shanties of other blacks. The house sat snugly between Lawson Bottom Road to the front and a 900-foot forest ridge to the rear. Its rough-hewn logs were sealed with wattle and daub and its roof was covered with foot-long split hickory shakes. Inside, the house was dominated by its massive, gray stone fireplace—five feet high with a hearth big enough for a six-foot backlog and guarded by heavy dog irons that Berry Lawson had tempered in his own blacksmith shop in the barn.

The Lawsons had plenty, little cash, but plenty. They had nice clothes, and my wife's grandmother Stella would give her old dresses to poor blacks—even to poor whites. For the winter, Berry Lawson stored mountains of 100-pound sacks of flour from wheat grown in his own fields. He grew corn, hay and tobacco; he raised cows, hogs, horses, mules, chickens and ducks. Each year, he put up ten 50-pound stands of lard. "Not even white folks had that much lard," Aunt G boasts. What the farm didn't produce, the steamboats on the Cumberland River delivered for barter—candy, coffee and Red Rolling Fork whiskey packed four quart bottles to the cardboard box. Such affluence among blacks didn't go unnoticed.

As a girl, Aunt G once picked up the phone—yes, the Lawsons had a phone—and overheard two white women gabbing on the party line: "What're you eatin' tonight?" one white woman asked the other. "I don't know," came the reply. "The only person who's got anything is Ada Lawson. She's got everything." Aunt G laughs at the memory, a joyful little cackle that she mutes with a hand put discreetly to her mouth. "Of all the Negroes over there," she says, "we was the only ones with land and horses and wagons. All the others would be walkin', and we'd be ridin'." She laughs again. "They said we thought we was better, rich, because we were Berry Lawson's kids." Well, truth is, Aunt G *did* think she was better than the other Lawson Bottom blacks. "I thought it was their fault they were poor," she says with uncertain contrition. "I don't guess it was, lookin' back."

Even then, polite whites referred to blacks as "coloreds," which was Aunt G's preference. But for all her affluence, when some "poor white trash" would call her a "nigger" or a "blackbird" or a "darkie," there was nothing she could do about it, except seethe. Black and white children played together and ate lunches at each other's houses, became good friends, but it was a rare white child who didn't, when angered, resort to his ultimate weapon, racial slurs. The black kids would respond—calling the white kids "peckerwoods," a slur against whites that they had often heard their parents use privately. But it never had the same sting: Without raw power to back it up, a slur is only a pinprick.

Aunt G especially hated the name-calling. She was so proud of her light skin and straight hair, and she hated being called a darkie. "I'd rather have been called a 'nigger,'" she says bluntly. "We had lots of white blood." Aunt G's grandmother—my wife's great-great grandmother—was the light-skinned child of a slave-slave master union, but she married a very dark man. Sadly, Aunt G says, "All her kids had nappy hair. They had bad hair. She'd say, 'I don't know nothin' about combin' those nappy-headed children.' She made Grandpa tend their hair." It was a sentiment Aunt G would carry into her generation: "I just had a horror of little black children, just thought I couldn't tend to them. I don't know why. It's something within me." Aunt G says this matter-of-factly, without guilt or self-reflection. For her, as for so many, race and social class and skin color were hopelessly intertwined. For Aunt G, light skin became a stand-in for the respectability she craved, just as surely as other blacks' resentment of her light skin was in part a stand-in for their resentment of her prosperity.

It is time for Reid to go to work. Outside, the sun has warmed the morning and I unzip my coat as we walk to the tobacco barn several hundred feet toward the ridge—past overturned and rusted trucks and automobiles, ancient and abandoned farm equipment, oil tanks and feeding troughs. In the barn, made of vertical, unpainted splinter wood, sweet-smelling tobacco stalks hang, curing, from three layers of cross-beams. Reid says, "Be sure to duck," but I hit my head hard anyway. He lights the kerosene heater and begins stripping the "trash" and the "lugs" from the three-foot-long tobacco stalks, leaving the lowest-quality leaves—the "tips"—for me to strip and bale for the burley market, where tobacco is bringing $1.67 a pound. "Ain't been much changed up here," Reid says finally, his breath hovering like a cloud in the windless barn. "Except whites and blacks go to school together and eat together." He laughs and hands me another stalk: "We'll make a farmer out of you yet." Reid and I strip and bale, strip and bale silently for a long time, until Alex has the well pump running again. Then Alex and I say goodbye, see you soon, Reid, and drive off, back into the 20th century, leaving the last Lawson in Lawson Bottom in the cold barn, still stripping tobacco.

I have no memory of ever talking to a black person until I was recruited to play with an all-black baseball team from Chicago Heights. I remember that, despite Big Grandma's biases, my working-class parents preached right-thinking attitudes about race: People are people and everyone should be treated the same. It was easy to think right on race in my midwestern suburban home town—with no blacks, no Hispanics, maybe an Italian or two. As far as I knew, the platitude that people were people was correct—people *were* people just like us, like me. I vaguely remember fat southern cops and vicious dogs on TV. I remember the Rev. Martin Luther King Jr. being pelted in Cicero, which was only an hour's drive away. I remember thinking those Polacks were really ignorant.

Despite learning all these proper notions, though, I also discovered that I could make my parents vaguely uncomfortable if I spouted off too liberally about race. My sister even recalls a time in high school when I asked my mother, "So what would you do if I married a Negro girl?" I don't recall the taunt, but it sounds like me. I remember also that when Moses Turner, the coach of the all-black Chicago Heights baseball team, asked me to play for him the summer I turned 16, I was happy to agree. Big Grandma thought I'd gone mad. But I relished the renegade image I got playing on Moses Turner's team. I loved it when an umpire from my suburban league pulled me aside and asked angrily, "Why are you wasting your time with these niggers?" My little step across the color line seemed to make everybody uncomfortable, which I enjoyed immensely.

But that summer, I also learned something else. I became friends with the team's 6-foot-4 pitcher, Pee Wee—a dark, strong kid who was an imposing athletic hero in his neighborhood. I often drove Pee Wee home after the games, and I can still see his street: wide and tree-lined and gray, with mangy dogs and broken bicycles, with grassless yards, tarpaper roofs, unpainted picket fences and missing screen doors. Kids were everywhere. The summer was 1967, and all around Chicago racial violence was breaking out. It was an angry time, and one day, as I turned onto Pee Wee's street, he said, in a voice husky and slow, "Whatever you do, don't hit one a these kids. There won't be nothin' even I can do for you." This wasn't a threat, but good advice, and you have never seen a person drive more carefully. After Pee Wee got out, I drove around the block and back to the highway so slowly people were staring at me. I smiled and nodded. I think I held my breath.

After that, I wasn't so eager to give Pee Wee a ride home.

The signs on the gas pumps at the Gulf station in downtown Burkesville read: "You may have won a BMW." Driving past the station into town, it seems that nothing could be more out of sync with Burkesville. It's a town of pickup trucks, of old men with leather faces and weathered jackets standing outside the county courthouse across from the Dollar Store. When I stop a delivery man to ask directions, I see a large knife and a holstered pistol on the dash of his truck. Nope, this is *not* BMW country.

Alex has suggested I stop in Burkesville to talk with his cousin Nell, because at 55 she's the last Lawson Bottom native of her generation still in town. I've met Nell before, at Alex's home, and I'm embarrassed to admit the prejudices I revealed that day. Nell wore modest clothes, and her hair was parted in the middle and turned up with simplicity. She said, "Hello, nice to meet you." At least I suppose she did, because I couldn't understand a word. She was, it seemed to me, strictly backwoods. I imagined her as a character out of Alex's story about Lawson Bottom: "*Paee*-tehr, go out and kill a *chai*-kin."

Only after Nell left did Alex tell me she was a schoolteacher with a master's degree. I felt stupid, though in my defense, it also was the beginning of my realization that what I had assumed was poor, uneducated, *black* Kentucky dialect was simply Kentucky country dialect. As meeting Nell had reminded me, things aren't always as they seem. Tonight, as I sit down with Nell and her 25-year-old daughter, she is about to remind me of this again.

I ask innocently, "Who was your father?"

With hesitation and a deep breath, Nell says: "I'll be honest with you. My father was white and he never did pay me any attention. He would come to my mother's father's house and sit out, and I'd jump flips, but he paid me no attention." His attitude, Nell says, was, " 'Yes, I did this to your daughter and there's nothin' you can do about it!' " Nell's white daddy, it turns out, was the same rich white man who complained that no "colored" should be allowed to own land as fertile as

Berry Lawson's. "I remember a kindly, round face with dark reddish hair," Nell says. "Maybe your height and a little chubby. When my father died, I didn't even go see him. I thought: 'If you don't care, I don't care either.' But I did care. I still do."

She pauses and no one speaks.

"I guess I didn't realize I really cared about my father just until you asked. I guess he's still controlling me from the grave. He never even spoke to me. I think he could have at least done that. I was called 'half-white' and 'bastard' by my own people. I don't know which was more painful. Just not being accepted by anyone, really. I've got a white half-brother right here in this town, and he does not acknowledge me. I've thought sometimes about calling him, but some things you just have to keep in the closet."

Nell's eyes are filled with tears now, as are mine. What to say? I think of good-hearted whites I know, even young affluent blacks, who would like this *race thing*, this ever-present *race thing* to disappear, go away, because life is different now, changed, better. Yes? Then I look at Nell, who is only 55, but who—like any abused or beaten or abandoned child—will carry this *race thing* forever. And beyond . . .

"I tell my daughters to stay away from white men," she says. "I'd be afraid they'd be using them the way we were done."

"But what about me?" I ask. "I'm a white man."

"I knew you were different," Nell says. At first, I think she's talking about my wife and me. But as she speaks, I realize she's talking about someone else too. "I knew that you wouldn't be ashamed to be seen walking down the street with me, that you'd do more than take me behind closed doors. You married her." I look at Nell's daughter, Donna, who is only 25. She says, "White men usually want one thing." What to say? Normally, this attitude would strike me as quaint, a throwback to another time and another place.

But not tonight, not in this town, this room, not in Nell's house.

I went to college in 1968 thinking I didn't have a racist bone in my body. Then this happened: At the height of the Black Power movement, black students circulated a petition to turn a little-used building on our small midwestern campus into a meeting place for black students, which meant they'd be the only social group on campus with a building of their own. I didn't speak against this idea. I didn't campaign against it. But I did decline to sign the petition when it came my way, because I thought the idea was unfair to everyone else. I did not think this was a big deal. I was wrong.

Overnight, the several black members of my dormitory basketball

team—with these guys we were expected to be campus champs—
announced they wouldn't play as long as I was on the team. Shell-shocked
and embarrassed, I offered to quit. But the team captain—a big white
guy with definite racist tendencies—declared I would not resign. *We*
would not be bullied! *We* would play without *them*! And that's what *we*
did. To keep the peace, the college broke its own rule and allowed the
black guys from all the dorms to form a team and play in the dormitory
league. It was something of an event when my dorm played them, with
me as point guard. We won that game, although it was little consolation. I'd been tarred as a racist, which was, I believe even 20 years later,
too simple. I didn't know then that most blacks see the world as black *or*
white, one *or* the other, and that to them the whole campus belonged to
white students, while all they were seeking was one small, ramshackle
building.

I was guilty, all right, but of believing people were people—just like
us, like me. I was guilty, all right, but of seeing the world through my
own eyes, guilty of not yet knowing that justice isn't always fair.

Lewis Street in the Kingdom . . .

The black places are gone today—King's Restaurant, the Royal
Cafe, Mr. Troop's barbershop, the pool and dance halls, Kurd's cab
stand and, of course, the little gypsy restaurant Alex's father, Shed, ran
in a tiny wooden trailer on rubber-and-spoke wheels near Lewis and
Brown streets. In dry Glasgow in dry Barren County, Shed sold hooch
from that trailer, as he also did from his kitchen half a block away at
506 Lewis, as his teenage sons Alex and Bobby later did on the streets.
Shed's house has fallen to a modern brick funeral home today, and vacant lots and a B-Kwick Food Mart have replaced the rest. Alex can't
help but be saddened by these changes. But he doesn't get too nostalgic,
because the rats—bold rats made fat and healthy at the feed mill on the
corner of Lewis and Back streets—also are gone. So is Red Row, a
dozen or so leaning and dilapidated board and batten shacks, desperate
even by Depression standards, that sat across and just up Back Street.

But the old Kingdom, the nickname for Glasgow's original few
square blocks of black neighborhood, was the world as my children's
mother's father's family knew it after they migrated from Burkesville
to Glasgow in the 1920s. My children's great-grandfather was king of
the Kingdom's bootleggers. Whites and blacks, rich and poor, visited
Shed's kitchen with the devotion of churchgoers—especially on Satur-
days, when Glasgow's town square, only a few blocks north, would be
packed with gawkers and talkers in from the fields. Shots of moonshine
cost 3, 5 or 10 cents; pints 35 cents. Demand was great and Alex's job

was to wash the Pepsi bottles, the old ones with the brown and green paper labels, so they could be filled with bootleg beer. Shed was a rough man, short and dark with a hard, cocky look in his eyes. He wore a skimmer hat and string ties. He told his sons he was a blacksmith, but Alex can recall seeing him with a horse only once. He worked as a janitor, a busboy, a carpenter, a bellhop and, for a long time, as a dishwasher at the Spotswood Hotel on the square.

But always, Shed was a bootlegger—until the day Alex, 8 years old, watched as the police lugged jug after jug from beneath the house. Shed went to prison. He died soon after his release. For a time, my children's great-grandmother, Stella—radiant, kind, gentle, religious Stella—took over the family enterprise. "I got these five boys," she told Aunt G. But she too was busted. Finally, Stella retired from the business to do what respectable blacks did in her day: She worked as a housekeeper and nanny and as a maid in Glasgow's hospital. Before she died in 1981, Stella soberly described her predicament by telling me this story: A friend of hers once applied for a good factory job. The boss called her in and told her apologetically that he knew she could do the work, but that he also knew she was Mrs. Richardson's cook. And the boss, with a friendly laugh, said he couldn't have Mrs. Richardson mad at him for stealing her favorite cook, now could he?

The men I hunt rabbits with each year in Lawson Bottom—Alex and his younger brother Bobby, who is 56, and their friend Carl, who is 55—all were bootleggers in the 1940s. In those days, Lewis Street was much like the corner drug markets that proliferate in American cities today. On weekends, a horde of young black males would mill about waiting for mostly white customers to drive through, roll down their windows and buy whiskey. Today, Alex, Bobby and Carl aren't embarrassed that they were bootleggers. They're proud of it.

"A black man couldn't get a good job in those days," says Bobby, a short, round man who absently lifts his blue cap and smooths his hand lightly over a bald head. Bobby, in Toughskins bib overalls and a gray hooded sweatshirt, is working at his barn today, creating a small corral of electric wire to enclose two black steers he plans to fatten for slaughter. Normally, Bobby leaves the castrated males in the cow herd as "markers"—they mount and ride a cow when she's in heat, thus notifying the farmer it's time to mate her with a fertile bull. "Them steers got pistols," Bobby quips, "but they ain't got no bullets." We lift an old Agstar water trough into the barn and Bobby goes to get the hose to fill it. The late autumn afternoon is warm and bright, 51 degrees, and a white cat suns itself against the concrete foundation of the red rackside barn. In odd juxtaposition, the trees in the pasture are naked for the winter while the Kentucky grass still is green and growing. "Nope," Bobby says, picking up the thread again when he returns with the hose, "the best job a black could get was being a janitor, and there weren't many of them."

Bobby had a respectable job for a while after he dropped out of high school: He was a janitor at Glasgow's hospital, where his mother worked. He earned $100 a month and bolstered his income with light bootlegging. Then one day, Bobby saw the paycheck of a white kid whose job was to scrape gum off the hospital floors. "It was more than mine!" Bobby says, still incredulous. Bobby went to the hospital chief, a white man who was one of his best bootlegging customers, and asked for a raise. "Bobby," the chief said, "they won't let me pay coloreds what I pay whites." So Bobby quit and took up bootlegging full-time. At his peak, between the ages of about 16 and 19, three men sold whiskey for him. Bobby would drive the 32 miles to Bowling Green, where liquor could be bought legally, and pay $1.25 for a half pint, which he sold for $2.50. In his heyday, Bobby sold six cases of half pints, 288 bottles, a week. After paying his salesmen, that was $216 a week for Bobby, more than $800 a month—compared with $100 at his respectable hospital job. He bought his mother clothes, gifts and groceries.

"Let me tell you," Bobby says, "you won't find a black in Glasgow who's got anything that somewhere along the line, bootlegging didn't touch their lives. Very few. Because the people workin' weren't paid anything. It was either work and be dirt poor, or risk going to jail and be a bootlegger." Bobby finally did get arrested and went to court. But the Glasgow police chief had broken up the bootleg transaction before Bobby was paid, meaning no illegal sale had taken place. When Bobby's lawyer pointed this out to the all-white jury, the prosecutor was flabbergasted. "I'll never forget it," Bobby says, laughing. "He said 'I guess we should put the chief of police in jail and turn this nigger loose.'" Bobby was acquitted. And eventually, he—like Alex before him—joined the military and got out of town a hot-step ahead of the law.

In those times, race was everywhere and nowhere. The movies, restaurants and public bathrooms were segregated, of course, as were the downtown Glasgow water fountains. As boys, Alex and Bobby gleefully rubbed their spit onto the spout of the whites-only fountain. Yet neither Alex nor Bobby can recall a single time anyone in Glasgow treated them rudely because they were black. Race was like a colorless, tasteless, odorless gas in the air. Alex remembers noticing that the football goal posts at his black school were always broken. He didn't question this. He remembers that he was once sent to a white school to pick up his teacher's paycheck and he noticed something amazing: On the tables in the white cafeteria sat entire bowls of fresh apples. Alex didn't think this was unfair, only that it was strange and mysterious. Bobby then tells this story: As he would walk to school, the white kids would ride by in their bus and make faces at him, but he would think nothing of it. "It's like the old joke about the Indian riding a horse with his squaw walking next to him," Bobby explains. "A guy asks the Indian, 'Why are you ridin' and your squaw's walkin'?' The Indian looks up at the man, thinks and then says, 'She no have 'em horse.' " We both laugh at the punch line.

"Well, it was like that," Bobby says. "We didn't have a horse."

Yet it's eerie how things no one seemed to notice can live so long, as in the mind of Alex and Bobby's friend and my hunting companion, Carl, who grew up outside Glasgow in a barn-wood shack. These days, Carl is never without at least the stub of a cigar working in the corner of his mouth. He's big as a bear, thick everywhere—stomach, chest, neck, legs, arms, even his fingers. Not fat, thick. This morning, he's out checking on his cows, breaking the ice in their water trough with a shovel. He wears insulated camouflage overalls and green rubber boots. He has a deep, bass voice and a head that seems to sit directly atop his massive shoulders. He is gentle and threatening at once. As a boy, there was no black school near Carl, so he didn't start until he was 9. "I'm still awful proud I graduated high school," he says, "considering where I began." Next door was a nice white family who let Carl ride their pony. He took the rides but deeply resented the family. Carl believed then that he resented them so much because they were white. But looking back, he knows that skin color was only a stand-in: As the black kids in Lawson Bottom had resented Berry Lawson's kids because they were rich, Carl resented his white neighbors because they too were rich.

Unlike Alex and Bobby, who got out of town for decades, Carl has lived in Glasgow all his life. He worked at the Texaco station for 12 years—as a "wash boy," scrubbing cars, cleaning the grease pit. He earned $60 a week, far less than his white co-workers. One day, Carl noticed that a white mechanic had worked on a car all morning and gone to lunch still unable to get it started. Carl got it started. The boss was so happy, he bought Carl a Coke. Finally, in 1965 Carl got one of the first area factory jobs that went to a black man. For the first time in his life, at 31, he was paid a white man's wage. He now drives a forklift at another factory and makes good money. He's now got good white friends. Thirty years ago, Carl would have said that was impossible. He marvels when he hears young black and white men at work bantering back and forth with racial digs. Even today, Carl couldn't do that without getting mad. He doesn't know exactly why.

Just the other day he was listening to a couple of young white men bragging about the University of Kentucky basketball team, and Carl felt as if they were pulling an invisible thread in his brain. He thought about the time three decades ago when he happened to sit down fishing next to UK's venerated coach, Adolph Rupp. That year, a local black basketball star was trying to get into Kentucky, which had never had a black player, and Carl asked Rupp if he was going to take him. "He can't pass the academic tests," Rupp said smugly. "Some schools will lower their standards to take him anyway, but not Kentucky."

Then Carl thought about all those years at the Texaco station, how he acted like "a nice colored man" when he sometimes wanted to slug the white men making more money for no more work. And about the day he got that car started and the boss bought him a Coke. *A Coke!* He thought about how they wouldn't let him go to school till he was 9, how far behind he was, how foolish he felt. He thought about the days when banks wouldn't lend a black $500 without a white co-signer, how as a boy he had to stand in the store and wait until all the whites were served, how even his daddy had to wait patiently, like a nice colored man.

And he got hotter and hotter.

"I had to catch myself not to say anything," Carl says. "These are good guys. They're 30 years old. They didn't know Adolph Rupp. But all that brings back through your head everything else that came before. It can eat at you. And you start lookin' for each and every thing. It eats you up. The next thing you know, you're angry and you don't know what you're angry about."

The summer after the last season I played baseball with Pee Wee, after my first year in college and who-knows-what for Pee Wee, I was with a girlfriend driving through Chicago Heights on the way to the Indiana dunes on Lake Michigan. I had what for me was a lot of money in my pocket. We stopped at a Tastee-Freez, and as we stood licking our cones in the sunlight, about a dozen black kids, maybe 13, 14 years old, rode up on their bikes and surrounded us in a shrinking half-circle against the shiny white wall.

"Got any change?"

Then, "Got any folding money?"

The next question seemed inevitable. So as I dug into my pocket, I asked, "Hey, any you guys know Pee Wee?" The boys glanced around at one another.

"You know Pee Wee, man?"

"Oh, yeah, Pee Wee and me, we go way back, man, played ball together."

Before long, we were laughing and swapping Pee Wee stories. Before long, I'd gotten away for small change. I drove carefully. I think I held my breath.

The Kingdom through a different lens . . .

As children, my wife and her two younger brothers saw Glasgow as a foreign land. They were military brats, kids who'd spent half their childhoods in West Germany, France, England, on the West Coast, always in military housing, always attending military schools. Alex can tell some pretty grim tales about his early days in the military. The black soldiers' breakfasts were always cold because they were trucked over from the white kitchen. The only day blacks could use the swimming pool was Wednesday—after which they changed the pool water for the week. He can't help chuckling at the memory. But by the middle 1950s Alex believed that no place in American society gave blacks a better shake. By then, everything in the military was integrated—housing, clubs, jobs, schools.

Into this brave new world came my wife and her brothers. Their playmates were mostly white, and out of, say, 20 kids in a military school classroom, only one, two, maybe three, would be black. In Europe, there were no "Whites Only" signs and no one was turned away at a restaurant door. Keran and her brother Alex Jr. can't recall a time when they were overseas that race seemed to make a difference in their lives. Keran was wild about the Beatles and thought she'd really die if she couldn't marry Paul. Alex Jr. was always the most popular kid in his class. "I didn't know race was supposed to be a handicap," he says. Howard, the youngest, does remember that when the family went to the Oktoberfest in Munich, people stared awfully hard. He remembers noticing at picnics that children with southern accents seemed not to play with him much. But Howard must rack his brain for these memories.

So when the kids visited Glasgow, it was culture shock. Blacks and whites didn't mingle, and that was odd enough. But the rural poverty was shocking. Two generations out of Lawson Bottom, a generation out of the Kingdom, the kids would sit on the porch of the house Grandma Stella shared with Aunt G since their husbands had died, and look across Back Street at mind-boggling destitution. "It wasn't race," says Howard, who, after flying jets in the Air Force, is now a pilot for UPS. "It was poverty. It was poverty like in Africa." He remembers the nights they would listen to the people across Back Street chasing rats from their bedrooms. "We used to make fun of those people," says Alex Jr., now a casino executive in Las Vegas. "I just couldn't comprehend them." Of his father's beloved Kingdom, he says: "The whole area around Aunt G's was a craphole. And all the black kids had these strange accents. It was hillbilly to me. I had the sense of not wanting to be associated with them."

My wife and her brothers all went to college. Today, they all have good jobs. And they all say that, as far as they know, being black has only helped them. My wife always jokes that as a black woman she fills two quota slots as a manager at Cigna Corp. Alex Jr. figures he got shots at the two biggest jobs in his career because he's black. Howard says UPS didn't even answer his job letter until he sent a picture. "Maybe I'm going through life with blinders," he says, shaking his head, "but when I hear people crying, 'Racism, racism,' I say, 'What are you talking about?' I just haven't seen it." Yes, there were occasional racial slurs at the mostly white Mascoutah, Ill., high school they attended when the family finally moved off base. Yes, they remember family vacations in the 1950s when motels in the States turned them away. Yes, they remember some mean redneck stares. And, yes, they also remember stares from black kids, who seemed angry and resentful of their white friends. "I noticed it, but I didn't let it bother me," Howard says. "I've been stared at all my life—at the Oktoberfest, in Mascoutah and years later when I'd take planes into Iceland. People stare for a minute and then they come up and talk to you. It hit home very early that through hard work you can make it too. That wasn't true in my dad's day. And that's different."

I think of what Bobby had said about his emasculated cattle: "Them steers got pistols, but they ain't got no bullets." Today poverty, poor education and lack of opportunity—the ageless barriers of class— are formidable obstacles to black achievement. But the power of racism, though still strong and ugly, is greatly diminished. For my wife and her brothers—for an entire generation of well-educated young blacks and their children—racism, like Bobby's steers, is more and more a pistol without bullets. A slur or a stare, yes, but they're not being turned away because Mrs. Richardson needs a cook.

I didn't know exactly *what* Keran was when we first met. She's got rising cheekbones, electrified hair and a nose that isn't European, but she has no accent except middle American and her skin is the color of honey. "Maybe," I told a friend, "she's part Filipino." He said, "No, she's black." I didn't think much about it, and when I first met her parents a month later and saw that she really was black, I didn't think much about it then either. Keran was the only black woman I'd ever dated, and I simply told myself that I would not let race matter, that I was beyond it. Besides, marriage wasn't on my screen in those days.

My mother, it turned out, was more farsighted. When my sister told her I was dating a black woman, I got an anguished late-night call from my mom, asking me, please, to think about what I was doing, please, think about the children. I told her not to worry, that I hardly knew the woman, that I wasn't marrying anybody for a long time.

She said, "But this is how these things start."

My mother the prophet. Five years later, Keran and I were married. In the years we had dated, strange as it seems, we never had a problem with race that I knew of. I never heard a slur. I didn't notice stares. Nobody seemed to care. I was amazed at this and always figured it had to do with Keran, who didn't wear race as a badge, who talked middle-class talk, and who was light-skinned enough that whites weren't knee-jerk threatened by her.

But I never forgot my mother's phone call, and, about a year before we married, I broke off with Keran. I told myself it was because I wasn't ready to get married, but I knew even then it was also because I feared my parents' reaction. If I were going to marry Keran, I reasoned, I'd better be awfully sure about it. After a few months apart, I was sure.

My parents, who had always taught me to think right about race, freaked out. I'd always been a rebellious kid, and in the '60s—with marijuana, long hair, strange clothes and radic-lib ideas—my folks saw me purposely rejecting their beliefs. Keran knew better. She joked, "You have to marry a black woman—to prove you're not hopelessly middle class." Indeed, it was my hopelessly middle-class sensibility that attracted her. "I can't marry a jive man," she said. But my folks believed my marriage mocked their values and squandered their sacrifices. "I'm sure Keran is a nice girl from a nice family," my mother said. "This has nothing to do with her." In their minds, as in the minds of so many, race and social class and skin color were hopelessly intertwined.

My parents were dirt poor as children. They struggled all their lives, sacrificed, to keep me in a decent home, decent schools. They struggled to move me up and out. In their view, my marrying across the color line was moving down, not up. I was throwing away all their sacrifices. Who'd hire me? Who'd have me to dinner? What nice neighborhood would take me? We didn't talk for years after my marriage. Then one day, as my mother looked through photos I'd sent—photos of my nice home, my nice yard, my nice kids—she made this telling remark to my sister: "It looks like your brother has built a life for himself." Soon, we were a family again.

Keran's parents had a different reaction: They said not a word about race. Alex asked, "You mean you're marrying that scrawny guy?" They remained true to their lifetime belief that race shouldn't matter, that it should never be an excuse or an explanation, that it should be ignored, pretended away. Their philosophy was simple: Blacks must act as if they can control their lives, whether or not they can. Otherwise their ambition is sapped and their lives consumed by self-pity. It is the way they have lived their lives, the way they have raised their children.

Alex's advice: Ignore the idiot in the dentist's office. He takes too much energy. He's a jerk, and there are few enough like him today that he can be ignored. Perhaps this was once an illusion, a psychic defense for blacks, but not by the time my wife and her brothers were growing up. And certainly not by the time of my children. I feel like Howard does. Maybe I'm going through life with blinders, but I can't think of a time when I or my wife or our kids have been mistreated because of race. Oh, I know the neighborhood was abuzz when we moved in. Since my revelation in the dentist's chair, I've heard my son's little league coach talk about the "niggers" and a neighbor joke about the "coons." I hate this. But in the end, these things are pistols without bullets. As it was even in Aunt G's day, a slur without the power to back it up is only a pinprick. My wife and I can work, live where we want and send our kids to the schools we choose. This is not true for all blacks, but it is true for us, with our power of affluence.

It turns out I'm not the pioneer I thought I was. Because it wasn't me or even my children who first crossed the color line. It was Alex and Celeste, my wife and her brothers and so many other blacks, all of whom ventured into the mainstream white world to face stares and slurs from whites as well as blacks. Thanks to them, not me, life is nearly normal for my children. About that I breathe easier.

But not too easy: The worst barriers are gone, but the confusion about race, class and color lives on in all of us, as I'm forever reminded.

With my kids, I pull into the McDonald's drive-through. We are in a hurry, and as I come to the squawk box, I see that the car ahead of me has four black people in it. In an instant, my mind makes its unconscious and racist calculation: We'll be sitting here forever while these people decide what to order. I literally shake my head at the awfulness of this thought. I laugh at my own deep prejudice. Then I wait. And wait. And wait. Each of the four people in the car ahead leans out the window and orders individually. The order is changed several times. We sit and sit, and now I am shaking my head again. I know that the buried sentiment that made me predict that these people would be disorganized on the basis of race alone was wrong—bad, not nice, racist. I know there are dozens of other reasons for their behavior, that race was only a convenient stand-in for social class or education or individual stupidity or rudeness. But the prediction was right. So now I chide myself for my racism, then I laugh to myself at my racism's unfortunate predictive power, then I shake my head again, this time at the conundrum that is race in America.

I think of Winston Churchill's line: "A riddle wrapped in a mystery inside an enigma."

That riddle is especially confusing to the young. My 4-year-old daughter, for instance, came home from Kinder-Care one day recently and announced that she didn't like the black boys in her class. They were too rough. I'm always fearful of my children being trapped somewhere between black and white, and I try again and again to make them see that race is only a stand-in for deeper explanations. As we talked, it became clear that Kyle didn't really like *any* of the boys in her class, white or black, which is all I wanted her to understand. In our family, when we talk about how someone looks, my wife and I always ask if the person is tall or short, hefty or thin, dark-haired or light-haired, blue-eyed or brown-eyed, light-skinned or dark-skinned. It was not until my son was in first grade that we saw the impact of this. Matthew came home the first day of school and said there were no black kids in his class. Concerned, I went to his classroom—and found about a dozen black kids.

"What about him?" I asked, nodding toward a black child.

"He's not black," Matthew said, as if I were blind. "He's dark brown."

Yet the seductive power of race as an explanation, as a predicter of behavior, is great. One day, Matthew came home and asked why the dark-skinned kids in his class didn't know as much as the light-skinned kids. As we talked, he realized that he didn't really mean *all* the dark-skinned kids, but a lot of them. What to say? I gave a little history lesson about slavery, about bad schools, about being locked out of good jobs, about how parents with good educations often start their children reading earlier, about how just because a child doesn't read or add well doesn't mean he isn't smart, only that he's behind in reading or adding. Matthew interrupted.

"Dad, Dad!" he said. "This is *booor*-ing!"

Okay, okay, but sometimes I think, I hope, the message is heard. In psychology, there's a classic experiment in which black kids are asked whether a white or a black doll is prettier. For decades, black children have more often picked the white doll. I once played a game like this with my light-skinned, sandy-haired, hazel-eyed daughter. I laid out five of her dolls—a dark brown Cabbage Patch doll; a pale white cloth doll; a light tan doll from Mexico; a white, blond-haired Barbie doll; and a black friend of Barbie's named Dee-Dee. I asked Kyle to pick the prettiest dolls: In order, she selected the blond Barbie, the black Dee-Dee, the pale white cloth doll, the tan doll from Mexico, and the dark brown Cabbage Patch doll. I asked why.

Barbie? "She has dangly earrings."

The black Dee-Dee? "She has pretty lipstick."

The pale white cloth doll? "She has a diaper."

The tan doll from Mexico? "She has pigtails."

The dark brown Cabbage Patch? "I don't like him because he's bald."

Except that I am going bald, I liked her answers. I know that many blacks don't judge racial progress on whether people are increasingly colorblind and whether blacks and whites mingle together more in society. But I do, and for obvious reasons: My children stand at a doorway to two worlds. I want them to feel comfortable in both, and I want their world—the world between the races—to grow and expand, for the races to melt together, for either-or to disappear. Blacks and whites work together now. We live as neighbors, go to school together, dine together. So much has changed.

My wife's living family encompasses this great arc of race history and psychology, of change and sad similarity: Reid, still stripping tobacco; Aunt G, still proud of her light skin; Nell, still anguished over racism's oldest crime; Carl, still stoically fighting his silent anger; Bobby, still proud that he bootlegged rather than work for next to nothing; Alex and Celeste, still bridging the old world of their childhoods and the new world of their children; my wife and her brothers, learning to live between two worlds long before I came along. Before my journey, I'd known my wife's family and friends for a decade, but rarely had we really talked. After my journey, I will never again think they are just like us, like me.

It's hard not to see the story of my wife's family as an American triumph. So much has changed. What remains, though, is the taboo of men and women and marriage across the color line.

I've often thought one of the reasons blacks haven't melted into the American melting pot is because they've been unable to marry across the line, as have Italians and Irish and all the other once-despised immigrant groups. Blacks haven't been able to marry the boss's daughter and move into the house on the hill, which has had a very real impact on their wealth and opportunity. Remember, Berry Lawson began with the luck of birth and inheritance. But the marriage taboo also exacts a deeper price. It means that the lives of blacks and whites rarely cross in the intimate, human ways that make the burying of differences among people not just a noble social goal, but an emotional necessity. To this day, for instance, Aunt G—chatting from the recliner in her sitting room, with the TV ignored and glowing orange beside her—tells me she will not eat meals with white people. For years, they wouldn't eat with her, and now she will not eat with them.

Surprised, I say, "But you eat with me."

"Oh, that's different," Aunt G says pleasantly. "You're family."

My last visit with Aunt G . . .

The sitting room is a shrine of photographs—her sister, her brothers, daughter, grandchildren, great-grandchildren, nephews, a great-nephew. Every inch of wall is covered. People of all shapes and shades. From here, Aunt G holds court. As a young woman, she moved to Glasgow from Burkesville and married the whitest, richest black man she met. This made sense to her, a woman proud of her light skin and straight hair, a woman accustomed to being relatively well-to-do. She and Mr. Troop, a barber and businessman, had a daughter—beautiful Mackiva, with soft, pearly skin and flowing, wavy hair. Aunt G, who feared she simply couldn't care for a dark-skinned child, was elated.

Her daughter felt differently. "The kids would call me a half-white, stringy-hair bitch," says Mackiva, who today is 56. Mackiva, who was so light-skinned that when she rode the bus to college in Nashville she sat in the front with the white people, did a 180-degree turn on her mother's outlook. "I decided I'd never marry a bright-skinned man," she says. "My kids would never go through what I went through." And that's what Mackiva did: Her husband, Evans, is handsome and dark-skinned, as are their three grown sons, as are their grandchildren, who are Aunt G's great-grandchildren.

Aunt G turns to me. "Your children are white," she says rather abruptly, using her own either-or standard to describe my tan-skinned children. "So many whites have a horror of black babies. You didn't know what you'd have. How could you have coped if you'd had a black child?"

I can't help but smile. The query brings me full circle, because today Aunt G is baby-sitting her great-grandchildren, Brittany, age 2, and Michael, 6 months old, who are on the floor before us. They are, in Aunt G's vocabulary, black children. "Aunt G," I say, "you were the woman who was terrified to have black babies. You married a bright man. Then your daughter goes off and marries a dark man and has dark children, who then go off and have these dark grandchildren. Let me ask you, How do you cope?" Aunt G looks startled for a moment, and then she lets out that joyful little cackle that she mutes with a hand put discreetly to her mouth. "I got one as black as July jam and another with hair nappy as a sheep's back," she says, cackling freely now. "And I just love 'em better than anything! I just love 'em!"

And that, really, is the heart of the matter.

Brent Staples

James White

"**M**r. Bellow's Planet"—an extract from Brent Staples's book *Parallel Time* (1994)—opens with Staples on his way to the University of Chicago. Staples completed his studies in psychology there, earning a Ph.D.

He then became not a psychologist but a staff reporter for the *Chicago Sun-Times*. He also wrote features for *The Chicago Reader*, a weekly newspaper that, like the *Village Voice* in New York, the *Phoenix* in Boston, and other urban weeklies, has been an outlet for developing literary journalists. Staples went on to the *New York Times* in 1985 as a book review editor. In 1990 he moved to the newspaper's editorial page staff.

Staples has written for *Harper's*, the *New York Times*, *Ms.*, and *Chicago* magazines. His work appears in many anthologies.

"I'm a lucky writer," he says. "The *New York Times* pays me to write from the heart about politics and culture for the editorial page. Book publishers pay me to write from the heart about my experience as an American abroad in the brawling, Whitmanesque nation in which we live. I enjoy writing argument for the editorial page. I also believe deeply in the personal essay as a form. It reaches people, touches them emotionally."

Mr. Bellow's Planet

I flew to Chicago holding the rucksack on my lap. At takeoff the stewardess had forced me to stow it under the seat, but I snatched it back as soon as she walked away. To let it out of my sight was to risk losing it, and that would be disastrous. The papers inside were proof of who I was.

I was certain that the University of Chicago had already forgotten me and that deans and registrars would greet me blank-faced, without a clue. The germ of this hysteria came from a Ford Foundation communiqué advising me to take along the award letter in case of a mix-up. That was one sentence in one letter in a ream of correspondence. I worried that sentence until it was a hundred pages long. To the cache of letters and newspaper clippings I had added my college transcript just to be on the safe side.

I was certain that my luggage would be sent to a distant city and not returned to me until who knew when. In the rucksack along with my documents I'd packed a shirt and toiletries so I could keep clean until my clothes turned up. All through the flight I worried about the can of spray starch in my duffel bag. It was an aerosal can; surely atmospheric pressure would cause it to explode. The can bore the likeness of an Indian maiden in a buckskin dress, standing beside an ear of corn as tall as she was. As the plane hurtled toward Chicago, I envisioned the can swelling toward explosion, the maiden and the corn growing larger and larger until, *Boom!*, the can blew up, making a jagged, flowering hole in the baggage compartment. When the plane hit a bump in the air, I assumed that the explosion had happened and pressed my nose to the window. There I saw my luggage as clear as day: my army duffel bag and my brown plaid suitcase falling down the sky.

Lake Michigan would better have been named the Michigan Sea. It was the first lake I'd known whose opposite shore was not seeable with the naked eye. The view toward Michigan offered only water and sky. Later I saw that the lake changed its coat with the weather: slate gray, sea green, arctic blue. Some days it was as glutinous as Jell-O congealing. Some days it rammed its shoulder against the rocks and slammed fist after fist onto the jogging path and into the outermost lane of Lake Shore Drive. At the very tip of The Point were concrete breakers shaped like coffins. On nasty days the coffins were submerged in angry surf. In fair weather the lake lapped gently at the coffins while people lay upon them taking the sun. Guerrilla winter was evident along the water. On balmy days the wind would suddenly shift, bringing The Hawk in from Michigan to rake your bones.

I liked walking at night. During this first week I found the quadrangles tranquil and beautiful after dark, the turrets and towers lit by the autumn moon. On one of these nights, I was nearly given a heart attack when the lawn sprinklers burst into life. The Midway had a separate weather system. When the air on 57th was as still as death, The Midway, two blocks south, was alive with breezes. At night the quiet beauty was mine alone. If I had attended the official tours and lectures of orientation week, perhaps I'd have found out why. People were frightened of crime, and with good reason. Hyde Park was an island of prosperity in a sea of squalor. To the south, beyond the last university buildings, lay what Saul Bellow would later describe as "the edge of rat-shit Woodlawn." To the north lay Kenwood, a sliver of rambling Victorian houses, some of whose porches looked out onto the burned-out hovels of 47th Street. Across Washington Park to the west, the ghetto picked up again. Since I'd skipped the tours and lectures to wander on my own, I was ignorant of geography and danger. I had yet to notice the high-rise housing projects marching along the western horizon. My only certainties were that the lake was east and that everything was exhilarating, redolent with possibility. The newness excited me to the bone. I sang out loud, leaped and punched at the air. I was hopped up, manic, flying.

I took an apartment across The Midway at the edge of Woodlawn, where nearness to the ghetto had driven down the rents. Five sunny rooms, with a sun porch and a walk-in pantry. I got the apartment illegally. The university had set aside this building and several others for married students and decreed that the single among us would languish in hotel rooms or in studios or in crowded shared apartments. I had not come a thousand miles to live in a shoe box. I needed *lebensraum*.

Brown-skinned Providence reigned at married student housing, too. I was clearly registered as single, but the angels who ran the office spared me the embarrassment of checking. They pointed out the best deals for the money. They cut me a break when the rent was late.

My building was a last outpost of university power. Under my windows middle-class Hyde Park ended and impoverished black Chicago began. The university police cruised east past my dining room and my bedroom, then turned north at my sun porch, back into Hyde Park.

The sun porch was my favorite room. Its windows looked east, along the dead-flat plane of 61st Street, and south on Ingleside Avenue into Woodlawn. I studied there, I ate there and sometimes slept there. The days were punctuated by the screams of children at the elementary school just across 61st Street. At the start of recess they burst from the building as though from jail. First there was a trickle, then a rivulet, then eddies of boys and girls swirling around the school yard, coats and ribbons flying.

At night I let the house go dark so I could watch the street without being seen. The French windows were only eight feet above the ground, and when it was warm I threw them open and listened in on the conversations of passersby. When lovers paused below me I heard the wet sounds of their kissing and the breath coming out of their noses, the rustle of clothing as they rifled each other's bodies. I was invisible to them, but only an arm's length away in the dark.

On the school playground, basketball players carried on after dark. It was too dark to see the game from my porch, but I could hear the ball bouncing on the macadam court, banging off the metal backboard. Eventually the game petered out. Traffic died down on 61st Street. The neighborhood went to sleep.

One morning before dawn I was startled awake by the voice of a man who sounded like he was in the room.

"You fucked them? You fucked them? They could kill me, you understand that? They could fuckin' kill me!"

Then I heard the muffled cries of a woman, the flat of his hand on her face and head. As I moved in a crouch to the window, I heard people in the apartment above me doing the same.

The woman stumbled backward into 61st Street, her forearm raised against the blows. The pimp was small but squarely built, an inverted triangle from the waist up, in a tight-fitting shirt and pants.

"Where's the money! Where's the money!" There wasn't any. They were detectives. She'd fucked the cops, and hadn't been paid. The pimp batted her around the intersection, then hauled her up Ingleside Avenue. Exit, shouting, stage south.

The pimp was a regular performer at my intersection. On another night I heard his voice. "I want my money! I want my money!" This time he was beating a man with a stick. The stick was big enough to cause pain, but too slight to bring the man down. The man retreated backward into 61st Street, warding off the board. Suddenly he raised his hands into the air and sank to his knees. The pimp dropped the plank and ran back into Woodlawn. The beaten man kneeled like a Muslim at prayer, his palms on the pavement, his bald pate glistening in the headlights of an approaching police car.

The pimp was also a seller of heroin. From my sun porch I watched the buyers who double-parked in front of his building every evening beginning at dusk. The cars queued up on Ingleside Avenue with blinkers flashing, like planes awaiting takeoff at O'Hare. On my side of 61st Street the dealer would have been taken down in no time at all. On my side of 61st you couldn't sneeze without arousing suspicion.

On the other side and southward the crime was worse and so was the supermarket. At the Hyde Park Co-op the food was impeccable and fresh. At the 63rd Street market the meat was unfit for consumption. The produce stank of rot. The 63rd Street "shopping" strip was composed of vacant lots, burned-out buildings. This dismal scene was cast in shadow by the tracks of the Jackson Park el.

At night, I walked to the lakefront whenever the weather permitted. I was headed home from the lake when I took my first victim. It was late fall, and the wind was cutting. I was wearing my navy pea jacket, the collar turned up, my hands snug in the pockets. Dead leaves scuttled in shoals along the streets. I turned out of Blackstone Avenue and headed west on 57th Street, and there she was, a few yards ahead of me, dressed in business clothes and carrying a briefcase. She looked back at me once, then again, and picked up her pace. She looked back again and started to run. I stopped where I was and looked up at the surrounding windows. What did this look like to people peeking out through their blinds? I was out walking. But what if someone had thought they'd seen something they hadn't and called the police. I held back the urge to run. Instead, I walked south to The Midway, plunged into its darkness, and remained on The Midway until I reached the foot of my street.

I'd been a fool. I'd been walking the streets grinning good evening at people who were frightened to death of me. I did violence to them by just being. How had I missed this? I kept walking at night, but from then on I paid attention.

I became expert in the language of fear. Couples locked arms or reached for each other's hand when they saw me. Some crossed to the other side of the street. People who were carrying on conversations went mute and stared straight ahead, as though avoiding my eyes would save them. This reminded me of an old wives' tale: that rabid dogs didn't bite if you avoided their eyes. The determination to avoid my eyes made me invisible to classmates and professors whom I passed on the street.

It occurred to me for the first time that I was big. I was 6 feet 1½ inches tall, and my long hair made me look bigger. I weighed only 170 pounds. But the navy pea jacket was broad at the shoulders, high at the collar, making me look bigger and more fearsome than I was.

I tried to be innocuous but didn't know how. The more I thought about how I moved, the less my body belonged to me; I became a false character riding along inside it. I began to avoid people. I turned out of my way into side streets to spare them the sense that they were being stalked. I let them clear the lobbies of buildings before I entered, so they wouldn't feel trapped. Out of nervousness I began to whistle and discovered I was good at it. My whistle was pure and sweet—and also in tune. On the street at night I whistled popular tunes from the Beatles and Vivaldi's *Four Seasons*. The tension drained from people's bodies when they heard me. A few even smiled as they passed me in the dark.

Then I changed. I don't know why, but I remember when. I was walking west on 57th Street, after dark, coming home from the lake. The man and the woman walking toward me were laughing and talking but clammed up when they saw me. The man touched the woman's elbow, guiding her toward the curb. Normally I'd have given way and begun to whistle, but not this time. This time I veered toward them and aimed myself so that they'd have to part to avoid walking into me. The man stiffened, threw back his head and assumed the stare: eyes dead ahead, mouth open. His face took on a bluish hue under the sodium vapor streetlamps. I suppressed the urge to scream into his face. Instead I glided between them, my shoulder nearly brushing his. A few steps beyond them I stopped and howled with laughter. I called this game Scatter the Pigeons.

Fifty-seventh Street was too well lit for the game to be much fun; people didn't feel quite vulnerable enough. Along The Midway were heart-stopping strips of dark sidewalk, but these were so frightening that few people traveled them. The stretch of Blackstone between 57th and 55th provided better hunting. The block was long and lined with young trees that blocked out the streetlight and obscured the heads of people coming toward you.

One night I stooped beneath the branches and came up on the other side, just as a couple was stepping from their car into their town house. The woman pulled her purse close with one hand and reached for her husband with the other. The two of them stood frozen as I bore down on them. I felt a surge of power: these people were mine; I could do with them as I wished. If I'd been younger, with less to lose, I'd have robbed them, and it would have been easy. All I'd have to do was stand silently before them until they surrendered their money. I thundered, "Good evening!" into their bleached-out faces and cruised away laughing.

I held a special contempt for people who cowered in their cars as they waited for the light to change at 57th and Woodlawn. The intersection was always deserted at night, except for a car or two stuck at the red. *Thunk! Thunk! Thunk!* They hammered down the door locks when I came into view. Once I had hustled across the street, head down, trying to seem harmless. Now I turned brazenly into the headlights and laughed. Once across, I paced the sidewalk, glaring until the light changed. They'd made me terrifying. Now I'd show them how terrifying I could be.

Jimmy's Woodlawn Tap was the student bar by default, as it was the only bar that remained along the stretch of 55th Street that had once been thick with them. The most lamented of these was The Compass Bar, which had been home to the Compass Players, who had counted among their members Mike Nichols and Elaine May. Jimmy's walls were painted a depressing brown to discourage dirt. The piss smell of the men's room could be overwhelming. The barroom was dank with spilled beer. Here I shared a table with Aaron Rhodes and listened to his opinions on Thucydides and St. Augustine and Durkheim. Aaron was working on a Ph.D. at The Committee on Social Thought. Former University President Robert Hutchins had created The Committee and dedicated it to the study of eternal ideas. Hutchins had despised bean counters and number crunchers and academic specialists of every kind. He viewed education as a Socratic affair, in which students read the great books, pondered the great questions, and listened to conversations among the great minds. The Committee's professors were a modern version of Plato's Philosopher Kings. The Committee's students were Philosopher-Kings-in-Training.

Aaron was true to the mold. He pitied students whose work consisted of statistics and surveys and other things that Hutchins had looked on as ephemeral. People who failed to heed the classics were "philistines," a word Aaron used with finality and with relish. "A philistine!" he'd say, dismissing the person with a flip of his wrist. Aaron wore a rumpled trench coat and walked toes out. He was still in his early twenties, but his bearing made him seem older, much older.

He'd have been middle-aged if not for his talents at mimicry. He was splendid at it, particularly around the mouth. As a child, he had mimicked a bear from a children's book so well that his teeth had been thrust permanently out of line. As Aaron explained it, his father had

pried the teeth back into place with a dinner knife. This had been done
in laborious sessions each night after the evening meal. Aaron specialized in sneers. He didn't have a sneer of his own, but could reproduce
those of others. When he dismissed a philistine, he mimicked the set of
the person's mouth for the occasion.

Aaron slept at my house when he stayed late at Jimmy's. There was no
choice. He lived on the North Side; transportation in and out of Hyde
Park was impossible after rush hour. The el stops were in the ghetto, the
buses slow boats to China. The next morning he got up and trudged across
The Midway to the office of the journal where he worked. Passing
through my living room, he admired the glass bookcases overflowing with
philosophy's greatest hits. Plato through Husserl, Sartre, and Merleau-
Ponty, chronologically arranged. It pleased him that I was "going about
things the right way." Aaron took an interest in my case.

Saul Bellow was The Committee's most public figure. His novel,
Humboldt's Gift, had just been published. The dust jacket was screaming
yellow, and copies were placed in every one of the university bookstore's
several windows. Inside, on the front-most table, *Humboldt's Gift* rose in
an enormous yellow pyramid. Bellow signed copies by the gross. Even
clerks who mainly read romances sensed that something was up and got in
line for autographs. A signed copy was given to me as a gift. I still have it.

Humboldt's Gift generated endless gossip. Aaron's mentor, the soci-
ologist Edward Shils, had been kidnapped into the novel and was said
to be deeply angry. He and Bellow had known each other forever. Apparently Shils had asked in advance that Bellow not include him.

Aaron spoke of Bellow as "Bellow," and Arendt "Arendt." Edward
Shils he referred to as "Mr." Mr. Shils wrote about tradition and stability. The genius that Aaron saw in Shils's books eluded me. His writings
in the university *Record* were more accessible and certainly more interesting. The *Record* contained his evaluation of a popular young professor who'd been denied tenure, thus sparking a takeover of the
administration building. Shils was brutal:

> [Her] level of performance is at best unqualifiedly mediocre. She has
> not a single relatively original, or even bold idea. She has not pursued
> a central theme with rigor nor in depth. . . . She lacks analytical skill.
> She is unimaginative. Such perspectives and theoretic framework as
> she possesses belong to the problematic clichés of the present day.

Aaron looked up this passage whenever he needed a hoot. It impressed me, too. How could it not? Professors didn't speak this way;

they hemmed around, hid their disdain in euphemism. Shils was intellectual royalty with blue-collar tact. He came on like a boxer, aiming to break some ribs. The faculty accepted his assessment of the professor's work. The decision to deny the woman tenure was reaffirmed.

At other universities students took over buildings with little or no risk of reprisal. At Cornell students who laid siege to a building with guns endured not a single expulsion. Chicago was different. Faculty members walked among the demonstrators and identified them for disciplinary purposes. The sit-in ended without concessions. The participants were summoned to disciplinary hearings. Suspensions and expulsions followed. Shils had been the hub of power through it all. For this he was loved—and hated.

Aaron kept after me to attend one of Shils's seminars. Finally I gave in and went. The seminar met in a small oak-lined room not much bigger than the conference table it contained. Shils loomed at the table's head: a cannonball figure with beefy hands resting in front of him. The man radiated power. The space around him was his space; entering it placed you under his control. His eyes settled on me almost at once. He was probably just curious about who I was. The Committee had only one black student—a Caribbean character with dark glasses and a goatee—and clearly I wasn't he. Shils's gaze made me uneasy. His top lip curled upward and to one side, making him seem disdainful. Instead of merely curious he seemed to be sneering at me, objecting to me on principle. I tried to look away, but there was nowhere to look. The windows were well above eye level, quite near the ceiling. I stared into the wall and waited it out. I fled the seminar and never went back.

Mr. Shils had been kidnapped as Professor Richard Durnwald into *Humboldt's Gift*:

> Durnwald was reddish, elderly, but powerful, thickset and bald, a bachelor of cranky habits but a kind man. He had a peremptory blunt, butting, even bullying manner, but if he scolded me it was because he loved me—he wouldn't have bothered otherwise. A great scholar, one of the most learned people on the earth, he was rationalistic. Not narrowly rationalistic, by any means. Nevertheless, I couldn't talk to him about the powers of the spirit being separated from a body. He wouldn't hear of it.

It amused me that Bellow seemed frightened of Shils, too.

The curl in Shils's lip Bellow had given to the character Mickey, a concessionaire in the Division Street Steam Baths:

Mickey had a twisted lip. During the Depression he had to sleep in the parks and the cold ground gave him a partial paralysis of the cheek. This makes him seem to scoff and jeer. A misleading impression.

I scribbled "Shils!" in the margin. The theft didn't end with *Humboldt's Gift*. Shils was a thread that ran through several of Bellow's novels, a stolen essence that popped up everywhere.

Bellow's people leaped more vividly from the page than any I'd encountered. Often he reduced them to a single bodily feature that carried their entire person in its wake: the set of the butt, the cleft of the upper lip, a gap in the teeth. He preferred a sexual organ if he could get it. At the Division Street baths he had waited vulturously for the steam room attendant to bend over so that he could record the squeaky-clean anus, juxtaposed with the "testicles swinging on a long sinew." If no sexual organ was available, anything would do. He sometimes snatched bodies whole, but mainly he cannibalized them, taking only the choicest parts. He stole from himself as well, giving characters his own enormous eyes and unflatteringly spaced teeth.

I lost the thread of his story when he paused to reflect on philosophy and metaphysics. The references were often oblique to the point of nonsense. Students from The Committee referred to them as Saul "Belching." This belching aside, the man was an alchemist. He could make the folds in a bald man's head seem like a window on the soul.

This was one of the first novels I'd read on my own. Most of the others had been assigned in college, and I'd ransacked them for facts to use in term papers and essays. Those novels had the added liability of being merely fictional: Their characters were elsewhere, living otherwise. *Humboldt's Gift* was local geography, people included.

The novel was cast as a farce. Its self-mocking star was Charlie Citrine, a middle-aged writer and Hyde Park egghead. Charlie is school smart but life dumb. Cannier types constantly exploit him. His fortune is being slowly extracted by a vindictive ex-wife and her lawyers. He hangs out with lowlifes who cheat him at cards. One of these lowlifes is a would-be mafiosi named Rinaldo. Charlie stops a check on Rinaldo. Rinaldo bludgeons Charlie's Mercedes with a baseball bat. When Charlie pays up, Rinaldo rips up the money and throws it away. Rinaldo wants humiliation. He drags Charlie into the shit stall and forces him to hold the toilet roll while he, Rinaldo, takes a dump.

The novel ceases to be a farce when a black man steps out of the shadows and, with no motive, slits a white woman's throat. Black people in the book were sinister characters. Rinaldo refers to them as "crazy buffaloes" and "pork chops." Crazy buffaloes populate the slums that surrounded Hyde Park. A pork chop chases Charlie down the middle of his street, presumably at night. These passages made me angry. It was the same anger I felt when white people cowered past me on the street.

Barbarousness in *Mr. Sammler's Planet* is a pickpocket who preys on the old and feeble as they ride the public bus in New York City. The pickpocket works in broad daylight. He manhandles bleary-eyed old men, rifles their pockets, and leaves them too terrified to speak. After spying this fellow at work, Mr. Sammler is chased down and cornered. The pickpocket says nothing, but shows Mr. Sammler his dick. What followed was the book's most vivid description:

> It was displayed to Sammler with great oval testicles, a large tan-and-purple uncircumcised thing—a tube, a snake; metallic hairs bristled at the thick base and the tip curled beyond the supporting, demonstrating hand, suggesting the fleshy motility of an elephant's trunk, though the skin was somewhat iridescent rather than thick or rough. Over the forearm and fist that held him Sammler was required to gaze at this organ. No compulsion would have been necessary. He would in any case have looked.

Bellow wanted the dick remembered. He returned to it again and again as a symbol of spiritual decay, of the "sexual niggerhood" that "millions of civilized people" had deluded themselves into wanting.

I expected more of a man who could see to the soul. I expected a portrait of myself, not as the beast I'd been made out to be, but as who I was at heart. I'd given up on this when Aaron lent me his dog-eared copy of *Dangling Man*, Bellow's first novel, written in 1944. "Read it," he said. "It speaks to our situation." The novel was written as a journal. The first page was an eloquent defense of the form:

> There was a time when people were in the habit of addressing themselves frequently and felt no shame of making a record of their inward transactions. But to keep a journal nowadays is considered a kind of self-indulgence, a weakness and in poor taste. For this is an era of hard-boileddom. . . . Do you have feelings? There are correct and incorrect ways of indicating them. Do you have an inner life? It is nobody's business but your own. Do you have emotions? Strangle them. To a degree everybody obeys this code. And it does admit of a limited candor, a closemouthed straightforwardness. But on the truest candor, it has an inhibitory effect. Most serious matters are closed to the hard-boiled. They are unpracticed at introspection and therefore badly equipped to deal with opponents whom they cannot shoot like big game or outdo in daring.

I sat up when I read this, and read it again. I was carrying a journal with me everywhere. *Humboldt's Gift* had given me the idea. I wrote on buses and on the Jackson Park el—though only at the stops to keep the writing legible. I traveled to distant neighborhoods, sat on their curbs, and sketched what I saw in words. Thursdays meant free admission at the Art Institute. All day I attributed motives to people in paintings, especially people in Rembrandts. At closing time I went to a nightclub in The Loop and spied on the patrons, copied their conversations and speculated about their lives. The journal was more than "a record of my inner transactions." It was a collection of stolen souls from which I would one day construct a book. Bellow had made it seem easy enough: Kidnap people onto the page, stir in stories from the papers and from your life, and *voila!* you had it made.

A journal of Chicago is a journal of weather. Winter lasts forever there. Dirty gray ice hangs on in the gutters through Easter. June suckers you outside in shirtsleeves, then shifts its winds, bringing January to rake your bones. Warm weather smells of an ambush until August. Then the lake heats up, the breeze stops, and it's too hot to breathe.

In deepest winter, arctic winds dipped down from Canada and froze every bit of moisture from the air. Indoors the air was so dry that it split your lips and gave you nosebleeds. The cold slipped its knife through the bathroom window and cut you as you showered. Outside, the storm drains along the street vented steam, as though boiling. As you walked to the corner store, steam flared from your tearducts and from the surface of the eye itself.

The beauty of the nights compensated for this cruelty. The wind that punished had also swept the sky clean and left it breathtakingly clear.

In the fiercest cold the lakefront fell exclusively to the runners. Trotting through the arctic waste by the lake, I imagined myself an explorer, racing to the Pole. Occasionally another runner appeared in the distance, steamy breath curling around his head. As we drew closer to one another we could see the sweat frozen into icicles hanging from our woolen caps and from our beards. We smiled at one another through ice-coated whiskers, then steamed on. Back at my apartment, I lazed in a hot bath, then wrapped myself in Miles Davis. "Miles Smiles." "In a Silent Way." "Kind of Blue." "Live in Stockholm." Then I turned to writing in the journal.

I suffered lung burn from running in subzero weather. The lung tissue was frozen and scarred and could no longer transfer oxygen. I lay in bed for days, too weak to sit up. My face was ashen, as pale as death. The doctor said the condition was temporary, but it still had scared me. It taught me respect for the cold.

The winter was one of the cruelest on record. The temperature stayed below freezing for the entire month of January, with several consecutive days well below zero. Sunday, January fifteenth, started out at 19 below zero, far too cold to run, too cold even for a walk around the block. An icy frost was covering the sun-porch windows faster than I could scrape it away. Finally, I gave up and let it wall me in.

By nightfall I was crazed with cabin fever. I decided to go to the movies. This meant taking the el to the North Side, to the Biograph Theatre. The trip was punishing, especially with the Jackson Park el on its Sunday schedule. A wait of forty minutes was not uncommon. Some el platforms offered the mercy of enclosed waiting areas. But mainly you stood in the open while the guillotine winds cut you to pieces.

I set out for the el stop at 63rd Street and had just crossed 62nd when the northbound train roared across the horizon and disappeared into the night. This had happened many times. Ordinarily I beat it back to my apartment, waited twenty minutes, then started out again. This time I pressed on to a diner under the el tracks. I ordered tea and a Danish and filled the time writing.

The journal notes that the tea was served in a disposable cup and that the restaurant was dimly lit and nearly empty. The waitress behind the counter stared out at the night and hugged herself against the chill. There were two other people in the place: a man using the phone in the foyer and a woman sitting at the counter. The woman wore a strawberry-blond Afro wig. It was an enormous wig, its curls obscuring her face. Her coat, draped across her lap, was thin and trimmed in fake fur. I wrote first about the man at the phone:

> There's a reason for placing a phone in the foyer of a restaurant; in a place like Chicago there's a better than even chance that the patron won't spend hours out there pleading his case. This joker in the foyer is probably explaining to his wife why he's late, telling her he's in a phone booth. It's so cold that the call doesn't take long.
> I sit down to order my tea and Danish, really to get the change for the train because the CTA doesn't take twenties. I look right and see her: the archetypal underdressed party girl: Her strawberry-blond wig is about the size of a basketball and droops around her taffy-colored cheeks. The wig is too big, slides way down around the outlines of her face. She wears one of those bare-shouldered Jane Russell blouses, spanning the skin from shoulder to shoulder (including the bruises bitten into her by some passionate lover). Her coat! Cheap. Superthin. Fake to the Chicago wind, trimmed in fake fur.
> He comes in from the phone. Wrinkled and kinky from a week-

end out in the same clothes (it's Sunday), and sits down with the lady who is by now ravenously biting into her cheeseburger deluxe.

"How's the food?" he says.

"OK," she says.

"You know what happens after this?"

"Mmmm." Mouth full of burger.

"You know what happens next?"

Inaudible response.

"We goin' to the crib, right?"

She sees me looking at her, peeks around the edges of her wig. (I wonder if she suspects that I'm writing this down.)

He's loud. He bought the pussy for a cheeseburger deluxe and hasn't the decency to keep quiet about it. I feel myself hating him.

"We goin' to the crib, . . ." she says.

"Then what's gonna happen?"

Inaudible.

"Yeah!" he says.

Then he gets off his stool and walks back to the pisshole. By this time I've finished my stuff. I slip my journal and pen into my rucksack and wrap up to split. At the door I do my classic full turn before moving offstage. Her eyes catch mine. They admit humiliation, desperation, and unhappiness . . . I pay my fare, and up the stairs to wait for the train. God, it's cold out tonight.

The tale of the prostitute and the burger deluxe typifies the journals in winter. The stories are gray and sad, like the weather. In Chicago I learned that weather made me who I was. Successive gray days left me on the verge of tears. The mood was impenetrable. I didn't know it was a mood until the sun came shining to the rescue. The lesson was new each time.

Dangling Man captured it all. The chrysalis character of graduate school. The idleness and sterility of Hyde Park. The vast emptiness of the wintertime streets. The ice clinging to the gutters into spring, and the desperate longing for warmth. This novel was the ground beneath my feet.

I felt for Bellow what the young Charlie Citrine had felt for Von Humboldt Fleisher: I envied his luck, his talent, and his fame. I wanted to be near him—but not too near. His sentiments about black men made me wary. So did the way he dissected people with his eyes. You had to protect yourself in Bellow's presence. He went over you like you were some kind of phenomenon.

Bellow lived in an apartment tower just off The Midway on Dorchester Avenue, next door to International House. I knew from the novels that his apartment faced the lake and that it therefore over-looked my running route at the eastern end of The Midway. When passing that spot, I concentrated on the upper windows of the tower. I envisioned him staring down at the lone runner trudging along The Midway. I raised my arm and waved.

I added the tower to my evening walks. The intersection at 59th and Dorchester was the dark stretch of sidewalk where I had played the cruelest innings of Scatter the Pigeons. The night walkers there were either students scurrying toward International House or gray-haired couples rushing from their cars into Bellow's tower or into the Cloisters, an apartment building just north of it.

Now and then I bounded up the tower stairs to make sure Bellow's name was still on the bell. A security gate cut you off from the base of the tower itself, which was too bad, because there were shadows there to linger in. His neighbors suffered mightily from my visits, especially when they encountered me descending the stairs in the dark.

What would I do when I caught him? Perhaps I'd lift him bodily and pin him against a wall. Perhaps I'd corner him on the stairs and take up questions about "pork chops" and "crazy buffaloes" and bar-barous black pickpockets. I wanted to trophy his fear.

I stalked Dorchester Avenue for months before I caught him out. The night it happened I had almost given up hope. I turned out of 58th Street and was passing in front of the Cloisters when I saw him: a little man in an overcoat, hurrying along the sidewalk about twenty yards ahead of me. I cursed my timing. Ten seconds earlier would have put me right on his heels. I could easily have run him down, but that wasn't the game. The game was to wait for chance to place me squarely be-tween the tower and him. That way he'd have to face me in the dark. This was not to be the night. He threw back a glance, wisps of white hair flying, then picked up his pace. He showed surprising bounce get-ting up the stairs. When I reached the tower, I saw only his shoe disap-pearing through the gate.

I finally got the advantage of him in broad daylight, in an afternoon crowd in front of the Hyde Park Bank. The crowd wasn't as good as darkness, but it provided camouflage. I could watch him without being seen. He was walking toward me, his khaki cap pulled low to protect his eyes from the sun. Even squinting, the eyes seemed saucerous, huge, the skin around them slack from heavy use. Spider-legged squint lines radiated from the corners of his eyes, upward into the temple and downward into the jaw. The skin over these squint lines was translu-cent, like the membrane of an egg, so luminous in the sunlight that I nearly reached out to touch it. He moved through the crowd looking downward, hungrily scanning asses, hips, and crotches. This was how he did it. The rest of us were a junkyard where he foraged for parts. I wanted something from him. The longing was deep, but I couldn't place it then. It would take years for me to realize what it was. I wanted to steal the essence of him, to absorb it right into my bones. After I passed him, I felt faint and reached out for a wall. That's when I realized that I'd been holding my breath.

David Quammen

David Quammen has for a dozen years written a monthly column, "Natural Acts," for *Outside* magazine. Quammen says he has had "unimaginable freedom and opportunity" as the magazine's natural science columnist. Literary journalists thrive in environments where they are given time and editorial encouragement for their imaginative work. The habitat at *Outside* apparently is rich in those nutrients. In its sixteen years a number of journalists have produced excellent work there, including Chip Brown, Tim Cahill, E. Jean Carroll, Donald Katz, Jon Krakauer, Mark Kramer, and Randy Wayne White.

Quammen's articles and columns from *Outside* have been collected in two volumes: *Natural Acts* (1986) and *The Flight of the Iguana* (1988). His nonfiction has also appeared in *Harper's, Audubon, Esquire,* and *Rolling Stone.* He has published three novels and a collection of short fiction. *The Song of the Dodo*

(1995), which required eight years of research, deals with what biological scientists have learned about evolution and the extinction of species while studying islands. His research for the book took him to Madagascar and the Malay Archipelago in Indonesia, which he described as "the most remote place I've ever been." Considering that he has traveled all over the world for *Outside* during the past several years, that's saying something.

In his introduction to *The Flight of the Iguana*, Quammen offered his perspective on natural science. "Walt Whitman never met a snake or a sea cucumber that he didn't like, and this Whitmanesque attitude toward nature is exactly the one that seems to me exemplary," he wrote. "It is highly unscientific, it tends toward anthropomorphism, but then scientific objectivity and abstention from the anthropomorphic metaphor are not absolute virtues; those two forms of cold intellectual purity can help us understand nature, sure, but they shouldn't necessarily define our relations with it." His columns reflect that view, although, he says, "Some of us come to the sticking point over spiders, some over grizzly bears, some over rattlesnakes, or cocker spaniels, or house cats. But we can try."

"Strawberries Under Ice," which first appeared in *Outside*, illustrates the enhancement of science writing by a literary journalist.

Strawberries Under Ice

1. The Gradient of Net Mass Balance

Antarctica is a gently domed continent squashed flat, like a dent in the roof of a Chevy, by the weight of its ice. That burden of ice amounts to seven million cubic miles. Melt it away and the Antarctic interior would bounce upward; Earth itself would change shape. This grand cold fact has, to me, on the tiny and personal scale, a warm appeal. Take away ice and the topography of my own life changes drastically too.

Ice is lighter than water but still heavy. The stuff answers gravity. Ice is a solid but not an absolute solid. The stuff flows. Slowly but inexorably it runs downhill. We think of iciness as a synonym for cold, but cold is relative and ice happens to function well as insulation against heat loss: low thermal conductivity. Also it *releases* heat to immediate surroundings in the final stage of becoming frozen itself. Ice warms. On a certain night, roughly thirteen years ago, it warmed me.

When a tongue of ice flows down a mountain valley, we call it a glacier. When it flows out in all directions from a source point at high elevation, like pancake batter poured on a griddle, we call it a sheet. Out at the Antarctic circumference are glaciers and seaborne shelves, from which icebergs calve off under their own weight. Both sheets and glaciers are supplied with their substance, their impetus, their ice, by snow and other forms of precipitation back uphill at the source. While old ice is continually lost by calving and melting in the lowlands, new ice is deposited in the highlands, and any glacier or sheet receiving more new ice than it loses old, through the course of a year, is a glacier or sheet that is growing. The scientists would say that its net mass balance is positive.

The Antarctic sheet, for instance, has a positive balance. But this is not an essay about Antarctica.

Each point on a great ice body has its own numerical value for mass balance. Is the ice right here thicker or thinner than last year? Is the glacier, at this spot, thriving or dying? The collective profile of all those individual soundings—more ice or less? thriving or dying?—is called the gradient of net mass balance. This gradient tells, in broad perspective, what has been lost and what has been gained. On that certain night, thirteen years ago, I happened to be asking myself exactly the same question: *what's been lost and what, if anything, gained?* Because snow gathers most heavily in frigid sky-scraping highlands, the gradient of net mass balance correlates steeply with altitude. Robust glaciers come snaking down out of the Alaskan mountains. Also because snow gathers most heavily in frigid sky-scraping highlands, I had taken myself on that day to a drifted-over pass in the Bitterroot Mountains, all hell-and-gone up on the state border just west of the town of Tarkio, Montana, and started skiing uphill from there.

I needed as much snow as possible. I carried food and a goose-down bag and a small shovel. The night in question was December 31, 1975.

I hadn't come to measure depths or calculate gradients. I had come to insert myself into a cold white hole. First, of course, I had to dig it. This elaborately uncomfortable enterprise seems to have been part of a long foggy process of escape and purgation, much of which you can be spared. Suffice that my snow cave, to be dug on New Year's Eve into a ten-foot-high cornice on the leeward side of the highest ridge I could ski to, and barely large enough for one person, would be at the aphelion of that long foggy process. At the perihelion was Oxford University.

At Oxford University during one week in late springtime there is a festival of crew races on the river, and girls in long dresses, and boys in straw hats, and champagne and strawberries. This event is called Eights Week, for the fact of eight men to a crew. It is innocent. More precisely: it is no more obnoxious, no more steeped in snobbery and dandified xenophobia and intellectual and social complacence, than any other aspect of Oxford University. The strawberries are served under heavy cream. Sybaritism is mandatory. For these and other reasons, partly personal, partly political, I had fled the place screaming during Eights Week of 1972, almost precisely coincident (by no coincidence) with Richard Nixon's announcement of the blockade of Haiphong harbor. Nixon's blockade and Oxford's strawberries had nothing logically in common, but they converged to produce in me a drastic reaction to what until then had been just a festering distemper.

It took me another year to arrive in Montana. I had never before set foot in the state. I knew no one there. But I had heard that it was a place where, in the early weeks of September, a person could look up to a looming horizon and see fresh-laid snow. I had noted certain blue lines on a highway map, knew the lines to be rivers, and imagined those rivers to be dark mountain streams flashing with trout. I arrived during the early weeks of September and lo it was all true.

I took a room in an old-fashioned boarding house. I looked for a job. I started work on a recklessly ambitious and doomed novel. I sensed rather soon that I hadn't come to this place temporarily. I began reading the writers—Herodotus, Euripides, Coleridge, Descartes, Rousseau, Thoreau, Raymond Chandler—for whom a conscientious and narrow academic career had left no time. I spent my nest-egg and then sold my Volkswagen bus for another. I learned the clownish mortification of addressing strangers with: "Hi, my name is Invisible and I'll be your waiter tonight." I was twenty-six, just old enough to realize that this period was not some sort of prelude to my life but the thing itself. I knew I was spending real currency, hard and finite, on a speculative venture at an unknowable rate of return: the currency of time, energy, stamina. Two more years passed before I arrived, sweaty and chilled, at that high cold cornice in the Bitterroots.

By then I had made a small handful of precious friends in this new place, and a menagerie of acquaintances, and I had learned also to say: "You want that on the rocks or up?" Time was still plentiful but stamina was low. Around Christmas that year, two of the precious friends announced a New Year's Eve party. Tempting, yet it seemed somehow a better idea to spend the occasion alone in a snow cave.

So here I was. There had been no trail up the face of the ridge and lifting my skis through the heavy snow had drenched and exhausted me. My thighs felt as though the Chicago police had worked on them with truncheons. I dug my hole. That done, I changed out of the soaked freezing clothes. I boiled and ate some noodles, drank some cocoa; if I had been smart enough to encumber my pack with a bottle of wine, I don't remember it. When dark came I felt the nervous exhilaration of utter solitude and, behind that like a metallic aftertaste, loneliness. I gnawed on my thoughts for an hour or two, then retired. The night turned into a clear one and when I crawled out of the cave at 3:00 A.M. of the new year, to empty my bladder, I found the sky rolled out in a stunning pageant of scope and dispassion and cold grace.

It was too good to waste. I went back into the cave for my glasses.

The temperature by now had gone into the teens below zero. I stood there beside the cornice in cotton sweatpants, gaping up. "We never know what we have lost, or what we have found," says America's wisest poet, Penn Warren, in the context of a meditation about John James Audubon and the transforming power of landscape. We never know what we have lost, or what we have found. All I did know was that the highway maps called it Montana, and that I was here, and that in the course of a life a person could travel widely but could truly open his veins and his soul to just a limited number of places.

After half an hour I crawled back into the cave, where ten feet of snow and a rime of ice would keep me warm.

2. Ablation

Trace any glacier or ice sheet downhill from its source and eventually you will come to a boundary where the mass balance of ice is zero. Nothing is lost, over the course of time, and nothing is gained. The ice itself constantly flows past this boundary, molecule by molecule, but if any new ice is added here by precipitation, if any old ice is taken away by melting, those additions and subtractions cancel each other exactly. This boundary is called the equilibrium line. Like other forms of equilibrium, it entails a certain cold imperturbability, a sublime stasis relative to what's going on all around. Above the equilibrium line is the zone of accumulation. Below is the zone of ablation.

Ablation is the scientists' fancy word for loss. Down here the mass balance is negative. Ice is supplied to this zone mainly by flow from above, little or not at all by direct precipitation, and whatever does come as direct precipitation is less than the amount annually lost. The loss results from several different processes: wind erosion, surface melting, evaporation (ice does evaporate), underside melting of an ice shelf where it rests on the warmer seawater. Calving off of icebergs. Calving is the scientists' quaint word for that event when a great hunk of ice—as big as a house or, in some cases, as big as a county—tears away from the leading edge of the sheet or the glacier and falls thunderously into the sea.

Possibly this talk about calving reflects an unspoken sense that the larger ice mass, moving, pulsing, constantly changing its shape, is almost alive. If so the analogy doesn't go far. Icebergs don't suckle or grow. They float away on the sea, melt, break apart, disappear. Wind erosion and evaporation and most of those other ablative processes work on the ice slowly, incrementally. Calving on the other hand is abrupt. A large piece of the whole is there, and then gone.

The occurrence of a calving event depends on a number of factors—flow rate of the whole ice body, thickness at the edge, temperature, fissures in the ice, stresses from gravity or tides—one of which is the strength of the ice itself. That factor, strength, is hard to measure. You might never know until too late. Certain experiments done on strength-testing machines have yielded certain numbers: a strength of thirty-eight bars (a bar is a unit of pressure equal to 100,000 newtons per square meter) for crushing; fourteen bars for bending; nine bars for tensile. But those numbers offer no absolute guide to the performance of different types of ice under different conditions. They only suggest in a relative way that, though ice may flow majestically under its own weight, though it may stretch like caramel, though it may bend like lead, it gives back rocklike resistance to a force coming down on it suddenly. None of this cold information was available to me on the day now in mind, and if it had been I wouldn't have wanted it.

On the day now in mind I had been off skiing, again, with no thought for the physical properties of ice, other than maybe some vague awareness of the knee strain involved in carving a turn across boilerplate. I came home to find a note in my door.

The note said that a young woman I knew, the great love of a friend of mine, was dead. The note didn't say what had happened. I should call a number in Helena for details. It was not only shocking but ominous. Because I knew that the young woman had lately been working through some uneasy and confusing times, I thought of all the various grim possibilities involving despair. Then I called the Helena number, where a houseful of friends were gathered for communal grieving and food and loud music. I learned that the young woman had died from a fall. A freak accident. In the coldest sense of cold consolation, there was in this information some relief.

She had slipped on a patch of sidewalk ice, the night before, and hit her head. A nasty blow, a moment or two of unconsciousness, but she had apparently been all right. She went home alone and was not all right and died before morning. I suppose she was about twenty-seven. This is exactly why head-trauma cases are normally put under close overnight observation, but I wasn't aware of that at the time, and neither evidently were the folks who had helped her up off that icy sidewalk. She had seemed okay. Even after the fall, her death was preventable. Of course most of us will die preventable deaths; hers was only more vividly so, and earlier.

I had known her, not well, through her sweetheart and the network of friends now assembled in that house in Helena. These friends of hers and mine were mostly a group of ecologists who had worked together, during graduate school, as waiters and bartenders and cooks; I met them in that context and they had nurtured my sanity to no small degree when that context began straining it. They read books, they talked about ideas, they knew a spruce from a hemlock, they slept in snow caves: a balm of good company to me. They made the state of Montana into a place that was not only cold, true, hard, and beautiful, but damn near humanly habitable. The young woman, now dead, was not herself a scientist but she was one of them in all other senses. She came from a town up on the Hi-Line.

I had worked with her too, and seen her enliven long afternoons that could otherwise be just a tedious and not very lucrative form of self-demeanment. She was one of those rowdy, robust people—robust in good times, just as robust when she was angry or miserable—who are especially hard to imagine dead. She was a rascal of wit. She could be hilariously crude. We all knew her by her last name, because her first seemed too ladylike and demure. After the phone call to Helena, it took me a long time to make the mental adjustment of tenses: She *had* been a rascal of wit.

The memorial service was scheduled for such-and-such day, in that town up on the Hi-Line.

We drove up together on winter roads, myself and two of the Helena friends, a husband-and-wife pair of plant ecologists. Others had gone ahead. Places available for sleeping, spare rooms and floors; make contact by phone; meet at the church. We met at the church and sat lumpish while a local pastor discoursed with transcendent irrelevance about what we could hardly recognize as her life and death. It wasn't his fault, he didn't know her. There was a reception with the family, followed by a post-wake on our own at a local bar, a fervent gathering of young survivors determined not only to cling to her memory but to cling to each other more appreciatively now that such a persuasive warning knell of mortality had been rung, and then sometime after dark as the wind came up and the temperature dropped away as though nothing was under it and a new storm raked in across those wheatlands, the three of us started driving back south. It had been my first trip to the Hi-Line.

Aside from the note in the door, this is the part I remember most clearly. The car's defroster wasn't working. I had about four inches of open windshield. It was a little Honda that responded to wind like a shuttlecock, and on slick pavement the rear end flapped like the tail of a trout. We seemed to be rolling down a long dark tube coated inside with ice, jarred back and forth by the crosswinds, nothing else visible except the short tongue of road ahead and the streaming snow and the trucks blasting by too close in the other lane. How ironic, I thought, if we die on the highway while returning from a funeral. I hunched over the wheel, squinting out through that gap of windshield, until certain muscles in my right shoulder and neck shortened themselves into a knot. The two plant ecologists kept me awake with talk. One of them, from the back seat, worked at the knot in my neck. We talked about friendship and the message of death as we all three felt we had heard it, which was to cherish the living, while you have them. Seize, hold, appreciate. Pure friendship, uncomplicated by romance or blood, is one of the most nurturing human relationships and one of the most easily taken for granted. This was our consensus, spoken and unspoken.

These two plant ecologists had been my dear friends for a few years, but we were never closer than during that drive. Well after midnight, we reached their house in Helena. I slept on sofa cushions. In the morning they got me to a doctor for the paralytic clench in my neck. That was almost ten years ago and I've hardly seen them since.

The fault is mine, or the fault is nobody's. We got older and busier and trails diverged. They began raising children. I traveled to Helena less and less. Mortgages, serious jobs, deadlines; and the age of sleeping on sofa cushions seemed to have passed. I moved, they moved, opening more geographical distance. Montana is a big place and the roads are often bad. These facts offered in explanation sound even to me like excuses. The ashes of the young woman who slipped on the ice have long since been sprinkled onto a mountain top or into a river, I'm not sure which. Nothing to be done now either for her or about her. The two plant ecologists I still cherish, in intention anyway, at a regrettable distance, as I do a small handful of other precious friends, who seem to have disappeared from my life by wind erosion or melting.

3. Leontiev's Axiom

The ice mass of a mountain glacier flows down its valley in much the same complicated pattern as a river flowing in its bed. Obviously the glacier is much slower. Glacial ice may move at rates between six inches and six feet per day; river water may move a distance in that range every second. Like the water of a river, though, the ice of any particular glacier does not all flow at the same rate. There are eddies and tongues and slack zones, currents and swells, differential vectors of mix and surge. The details of the flow pattern depend on particularities to each given case: depth of the ice, slope, contour of the bed, temperature. But some generalizations can be made. Like a river, a glacier will tend to register faster flow rates at the surface than at depths, faster flows at midchannel than along the edges, and faster flows down toward the middle reaches than up near the source. One formula the scientists use to describe the relations between flow rate and those other factors is:

$$u = k_1 \sin^3 a\, h^4 + k_2 \sin^2 a\, h^2.$$

Everyone stay calm. This formula is not Leontiev's Axiom, and so we aren't going to bother deciphering it.

Turbulent flow is what makes a glacier unfathomable, in the sense of *fathoming* that connotes more than taking an ice-core measurement of depth. Turbulent flow is also what distinguishes a river from, say, a lake. When a river itself freezes, the complexities of turbulent flow interact with the peculiar physics of ice formation to produce a whole rat's nest of intriguing and sometimes inconvenient surprises. Because of turbulence, the water of a river cools down toward the freezing point uniformly, not in stratified layers as in a lake. Eventually the entire mass of flowing water drops below 32 degrees F. Small disks of ice, called frazil ice, then appear. Again because of turbulence, this frazil ice doesn't all float on the surface (despite being lighter than water) but mixes throughout the river's depth. Frazil ice has a tendency to adhesion, so some of it sticks to riverbed rocks. Some of it gloms onto bridge pilings and culverts, growing thick as a soft cold fur. Some of it aggregates with other frazil ice, forming large dollops of drifting slush. Meanwhile huge slabs of harder sheet ice, formed along the banks and broken free as the river changed level, may also be floating downstream. The slabs of sheet ice and the dollops of frazil ice go together like bricks and mortar. Stacking up at a channel constriction, they can lock themselves into an ice bridge.

Generally, when such an ice bridge forms, the river will have room to flow underneath. If the river is very shallow and the slabs of sheet ice are large, possibly not. Short of total blockage, the flow of the river will be slowed somewhat where it must pass through that narrowed gap; if it slows to less than a certain critical value, more ice will collect along the front face of the bridge and the ice cover will expand upstream. The relevant formula here is:

$$v_c = (1 - h/H)\sqrt{2g\left(p - p_i/p\right)}\,\mathrm{h},$$

where V_c is the critical flow rate and h is the ice thickness and everything else represents something too. But this also is not Leontiev's Axiom, and so we can ignore it, praise God.

The Madison River where it runs north through Montana happens to be very shallow. Upstream from (that is, south of) the lake that sits five miles north of Ennis, it is a magnificent stretch of habitat for stoneflies and caddisflies and trout and blue heron and fox and eagles and, half the year anyway, fishermen. The water is warmed at its geothermal source in Yellowstone Park, cooled again by its Montana tributaries like West Fork, rich in nutrients and oxygen, clear, lambent, unspoiled. Thanks to these graces, it is probably much too famous for its own good, and here I am making it a little more famous still. Upstream from the highway bridge at Ennis, where it can be conveniently floated by fishermen in rafts and guided Mackenzies, it gets an untoward amount of attention. This is where the notorious salmonfly hatch happens: boat traffic like the Henley Regatta, during that dizzy two weeks of June while the insects swarm and the fish gluttonize. This is the stretch of the Madison for fishermen who crave trophies but not solitude. Downstream from the Ennis bridge it becomes a different sort of river. It becomes a different sort of place.

Downstream from the Ennis bridge, for that five-mile stretch to the lake, the Madison is a broken-up travesty of a river that offers mediocre fishing and clumsy floating and no trophy trout and not many salmonflies and I promise you fervently you wouldn't like it. This stretch is called "the channels." The river braids out into a maze of elbows and sloughs and streams separated by dozens of small and large islands, some covered only with grass and willow, some shaded with buckling old-growth cottonwoods, some holding thickets of water birch and woods rose and raspberry scarcely tramped through by a single fisherman in the course of a summer. The deer love these islands and, in May, so do the nesting geese. Mosquitoes are bad here. The walking is difficult and there are bleached cottonwood deadfalls waiting to tear your waders. At the end of a long day's float, headwinds and choppy waves will come up on the lake just as you try to row your boat across to the ramp. Take my word, you'd hate the whole experience. Don't bother. Give it a miss. I adore that five miles of river more than any piece of landscape in the world.

Surrounding the braidwork of channels is a zone of bottomland roughly two miles wide, a great flat swath of subirrigated meadow only barely above the river's springtime high-water level. This low meadow area is an unusual sort of no-man's-land that performs a miraculous service: protecting the immediate riparian vicinity of the channels from the otherwise-inevitable arrival of ranch houses, summer homes, resort lodges, motels, all-weather roads, development, spoliation, and all other manner of venal doom. Tantalizing and vulnerable as it may appear on a July afternoon, the channels meadowland is an ideal place to raise bluegrass and Herefords and sandhill cranes but, for reasons we'll come to, is not really good for much else.

By late December the out-of-state fishermen are long gone, the duck hunters more recently, and during a good serious stretch of weather the dark river begins to flow gray and woolly with frazil ice. If the big slabs of sheet ice are moving too, a person can stand on the Ennis highway bridge and hear the two kinds of ice rubbing, hissing, whispering to each other as though in conspiracy toward mischief, or maybe revenge. (Through the three winters I lived in Ennis myself, I stood on that bridge often, gawking and listening. There aren't too many other forms of legal amusement in a Montana town of a thousand souls during the short days and long weeks of midwinter.) By this time the lake, five miles downstream, will have already frozen over. Then the river water cools still farther, the frazil thickens, the slabs bump and tumble into those narrow channels, until somewhere, at a point of constriction down near the lake, mortar meets brick and you begin to get:

$$v_c = (1 - h/H) \sqrt{2g\,(p - p_i/p)\,h}.$$

Soon the river is choked with its own ice. All the channels are nearly or totally blocked. But water is still arriving from upstream, and it has to go somewhere. So it flows out across the bottomland. It pours out over its banks and, moving quickly, faster than a man can walk, it covers a large part of that meadow area with water. Almost as quickly, the standing floodwater becomes ice.

If you have been stubborn or foolish enough to build your house out on that flat, on a pretty spot at the edge of the river, you now have three feet of well-deserved ice in your living room. "Get back away from me," is what the river has told you. "Show some goddamn respect." There are memories of this sort of ice-against-man encounter. It hasn't happened often, that a person should come along so mule-minded as to insist on flouting the reality of the ice, but often enough for a few vivid exempla. Back in 1863, for instance, a settler named Andrew Odell, who had built his cabin out on the channel meadows, woke up one night in December to find river water already lapping onto his bed. He grabbed his blanket and fled, knee deep, toward higher ground on the far side of a spring creek that runs parallel to the channels a half mile east. That spring creek is now called Odell Creek, and it marks a rough eastern boundary of the zone that gets buried in ice. Nowadays you don't see any cabins or barns in the flat between Odell Creek and the river.

Folks in Ennis call this salubrious event the Gorge. The Gorge doesn't occur every year, and it isn't uniform or predictable when it does. Two or three winters may go by without serious weather, without a Gorge, without that frozen flood laid down upon thousands of acres, and then there will come a record year. A rancher named Ralph Paugh remembers one particular Gorge, because it back-flooded all the way up across Odell to fill his barn with a two-foot depth of ice. This was on Christmas Day, 1983. "It come about four o'clock," he recalls. "Never had got to the barn before." His barn has sat on that rise since 1905. He has some snapshots from the 1983 episode, showing vistas and mounds of whiteness. "That pile there, see, we piled that up with the dozer when we cleaned it out." Ralph also remembers talk about the Gorge in 1907, the year he was born; that one took out the old highway bridge, so for the rest of the winter schoolchildren and mailmen and whoever else had urgent reason for crossing the river did so on a trail of planks laid across ice. The present bridge is a new one, the lake north of Ennis is also a relatively recent contrivance (put there for hydroelectric generation about when Ralph Paugh was a baby), but the Gorge of the Madison channels is natural and immemorial.

I used to lace up my Sorels and walk on it. Cold sunny afternoons of January or February, bare willows, bare cottonwoods, exquisite solitude, fox tracks in an inch of fresh snow, and down through three feet of ice below my steps and the fox tracks were spectacular bits of Montana that other folk, outlanders, coveted only in summer.

Mostly I wandered these places alone. Then one year a certain biologist of my recent acquaintance came down for a visit in Ennis. I think this was in late April. I know that the river had gorged that year and that the ice was now melting away from the bottomland, leaving behind its moraine of fertile silt. The channels themselves, by now, were open and running clear. The first geese had arrived. This biologist and I spent that day in the water, walking downriver through the channels. We didn't fish. We didn't collect aquatic insects or study the nesting of *Branta canadensis*. The trees hadn't yet come into leaf and it was no day for a picnic. We just walked in the water, stumbling over boulders, bruising our feet, getting wet over the tops of our waders. We saw the Madison channels, fresh from cold storage, before anyone else that year. We covered only about three river miles in the course of the afternoon, but that was enough to exhaust us, and then we stumbled out across the muddy fields and walked home on the road. How extraordinary, I thought, to come across a biologist who would share my own demented appreciation for such an arduous, stupid, soggy trek. So I married her.

The channels of the Madison River are a synecdoche. They are the part that resonates so as to express the significance of the whole. To understand how I mean that, it might help to know Leontiev's Axiom. Konstantin Leontiev was a cranky Russian thinker from the last century. He trained as a physician, worked as a diplomat in the Balkans, wrote novels and essays that aren't read much today, and at the end of his life flirted with becoming a monk. By most of the standards you and I likely share, he was an unsavory character. But even a distempered and retrograde Czarist of monastic leanings is right about something once in a while.

Leontiev wrote: "To stop Russia from rotting, one would have to put it under ice."

In my mind, in my dreams, that great flat sheet of Madison River whiteness spreads out upon the whole state of Montana. I believe, with Leontiev, in salvation by ice.

4. Sources

The biologist whose husband I am sometimes says to me: "All right, so where do we go when Montana's been ruined? Alaska? Norway? Where?" This is a dark joke between us. She grew up in Montana, loves the place the way some women might love an incorrigibly self-destructive man, with pain and fear and pity, and she has no desire to go anywhere else. I grew up in Ohio, discovered home in Montana only fifteen years ago, and I feel the same. But still we play at the dark joke. "Not Norway," I say, "and you know why." We're each half Norwegian and we've actually eaten lutefisk. "How about Antarctica," I say. "Antarctica should be okay for a while yet."

On the desk before me now is a pair of books about Antarctica. Also here are a book on the Arctic, another book titled *The World of Ice*, a book of excerpts from Leontiev, a master's thesis on the subject of goose reproduction and water levels in the Madison channels, an extract from an unpublished fifty-year-old manuscript on the history of Ennis, Montana, a cassette tape of a conversation with Ralph Paugh, and a fistful of photocopies of technical and not-so-technical articles. One of the less technical articles is titled "Ice on the World," from a recent issue of *National Geographic*. In this article is a full-page photograph of strawberry plants covered with a thick layer of ice.

These strawberry plants grew in central Florida. They were sprayed with water, says the caption, because subfreezing temperatures had been forecast. The growers knew that a layer of ice, giving insulation, even giving up some heat as the water froze, would save them.

In the foreground is one large strawberry. The photocopy shows it dark gray, but in my memory it's a death-defying red.

Adrian Nicole LeBlanc

Kristine Larsen

Adrian Nicole LeBlanc prefers to write stories about disenfranchised urban kids. She says she thrives on the humor and resilience of streetwise teenagers and can "chart the strategy of my fieldwork by how it feels."

At first she hangs out in the neighborhoods where her subjects work and live. "I feel like an idiot, and I should. I don't know anything. Given the close-knit communities that interest me, there are plenty of knowing people watching, aware when I trip up. But usually, it's like the first day of school. Someone inevitably seeks you out—a busybody or prankster or macho boy."

LeBlanc follows whatever introductions present themselves. They lead her to interesting people. "At this stage I tend to see my subjects as only victims or heroes. As I smarten up, the complexities surface, and I begin to call certain shots. A subject's reactions to my growing hunches reveal as much as any straightforward question could. I put off asking a roster of questions until the end because I find it embarrassing and not particularly helpful. Most of the relevant biographical details present themselves over time. To me, the omissions in someone's self-presentation are just as interesting."

LeBlanc wants readers to be able to assume the internal logic of her subjects and to feel the routine of a neighborhood. She met Trina on an assignment about crack prostitution. "Perhaps my early blind faith in Trina's strength tugged her strength out. My gullibility may have encouraged more flamboyant lies. Luckily, the sheer number of hours and tedium of our time together wore us both down. When we retreated into ourselves after all that, the crack use and prostitution became secondary, and a more resonant story emerged."

LeBlanc took a literary journalism seminar while at Smith College; studied literature at Oxford, law at Yale, and was a Bunting Fellow at Harvard; was fiction editor of *Seventeen* magazine; and has written for the *New York Times Magazine* and *Esquire*. She is completing her first book, about a young Latino family in the South Bronx.

Trina and Trina

$\mathbf{O}$n weekends, the buses pull up to the eastern tip of Richmond Terrace around 3:00 P.M. The drivers park end to end. From my car, I watch in resigned horror as Trina jumps into the first bus. She scrambles down the steps a few minutes later, vaults out the accordion doors, and climbs into the next bus. In less than twenty minutes, she's done the line. Each driver has paid her two dollars. She makes herself vomit before she climbs South Avenue to the Mariner's Harbor Project Houses to buy more crack. Vomiting, she believes, helps to prevent AIDS. "Cuz you get it through holes in your stomach if you let it stay theah," Trina says.

I first met Trina on New York City's Staten Island in the fall of 1989, while working on a story about teenage prostitutes. She was sixteen, six months into crack, holing up in a housing development with a thirty-two-year-old night security guard named Joe. Just released from nine dull years in state prison, Joe was as grateful for Trina's wired company as he was for the damp cellar that served as both building security base and crack house. The sanctuary stood in the shadows of the Mariner's Harbor project, home to a blooming crack trade. Trina had already earned a local reputation as the white girl pipehead.

An academic friend who studied crack houses pointed me toward her. It was a vague referral. An acquaintance had asked if he knew of an agency that could help a teenage girl who used crack and lived on the streets. I phoned and learned her name. Trina was white, Italian, watchful, unyielding, and working class. These attributes not only distinguished her from many urban crack streetwalkers, but also made her like me. Our shared attributes would blind me, delude me into the sort of sturdy plan of action that seems possible when you and the person you are trying to help share common ground.

After the first time—two weeks of wooing, with Trina's round brown eyes staring down on me from an upstairs window, while Joe swore she wasn't home—it never took me long to find her: she was sleeping at

Joe's, lingering on the Terrace or on South Avenue, climbing in or out of some car, or heading for a crack house. On Staten Island, crack houses are project or tenement apartments where crack users pay the owner at the door, in kind, for a place to cook up and get high. When Trina was on a mission in search of crack, I would leave and return later. Unless she had been beaten up for money she'd hustled, robbed, or borrowed, she wouldn't—couldn't—stay talking in my car for more than fifteen minutes at a time.

Whenever I could catch her before she was chasing a high, we would sit in the doorways of the abandoned stores on Richmond Terrace, talking between johns. "I'll be back in ten minutes, Adrian," she would say cheerfully, but with eyes lowered, then duck into a car. If business wasn't good, the long hours of the days bore down, exposing her sadness. With prodding, she'd jump into my car then, to warm up. We'd drive a little—but usually only to the projects on South Avenue, with no real questions asked. I didn't want to rummage through the details of her life yet, and my hesitation about even innocuous information let her know I respected her caginess. The courtship was slow.

Throughout the months, her sass and antics kept our spirits up. She was my teacher, training me in street smarts. The role flattered her quirky expertise. She showed off and pronounced verdicts on the neighborhood regulars ("That's a junkie shuffle, there!" or, "Look at Patty. I ain't *that* messed up!"); crunch up under the dashboard if we passed one of her drug dealers; parcel out advice on how to pick up men ("Sunglasses on. Radio up. Windows open."); and chastise me for smoking, for grubbing her cigarettes. Each time I bummed one from her, she would inhale her own as deeply as she could, ten times, to punish me, and eye me sternly. Without a trace of irony, she would say, "Get off the drug thing. Youse too smart for that." The inevitable inverse question met her most durable answer: "Youse a grownup, Adrian. A reporter. I know you like axing all kinds of questions. But remembah I'm a kid."

Too much closeness and too much distance both made her jittery. Her jitters ruled her. I learned their idiosyncratic triggers (little boys that reminded her of Dominick, her younger and favorite brother; a radio station; certain bakery cookies; the dusky late afternoon), and I paced my comments and suggestions to spur them or avoid them. Sometimes we went to a nearby Italian bakery or made it as far as the McDonald's Drive-Thru on Forest Avenue, not even a mile away. She would eat infrequently, and then she'd binge—two Quarter Pounders, a cheeseburger, a strawberry shake, two large fries, an apple pie, cookies, and a large Coke. She hoarded sugar and ketchup packets, stuffing her pockets full, and poured handfuls of half-and-half cups down her throat, two at a time.

Bolstered by our companionable road trips, I took a shortcut in trying to make sense out of her crazy life and mistook her traits for mine.
Her scrappiness, I thought, was mainly working class, her evasiveness
due to the intense family privacy of the Italian sort I'd known. The
most important difference between us was that I'd been tracked for
luck: I stayed dutiful and took the fight to my writing, while Trina,
more feisty, less well-loved, and less well-equipped, took it to the street.

Unsurprisingly, the shortcut left me stranded. I was trying to rescue
an abandoned child and she was an entrenched adult. She fought off my
attempts until I saw what made her grow: she'd already rescued herself—from her home—and the refuge was the street. I learned this
when we became friends, months later. Until then, I figured in her life
only to the extent I helped her continue to survive.

A mid-November Sunday, 1989. Trina's skinny, scabby arms grope out
from under a stained blanket that reeks of rotten meat. It's 11:00 A.M.
"Cigarette!" she grumbles. Joe lights a Newport for her, takes a gulp of
vodka and swishes it around in his mouth before swallowing. He
watches TV and applies mayonnaise to his thick dark hair as styling gel.
Trina pokes her head out and fights her way up mad. She drags the
blanket around her, heads for the toilet, a bucket in the otherwise
empty sheetrock room. Trina, hunched up teenage queen, reigns over
McDonald's trash, broken cookies, the slab of spoiled meat for Joe's pit
bull, Dood. "She pukes every day," Joe says, nonchalant, picking his
teeth. He preens in front of the cracked slice of Budweiser bar mirror
propped atop the TV. "I am so gorgeous, right?" he jokes.

"You're ugly," Trina says, slouching back onto the couch. "Don't
mind me if I fall asleep." She wraps her gawky arms around her knees
and rocks back and forth.

"Are you all right?" Joe asks.

"Yeah."

"You cold?"

"No, I'm tired. And hungry!" He changes channels and walks off.
Trina inspects an old McDonald's bag, tosses it, and reaches for the
mayonnaise, alternating fingerfuls for herself and Dood. She picks at
the scabs on her legs, circling the faded purple marks with a pen.
"Crackpocks!" she laughs until her laughter turns into a hack. "I have
bronchitis!" she gasps. She settles in with another Newport, bleary-
eyed, and watches cartoons.

Joe returns, a Santa Claus without a coat, carting in the cold and
Devil Dogs, ice cream sprinkles, orange soda, a pack of Newports,
Reese's Peanut Butter Cups, chocolate milk, hot chocolate, and more

meat for Dood. "I want Dunkin' Donuts," Trina says, grabbing the bag. Joe places half of the fresh meat on the floor for Dood and puts the other half on the TV. Trina eats the junk food, offering Joe nothing.

"I know a place where we can go and get a shower," he says.

"I don't need no shower," Trina snaps. The suggestion interferes and the interference sets her moving to her knees, on a pile of dirty clothes on the cement floor. She tugs on layer after layer of what she wants of what she finds: pink longjohns, a sweatshirt, three T-shirts, mismatched socks, a scarf, a pair of men's boots, oversized. She tosses what she doesn't want into a musty puddle, then she's off through the sliding glass door, toothpick legs tromping through the muddy snow.

The short afternoon rolls into night. From the upstairs window, Joe and I watch Trina again. She straddles the fading yellow line, arms waving like a windmill, so she won't miss a customer driving either way. The cars—a Subaru, a Volvo with handicap plates—pull over by the church or into the shadows of the side street, and Trina disappears.

"I like to think I'm providing shelter from the storm," Joe says. The very chance of a routine out here is privilege. Still, Trina doesn't always return to him. She sleeps in the pool room of a nearby bar some nights. Others, she stays with Ken and Lisa, a couple from the projects, who agree to take her in if she agrees to watch them have sex. Occasionally they give her food. "Those guys are in their sixties," says Joe, incredulous. "I don't get how she can stay there."

Trina wouldn't talk during the depressions that inevitably followed her crack bouts. At first, I was grateful for the silence. The roughness of her life made my curiosity feel too much like voyeurism and in spite of my professional mission, I felt a little guilty about seeing her in a light she couldn't remember let alone understand. I mostly watched. Early one morning, though, I asked Trina straight out how she'd ended up on the Terrace. I'd spent hours looking for her the night before. I was sick with coffee, cramped from my car, weary from my vigilance to night-time threats. She'd been on a weeklong binge, had woken up at dawn and shuffled out of the scrub woods slowly, scratching, toward my car. I took in the dreary gray of her broken-down street, the stillness, and imagined the working people in the tenements rallying themselves to get beyond it one more round. I realized it wasn't so different from the streets I grew up on and that I knew the rules already. The climbing sunshine cleansed the tragedy from Trina's hooking. Standing near my car door, she looked clownish to me. Her cageyness wasn't pride, but rejection of what I had to offer, and in that stretched out moment, I impudently blamed her for her damage and she climbed into the car.

I met her sarcastic comments about commuters with my silence. I
went off and bought my own cigarettes instead of mooching; she didn't
flee. She knew at once the deal had changed and warmed to the new
terms. Trina offered me her story in exchange for something she knew
I could deliver: a notebook and a pen. "I can't talk about it," she said,
"but I can write it down." The request was her interpersonal specialty, a
low-stakes call. That afternoon I bought her a chrome green and pink
flowered journal and I took my notebook back.

> Hi my name is TRINA
> Life as A kid:
>
> I grew up as a frightened child always scared of older men & women
> the only one I went to & I wasn't scared or frightened of was my
> mother, Joanne, but as I grew older, like by the age of 3 & 4, I got
> more attached to my father, (Sal) which disappointed me by the age
> of 5 going on 6, because I was abuse by him, on day, 3 days before
> my Birthday, which is on July 26, 1972. So my father Sal, brought
> me into my Bathroom up Stairs when no Body was home & tide a
> Blanket around my eyes & said here's a lolly pop it a good one to then
> he forsed it into my mouth & I untied the towel off my head by stug-
> gling & I bit what ever was in my mouth. And Sal screamed at me &
> hit me, & after he sent me to my room ... [he] said he was sorry for
> screaming & hiting on me, [and that] he was only putting his finger in
> my mouth. (but I really new he wasn't) ... so when I was about 13
> years old I started to cut school never care about anything & also
> stared to run away too.

When she was eighteen months old, Trina had been placed with Sal
and Joanne. They were a young working family and wanted the few
dollars she brought in (the names of Trina's foster parents and siblings
are pseudonyms). "It was a short-term thing that turned out to be long-
term," says Sal. "We became attached." At six, they adopted her. At
eleven, she was hospitalized for alcohol abuse. Junior high brought out
violence; Trina would physically attack her foster mother, who was forever sick. They always argued. She'd get grounded and run to her best
friend, Michelle, who'd hide Trina in the cellar. "There were times I'd be
taking a shower and she would take my car," Joanne, Trina's mother,
once told me. "I had no control over her. She did what she wanted to
do." One joyride ended in an accident, and Trina's junior high school
guidance counselor stepped in, beginning Trina's long career of failed
attempts to accept care.

Here, accounts by Trina and her parents diverge. Trina told her social worker that she'd been sexually abused by Sal and Special Services

for Children placed her in a group home. For six weeks, Trina refused to discuss the charges, so they were dropped (Trina says Joanne told her that Dominick would be taken away if the charges stuck). Sal told me he'd never abused Trina. Said Joanne, "Everything Trina says is a lie." A family court judge ordered Trina to a psychiatric center for evaluation. She checked in for two weeks of treatment in 1988.

The hospital termed her "antisocial behaviors as secondary to underlying emotional problems," which doctors felt was conflict with her biological mother. Trina's mother was an Italian-American high school graduate who'd worked in bars and been diagnosed as a "depressed psychotic type." Trina's maternal grandmother was mentioned in the records as having severe psychological problems. "If I look at Trina from the outside, I think, *This can't be*," says Sal. "We went through the counselors, psychiatrists, family meetings. We didn't want to lose her and we lost her. She was thirteen or fourteen at the time." In fact, she was 15 when she ran away for good.

Sal talks about his daughter in bursts of rhetorical questions he asks himself. "Is she capable of being manipulative?" he asks. "Yes," he answers. "Is she capable of being vicious? Yes. Is it her? I really don't believe it's her. There's something wrong. What went wrong? All I know is that when she had problems we did everything humanly possible to help her. Did we fail her? If we failed, we failed. If she failed, she failed. But the bottom line is that she still needs help."

"I'm just a normal housewife here, trying to raise a family," Joanne told me. "I don't know what went wrong." And a social worker of Trina's said, "Whatever happened to that child before seventeen months, she was so traumatized, so devastated, it was so horrific, losses so acute, such narcissistic losses, she can't get beyond that point and relate. There is an empty spot in this child that you can't fill. You can't move past that spot."

My friend Artie met Trina earlier that fall, at seven o'clock one cold morning. He'd climbed out of his pickup and seen her crouched in his office doorway, wearing a slip, knobby knees up to her ears. He saw that she was just a kid and asked, "You wanna bagel?" She'd nodded. He'd come out of Aunt Dee's store carrying food for her, and saw her hop in an idling car.

Fall passed into winter—he'd wave, she'd wave, she'd hit him up for money, he'd buy her food and cigarettes. She'd come up to his office and he'd send her out for coffee and let her keep the change. She'd use the office bathroom to wash up. Artie noticed that she'd started gabbing with his office mates. He hoped, as he began a search to locate professional care for her, that such civil contact might hold her over until he'd found proper help.

Two days before Thanksgiving, Artie drives through the Mariner's Harbor Houses on his way home. A storm is coming. Only the drug dealers and buyers are out. He will ask Trina to dinner one last time. All week, he's invited her home for Thanksgiving and she's said no. He bets the snowstorm and the inevitability of holiday blues will change her mind. "Heat!" she commands as she clambers into his pickup. "It's cold!" Does she want to come over? "I gotta change my clothes for dinner," she says, then pauses. "Take me?"

Trina bolts into Joe's and runs out again wearing five new layers and carrying a shoe box full of makeup and probably her pipe and crack. They drive and she says, "Turn back. I gotta go! I can't leave Joe alone for Thanksgiving." She asks Artie to wait. She is frantic. Watching her makes Artie think of pinball. She runs back in, then returns, runs back three more times, changing outfits each time, and finally jumps back into the truck. At the Verrazano Bridge, she breaks into sobs. The thirty-minute trip stretches into four and a half hours. Then, Trina sits shivering in the truck in front of Artie's house for another hour, refusing to go inside. I come out. She agrees, if his family will promise not to stare. They promise. Once safely in, she darts for the cellar. It takes two more hours for her to make her way upstairs.

"This is how you do it," Trina chirps, chopping vegetables for the salad. "My family used to have Thanksgiving just like this, everybody eatin'. This is how you do it." She clomps over to the long buffet table and gently places down the bowl.

Dinner's ready. Trina circles the twenty-three-foot banquet of food, plate positioned, heaping on baked zucchini and ham and sausage and peppers and macaroni, scalloped potatoes and salad and turkey and stuffing and gravy and cranberry sauce and beans. At this Thanksgiving table in Bensonhurst, Trina does look a little freakish. She is eighty pounds and five feet nine in a pair of baggy pink pajamas, with black pumps. She's sprayed her hair straight out and up a good foot, become a Brooklyn lioness, but the warm good manners of the guests keep Trina comfortably in the family fold. She eats four servings, dumps herself by an electric heater, rubs her bloated belly, and burps. A lanky, wide-eyed twelve-year-old stands near her, forgets the family oath, and stares.

"You cold?" Trina asks. The girl nods. "Come ovah heah where it's warm then." They sit in silence. "Are you good in school?" Trina asks ten minutes later; the girl nods again. "I was too. I was smart even though I nevah went to school. I only finished up until eight grade." Through their silence they decide to eat chocolate pie. Then they circulate, screening the relevant parts of the party through their bright eyes, taking in the busy living room, the messy kitchen, stopping halfway upstairs. They linger on the steps, near each other, for a good ten minutes. Above them, behind a bedroom door, in blasting music, teenage boys sit. Trina leads the way back down clomping, the younger girl hopping, two nervous, chatting, slim-hipped girls.

By eight o'clock, the house quiets down—conversation softens, the dishes have been washed. Coffee cups and forks still clank against cake plates. Trina and the girl sleep in a downstairs bedroom on the pile of coats. The girl wanders out, blinking and rubbing her eyes with small fists. She whispers into her mother's neck, squinting from the light: "Mommy, Trina is having a bad dream." Her mother brushes the child's dark hair from her forehead. "Trina kept yelling in her sleep. *'Cover yourself up. Just go to sleep and cover up. It's so cold.'* "

The next morning Trina blinks awake and finds herself on the sectional beige leather couch. She's in a fury. "Artie left without me?" she mutters, long legs kicking off the crochet cover as if it's attacking her. "There's no more chocolate cake!" she barks from the kitchen as she slams the refrigerator door. She's quick and restless, yelling, "Gimme-my-cigarettes!," nasty, thirty-six hours from her last crack high. She's diving toward a panicky tantrum, throwing her clothes and makeup into a plastic garbage bag she's found, lurching through the house, lunging for her lighter, hating the world. I represent the world today, so she snarls at me. Artie interrupts the storm, returning, snow dusted, from the store.

"I want to go home!" Trina screams. "Take me home!"

"Let's go then," Artie says in monotone. He doesn't take morning rudeness well. "Move it." Trina, coatless, runs behind him, dragging her bag, slipping and cursing through the snow. "I gotta go and get Joe," she says, breathless. Artie starts the pickup. "Then we'll come back." Artie drives silently. I sit between them. "I'd stay, if I knew where I could get some," she says in a small voice.

"Why don't you look in the Yellow Pages," Artie says, "under *crack*."

"You don't have to call it that. It's base. Black people call it crack." She pulls out her lighter, pretends to set fire to the seat. She mutters swears to the window, blows on the glass, and looking through the world of fog, crosses them out. "Take me to Mariner's Harbor."

"I'm going to drop you off at the most low-life scumbag scuzziest place you can think of so you won't have nowhere to go down from there," Artie says, as they turn off the Staten Island Expressway to the South Avenue exit. "Name it."

"The projects," Trina says. He leaves her on South Avenue. She slams the door and grabs a broken brick from the ground, hurling it at the truck. A girl approaches her on the sidewalk and Trina shoves her.

"Get outta my way!" we hear her screech. She sobs deep-hearted, coughing cries. And we drive off.

Often Trina hooks in front of an empty lot that her father owns. She climbs in and out of cars and buses on Richmond Terrace only a mile from the offices of his shipping firm. To publicize her desperation is the deepest assault on family she can muster. What she'll say is that she's too scared to move farther from the neighborhood she knows. What she can't admit is that she hopes, deep down, that Sal will stop on his way to the office and out of love or at least embarrassment, scoop her up in his arms and save her. For all her hope and hate, she identifies herself by family, adamant that her degradation is also theirs. Inversely, she assumes the objects of their pride and asserts herself as the daughter of a self-made man who has a boat and drives a classy car. She beams at the whir of Sal's Mercedes, even though when he sees her standing, flagging, crouching, heaving, waving, he drives on by, blank-faced. She is so expectant, Trina, dirt smudged on her face.

December 1989 and Trina is with me. I think I really know her because I think I've seen her broken, so I am unknowingly and exorbitantly out of bounds. She has been staying with Artie's family, claiming she is ready to keep clean. There's no open bed for her to start treatment, but Artie's family needs a break. I exceed my role as reporter, convinced I am going the limit as a reporter, and I take her, fully, in.

She refuses to leave my apartment alone. "The city scares me," she says. I maneuver her eighteen blocks to Covenant House, a shelter for teenage runaways, and convince a doctor to give her a physical and a TB test. We chainsmoke after dinner, waiting for Raphael Flores, a counselor who has agreed to pay the rehab version of a house call. He arrives, a tired Spanish man, and Trina glowers at him.

"How you doin?" he asks her, offering a cigarette.

Trina growls, "Spic."

Flores cuts straight to her options: Go to rehab or return to the street. She has twenty-four hours to decide. She draws a circle around her TB shot in pen and colors in the tiny hole from which her blood was drawn. She bears down hard on her skin. "Can I go now?" she spits. She walks away in an angry huff. Flores says young beautiful girls get more mileage from the street; the leverage dupes them into thinking they can beat it. They don't yet know the street is who they become. Trina has the further disadvantage of her status as a coveted hooker on the Terrace, because she's so skinny that she looks androgynous and also, she is white.

In the middle of the night I smell cigarette smoke. "Sshh," Trina says. "I'm asleeeeep." I turn on a light. She's written more in her journal:

> Once upon a time, I was at a place in the city with . . . I don't want to stay here. When a guy has a business it takes over one way or another. It took over my father. That's why I hate Big Important businesses. They take over everything like that.
>
>   Every night I've been here I wet the bed when I sleep. I don't want to tell anyone because I don't want to be lectured.

"I don't want to go back to Richmond Terrace," she says into the night's silence. "I don't wanna go back there." Then she starts to bawl, her mouth a gooey sore. She is frail here, so she won't stay. An hour later, I leave her propped up on the bed, drawing her younger brother's name and Magic Marker hearts and flowers on her arms and legs. She draws two tits on her T-shirt over her own.

The next day she asks for the counselor's phone number. She jots it under "Dickhead," street sass returning. "Don't worry about me, I'm a survivah," she yells into the lobby intercom as she leaves.

A new consciousness fills the space left by her departure and through it, I interpret the good parts of my days—coffee with a friend, napping with my boyfriend—in terms of Trina's future, the kind of future that both she and I aren't sure she'll ever have: Will Trina ever enjoy coffee with a friend? I wonder. The comfort of a nap with a good man? She lingers everywhere in the apartment. She's written REMEMBER ME on the dishwashing gloves, and TRINA on the roll of paper towels and on the corner of a sheet, TRINA C. and DON'T FORGET ME on boxes of cereal and crackers and croutons, and TRINA AND TRINA in hearts on the binding of books and inside pages of magazines.

A woman from Covenant House clinic calls a few days later. They need to track down Trina. She cannot release any information, but it's urgent and involves Trina's health. I tell them where to go on Richmond Terrace. They look but never find her. I don't go looking myself.

Trina resurfaces in five months and is unconcerned about the call. "Oh yeah?" she says over the phone, politely. "If it was important, they woulda tracked me down." She declines help again. She won't be diverted.

An anonymous supporter circulates a letter in Trina's childhood neighborhood around this time, referring to her allegations of sexual abuse, her prostitution and addiction:

> Someone must get them to make good and help there daughter possibly get back from the selfdestruct course she is on . . . HER LIFE CAN STILL BE SAVED!

Memorial Day 1990, Trina's on the Terrace, flying. "I need something to get me awake, I need to stay awake, all right!" she hollers in the direction of my car. She wears a cut-off Benetton T-shirt that exposes her midriff, black tights, yellow socks, and Reeboks. She pants, her concave stomach heaving up and down. She twists her head dramatically, spins her wrists in circles—"I'm being followed by a cop! I'm messed up because I watched these kids all night, I babysat. I ain't working on the Terrace no more." A man walks by. "You can tell he does crack," she says, pointing impudently, "by the way he holds his jaw." She gets into the car. "Patty died of AIDS," she announces. "I'm gonna be seventeen soon."

She turns my radio up until it's blasting. She's skittish, yanking her socks up, shoving them down, thrashing in the passenger seat. She wraps her arms around her chest as if she's in a straitjacket, flicks imaginary crumbs off her tights. She says she doesn't want to eat. "The food is too hot!" she screams, spooked. She asks for coffee. I pass it to her. She gropes for the cold, old danish on the dashboard.

"I would never get high in front of the kids I babysit for," she says, lighting her crack pipe. "I ain't no maniac." She wants out. The encounter lasts ten minutes. I slow down. She leaps out while the car is still moving and hits the pavement running, arms flailing in that awkward warped pinwheel motion. She's left her cherished crack pipe on the seat. She's slipping up, I think. The addiction closes in.

A late July afternoon, Mariner's Harbor Houses, a crowd hanging out. I find Trina walking on the Terrace. She wants to go for a ride. She is willing because she is straight and she's straight because it is just a few days before her birthday and that marker always gives her hope an unreasoned, pure adolescent push. "I don't wanna be no crackhead when I turn seventeen," she says.

We drive to the Smart Shop, an immaculate convenience store. Trina barrels to the freezer. She hums and slaps her legs in time as she flips frozen pops and ices about, making a quick mess. She finds a Bomb Pop, drops the sticky wrapper on the floor. She takes a big bite then tosses the pop on the counter. "A worm," she says, disgusted. She grabs a grape drink from the fridge. She likes cold things because they soothe the sores in her mouth. She knows she's being rude and explains away her bad manners. She calls her bad mood a crack ache.

July 26, her birthday and a sunny day. Trina is depressed. I take her clothes shopping. She's searching for something she calls "classy." "I don't want to look like no slut," she says, whizzing through rack after rack. Artie's office mates have a little party planned for Trina at 4:00 P.M.

It's not the same, she moans, as birthdays at home. She has just one birthday wish—"I wish I was dead." We park in front of Artie's office on the Terrace. A man in a Camry spots her and stops. By the time I lock the doors of my car, she has moved toward him. They drive off. I'm surprised I still feel disappointed. Artie hands pieces of pizza and cake out to the neighborhood kids.

Dusk falls. Trina stumbles back, wavering, shoving off air, in the middle of the potholed road. Her face is smeared, her new blouse hangs from her bony shoulders, stained. She tosses a handful of pebbles at my car. "I hate you all!" she yells at the sky. "Youse ate my birthday cake! I hate you all!"

Trina stands in court for her arraignment at the end of August, looking burnt-out and poor, not much different from any of the other skinny women in criminal court on the same small-time drug charges. Except that Trina is young, with a team of well-wishers on her side. It is her sixth arrest. She says her last trip to Rikers Island prison convinced her she's ready to accept help and to stay straight for good.

A place called Staten Island TASC dispatches a caseworker to collect her from the bull pen at criminal court. John Kain is a gentle, older man, a pro. Trina clutches baby-blue plastic rosary beads and laughs, through her sniffles, at John's corny jokes. A man whistles at Trina as they enter the TASC office. "Hormones," she shrugs. She sits for the next four hours while caseworkers try to convince her father to help and call facility after facility in search of a bed.

"What you gonna do when you get the urge?" the caseworker calls out. "I'm gonna think twice," Trina chirps dutifully. The caseworkers leave several messages for her father. They know they will lose Trina if they put her in a shelter for the night. Trina calls Artie to say hello: he says she can stay with him. TASC promises an open bed tomorrow.

The delays continue for a month—insurance obstacles, a mandatory pregnancy test. They make a temporary arrangement with an outpatient facility near McDonald's. Artie drops her off on his way to work in the morning and picks her up again at night. Her willingness and pride in having a schedule—"a life," Trina calls it—sustains Artie's hope that she'll straighten out. "The kid's doin' everything she's gotta do," he says.

When she's not sleeping on Artie's couch, Trina eyeballs his sons' teenage friends from a cautious distance, recites the twelve-step credo, chainsmokes, watches TV, and folds piles of family clothes—her designated chore. Weeks pass. She'd like to hang out with the teenagers, but, she says, "I fahget how tah be with kids my own age." Later, she admits,

"They treat me like I'm weird." TASC finds Trina a bed upstate at a place called Daytop. I drive her there.

"Is this fresh air?" she asks when we merge into the New York Thruway, "cuz if it is, I'm chokin'." She shouts out the lyrics to her favorite songs, then looks wistful as we near the place, then turns scared. "I'm going to a place where I don't know nobody," she says. "When I meet new people, at first I don't like them and I start fights." TASC's evaluation is more optimistic: Trina is "highly motivated toward treatment" and appears to be "nonsuicidal and nonviolent."

The adolescent unit receptionist directs us to the cafeteria. Two dull-eyed attendants process us. The girls, one tall, one short, shuffle in and escort us to the dorm, a rustic A-frame tucked in the woods, immaculate and sparse.

"You haveta strip," the tall girl says to Trina, bored. The short one instructs Trina to wash her hair with Joannene shampoo and both watch her shower (so she doesn't pull anything cute). They weed out traces of drug culture and sex from her wardrobe—a T-shirt with heavy metal slogans, a short Lycra skirt, leopard underpants, her leggings. Trina gives me the leftover clothes. The tall girl tells Trina to squat, legs spread on the bathroom floor. Trina coughs out all remaining suspicion while they trace every seam for hidden drugs. The sad-eyed girls recite the Daytop rules.

Sal will let his insurance pay the bill. But he and Joanne refuse to participate. "When your child destroys the family, it's hard to get into family counseling," he later tells me. "You just can't get *into* therapy." Trina asks me to act as a substitute family for one session, but we know we are friends.

I arrive for the session at the end of October. Trina bolts out the door and jumps on me. She beams and shakes with excitement—her face and eyes and clothes look fresh. She takes the long way to the director's office, proudly touring me through the halls and pointing out the details of her new life—the Coke machine, the Clorox she uses to clean the bathroom after use ("I have hepatitis!" she announces, authoritatively), the cafeteria, the classroom, the nurse, her new young friends.

The clinical director, in a starched striped shirt, is a tiny man, who speaks slowly, with a lisp. The affect of his cadence is ambiguous—concern or condescension. Trina smells bad news instantly. "I don't want to go nowhere else," she says quietly, looking at the ground. The director smiles. "Trina, this is not rejection," he says. "How come it feels like rejection, then?" she asks, in tears. We drive three hours home.

For the next week, rejection pours in. We try every adolescent facility and find no open bed. The obstacles amplify her obvious longing, at this point, to continue treatment, until she can't absorb plans of any kind anymore. I don't pretend to have an answer now and she doesn't dare ask for one. One morning, she heads for Staten Island, hoping to return to her old outpatient center until we figure out what to do. She calls crying from a pay phone—they won't let her in—and I don't hear from her for seven months. I stay put.

The sounds of the Good Samaritan Hospital in suburban Long Island are of soft purring. I find Trina hunkered over in the corner of Room 108, praying with a chubby volunteer with long brown hair and zits. The Samaritan gathers her prayer cards. Trina won't let her go and whizzes through the Our Father as an offering to her new pal. The medication melts her sentences into a slur. The woman says, "Sometimes it's hard to have faith, but we have to have faith in Him."

Trina doesn't have faith. "What time you gonna come tomorrow?" she asks. "I'll keep praying till then." A sign on the door warns of Trina's contagious hepatitis. The Good Samaritan is a pit stop in yet another adolescent program called Hope House. When she gets her hepatitis under control, the treatment will begin.

On the crazy streets, Trina's mischievous beauty shines. Today the awkwardness of her lost adolescence surfaces: I see the ugliness of her pain in the too-tight chest of her black jumpsuit, in the way the material bunches around her thighs, the way her hands shake, in her face, bloated, without expression. She is still a girl but she seems beyond repair, her bloodstream coursing with the tranquilizer Atavan.

To reach treatment at Hope House is Trina's second wish: the first is to go shopping for her eighteenth birthday. "I'd go to the teen section of the store, and ask a teen girl what she would wear, and that's what I want," Trina says. Sal's insurance will cover her treatment. To Trina, this is auspicious. In the rush of optimism, she writes her mother:

> I remember us together—talking, arguing, and fighting. You told me I was your chosen child, that is still the same. I always let you down by running. Now you're going to see what a different person I am. I think I changed. I remember when I was younger. Tell my sister and brothers that someday when I come home, we can get cake and cookies from the bakery on Holland Avenue that we all love. From this day on I'm going to be waiting for a response. Please write me back no matter how many make up families I make up you are my family and this is the only way we can talk unless you give me your phone number, anything is better than nothing.

I check in every few days.

Early May: I ask her how she feels about her family. She says, blandly, "Disowned."

Mid-May: "What are you going to do tonight?" I ask.

"I'm going to go in a straitjacket. I got nothing else to do."

She leaves a message on my machine: "I feel drugged up and I'm running out of journal. That's all. Good-bye."

Late May: A boy answers the patients' pay phone. I ask for Trina. He says, "The hall. Flight deck. Depression drugs. They bugged her out too much. The lotion will do it." I cajole him to get her, to please bring her to the phone. The boy laughs sweetly. He giggles and says, "TLC. What's gonna happen if *everyone* slips? I got to go now. I got smoke in my face."

Irony laces Trina's first adult act. On the warm July day of her eighteenth birthday, she signs herself out of Hope House. "They ain't doin' nothin'," she'd said the day before, by phone. "I'm ready to start my life now. I'll go to Covenant House, drop my stuff off, go walk around the city, and get a job." She departs with a halfway house referral that doesn't pan out. We run through the list of rejections again. Trina's hepatitis makes placement hard and now that she's not a minor, social service options are thinner. She stands by a pay phone somewhere, impudent and insecure, working collect calls, readiness for treatment evaporating.

I don't believe she'll make it and this doesn't hurt me, now. I've long since prepared for the news that she's died, so that any other outcome seems manageable, almost upbeat. She calls again. She's headed for Mariner's Harbor and promises that she will stay straight this time. "Just be careful," I say. "At least I know people in the Harbor," Trina says.

I don't hear from Trina again until February. She calls from the Terrace and jumps into a confused story about a down jacket that's been knifed. "It's someone else's coat," she says, her voice cracking. "I'm tired of paying." She says that she has four sweatshirts on underneath, that she ate egg and ham on a roll. She cries and hangs up. She calls back. "Adrian, do me a favor? Give me $50. I've gotta put food in the refrigerator." I say no. "Forty dollars? It's winter and I'm pregnant." She hangs up again.

The next call comes from Rikers Island prison. The sadness and the echoes of the bull pen wash in with her voice, which has thickened and turned tough. Heading into spring, every other word is a curse. The phone wrestling and background screeches of Rikers become familiar, part of her voice. She has been fighting with a girl over a pair of shorts and sounds shameless, proud. "Now everybody will respect me in here," she says. "You know. Knowing that I'm not a punk white bitch." But she is. The charge this time is prostitution. The police pick her up again for it in August and in September.

Trina struts out of the main door on Rikers Island in late September, a bright fall day, her neck thin as a pipe cleaner, those arms swinging, swearing loudly and smiling, two new homegirls by her side. She has just been released. "I'm gonna fly!" she shouts. "I'm gonna go see Pockets! Gotta get my welfare check and bail Mabel out for $1,000." Trina's not on welfare. She is pumped up. She adopts the commanding voice of broadcast news: "Discharge! Trina C.!" The homegirl to her right looks on, pained; the one on the left, whose name is Lucky, looks awed. "Then I wanna go to the Terrace. I gotta say hello to a few people and get my stuff." I chauffeur.

We cram into the bus from the complex to the parking lot, $1.25, for a minute's run. Trina gobbles three hot dogs with lots of ketchup and mustard and downs two Cokes from the hot dog stand in the Rikers lot. "Jail is not for me, am I right or am I wrong?" she asks. She belches and flops into the car. "You didn't park straight," she says, and smiles.

She turns quiet and reflective until traffic jams up. Then the radio sucks, the car's too hot, I suck, the city sucks, jail sucks, her sister is an asshole. Her skittishness increases near the Harbor. Trina jumps out the door. "Hey, Sheila!" she yells, running.

"Hey, Trina! Where you been?"

"Hey, Trina, whatsup?"

"Trina girl, ehhyo, Trina!"

She waves and smiles shyly into the breeze and the chorus, sauntering—her grin breaking—into a little crowd. My anger at her weakness evaporates as I see how she is loved, for a moment, here. She is home. She punches Sheila playfully. They walk through the entrance to the building where Trina usually cops her crack. That night, hooking, she looks defeated, sinking in someone else's dirty clothes. "Oh, just go *on*," she says, swatting air, waving me away. But even her anger at me is uninspired. "I been here ten minutes and I may as well stay out here."

Nineteen-ninety-two, 5:30 on an April morning, she checks in. Her voice is quiet—How are you doing? What's up?—and she sounds as if she has faded. She doesn't have anything special to say. "I just wanna say hi. I gotta go."

"I quit on my own," she announces in mid-April. "I don't know. I was being good on the street, Adrian. I can't say I was being good good good, but I was being good to a point. Now I'm in front of McDonald's, it's really weird. Three days I ate sleep ate sleep I didn't have the urge or nothing. I think I did really need to do it on my own, cuz all that time in jail I was fooling myself. Now when I smoke, I don't go on a mission for seven or eight days. Now I just fall asleep." She is living with an older guy named Danny and she doesn't even have sex with him. "Can you come see me?" she asks. "Cuz I gained weight."

As soon as I pull into McDonald's, Trina is at the car door, her face thin, the veins in her forehead visible through her pale skin. It seems a surface touch could make her features break. We talk about nothing, then about rehab, then squat in the parking lot, on the tar. Her eyes well up. "I just sit around and do nothing all day long. This can't be good for me," she says. Her narration starts up slowly, in a whisper. "I called my mother two months ago? And I asked her how old my younger brother was and she said, 'He's not your brother. I'm not your mother. Why do you bother us? Why do you do this? Do you want to destroy my life?' " Trina's never been as candid. I can finally see that I have become in her conscience what she's long been for me: a marker, a yardstick of my distance from the rocks below. "I wouldn't be sitting in this parking lot talking to you about what to do with the rest of my life if it wasn't for what my father did to me," she says. A police cruiser pulls in the Drive-Thru. She places her slender hands on her knees and boosts herself up, like an old woman. "Time to go," she says.

She lives in a tiny bungalow. We sit for a moment in the car. All the sociology and psychology and misplaced affection wilts into her unfair choice. She has to save herself again. Only I know how unreasonably strong she must be to manage it, to push her way through the blurry rage of having been a cheated kid. "What do you want to do?" I ask.

"I don't think that way, Adrian," she says, warmly chiding, as if I should know better than to pose a question in the safety of our quiet car. She slips out into the darkness, past the shadow of a small porch. It's not optimism I feel but relief, because she's said out loud that she knows she's alone and that there's further for her to go.

I stop by a week later to pick her up. We've planned to see a movie. I find this note stuck in the broken screen door:

Danny,
Listen. This is frankie Johns friend. I'm sorry about the other day but its because of Trina, I got locked up, she took $40.00 from me I'm a nice person. All I wanted to do was show her a good time take her to

dinner hang out and get high I came to your house today to say I'm
sorry, the cops took my car now I can't even work and take care of my
kids. Tell Trina I want to talk with her, she is a very nice girl, If you
see her tell her I said be safe and I'll see her soon. Tell her I'm not
mad, I just want to talk.

Frankie

Trina. If you get here before Danny, Trina I'm not mad, I just want
to talk to you. Your a very sweet girl. I don't want anything bad to
happen to you.

Frankie

Just hours earlier, Trina'd been arrested again for possession for the
umpteenth time. She stays in jail. Talking is the only way we can stay
friends.

May 4: "Let's talk about your life," I say. "My life? I don't have no
life," she says.

May 13: "I met this girl. Her name is Zeno, but they call her
Mickey. She's a she but she's a he. She's an aggressor. It's a girl, but she
dresses like a guy. I'm working my ass off! I got a job in the bakery."

May 19: "I got adopted by Reverend Pat Green. Even if there's no
bed. Even if I have to sleep on the floor or the couch, they can't say no,"
she says. She sounds happy, excited, girlish. She has got a girl, too. "I got
another girl I got to meet tonight," she says. She's phoned her mother
again. "She said she didn't want to see me in jail." Her friend Lucky is
back in, for sucking tokens out of a turnstile.

Somewhere hidden on Richmond Terrace stands the Rose of Sharon
Ministries, a shelter for battered women, run by the Reverend Patricia
Green. "We get the ladies in here," says Reverend Green. "Two Bible
studies a day . . . It helps them to feel super about themselves."

They write a letter for Trina's swollen legal file, saying the ministry
helps girls like Trina "re-enter the community as a self-constaining (sic)
person." Trina's got nothing else, and the court will let her try it out.

I call to arrange a visit. "Jesus loves you," Ruth Ann Bott, the
founder, says. "Call back in the morning. By then I should get the word
on you from the Lord."

The next day Trina calls me. "I couldn't stay there," she says,
breathlessly. "Them people are weird!" The next day, I call the Reverend Green, who says that Trina has stolen her ID cards and money
and bolted. "I saw her passed out on the sidewalk," says the Reverend.

"There's not a time I go out that I don't see her staggering around on some kind of drug and I say, *'Oh God, don't let her be hit by a car.'* "

"I'm crying," says Ruth Ann Bott. "The girl just don't listen to us. Now there's a warrant out for her arrest. This really hurts me. I went to court for this girl. And I can't do anything now. My heart goes out to her. I prefer to work the love angle in this home. This young lady is going through a rebellious stage." In Ruth Ann's outraged self-absorption, I hear a novice, whose need has little to do with Trina's raging self, and I think of my own bull-headed intervention.

June, on Brabant Avenue, by the Mariner's Harbor Houses. Today Trina is an entertainer. Her fair skin is street-tanned and she's running sloppy, whirring, free. "My family is here!" she squeals, hopping off the sidewalk. She sticks her head in the driver's window of my car and gives Artie a kiss. "I ain't doin' crack no more," she reports. "Look at me! I ain't doin' crack no more, see? I'm drinking, I'm so drunk!" She runs around to the passenger side, swings herself onto my neck, and smacks her brow on the roof. She laughs then twirls on the hood, like a top. She spills onto the sidewalk. A fat black girl grabs her arm and jerks her so abruptly that Trina freezes. "I got one thing to say to you," the girl seethes. "You suck my boyfriend's dick again and you're dead." "Owww! Owww! Allrightall *right*!" Trina says, amiably, rubbing her thin arm. She accepts a slice of pizza from the car, but trips and drops it on the street.

Two days after her nineteenth birthday, in late July, she phones in from Rikers again. In August she pleads guilty to possession and loitering. In September, I visit. She hunches over, bloated, her legs wide open, wrists crossed with elbows on her knees, eyeing the femme inmates to whom she plays butch. She's rolled up her prison jumpsuit sleeves to show a tattoo she's given herself—TRINA. "Indian ink," she says in a hoarse monotone. She thinks she might be gay.

We talk on the phone. Her plans change daily. She claims she's pregnant. "My head's in too much of a puzzle and I can't put it together," she says another day. "It's like I'm living in a fairy tale, hoping that everything is going to be all right." Of course, it can't be. But the commotion of her life defers thinking much about it.

She's freed in October and mails me a letter she'd written weeks earlier, from her cell: *These days are going by quick, little do I even know it.* The weeks of enforced sobriety and the words bring out the best in her—a hint of entitlement, the huge questioning of an undamaged kid.

She'd decorated the page with hearts and drawn kisses and Dood the
pit bull and hugs:

> These are the things I think about at night: 1) will i ever be a normal
> person again 2) will i ever stop doing drugs 3) do i really Forgive my
> Father 4) will i ever love a man 5) will I always be gay 6) Do i be-
> trayed my mother & sister 7) will i ever stop pushing people away
> From me who care for me. 8) will i ever stop prostituting 9) do I really
> love myself or can i 10) will i ever stop comming to jail 11) will i ever
> stop being a criminal & robbing 12) will i ever be me again.

I keep track of the sequence of arrests—over thirty. At the end of
Trina's 1991 comes a grand larceny charge, two counts. In January
1992 she begins serving real time for a middleweight street scam that
went like this: She'd get a john into a secluded parking space. A buddy
of hers would stage a fake mugging and as he held the unsuspect-
ing, scared john outside, Trina would scoot over into the driver's
seat and drive off. The buddy copped a plea, ratted on Trina, and
returned to the street. Trina stewed for months, then gave up. She's
resigned and politely urges her attorney to bargain her sentence down
to three years.

There are many calls, and they all share a shape, opening with the
easy rhythm of old friendship, then collapsing awkwardly because I
can't carry the optimism for us anymore. I've been disappointed so often that—like her—I've become tough to the suggestion of new hope,
weary, even annoyed.

The casual chats about jailhouse gripes, tales of wronged friend-
ships, intrigues over jewelry and food, TV-movie updates, all in her
vibrant slang, are over. For the most part, she's given up, too. Matter-of-
factly she reports that she has seizures, almost every day, and that she
cries a lot at night. On her birthday, she phones from a criminal psychiatric ward, sounding lively for a change. She's tried to hang herself. "I know I shouldnta done it, Adrian, but I don't belong heah! You
know me! These people heah are really really crazy! I was just feeling
really bad."

Sometimes I get messages. I play back her voice on my answering machine and I miss Trina in those minutes—the irascible charm, the oddball
wisdom, her hard honesty. Her words waft through my apartment:

"Hi, Adrian. You know it's me. And you know it's ridiculous talking to an answering machine. I know you don't got time to visit, but at
least you could tell me that you are gonna try to visit. I'll understand if
you can't. You remember how bored I get, right? I'll call back later."

"Hi, Adrian. I know you are in the Bronx tonight. Be careful. It ain't like Richmond Terrace. These people from the Bronx are for real! Believe me, I know them from heah. Don't be axing so many questions like you did with me."

"Hi, Adrian, it's Trina. You know it's very tiring calling you when you ain't home. Especially from prison. I'll try again latah. I love you. Bye."

Joseph Nocera

Mary Schjeldahl

Joseph Nocera says it took months to write "The Ga-Ga Years" because he had another job and could work on it only in bits and pieces.

The assignment began during a conversation with *Esquire* editor Lee Eisenberg in January 1987 during the stock market boom. "We came up with the idea together one day sitting around his office talking about the craziness of the stock market," Nocera said. "He was talking about how crazy it seemed at the Fidelity Center on Park Avenue, and I had my own thoughts about Fidelity Investments. One thing led to another. It was not an *Esquire*-type idea because it didn't have a big star at the center of it. It was not a profile. From that point on, I was on my own."

By the end of September, Nocera had completed his research and spent three weeks writing the article. Then a disconcerting event jostled his plans. He had shaped the article to reflect the stock market boom, but in October the market took a historic crash. Nocera felt his article might be going down the drain with the market. He drove to the Fidelity Center in Boston and watched investors whose bubble had been burst milling around, stunned. He decided all was not lost. On deadline, he spent a long weekend recasting the piece.

Nocera started his journalistic career at the *Washington Monthly*, and later joined *Texas Monthly* when it was edited by William Broyles, Jr., and Nicholas Lemann. After four years in Texas, he moved to western Massachusetts as executive editor of *New England Monthly* magazine. Following publication of "The Ga-Ga Years," Nocera began a book on the penetration by what he calls "the money culture" into middle-class life, in the form of the credit card, the mutual fund, the money market account, and stock trading services such as Fidelity. During the long process of writing this book, *A Piece of the Action: How the Middle Class Joined the Money Class* (1994), he wrote columns on business culture for *Newsweek*, *Esquire*, and *GQ*.

The Ga-Ga Years

January 28, 1987.
Dow Jones Opening Average: 2163.39

It's 10:00 in the morning, and the Dow has already risen 18 points. Amazing. Like everyone else, I've become transfixed by the astonishing upward spiral of the Dow, up almost 250 points since New Year's Day, four and a half years into the greatest bull market in history. Usually, though, I try to wait at least until the evening news. Today, I am standing in a posh storefront in Manhattan, at the corner of Fifty-first Street and Park Avenue, a vantage point from which it would take a supreme act of will *not* to keep track of the Dow's every tick. This is the New York beachhead of Fidelity Investments, the giant Boston-based mutual-fund company that manages more money for more people than anyone else in the world.

It's quite a spectacle here at Fifty-first and Park. Right now I'm staring up at an electronic board that resembles one of those overhead scoreboards you find in modern arenas. Only instead of scores, it is spewing out the current value of Fidelity's Select funds—high-risk mutual funds that invest in only one industry. A light show for the 1980s. Amber numbers flicker across the screen, disappear, and then blip back up again. Every hour the numbers are updated. Hourly pricing, a Fidelity exclusive, has almost no real purpose: it is little more than a dazzling prop. At the bottom of the board flashes the most dazzling prop of all: the Dow itself. Which, by the way, has just gone up another 6 points.

If money is the new sex—and isn't that what everyone is saying these days?—then this place is the whorehouse. The scent of the market is powerful here, intoxicating. Stretching across a long expanse of pink marble wall is one of those digital tapes that announce block trades. Does anyone here have the slightest idea how to read the thing? So why are we all staring at it so shamelessly? Above the tape, a mural depicts pleasant scenes from the bull market. Multiracial investment bankers peering at Quotron machines. That sort of thing.

All around me I can see the blandishments of money, the seduction of wealth, the lure of financial security. A recorded voice entices: "Choosing an investment should be as easy as watching TV." The aisles are lined with fund prospectuses. "Fidelity Magellan," it says in front of one big stack, "one of America's most popular funds." "Municipal bonds," it purrs a few aisles over. "They're not just for the wealthy anymore." I leaf through a few prospectuses. Is it my imagination, or is there a certain furtiveness to this act, like the way men thumb through *Penthouse* at an airport newsstand?

I see a woman outside, her face pressed hard against the window. She is a meter maid, young and black, and to judge from her expression, this place might just as well be Tiffany's. "She comes by every day," whispers a Fidelity saleswoman. "She really wants to make an investment, you can tell." Just then, the woman steps haltingly through the revolving door. Once inside, she looks ga-ga at all she sees. This strikes me as the only appropriate response in the face of such irresistible come-ons. If the late 1960s bull-market were the Go-Go Years, then surely these are the Ga-Ga Years.

The lunch hour approaches. The Dow is up 30 points. The place begins to fill up. Many come to transact business, but just as many are here for the same reason I am: to browse, to gawk, to stare ga-ga at the Dow as it makes its relentless climb upward. I watch a young man named Jeff Goddard, one of a dozen Fidelity "reps" working the room. He is earnest and cherubic and twenty-four years old. People tug at him, wanting information. A middle-aged man in a driver's uniform pulls out a pamphlet and waves it at Jeff. He is holding a prospectus for a bond fund. "They're offering 12½ percent. Can you do better than that?"

"Our highest is 10 percent," admits Jeff. The driver snorts audibly and walks out. Another man takes his place. "Jeff, remember me? I'm ready if you are!" The man writes out several checks to put into Fidelity mutual funds. Next to him, a woman in tattered jeans who might be, oh, nineteen years old is doing likewise. She writes three checks in all, each for—am I seeing this right?—$50,000. Behind her, a woman in a mink coat says loudly, "I want to put another $65,000 in my account. Can I sit down with someone?"

I wander over to a bank of computers to punch up a few stock quotes but become distracted by a couple standing next to me. Complete strangers, they are deeply engrossed in conversation. The man looks like Robin Williams, only twenty years older; the woman is that classic type, the "little old lady" who dabbles in the market. In any other setting, it would be impossible to guess that these two are part of the Ga-Ga Years. Yet this is what I hear them say:

She: "My biggest mistake was selling my Carter-Wallace. You know, because of the AIDS thing. Sold it over a year ago."

He: "I hear Pan Am is supposed to be sold."

She: "A Philip Morris man said to me, 'Helen, you will never go wrong investing in Philip Morris.' " She sighs. "But I didn't."

He nods in sympathy. "Philip Morris is the finest of the tobacco companies." Then he asks, "Why don't you consolidate?"

She: "Oh, I couldn't. I love to play with my stocks. I have over $1,000 in newsletter."

They dawdle for most of the afternoon, talking, comparing investment notes, calling up stock quotes. Finally, they walk out together. They are friends now. They met at Fidelity. They have the market in common.

So did we all.

It seems so long ago, doesn't it—those days of ga-ga, when the market looked as if it would never stop rising? Black Monday, it is safe to say, will mark the end of the Ga-Ga Years. And what images will remain? After the Go-Go Years of the 1960s, the names that stuck were Gerry Tsai and Bernie Cornfeld. This time, the symbols will undoubtedly include Drexel Burnham and Boone Pickens and Ivan Boesky. And Fidelity. Just as Drexel will stand for the rise of the junk bond, and Boesky for the wages of greed, so will Fidelity conjure up the return of the equity mutual fund.

Fidelity was everywhere. You couldn't open a newspaper without seeing a Fidelity ad. You couldn't pick up the phone without knowing that Fidelity was ready to respond. At its peak, Fidelity had $85 billion in assets, making it a larger investor of people's money than even Merrill Lynch. It had the most funds—more than one hundred—and in Magellan, the largest fund, too, run by the most famous portfolio manager, Peter Lynch. Fidelity became such an icon of the Ga-Ga Years that on Black Monday reporters scrambled not to the stock exchange to get reactions but to Fidelity.

The last time mutual funds were hot, at the height of the Go-Go Years, 3 percent of American households had money in them. This time around, more than half the households in America had some stake in one—if not an equity mutual fund then at least a money-market fund. That one fact, I think, indicates a sea change in the way people thought about their money during the Ga-Ga Years. Almost alone, Fidelity understood people's evolving feelings about money, and played to those feelings. That was, and is, its secret.

I spent much of last year hanging around Fidelity, seeing in this exercise both a means of coming to terms with the Ga-Ga Years and a way to get at the modern history of money in which Fidelity played such a crucial role. I was at Fidelity when the Dow made some of its great gains. I was there when the crash came, too. Fidelity was always moderately enthusiastic about my endeavor, allowing me considerable access, though never so enthusiastic as to give me free rein of the place. This, I was told, was the way things were there, the way Mr. Johnson wanted it. Edward Johnson III, a reserved and somewhat eccentric Boston Brahmin, had run Fidelity since 1972 and was universally credited with being the genius behind the company's rise. As I began my trip, I wanted to learn more about him, too. Not least, I wanted to know how he saw the Ga-Ga Years coming and got there first.

The History of Money: A Preamble

Gerry Tsai began his career at Fidelity—he not only got his start there but became famous there: the first portfolio manager to get the press of a rock star. It was a different world then, a world in which the middle class still squirreled its money away in bank savings accounts, and small mutual-fund companies such as Fidelity were easily dwarfed by a superstar fund manager. Fidelity was also run by a different Mr. Johnson—Edward Johnson II, who left behind a career as a fairly substantial Boston lawyer when he bought Fidelity and its two small funds in the 1940s.

Johnson was a Boston Brahmin in a profession dominated by Boston Brahmins. But though he was one of them by virtue of class and bearing, he had nothing but scorn for the way they approached money management. Before Johnson, investment management was an overwhelmingly defensive profession, dedicated to preserving capital. Johnson hated the idea that the goal was to avoid losing money instead of making money. He hated the fact that mutual funds were managed by committees, which dithered instead of buying and selling. He believed that mutual funds should be managed by one person, using his own instincts and knowledge to trade stocks. And of course he was right. By the early 1960s, Johnson had created an entirely new species, the fund manager, and charged it with one simple (and radical) mission: to beat the market by as much as possible. Fidelity was the first company to sell not its cachet (for it had none) but the performance of its funds.

Because Johnson believed that money management was too important to be left to Brahmin money managers, he wasn't afraid to hire Gerry Tsai, a young, untested immigrant from Shanghai, as a stock analyst in the early 1950s. When Tsai began running a fund in 1957, he became the embodiment of Johnson's theories. Tsai's fund was called Fidelity Capital, and it was, as John Brooks would later write, "the company's first frankly speculative . . . fund."

No one had ever run a fund the way Tsai did. He bought all the glamour stocks of the day: Polaroid, Xerox, the conglomerates with their bloated P/E ratios. The turnover in his portfolio was dizzying: 120 percent in 1965 alone. That same year, Capital Fund gained an unheard-of 50 percent. Tsai's performance made him famous, and his fame brought him customers; by the mid-1960s, he was managing well over $1 billion.

And then he was gone. Legend has it that the departure was precipitated by a meeting with Mr. Johnson, in which the younger man asked about succession, and the older man replied that he expected his son to take over when he retired. Edward Johnson III, known as Ned, was running Fidelity's Trend Fund and (it was much noted afterward) outperforming the master as often as not.

Tsai moved to New York to start a new fund, called the Manhattan Fund, hoping to raise $25 million. But so many people wanted to bottle the Tsai magic that when his new fund began life, in February 1966, it had an incredible $247 million. And of course that's when Tsai's touch deserted him. In 1968 the bottom fell out of the Manhattan Fund, and Tsai's humiliating fall from grace became the parable for the Go-Go Years. Shortly thereafter, the bottom dropped out of the Dow itself, and everyone got a similar comeuppance. But Tsai went first, and loudest, and for that he would be forever remembered.

Fidelity itself was hardly immune to the market downturn. Mutual funds can never gain while the broader market is losing; the best a portfolio manager can do is lose less than the market. But during the Go-Go Years, funds had been spectacularly hyped; now, as profits turned to losses, people felt burned, and they began doing exactly what you'd expect: redeeming their mutual-fund shares with a vengeance and putting their money back into the bank, where (they now thought) it should probably have been all along.

The result was that when Johnson II finally handed the baton to Johnson III in 1972, Fidelity was in trouble. The Dow, which had once stood near 1,000, was closing in on 600. Some of Johnson's first acts as boss included firing people he had worked with for years. It wasn't enough. He needed something else, something more dramatic to reverse Fidelity's course. And then he saw it. A man named Bruce Bent, operating out of a tiny office in New York, had invented a strange new fund. It was called the money-market fund, and its creation marked the start of the modern history of money.

March 5, 1987. Dow Jones Average: 2276.43

"The idea first came to me in the summer of 1969," Bruce Bent is saying. It is late on a brisk afternoon in March, and the market has closed for the day. (Up 20 points today! More than 300 on the year!) We're sitting in Bent's corner office on the thirty-fifth floor of a slightly seedy Manhattan office building. He is a trim, handsome man, fifty years old now, with a face like Jack Kemp's—a face enhanced by the first few creases of age. Yet there is a certain prophet-without-honor quality about him. The carpet is faded. The furniture is old—not antique old but 1950's old. Bent's company, called the Reserve Fund, only handles money-market funds, which puts it at one remove from the bull market. While I was waiting in the lobby, I took a look at Bent's prospectus. His funds have only $2.7 billion in assets—peanuts compared to even a small mutual-fund company. If this bothers him, he hides it well.

"It was the summer of 1969," he begins again, smiling as he recalls the time he changed the world. "My partner and I had started our own investment firm. We didn't have any capital, and I was stuck on one question: How do you get money to come to you? Well, the answer was plain as day. *You had to pay higher interest rates than anyone else!*"

In those days, bank savings accounts were limited to 5¼ percent because of something called Regulation Q, a government-imposed ceiling on the interest a depositor could earn. Banks loved Regulation Q because it meant they took in money at an artificially low rate and then turned around and loaned that same money at whatever the market would bear. Bent wanted to find a way around Regulation Q, which he did by inventing the money-market fund. A money-market fund uses "deposits" from investors to make extremely short-term loans to corporations or the government. Like a bank, a money fund could charge market interest rates for those loans. But since it wasn't a bank (no Regulation Q!), it could also grant those same rates to its investors. The fund itself would make money by charging a management fee. Like all great leaps forward, it was both simple and elegant—or at least that's what everyone said once they began stealing Bent's idea.

"In February 1970," Bent says, returning to his story, "we filed with the SEC. The guy said, 'I think we're going to have a problem with this thing.' For the next year and a half we went back and forth with them on it. They just didn't get it. Finally, in November 1971, they let us go ahead. I'm sure they only let us do it because they thought it was going to die."

Can you guess what comes next? Our prophet is rebuffed at every turn. Bent pitches his fund to corporations as an efficient way to manage cash. They show him the door. He talks up the idea among brokers. They yawn. Meanwhile, Bent is trying to support a wife and two small children on zero income. "On bad days, I ate franks," he recalls giddily. "On good days, I ate in the J.C. Penney cafeteria. I took out a home-improvement loan and used it to buy food. I started having trouble handling it, to tell you the truth. My wife, thank God, she understood I had this vision."

On January 7, 1973—more than a year after the SEC gave its approval—Bent got a big break. A *New York Times* reporter, after months of badgering, wrote a short article about the fund. "The next day we got a hundred phone calls," says Bent. "By the end of the year we had $100 million in assets. People I knew on Wall Street would send their mothers to me. Little old ladies would say to me, 'My son told me you have a good thing.' Then they'd say, 'I'm nervous and I don't want to lose my money.'"

And, as we all know by now, they didn't. Money-market funds turned out to be great investments for little old ladies, for unless the fund manager was stupid beyond belief, the principal was never at risk. Only the interest fluctuated. However, since most of us didn't have sons working on Wall Street, it took a long time to figure that out.

It did not, however, take the mutual-fund industry long to see what the money funds were: salvation itself. Here was the means to win back some of those dwindling assets.

"And then," says Bent, finishing his story, "Ned Johnson figured out how to let people write checks against a money-market fund. That really added value."

The History of Money: The Early Years

Do you remember 1974? Do you remember any of your friends investing in money-market funds? I do. I remember exactly one couple. I thought they were out of their minds. So did all their other friends.

Actually, the mutual-fund industry thought Ned Johnson was pretty crazy back then too, what with this check-writing nuttiness. Check writing violated the principle the industry held closest to its heart: make it simple to get into a fund but hard to get out of one. But somehow Johnson saw what no one else did. The money fund wasn't just a temporary stopgap: rather, it marked the beginning of a new era, an era in which people would have options for their hard-earned money. To get people to hand their money to Fidelity, Johnson realized that he would have to treat the buyers of Fidelity "products" the same way McDonald's treated the buyers of hamburgers. Like *customers*. This was his revelation.

Ned Johnson's check-writing feature was the second great invention in the modern history of money. The addition of checks gave the impression that money-market funds were like banks—they felt *safe*. People who invested in them could still think of themselves as savers. In effect, Johnson had begun to blur the distinction between investor and saver.

Fidelity's money-market fund opened for business on June 12, 1974, and was an immediate hit. It was called the Fidelity Daily Income Trust, or FIDIT. Its logo was a frog (fidit, ribit—get it?), and Johnson began scattering frog images about his office. This only reinforced his image as an eccentric, which was then approaching legendary proportions.

He looked a little like Wallace Shawn in those days, vaguely nerdy, with an air of distraction that could rival the most absentminded professor. Whatever big picture he saw remained trapped within the confines of his own mind, escaping from time to time only in little wisps of sentences that came seemingly out of the blue. To the uninitiated, talking to him could be a disconcerting experience, and within Fidelity there developed one school of thought that said Ned Johnson wasn't really a genius at all. He was a flake.

Certainly what he was doing to Fidelity seemed flaky, even to the people on the inside. *Especially* to the people on the inside. Check writing wasn't the half of it. Here was this company still starved for cash, and the boss was spending millions upon millions of dollars. And on what? Well, there were all the fancy new computers Fidelity suddenly had. Now, no one was saying that Fidelity didn't need computers. But the computers Johnson bought were so full of bells and whistles they seemed all out of proportion to Fidelity's needs. Another thing: advertising. Johnson decided Fidelity should do its own selling and began advertising in *The Wall Street Journal*—slick ads with headlines and a sales pitch. The budget was $30,000 a month—shocking!

And the telephones! Fidelity employed six "reps" who worked in an awful windowless room answering calls at random. The six had been hired after Fidelity started running its ads and quickly discovered—and my, wasn't *this* interesting—that people would phone in with questions. Well, six wouldn't do at all! No sirree. Overnight, Fidelity had as sophisticated a system as an airline.

Are you getting the picture here? Ned Johnson remade Fidelity. It became completely self-sufficient, with its own systems company and its own service company, and eventually, its own taxi company. This last, it was said, was the result of Johnson's eccentric inability to flag down cabs during the Boston rush hour. By 1978, Fidelity had gone from being a company that could monitor phone calls weekly to one that could monitor them hourly. But *why?*

Do you remember 1978? You should; that was the year you started to think about your money again. Not that you had much choice; inflation was approaching double digits and interest rates were already there. Both were gnawing away at your standard of living. By then, though, the revolution had come. The money revolution. As you looked around, you suddenly realized that there were ways to outsmart inflation. If you owned a house you felt great. Houses were great inflation beaters. You hired an accountant for the first time, and he told you to borrow as much as you could against your Mastercharge, where the interest was fixed by law, and put that money in a money-market account earning a few percentage points more. And you did it. And it was a real kick: you were making money on the spread. And then there was the night you woke up with a start and realized what an absolute idiot you'd been to keep your savings in the bank, where Regulation Q and inflation were robbing you. This was a truly terrible moment. You felt a little panicky, and your palms were sweaty, and you vowed that the very next day you would switch to a money-market account, the way all your friends were doing.

Do you remember that moment? That is the moment Ned Johnson had been planning for.

May 14, 1987. Dow Jones Average: 2329.68

"Fidelity Investments. This is Wendell Weaver. How may I help you?"

Wendell Weaver, who is twenty-three years old, who is wearing a pair of oversize glasses that make him look like a character out of a Jeff MacNelly sketchbook, who exudes a naive wholesomeness and frothy effervescence that would do Jimmy Stewart proud—Wendell Weaver is sitting in a tiny cubicle on the eighth floor of a banal Dallas high-rise answering the phones. He is joined, on this hot Texas night, by twenty-seven other phone reps manning similar stations along a long, open room. Wendell sits erect, his gangly frame on red alert as he awaits the next call. They come with some frequency.

"Let's see," he says into the receiver, glancing over at a sheet filled with the day's closing prices. "Magellan, up .15. Puritan, down 1. Overseas Fund down .59 to 40.88. Looks like there was some profit taking in the Japanese market." Next call: "Yes, sir. The Ginnie Mae Fund has been taking some substantial losses. Why? Well, when interest rates go up, bond prices go down." Next call: "The price of the yen? Just a minute." He pulls out his copy of *The Wall Street Journal* and rattles off the price of the yen. The calls stop coming for a minute, and he glances at his watch. It's a little after midnight. Welcome to the graveyard shift at Fidelity.

It's May. The Dow is still going up, though it's had a few little tumbles lately—those triple witching hours are murder. No one seems too worried, though. Certainly, there is no sense of worry here on the eighth floor. Off in the distance, I can see downtown Dallas, giving off the illusion of quiet that big cities often emit at night. Things are quiet in here, too, despite the low buzz of telephone talk.

If the portfolio managers in Boston are the beating heart of Fidelity, then this phone operation in Dallas is the belly of the beast. When Ned Johnson put those six people in that little room, the phone became the company's weapon of choice. People who want to switch from one fund to another can do so by picking up the phone. They can call to make stock trades through Fidelity's discount brokerage. They can call just for the hell of it, twenty-four hours a day, seven days a week.

And Lord knows, they do. In a way, the Fidelity phone centers— there are similar setups in Boston and Salt Lake City—are the belly of the Ga-Ga Years, too. Especially at night. Why, I wondered, were people calling Fidelity instead of going to bed? In February 1986, when Fidelity began answering the phones all night, it didn't even bother doing market research. It just *knew*.

Neither Wendell nor anyone else in Dallas can ever recall the phones shutting down completely, except on the day the space shuttle blew up. Then, as the shock wore off, the lines were suddenly jammed, the callers all asking the same warped question: *"What's it going to mean for the market?"* Here in the middle of the bull market, one can see how firmly the ga-ga mentality has taken hold. Wendell detects a certain frantic tone from callers lately, as people who know nothing about the market try to climb aboard, worried that the train is leaving the station. "I spend a lot of time explaining what a dividend is," is how he puts it.

I had come to Dallas because I was simply curious about what people asked about their money at 2:00 in the morning. But nothing at Fidelity is ever so simple as that. Most of the afternoon was devoted to an extravagant tour of the entire Dallas operation. It was, as Fidelity tours always are, impressive. Most of Fidelity's mailings are done from Dallas;

in the huge mail room, I saw a figure written on a blackboard for the number of mailings sent out in the first four months of 1987: 8,358,146. Then on to the phone operation: two enormous aisles filled with more than two hundred little phone cubbies. More than six hundred people answering the phone in Dallas. More than a thousand phone lines open during peak hours. If one center is overloaded with calls, the system transfers calls to another location. And on, and on.

By the time Wendell came on duty at 11:00 P.M., the day's market headline was obvious. So jaded had everyone become by big gains that the Dow's rise on this day, a "mere" 7 points, was a snore. Instead, most callers wanted to talk about the *Japanese* market, which had dropped 172 points, a fact of passionate concern to the many shareholders of a fund called Fidelity Overseas. Overseas was the number-one fund in the country in 1986, due in no small part to its Japanese holding. As a result of that record, it now has some hundred thousand shareholders, most of whom seem to be on the other end of the phone tonight.

At 1:00 in the morning an anxious shareholder calls to say that he has $36,000 in Overseas and what should he do? Wendell gives him a by-now practiced speech. "It's not nearly as bad as two weeks ago," he says. "There's some profit taking. And they're trying to stabilize the dollar. You're still looking at a 34-percent gain since the beginning of the year." Then, a note of caution: "There is some instability in the for- eign markets. You need to be aware of that."

It seems a little strange to me that this twenty-three-year-old kid, not long out of the University of Texas, is discussing the market with doctors and lawyers making ten times the $20,000 or so he makes. Or maybe it's not so strange. The doctors and lawyers can't see Wendell after all; they can only hear him. They hear his reassuring voice offer- ing, in some weird way, comfort. "People want me to say it's okay," ad- mits Wendell. But do you know what the whole thing reminds me of? It reminds me of the phone-sex business, in which women in curlers iron their husbands' shirts while talking dirty to some desperate soul in a hotel room.

One-thirty: a sudden upsurge in calls as Salt Lake City closes down, leaving only Dallas open. Wendell takes one from Fresno. A woman wants to close out her position in Magellan. New Mexico calls; a poten- tial customer wants information about rolling over an IRA. At 3:00 Al- abama calls, wanting to talk about the downturn in the Japanese market. After Alabama hangs up, Wendell tells me that he could hear the man eating breakfast.

"I talk to people with toast in their mouth every day," he says.

The History of Money: The Middle Years

Early in 1980 there occurred one of those small, seemingly ho-hum events that later turn out to be fraught with significance. The event was the announcement by Time Inc. that Marshall Loeb had been named managing editor of *Money* magazine; its importance, in terms of the Ga-Ga Years, was that by some happy accident, Time Inc. had managed to put precisely the right man in the right spot at the right moment.

Loeb, a nattily dressed man who resembles nothing so much as a leprechaun, was (and is) on the fast track at Time, while *Money* was the company's most snakebit publication, having done nothing but lose millions in its eight-year existence. Loeb's mandate, plainly, was to turn things around, which he did in classic golden-boy fashion, doubling the circulation within two years. He did it by openly and shamelessly selling money as the new sex.

Nineteen eighty: time for another trip in the wayback machine. Interest rates have come down just a bit, but oddly, no one seems to be happy about it. Why is this? It's because, thanks to the money-market fund, we've become a nation of interest-rate junkies, where little old ladies move their money around to feel the thrill of an extra quarter of a point.

Nineteen eighty was also the year the banks tried to put the clamps on the money funds, having finally realized that Regulation Q was killing them. Congress was so flooded with outraged mail that the banks never had a chance. The secret was out. Only suckers put their money in savings accounts.

As interest rates declined, the fund pushers showed us their other wares. We were interested now. We were curious. As we looked for ways to keep making double-digit gains, we saw . . .

"Choices!" Marshall Loeb practically leaps off his couch in the Time-Life Building, where he now edits *Fortune.* "Just *think* of all the choices you had by then," he exclaims. "You had bond funds. You had tax-free bond funds. You had money-market funds. You had *tax-free* money funds."

You also had Merrill Lynch's Cash Management Account. You had the new Select funds from Fidelity. On the horizon, you had a little retirement idea called an IRA, ready to explode. And of course you had the bull market. When the market took off in August 1982, it became the new fix. Money streamed into stocks, and into their surrogate, the mutual fund. This influx dwarfed anything that had come before because so many more people were thinking about money now. Here was the moment that the transformation from saver to investor—begun by Bent, nurtured by Johnson, championed by Loeb—was complete.

Loeb believes that money became, in his words, "the most discussed topic among consenting adults," as two-income couples began talking about their money over dinner; it was only a matter of time before those private conversations became cocktail-party talk. My own belief is that Loeb had a microphone in the saltshaker, so sure was his feel for those conversations. "*Money* did good journalism," Loeb insists defensively. But who was buying it for the journalism? People were buying it for the fantasy—for the sex.

No one was more ga-ga during the Ga-Ga Years than Loeb. His trademark was his cover, where he regularly put a wholesome young couple next to a headline that read: HOW TO TURN $50,000 INTO $250,000 IN JUST FIVE YEARS. What was this conceit if not the equivalent of *Playboy*'s centerfold? That you had as much chance of getting rich by following the example of the *Money* centerfold as you did of sleeping with a Playmate scarcely seemed to matter. People bought the magazine, took it home, and drooled.

Inevitably Loeb's magazine began intersecting regularly with Johnson's company. The first and most revealing incident came in April 1983, when *Money* chose a wholesome young Fidelity fund manager named Michael Kassen for its cover. The headline read: HOW TO MAKE MONEY IN MUTUAL FUNDS. Underneath that: THEY'RE THE SUREST, SAFEST WAY TO INVEST IN A SURGING MARKET. And finally, the clincher: KASSEN, THIRTY, RUNS A TECHNOLOGY FUND THAT HAS JUMPED 131 PERCENT SINCE AUGUST. A hundred and thirty-one percent! Wow!

Kassen's appearance in *Money* marked a kind of coming out for Fidelity. Ever since Tsai had left, portfolio managers had been forbidden to talk to the press, the lone exception made for Peter Lynch, who was allowed guest appearances on Louis Rukeyser's television show, *Wall Street Week*. That Johnson would now allow Kassen to speak freely to a *Money* reporter about his stock choices, allow him to spend five hours in the freezing cold being photographed in his tennis togs, allow him to talk about his upbringing in Cleveland and his affinity for squash—all of this spoke volumes about how the world had changed. Fund companies needed every little edge now. In this new world, Johnson's decision to open Fidelity to the press, however distasteful personally, was a given.

What was not a given was *Money*'s choice of Kassen to represent the "safety" and "sureness" of the mutual fund. Despite his undeniable talent for picking stocks, he was, in fact, probably the worst choice imaginable. His fund was anything *but* safe. It was called Fidelity Select Technology, and it did not invest broadly in the market like most funds, but only in one segment: high technology.

During the Ga-Ga Years, every modern investment company was

also an entertainment company, and with its Select funds Fidelity was playing deliberately to the entertainment side of the market. It always assumed that the constituency for the Selects would be the most active amateurs, people who enjoyed guessing which industries were poised to go up, people who could afford to guess wrong. This caveat, however, never made its way into the *Money* article.

Kassen wound up feeling a little embarrassed by the publicity, but for Fidelity the experience exceeded its fondest hopes. When the article hit the newsstands in April, Kassen's fund was already an established hit, with a little more than $200 million. By *July*, it was closing in on $650 million. Millions of dollars were poured into the fund every day, thousands of checks for $3,000 and $4,000. "It was like watching time-lapse photography of a flower," Kassen recalls. "Surreal."

And then—*poof!*—the joyride was over. In August, technology stocks crashed, and so did Kassen's fund. He was working furiously now, trying to keep his head above water. And by any objective measure, he succeeded brilliantly. "Technology stocks were down 20 percent," he recalls, "and I was only down 10 percent."

Unfortunately, this was not much consolation to all the people who had first learned of his walk-on-water mutual fund from *Money* magazine. As Select Technology fell back during the second half of 1983, a lot of people discovered something about mutual funds they hadn't quite comprehended before. They were not necessarily "sure." To be an investor, rather than a saver, meant accepting risks; and funds like Kassen's, geared to make the quick, spectacular gain, also involved the most risk. But the lesson had not been learned from *Money* magazine. It had been learned with cold, hard cash.

July 28, 1987. Dow Jones Average: 2493.94

"Quite a paper this morning," says Peter Lynch, shaking his head in mock wonder. He is leaning back in the chair of his small corner office, leafing through *The Wall Street Journal*. Lynch, who is rumored to make $3 million a year managing Fidelity's Magellan Fund, is wearing a light-blue seersucker suit, slightly worn and in desperate need of dry cleaning. It is 8:00 in the morning. Late July: as the bull market closes in on its fifth anniversary, the gains keep coming—up more than 500 points so far this year. Incredible.

"Did you see what Boone did today?" Lynch asks. Pickens has announced plans to buy a $15-million stake in the giant airplane manufacturer Boeing. "I've got twenty thousand shares of Boeing," he says—a position worth a little more than a million dollars, pocket change for the $11-billion Magellan fund. Like most portfolio managers, Lynch tends to refer to himself when he means his fund. "Someone forgot to tell that whole sector there's a bull market going on," he shrugs.

As Lynch makes his way through the paper, he finds a story on almost every page that affects his life. He groans over a report that American Express intends to buy back some of its shares. "Look at this." He shows me a printout that lists the previous day's performance of Magellan's 1,700 stocks. At the top of the sheet, written in pen and underlined for emphasis, are the words "Buy AmEx." "I wrote it on the way in this morning. If only they had waited a month."

"Yup," says Lynch, shaking his head again. "It's quite a paper today."

Peter Lynch may be the most famous portfolio manager of the Ga-Ga Years, but he's not famous the way Gerry Tsai was twenty years ago. There is nothing flamboyant about him, nothing exotic, nothing larger-than-life. He is forty-three years old, tall and thin, his hair completely white, with classic Irish features. The only thing that sets him apart is this: for ten years now, he has been the best mutual-fund manager alive.

Of all the smart moves Ned Johnson made in the 1970s, the smartest may have been giving Magellan to Lynch. When he did so, back in 1977, Magellan was a nice little $22-million fund, and Lynch was head of research. Ten years and $11 billion later, Lynch could lay claim to one of the most fabulous statistics of the Ga-Ga Years: if you had put $10,000 into Magellan on the day he took it over, you'd have made $175,000.

The result of Lynch's performance is that Magellan was a symbol of the Ga-Ga Years even before they were over: a few years ago, it was an answer on the game show *Jeopardy*. Just in the time I've been hanging around Fidelity, the fund has grown by $3 billion, as people scramble to get in before it's too late. It is the greatest marketing tool Fidelity has ever had, a powerful magnet pulling people into the company, making it the single biggest mutual fund in America. "Around Fidelity," says one former marketing aide, "Peter Lynch is God."

Well, maybe not *God*. But as the man who manages the franchise fund, his influence on the other portfolio managers is enormous. His lack of flash is part of the ethos of the equity shop. The suspender quotient is low here. Nor is there any flamboyance in the way Lynch and his colleagues buy and sell stocks. There is no worse sin at Fidelity than buying something simply because it is "hot." Back when everybody was in technology stocks, Lynch was a guest on *Wall Street Week*, and Rukeyser asked him which high-tech companies he was buying. None, he replied; they weren't his kind of deal.

On this day in late July, fifteen companies will visit Fidelity; Lynch will see as many as he can. Frank Lorenzo touted Texas Air at breakfast. The officers of a small company in which Magellan holds a large position are scheduled for lunch. An oil analyst is coming by. A huge foreign conglomerate. When you have 1,700 stocks in your portfolio, your job can be defined rather simply: you have to know everything about everything.

At 10:00, Lynch goes to his first meeting. "I bought a lot of your stock," he begins in a surprisingly soft voice. "Thanks for making me some money." Although there are a dozen people in the room, Lynch asks almost all the questions. He rubs his forehead with his free hand: a little tick. As everyone settles into their chairs, the CEO says, "We've had a good quarter, which we're reporting in three days. As you are valued shareholders, we'll trust you . . ." Lynch cuts him off. "We don't want to know that stuff," he says. "Just tell us about the company."

Lynch dashes out of the meeting and heads back to his office. Rummaging around his desk, he yells out to one of his assistants, "Do you know where my Ford file is?" Ford Motor Company is Magellan's largest holding, with some eight million shares—an $800 million position. When Lynch first started buying it heavily a few years ago, Ford was just beginning to show signs of turning around. Now, of course, it is making more money than General Motors.

Everything seems to be happening at once. The phone rings—it's a company he's been trying to reach. The oil analyst has just arrived. A young Fidelity hand pops in to announce some second-quarter results. Lynch's secretary reminds him about the lunch. In the middle of this low-level chaos, Lynch suddenly looks at me and says, "You know, the last two and a half years have been the worst in the last twenty." What's he talking about? The last two years have been *great*. Sensing my disbelief, he adds: "Eighty percent of the pros have lost in this market."

Well, sure. But to me, all that proves is the difference between the way Lynch thinks about money and the way the rest of us do. His goal is to beat the S&P 500, while ours is to make more money than we could make in a bank or a money-market fund. Because of its enormous size, Magellan can no longer beat the market the way it once could; Lynch himself advises people looking for big gains to try another fund. But they don't. Magellan is where people want their money in the Ga-Ga Years. And when they look up later and see that he's made them 20 percent, they are very happy. Who cares if he hasn't beaten the S&P 500?

Though most of the time, he has. "I'm just a little behind it right now," he says. So far this year, the S&P 500 is up 33.8 percent. Magellan is just a shade behind, up 32.2 percent. So I take it back. Maybe the guy is God.

Late in the afternoon Lynch turns his attention to me again. He has a few standard speeches for the press, and now I get one of them. "Economics to me," he says, "is when a company had seven losing divisions and now it only has five. I don't know how long this bull market will last. We had the worst recession since the Depression in 1982. Nobody told me. What I'm trying to do here is find out: Is Zayre getting better? That's how you make money over the long haul."

He has another standard speech, about the worth of mutual funds, and the time has come for me to hear it as well. In the past few months, the mutual-fund backlash has been gaining ground. Magellan has been criticized for its high management fee. The industry has been criticized for peddling funds without explaining the risks, not unlike the excesses of the Sixties. But the worst cut of all came in May from the novelist Michael M. Thomas, who predicted a crash of the bull market triggered by the mutual funds. "When mutual-fund shareholders hit the panic button, and start clamoring for redemptions of their shares," he wrote in *The Nation*, "the funds have no legal recourse but to come up with the money, and that could trigger a selling panic."

Has Lynch heard the criticism? I have no doubt. "My mother used to say, 'Never play the market because you'll lose it all,' " he tells me now, with more passion than I've heard from him all day. "But people don't have any choice anymore. They've been pushed into the market. I'm happy to beat the market by 4 or 5 percent. Last year I was up 23.7 percent, or whatever the hell I was up last year. That's after the management fee, after the commissions—after everything." His voice is rising. *"This is a very efficient method for the public,"* he says with finality. He gives me a steely look that says, "This is not a point you want to argue with." Not today, anyway.

August 13, 1987. Dow Jones Average: 2669.32

The whole thing is starting to get a little weird. The Dow was down today, 11 points, but it's been going up so far and so fast—up 44 yesterday; up 43 the day before, a new record every day—that there is a lot of nervous talk that we're due for a big correction. Or worse. Surely it can't go on forever. One of these days I'm going to start worrying about it.

Right now, though, I've got other things on my mind. I'm sitting in the office of Ned Johnson. Johnson, I've been told, does not grant many interviews, and there was some question as to whether I'd be granted one. But at long last the moment has arrived.

Johnson's office is full of perfect Brahmin touches—tasteful painting, discreet antiques—and also, I notice, the odd frog here and there; he likes to keep a few reminders of the old days. I spot a Quotron machine by his desk. Although Johnson hasn't managed a portfolio in years, I've heard he still loves the market. A few years ago, when Gerry Tsai joined American Can Company, Johnson called the person who manages his holdings and said: "I worked next to Tsai for five years. Buy twenty thousand shares of American Can."

He does not look like Wallace Shawn anymore. At fifty-seven, his hairline is long gone, but over the years his face has gotten thinner and longer, more dignified. There is still that sense about him that though his body may be here, his mind is a million miles away. He is wearing an expensive tie, but when he crosses his legs, I can see that his shoes need new soles.

After some preliminary chitchat, I start the interview. "Mr. Johnson," I begin, "how did you come up with the idea of adding the check to the money-market fund?"

He seems instantly uncomfortable. "Oh, I don't know," he replies with a sigh. "Ideas bubble up and down, and the ones that keep coming back up usually have the most merit." That's it. That's the whole answer.

Oh boy, I'm thinking. He's not going to make this easy. One more try. "Sir, what compelled you to do what you did in the 1970s? What did you see that no one else saw?"

This time he gives a helpless shrug. "I just assumed the equity market would eventually come back. It always has before."

Do you know how I'm feeling here? I'm feeling like Dorothy in *The Wizard of Oz*, and I've just pulled back the curtain. *This* is the insight that changed the world? That the equity market was going to come back?

We talk for an hour, but the interview never really gets off the ground. Finally, I thank him for his time and flip my notebook shut. And then a funny thing happens. Ned Johnson becomes comfortable again. The act of closing the notebook has somehow freed him to talk. I can see it now: the wisps of sentences, the flash of ideas. I'm not saying I see genius, not in a ten-minute conversation, or even that I have any better understanding of where this very private man learned to see the future. But I am willing to concede now that he is capable of such a feat.

Just before I leave, I pop one last question. I ask him how long he thinks the bull market will last. But immediately Johnson reverts to his previous Dalai Lama–like pose. "How do you ever know when you've reached the top?" he replies elliptically. "Each crash is a little different from the one before it." He stares off into space. "They're all a little different," he repeats.

The History of Money: The Late Years

How do you know when you've reached the top? It's mid-August now, and the question is being asked with increasing frequency. I saw Marshall Loeb on television the other night pooh-poohing the bears. Then I saw Elaine Garzarelli of Shearson Lehman Brothers on CNN, making it sound as if collapse is imminent. It's hard to know what to think anymore.

And what is Fidelity saying about the market—Fidelity with its hundred delicious options for making money? Fidelity isn't saying anything. Fidelity believes that its job is simply to provide the choices. "There are huge attitudinal changes in this country," Rodger Lawson told me in August. Lawson heads Fidelity's giant marketing operation, and he was outlining Fidelity's official world view. "People want control," he said. "They want to make their own decisions."

But I'm not so sure. I think back to my night with Wendell Weaver, listening to callers practically plead for help. And I recall, too, an investing seminar I attended in Cambridge early in the summer, well before the bull market started to get the jitters. The most memorable speaker that day was a charismatic man named Dick Fabian, described by the master of ceremonies as "the father of mutual-fund switching." Flailing his arms like an evangelist preaching salvation, Fabian had proclaimed that everybody should be able to attain "20-percent-annualized-compounded-growth-with-no-downside-risk-as-measured-over-a-five-year-period." He kept repeating these words over and over like a mantra, until they hypnotized.

When Fabian left the podium, he was blocked by a mass of people who had raced to the front of the hall and had surrounded him. To watch these people crowded around Fabian, to see the longing in their eyes, to listen to the desperate quality of their questions, was to realize that they did not feel freed by the new financial marketplace. They felt paralyzed by it. They were drowning in an ocean of choice, and they wanted Fabian to throw them the life preserver. *They wanted him to tell them what to do.* This, I think, is what people most crave as the Dow approaches 2,700. But it is the one thing Fidelity won't provide.

On the eve of the fifth anniversary of the bull market, a balmy day in August in which the market had opened 44 points up (again!), I sat in on a meeting of a group of Fidelity portfolio managers. More than sixteen people jammed into a small conference room, all members of the "income-growth" group, which consists of more conservative funds than pure growth funds such as Magellan.

Leading the meeting was Bruce Johnstone, who manages both this group and his own huge fund, Equity-Income, which had returned 600 percent in ten years and bulged with $4.5 billion worth of conservative money. As he stood at the front of the conference table, Johnstone held five different colored markers with which he kept notes on a board behind him. Short, balding, quick to laugh, Johnstone so overflows with guileless enthusiasm that he can get away with saying things like, "I can't *believe* I've been so *lucky* to work with a genius like Ned. It's been *great!*"

The meeting was a freewheeling discussion of the market: where it had been, where it was going, what was on people's minds. "Salomon Brothers is predicting 6½ percent inflation for 1988," a young analyst began. Johnstone winced skeptically. "Gee whiz, that sounds high," he replied finally. "Where are wages going up?" Everyone clamored to answer at once. "New York just settled with its union workers—three years, 18-percent raise," someone said. "Autoworkers, steel workers, and mine workers all have contracts coming up this year," added someone else. "The auto companies have made a snootful of money," chimed in a third voice. "What can Ford possibly tell its workers?"

Eventually the discussion turned to the mood of the investing public. Someone mentioned that the *Boston Herald*, the local Murdoch paper, had begun carrying a stock market game. I'd noticed that, too. What could it mean, I wondered, when the lure of the Ga-Ga Years had become so pervasive that Rupert Murdoch could use it as a circulation booster? Maybe it meant the end was near.

Certainly most of the people in this room felt that way. "You simply cannot justify this market on the fundamentals," I heard Francis Cabour say vehemently. Cabour is a legendarily conservative portfolio manager who is always predicting doom. But today everyone agreed, Johnstone included. "Four or five months ago, we thought we were in the ninth inning," he said. "Now it looks like we're in extra innings." Everyone laughed, but it was a nervous laughter—the kind that means the joke has hit home. I looked around the room at this handful of fund managers, all furiously working the bull market for every last dime, and the thing I noticed most was the complete lack of euphoria, that giddy sense of jumping in head first that had characterized the Go-Go Years, or the Roaring Twenties, for that matter. And it suddenly occurred to me that these portfolio managers were feeling what I was feeling—whatever everyone was feeling. In the last few months, as the Dow made some of its most majestic gains, there was none of the joy that usually accompanies such gains. We watched the Dow in awe, not understanding, and not really believing either. We were just ga-ga.

In five years, the Dow has risen 2,000 points, and everybody is sup-

posed to have had such a great time. And it *has* been fun. It's been exciting. So why isn't anyone smiling? I think it's because although we've
become investors, in our heart of hearts, we wish we were still savers. We
wish we didn't have to worry about whether to stay in or get out. We wish
we didn't have to learn about the effect of interest rates on bonds, or the
difference between a growth and an income fund. We wish the world
were simple again.

As the meeting drew to a close, a young woman, newly hired and
not yet in sync with the rhythms of Fidelity, asked for a straw poll on
how long the bull market might last. It was an embarrassing moment.
People looked in the other direction, or waved her request away. I
thought: here I am among some of the smartest money managers in the
world, and not one of them is willing to look the bull market square in
the eye. They are too nervous, just like the rest of us.

October 20, 1987. Dow Jones Average: 1738.74

Is this how it ends? Not with a whimper but with a bang—a huge,
amazing, horrifying bang? Yesterday was Black Monday: the Dow
Jones lost 508 points, 22 percent of its value, on a staggering 604 million
shares. The worst day ever. A year's worth of gains wiped out. Those
tremors I felt in that meeting with Johnstone have suddenly turned into
a terrifying earthquake.

And here I am right back where I started, at a Fidelity investment
center, in Boston this time. I am transfixed by the Dow again, just as I
was that January day in New York. Now, as then, I am staring at that
magical Select scoreboard, which in Boston is placed in the window so
people can see it as they walk by. Except no one is walking by. They
can't walk by. They stop, and they stare, their mouths hanging open.
They—we—look like zombies, unmoving and uncomprehending.

It is a strange and frightening scene. The crowd has grown so large
that it has spilled onto the street, blocking traffic. Truck drivers honk
their horns angrily. I hear someone say, "It just dropped another 2 points
in two minutes. It's all over now." I see a tourist taking a picture of the
Select board—something to show his grandchildren in fifty years? I hear
someone else say, "I thought it would recover today. Wishful thinking."
It seems, somehow, a fitting end to the Ga-Ga Years, if indeed this is the
end. What can be more ga-ga than the greatest crash in history?

I had driven into Boston early yesterday on other business, but by
8:30 this morning, I was in Fidelity's public-relations office. "We're not
doing any selling on the phones," the press guy told me. "We're strictly

trying to reassure people." Eighty thousand people had called over the weekend, after the market dropped more than 100 points on Friday. Top officials met all weekend and met again after Monday's huge loss. At one meeting, Johnson, surveying the wreckage, concluded that there were a lot of great stock buys out there. Oh, that Ned Johnson.

Fidelity, of course, was hit hard by Black Monday. By the end of the week, its $85 billion in assets will shrink to $76.7 billion, and the company will consider it a victory just to keep that much money in the "Fidelity family"—much of it now residing in money-market funds. Although no one will give out redemption figures, it is clear that shareholders were bailing out like crazy, and that mutual funds played at least some role in creating Black Monday, just as Michael Thomas had predicted. On Wednesday, *The Boston Globe* will describe Magellan as a $7.7 billion fund.

And yet, and yet. Virtually every Fidelity equity fund beat the market on Black Monday. Beat it by a lot. Magellan was down 17 percent, compared with the Dow's 22 percent. Balanced, the fund Cabour now manages, was down only 6 percent. To paraphrase that famous 1960s slogan: Are mutual funds part of the problem or part of the solution? Who can say anymore?

The market opened 200 points up this Tuesday morning, but by the time I get to the investment center, around 11:30, most of the gain is gone. As it drops the crowd keeps growing, making the street ever more impenetrable to traffic. Who has time to worry about traffic? Every time the Dow makes another downward blip, there are audible groans.

At 12:30, with the market down 20 points, the police arrive. They want Fidelity to shut off the Select board so that people will get out of the street. Fidelity complies—and everyone moves twenty feet to stare at the block trade tape in the other window. Fidelity shuts that off, too. No one moves. People are now staring at two blank screens. An old man on a bicycle rides by and asks, in a thick foreign accent, "How's the New York?" Down 20, I tell him. "I hear up 50," he says.

I go inside and walk down a flight of stairs where the Quotron machines are. There must be twenty people crowded around the two machines. The hard core in this group first got here early yesterday. They look dazed and tired as they stare at the Dow. It reminds me of a poker game at 4:30 in the morning—you're sick of playing, and the games all seem stale, and you want to quit. But you can't. You're too deep into it. Clearly no one here will leave before 4:00, when the market closes. When I go back upstairs a half hour later, the Dow is up 90 points.

Upstairs, I notice another cluster of people. They are waiting patiently on the phone to get through to a Fidelity rep. "I want to buy some IBM," says a man who, judging by the splotches of white paint on his work clothes, appears to be a house painter. IBM closed yesterday at 103, down nearly 32 points. "I'll never get another chance like this." I'm thinking: Ned Johnson strikes again.

I wander back downstairs. "Where's the Dow?" I ask. "Up 10," someone says. "It was just up 90," I say.

"That was ten minutes ago," comes the reply. "Where have you been?" Everyone laughs, myself included. But it's all too crazy. I can't take it anymore. About 2:00, with the Dow creeping up again, I leave Fidelity and retrieve my car from the parking garage. For most of the drive home, I resist the impulse to find out how the market is doing. But then 4:00 arrives, and the market closes, and the impulse is too strong to resist. "For those of you who haven't heard," the announcer says, "the stock market closed up a record 102 points." Good God: 102 points! Now what do I do?

Mark Singer

Anne Hall

Errol Morris got in touch with Mark Singer at *The New Yorker* and asked him to write a book about Randall Adams, a man jailed in Texas for murder. Singer refused. For one thing, Morris was already making a documentary film about Adams. For another, Singer looked at Morris's films and decided to write about Morris instead.

Characters in Morris's films rambled on about seemingly inconsequential subjects that eventually started adding up. Singer sensed a connection to his own writings about people who operate dog washes, repair zippers, or attend murder trials as entertainment.

"I was interested in the same issues," Singer said. "His view of the world is, I think, a highly evolved and refined version of what my view of the world had been up to that point. You deal with people and their stories in an ironic way, or you can even deal with abstract ideas if you then try to fix to a human narrative in an ironic way. I'm as proud of the Morris piece as anything I've done, for that reason. I was really caught up in that whole story."

Mark Singer's "Talk of the Town" pieces and major articles from *The New Yorker* are collected in *Mr. Personality* (1990). His other book, *Funny Money* (1985), tells about the failure of a small bank in Oklahoma that had brokered so many oil loans to big financial institutions that it almost dragged the huge Seafirst, Northern Trust, and Continental Illinois banks down with it.

"Predilections" took a long time to write, Singer said. When he started the reporting, Morris was still filming *The Thin Blue Line*. "I had the time to wait and see what happened with the film, to see what happened to Randall Adams. I did have to write a little epilogue, because Morris was later sued by Randall Adams. It was totally fitting, in a way. It added a wonderful ironic touch."

Singer generally has avoided portraying celebrities—although Morris became a minor celebrity after *The Thin Blue Line*—because, as he says, "I wasn't going to ask them a question they hadn't been asked before and they weren't going to give me an answer they hadn't given previously." However, he's currently writing an investigative report, and a social history of the late 1960s, about someone involved with a celebrity: Brett Coleman Kimberlin, resident of a federal prison, who says he sold marijuana to former Vice President Dan Quayle.

Predilections

Among the nonfiction movies that Errol Morris has at one time or another been eager to make but has temporarily abandoned for lack of investor enthusiasm are *Ablaze!* (or *Fire From Heaven*), an examination of the phenomenon of spontaneous human combustion; *Whatever Happened to Einstein's Brain?* (portions of the cerebellum and the cerebral cortex are thought to be in the possession of a doctor in North Carolina, other parts are floating around here and there); *Road*, the story of one man's attempt to build across northern Minnesota an interstate highway that no one else wanted; *Insanity Inside Out*, based on the book of the same title, by Kenneth Donaldson, a man who, in his forties, was wrongly committed by his parents to a mental hospital and got stuck there for fifteen years; *Weirdo*, about the breeding of a giant chicken; *The Wizard of Wendover*, about Robert K. Golka and his laser-induced fireball experiments in Utah; and a perusal of Yap, a South Pacific island where stone money is the traditional currency.

Some months ago, Morris attended a meeting with executives of Home Box Office, his primary motive being, as they say in the movie business, to pitch an idea—in that case, the one involving Einstein's brain. The meeting did not go particularly well. An HBO person at one point said admonishingly, "You know, your movies are ironic. Our viewers just don't like irony."

Groping for a more tactful evasion, another HBO person said, "We're already doing a transplant movie."

"But wait a second," Morris replied. "This brain hasn't *been* transplanted—*yet*."

Unapologetically, Morris draws his films fresh from the substance of the real world, where irony has a way of running riot. Describing his work, he goes to some lengths to avoid using the term "documentary" ("the 'D' word," he will say, in a pinch), but he has not yet coined an alternative label that a Hollywood publicist might use to characterize a generic Errol Morris movie. During the past twelve years, he has directed and released three films: *Gates of Heaven*, about two pet cemeteries in northern California; *Vernon, Florida*, a series of interviews with several residents of a swamp town in Florida; and *The Thin Blue Line*, which arrived in theaters around the country last summer and fall, and which Morris has described, not immodestly, as "the first murder mystery that actually solves a murder." An Errol Morris movie features real people talking uninterrupted, mainly about literal objects or events, only occasionally about feelings or ideas: trafficking in entertaining truths as well as in equally entertaining transparent prevarications; free-associating, it often seems, as if the camera were a psychotherapist whose expensive time it would be a pity to squander on silence.

Near the midpoint of *Gates of Heaven*, which was completed in 1978, a woman with a pinched mouth whose age might be anywhere from seventy to eighty-five sits in a chair before an open doorway. She is never identified, but, it happens, her name is Florence Rasmussen. In a manner that alternates between passive and bold, accented by facial expressions that range from beatific to sinister, Florence Rasmussen soliloquizes elegiacally:

"I'm raised on a farm, we had chickens and pigs and cows and sheep and everything. But down here I've been lost. Now they've taken them all away from here up to that—What's the name of that place? Up above here a little ways? That town? Commences with a 'B.' Blue. It's— Blue Hill Cemetery, I think the name of it is. Not too far, I guess, about maybe twenty miles from here. A little town there, a little place. You know where it's at. But I was really surprised when I heard they were getting rid of the cemetery over here. Gonna put in buildings or something over there. Ah well, I know people been very good to me, you know. Well, they see my condition, I guess, must of felt sorry for me. But it's real, my condition is. It's not put on. That's for sure! Boy, if I could only walk. If I could only get out. Drive my car. I'd get *another* car. Ya . . . and my son, if he was only better to me. After I bought him that car. He's got a nice car. I bought it myself just a short time ago. I don't know. These kids—the more you do for them . . . He's my grandson, but I raised him from two years old. . . . I don't see him very often. And he just got the car. I didn't pay for all of it. I gave him four hundred dollars. Pretty good! His boss knows it. Well, he's not working for that outfit now. He's changed. He's gone back on his old job—hauling sand. *No*, not hauling sand; he's working in the office. That's right. He took over the office job. His boss told me that on the phone. But, you know, he should help me more. He's all I got. He's the one who brought me up here. And then put me here by myself among strangers. It's terrible, you stop and think of it. I've been without so much, when I first come up here. Ya. It's what half of my trouble is from—him not being home with me. Didn't cost him nothing to stay here. Every time he need money, he'd always come, 'Mom, can I have this? Can I have that?' But he never pays back. Too good, too easy—that's what everybody tells me. I quit now. I quit. Now he's got the office job, I'm going after him. I'm going after him good, too—if I have to go in . . . in a different way. He's going to pay that money. He's got the office job now. And he makes good money anyway. And he has no kids. He has not married. Never get married, he says. He was married once—they're divorced. Well, she tried to take him for the kid, but she didn't. They went to court. It was somebody else's kid. She was nothing but a tramp in the first place. I told him that. He wouldn't listen to me. I says, 'I know what she is.' I said, 'Richard, please, listen to me.' He wouldn't listen. He knew all, he knew everything. Big shot! But he soon found out. Now that's all over with. I've been through so much I don't know how I'm staying alive. Really, for my age . . . If you're young, it's different. But I've always said I'm never going to grow old. I've always had that, and the people that I tell how old I am, they don't believe me, because people my age as a rule don't get around like I do."

With an arresting instinct for symmetry, Florence Rasmussen manages to contradict most of what she has to say. It seems that she knows certain things, but then, in the next moment, she trots out contrary information: I have roots with the earth; I'm lost in this world. People have been very good to me; I'm all alone, surrounded by strangers, my own flesh and blood treats me badly. I have a health problem that's real; I protest too much. I'd like to drive my car; but I might not even have a car any longer, might have to buy a new one. I bought my son—O. K., he's not my son, he's my grandson—a new car; well, I didn't pay for the whole thing, I gave him four hundred dollars, but anyway I want my money back. His boss—Hold on, he has a different boss. He hauls sand for a living; nope, he's got that office job now. He's not the marrying kind; he was married once. He has no children; he's been involved in a paternity suit. I'll never grow old; I'm so old people can't believe it. Even though I can't walk, people my age as a rule don't get around like I do.

Gates of Heaven gives an account of a pet cemetery that fails and one that succeeds; Mrs. Rasmussen refers to each in only a glancing manner. The first day that Morris set out as a bona fide film director with an actual film crew was the day the residents of the failed pet cemetery were being exhumed, so that they could be transferred to the other cemetery. The cinematographer Morris had engaged to shoot *Gates of Heaven* he fired that same day—a consequence of serious philosophical differences that culminated in a physical struggle for the camera. ("It's *mine*!" "No, it's *mine!*") Day Two, Morris met Florence Rasmussen, and she became the first person with whom he ever filmed an interview. The footage from that interview didn't make it into the final cut, however, because the replacement camera operator, a woman, felt compelled to engage the interviewee in a dialogue. When Mrs. Rasmussen mused "Well, here today, gone tomorrow. Right?" the camerawoman said "No. Wrong." Morris couldn't decide which made him angrier—that the camerawoman had interfered with the interview or that her notions about death and the hereafter were so misguided. In any event, he fired her on the spot and hired a replacement, who lasted three or four days.

One of Morris's techniques is to situate his interview subject in a chair (when possible, a specific chair: a lightweight canvas-and-metal-frame low-back Regista) that is a precise distance (forty-nine inches) from the camera, which is equipped with a 25-mm Zeiss high-speed prime lens—a lens of fixed focal length, which is one that cannot zoom—and is secured to a tripod, so that the camera cannot pan. When Morris went back to reshoot Mrs. Rasmussen—accompanied by Ned Burgess, his fourth, and final, cinematographer—she rewarded him with what has become the emblem of the Morris style: a seamless monologue from someone who has been allowed to talk until the truth naturally sorts itself out. Quotidian lies, the little fabrications that make the commerce of daily life possible, if not always palatable, are laid on the surface by the speaker. A muted strain of implicit skepticism—the silent voice of the filmmaker—bubbles along just beneath that. Peripheral stuff turns out to matter. "I like the idea of making films about ostensibly absolutely nothing," Morris says. "I like the irrelevant, the tangential, the sidebar excursion to nowhere that suddenly becomes revelatory. That's what all my movies are about. That and the idea that we're in possession of certainty, truth, infallible knowledge, when actually we're just a bunch of apes running around. My films are about people who think they're connected to something, although they're really not."

Gates of Heaven is the only one of Morris's films that can be said to have emerged with its original subject matter intact. *The Thin Blue Line*, which at its inception was to have been a study of Dr. James Grigson, a Texas psychiatrist who regularly testifies for the prosecution in death-penalty cases, instead became a horrifyingly satiric examination of the wrongful murder conviction and near-execution of an innocent man. *Vernon, Florida*, which is essentially plotless—a pastiche of interviews with a turkey hunter, a policeman, a retired couple who are convinced that a glass jar in their possession contains radioactive sand that grows, a wild-animal collector, a Holy Roller preacher, a worm farmer, and others—evolved haphazardly, almost desperately, from an unwieldy idea Morris had of making a fiction film based upon a bizarre insurance scam. A loquacious man named Albert Bitterling, who appears intermittently throughout *Vernon, Florida*, has held a pair of opera glasses against the lens of a camera and photographed the night sky. In one scene, displaying the opaque result, he says, "Of course, as you can see that picture ain't too good, it's a cheap camera, you get a cheap picture." Then, speaking literally and in metaphor, he encapsulates the filmmaker's dilemma: "Well, of course, you see, when you have a camera . . . You have a camera and you point it at a certain—Just like if you had a gun. You don't shoot, do you? Well, if you had a gun and you pointed it at something, you're liable to hit what you're pointing at, and then again you might not."

Vernon, Florida has been, as a practical matter, the least accessible of Morris's films; it was completed in 1981, but a commercial videocassette version of it has just been released. Videocassettes of *Gates of Heaven* became available only a few months ago. *The Thin Blue Line* is the first of Morris's films to be widely distributed in theaters. A word that regularly comes up when Morris discusses the until quite recent low-orbit trajectory of his career is "disturbing." The frustration of making movies that only modest numbers of people have seen, or even heard of, has encouraged Morris to cultivate a melodramatic haplessness. In a less ironically disposed person, this tendency might be taken for neurotic self-indulgence. When Morris consents to be the interviewee—when it becomes his turn to sort the truth out—he ends up quoting Shakespeare ("But since the affairs of men rest still uncertain, let's reason with the worst that may befall") or himself ("The fact that the world is, like, utterly insane makes it tolerable"). Once, when I made the mistake of asking, in an offhand manner, how he'd been feeling lately, he said, "I've been horribly depressed, which, as you know, can be terribly time-consuming. I mean, if you're going to do it right, that is." Another time, en route to a preview screening of *The Thin Blue Line*, he said, "I hope this won't be terribly embarrassing." A pause, then: "No, actually, I remember, when I was a teenager, thinking there was no point in going on, but then I realized that life is just an endless series of embarrassments and I'd hate to miss out on all that."

The first time I met Morris was in an airport, on a day in early 1987, when he was still working on *The Thin Blue Line* and was flying to Dallas to attend a federal-court hearing. He wore a navy pin-striped suit, carried a briefcase, and could easily have masqueraded as a typical traveling litigator except that he was not flying first class. Days when he doesn't wear a suit, he dresses like a permanent graduate student—

khakis, Black Watch blazer or tweed jacket, button-down shirt, dark-framed Clark Kentish eyeglasses. He has short dark-brown hair, which often looks as if it had been slept on the wrong way, and a rueful, asymmetrical smile. Although he is six-one, imperfect posture renders his presence less than imposing. Photographs make him appear either darkly handsome or dolefully goofy. Morris is now forty-one years old. He grew up in Hewlett, on the South Shore of Long Island. His father, a doctor, died when he was two, and his mother, a Juilliard graduate, who did not remarry for more than twenty years, supported him and an older brother by teaching music in a public school. Errol studied cello, read with a passion the forty-odd "Oz" books, watched a lot of television, and on a regular basis went with a doting but not quite right maiden aunt ("I guess you'd have to say that Aunt Roz was somewhat demented") to Saturday matinées, where he saw stuff like *This Island Earth* and *Creature From the Black Lagoon*—horror movies that, viewed again thirty years later, still seem scary to him. "I don't really understand how Errol got drawn to these themes that interest him—maybe that he lost his father," his mother, Cinnabelle Esterman, told me not long ago. "I remember the first time we went on a trip out West. We had to take a flight to Chicago, and a friend drove us to the airport. And I noticed that along the way, in the car, Errol was reading the *World Almanac*, studying about air crashes." In the tenth grade, he was enrolled in the Putney School, in Vermont. Part of what had drawn him to Putney was its highly regarded music program. Morris's most vivid memories, however, include having a forbidden radio confiscated because one evening he made the mistake of loudly singing along while listening to Birgit Nilsson perform the immolation scene from *Götterdämmerung*. On another occasion, for an offense that he cannot recall, a dormitory proctor deprived him of his cello.

Next came the University of Wisconsin, where he excelled academically ("the first time I did really well at anything, except elementary school") and, in 1969, received a degree in history. For a couple of years, he drifted about, earning money as a cable-television salesman in Wisconsin and as a term-paper writer in Massachusetts and "trying to get accepted at different graduate schools just by showing up on their doorstep." This strategy, which did not succeed at Oxford and Harvard, finally worked at Princeton, but graduate school soon proved to have been not such a hot idea. Morris's mistake was in pursuing academic disciplines—at Princeton, the history of science—in which he had "absolutely no background."

"I did enter Princeton actually thinking I was going to get a doctorate," he says. "I was wrong. I had big fights with my adviser. I was supposed to be concentrating on the history of physics. And, naturally, my adviser expected me to take all these courses in physics. But the classes were always full of fourteen-year-old Chinese prodigies, with their hands in the air—'Call on me! Call on me!' I couldn't do it. I reneged on some of my commitments. At the end, my adviser actually assaulted me. He was on sabbatical and had an office at the Institute for Advanced Study. I remembered thinking, This is the Institute for Advanced Study, and he's *assaulting* me. I'd written a thirty-page double-spaced paper, and he produced thirty single-spaced pages of his own criticizing it. The bile just flowed out of him. I accused him of not even finishing reading what I'd written. It turns out I *was* a problem, but at least I wasn't a drudge, and that school was filled with drudges. I remember saying to my adviser, 'You won't even look through my telescope.' And his response was 'Errol, it's not a telescope, it's a kaleidoscope.' "

In 1972, Morris moved to Berkeley, where he had been accepted as a Ph.D. candidate in philosophy at the University of California. His recollections of that experience also lack a warm glow, but something fundamentally positive did take place, which was that he discovered the Pacific Film Archive, a cinémathèque/library/revival house/symposium center, and the only place in the Bay Area with the ability to devote several days to a retrospective of, say, the cinema of Senegal. Tom Luddy, a film producer, who was then the director of the Archive, recently said, "There were a bunch of regulars and a bunch of eccentric regulars, and Errol was one of the eccentrics. I often had to defend him to my staff. What made him eccentric? Well, for one thing, he dressed strangely. Remember, this is Berkeley in the early seventies. And Errol was wearing dark suits with pants that were too short, white dress shirts, and heavy shoes. He looked like a New York person gone to seed. Then, I let him use our library for research, and he was always getting into little frictions with the staff. He felt he could both use the Archive and put it down. He would leave messes. He never bothered to reshelve books. I found myself defending him, which was often difficult, because he would attack me for the programming. He was a film-noir nut. He claimed we weren't showing the *real* film noir. So I challenged him to write the program notes. Then, there was his habit of sneaking into the films and denying that he was sneaking in. I told him if he was sneaking in he should at least admit he was doing it."

The Archive opened each afternoon at five-thirty. Among the other eccentric regulars were a superannuated Berkeley professor who had a habit of showing up at 5:30 A.M.; the narcoleptic who used to come for the first show, immediately fall asleep, and remain that way through the final feature; a disconcertingly loud laugher, known as the Cackler;

and a misanthropic woman who, with her dog, lived in a van outside the Archive.

Meanwhile, Morris's academic career failed to thrive. "Berkeley was just a world of pedants," he says. "It was truly shocking. I spent two or three years in the philosophy program. I have very bad feelings about it." His own flaw, he believes, was that he was "an odd combination of the academic and the prurient." While he was supposed to be concentrating on the philosophy of science, his attention became diverted by an extracurricular interest in the insanity plea. A quotation from "The Black Cat"—a story in which Edgar Allan Poe writes of "the spirit of perverseness . . . this unfathomable longing of the soul *to vex itself* . . . to do wrong for the wrong's sake only"—had become resonant for him, and he began to ponder the metaphysics of mass murder. In 1975, he returned to Wisconsin long enough to have several interviews with Ed Gein, the real-life prototype for the Norman Bates character in *Psycho* and a midwestern legend. "You couldn't spend long in Wisconsin, especially with my predilection, without hearing a lot about Ed Gein," Morris says. Gein was then confined to Central State Hospital, in Waupun, a maximum-security institution for the criminally insane. Evidently, Morris was the first person in quite a while to make a special effort to talk with him. What perhaps discouraged other potential visitors was that Gein not only murdered people but also was a cannibal, a grave robber, and an amateur taxidermist. Morris found his way to Dr. George Arndt, a Geinologist and the author of a study—a catalogue of Ed Gein jokes, basically—titled *Community Reaction to a Horrifying Event.*

"I go and meet Dr. Arndt," Morris says. "Almost from the beginning, I entertain serious doubts about the wholesomeness of Dr. Arndt's interest in the Gein case. Dr. Arndt seems real excited that there's this kindred spirit interested in the Ed Gein story. I tell him I've been spending a lot of time in Plainfield, Wisconsin, where Ed Gein lived and committed his crimes. I tell him I've been to the Plainfield cemetery to look at graves. I had the names of the graves whose occupants Ed had exhumed. I noticed that those graves made a circle around his mother's grave. Dr. Arndt looks at me and says, 'You know what that means, don't you?' I say, 'No, sir.' He says, 'It's a kind of sublimation. Transference. He couldn't go down directly after his mother. He had to go down through the other graves.' He says, 'There may be underground tunnels leading to his mother's grave.' So we go in his Cadillac to the Plainfield cemetery. When we're almost there, he pulls over and starts looking around in the brush for something, and he comes up with a big thick stick. We get to the cemetery, we find the graves where the exhumations took place, and he has me put my ear to the ground near

Mrs. Gein's grave. While I do that, Dr. Arndt walks around beating the ground, searching for hollow sounds. I hear nothing. Finally, I ask, 'Dr. Arndt, why didn't he just dig straight into Mrs. Gein's grave?' And Dr. Arndt gives me this look and says, *'Too devious.'* "

During his research, Morris stumbled across the provocative fact that Plainfield, with a population of seven hundred, had within a ten-year period been home to several multiple killers, and that Gein's depredations had antedated the others', almost as if he had driven the town mad.

"One of the things that have always fascinated me about abnormal behavior is that we can't really explain it to our satisfaction," Morris says. "Almost everything I do now in my work is about epistemic concerns: how do we come by certain kinds of knowledge? Take the insanity plea—we talk about insane acts and insane people. When we talk about insane acts, we're saying we don't understand something about the act itself. When we say someone is insane, we're either saying, one, 'That person could be mentally ill,' or, two, 'I don't *know* why that person does what he does.' Rather than expressing a knowledge, we're expressing a *lack* of knowledge. I wrote an essay on the insanity plea and movie monsters and certain mechanistic fantasies we have about criminal behavior. I very much wanted to write a doctoral thesis on this stuff, and it hurt my feelings when Berkeley just sort of kicked my ass out of there."

The demise of Morris's academic career was a protracted matter, and he stayed at the university long enough to get a master's degree in philosophy. All the while, he was a devotee of the Pacific Film Archive. Tom Luddy introduced him to Werner Herzog, the German director, whose fascination with fanatics, losers, Nazi supermen, and dwarfs dovetailed with Morris's outside-the-mainstream preoccupations. Once, making the film *Even Dwarfs Started Small*, Herzog inadvertently set a dwarf afire; the dwarf survived, and Herzog did penance by throwing himself onto a cactus. At the time he and Morris met, Morris's reading diet included, in addition to his academic texts, the *National Enquirer* and *Weekly World News*. For listeners whom he deemed worthy, he had assembled an endlessly digressive repertoire that included eyewitness tales of Geinology and other vignettes of American dementia.

"Werner was very taken with Errol," Luddy recalls, adding that, despite Morris's never having shot a single foot of film, "Werner treated him as an equal."

Morris and Herzog discussed the question that Morris and Dr. Arndt had left unanswered—whether or not Gein had disinterred his mother—and they set a date for a rendezvous in Plainfield in the summer of 1975. The idea was that, with shovels, in the moonlight, they

would satisfy their curiosity. When Herzog arrived in Plainfield, however—he had been working on a film in Alaska and was now driving
toward New York—no familiar face was there to greet him. He made a
phone call to California and learned that Morris had had second
thoughts. A few months later, Morris did return to Plainfield, alone,
and rented a room from Ed Gein's next-door neighbors. This time, he
stayed almost a year, during which he conducted hundreds of hours of
interviews with some of the other homicidally inclined local talent. He
had no focused idea of what to do with the material. Maybe he would
make a film about Ed Gein called *Digging Up the Past*, or maybe he
would write a book. Although he still had a fellowship at the University
of California, he didn't have enough money to transcribe all his interview tapes. Some supplementary financial support came from his family, but it was not unqualified support. "My mother was worried about
what I was doing," he says. "She has this wonderfully euphemistic way
of talking to me. At one point, she said, 'Errol, can't you spend more
time with people your own age?' And I said, 'But, Mom, some of these
mass murderers *are* my own age.' "

It didn't do Morris any good when, in order to talk to one of the
Plainfield murderers, he made his way illegally into a state mental hospital, got caught, and was reported to his academic supervisors at
Berkeley. In the fall of 1976, while Morris was still in Plainfield, Herzog
unexpectedly returned. During Herzog's visit the previous year, his car
had broken down, and he had discovered an automobile-repair shop—
a grim place set against a grim, flat natural backdrop—that struck him
as an excellent movie location. So now he had come to finish a film,
Stroszek, most of which had been shot in Berlin. He asked Morris to
work with him, but Morris felt that he had been abused. "Stealing a
landscape," he complained. "The worst kind of plagiarism." On the other
hand, he had never made a film himself, and here was a chance to observe
a master. So he stuck around, and when the shooting was completed Herzog, afflicted with some measure of guilt, handed him an envelope
stuffed with cash. They were in a motel room. Morris went to a window
and tossed the envelope into a parking lot. After retrieving the money,
Herzog offered it once more, saying, "Please don't do that again."

The envelope contained about two thousand dollars—more than
enough to finance a two-week trip Morris had been planning. Recently,
he had read a newspaper article about an insurance investigator which
mentioned, in passing, how several people in an unidentified Southern
town had tried to collect benefits after "accidentally" losing limbs. Morris had tracked down the insurance investigator and learned that the
town was Vernon (pop. 883), in the Florida panhandle. Vernon's unof-

ficial nickname was now Nub City. In the hierarchy of nubbiedom, the supremely rewarding self-sacrifice was the loss of a right leg and a left arm, because, so the theory went, "afterward, you could still write your name and still have a foot to press the gas pedal of your Cadillac." Morris stayed in Vernon long enough to read some files at the courthouse, talk to an insurance broker and several nubbies, and receive at least one unambiguous death threat. At the Cat's Eye Tavern one night, a citizen twice Morris's size smiled as he extinguished a cigarette on the lapel of Morris's blazer. Morris remembers thinking that perhaps he had packed the wrong clothes. Also, "I remember it hurt my feelings, because it seemed that, you know, maybe the people in Vernon didn't like me." Rarely did murders take place in Vernon, because, someone explained, "down here, people don't get murdered—they just disappear."

Back in Berkeley, Morris tried to write a script for a fiction feature to be called *Nub City*. Mainly, he had a pitch line—*Nub City* would be "about people who in order to achieve the American dream literally become a fraction of themselves"—but the plot elements were still gestating. Months went by and he made only slight progress. One afternoon while waiting for inspiration to descend, he was eating lunch in the Swallow, a restaurant in the same building as the Pacific Film Archive, and he saw a headline in the *San Francisco Chronicle* that said, "450 DEAD PETS GOING TO NAPA VALLEY." Suddenly, he had an altogether different idea for a film; *Nub City* would have to wait.

It was enough that in deciding to make *Gates of Heaven* Morris selected a subject that, on its surface, seemed highly likely to repel. He also insisted on making a documentary film "the opposite of how you were supposed to." That meant being static and obtrusive—using artificial light and heavy, earthbound equipment rather than the standard handheld, mobile tools of cinema verité. After Morris hooked up with Ned Burgess, a compliant cinematographer, the making of *Gates of Heaven* progressed in a straight-forward fashion. The film was shot in the spring and summer of 1977 and cost a hundred and twenty thousand dollars to make; the money came from a wealthy graduate-school classmate and from Morris's family.

Getting to know mass murderers and their relatives in Wisconsin, Morris had developed an interview technique that, reduced to basics, amounted to: Shut up and let people talk. "Listening to what people were saying wasn't even important," he says. "But it was important to *look* as if you were listening to what people were saying. Actually, listening to what people are saying, to me, interferes with looking as if you were listening to what people are saying."

The first half of *Gates of Heaven* explores the broken dream of a man named Floyd McClure, who lives in Los Altos, a peninsula town thirty miles south of San Francisco. In the opening frames, McClure describes, in a sincere but unmaudlin manner, how the accidental death of a beloved collie in his childhood inspired his vision of a pet cemetery. Choosing a site, he settled on what he calls "the most beautiful piece of land, as far as I was concerned, in the whole valley." (Never mind that the land was situated right next to a freeway; it also happened to be across the street from his house.) "A pet-cemetery business is not a fast-buck scheme, it's not a suede-shoe game," McClure says. "It's a good, solid business enterprise. And in order to have this concept it has to be in your heart, not in your billfold. And these are the type of people I wanted in business with me, in the pet-cemetery *concept*." His co-investors in the by now failed enterprise allow themselves to be interviewed, the owner of a rendering plant talks, families of departed pets have their say, Florence Rasmussen appears. Monologues tend not to parse. At one point, McClure says, "And this is the part of the inspiration of getting our little pets . . . into a cemetery. Something that we could be proud of, of saying 'My little pet did his chore here—that God has sent him to us to do a chore—love and be loved and serve his master.' And, boy, these little pets that did that . . . Like I said before—death is for the living and not for the dead."

The second half of *Gates of Heaven* focuses on the Harberts family—Cal and his wife, Scottie, and their sons, Dan and Phil—who are the proprietors of Bubbling Well Pet Memorial Park, the *final* final resting place of the displaced tenants of Floyd McClure's doomed pet-cemetery concept. Dan, the younger son, has been employed in the family business for a few years. Phil has recently given up selling insurance in Utah (his idol is W. Clement Stone, the Chicago insurance tycoon and an avatar of the Positive Mental Attitude) and has repatriated to the Napa Valley.

Cal Harberts says, "We created the Garden of Honor. And in this garden we will bury a Seeing Eye dog or a police dog killed in the line of duty at *no* cost—*if* it's killed in the line of duty. And for anybody else who wants to share this garden then we created a price which amounts to more than any other garden that we have."

Phil, who manifests what might or might not be symptoms of an incipient existential crisis—possibly a consequence of having listened to and delivered too many motivational lectures—says, "I have to say to myself: What does it mean to me? What does *this* mean to me? What is it going to mean to me? I recognize this and—A couple of things when I was instructing motivation back in Salt Lake City is that if we don't stop and ask ourselves a question once in a while to probe our subconscious or to probe our conscious . . . I used to teach it. It's a plain, simple formula. We reduced everything to a formula, memorized it, and therefore we were able to repeat it constantly. I used to call it the R2-A2 formula: Recognize, Relate, Assimilate, and put into Action! Like, I could be driving down the freeway and see a 450 SL. I could say, 'Hey, I like that. What does that mean to me? What would I have to do to get it? How can I do it?' And then go to work for it. And strive for it. It kind of makes life easy. I think that's why a lot of people don't—They get frustrated. They have emotional problems, it's that they don't know how to cope with their—*mind*. There are three things that I've got to do and that if anybody wants to do to be successful, to have the desire, the want-to. Why do you go to work in the morning? *Gee, why am I here?* Because you want to. But that's obvious. And then the next very important ingredient is something that a lot of people and a lot of businesses fail to delve into. It's the activity knowledge. It would be the equation to a mathematical problem. It would be equal to the chemist's ability to emulsify chemicals—you know, properly, the valences. But the knowledge of it, the whole scope. Everything in detail. And then the third element would be, of course, the know-how or the experience. I have the inspiration to action. I don't have the activity knowledge, but I'm getting the know-how before I'm getting the activity knowledge. As a matter of fact, I'm getting more know-how than I'm getting activity knowledge. But they can be correlated together. They can be overlapped."

Dan Harberts says, "As far as preparation—a hole has to be dug, prepared. We have to make sure that the hole is going to fit the size of the casket. Because you don't want to make it too large, because you're going to waste space. And you don't want to make it too small, because you can't get the thing in there."

Gates of Heaven was first shown during the 1978 New York Film Festival, which happened to coincide with a newspaper strike. In other words, *Gates of Heaven* sprang into a void. When the film opened in Berkeley, that same year, a glowing review by Michael Covino appeared in the *East Bay Express*. (Covino later retooled the essay, and it was published in *Film Quarterly*.) More than two years elapsed before *Gates of Heaven* was seen again, in New York or anywhere else—before anyone paid significant attention. In the spring of 1981, New Yorker Films arranged a limited national distribution. The notices were favorable—in several instances, extravagantly so. Perhaps the most ardent champion of *Gates of Heaven* across the years has been Roger Ebert, who includes it in his list of the ten best films of all time and calls it "compulsively watchable, a film that has engaged me as no other movie has in my twenty-one years as a movie critic." When Ebert is invited to give a speech and is told that he can screen a film of his choosing, he selects *Gates of Heaven*, which he regards as "a film about hope—hope held by the loneliest people who have ever been on film." Ebert estimates that he has seen it at least fifty times—often enough to have memorized long passages. "Every time I show this, it plays differently," he says. "Some people think it's about animals. Some people think it's about life and death. I've shown it to a group of bankers, who believe it raises all kinds of questions about success, about starting a small business. People think it's funny or sad or deadpan or satirical. They think that Errol Morris loved the people in the film, or that he was being very cruel to them. I've never yet had a person tell me that it's a bad film or a film that doesn't interest them."

Werner Herzog commemorated the Berkeley première of *Gates of Heaven* by eating one of his shoes—a poached desert boot—in a public ceremony. Though less spectacular than flinging oneself upon a cactus, this event was sufficiently momentous for the documentary filmmaker Les Blank to record it in a twenty-minute short titled *Werner Herzog Eats His Shoe*. A haze of myth enshrouds the genesis of the shoe-eating. Tom Luddy's version has Herzog, while one day arguing with Morris in a hallway of the Pacific Film Archive, saying, "You'll never make a film, but if you do I'll come and eat my shoe at the première." Herzog maintains that it happened in a more encouraging manner, as in "You are going to make a film. And the day I am going to see the film in a theater I will eat the shoes I am wearing." Morris, who claims not to recall any of the above, says the entire stunt was concocted by Luddy.

"I didn't make *Gates of Heaven* so that Werner Herzog would have to eat his shoe," he says. "It's not as if I decided to realize my potential as a human being in order to get somebody to ingest something distasteful. I specifically asked Werner *not* to eat his shoe." Morris was supposed to fly from New York to Berkeley to attend the screening and to appear in Les Blank's film. At Kennedy Airport, he boarded a plane, but when a mechanical problem forced all the passengers to get off he decided not to go. "As a result, I don't appear in *Werner Herzog Eats His Shoe*," he says. "I suppose I regret that reticence. Why be so prissy? Why try so hard to control things? I'm not even sure what that's all about. Probably, as a result of my petulant behavior, fewer people have seen *Gates of Heaven* than otherwise would have. In fact, I'm still surprised when anyone tells me he's seen it."

In the winter of 1979, Morris went back to Vernon, Florida, and for very little money he was able to rent one of the biggest houses in the county. Vernon was no less xenophobic than any other small southern town. When the locals asked Morris why he had come there and he gave vague, misleading answers, the typical response was "No, you're here because of the Nub City stuff." He spent much of his time attending revival meetings and driving around to places that had interesting names—Blackhead, Lizard Lake, the Ebro Dog Track. Although he was still enamored of the Nub City idea, he had not yet written a workable screenplay. If he were to try to make a nonfiction film about the Nub City episode, "it would turn into one of those bad investigative documentaries where people are slamming doors in your face." Finally, after several months of insisting "I'm not here about Nub City, I'm not making a film about Nub City," guilt overwhelmed him, he indeed became incapable of making a film about Nub City, and he left town.

A year later, he returned, rented the same big house, and spun his wheels some more. Now, however, vacillation carried a steeper price tag, because he had financial help from German television and from WNET, the public-television affiliate in New York. A crew of recent graduates from the New York University film school drove to Vernon in a rented van, bringing with them equipment so heavy that the van blew out two sets of tires on the drive south. When they arrived, Morris had still not decided what the film would be about. A controversy had arisen involving the firing and rehiring of one of the local police officers. Morris felt that the officer's travails were connected with "the Napoleonic ambitions of the king of the nubbies." The king of the nubbies had advised Morris to leave town within twenty-four hours or leave in a casket. When Morris failed to oblige, the king made what seemed a sincere effort to run down Ned Burgess, the cinematographer, with a truck. More or less in desperation—to get the king of the nubbies off his back, to give the public-television people something, *anything*, for their money—Morris began to film interviews with various interesting citizens of Vernon, among them Roscoe Collins, the cop; Joy Payne, the collector of wild animals (opossum, gopher, tortoise, rattlesnake); Albert Bitterling, the cosmologist with the opera glasses ("Reality—you mean, *this* is the real world? Ha, ha, ha. I never thought of that"); George Harris and Claude Register, two geezers who discuss how an acquaintance put a shotgun to his forehead and pulled the trigger with his big toe ("And he said, that day, he says, 'That'll be the last thing I ever do is to shoot myself.' Which it was"). *Vernon, Florida* contains not a single reference to Nub City. Rather, as with *Gates of Heaven*, the film's subjects are the American vernacular and the malleability of truth. Morris presents Vernon, Florida, as is—no special effects, what you see is what you get—as if he had stumbled across, and without editorial intrusion had agreed to share, an unexplored settlement full of Florence Rasmussens.

Howard Pettis, the worm farmer, says, "I've never studied no book on these wigglers. What I know about 'em is just self-experience. They got books on 'em, but them books is wrong. They don't teach you right. They don't teach you right on 'em. Teach you what kind of feed to feed 'em. How to do 'em and all, there. And it's all wrong, in my book." Henry Shipes, the turkey hunter ("I can't tell you how it feel. It's just a hell of a sport, that's all"), sits in a chair in his living room and, with enormous relish, recounts the gut-stirring thrills of each of a series of trophy kills. While the viewer is not prohibited from imputing deep meanings to the images or the monologues of Henry Shipes, one ultimately gets the feeling that if turkey hunting stands as a metaphor for anything it is probably turkey hunting. In the film's final scene, Henry Shipes, on a hunt, surveys a crowd of buzzards roosting on a cypress tree and counts them aloud—thirty-five. "Listen to that sound," he says. "That *fwoop fwoop*. Hear that sound? Getting in and out of the trees? That flop-flop sound? Mmm-hmm. That sound'll sure mistake you for turkeys. Listen! Hear that flop-flop? Limbs breaking. Hear that good flop then? Listening to that gives me the *turkey fever*. Mmm-hmm. I wish there's as many turkeys as there are buzzards."

Like *Gates of Heaven*, *Vernon* had its première at the New York Film Festival—the 1981 edition. Werner Herzog called it "an invention of cinema, a discovery of one side of cinema that all of us have not known yet." A review in *Newsweek* said it was "a film as odd and mysterious as its subjects, and quite unforgettable"—unforgettable, that is, for those who laid eyes on it. Because it had a running time of only sixty minutes, no national distributor materialized, and not until the summer of 1982, when it was shown on public television, did significant numbers of viewers or critics take notice. Meanwhile, Morris was, as usual, low on funds. He was living in Manhattan, occupying rooms in a series of not quite elegant hotels—the Carter, the Bryant, the Edison, the Wellington—before finally settling in a building in the West Fifties, where he still keeps an apartment. The more dire his fiscal circumstances grew, the better he got to know a Mr. Montori, an employee of a collection agency. Mr. Montori seemed to derive pleasure from gracing Morris's telephone-answering machine with one-a-day rhetorical questions like "Mr. Morris, have you no sense of shame?" and "Mr. Morris, were you really brought up to act this way?" Then the calls abruptly ceased. After several months had passed, Morris phoned the collection agency, asked "Is Mr. Montori O.K.?," and learned that his tormentor had moved on to a more rewarding position elsewhere.

In earnest, Morris sought backing for what turned out to be some of his most resistible film projects: *Road*, the story of the northern Minnesota interstate-highway folly; Robert K. Golka, the laser-induced-fireball wizard in Utah; Centralia, Pennsylvania, the coal town where an inextinguishable subterranean fire began burning in 1962. Morris concluded that "people who tend to be interested in documentary filmmaking weren't interested in my films, because they didn't look like documentary films." The theme of *Road*, in particular—a man wants to create a complicated and expensive thing for which absolutely no need exists—was, he says, "disturbingly self-reflective."

As his debts accumulated, his stepfather advised him that the time had come to "turn yourself in to the phone company." Instead, Morris permitted himself a brief Hollywood interlude. In 1983, Edward Pressman, a producer whose credits include films by Brian De Palma, Terrence Malick, and Oliver Stone, agreed to finance the development of a screenplay about the exploits of John and Jim Pardue, brothers from Missouri who, fifteen years earlier, had killed their father, their grandmother, and two accomplices and robbed five banks, in two instances using dynamite. Pitching the film, Morris would say, "The great bank-robbery sprees always take place at a time when something is going wrong in the country. Bonnie and Clyde were apolitical, but it's impossible to imagine them without the Depression as a backdrop. The Pardue brothers were apolitical, but it's impossible to imagine them without Vietnam." Pressman underwrote a sojourn at the Chateau Marmont, a Hollywood hotel that is famous in part because John Belushi died there (not because Errol Morris wrote anything memorable while in residence). Morris enlisted Tom Waits and Mickey Rourke to portray the Pardue brothers, and got as far as writing a treatment before the project derailed.

Next, Morris was set to direct a Pressman film called *The King Lives*, about an Elvis Presley impersonator; this venture proceeded not very far before Morris was fired. For Dino De Laurentiis, Morris agreed to work on an adaptation of a Stephen King short story. Then De Laurentiis changed his mind and asked him to adapt a different King short story. Then he changed his mind again and gave Morris two and a half weeks to write a screenplay based on King's "Cycle of the Werewolf." Around the time that De Laurentiis rejected the script—because it "wasn't frightening enough"—Morris's brother and only sibling, Noel, died suddenly of a heart attack, at age forty. "I was very depressed," Morris says. His apartment in Manhattan was a couple of blocks from the Ed Sullivan Theater, from whose studios fund-raising telethons were often broadcast. He found himself dropping in. "My favorite was the Stop Arthritis Telethon," he says. "When I would go to these things, I would always see the same people in the audience, and I'd look upon them with some pity, and then I realized that I was one of them."

In 1984, Morris married Julia Sheehan, an art historian, whom he had met in Wisconsin in the mid-seventies, during his Ed Gein phase. Julia had tried to get a friend to introduce them, but the friend "made such a mess of it I actually approached Errol to apologize," she says. "I wanted to meet him because I'd heard he had been interviewing murderers. I didn't know anyone else who knew any murderers. It was quiet in Wisconsin—the sixties were over, not much was going on—so somebody who had met murderers sounded good." Morris recalls saying to her, early in their relationship, "I was talking to a mass murderer but I was thinking of you," and immediately fearing that this might not have sounded affectionate. Julia, however, was flattered: "I thought, really, that was one of the nicest things anyone ever said to me. It was hard to go out with other guys after that." They share a vivid and fond memory of their wedding, which took place in the Criminal Court Building in Brooklyn.

"They frisked us on the way in, which was very romantic," Julia says.

"We got married between two prostitution cases," Morris says. "And we celebrated with a whale-shaped cake from Carvel."

They have since become the parents of Nathaniel Hamilton Morris, and Julia has come to understand her husband well. Some time ago, she stopped in at the Strand Bookstore to pick up an order for him. The clerk who was helping her couldn't find the books and asked whether she knew the subject matter. "I don't know any of the titles," she said. "But they're probably about either insanity or murder or Nazis." Indeed, there was one of each.

"The Nazis, of course, are interesting to me," Morris once told me. "I just finished reading Joseph Goebbels's diary. You know a movie director Goebbels really liked? Frank Capra. I have this heartwarming image of Goebbels sneaking away from the office in midafternoon to go watch *Meet John Doe* or *Mr. Deeds Goes to Town*."

What Morris likes to call his "predilections" led him, in early 1985, to Dr. James Grigson, a Dallas psychiatrist. Under Texas law, a jury cannot impose the death penalty unless it is confident that a convicted person will commit future violent crimes. To encourage juries to arrive at that conclusion, Dr. Grigson for more than fifteen years regularly appeared as a prosecution witness in capital cases. In almost every instance, Dr. Grigson would, after examining a defendant, testify that he had found the individual in question to be an incurable sociopath, who it was "one hundred per cent certain" would kill again. When Morris first went to see Dr. Grigson, it was with the idea of making a film titled *Dr. Death*. Grigson proved to be as obliging to Morris as he had been to the prosecutors he served, and encouraged him to interview several men who, helped along by Dr. Grigson's testimony, had received the death penalty. Don't be surprised if these fellows profess their innocence, Dr. Grigson warned; that, after all, is how sociopaths behave.

A number of the twenty-five or so inmates with whom Morris spoke made such a claim. One was a thirty-six-year-old man named Randall Dale Adams, who was an inmate of the Eastham Unit, a maximum-security prison in southeast Texas. In the spring of 1977, Adams had been convicted of and sentenced to die for the murder, the previous fall, of Robert Wood, a Dallas police officer. Wood had been shot five times by the driver of a car that he and his partner, Teresa Turko, had stopped in west Dallas for a minor traffic violation. Nearly a month elapsed between the murder of Wood and Adams's arrest. Adams told Morris that he had been framed, and that the actual killer was David Harris—"the kid," he kept calling him during that first conversation—who had been the principal prosecution witness at Adams's trial. Morris had not gone to Texas with the purpose of finding and becoming an advocate for innocent incarcerated men; he had gone there because of his fascination with Dr. Grigson. He didn't really believe the story Adams told him, because he had no particular reason to believe it. Nevertheless, he went to Austin three weeks later and read the transcripts of several trials. A number of passages in the Adams transcript aroused the possibility that Adams was telling the truth. After Morris met David Harris, two weeks later, in a bar outside Beaumont, his doubts about Adams's guilt and his curiosity about the case deepened.

This came at a time when Morris's film career was in another lull. Suzanne Weil, then the head of programming for the Public Broadcasting System and a generous believer in Morris and his work, had arranged a grant sufficient for him to begin his research on *Dr. Death*. (She once told me, "Errol is the one person in the world who, if he now came to me and said, 'I want to make a documentary titled *My Grandmother Remembers* or *So-and-So: Potter of the Southwest*,' I would tell, 'Go ahead.'") Morris's main source of income at that point was free-lance employment with a private detective agency that specialized in Wall Street securities and commodities cases. Most of the agency's referrals came from law firms.

"When I worked as a detective, I felt like this well-paid conceptual cleaning lady for lawyers," he has said. "It's like—There seems to be hair clogging the drain. My job was to clean it out and find out if it was really hair. I had one particular problem: people would start talking to me and when I'd leave I often couldn't remember what they had said. I wanted to use a tape recorder, but my employer was totally opposed. So I worried about whether I was getting valuable information. I also worried about getting stains on my clothes—I had to wear suits all the time. Because I couldn't use a tape recorder, my most important piece of equipment was my can of K2r spot remover."

The owner of the detective agency, who prefers anonymity, told me that what he valued most about Morris was his talent as a listener—the talent that has served him so effectively as a filmmaker. What happened next was that Morris began to employ in his film work certain skills he was honing as a detective. As a "director-detective"—a phrase Morris used to describe himself when he was promoting *The Thin Blue Line*— not the least of his accomplishments was cultivating Henry Wade, for thirty-six years the District Attorney of Dallas County. Instead of handling the Adams prosecution himself, Wade assigned it to Douglas Mulder, one of his most experienced assistants. After gaining access to the files in Wade's office, Morris became convinced that Mulder had seriously tampered with the truth and that Adams had received anything but a fair trial.

Randall Adams and David Harris met by chance the morning before Officer Wood was killed. Adams had run out of gas and was walking along a road in west Dallas when Harris, a sixteen-year-old with an extensive criminal record, driving a car that he had stolen in his home town of Vidor, Texas, pulled over and offered to help him refill the tank. They spent the rest of the day, a Saturday, together—bumming around a shopping mall, drinking beer, visiting pawnshops, shooting pool, smoking marijuana. That evening, they ended up at a drive-in theater that featured two soft-core-porn movies. Officer Wood was shot at twelve-thirty Sunday morning—almost three hours after Harris, according to Adams's testimony, had dropped him off at the motel where he was living. That became Adams's alibi: he was home asleep when the crime was committed.

Teresa Turko proved to be a poor eyewitness to the slaying of her patrol partner, and gave an inaccurate description of the car that the killer had been driving. The first break in the case came because David Harris, back in Vidor, told several friends that he had killed a policeman in Dallas. After being arrested and leading the Vidor police to the murder weapon, a .22-caliber handgun that belonged to his father, Harris was turned over to the Dallas police. At this point, he changed his story and said that he had only been bragging—that the real killer was a hitch-hiker he had picked up and spent the day with. Which is how Adams, who had no prior criminal record, came to be charged with murder.

Initially, Adams was represented by Edith James, a lawyer whose criminal-trial experience included no homicide-defense work. She brought in as co-counsel a general practitioner named Dennis White. In one of White's previous head-to-heads with Doug Mulder, things had ended badly for his clients—two brothers named Ransonette who had made the mistake of kidnapping the daughter-in-law of a Dallas newspaper publisher. At the sentencing hearing in that case, White argued that the victim had not been harmed by her captors, and suggested a lenient prison term of five years. The prosecution mentioned a term of five thousand years. The jury, aspiring to Solomonic wisdom, said, in effect, "O.K. Let's compromise," and sentenced each defendant to five thousand and five years. Dennis White was simply no match for Doug Mulder, who is said to have once boasted, "Anybody can convict a guilty man. It takes talent to convict an innocent man."

Testifying during Adams's trial, David Harris offered a chronology of the events surrounding the murder that varied from Adams's version by approximately two and a half hours. Adams and Harris agreed that they had left the drive-in theater during a movie called *Swinging Cheerleaders*. Mulder elicited from Harris testimony that their departure had occurred shortly after midnight; Adams said they left around nine-thirty. In the D.A.'s files, Morris discovered a memorandum from Mulder's own chief investigator stating that there had been no late showing of *Swinging Cheerleaders* that night and that the final feature had ended shortly after ten o'clock.

This was the sort of serious defect in Harris's version of the facts that Mulder apparently had no intention of allowing to interfere with his prosecution of Adams—who, at twenty-eight, was eligible for capital punishment, whereas Harris, at sixteen, was not. It was also, unfortunately, the sort of discrepancy that Adams's attorneys failed to make clear to the jury. Nor were Edith James and Dennis White prepared when Mulder produced three mysterious witnesses, all of whom testified that they had driven past the scene of the crime moments before Officer Wood was murdered and that Randall Adams was in the driver's seat—the position from which the shots were fired. The three witnesses, Emily Miller, Robert Miller, and Michael Randell, all of whom were aware of a five-figure reward for information leading to the conviction of the killer, appeared in court on a Friday and impressed the jury. White, outmaneuvered by Mulder's strategy of presenting his "eyewitnesses" during the rebuttal phase rather than as part of his case-in-chief, conducted an ineffectual cross-examination. That weekend, White received a call from a woman named Elba Carr, who knew Emily and Robert Miller and expressed the opinion that "Emily Miller had never told the truth in her life." When, back in court the following Monday, White asked to question the Millers and Michael Randell further, Mulder told the judge that all three had left town or were otherwise unreachable. Actually, all three witnesses were still in Dallas. The Millers, in fact, were ensconced in the Alamo Plaza Motel as guests of Dallas County. Not until nine years later, when Morris came along and found in the District Attorney's files bills for phone calls that the Millers had made from the Alamo Plaza, did Mulder's role in this apparent deception become evident.

Toward the end of *The Thin Blue Line*, Errol Morris asks David Harris, "Would you say that Adams is a pretty unlucky fellow?" and Harris responds, "Definitely—if it wasn't for bad luck, he wouldn't have had none." Ironically, of course, Harris's reply is accurate only up to the moment when Morris met Adams. Not only did Morris discover important evidence in the prosecution's files; he discovered the absence of some important documents—specifically, the official record of a police lineup at which, according to Emily Miller's trial testimony, she had positively identified Randall Adams. Most significantly, Morris tracked down the three rebuttal witnesses themselves and persuaded them to appear on film. Emily Miller, a bleached blonde, whose childhood ambition was to be a detective or the wife of a detective, told Morris that she had failed to identify Adams in the lineup but that a policeman had told her the correct suspect, "so that I wouldn't make that mistake again." Robert Miller told him, "I really didn't see anything." Michael Randell, who had testified in 1977 that he was on his way home from playing basketball when he drove past the murder scene, told Morris that in fact he had spent that evening in an adulterous endeavor and that he was drunk "out of my mind." Each of the state's rebuttal witnesses, it therefore appeared, had committed damaging perjury. Putting David Harris on film posed a significant challenge. The first interview appointment, Morris says, Harris missed "because he was off killing somebody"— Mark Walter Mays, a Beaumont citizen, whose apartment Harris had broke into, and whose girlfriend he had abducted. Another interview had to be postponed when Harris tried to use Morris in an escape attempt from the jail where he was awaiting trial for these crimes. The climactic interview finally took place in the Lou Sterret Jail, in Dallas, by which time Harris had been convicted and sentenced to death for the Mays murder, and it included this exchange:

MORRIS: Is he [Adams] innocent?
HARRIS: Did you ask him?
MORRIS: Well, he's always said he's been innocent.

HARRIS: There you go. Didn't believe him, huh? Criminals always lie.
MORRIS:Well, what do you think about whether or not he's innocent?
HARRIS: I'm sure he is.
MORRIS: How can you be sure?
HARRIS: Because I'm the one that knows.

On a straightforward, realistic level, *The Thin Blue Line* is the story of how Adams got railroaded, the story of an innocent man wrongly accused. Its aura, however, is that of a dreadful fantasy, a mixture of the ghastly and the absurd. By any standard, it breaches the conventional definition of "documentary." Tom Luddy has said that *The Thin Blue Line* illustrates Morris's belief that cinema verité is "too mundane—that there is a way to heighten the structure of the facts." To accomplish this, Morris combines straight interviews—his unblinking talking-heads technique, from *Gates of Heaven* and *Vernon, Florida*—with artful restagings of certain incidents. The restaged episodes correspond to conflicting versions of "the facts" proposed by the people who appear in the interviews. Also, inserted throughout the film are closeups—of a gun, a mouth and a straw, a milkshake spilling, popcorn popping—that have a fetishistic quality, an exaggerated objectivity (evidence of Morris's passion for film noir). The *Rashomon*-like result is something considerably creepier than the cold-blooded murder that *The Thin Blue Line* explores.

The day before the interview with Harris, which took place December 5, 1986, Morris appeared in the courtroom of John Tolle, a federal magistrate in Dallas, who was presiding over a habeas-corpus hearing—an effort by Adams to win a new trial. In addition to Morris's oral testimony, unedited footage from his interviews with the prosecution witnesses became part of the court record. Watching these interviews—either unedited or as they appear in the final cut of *The Thin Blue Line*—one marvels at Morris's ability to win the confidence of so many people so prone to self-incrimination. On film, the witnessess against Adams seem to suffer collectively from the actor's nightmare—an instinctive fear of silence, terror at the thought of forgetting one's lines. Talking to Morris, they managed to discredit themselves thoroughly.

Under oath in Magistrate Tolle's courtroom, however, Emily Miller and Michael Randell tried to recant their statements to the filmmaker. Among the questions raised by Adams's habeas-corpus motion were: Had Adams been denied due process because he had not been effectively represented by his attorneys during his original trial, because of certain evidence that was illegally withheld from the jury during that trial, and because in 1980, when the United States Supreme Court overturned his death sentence (on a technical point involving jury selection), he received from the governor of Texas a commutation of the death sentence to life imprisonment rather than a new trial?

Morris returned to Magistrate Tolle's courtroom a month later, for the second, and last, day of the habeas-corpus hearing. Doug Mulder, by now a highly successful defense attorney, testified, responding to unwelcome questions from Adams's appellate lawyer, Randy Schaffer, with mumbled replies and lapses of memory. As the hearing ended, reason dictated that the magistrate would rule on Adams' petition within a few weeks. Tolle, however, turned out to be an even more gifted procrastinator than Morris. The New York Film Festival committee had expressed interest in showing *The Thin Blue Line* in September of 1987, but Morris failed to meet the deadline. Finally, on March 18, 1988, *The Thin Blue Line* had its première, at the San Francisco Film Festival. Morris appeared to be in buoyant spirits that day, and I asked him what he expected to do after the screening. "Oh, I imagine the usual lithium treatments," he said. "Followed by a period of hospitalization." A month later, *The Thin Blue Line* led off the USA Film Festival, in Dallas. Magistrate Tolle had yet to be heard from. Two more weeks passed—sixteen months had elapsed since the conclusion of the habeas-corpus hearing— and Tolle at last rendered his judgment: "All relief requested . . . denied." As far as Morris's role in the case was concerned, Tolle wrote, "much could be said about those videotape interviews, but nothing that would have any bearing on the matter before this court."

A week later, Randy Schaffer filed a motion asking that Tolle's opinion be set aside, because an astonishing fact had come to light: In the spring of 1977, on the heels of Adams's conviction for the murder of Officer Wood, Dennis White had filed a five-million-dollar lawsuit against Doug Mulder and Henry Wade, alleging that the District Attorney's conduct during the trial had violated the defendant's civil rights. John Tolle then worked in the civil division of the Dallas County District Attorney's office. White's suit had been briskly dismissed by a federal judge. After the screening at the USA Film Festival, Dennis White mentioned to Morris that he recalled Tolle's having been involved in the 1977 civil suit. The records of that litigation were dredged from a file, and, sure enough, John Tolle's name was all over them: John Tolle had triumphantly represented Mulder and Wade. Somehow, not quite ten years later, Magistrate Tolle had decided that this coincidence did not disqualify him from rendering an opinion on Adams's habeas-corpus petition. Rather, he had chosen to hear the case, and had then sat on it for seventeen months before eventually ruling, in effect, in favor of his former client. The embarrassing revelation of Tolle's conflict of interest forced him to withdraw his recommendation;

thus, an additional year and a half of Adams's life had been consumed by a proceeding that ultimately yielded irrelevance. Rather than start all over again in federal court, before a different magistrate, Schaffer decided to formally withdraw the writ and refile it in state court, citing new evidence that Adams had never received a fair trial.

Officer Robert Wood was murdered Thanksgiving weekend in 1976. Twelve years later almost to the day, Adams and his attorneys returned to the room where he had been convicted of the murder and handed a death sentence—Criminal District Court No. 2, on the fourth floor of the Dallas County Courthouse. By Texas statute, the judge who presides at a trial—in this instance, District Judge Don Metcalfe, whose evidentiary rulings against Adams formed part of the basis for the writ—also presides at any subsequent appellate-writ hearing. Adams's bad luck, while consistent, was not absolute, however, and Metcalfe had since left the bench. In 1984, he was succeeded by Larry W. Baraka, a respected former prosecutor and defense attorney, whose special distinction is that he is the only member of the Texas judiciary who is black, a Muslim, and a Republican.

On the eve of the hearing, I had a phone conversation with Morris. In New York the previous day, he told me, his secretary had taken a call from a stranger who said, "An important message for Errol Morris: Stay away from the hearing in Dallas on Wednesday. You might disappear"—a forewarning that brought to mind his experience in Vernon, Florida, a decade earlier, where, he had been informed, unfortunate people had a tendency to "just disappear."

"My stepfather told my wife I should wear two bulletproof vests, so that one covers the seams of the other," he continued. "I don't mind a death threat, as such, but I do mind the idea of disappearing. That's like the 'delete' button on your personal computer—'We deleted that character.' Disappearing suggests a whole set of unsavory possibilities."

As it turned out, I couldn't be in Dallas the opening day of the writ hearing, and thereby missed a memorable striptease by David Harris. Testifying for three hours, Harris said that he had been alone in a stolen car and in possession of a stolen gun when Wood pulled him over. In a videotaped interview that was introduced as evidence, he said that he had had his finger on the trigger as Wood approached him. Judge Baraka, no quibbler, announced, "As far as the court is concerned, he's in fact telling me he did it." Randy Schaffer read aloud a letter from Harris to his mother, written in September, 1988—just two months earlier—that said, "It seems like my whole life is surrounded by 'wrongs' of some kind and it seems like I've never done the right thing when I could and should have. Absolving Randall Dale Adams of any guilt is a difficult thing for me to do, but I must try to do so because he is innocent. That is the truth."

Next, Schaffer called Teresa Turko, Robert Wood's patrol partner, as a witness. He wanted to make plain to the judge that Turko's initial description of the killer, recorded immediately after the shooting, differed measurably from the one she had offered at Adams's trial. Dennis White had not cross-examined Turko about the first statement, because, in violation of a cardinal principle of criminal-trial procedure, Mulder had not given him a copy. Nor would the document have come to light, of course, if Morris had not insinuated himself into the Dallas District Attorney's good graces and scrutinized Mulder's old files.

When I caught up with Morris, at the end of the first day of the hearing, his mood was upbeat but not entirely sanguine. The drama of Harris's confession notwithstanding, it did not, in a technical sense, really help Adams. In Texas, evidence of innocence is insufficient to win a new trial. What Schaffer had to prove was that Adams's original trial had been "unfair" on constitutional grounds. Even if Baraka were to grant Adams's writ, his ruling would have the effect only of a recommendation to the Texas Court of Criminal Appeals, a nine-judge panel, which in 1977 had unanimously upheld Adams's conviction. Harris's testimony was useful, however, in bolstering some of the other claims in the writ—most significantly, that Harris and Mulder had an understanding in 1977 whereby in exchange for testimony against Adams unresolved criminal charges against Harris in another county would be dropped. (Under cross-examination at the original trial, Harris had insisted that no quid pro quo existed—an avowal that Mulder has always maintained. Further harm to Adams was done when Judge Metcalfe refused even to allow into evidence the fact that Harris had such charges pending.)

Randall Adams wore the same outfit to court all three days of the hearing—a bright-orange jumpsuit with DALLAS COUNTY JAIL in black block letters stencilled on the back; leg irons; and handcuffs, which were attached to a chain around his waist. When Adams was escorted into the courtroom on Day Two, Morris had already arrived and taken a seat in the front row of the spectator section, between Adams's mother, Mildred, and his two sisters, Nancy Bapst and Mary Baugess. Two of Mildred Adams's sisters and their husbands had also come to Dallas for the hearing. George Preston, a lawyer who was assisting Randy Schaffer, leaned across a low partition that separated the spectators from the business end of the courtroom and showed Morris a printed sheet of paper, portions of which had been highlighted in yellow.

"This is from the Bar Association code," he said. "It regards tampering with witnesses and suppression of evidence."

"I'd like a copy of that," Morris said.

"Our Xerox machine broke, so I had to tear this page out of the book," Preston said.

"That page must have been missing from Doug Mulder's copy, too," Morris said.

The first witness on Day Two was Emily Miller. Randy Schaffer expected to score several points while she was on the stand: her failure to identify Adams in a lineup; the intervention of the Dallas policeman, who then pointed out to her the "right" suspect; her subsequent perjury regarding her performance at the lineup; and evidence that, like David Harris, she had struck an implicit deal with Mulder—specifically, her testimony against Adams in exchange for the dismissal of an outstanding robbery charge against her daughter.

A week after the murder of Robert Wood, at which time a twenty-thousand-dollar reward was being offered for information leading to the arrest and conviction of the killer, Emily Miller had given a formal statement to the Dallas police. According to what she saw while driving past the crime scene moments before the shooting, the suspect was "either a Mexican or a very light-skinned black man." That this description would divert suspicion from Adams, an auburn-haired Caucasian, perhaps explains why Mulder never showed the statement to Adams's attorneys. By the time of Adams' trial, Emily Miller's description of the killer had metamorphosed so that it matched the defendant. In Judge Baraka's courtroom, when Schaffer presented Emily Miller with a copy of her original statement she said that she had left her eyeglasses at home and couldn't read it. When Schaffer then read it to her and proceeded through a barbed interrogation, she said, "I don't remember nothing that happened back then. Specifics, I don't remember who asked me what or who said what or who did what. That was twelve years ago."

As far as the officer who had coached her at the police lineup was concerned, she said, "I didn't base nothing I said on anything anybody told me. It was what I seen. And I'm sorry I ever seen it."

"You're not the only one, I'm sure," Schaffer replied.

The subject of Errol Morris and his filmed interview with Emily Miller arose.

The witness turned to the judge and said, "May I get this clear on this videotape? This man [Morris] came to my house and told me that he was going to make a movie. . . . They were kicking it around in their heads about making a movie about the police shooting in Dallas. So I said O.K. He said, well, it would be interesting because, he said, 'In the first place, you're married to a black man.' This was his exact words. And I said, 'Well.' And he said, 'Do you mind? We're not sure we're going to film or anything. We're just going to kick it around.' And I said, 'Well, I don't exactly remember how everything went down back then.' And he said, 'Well, what the heck, it's just a movie, you know?' He said, 'Anything you don't remember . . . I'll remember for you.' Well, this went on . . . The movie wasn't accurate. It wasn't, you know . . . I went along because he said what the heck, it's a movie. . . . He . . . tried to make me look like trash."

During a recess, several reporters approached Morris—the courtroom was filled to capacity most of the three days of the hearing—and asked about Emily Miller's accusations. He pointed out that she had described the precise antithesis of his well-established interviewing style—his let-'em-talk-until-the-truth-flows technique—and he offered to roll the tape of the full interview for anyone who was interested. "She spoke extemporaneously, at length, without coaching, prodding, or interruption by me," he said. "It's quite clear that Emily Miller has no credibility."

Nevertheless, Emily Miller had accomplished something oddly significant: she had introduced the idea that *The Thin Blue Line* was a corrupt document. Months earlier, a reporter for *The Dallas Morning News* had said to Morris, "You know, Errol, there are two sides to every story," and he had replied, "Yeah, the truth and falsehood." Much as he still believed that about the Adams case, he also understood the mythology that attaches to movies, and he understood that in the iconography of this courtroom proceeding *The Thin Blue Line* had acquired a taint, as if it were some soiled version of the truth. Errol Morris, seated in the front row of the spectator section, wearing a blue plaid jacket, chinos, a white shirt, and a red paisley necktie, repeatedly heard himself referred to as "a filmmaker from New York"—a phrase chock-full of unflattering connotations. The word "movie" was chock-full of connotations. Robert Wood was dead, and Randall Adams had spent twelve years behind bars—those were virtually the only remaining unassailable truths. Almost every intervening fact had been tampered with by the police or lawyers or mysteriously motivated witnesses. In the immediate context, Randall Adams, in his jumpsuit, handcuffs, and leg irons, seated mutely with his back to the spectators, seemed more relevant to the proceeding than Robert Wood but less relevant than Errol Morris.

Other witnesses went out of their way to impugn Morris—most notably Gus Rose, a former homicide detective, whom Adams described in *The Thin Blue Line* as having pulled a gun on him during one inter-

rogation session. Rose had come to court as the District Attorney's witness. During the direct examination by Leslie McFarlane, the appellate
lawyer assigned to represent the Dallas County District Attorney, he
made several statements that had Morris squirming in his seat and
whispering to me things like "Don't these people get embarrassed lying? After all, this is only a man who was sentenced to death." Rose
complained that Morris had misrepresented his intentions in soliciting
an interview and then had been argumentative during the interview.
"You should *hear* this interview," Morris said to me. "I'm barely present." When Rose testified that Adams had never denied murdering
Robert Wood, Morris seethed, "That's a lie. He told me on film that
Adams had denied it. This is all lies, lies, lies."

During cross-examination, Schaffer gave Rose reason to regret this
particular portion of his testimony. Holding a transcript of *The Thin
Blue Line*—proof of Rose's failure to keep his own story straight—
Schaffer stood at the detective's side and read a passage in which Rose
recalled that Adams, shortly after his arrest, "almost overacted his innocence." A hubbub arose in the spectator section, not unlike the inevitable moment when Perry Mason's assistant, Paul Drake, shows up
with a previously elusive piece of physical evidence. A bearded man
seated two rows behind Morris suddenly produced a videocassette of
The Thin Blue Line, and Morris relayed it to George Preston, who passed
it to Schaffer, who was able to taunt Rose with it, asking whether he
wanted to see a moving picture of himself uttering words directly at
odds with the testimony he had just given.

Trapped, Rose turned to Judge Baraka and said, "Your Honor, if
the question is do I want to see the film the answer is no, I do not want
to see the film or anything Errol Morris has anything to do with."

Baraka called a recess for lunch. In the hallway, I passed Mildred
Adams, Randall's mother. A tall, broad-shouldered woman with light-
blue eyes, blue-gray hair, and a beauty-shop permanent, Mrs. Adams
was standing in a bath of bright light, being interviewed by a television
reporter, saying not for the first or the last time, "If Dallas County will
just admit that they made a mistake and let that boy come home . . ."

One evening, I went to the Dallas County jail to have a conversation
with Randall Adams. I rode an elevator to the eighth floor of the courthouse building, signed in, presented a guard with a letter from Randy
Schaffer authorizing my visit, and was directed to a pinkish-beige room
about twice the size of a prison cell, along one wall of which was a row
of telephone receivers and thick six-by-twelve-inch windows. Adams,
standing on the opposite side of the wall and holding two adjacent re-

ceivers—one to each ear—was concluding a conversation with Nancy Bapst and Mary Baugess, his sisters. A black woman who had three children with her was talking on one of the other phones. When Nancy Bapst handed me her receiver, a wall clock said 8:45—which meant that we didn't have long before the visiting hour would expire.

Adams and I discussed Randy Schaffer's aggressive style ("I need somebody who can intimidate. That's what you need") and Doug Mulder, who was scheduled to testify the next morning ("I know what those people did to me, but I have no personal animosity toward them"), and then I turned the subject to Errol Morris.

"If it wasn't for him . . . I sat down there in Huntsville and this man listened to me—I was pleading for somebody and this man listened," Adams began, in a flat voice, which, although it originated only a couple of feet away, sounded distant and disembodied, as if it had traveled through water. "Errol Morris, when I talked to him, I talked to him for one purpose and one purpose only: for the investigation of my case, whether good or bad. I told him, 'Whatever you want to do—you can dig into my closet if you will allow me to look at whatever you turn up.' I knew what these people had done to me, but I couldn't prove it. Randy Schaffer and Mel Bruder [another appellate lawyer], they didn't know. The only one who knew was Dennis White, but he was shook up entirely and he was devastated. I agreed to talk to Errol Morris on the condition that he would share with me what he found out. I like to call Errol the Easter Bunny. I needed somebody to gather up all these facts and put them in one basket. He went and did his investigative work, and everything we're doing now is because of what he did with his investigation of the facts. That is what *The Thin Blue Line* did for me."

The next morning, Doug Mulder gave a poised and self-assured courtroom performance. As Leslie McFarlane lobbed him across-the-letters questions, Mulder, a handsome man in his late forties with a squarish face, not much of a neck, and a stocky, athletic build, effortlessly swatted them out of the ballpark.

McFarlane: "Everything that you discovered and everything that you reviewed in preparation for this case indicates Adams's guilt, is that correct? . . . Did you find anything inconsistent with that?"

Mulder: "Nothing that comes to mind, no."

Schaffer, when his turn arrived, proved somewhat less ingratiating. His gambit, for instance went "Well, I guess today you've returned to the scene of one of your greatest crimes." Leslie McFarlane objected to the argumentative tone, and the judge agreed with her, telling Schaffer, "That's not the way to start." From there on, Schaffer and Mulder duelled for more than an hour—until it was apparent that the judge had had enough and that Mulder was not going to throw up his hands and declare, "O.K., ya got me, my legal career's a shambles, I'm finished in this town." The judge's impatience with Schaffer belied the fact that he had already made up his mind on the basic question. After a masterly summation by Schaffer—sufficient in its eloquence for McFarlane, when her turn came, to apologize, accurately, that her closing argument would be notably devoid of eloquence—Baraka said he was ready with his decision.

Of the thirteen grounds for relief cited in Adams's writ, Baraka agreed on six: that Metcalfe, the original trial judge, had erroneously denied the admissibility of David Harris's prior criminal record; that Teresa Turko's initial statement describing the killer had been illegally suppressed; that, similarly, Emily Miller's initial statement describing the killer had been illegally suppressed; that evidence of Emily Miller's failure to identify Adams in the police lineup and subsequent coaching by a police officer had been suppressed; that Emily Miller had later committed perjury regarding her performance at the lineup; and that Adams had been denied effective assistance of counsel.

It seemed that, because Baraka had rejected seven of the contentions cited in the writ, a final observation he made was designed to eliminate any remaining ambiguity: "I think over all, when we look at this trial, all the nuances that are involved, I think there's no question that the defendant did not get a fair opportunity to a trial. I would not go so far as to say that the defendant is innocent of this. I would go so far as to say that if the defendant were to be retried, considering all the testimony elicited and what would be presented to the jury or a court, that more likely than not the defendant would be found not guilty."

The ruling did not mean that Adams was now at liberty to walk out of the courtroom; it meant that one judge officially believed that Adams had yet to receive a fair trial. As a practical matter, Baraka's recommendation could languish with the Texas Court of Criminal Appeals for months before a final ruling came down. And the court could, of course, reject Baraka's recommendation. Imminent freedom for Adams, in other words, was by no means a foregone conclusion. Knowing that Baraka lacked the authority to grant Adams bail in the meantime, Schaffer asked for it anyway, and the motion was denied. On that note, the hearing ended. There was applause, and a call for order from the court officers, and then the television and newspaper people were ready with their questions.

Adams, seated in a wooden armchair and still wearing handcuffs and leg irons, said he felt "numb"—the same word he had used in *The Thin Blue Line* to describe his frame of mind when, twelve years earlier, he heard himself sentenced to death.

A woman with a microphone asked Adams if he had anything to say to David Harris. No, he did not.

A reporter from *New York Newsday* asked, "Do you think you'd be here today if it hadn't been for Errol Morris?"

"Without the facts that came from the movie, no, I wouldn't be here in this courtroom today. We needed the facts, and the film helped. It helped immensely."

Roughly the same question was directed to Schaffer, who was standing nearby: "Do you consider that if the file that Errol Morris got out of Mr. Wade's office had not been found, we'd be here?"

In his summation, Schaffer had belittled the Dallas District Attorney, saying, "They'll give their file to a moviemaker, because he'll go out and make a movie and they'll be famous, but they won't give it to a defense attorney." Elaborating, he now said, "No, if Errol had not decided on his own that this was a story worth telling, Randall Adams would have been buried forever. Yes, that was the linchpin."

Mildred Adams, between bouts of crying for joy and kissing Morris and Schaffer and any willing members of the press, said she hoped people would remember Robert Wood and his family in their prayers. When the excitement had lasted close to half an hour, Morris suggested to Mrs. Adams that she and her daughters and sisters and brothers-in-law should join him for champagne at the Adolphus Hotel.

"Did I tell you what Randall Adams said to me about my movie?" Morris asked me as we headed for the hotel, a few blocks east of the courthouse. "He told me another inmate asked him, 'How come your case is being argued in the entertainment section of the newspaper?' And you know what Randall's response was? He said, 'I'll argue my case anywhere I can, any way I can.'"

The Thin Blue Line made dozens of critics' lists of the ten best films of 1988; according to a survey by *The Washington Post*, in fact, it turned up on more ten-best lists than any other film. Both the New York Film Critics Circle and the National Society of Film Critics chose it as best documentary of 1988. Although its box-office receipts have not extended into the *Roger Rabbit* or *Crocodile Dundee II* vicinity—at the end of the year, it was playing in fifteen theaters around the country—Morris no longer faces the prospect that he will soon again be working as a private detective or dodging collection agencies. Immediately before the writ hearing in Dallas, he was in Italy, where *The Thin Blue Line* was shown at a festival in Florence. On the same trip, he made stops in London—where he screened it for some people from the London Film Festival—and in Munich, where he met with Reinhold Messner, the legendary

Alpine climber and the first man to have scaled all fourteen eight-thousand-meter peaks on earth (including Mt. Everest without oxygen). Messner was planning an ascent of Cerro del Toro, in Chile, and he wanted Morris—who happens to be an experienced rock climber—to accompany him and make a film. "I'm thinking of doing it," Morris said, in Dallas. "Messner's a terrifically interesting person. He told me he's been doing a lot of walking recently. You or I might assume he meant he was taking long strolls in his neighborhood. What he actually meant was that he had just walked across Tibet. And he's planning to walk across Antarctica. He told me some interesting stuff about meeting the yeti—you know, the abominable snowman. He's seen two—the red yeti and the black yeti. Messner was very reassuring. He said, "The only thing you really have to be scared of is when you hear the black yeti whistling—whistling through his nose.' "

Heading off to South America with Messner would mean delaying a couple of other projects that Morris was eager to carry forward. He still had plans to complete *Dr. Death*—the movie he had intended to make before the Randall Adams case sidetracked him. He also hoped to direct *The Trial of King Boots*, a feature-length examination of how an Old English sheepdog named King Boots—the most highly decorated performer in the annals of show-dog competition—became the only canine in Michigan history to be prosecuted, in effect, for homicide. Morris already had a vision of what the film's publicity posters would say: "Only Two People Know What Happened. One Is Dead. The Other Is a Dog."

If Morris could find the time to finish *Dr. Death*, he might at last tie together an odd mélange of material: interviews with Dr. Grigson himself; action shots of a lion tamer; scenes from lab research on a mammal called the African naked mole rat; archival footage from an Edison silent film called *Electrocuting an Elephant*; and a meditation on Zoar, an extinct utopian community in Ohio. After a previous trip to Europe, Morris had told me with satisfaction about finding the right music to accompany the Zoar material. "It's called 'Yodeler Messen,' " he said. "I'd been hearing this stuff on the radio in Zurich, and then I went into a record store and asked whether they had any liturgical yodelling. They came up with 'Yodeler Messen.' It's, like, based on the idea that God might be hard of hearing."

One afternoon, in his office near Times Square, Morris patiently tried to walk me through the connections between the elements that would compose *Dr. Death*, an exercise that struck me as analogous to a journey along the scenic route from the right side of his brain to the left. He told me that his fascination with Dr. Grigson's disturbing theories of sociopathy and recidivism had aroused an interest in lion taming, and that in 1985 this led him to the eponymous ringleader of a circus act called Dave Hoover's Wild Animals. Of the three basic schools of lion taming—what Morris delineated as "the persuasive, mutual-respect school, the behaviorist school, and the chairs-whips-guns school"—Hoover subscribed to the third. Having filmed Hoover at work for several hours—the soundtrack consists mainly of scary roaring noises and the determined voice of Hoover saying, again and again, "Bongo! Come! Come to Daddy! Bad girl! Caesar! Get home, *Caesar!* Good boy!"—Morris was uncertain what to do with the footage.

"After I'd looked at this stuff awhile, I decided, Oh, no, I can't use this. It's too goofy," Morris said. "Then I got interested in the mole rats. What's the connection between the lion tamer and the mole rats? I don't know if there even is one. Mole rats spend their entire lives digging tunnels. They have a rigid social system. They're like wasps or bees—there's a queen and workers. Mole rats dig at random, looking for tubers. Maybe they find a tuber, or maybe they don't. They just dig away. At one point, I had thought the mole rats addressed the utopian ideal of what it would be like if there were no crime or criminals, if you could say hello to your neighbor and your neighbor would say hello in return and we'd all be assured that no one would attack us with an axe. Is aggression innate in mammals? Well, supposedly not in mole rats. The mole rat was thought to be the only mammal that lives in harmony with its fellow-mammals, its fellow mole rats. *The* only. But it turns out that mole rats are nonviolent only under certain circumstances—that, in fact, they can be really nasty critters after all, who at times really do seem to hate one another. When one colony of mole rats meets another, they can be extremely vicious. Anyway, that was my original idea—Dr. Grigson, lion tamers, mole rats. I then decided to add to this compote *Electrocuting an Elephant*—which was, if anything, a miscarriage-of-justice story."

When it became clear that I was unfamiliar with the once popular habit—practiced during the first half of this century—of systematically executing "bad" elephants, Morris eagerly took a book from a shelf next to his desk and handed it to me. It was a prolifically illustrated memoir titled *I Loved Rogues*, by George (Slim) Lewis and Byron Fish. Lewis was a passionate lover of elephants who spent most of his working life in the employ of zoos and circuses, and Fish was a newspaperman whose interest in elephants was that of an involved amateur. The book had chapter titles like "They Are Not House Pets" and "Ziggy Tries to Kill Me" and "How to Feed and Water Your Elephant." The foreword included a reproduction of a painting labelled "George Lewis and Tusko"—Tusko being a vast bull elephant who came close to being executed for doing something deemed bad. A photograph on the facing page, captioned "Byron Fish painting Wide Awake," showed Fish perched on an elephant's shoulder, giving the animal a cosmetic treatment with a bucket of oil made from horse fat. The phone rang. While Morris took the call, I wrote down some more interesting captions and passages:

"Occasionally the victim of an elephant's attack is a man who was hated for reasons of the elephant's own" (p. 29).

"Black Diamond seemed to know that he was taking his last walk" (p. 47).

"After 170 shots by the firing squad, Diamond finally goes down" (p. 48).

"Joe Metcalf was another man Slim often met in his travels. The man with his head in the elephant's mouth was Alonzo Dever" (p. 62).

"Isn't that a wonderful book?" Morris said after he hung up. "I'd very much like to show you *Electrocuting an Elephant*. This elephant, Topsy, was, if anything, a *good* elephant rather than a bad elephant. Topsy was being electrocuted because, as I understand it, some guy was smoking a cigarette and gave the cigarette to Topsy, burning the tip of her trunk. Now, the tip of an elephant's trunk is the most sensitive part of an elephant. Topsy picked this guy up, tossed him in the air a couple of times, and hurled him onto concrete. I ask you: Does Topsy deserve the juice for this? The film of Topsy's electrocution is a 1903 Edison short—one of the first times electricity was used in capital punishment. And, coincidentally, the equipment malfunctioned and the person who pulled the switch almost electrocuted himself while he was electrocuting Topsy."

Morris paused. We could hear the traffic on Broadway, two floors below, and from the editing room, ten feet away, we could hear a litany of "Come, Bongo!"s and "Home, Caesar!"s.

"My favorite line in *Dr. Death*, I think, will be when the last living Zoarite is quoted as saying, 'Think of it—all those religions. They can't *all* be right. But they could all be wrong,'" Morris said. He looked down at his hands, massaged the tips of his little fingers—a characteristic tic—and then looked up, smiling his asymmetrical smile. "My two remaining ambitions are to have my picture hung up in my local Chinese restaurant and to have a sandwich named after me at the Stage Deli. And I guess I'll still keep making films. I always felt film was a good medium for me to work in, because if you don't finish, the level of embarrassment is so high."

Coda

At the time this Profile was published in *The New Yorker*, in February 1989, a decision about Randall Adams' legal fate, although imminent, remained unresolved. A further, unanticipated, development—an ironic postscript entirely worthy of an Errol Morris enterprise—was yet to come.

On March 1, three months after the habeas-corpus hearing in Judge Larry Baraka's courtroom, the Texas Court of Criminal Appeals unanimously overturned Adams's murder conviction. Three weeks later, Adams again appeared before Judge Baraka—this time for a bail hearing. John Vance, the Dallas County District Attorney, had at that point still not announced whether he intended to retry Adams. Confident that a new trial would result not only in acquittal and vindication but in humiliation for the District Attorney's office, Adams and his appellate lawyer, Randy Schaffer, made it clear that they hoped Vance would indeed pursue the case. Anything still seemed possible; from the time of Adams's arrest, in 1976, the conduct of the D.A.'s office in this matter had been characterized by a disdain for logic and due process. On the morning of the bail hearing, an assistant D.A. named Winfield Scott appeared before Judge Baraka. Scott, who had aided Douglas Mulder in the original prosecution of Adams, and had been incensed by Judge Baraka's ruling at the writ hearing, now sought to disqualify the judge, claiming that he had shown bias toward Adams. Although Scott ultimately did not prevail, he did perform a public service by rendering what many observers felt was an entertaining impersonation of a loose cannon.

Ignoring the fact that *The Thin Blue Line*, together with Schaffer's legal skill, had effectively impeached virtually all the state's witnesses, Scott told Baraka, "We have witnesses on standby and we are ready to try this case immediately," and then refused to participate in the proceeding. Scott's bombast brought to mind a declaration by John Vance to the *Dallas Times Herald* some months earlier that "as much as I'm convinced that Lee Harvey Oswald killed John Kennedy, I'm convinced that Randall Dale Adams is the man that shot Officer Wood." Since then, however, *The Thin Blue Line* had turned up in movie theaters, and Vance's assurance had been replaced by vacillation.

Judge Baraka released Adams on a $50,000 personal-recognizance bond. Within an hour, before Schaffer could physically escort Adams from the courthouse, Winfield Scott arranged a hearing before a more friendly judge who—evidently persuaded by rhetorical questions from Scott such as "What if Randall Adams isn't really going home to his mommy in Ohio? What if he tries to flee to Mexico or Canada?"—compliantly raised Adams's bail to $100,000, payable in cash or surety, pending a ruling on Judge Baraka's impartiality. Unable to make bail, Adams was forced to spend one more night in the custody of Dallas County.

The next day, a third judge reinstated the $50,000 personal-recognizance bond and Adams was released. Speaking to a reporter in

Houston the day after that, Adams said, "No offense, but I hate Texas."
The day after *that*, he flew to Columbus, Ohio, where his mother and
two sisters lived. As he walked off the plane, the reporters who had
gathered at the airport told him that John Vance, in Dallas, had just
held a press conference. Despite having said earlier in the week, "I don't
think Randall Dale Adams ought to be out on the street," Vance now
acknowledged that his office lacked "sufficient credible evidence" and
would therefore not retry the case.

Leslie McFarlane, the assistant D.A. who had been assigned to represent the Dallas County District Attorney in the habeas-corpus proceeding, apparently decided that the maladroitness of her colleagues
was more than she could bear, and she soon resigned from that office.
Around that time, the excitable and diverting Winfield Scott was fired.
Dallas County has never formally stated whether David Harris, who
since 1986 has been on death row in Texas for the unrelated murder of
Mark Walter Mays, will be tried for the murder of Robert Wood.

Errol Morris was in the crowd at the airport in Columbus when Randall Adams returned home, and Adams made a point of pushing his
way through the throng to warmly greet and embrace the person he
had come to refer to as "the Easter Bunny." At that moment, it probably
did not occur to either man that, within three months, Adams would be
filing a lawsuit against Morris—although Morris, who all along had described the *Thin Blue Line* murder as a "tale of error and confusion,"
perhaps should have seen it coming. The personal affection that Morris
felt for Adams did not extend to Randy Schaffer. Morris had often differed with Schaffer's tactics in the handling of Adams's appeal, and
Schaffer, in turn, did not really welcome Morris's freely offered advice
on legal strategy. The undercurrent of friction in the relationship blos-
somed into vindictiveness when, in the late spring, Schaffer sent Morris
a letter threatening to sue him on Adams's behalf.

At issue was an agreement reached in December 1986, a year and a
half after Morris had filmed an interview with Adams at the Eastham
Unit. The agreement, which granted Morris a two-year option to purchase the rights to Adams's life story, set forth a schedule of potential
payments—depending on the form in which his story was, as they say
in show business, exploited. If, for instance, Adams's experiences became the basis for a "dramatic motion picture intended for initial the-
atrical release," he would receive $60,000 plus a share of net profits. If
the medium of exploitation was a made-for-television movie, Adams
would receive $40,000—and so forth. In the event a documentary film
was made, Adams would receive ten dollars—the same amount he was

paid by Morris for the option. The object of these token ten-dollar payments was a mutual desire to eliminate any appearance of impropriety or conflict of interest. At the time of the agreement, neither Adams nor Morris was guided by mercenary motives. Rather, Adams was trying to win his freedom and Morris was making a documentary film that might be used in a courtroom to further that endeavor. Paying Adams to appear in the movie might create an unseemingly taint. Indeed, no one who agreed to appear in the movie was paid.

Beyond the pivotal role that *The Thin Blue Line* played in proving Adams's innocence, it also elevated him to celebrity status, an inevitability in the late eighties. Various book and movie offers immediately materialized—blunt attempts by the usual opportunists to further exploit what had happened to Adams. Morris, of course, was also approached with similar offers to tell, for a price, the story of how he got the story. By Texas statute, Adams could not sue Doug Mulder or any of the other parties who had helped bring about his twelve and a half years of unjust imprisonment. Recognizing that fact, and taking into account the 1986 agreement between Adams and Morris—and, above all, proceeding with the mistaken assumption that *The Thin Blue Line* had produced a profit and had earned Morris a lot of money—Schaffer sent his demand letter in May 1989. On the one hand, Schaffer insisted that Morris owed Adams $60,000, the amount that would have been due if Adams's life story had become the basis for a "dramatic motion picture intended for initial theatrical release." According to this logic, *The Thin Blue Line* was not a documentary film. Demonstrating that logical consistency was not his first concern, however, Schaffer also argued that Morris, having failed to exercise his option by paying the $60,000, no longer owned the rights to Adams's story. If within thirty days, Schaffer assured Morris, he did not agree to pay the money *and* release Adams from the agreement, he would be sued. As it happened, Morris was quite willing to return to Adams the rights to his story. But he deeply resented what he regarded as an extortion attempt by Schaffer, who, displaying an extraordinary imagination, alleged that the filmmaker had manipulated his client through "fraud and duress." In particular, Morris did not enjoy the passage in the lawyer's letter that went: "It seems to me that your public image is presently at its peak. You are perceived as a person who made a movie not for the money but to help another human being. . . . If you cause this matter to go into litigation your public image can only suffer as you will be perceived as a New York filmmaker who came to Texas and took advantage of a prison inmate to line your own pocket. If we go to court, for once I believe that Randall will be able to receive a fair trial from a Dallas jury."

Before the thirty days were up—during which time Morris and his lawyers thought they were fruitfully negotiating a settlement—Schaffer and a co-counsel went ahead and filed their lawsuit against Morris and Miramax Production Company, the film's distributor. The defendants' lawyer successfully removed the case from Texas state court to federal court, and before long the whole thing hit the newspapers. Unlike Schaffer's demand letter, the lawsuit did not ask for $60,000 or any other payment for alleged damages. Not insensitive to public relations considerations, Schaffer now made a point of telling anyone who asked that his client sought no money from Morris, but just wanted to control the rights to his own story. "They think they bought [Adams] lock, stock, and barrel for ten dollars, and that's unconscionable," he got in the habit of telling reporters. Nevertheless, the lawsuit attracted considerable publicity and much of it did not flatter Adams. "Now the envelope, please, for Ingrate of the Year," was the lead of an item in the New York *Daily News*.

As settlement discussions proceeded, Morris was good for a few colorful quotations of his own.

"Someone remarked that this started out as Kafka, then became Frank Capra, then Preston Sturges, then back to Kafka," he said to me at one point. "By the way, did I tell you the idea for my next film? I'm going to find an innocent man, frame him for murder, and then follow the case right up to and including the moment of his execution. What do you think of that idea? Do you like it?"

In a conversation a few days later, he said, "I've had a dream in which I'm on the witness stand in a courtroom and Randall Adams is sitting next to my mother in the spectator gallery, and as they're leading me away in chains to a period of indefinite incarceration, I see Randall lean over to my mother and say, 'Don't worry, Mrs. Morris, we're gonna get him out. I don't know how long it will take, but rest assured: I will spare no effort to win Errol's freedom.' "

I mentioned to Morris that I had been dining out on his fanciful description of the plan to frame and make a film about an innocent man. "And now I see you've modified that idea so that it stars yourself," I said.

"Yes, that's it," Morris replied. "I was determined to make a story about the framing of an innocent man, but because of my reluctance to do harm to an innocent person I'm being forced to make the movie about myself."

One could argue that, by making such a peculiar, hybrid documentary film as *The Thin Blue Line*, Morris brought Schaffer's lawsuit upon himself. Even Morris, however, with his gift for wry self-flagellation, was not pushing that line of reasoning. In any event, the issue became moot when, two months after the lawsuit was filed, a settlement was reached. Randall Adams got back the rights to his life story, Errol Morris got to keep the rights to his own life story, and no money changed hands. In the wake of the settlement, a Houston newspaper reported that Adams, twelve and a half years after being convicted of a murder that he didn't commit and five months after being certified, at last, a free man, had become a client of the William Morris Agency. Meanwhile, Errol Morris was not doing too badly himself: he had been named a recipient of a five-year "genius grant" from the MacArthur Foundation; he had won a Guggenheim Fellowship to support completion of *Dr. Death*; and the Stage Deli had decided to name a sandwich after him.

Ted Conover

Miriam Berkley

Ted Conover's first book, *Rolling Nowhere* (1984), took about a year of research riding the rails with hoboes. In an era of six-figure advances for long-term book projects, Conover says he had no advance and spent only about $300 on his research. This has made him something of a hero to writers just coming out of school—which is exactly what he himself was at the time. His research became an honors thesis at Amherst College, and later, the book. If you spend more than $300 a year doing participant-observer research on hoboes, Conover says, you're probably doing something wrong.

Conover's second book, *Coyotes* (1987), examined the lives of illegal Mexican immigrants who crossed the border into Arizona to pick oranges. Conover worked in an orange grove with one group of workers and lived in their hometown in Mexico for several months. At the end of his stay, he journeyed north and slipped across the border with them in the company of a *coyote*, a professional people-smuggler.

His next book, *Whiteout* (1991), captured the culture of Aspen, Colorado. It presented difficult research problems because the town has several subcultures, from servants to wealthy owners of multimillion-dollar homes. "It's interesting because of all the ways I pursued the story," Conover said, "from behind the wheel of a cab to being a reporter to going to parties to being an extra at John Denver's TV Christmas special. I can only write about what I have researched. I can only re-create a situation I have lived through."

Conover's article on truck drivers and AIDS in Africa was his first for *The New Yorker*. His research took him to Rwanda just months before the bloody civil war captured the world's attention. "Rwanda, when I visited in 1993, was already in a civil war and the most frightening place I have ever been," Conover said. "Tanks were in place in the center of Kigali, and rebel Tutsi forces were making sporadic night raids on the capital. Drunken soldiers roamed the streets of the city at night." It was the AIDS epidemic, however, that took him to Africa, not the fighting. "I suppose we all have our criteria for deciding what to write about next, at least our conscious criteria," he said. "For me, the perfect combination has a personal challenge, in terms of getting the story, that will require some ingenuity, dexterity, some difficulty. I prefer to go to places where there aren't so many journalists because there are more interesting stories in those places, and I prefer there be some socially compelling reason we should know more about this subject. The trucking piece is a case in point."

The Road Is Very Unfair: Trucking Across Africa in the Age of AIDS

The red dirt road is so slick with rain that the trucks stacked along either side look as if they might simply have slid off. Pools of muddy water fill the center. All thirty or forty trucks are pointed one way: toward the border crossing a few hundred yards down the road—toward Tanzania. Most have come to this place—a Kenyan settlement called Isebania—from Mombasa, where there is a port, or from Nairobi, where there is an oil depot. The weekend has stopped their progress: the customs offices are closed. There is no traffic except for the back and forth of turnboys attending to a group of four semi rigs with royal-blue tractors hooked up to long white shipping containers. The trucks have punctures, as they say in East Africa, and the turnboys must repair them. And when that's done there are mechanical problems, which the turnboys must attend to as well.

The four drivers of this small convoy sip tea under the narrow wooden awning of one of the many one-room restaurants that line the road, and watch the muddy proceedings. One of the perquisites of being a driver is that the driver gets to stay clean. Each driver's turnboy is responsible for their particular truck: he maintains it mechanically, guards it at night, warms it up in the morning (in colonial days, he turned the crank that started the motor, hence "turnboy"), and even does the cooking if there's no restaurant around. The turnboys with their trucks are like Masai with their cattle, constantly attentive. When the trucks are in a group like this, the turnboys help each other out.

On my left, Malek, the driver of the truck called Fleet 10, yells to his turnboy, Stephen, to be sure to check the tubes for more than one puncture each. (The names of some of the men have been changed.) Malek then explains to me that these flats could have been avoided if the armed escort, travelling with his truck from Nairobi, had allowed them all to rest. Escorts, provided by the national traffic police, are required for any truck hauling valuable imported goods—electronics, for example, or tires, as in the case of Fleet 10. This is because of the likelihood of theft or ambush, even in a country with the relative stability of Kenya. The convoys of escorted trucks—up to thirty or forty of them—tend to travel at night, when traffic is light, typically setting off around 2 or 3 A.M. But the traffic police, in a hurry to arrive, sometimes push the drivers too hard. A driver like Francis, whose jumbo rig, Fleet 37, is seventy-two feet long, with a payload of three containers weighing a hundred tons, needs to go quite slowly or else make frequent stops to let his brakes and tires cool off in hilly central Kenya. But on this trip the policemen had insisted that he keep going. The result was several burst tires.

I did not arrive with the three trucks in the escorted convoy but instead joined them in a fourth truck, Fleet 19, which was carrying empty beer bottles. Such a load, Malek explains, does not qualify as protected cargo. It is unlike auto parts, imported liquor, or "clothes from your dead people."

"What?" I ask.

"Yes, you know, the clothes—the clothes they sell at markets," he says.

"But what dead people?"

"You know, the clothes they sell that have been worn by your people who now are dead—*nguo za mitumba*."

It suddenly dawns on me. "Secondhand clothes."

"Yes!"

I see that Malek, though he is a worldly man, who has travelled on three continents, does not understand the discarding of clothes that can still be worn. In other words, he does not understand the Western practice of fashion. I don't have the heart to explain it.

"Those clothes are very valuable, then?"

"Oh, yes," Malek says. He takes the sleeve of his colorful print shirt between thumb and forefinger and holds it out toward me. Green stripes in the shirt match the color of his eyes; Malek has Arab blood. "Nice, isn't it?" (I speak with the men in English, since their English is much better than my Kiswahili, the language they prefer.)

The proprietress of the restaurant comes out to refill our cups with a pot of delicious *chai ya maziwa*, tea with milk. Refills aren't free, but everybody wants one. She then sets down the metal pot and leans against the doorjamb, and joins us in passing the time by watching the turnboys get filthy. A spider drops from a fold of her skirt and dangles above the concrete floor.

A week earlier, I had been shown around a truck stop outside Nairobi—the Athi River Weighbridge Station—by a medical doctor named Job Bwayo. In the early nineteen-eighties, when Bwayo, who also has a Ph.D.

in immunology, was at the University of Nairobi researching sexually transmitted diseases among prostitutes, his subjects started showing up with the symptoms of a new disease. After AIDS had been identified, Bwayo said, "I got interested in looking at the other side of the question—there must be a vector, somebody to be spreading it. There must be a man involved. Who are these men and what do they do? And it was thought that the truck drivers who cross the continent must have some role. So we went out to see."

Truck drivers were early suspects because they not only travelled constantly but had a reputation for sleeping with the "commercial sex workers," as researchers call them, who are a feature of wayside bars and restaurants all over sub-Saharan Africa. In 1989, Bwayo, who has received grants from the University of Washington and the University of Manitoba, opened a free clinic at Athi River for the use of drivers and others in the area—mainly women from surrounding shanties.

Blood tests on his patients found that twenty-seven per cent of the drivers were H.I.V.-positive; a later study showed that drivers coming from closer to central Africa had higher rates of seropositivity. Rwanda, for example, had a rate of fifty-one per cent; Uganda, thirty-six per cent; and Kenya, nineteen per cent. In similar studies of commercial sex workers, infection rates were found to run from thirty-four to eighty-eight per cent. Because AIDS is thought to have originated somewhere around the west side of Lake Victoria, in Zaire, Rwanda, or western Uganda (one theory is that it jumped to human beings from green monkeys, which carry a similar virus and are slaughtered for food in the area), and because long-distance trucking is this region's main link to the outside, it was hypothesized that truckers were unwittingly transporting the virus from central Africa to the rest of the world. Today, of the fourteen million people with H.I.V. worldwide, more than eight million of them are in sub-Saharan Africa.

International aid money began to be channelled through organizations like the African Medical and Research Foundation to educate the truckers and the women they sleep with. Getting the word out was not without its problems, however. Bwayo and the drivers ruefully remember headlines such as one on the front page of a Nairobi daily announcing to a frightened nation that TRUCK DRIVERS SPREAD AIDS! This reputation became a public-relations problem for the drivers, many of whom had enjoyed for years an aura not unlike that of the American cowboy: a man of carefree mobility who traverses unknown landscapes and survives by his wits—and, in the African case, is relatively well paid besides. But in the late nineteen-eighties the drivers started to become unhappy celebrities in the annals of AIDS research. "Oh, yes, the truckers!" said Dr. O. E. Omolo, the provincial medical officer in Mombasa, when I expressed a desire to travel with some of them in order to learn about their lives. "They are true museums of disease! Chancroid, gonorrhea, syphilis, herpes, AIDS—well, the list goes on and on!"

Before the concern with AIDS, I had known of African truck drivers through brief mentions in the books of a dozen travellers who had beaten their way across Zaire, or the Sahara, or war-torn Mozambique, by hitching rides with them. Especially in the poorest or most politically unsettled countries, trucks are the only means of getting in or out, public transportation being virtually nonexistent. As travellers, it struck me, the drivers probably had no equal in Africa.

Truckers almost never drive completely across the continent, from north to south or from east to west, since the condition of roads and the politics of Africa's fifty-three countries make it easier to ship by sea. Instead, most African trucking links the middle and the margins, plying routes from the coasts to the interior and back again. The principal ports of East Africa are Mombasa and Dar es Salaam, both on the Indian Ocean south of Somalia. From there, goods travel inland to Malawi, Zambia, Uganda, Burundi, Rwanda, western Zaire, to southern Ethiopia, Somalia, and, in calmer times, to southern Sudan. The so-called Trans-African Highway is merely a network of paved roads that link Mombasa to Nairobi, to Kampala, and then to Kigali, the capital of Rwanda, or to Kinshasa, in Zaire.

Some of the biggest competitors in this business are owned by international freight-forwarding conglomerates and are European-managed. Interfreight, a German trucking firm in Dar es Salaam, and Transami, a Belgian-run concern in Mombasa, are often favored by drivers, who say they're better paying and better run. Better paying, in the case of Transami, which owns the trucks I'm with, means compensation that ranges from twenty-six hundred to three thousand American dollars a year for a driver, and, for a turnboy, between five hundred and seven hundred dollars. In a country like Kenya, whose annual per-capita income is three hundred and sixty dollars, this is good money. But to Transami managers, dealing with the huge capital costs of imported trucks, fuel, and parts—a set of new tires costs nearly fifteen thousand dollars, for example—drivers' salaries are peanuts.

Salary, however, does not necessarily constitute all of a driver's income. Wherever there are customs rules and import duties, there is money to be made getting around them. Extra fuel taken on in Tanzania, for example, can net up to a month's salary if resold on the black market in a landlocked country. Gray parrots procured in the jungles of Zaire fetch a high price back on the coast, if they make it alive. Tanzanian maize meal increases in value over fifty per cent once it's smuggled into Kenya.

The four Transami trucks in Isebania will travel in a loose convoy at least as far as Rwanda. Besides Malek and Francis, who has a pot-belly, wears colorful silk-screened T-shirts, and loves to listen to the news on his small short-wave radio, the drivers are Sammy, a beanpole-thin member of the Kalenjin tribe, famed for its distance runners, who sports long beatnik sideburns and begins every day with a couple of wind sprints, and Bradford, the driver of Fleet 19.

A fifty-year-old veteran of the Kenyan Army, Bradford is a soft-spoken man who is meticulous in his grooming: every day, he shaves, puts on a clean button-down shirt, and polishes his black metal-toed ox-fords. Unlike Malek and many other drivers, Bradford drives cautiously, which is all right with me. It is not all right with Obadiah, the turnboy. Occasionally, as we rumble out of a turn and onto a straightaway, Oba-diah will shift restlessly in his seat, then wave his long arms in the air, and finally say, "O.K., now you can go faster. Faster! *Haraka-haraka!*" As the driver, however, Bradford rules. He tells me he has not had an accident in twenty years. He responds to Obadiah's exasperation the same way he responds to practically any perturbation: silently, almost stonily.

Obadiah is the opposite. His liveliness, humor, and occasional swings of mood can all be seen in his animated face and in the way he moves. A man of thirty-four with a rangy build, he is better educated than his driver, having completed the Kenyan equivalent of high school. One of the things, besides my cigarettes, that pleased him most when I joined Fleet 19 was my copies of Chinua Achebe's "Things Fall Apart" and Ngugi wa Thiong'o's "Petals of Blood": he quickly borrowed and con-sumed both.

Fleet 19 is a white-and-blue British Leyland Landtrain. The num-ber "19" is roughly hand-painted in white on the big black front bumper. Inside the cab are hand-painted the following notices: on the dashboard, NO SMOKING and WEAR SEAT BELT; across the glove com-partment, SPEED LIMIT 60 KPH; and, behind the driver's head—the only one that Bradford and Obadiah pay any attention to—ENGINE MUST BE ALLOWED TO RUN 5 MIN BEFORE SHUTDOWN—200 SH. FINE. There is no radio, CB or other. The steering wheel and a single seat are on the right; on the left is a double seat for passengers. In between is the gearshift. The horn works from a button on the dash. The speedometer does not work. Though the passenger-side rearview mirror was smashed long ago, enough shards remain to deliver a serviceable rear view. The door it's attached to doesn't open from the outside and can be opened only with difficulty from the inside. The vent-window locks are broken, but that's fine, because Obadiah and I can reach in through them and un-lock the truck if Bradford is not around with the key. Stuffed under-neath and behind the seats are all the clothes that Bradford and Obadiah have brought on this trip, and in the narrow slot between the seats is jammed my small duffel.

The truck is no longer than an American eighteen-wheeler: the tractor has ten wheels, and the forty-foot trailer twelve more. On our trailer is a forty-foot container, which holds, along with a small amount of sheet metal, a great quantity of new Belgian beer bottles bound for a brewery in Rwanda. They make a good strong beer in Rwanda, but they do not make bottles; thus, this critical import from Rwanda's for-mer colonial master.

Though there is much to do before the reopening of the customs offices, on Monday morning, the work doesn't weigh too heavily on anyone's mind, because Kenya is the easy part of the journey. In Kenya, the roads are paved and repair facilities are close at hand, so you can tra-verse the country in three or four days. Communication with others, in Kiswahili or in English, is seldom difficult. Good food is available, and friends are never too far away. Travelling in convoys is nice but not es-sential. In Kenya, the road is known.

But at Tanzania the pavement ends, the shilling notes change from blue to red, the prices plummet. The danger quotient rises. It is like driv-ing from Texas into Mexico. The four Transami trucks will try to travel close together. And, this being Africa, there is one major added effect: in Tanzania, the drivers and the turnboys, from multiple rival tribes and subtribes, all become Kenyans.

Obadiah, his elbow out the window, looked as hip and natural in my sunglasses as Bradford did awkward. I was sharing the glasses because the sky had cleared as we rolled away from the border, and neither had any. "Such fine goggles!" Obadiah exclaimed. "Very yellow! So nice!"

Our plunge down a hill into Tanzania was insanely bouncy. The smooth roads of Kenya had yielded to something worse than dirt: a paved road in advanced decay, its remaining islands of asphalt rising randomly to form a thousand speed bumps. For much of the afternoon, our progress varied from five to fifteen miles per hour, Bradford per-spiring as he wrestled the wheel left and right, bouncing off his seat when the old pavement lifted the truck, and Obadiah wincing to think of the tires he'd have to repair. "The road is very unfair, very harsh," he said, shaking his head.

At the first town, we pulled over to await Malek, who had stayed back to avoid our dust. Next to a shop where we bought soft drinks

stood the town's unusual wooden welcome sign: at the top, in Kiswahili, was a pleasant WELCOME TO TARIME! and then came a skull and
crossbones and the legend DANGER—PROTECT YOURSELF. THERE IS
AIDS HERE! Tarime, Obadiah said when we were back on the road, had
Tanzania's second-largest AIDS problem. Another afflicted locale was
Mwanza, a city at the south end of Lake Victoria, which we hoped to
reach by the next night. The corner of Tanzania that we were entering
was one of the places worst hit by AIDS in the world.

I tried to gauge Obadiah's reaction as we talked about this situation.
Four drivers he knew had probably died of the disease, he said. But it
was hard to be sure. Even if there were a way for drivers to be tested, he
explained, most drivers would probably not want to be: "It would only
make them sad to know." But this talk did not seem to sadden Obadiah.
Instead, after a while he became philosophical. "People must die," he
told me. "If they did not, the world would be overcrowding. You could
not drive. You see, when people die, other people get their jobs. If nobody died, there would be too many drivers." Obadiah, a smart man
who was the son of a truck driver, was probably well qualified to drive.
But in the deteriorating economy of Kenya he was not likely to be promoted any time soon. Some turnboys were now in their forties. Then,
again, if Bradford were to die . . .

I mentioned that friends of mine in the United States had died of
AIDS, and said that it was not a nice way to go.

"No, it is not," Obadiah agreed. "But there are many other ways to
die." I believe he meant that people in East Africa died of malaria,
dysentery, and truck wrecks, and, of course, he was right. But to down-
play the AIDS threat, and even to mention its positive side, was not the
reaction I had expected.

Bradford, fifty years old in a region where the life expectancy was
fifty-seven, listened to everything but said nothing.

Together, our truck and Malek's dwarfed the five or six buildings in a
village called Utegi. Sammy and Francis were somewhere behind, but
Bradford said not to worry—they would catch up in a day or so. I was
surprised when we pulled over at dusk, having expected us to travel
through the night, with Obadiah to share the driving. But Obadiah and
Bradford shook their heads. "Many bad men in Tanzania," Bradford
said, making a gun of his thumb and index finger. "You break down at
night, they shoot you."

But they had stopped at night in Kenya, too; bad men were only
part of the story. The rest, I thought, was simply that the trucking culture they were a part of considered sleeping at night the civilized thing

to do. In Utegi, Bradford and Malek paid local boys a hundred shillings (twenty-five cents) each to guard the trucks overnight, and then they and I took tiny rooms in the village's only hostel, while the turnboys laid sleeping pads across their trucks' front seats.

We left in the morning for Mwanza, and Bradford said we would make it that evening if all went well. The dirt road, though seemingly empty, was full of wonders. Winding its way through tall brown brush on our left was a procession of people led by an old man with a big spear. "They are Luo, going to a funeral," said Obadiah, who was himself a Luo. The spear was "to chase away death," he explained as we passed. A few kilometres further on, where the roadway doubled as the eastern border of Serengeti National Park, we came upon baboons seated by the roadside, and soon afterward we were passed by several of the open-backed safari vehicles called "overlanders," all of them filled with white people.

"*Wazungu!*" Obadiah cried out the window, and turned to me, grinning. This was a joke, because I was already known less by my name than by the term *mzungu*, the singular of *wazungu*, which is basically Kiswahili for "gringo," with about the same hint of deprecation.

It was September, and the land, a month or two from rainy season, looked too sere to support any human life. But Africa was deceptive. Life lurked around every bend. In the seeming middle of nowhere, we saw propped up at the side of the road tall sisal bags full of charcoal. Though we had brought one bag from Kenya, to cook with, Bradford decided it would be a good idea to pick up another—prices would never be lower. We pulled over and waited. It took about five minutes for a teen-age boy to emerge from the landscape of dry grass and leafless trees to discuss the price. An hour or two later, we stopped for woven bamboo mats, a sample of which hung from the only tree for miles. Bradford explained that these were good for sitting on and for sleeping on. Carved wooden stools, the truck drivers' lawn chairs, were next. Obadiah secured all the stuff to the front of the trailer.

Mwanza was not the lakeside oasis I had hoped for. A small port, it appeared to be built on a huge foundation of pink dust. We kicked up clouds of it wending through town to the filling station on its far side, over principal roads, all of them dirt. The heat was oppressive, so we rolled the windows down, and our damp bodies immediately became coated, like every two-story building in town, with a layer of pink powder, which left me looking darker and Bradford and Obadiah looking lighter.

Our destination was a lone Esso station, where we would refuel with a thousand-odd litres of diesel. Much of this was to be stored in the two main tanks of the tractor, and the rest would go into tanks fitted under the sides of the trailer. But when we arrived at the station—a single working pump at the edge of a big dirt parking lot—we discovered that trucks had been lining up there for three or four days. The station was out of fuel. Bradford, maneuvering with Obadiah's help, added Fleet 19 to the several rows of behemoths ahead of us and shut down the engine.

A few hours remained until dusk. The bamboo mats were unrolled beneath our trailer, providing a cool place to lie in the shade. In many parts of Africa, men who are friends hold hands; in a similar spirit, some of the turnboys lay with their arms across each other and snoozed. Some of the drivers sat on stools and talked. Obadiah picked up a copy of the Tanzanian weekly *Business Times* which he had found and soon came upon a news item that told of a crisis at one local factory: two top employees had died of AIDS, and the owners were having trouble finding replacements. (In Africa, it often happens that wealthier men, who can afford more prostitutes, are harder hit than poor men.)

"AIDS," Obadiah said. "It is very bad around here. This part of Tanzania, all the way to Uganda, it is the worst place in the world for AIDS. I know people who work at this factory." "UKIMWI," as the acronym reads in Kiswahili, was a word constantly on the lips of the turnboys.

Bradford and I went to buy food in the town market. He bought small bags of a number of exotic spices, and then lingered for quite a while over the apothecary stall. Nearby, several men stood next to bathrooms scales; I paid to climb aboard, was told my weight, and then continued to a small shop to buy a Coke. Through the shop's glass countertop was visible a box containing perhaps a gross of condoms in plain white cellophane wrappers. The box had no markings and no brand name, which made me think it had been donated by an AIDS program. "Are they free?" I asked. "No, they are two hundred shillings," the shopkeeper replied. This sum took on meaning in the coming days, as I saw that a room for the night generally cost four hundred shillings, a woman for the night cost four hundred to six hundred shillings, a filling meal cost from eighty to a hundred and fifty shillings, and a bottled soft drink seventy shillings. In other words, these condoms cost a local the equivalent of seven or eight dollars apiece—a sum that would buy you a dozen in the United States.

After dropping off our groceries for the turnboys to deal with, we set about finding lodgings for the night. Malek, who said he had a local friend in whose house he could stay, offered to help us look, because he knew Mwanza. Many hotels were full, and almost all displayed AIDS-warning posters in the lobby. When the only vacancy we could find turned out to be slightly expensive, I suggested to Bradford that he and

I take a double and split the cost. He wasn't interested. This surprised me until, on our way down the stairs from the fifth floor, Malek loudly explained, "He wants his own room so he can take a woman!"

Bradford was typically silent, but once Malek had departed he struck back. "His friend here is just a woman," he said fiercely. "He sleeps with her every time he comes here."

It took me a while to understand that in this situation "woman" automatically signified "prostitute." Women here didn't sleep with you just for the fun of it. But the guys never used the word "prostitute." To say, in a strange town, that you were sleeping with a woman was to say it all.

Bradford and I went out on the town that night. In the near-empty bar of our hotel, we had a beer and a chat with the bartender, a woman whom Bradford seemed to like. Then, at a place lit by blue lights down a side street, we sat at the bar and drank Tanzanian beer and watered-down cognac. I noticed the care with which our waitress served us the beer—a method that all waitresses in Tanzania used. Her job wasn't just to set the bottle in front of us and rush off to the next customer. It was to place fresh glasses before us, then to set out the bottles of beer, then to wipe the dust off the necks of the long-necked bottles by putting her hand around the neck and pushing it down the bottle. (After my third beer of the night, this began to look erotic.) The waitress then tipped the glass, and poured the beer. You watched while she served you; you were meant to watch.

"Which one do you like?" Bradford asked me. He was referring to the women. I nodded toward our waitress. "You can have her, then." I lifted an eyebrow. "She likes you." I gave a little snort at this, but knew that what he meant was that they were all available, or probably were. Though increasingly drunk, I explained to Bradford that I was happily living with my girlfriend in New York, and wouldn't be interested in sleeping with the waitress. I took out my wallet and showed him Margot's picture. She was sitting on her red Schwinn Hollywood on East First Street on a hot July night, flashing a big smile. Bradford reached into his wallet for a photograph of his wife. "She is at work," he explained. The picture showed a middle-aged woman sitting at a large, neat desk. On it were a telephone and huge rubber stamp. She was not smiling; smiling was not the custom in photographs here.

"Did you say she is your girlfriend?"

"Yes."

"Then it is fine! She is not your wife."

How to explain this? "But she is like a wife."

Bradford looked at me pityingly, as though I had chosen a very early retirement.

I sought another approach. "Besides, you heard what Obadiah said, right? This is one of the worst places in the world for AIDS."

Bradford agreed with me on this. "Yes, I know," he said. "To bring that home to your wife, to then pass it on to your children—very bad." He had a daughter and two sons, he said. He waved his hand and shook his head. So he did understand AIDS. I felt glad, and bought us another round.

As we entered the lobby of the hotel, I was surprised by Bradford's desire to have just one more at the hotel bar. I did not have the stamina, and so climbed the stairs to go to bed. But the wall between our rooms did not extend all the way to the ceiling, and an hour or so later I awoke to the noise of whispering voices as Bradford and someone else entered his room. The only other sound was the rhythmic, almost ultrasonic peeping of an Abyssinian nightjar. I listened to the little bird and I listened to Bradford, and I wondered, Does he use condoms? In the morning, I heard a woman speaking softly again, and as I came back from the bathroom saw her rounding the corner of our corridor, the hotel bartender, skirt whirling behind.

Sammy and Francis and many more trucks had arrived overnight at the Esso station, wedging themselves into any unclaimed space in the parking lot, of which there hadn't been much to begin with, and lining the road on either side. Approximately thirty trucks were now waiting for the fuel, which, when it arrived, would be pumped out of the single pump. I took out my books and prepared for a long wait.

The drivers and turnboys chatted, smoked, drank tea, went on errands, and sat guard, some of them on mats under the trailers, some of them seated in the cabs. Obadiah took his work clothes, still mud-caked from Isebania, to the communal spigot by the Esso office and washed them by hand. Half an hour later, jeans were draped over the rearview mirrors of Fleet 19, shirts over the windows, and socks and underwear over the windshield wipers, which were flipped away from the glass. So hot and arid was it that everything dried in about fifteen minutes.

The captive drivers attracted a stream of venders, selling everything from used clothing to pencils and spare parts. What caught my eye, looking down from the cab, was slices of freshly cut pineapple being paraded by on platters on the heads of young women; the mouthwatering fruit passed by inches from my face. Malek saw me staring and bought several slices. He also bought a thick bunch of succulent, sun-warmed grapes. I had the confidence born of a month of health in unhealthy places, and my hunger for produce was so fierce that I bent my rule against it: the grapes, I concluded, might be O.K. if I just squeezed their innards into my mouth, avoiding the skins, and the pineapple should be fine, assuming it had been cut by clean hands.

Other young women we saw evidently had nothing to sell. Two joined Malek in his cab, and I thought they might be old friends of his until he gestured at them and said, "Do you like these pretty girls, Mr. Teddy?"

"Very pretty, Malek! No, thanks!"

They left after a while, Malek deciding against further involvement, but others filtered through the tall maze of trailers all day long, smiling, climbing in to have a chat, going on their way. You did not need to seek the women out.

Just as I joined Stephen, Malek's shy, retiring turnboy, to do my wash at the communal spigot, two fuel trucks drove up to the pump. All talking in the area seemed to cease as their drivers began to unreel their hoses to replenish the station's supply of diesel. The lull was followed by the roar of engines being started in anticipation of the new fuel. Within minutes, Stephen and I could no longer speak, because of the epic rumbling coming from the grand ignition. A dark cloud of smoke gathered over the compressed mass of dirty trucks. There was a generalized jostling as those nearest the pump began inching forward, and those in the rear inched after them.

Perhaps three of the thirty trucks had fuelled up when, as quickly as it had started, the whole thing shut down. Obadiah had joined us by then, and I saw him sigh.

"What's going on?"

"They have shut down the electricity," he answered.

"What do you mean? Did they blow a fuse?"

"No, no, it is shut down everywhere." He waved his arms to indicate the surrounding neighborhood. No darkened electric signs were available to corroborate his statement, but I remembered an advertisement I'd seen in the *Business Times*, announcing strategic power rationing. This was what it meant.

Delay, I was beginning to appreciate, was one of the few certainties of this life. There was the delay of breakdown, and of border-crossing hours. There was the delay of refuelling and the delay of bad roads. And then there were the delays that to the Africans were simply life lived reasonably; namely, twelve or more hours a day spent sleeping and resting and stopping to eat.

The drivers, because of their freedom, seemed to handle the delays better than the turnboys, who were tied down by poverty and job description. Obadiah moped, but Malek wasted no time in reverting to pleasure mode once the pump went off. "Boss! Mr. Teddy!" he called as I walked back to Fleet 19. "You will come join us? This is my friend in Mwanza!" He gestured at a shapely woman standing near him, whose dark skin was set off by a brilliant-yellow dress. She wore yellow flip-flops.

"Sure," I said.

"We will be down the road. Bradford knows where."

An hour or two later, as the sun was starting to set, Bradford and I were on our way to the New Gardenia, a bright-blue two-story building with a pleasant front porch set back a little from the dusty street. I had already noticed this place; it always had a good crowd. Drinking beer at a table on the porch were Malek and his friend.

"They still have rooms!" he said encouragingly. "Go inside now!"

Bradford and I walked in. The bar was full of men and women, and other women sat in upholstered chairs. Most of the lighting came from red bulbs. Bradford spoke to the bartender about rooms, and a woman appeared to show them to us.

The rooms were as run-down as the public areas were nice. On our way to the last available single, we walked through a cloud of mist from a shower stall with a broken pipe; water was hissing out loudly. The single was next door to this shower stall. The only other available room was a nearby double, with two small windows looking onto a small second-floor patio that got a lot of foot traffic, and this was more expensive. But tonight Bradford wanted to share it. The woman had us sign the register, and I puzzled over what to put under the heading "Tribe."

"Put 'Europe,'" Bradford suggested.

"Norway," I wrote, the land of my ancestors.

The flimsy door to the room was held shut by the meagrest hook; to judge from the doorjamb, the door had been kicked or pushed in two dozen times. The beds had mosquito nets, but these were badly torn. As we unpacked a few things, I noticed a thin column of tiny ants marching across my bed.

Bradford and I went out to find dinner, but I could hardly eat what looked like a delicious omelette, because of sudden stomach cramps: it was the revenge of the fruit. We returned to the New Gardenia, where my experience of the rest of the night was aural. From my bed I picked out the voices of Malek, Bradford, and Sammy amidst the general laughing, squealing, and hollering from the bar. From the second-floor patio there came the occasional whispering of women and the bellowing of men. Near my head, mosquitoes buzzed faintly, seeking the holes in the netting over my bed; I lit a mosquito coil. Periodically, when the cassette tape at the bar was being changed, the amplified call to prayer from the local mosque drifted in the window. Around midnight, I was awakened by Bradford's return. Soon after that, some stupid drunk began pounding on our door and yelling, "Ishmael! Ishmael!"

"He's not here," Bradford replied in Kiswahili. "You've got the wrong room."

"Ishmael, Ishmael!" Again the pounding. Once more, I thought, and the door would fly open.

"He's not in here!

"Ishmael!"

Finally, there came silence. Then the same voice, this time yelling through the shutters from the patio: *"Ishmael!"*

"My name is not Ishmael!" I yelled back.

By noon the next day, because of some aggressive creeping forward by Bradford, we were pumping our fuel, hoping against hope to make it by the power-off time. "If it goes off now, we can pump the rest by hand," Obadiah said. Using a hand pump that adjoined the electric one, he explained, a man (alternating with another man) could pump seven hundred litres in three or four hours. But we finished under electric power, and so did the others in our convoy. As a small truck from the national electric utility cut into the line at the pump right behind us, we had the last laugh: two minutes into the fill-up, the electricity went out on *them*.

The next night's destination was Shinyanga, and Malek was excited. He was Tanzanian by birth, he explained when we stopped for tea in the village of Mabuki, and much of his family lived in this region. We had to wait for our tea, and, while Bradford washed his hands in a corner of the restaurant, Malek went on to say that he was way overqualified to be a truck driver but had been reduced to it by a confidential "controversy" in his life. "You know, I used to play guitar in a band," he said. "We played in all the clubs in Dar, all the clubs in the country. We made records! We played rock and roll, and we played *soukous*. We did everything."

I somehow knew that this was true. "But then what happened?"

Bradford returned. Malek said he would tell me later. He flirted in the local language with the young woman who brought us our tea, and finally she turned away, blushing.

"See? She would!" he told Bradford. "I asked her if she would like to pack her things now and come with us," he said to me jubilantly. He was famous in these parts, he assured me. "If someone is coming from the bush, like a monkey, he will still know me. I am like their president." Moreover, he continued, "I know all the women! They love me here!" We might stay in Shinyanga, he added, for a day or two.

"O.K.," I said. "For the women?"

"No, no. In Shinyanga, I get my parents' bless on me, then I feel much better. You cannot go through the country without stop at your parents."

Around midday, we pulled over again, in a village called Maganzo. It resembled a score of other places we had stopped in for tea: a handful of one-story buildings set far back on either side of the dirt highway, to give trucks plenty of maneuvering space. A small stand of trees wilted in the sun at one end of town. As Bradford eased the truck off the dirt road, our own wake of dust engulfed us and the venders who besieged our convoy, climbing up on the trucks' steps to offer us the usual bread, soft drinks, and dried fish. Malek, increasingly animated at being back on his home ground, beckoned for Bradford and me to follow him.

We took seats on benches in a smoky barbecue shed. Beams of light slipped in through the slats, illuminating sides of goat hanging from hooks on the back wall. Hosts of flies jumped from the meat to us and back again. A man with a cleaver stopped hacking away at a beef carcass long enough to hear Malek order three skewers. The flies landed. He started hacking again. The flies took off.

Three men already there knew Malek, and one shook his hand, and then mine and Bradford's; the others, who were eating, offered their forearms, and we grasped them. A boy appeared with a dish of water, and we dipped our fingers in and used a towel he offered. A bowl of salt was set down, and a bowl of chili powder. In the background, the skewers sizzled. The men licked their lips. One wiped his mouth on a sleeve and began to chat with Malek in Kisukuma, the local tongue. Malek asked me in English if I knew that there were diamond mines nearby, and explained that the mound of earth we had seen in the distance was part of them. The man spoke with Malek some more and then peered behind him and out the door. He put an oily finger back between his cheek and lower molars and withdrew something very small. He put it in Malek's hand. It was an uncut diamond, translucent, irregular, like something you might find on the beach. He described it to Malek in low tones. Malek handed me the stone and said, "He wants twelve thousand dollars. Are you interested?" The diamond was a little larger than the seed of a grape.

Our dish of hot goat was set in front of us, and the diamond went back into the mouth.

Normally the turnboys went their own way during these rests. They found tea, or bought a few cigarettes, or just sat in the shade. They weren't supposed to go too far, because always they were responsible for the safety of the truck. We left when the drivers decided it was time to leave, and the turnboys were to be close enough at hand to know when that was.

Bradford climbed up, restarted the engine, and then took a walk around the truck, examining the tires and everything else. I climbed in. Obadiah was not yet there, and neither was Stephen. Malek, parked in front of us, started his engine. He waited a moment. No turnboys. He started to drive off. It was a slow process. Bradford engaged first gear, too, then second. We were now going walking speed. Stephen and Obadiah suddenly appeared, smiling broadly, sprinting toward the trucks. Obadiah grabbed the tractor like a hobo grabs a boxcar, swung his door open wide, and landed in his seat. I wondered whether he wasn't a little annoyed by the implication that Bradford would drive off without him, but that was the last thing on his mind.

"We found milk," he said. "It was *sooo* delicious. We had a big glass of it." I picture Obadiah with his large hand wrapped around the glass of milk. He sat back and closed his eyes, then abruptly sat back up.

"Oh! And it was cold!" He gazed back at the shack where they found the precious milk.

"*Sooo* delicious!"

Malek's next stop was in the middle of a wide and barren plain. No human settlement was visible, nor, indeed, was any human until Bradford and I made it around to the front of Malek's truck. There we found Malek deep in discussion with a very thin man who had been riding his bicycle on the dirt road when the monster trucks overtook him. The bicycle itself was practically invisible because of the number of live chickens tied to it: they hung upside down from the handlebars, from the tube between the handlebars and the seat, and an indeterminate number of them were stuffed into a big wooden cage over the back wheel. There were easily sixty pounds of chicken on the bike, probably closer to seventy-five. The man removed some from the cage to show to Malek. Malek wanted to see even more. "Hold these," he instructed me, and I grasped two flapping birds around their scaly legs.

The man and Malek finally struck a bargain; Bradford bought three more. Malek handed his five chickens to Stephen, who disappeared under the trailer with them. Uncomprehending, I followed. Stephen was on his knees. He had lain the chickens in the dust. He was reaching up to open a wooden cage that had been built into the undercarriage of the trailer. "*Kwa kuku,*" he explained to me. "For chickens." One at a time, the birds were untied and placed in the cage.

Obadiah, meanwhile, was tying our *kuku* onto the back of our cab. Three-foot cords led from their legs to the exhaust pipes; the birds were meant to stand on the flat black fuel tank. Despite my disbelief, Obadiah assured me that was what they'd do. I pictured them on the bumpy roads, pictured Malek's in the sea of dust that would be kicked up by the wheels. "How long will they live?"

"Oh, they will live a long time," he said. "They will live until we eat them."

Late in the afternoon, we arrived in Shinyanga. As usual, the road had taken its toll: Malek's trailer listed to one side, and he had turbocharger ills besides. "We might be here two or three days, getting these fixed," he said happily.

The people of Shinyanga looked like Malek—lighter-skinned than Bradford or Obadiah, with a lot of Arab blood and sometimes blue or green eyes. Malek took Bradford and me on a walking tour of town and did, in fact, seem to know everybody. Assuming the role of host, he even installed us in a hotel costing a thousand shillings a night—two dollars and fifty cents, or more than double our usual tariff. Dinner, he announced, would be at the home of his cousin Walid. There was time before that to rest, and I bought a couple of beers for the turnboys.

Joining Obadiah and Stephen, I met Cromwel, a mechanic. Cromwel, aged twenty-nine, roamed Transami country in a radio-equipped Toyota Land Cruiser driven by a rotund "convoy leader" named Mwalimu. Mwalimu, a former truck driver, was now one of four lower-management trouble-shooters who zipped from country to country attending to the mechanical breakdowns, bureaucratic snafus, and other difficulties experienced by Transami drivers. The two had caught up with us that afternoon, and would provide an escort all the way to Rwanda. Though Cromwel in a way served as Mwalimu's turnboy, he was a skilled and highly paid one. With the first beer, we talked about the trucks (of course) and the books we all were reading. Obadiah had finished the Ngugi and the Achebe and was into the Tolkien I had brought from Nairobi. He confessed he really did not care for that one. Cromwel was a fan of the thriller novelist Nelson DeMille, and was currently reading "The Charm School."

With the second beer, the conversation turned to women, and Malek's prodigious appetite. Obadiah and Cromwel debated whether it was natural to have a strong sex drive, and, if so, whether you should try to control it. The terms of this talk confused me. If a strong sex drive was natural, they both indicated, one should not try to control it. But if such a drive was unnatural one should control it. "Natural," apparently meaning God-given, was the operative concept. Was Malek's randy behavior, they asked me, natural or unnatural?

I had to shrug: I didn't know. They debated this and other matters, finally agreeing only on the perils associated with amorous pursuits.

"I tell you, my friend!" Obadiah cried, waving his hands in the air. "You are fine until you are in a bar and drinking one or two beers, and then a woman with big buttocks walks by, and—oh my God!"

At the home of Malek's cousin Walid, we were served a huge quantity of good food—chapati bread, fried fish, curried-chicken stew, and lamb-and-egg pie. Afterward, over small cups of strong coffee, I asked Malek to tell me more about the controversy in his life. He turned serious, and we scooted back a little from the circle of men seated on a thin rug. In a low voice, he told me that when Tanzania invaded Uganda to unseat Idi Amin, in 1978–79, he had entered the Army and become a captain in the military police. He received training in Israel and Cuba and then participated in the campaign. In its late stages, he was put in charge of some important prisoners. But, in what sounded like an admission of guilt, he said, "I made an arrangement and they escaped." The Tanzanian Army charged him with corruption. A United Nations inquiry, however, determined that the escapees were political prisoners who had been unfairly held, and arranged for Malek to receive asylum in Kenya. That was how he and his family had come to live in Mombasa, though Tanzania was home.

This tale of exile and redemption had an epic quality that made Western life, or my life, seem humdrum. He filled in more details later, in the courtyard of our hotel, but soon became distracted by a flirtation with the waitress, and by the drinks she brought. When mosquitoes started to get bad, Bradford and I turned in.

In the morning, I asked Malek how he'd done.

"Do you know the word *hanjam*, Mr. Teddy?" I did not. "It means a lot of sweet nothing. It can also mean lots of work but no pay. You understand?"

"It means you struck out."

"Yes!"

Mwalimu, the convoy leader, dispelled Malek's hope of a prolonged stay in Shinyanga by insisting that we leave by the following afternoon. Dusk found us in a market town called Kahama, whose dirt square was filled completely with about twenty overnighting trucks. A fierce old man wielding a bow and arrow and a receipt book approached, eying me suspiciously. He was the *askari*, or night guard, of the square, and his services were compulsory. Bradford and Malek anted up. Then, after some searching, Bradford, Malek, and I secured the usual sort of lodging, and within a couple of hours Bradford and I were seated in the usual sort of bar.

This one was swarming with mosquitoes. It was off a side street near our lodging and was lighted with blue fluorescent bulbs. There was a bartender, whose bar was secured against robbers by bar-to-ceiling bars, and there were two waitresses, who wore flowing blue muumuus and, over their heads, the lovely beaded scarves known locally as *kik-wembe*. They did not have much to do; we were about the only customers. We sat on low couches around the far, dark end of the room and stretched out our legs around low tables in front of us. For the first time, we were able to order Primus, the Rwandan beer whose bottles we were hauling. It cost nearly as much as our room, and was quite strong. As our waitress went through the serving ritual, she bent forward. Underneath the muumuu she wore nothing.

Bradford was characteristically quiet, and things were starting to feel a bit dull, when Malek entered with Sammy. Malek's appearance somehow electrified the room. It put me in mind of his earlier incarnation as a rock and roller. Within moments, he had made Christina, our waitress, smile, blush, and then burst out laughing with some little remark. He sat down. She returned with a drink for him. He talked to her some more. "I am discussing with her how much I will teach her sexually," he informed me. Christina's English was not so good, so he repeated the quip in Kisukuma, and she cracked up again. "She already loves you very much," he continued, to me. "She wants to do anything you want. I have told her that you are afraid of AIDS, and that she must just suck. She says fine." Christina did not appear to have followed this, which was O.K. with me.

Malek and the others had by now become skilled at running interference for me with the women in bars. They explained what I felt they had come to believe—that I was overly concerned with AIDS—and they told the women not to take it personally, because this was a typical *mzungu* fear. Sometimes I would buy drinks for the women to show that it was nothing personal.

Outside, I asked Malek about exactly what went on when you paid to be with a woman. Did he wear protection?

"*Soksi?*" (That is, "socks"—slang for "condom.") "No. But I do not put it in them. I only have them suck. You are paying them, they'll do what you want." The usual price was between five hundred and a thousand shillings, he said, but since he spoke their local language they'd do it for three hundred, "and sometimes they'll even pay me."

I liked Malek, but the subject was depressing. Often the castoffs of men who had other wives and discovered that they couldn't afford them, these women had children to feed and no skills. Engaging even briefly in prostitution could mean that their village would refuse to take them back. A given evening at a truck stop provided only so many po-

tential clients; if a woman were to displease them by insisting on condoms—well, plenty of other girls were willing. The same held true for
anal intercourse, which many drivers requested.

We walked into another bar, nearer our hotel. Malek was immediately recognized by the bartender ("Everybody knows me!") and bought
us a round. No sooner had he told me he needed someone for the night
than a woman in a silver dress appeared and jokingly upbraided him
("She is asking why I didn't see her the last time I came through") until
he calmed her down with the usual cajoling and "words to make her
laugh." Also, apparently, a request for a date. Bradford, too, soon settled
on a girl, and I went to bed.

In my room, I thought about a conversation I had had in the truck
that day with Obadiah. He had been angry again at Bradford, this time
for going too fast over bumps. We were smoking. Obadiah was also
worried about AIDS. Whether his worries about the disease were pre-
existing or were partly brought on by me, I didn't know.

"A truck driver I know said some people don't get AIDS and some
people do, and there is no reason for it," he said. "It is like the way some
people have car crashes and some do not. Some get sick from smoking
and many do not. It is life."

"You mean you just live with it—it's your fate."

"Yes."

"But isn't this true—that you can smoke less, drive slower, and
wear a condom?"

"Yes, that is true."

"So it's not all black-and-white."

"No." He paused. "But life with precaution is no life."

That one I had to think about. Obadiah—who if he had been
brought up as I had would probably occupy some executive position—
had to spend most of his best years away from his wife and kids, and
within about a fifty-foot radius of a semi rig. His pleasures were smoking
and, much less frequently, beer and women. "Life with precaution"
would subtract from his life the two cheaper principal pleasures—and
probably all three, because of the difficulty of restraint when you had a
beer in your belly and a "woman with big buttocks" on your lap. His attitude of recklessness pained me, but I found it hard to condemn him for it.

On a recent flight in Africa, I had sat next to a sixty-year-old Canadian who smoked, drank, and told me he didn't take his heart medication even though he had suffered a near-fatal heart attack the year before.
This man held a doctorate in engineering. At my hotel in Nairobi, I had
met a foreign correspondent for a North American daily. He was an
ambitious, smart fellow who was particularly interested in the subject

of AIDS, because, he explained in the bar, he had slept with women all over the world. "But I'm cutting down on the fucking now, and trying just to stick to blow jobs," he said. Cutting down, it turned out, meant that he had had unprotected intercourse with "maybe six or seven" different women in the past three months. I said that that probably wasn't a good idea, and he said yeah, he knew.

The next morning, on a remote stretch of road, Malek's truck suffered a breakdown—cylinder-head problems. We pulled up behind him. Malek was anxious because this meant a major repair. He sketched out a plan of action: If the others didn't appear soon, he would hitch a ride to the next town and dispatch a policeman to join us by the roadside. Then he would go on to the Rwanda border where Transami had a radio transmitter, and call for help. Bradford concurred; we would watch the trucks while Malek was away, but getting a guard was essential—bandits were commonplace, and drivers could not be armed. As in most of Africa, only police and soldiers were permitted to carry guns.

Obadiah lay out the bamboo mats we had purchased earlier, and also some stools Bradford had bought. I untied the chickens, for which I had taken informal responsibility, from their attachment point at the exhaust pipe. There wasn't much to it—a few times a day the three needed a bowl of water to drink from, and some corn or rice grains scattered in front of them. Obadiah put them on the ground and showed me how to tie the ends of their three tethers together so that they could wander, but not too far. The freedom seemed to brighten them up a bit.

Malek was calculating the odds of making it to a town by nightfall when Sammy and then Francis roared down the hill and parked behind us. Mwalimu and Cromwel were not far behind, they said. *"Al-hamidulillah!"* exclaimed Malek. "I must be a holy man! I have been to Mecca! Because when I break down I don't have to wait six days, the mechanic comes!" Everyone was relieved; there was a sense of power in seeing the four huge trucks lined up along the side of the road.

To celebrate, Malek announced, we would eat. Removing a long knife from under his floormat, he bent down to the tarmac and sharpened the blade by pulling it across in long strokes. Malek put the knife between his teeth, and held out his hands; Stephen, ducking out from underneath the trailer, handed him the legs of two upside-down chickens. Malek walked over to the small trees where snakes lurked and lay each chicken on the ground, a foot over each neck.

With smooth, slicing motions, he dispatched them. Then he stood up and waited for them to stop twitching. Next he carried the headless birds to Obadiah, who plunged them into boiling water. They came out after a minute, and he and Stephen plucked them.

The two days that followed our breakdown were like camping. The men spent a lot of time seated in circles beneath or next to a trailer, telling stories and drinking tea. Francis sat in his cab, listening to the BBC foreign service on his shortwave radio.

A group of drivers paid a diplomatic call on the local goatherds, who lived in huts just around the bend. With a little warming up, they sold us delicious fresh milk for our tea, directed us to their well and to a muddy livestock-watering pond about a mile into the woods, in which we bathed, and even supplied us with chickens to augment those Malek kept in the wooden cage built into the underside of his trailer—emergency food, for occasions like this. In the morning, we heard the pipes of the boy goatherds, steering their goats around our encampment. At night, we climbed up on top of the containers, away from snakes, to lay our blankets out. And the turnboys, though they did not make a big deal about it, all slept with weapons at their sides, ranging from hatchets to tire irons. Their caution belied the idyllic look of the countryside.

All the work was done by the turnboys—they were kept busy cooking (mostly chicken or goat stew and *ugali*, a chunky starch dish, at which Obadiah excelled)—and by Cromwel, the mechanic. Replacing the *silinda hedi* was a time-consuming job for skilled hands, and Cromwel seemed to have them. The more covered with oil he got, the happier he seemed to be; there in Malek's engine compartment, he had no boss but himself. Bad cylinder heads, he explained to me, were a fairly common problem. "Transami has a shop that does nothing but recondition them—I used to work there. But the reason these trucks break so much is that everything in them is reconditioned. You see, we do not buy new parts. They are costly and must be imported. We fix the old. They last for a while, then they break again." He called out to Stephen to pass him a *tork renchi* from the *tulboksi*.

Part of the *mzungu* mystique, I came to realize, was that the far-away lands where people like me lived were the source of all this machinery—of its manufacture and design. Trucking companies there got their parts new, "factory fresh." Somebody in *mzungu*-land actually got to drive trucks when they were new. Perhaps most essential, I thought, taking an unexpected pride in the fact, was that we named the trucks and named the parts.

The first afternoon, it rained, but Cromwel worked on; the truck "bonnet" provided him with a roof, and he was so coated in oil he looked waterproof. I sat in the cab and read and was tutored in Kiswahili by Francis and slept. Early the second afternoon, the skies cleared, the clothing dried, Cromwel finished, and a large hawk landed on a snake crossing the road by the trucks. It stood there for a long time, pecking away at the snake, as we watched from the cabs.

Runzwewe, our last stop before Rwanda, was another collection of small, low buildings at a crossroads in a barren landscape. All had roofed front porches and rear courtyards and were set back far enough for rows of trucks to park in front. We arrived in midafternoon, famished, and entered a café.

The tall, thin Somali men who ran the place wore skirts. Our waiter spoke the menu: chicken, goat meat on rice, or beans. Most ordered goat meat. On the wall across from us was a portrait of Saddam Hussein; directly above our heads was an AIDS poster. It conveyed its message graphically, showing, left to right, a man in four phases of emaciation. He was practically dead in the last drawing; a cemetery with headstones underneath made the message clear. Mwalimu read the caption out loud—"*Utapunguza uzito kwa muda mfupi*"—and cracked a joke in Kiswahili, which I missed.

"What does it say?" I asked as the others chuckled.

"It says, 'You'll lose weight in a short time,' and I said, 'They should call it the Truck-Driver Diet.' "

Though it had clearly been drawn by an African hand, the poster carried a very Western message. The idea behind it was that a simple dose of correct information could make a huge difference in people's lives. The challenge was to print up enough posters, and hang them in enough public places.

But already I could see the barriers.

"You know," Cromwel said, musing on the poster. "Some people are immune from AIDS."

I told him that was not known for sure.

"But they are not certain? Then I think it could be true!"

Francis said that he had heard many different stories about AIDS. "First, we were told the *wazungu* brought it," he said.

"*Mzungu* scientists were the first to identify it, but they think it came from here," I replied. Francis looked at me as if to say, *Well, of course they do.* "Then they said that truck drivers brought it!" he continued. "There was a time when the women wouldn't sleep with *wazungu* or drivers. Now they will, but they want condoms with people they don't know."

"Yes," Cromwel said. "They want condoms with unmarried people. But if you talk with them and they come to trust you, then you don't have to."

"That's right," Francis agreed. "If you're married, with kids, it's much better. And if you are healthy."

"You mean looking healthy," I said. "You can look healthy but still have the virus that causes AIDS."

Though Obadiah understood this, the others were less familiar with the idea of being infected but showing no symptoms. I explained it, realizing as I did that understanding H.I.V. infection really required a rudimentary knowledge of biology, of how infections occur—and not only an understanding of it but a belief in it, for, as they listened and I talked, I could see my words getting filed in the mental drawer labelled POSSIBLE EXPLANATIONS.

"And anyway," said Francis, moving to end this inconclusive conversation, "if you get it you can just take some Kemron." Francis explained that though *mzungu* doctors said AIDS was incurable, Kenyan doctors had recently invented Kemron, a drug that cured AIDS. (Later I looked into Kemron, a form of American-made alpha-interferon that a team of Nairobi medical researchers had used on patients, with encouraging results, in 1990. Within weeks, and before corroborating studies, no less a personage than Kenyan President Daniel arap Moi had announced to the world Kenya's new "miracle drug" and the country's plans to manufacture it. Unfortunately, the results could not be duplicated by other researchers and Kemron, in the international health community, bit the dust. But it continued to give false hope to those who never heard the discouraging follow-up.)

"I've never heard of that drug," I told him. Oh yes, they both assured me. And if that didn't work, said Cromwel, there was always a virgin.

"What?"

"'Yes, you know, if you sleep with a virgin it will often take away your AIDS," Cromwel assured me. He knew people who had done it. I winced, and told them it wasn't true. If you slept with a virgin, you would probably just give H.I.V. to the virgin. They didn't argue with me, but I doubt whether they believed me. Modern medicine, which I took to be a challenge to traditional beliefs, they saw as merely a complement to them. My rebuttal of every African idea about AIDS probably sounded closed-minded to them.

Stretching my legs after the meal, I was relieved to run into Obadiah by the truck. Obadiah was educated—in other words, he saw things my way. As I walked toward him, I saw him looking warily at a mentally disturbed woman weaving around the parking lot, jabbering and shouting to herself.

"She is bewitched," he whispered to me. I gave him a look of incomprehension. Was this a joke? But neither Obadiah nor any of the others tended to be ironic. "Yes, it is a spell. It happens often in these small places."

I felt despairing, and the feeling was increased by the rooms we rented. They were the worst yet. There was no light—Runzwewe had no electricity—but even in the dimming daylight the sheets were obviously dirty, and the filthy pillow had no pillowcase. Bradford said his room was the same. I rested awhile and checked my watch: only 8 P.M. Maybe I could get a drink.

When I went out on the hotel porch, I could hear the faint noise of a generator and of American voices arguing: somebody had a TV. Around the trucks, it was dark, but I heard laughter on the other side and wandered over to some lantern-lit tables in front of one of the small places across the road. There a round innkeeper named Bora was joking with the drivers. They introduced me, and she continued with a story she'd been telling. It turned out that when the authorities went to the house of this man in Uganda who'd died of AIDS they found dozens of packages of unused condoms. Ah, I thought, there's a moral here, of the right kind. But Bora went on, "And all the condoms had dates that had expired!"

Knowing murmurs circled the table, and I asked Francis to explain. "These condoms, when they are too old, contain germs," he said. "And that's how he got AIDS."

"From expired condoms? That's ridiculous."

The woman asked Francis to translate my English. She looked hurt and offended, and replied sharply to him. "She says you should not doubt her. She knows—she is from Uganda," Francis said.

I touched her arm and tried to have Francis explain that I did not doubt her word, merely the interpretation of the facts. I could see that this was a losing day for Western medicine. I ordered a beer, quickly drained it, and returned to my bed.

The route to Rwanda took us over a brief but sudden ridge of red-soil mountains. The trucks groaned up the steep grades, and whined slowly down their far sides, the drivers taking it very easy: littered at every sharp turn and at the bottom of every hill were the wrecks of trucks whose drivers had been careless. Some of the wrecks were recent and spectacular. This time, Obadiah didn't complain about Bradford's snail's pace.

Malek, as usual, drove the fastest, and soon he had the punctures to show for it. We all pulled over on a shoulder behind him as it started to rain, and the turnboys paired up to attend to the tires.

Francis was the last in line, and he walked up to our truck carrying a chicken with a loose cord around its leg. I looked at my charges on the back of our tractor—one was missing! "He got away," said Francis, smiling. "He was trying to escape. I stopped to get him." This chicken had somehow foiled my knot. I retied him to the exhaust stack as Bradford looked on disapprovingly.

"You know what they say, when you get punctures?" Francis asked me.

"No."

"They say you forgot to pay your girl this morning."

"So who do you suppose didn't pay today?" I asked, playing along. We had discussed this subject before, Francis explaining that, with women you knew, the gift of a "compact" (cassette tape), a bottle of perfume (Francis had gestured to his underarms), a nice T-shirt, a pair of shoes, or a length of fabric was as welcome as money. "Did Malek cause this?"

Francis shrugged. "Could have been anybody," he said.

The final drop, into the river valley that marked the border, was scenic, and excruciatingly slow: the grade was ten per cent, and the drivers were hypercautious. Eventually, we rounded a bend that presented us with a view of a small Tanzanian customs station perched on the steep hillside, a compound of Rwandan customs buildings, across the valley, and, between them, a bridge over a wild and glorious cascade of water, identified on my map as the Chutes de Rusumo. Mist rose from the churning waters, partly obscuring dense semitropical foliage that listed toward the river from its banks. Leaving Tanzania proved to be a simple matter, but when I saw the drivers blocking their wheels and parking for the night, planning not to cross till morning, I told them I was going to walk down to the bridge and take a look.

As one, they warned me to stay. "The soldiers will shoot you," Bradford said.

When I expressed my doubts, Francis told me what had happened to another truck he had driven in Rwanda. I suddenly remembered that at the Transami office in Mombasa, Harry Hanegraaf, a white Kenyan who was the manager of land transport, had shown me a pile of snapshots of various trucking mishaps from the past two years. There were several impressive wrecks, but the most memorable was the picture of the cab of what had evidently been Francis's rig. It had been heavily sprayed with machine-gun fire and, from what I recalled, set ablaze. Francis told me that two years earlier his truck, as part of a convoy of government-escorted trucks travelling on the road west of the northern Rwandan town of Ruhengeri, had been ambushed by a squad of guerrillas. After stopping the trucks by blocking the highway with debris, the guerrillas told the drivers to run; they then looted the trucks and, to underscore their message, destroyed them.

Bradford had a way of dealing with officials that drove Obadiah crazy. "He is so stupid!" he whispered vehemently as Bradford got down from the cab to open the container for the Rwandan customs man. "He sits with a face like this"—he did a good impression of Bradford's pugnacious stare—"and pretends he doesn't understand anything. And he thinks this will work. Well, let me tell you, it doesn't work!"

All the paperwork had gone smoothly, if slowly, that morning, the drivers presenting their thick sheaves of bills of lading, export certifications, and identification documents at the single window. Around the side of the building, at the same time, Obadiah had helped me negotiate with the black-market money changers who swarmed around us in their furtive way. All that remained was to drive away.

But, even with the paperwork in order, the guard who controlled the barrier gate across the road had to be dealt with. Bradford's stone-faced truculence had worked at the Tanzanian border—he had had to pay only the official duty, which Transami advanced him. But that was not going to cut it here. "You have to talk to them, to show them you are not afraid," Obadiah said, looking in his rearview mirror. "You have to compliment them, and then you have to insult them for wanting money that is not their due. Bradford does not understand this."

Bradford hoisted himself into his seat a few moments later, livid, and jerked the truck into gear. He had had to pay the guard twenty dollars, he said. "Out of my pocket! Transami should pay for this! But they pay me nothing!" Obadiah, wisely, kept quiet. Bradford was so mad that he ignored the gestures of two more soldiers, who rose to their feet as we approached, apparently signalling us to pull over. It was not until a third soldier, waving menacingly, made us understand that we were supposed to be driving on the other side of the road—in Francophone Rwanda, you drive on the right, and not on the left, as in Kenya, Tanzania, and Uganda—that Bradford veered across the tarmac, still muttering. "These people! Rwanda!"

During an afternoon of low-gear rises and drops, Bradford, the tension showing on his face, swerved and shook his fist to keep kids from grabbing rides on the trailer. He even stopped the truck, ordering Obadiah to chase them away. The reason, he said, was that kids would drop off and then cross the road without looking—many were killed this way. But I also sensed that Rwanda annoyed him in general, and that keeping kids off the truck helped him keep the country at bay.

Late the second day, we reached the hilly capital, Kigali. We passed near the modern-looking center and then continued out of town to a dingy suburb, where industry and low-grade housing were mixed. This district, Gikondo, was the home of the Magasins Généraux de Rwanda (MAGERWA), the national warehouses. In order to protect international trucks from the depredations of local thieves while they awaited customs certification and did their loading and unloading, the government had carved from a hill two huge holding yards, surrounded by red cliffs and by fences topped with barbed wire. The rear yard was for flammable loads, most of them twin-trailer petrol trucks returning from fuel depots in Tanzania and Kenya. The other was for general cargo, and we pulled up at its entrance. Obadiah dropped off with our documents as armed guards unchained the metal front gates, raised a traffic boom, and waved us in. Bradford headed for a corner of the great space where one Transami truck was already parked.

As the drivers parked their trucks, I took a walk around. The surface was not pavement but hard-packed, oil-saturated soil. A concrete building housed some fetid toilets and some overflowing sinks for washing dishes and clothes. The hundred-odd trucks in the lot were divided into national ghettos, the brand of truck varying with the nationality: the largest cluster, driven by Somalis, consisted mostly of old orange Fiats, Italy having administered parts of Somalia; the next largest consisted of Mercedes-Benz ("Benzi") trucks, operated by the big German-owned Tanzanian shipper Interfreight (Germany ruled Tanzania early in the century); trucks of Rwandan, Burundian, or Zairean registration were usually Renaults; and our vehicles, of course, a legacy of British empire, were Leyland. (One had even been used in the Falklands War, Harry Hanegraaf said.) The only other *mzungu* in the area was a vender of frozen Lake Victoria perch from Mwanza, who was selling the big fish from a refrigerated trailer.

The length of our stay in Kigali depended on the actions of two parties. Transami's sister company in Rwanda, Transintra, had to supply paperwork for the loads we were dropping off and picking up; and the MAGERWA customs personnel had to accept the paperwork. The order from Transintra to unload didn't come until the third day, Friday, and Bradford and Obadiah returned from the MAGERWA warehouses in dark moods, the container still on the trailer. There was a huge line, Bradford explained, and they didn't come close to making it to the front. And they couldn't try again until Monday.

There was more to it, Obadiah told me later, when his fury had somewhat subsided. To unload in any reasonable amount of time, you had to tip the clerks, had to tip the crane operator, had to tip the *askari*—

you had to play the game. Bradford stonewalled, as usual, with the result that they got nowhere.

"I guess maybe that's the price of being honest," I suggested, looking for a positive side.

"It is not a question of honesty. He is just stingy!" Obadiah said.

Malek, Sammy, and Francis did unload, and Sammy and Francis took on new containers to take further into Rwanda and into Zaire, respectively, on Monday. In the meantime, we waited. Life in the yard had its interesting aspects, most notably the commercial ones. After we washed our shirts, boys came by to iron them. There were no electrical outlets around; the boys used portable black irons that had hot coals in an internal compartment. Venders of used clothing, *nguo za mitumba*, made the rounds night and day. Flyers advertised a showing of the film *Pretty Woman*—not in a theatre, Bradford explained, but in the house of someone who had procured a VCR and a bootleg tape. Scores of venders not so favored by the gatekeepers offered their wares right outside the front gate, besieging the drivers as though they were tourists emerging from a fancy hotel.

The turnboys switched from maintenance mode to culinary mode and our chickens, alas, were one casualty. (Obadiah, perceiving my unnatural attachment to them, dispatched two one day when I had stepped away.) Hours were spent preparing food (the rice we used, from Tanzania, had to be sifted to remove tiny pebbles and husks), cooking it over the charcoal stove, eating, and then sitting around. Mwalimu at night turned into a master storyteller. Standing amid the circle of men seated between two trucks, he created gales of laughter as he imitated Francis drunk, berated colonial powers for getting African farmers to grow something as useless as tea, and mimicked a Transami driver they did not much like, who had so far spent two fearful weeks stranded by the side of the road in wild Zaire, waiting for a rescue.

At night, the drivers and I would generally escape MAGERWA for a hotel known as the Snake. This was a nickname; on the room receipts it said "Logement Kalibu Gikondo." Except for Mwanza's New Gardenia, it was the most brothel-like of the cheap hotels we stayed at.

There were no signs. To get to the Snake, we walked up a steep road rutted by rain to the top of the Gikondo hill. Here, amid small houses, were two tall white iron gates opening onto a brick patio, the beer garden of the Snake. These gates were the sole entrance to the compound. The rooms all opened off two small courtyards farther in, past the office, and these, too, could be sealed off with iron gates. I didn't like the place at first. A drunk yelled at me as we walked through the crowded beer garden to get to the office. A crowd gathered as we registered. I was the first *mzungu* they had ever had, an unsavory-looking man in an unbuttoned shirt, who was named Alphonse, explained. He handed me a receipt and a carbon copy of it. "That one you give to the girl," he said, in French, "so that she knows what room you're in."

Another employee then asked gaily, "You want to fuck my wife?" His name was Andrew, and I think now that he was just giddy at his first chance to pander to a *mzungu*, because later he became friendly and quite helpful. The woman in question, who stood smiling, turned out to be Zairean and a great favorite of Malek's, and of course was not Andrew's wife at all. To my surprise, the room was clean and better than average: the Snake, I came to appreciate, was underpriced in the way of Las Vegas hotels, which make their real money off you in other ways.

Apart from Andrew and Alphonse, the personnel seemed to be women. They would serve you your Primus, then sit with you while you drank it. They would come to your room if you wanted, but there was no obligation—the usual arrangement. In the morning, the tiled showers had hot water—a miracle—the sun shone down on the courtyards, and the women became maids, who would sing as they washed up. There were good mirrors, each with an Afro comb hanging from a string. The Snake was a favored spot of the local military commanders, Andrew told me, and no one ever bothered you there.

Well, almost no one. As Cromwel, Sammy, and I were having a few beers the first night, a drunk guy stood up and insisted on sitting next to me. He wanted to thumb-wrestle. I consented, and each of us won a round. But then he wanted to yell loudly in my ear. He was high on something besides beer. Andrew interposed, telling him to lay off, and he did for a while; Andrew then said to me that the man had been smoking some kind of dope, and this was why he was so aggressive. Finally, escorted by my friends, I retired to my room. A while later, there was an insistent knocking at the door and then an *"Ouvrez la porte!"* I opened it. Alphonse, silk shirt unbuttoned to his waist, stood there with a young woman, who looked far more virtuous than he.

"You want?" he asked, with a big grin.

"Non, merci. Elle est très jolie, mais non. Bonsoir." I bolted my door. The knocking resumed. I ignored it.

But after that first night things calmed down. We checked out every morning, as was our custom (you never knew what the day would bring), but every night we returned, becoming regulars at the Snake.

After the convoy had spent nearly a week in the yard, however, everyone's spirits began to deteriorate. Various incidents set them back. Obadiah had a pair of jeans stolen from where he had hung them to dry over the chain-link fence. Cromwel had his flashlight (*torchi*) stolen

from the Land Cruiser while Mwalimu was inside the Transintra office. MAGERWA's immigration officers, whom Obadiah had told that
I was *bwana*, the boss, apparently had begun to doubt it and were looking for me. Malek started getting fevers, which reduced him to spending most of the day lying in his cab; he said it was malaria. Obadiah got
diarrhea—underripe bananas, he thought. And I was with Mwalimu
when he got into a fender bender with a reckless-driving government
official, and had to go to the police station. There he was informed that
the accident was being judged his fault.

"How could that be?" he asked.

"It would never have happened if you had not come into the country," the policeman said.

I started noticing coffins everywhere. About eight were stacked up
outside a craft shop in Gikondo, and it seemed that a small funeral
procession with a rough-hewn, unfinished casket held aloft passed
MAGERWA every other day. Was it AIDS or the civil war? Kigali,
where between thirty and thirty-four per cent of the adults of reproduc-
tive age were infected with H.I.V., was the closest thing to an epicenter
that the epidemic had. But at night we would sometimes hear shells exploding, and automatic-weapons fire. Then, one morning, a man at the
Snake said he had heard on the radio that peace talks between the government and the rebels had broken off, and an invasion of Kigali was imminent. I decided it might be a good time to visit the American Embassy.

The center of Kigali, while more lively than the yard, was also
much more frightening. Soldiers were everywhere; streets were sealed
off for security reasons; a manned tank surrounded by foxholes was
parked at a main intersection. I ate lunch at a restaurant overlooking
the street, and stood up when everyone else did to watch a demonstration of perhaps forty people waving blue banners and singing. This, I
was told by an American woman standing nearby, was not the rebel insurgency but a political demonstration by the newly constituted Social
Democratic Party—one result of the simultaneous "opening" of Rwandan politics toward a multiparty system.

The marchers turned the corner, and we started to sit down, but
then shots were fired and people outside screamed. Demonstrators began running back down the street past the restaurant. I hastened to the
door, but the American woman told me to sit down. She lived in Kigali,
she said, and explained that the soldiers were very nervous. A week before, she and a friend were being interrogated on the street by a soldier
when the soldier's rifle accidentally went off, sending a bullet through
the narrow space between their heads. They had escaped with only a
nicked ear. Today, things sounded different.

Half an hour later, she directed me to the American Embassy. Officials there gave me some details about the insurgency, showed me maps, and indicated the location of the nearest rebel stronghold, about forty-five miles away.

"Is that all?"

"Well, they were here in the city two months ago," one official said. At least, they thought so: the possibility existed that the government had staged the gun battles for its own purposes.

An Embassy official named Larry Richter took over, and assured me that the rumor that the talks had broken down was a result of a misunderstanding; the two sides had merely concluded the latest in a series of negotiations. Richter was candid and friendly. The shooting at lunch, an employee told him, had resulted in the death of a demonstrator—nervous soldiers had fired on the procession. He thought I had more to worry about in Gikondo, where burglars dressed as policemen were said to be entering houses and beating the occupants, and where other opposition demonstrators had been brutally attacked. He warned me to be careful, and wrote down the phone numbers of his Embassy office and his residence. "Give a call if you're still here on Sunday—we play volleyball at my place," he said. I tucked the numbers into my back pocket.

A red motorbike-taxi took me back to the yard through an afternoon shower. But where the trucks had been there was only empty space. A driver who was parked next to the empty space told me that Fleet 19 had unloaded its beer bottles and been sent to a yard owned by Transintra, to take on cargo, and the driver's turnboy said he'd show me where.

We walked for an hour and entered another industrial neighborhood—this one, for better or worse, largely devoid of people. The Transintra yard had an open-air repair shop and a grassy space on which were parked Fleet 19 and another Transami truck, driven by a veteran Swahili driver named Zuberi. Resting near a brick wall in the back, slowly being absorbed by vegetation, were the components of a large building crane—engine, swivel, boom segments, everything. This was to be our load, Obadiah told me sullenly—not the bags of coffee they had hoped to get for a quick trip back to Mombasa. The crane, bound for tiny Burundi, to the south of Rwanda, would add days to what already felt like a lengthy trip.

We talked until the sun began to set and swarms of mosquitoes wafted over from the marsh next door. Cromwel and I, it was decided, would go to the Snake to reserve rooms for all of us. Mwalimu offered to drive us over.

We alighted at the entrance to the MAGERWA yard, and Mwalimu sped away. When we had walked no more than twenty paces toward the steep hill leading to the Snake, two soldiers armed with carbines stopped us. They were dressed in fatigues, with jackboots and berets. One bore his rifle properly, with the barrel behind his shoulder, but the shorter one had his reversed, so that the barrel pointed up into the nose of anyone he spoke to. They appeared to be sixteen or seventeen years old, and both, it soon became evident, were drunk.

Thus began a fearful several-hour saga in which the soldiers, illiterate and unable to speak any language but Kinyarwanda, followed us to the Snake, harassed Alphonse and Andrew, and demanded that I surrender my passport and accompany them to an undisclosed location. That seemed like a bad idea, so I stalled, and took refuge in my room. Once, when they had left momentarily, Andrew came running in to say he'd heard that the surlier of the two planned to return and stab me. (Cromwel said it was too bad we couldn't get the soldier alone "and bash his face in.") Andrew first changed my room and later persuaded the owner of the Snake, the fattest man I had met in Rwanda, to seclude me in his personal wing of the compound. Bradford came in, too.

Several soldiers had by this point gathered at the gate to the Snake. I used the owner's phone to call Larry Richter at his home. Not long before midnight, the owner opened his door to a small, armed contingent of tall blond men from the Embassy who grabbed me by either arm, brushed past the Rwandan militia, and spirited me away in a Mitsubishi Montero that had been left running at the gate.

For four days, I lay low at an Embassy residence, emerging only to check on the progress of the crane loading. It was delayed, in an irony that escaped none of the drivers, by the lack of a small mobile crane needed to lift the pieces of the big one onto the trailers. Then, once everything was loaded and secured, departure was delayed again by Transintra's failure to provide a new freight manifest and other customs paperwork. In the end, we left without the paperwork, carrying only Transintra's promise to send a courier to intercept us before we made the Burundi border.

I had nothing physical to show the drivers of my ordeal—no black eye, no stitches from a stab wound. However, filling in at an Embassy volleyball game, I had managed to mangle my right ring finger; it could no longer extend itself. A doctor at the game couldn't diagnose the injury but said she didn't think that the finger was broken. Seeking sympathy, I showed the injury to Obadiah, who had played volleyball at the national level in Kenya. Maybe he had seen something similar, I thought.

Obadiah looked at my hand, and then I noticed his: *He didn't even have a right ring finger.*

"A container landed on it when we were loading three years ago," he explained. "I had to miss four months of work."

For a long time, I did not worry any more about my finger.

To fly from Kigali to Bujumbura, the capital of Burundi, takes half an hour. To drive by car usually takes five to six hours—"which tells you a lot about the road," Larry Richter had said to me. But to go by truck took us from Sunday morning to midday Wednesday, or roughly seventy-seven hours—which tells you a lot about truck driving in Africa.

The big delays, for trucks, are the border crossings, but so snail-slow were we and Zuberi, with our trailers overloaded and the roadway nothing but hills, that we also had to spend three nights en route. The first was the provincial southern capital of Butare, 81 kilometers from Kigali. Butare had signs warning truckers they would be fined if they parked on its streets overnight; but after some hanging around at dusk we learned of a lot off the main drag where we could park if we left before dawn.

Zuberi, Bradford, and I then sought out dinner at one of the town's three restaurants. Two female *wazungu* sat down shortly afterwards with a local man, and we got to talking. The women were Peace Corps volunteers, one involved with a fisheries project and the other with a health program. They said AIDS was a big problem in Butare—Rwanda's cities are much worse off than its countryside. They blamed the soldiers, who had attracted legions of prostitutes to town when first they were quartered there. Attitudes toward sexual behavior were changing, but slowly. Why, just the night before, across the street at the restaurant-club called the Ibis, Adrienne had been dancing to Zaireian *soukous* when the soldiers and men she was with all started chanting along with the refrain to one song. The words were in Lengala, the Zaireian tongue most used in music and by the army. "And they said, 'It's about how fun sex is without condoms!' "

Their shy African friend was a truck driver, too, and Adrienne told us that he aspired to do the kind of long-haul driving my companions did. The man knew a little Kiswahili, and Bradford and Zuberi shared some words with him. But afterwards when I asked, Bradford sniffed to me that the man "drives a fish truck of only ten tons." Though the Transintra manifests claimed less, we were each hauling around 60 tons. To my friends it was the difference between a tricycle and a ten-speed. The man had no stature.

By noon the second day, we had reached the remote, mountainous border. "Here is very far, very deep," Obadiah said as we parked. A river marked the actual line, with tiny settlements on either side and lush vegetation all around. We wouldn't be crossing right away—Transintra still had not caught up to us with the customs papers. Instead, we would wait at the border until the messenger arrived.

There were no lodgings, no real restaurants, and not much to do. Across the road from us was the dormitory of a small detachment of soldiers. I shied away from them, but Obadiah made friends. It was more peaceful here, he said, and the soldiers were nice. Bradford slept in the truck that night, and Obadiah and I underneath. When Obadiah slept outside, he put his shoes right next to his head, to keep them from being stolen. I did the same, and was awakened in the morning by a goat tugging on the salty, smelly leather of my cross-trainers.

Obadiah and I ended up the next evening in the small dark room of a woman who served us charcoal-broiled goat, unleavened bread, and tall glasses of a locally brewed banana wine called *urwagwa*. I had offered to buy him dinner, because I had seen his discomfort the night before when a crowd of hungry children gathered around the meal he was preparing by the side of the truck. "I cannot eat if hungry people are watching," he said, and, in fact, he hadn't. So now we were in a dark room, where hungry people couldn't see us.

He was, I was concluding, a very moral man. I remembered the afternoon at MAGERWA when through the fence we watched the driver of a flammable liquids truck kill two chickens. Unlike Malek, who held the birds down till they were really dead, this man had lopped off their heads and allowed the bodies to run around, spurting blood and attracting the attention of other chickens, which began attacking the headless ones. Obadiah had shaken his head in disgust.

"That is how they do it in the big hotels," he said, "when they have to kill many, many chickens. But he was only killing two.

"You know, Ted," he had said, touching my arm, "how you kill is how you will die."

We drank more *urwagwa*, and Obadiah said that it was probably what the soldiers were drinking before they hassled me—it was common in Rwanda, and cheap. I wondered as I drank if *urwagwa* normally brought on that kind of ugly response, but concluded that the general situation in Rwanda—AIDS, and a civil war that had killed tens of thousands of people and displaced nearly a million—was a more likely cause. The wine engendered a certain congeniality, and Obadiah and I sat for a long while. I had told him about some pretty *mzungu* women at the volleyball game in Kigali, and he now asked me, knowingly, if I had "made friends" with them. No, I told him, I hadn't, and he suggested, "They are worried about AIDS, like you!" No one, he assured me, could stop sleeping with people forever. "One day—after a month—they will want to do it," he said. We laughed, and he lowered his voice. "Ted," he said earnestly, "a friend of mine is sick. Are any of your pills for gonorrhea?"

What friend could it be, I wondered. And what pills were for gonorrhea? "Like penicillin?"

"Penicillin, yes, but better is amoxicillin, or tetracycline. Ampicillin, too, will work."

I was surprised to hear the names. "No, I'm sorry," I answered. "I don't have those." He didn't bring it up again for three more days, but I started wondering just how Obadiah had got gonorrhea, if that was what had happened. Gonorrhea is one of the diseases linked with a high risk of catching H.I.V. If Obadiah had it, that meant that even the best-educated people probably weren't using condoms. This, in turn, implied, of course, that they could well die, and along the way perhaps their wives and children. The impulse to lecture all the men, instead of just inform them, was practically overwhelming.

The next afternoon, the messenger arrived with the papers, and two days later we reached Bujumbura. Some of the hills en route had been extremely steep; as the convoy crawled down one, Bradford and Obadiah told me about a Transami driver who, a year before, had descended too fast, lost his brakes, and killed seven people, many of them squashed by his container; it had been filled with mattresses, and they were strewn everywhere. An ambulance rescued the injured driver moments before an angry mob of villagers would have torn him to pieces.

Bujumbura lay at the bottom of the biggest and final hill, and had a far more relaxed atmosphere than Kigali, which was in some ways its sister city. It was a city at peace. Also, it enjoyed a site on the shore of Lake Tanganyika—a wide, murky sea, across which the dark mountains of western Zaire were sometimes visible. Even Bujumbura's equivalent of MAGERWA was situated on the lake. From its black-topped surface and through its high chain-link fence we could hear the lapping of water on the beach and see the tips of waving palm trees. At night, we heard the snuffling of hippos, which trundled up from the beach in search of choice garbage in the dump across the street. The sky, early in the morning, was filled with thousands of bats above a large tree half a mile away from us.

Bradford was annoyed at me for having done what I thought was a good deed—giving Obadiah a little money. "How much did you give him?" he demanded when he saw Obadiah smoking from an entire pack of cigarettes. (Turnboys normally bought them singly.) I told him half the actual amount, and he was still annoyed. "He will use it to get drunk!" he said angrily. "You should not give him money." The real problem, I figured, was that their poverty was one of the things that kept turnboys near the trucks—without money, there was really nowhere else to go—and also made them beholden to the drivers. Money was the drivers' control. I had stepped into the balance and, at Obadiah's behest, distorted it.

I had given him nine hundred Burundi francs—the equivalent of about four dollars. With a certain amount of misgiving, I watched as he left the lot with a local driver at about 4 P.M., and waited to see if Bradford's prophecy would come true. Would he just use it to get blasted? But an hour and a half later the two returned, a nice, sober spring to their steps. Obadiah had spent his remaining seven hundred francs, he told me without being asked, on a meningitis shot. Hadn't I heard? There was a big outbreak of meningitis in Burundi—two hundred people had died so far. Bus transportation between cities had been halted to try to slow its spread. I had received such a shot before coming to Africa but hadn't dreamed that I might need it. I secretly congratulated Obadiah on his caution—I hadn't known him as well as I thought.

Though the Transintra agent had visited us and promised to try to expedite things, it looked as if this were going to be another long wait. After unloading the crane, we would have to load thirty-odd tons of coffee. But first the agent would have to locate a container to put the coffee in, and he didn't know of any in the vicinity. The drivers rested, talked, slept.

The second day, Bradford offered to show me the way into town, but Obadiah pulled me aside as we prepared to leave.

"You know the gonorrhea?" he asked when we were alone. Not having heard more, I had assumed it had got better. "Well, it is much worse. You know—pus, and everything. That girl in Kigali was so very pretty, but—"

"What girl in Kigali?"

"I told you, the night the soldiers came and you gave me your key." I had tossed him my room key on the way out.

"Oh, no! That was when you got it?"

"Yes! So here is what I need—tetracycline, amoxicillin, or ampicillin." He even seemed to know the dosage in milligrams, so I had him write it all down in my notebook. And off I went.

Visiting the pharmacy put me in mind of my own health. I went by the local United States A.I.D. office, where a doctor agreed to look at my finger. By now, it was red and sore, still couldn't extend itself, and had assumed an odd gooseneck shape. He manipulated it, said he thought I'd snapped a tendon, and suggested I consult a hand surgeon.

"Can you suggest anyone locally?" I asked.

He looked at me as though I were joking. The country didn't have X-ray machines with the definition needed to diagnose my injury, he said, much less a specialist. "But maybe in Nairobi," he added. I thanked him and returned to the lot.

Obadiah was thrilled to see the packets of amoxicillin capsules I had picked up for him. "Oh, you are such a nice *mzungu*!" he exulted. Then I handed him another purchase from the pharmacy—a small package of Prudence condoms, price twenty Burundi francs, or less than a dime. "Next time, use these," I said, in a mock man-to-man tone. Looking at the box, he didn't know what they were. "Open it," I said. He pulled out the four cellophane-wrapped condoms. He still didn't know what they were. "You don't know?" They didn't look any different from condoms you would buy anywhere. I opened one and removed the latex circle.

At last, there was a sigh of recognition. "Oh, yes."

Obadiah had finished reading a well-thumbed Perry Mason mystery, "You Find Him, I'll Fix Him," and left it for me. I lay on my side and opened the paperback to a small card that he had used as a bookmark. On it was a paragraph in his handwriting: "Short, fat, and built like a barrel, but all the same the best description I can give her is that she reminded me of Mussolini in her size, same ruthless, jutting jaw, dark complexion . . ." This was not, I would later confirm, a passage copied from the book. Obadiah admitted sheepishly that he had written it while he was sitting, bored, in the yard that afternoon. He said the Perry Mason book had inspired him, and so had the way I was always writing things down. I told him he should write the whole book.

The winds the first night had been hot, but dry and strong enough to keep us cool. This second night, though, the breeze slowed and reversed direction; humid air from the lake poured in and soon had us soaked. It also brought a huge quantity of mosquitoes. Everyone started slapping himself and pulling a blanket or a shirt over his head, despite the swelter. Though my malaria medication was supposed to be good, it wasn't fail-safe, so I reached into my bag and dug out mosquito repellent. Because this was the dry season, I had hardly used repellent up to this point; tonight would be a test. Others gathered around as they saw me slathering on the pungent lotion.

"What medicine is that?" Obadiah asked.

"Mosquito repellent," I said matter-of-factly, passing some to him. He asked for directions. "You've never used it?" He shook his head.

The others, waiting their turn, regarded the little red bottle with such amazement that I felt like Aladdin demonstrating my lamp. Only

Zuberi looked on with any recognition. "We used this in the Sudan," he said to me. "In the Army."

I felt a prick in my shoulder and reached back to slap it. The action left a stain of blood on my white shirt. Shit, I thought—it was one of the few "confirmed hits" I'd had since coming to Africa. And this was moments after applying the repellent. No precaution, I supposed, was a hundred per cent foolproof. Under the trucks, even with the lotion, there was still a lot of swatting going on. One unlucky mosquito bite, I thought, trying to take the drivers' point of view, could perhaps be likened to one unlucky fuck: you'd probably already had it, and what was the incremental risk of just one more? I wondered if what had been called Africa's fatalism wasn't just a reasonable response to the fact that there was only so much you could do.

I left three days later. That morning, a crowd of people had gathered on the beach of Lake Tanganyika, across the road from the truck yard. Obadiah was among them. He had an uneasy look on his face as I approached. There at his feet, water lapping over its bloated limbs, lay a corpse that had just washed up. "He was a sailor on the lake," Obadiah reported. "They say he fell overboard three days ago when he was drunk." I had never seen a drowned man before. He was gray, and very dead. Nobody touched him.

The crane had still not been unloaded—"Some of these shippers use our trucks to store things for free," Bradford explained—and I had caught my bad finger on some clothing and further torn something inside it. We guessed that it could be another ten days before the truck left Burundi (it turned out to be even longer). I said my goodbyes, traded addresses, took orders for presents. Obadiah and Bradford walked me to a taxi stand, and I left for the airport.

I made it to Mombasa in a day; Bradford and Obadiah's return trip took three weeks. Bradford's truck and Zuberi's, I later learned from Transami, reached home without incident; they had left Bujumbura two weeks after I did, and in the provincial town of Gitega they each loaded about thirty-five tons of coffee packed in sisal bags, like our charcoal. Other trucks from the convoy returned earlier and later. Sammy was back from Ruhengeri, Rwanda, on the twenty-third of October, soon enough to receive a promptness-incentive payment (fifteen dollars). Francis didn't return from Goma, Zaire, until the twelfth of November. And Malek had somehow managed to break down again in Shinyanga, and would be there a while. I knew that would make him happy.

I had several questions to ask Harry Hanegraaf, of Transami, among them details of a story I had heard when we were waiting at the MAGERWA yard in Kigali. A turnboy of Zuberi's had died there two years before, of malaria, Zuberi had told me. Malaria, of course, is endemic to the area, and everyone suffers bouts of it; women and children sometimes die of it, but grown men seldom do. Since Zuberi's English was worse than my Kiswahili, I had had to collect this story secondhand and had heard many versions. What, I asked Hanegraaf, had really happened?

Hanegraaf said the turnboy had been dead several days when drivers brought him to the Kigali hospital from Gisenyi, on the Zaire border. The body was so decomposed, the morgue there claimed, that it could not be put in cold storage; instead—and this outraged the drivers—it was left outdoors. Transami dispatched a truck to recover the body but, realizing the awful shape it was in, finally paid to fly the corpse to Mombasa. ("It's Africa," Hanegraaf said, explaining the expense. "The family refused to allow the remains to be buried in Kigali.") The family came for the corpse at company headquarters, and the casket it had been shipped in was buried at the back of the yard. ("Nobody here would touch it.") Of course, no autopsy was done—who would ever pay for such a thing?—but Hanegraaf had an opinion about the death which differed from Zuberi's. "That turnboy didn't die of malaria," he said. "He died of AIDS."

Mark Kramer

Peter Vandermark

Mark Kramer's plans to write about bureaucracy and agriculture in the Soviet Union expanded in 1988, during an assignment there for the *New York Times Magazine*. He eventually made six trips, traveling for up to two months at a stretch with friendly informants who knew the Communist system.

"It was exhausting working with translators week after week. Imagine doing an intricate cabinetmaking job, using only tools that have handles ten feet long. Every chat, every glance at a factory bulletin board, was clumsy and slow, but it was still possible to do the work," Kramer said.

Literary journalists who take on long-term projects risk time and money until their books are published. Kramer had a 500-page manuscript written by

August of 1991. Then the Soviet Union fell apart and the Party collapsed—some of the most astonishing and unpredictable events of the twentieth century. "John McPhee had the right idea about topic selection when he chose to write about rocks and mountains," Kramer said. "Those writing about Russia in the past few years know they're describing the configuration of quicksand."

The heroes of his first draft had been the "reform Communists," who appeared to be the only hope for progress. After the fall of the Communist regime, Kramer made two more long trips to Russia, where he at last gained access to emerging "capitalists, artists, and whimsical freethinkers." They had no love for the "reform Communists" who had wanted only slow change and to preserve the Party.

Kramer has written two other works of literary journalism. *Three Farms: Making Milk, Meat, and Money from the American Soil* (1980) brought the reader to a New England dairy farm, a midwestern corn and hog farm, and a huge corporate farm in California. *Invasive Procedures* (1983) chronicled the lives of two surgeons, for which Kramer spent a year of research in medical offices and operating rooms. The title of his latest book, from which "Access" has been excerpted, is *Travels with a Hungry Bear.*

"I'm drawn to intricate subjects," Kramer said. "In *Three Farms*, it was farmers navigating the arrival of big business and high technology. In *Travels with a Hungry Bear*, it was Soviet country folk dealing with (sometimes by being part of) a government that bridled every transaction, financial and interpersonal, public and private. Finally, the regime collapsed, and then I had even more explaining to do. Readers of both books need lots of background before the dramas in everyday lives seem crucial. I mostly give this in brief asides—sometimes a paragraph or two, sometimes just half a sentence—as the stories flow. In *Invasive Procedures*, the drama of surgeons' lives was immediate—stories about blood, cutting, sewing, and healing need less explaining."

Kramer teaches a literary journalism seminar at Boston University, where he is writer-in-residence and professor of journalism. He has written for many magazines, including *The Atlantic, National Geographic, New England Monthly,* the *New York Times Magazine, The Nation,* and *Outside.*

Access

Outside a neighborhood food shop in Moscow in 1988, at the height of *perestroika*, a young, scowling truck driver lazed about watching a store clerk. From a slanting pile of cabbages that had rolled around the battered truck bed, the clerk pawed a few dozen into a crate. He dragged the crate inside, nudging open the door with his hip. Then, he did it all again, many times.

I redesigned the scene in my mind: I rewrote job rules and put the driver to work beside the clerk, and got them one of those conveyors with roller bearings, and packed the cargo of loose cabbages into lugs, and conjured up a loading bay for the back of the shop. Just those changes might have reduced cabbage-unloading time from an hour to six minutes, multiplying the driver's productivity tenfold. I quadrupled the truck's size, so there'd be cabbages enough to occupy his new time, and remapped his route to reach more shops, probably doubling efficiency again.

While I was at it, I repaved the bad road from the new loading bay clear back to the cabbage farm. I instituted similar changes to all the cabbage shops, trucks, and routes to Moscow. That made things pretty complicated, so I materialized a few competing cabbage brokers and found them working telephones and fast computers equipped with programs that juggled cabbage bids. I delivered them sound and wise bankers who'd lend hard currency to smooth the funding of the various parties. I threw in a contract, and made it enforceable under a reliable code of contract law. I was just getting around to the consequences of adding some boiled beef to eat with the cabbage, when the kid drove away.

While I stood there, conjuring up this tall tower of improvements, Gorbachev presided over a glum near-equality of poverty and isolation. The Communist Party had long invested only in state monopolies. The Party stifled foreign news that made it look bad, so few citizens understood how much better factories and farms elsewhere ran. Gorbachev had recently slackened press control and enterprise management, in what appears now to have been a doomed final attempt to rescue Party control. Instead, he triggered the inevitable, gradual toppling of Lenin's grand ideological experiment. Between 1985 and 1991, dispirited Soviet citizens, mostly unknowingly, shouldered a colossal, intricate undertaking, not one that just followed from their reluctant turn of conviction. The transformation would cost all the political and financial and human pains that go along with rearranging basic beliefs, habits, and alliances. It was a fascinating time for a Westerner to visit. The structures of central control were still mostly in place.

Yuri Dmitrovich Chernichenko—a formidable and cheery Russian writer and agricultural reformer who'd regularly strolled right to the cliff-edge of dissidence—had accepted my suggestion that we trade tours. We didn't know much about each other, but because I'd written about American farming, friends had put us in touch. Just as soon as the Soviets eased travel controls, we arranged to visit farms across America and the Soviet Union. Chernichenko could, for the first time, write quite freely about how the Western world worked; and American newspaper editors wanted to know why there were long lines in Moscow's bedraggled food markets. As I write this, six years and five trips after our first exchange of visits, Chernichenko has a new trade. He's a democratic politician, the oldest congressman in the Russian parliament's upper house, still pushing his dream of putting Russian farms into farmers' hands.

One moment during our journey across America sealed his conviction that Soviet collective farm laborers, working nobody's land, controlled by giant ministries, could never feed his hungry country. It was a hot Missouri afternoon. By the fat cylinders of a Bunge Corporation grain elevator on the Mississippi's shore, we watched a torrent of golden wheat tumble into a barge—a businesslike, mundane scene, duplicated at busy elevators up and down the river that harvest season. Yuri saw how ordinary this efficiency was, and both wonder and dismay played on his face.

The barge would carry the grain downriver from Missouri to a freighter that would cross the Gulf, the Atlantic, the Mediterranean, Aegean, and Black seas. In Odessa, in a few weeks, a train would transport it to a central mill, then trucks would bring flour to regional bakeries. Baked to conform to a national "state standard," the bread would be sold at a fixed price in state shops—perhaps even the shop on Yuri's street. He'd be home in time to buy a loaf.

Meat and potatoes—and cabbages—had gotten scarcer, but the state shops still stocked bread, paid for almost entirely by the government. Cheap bread was the price of public docility. But Soviet collective farms couldn't manage to grow enough wheat to supply the country. That reflected embarrassingly on the validity of central planning—a fundamental piety of the Communist government. For decades, they'd compensated by importing a lot of Western grain.

The inefficiency of collective farming was not widely known— until Chernichenko, in 1987, had been permitted to publish a major magazine essay announcing this fact: *Every year the Soviet government bought, from private farms in the capitalist West, half the grain in every loaf of bread.* They'd paid out billions in hard currency to the free world's biggest grain companies. The Soviet breadbasket was as much Kansas and Texas and Oklahoma as it was the Ukraine and the Virgin Lands, readers had learned.

The wheat barge was long and black, like dozens headed down-river past the dock. Chernichenko studied it and muttered a few frowning Russian sentences into his tape recorder. He was planning heretical new pro-Western articles—he kept asking me to show him more of the strong supply and marketing infrastructures that service our farms. He was sturdy and balding, and his luminous smile usually started way back at the corners of his wide-set, knowing eyes. But the barges glided past and he glowered.

As a young journalist on the rise, he'd volunteered to live in Siberia; he'd written critically about Khrushchev's campaign to plow up millions of acres of virgin prairie in Kazakhstan and Siberia. Gorbachev took over in 1985 and started his last-ditch technocratic effort to make Communism efficient. He had installed the new, liberal editors who published Chernichenko's criticisms. Four book manuscripts had come out of the closet and gone to press.

Chernichenko had a following of urban intellectuals and a few reform-minded collective farm chairmen. But most of the hundreds of thousands of Soviet bureaucrats who produced bad combines and tractors by the million, who directed farms often a tenth as productive as equivalent Western farms, who botched grain storage, and who had barely developed a food-processing industry, knew of and detested him for wittily proclaiming their inefficiencies. Access to bread was universal, but access to Chernichenko's sort of perspective on any state enterprise was still discomfiting heresy—they'd banned him from the combine factories, and he'd responded by writing about being banned.

He studied the barge-loading machinery, peered down the churning brown river, and muttered more Russian ruminations into the tape recorder. We strolled back up the dock, past a railway car on a siding, into the waiting room. A few truck drivers sat restlessly on orange Naugahyde couches, drinking black coffee. Through a picture window they watched a big hydraulic piston tip eighteen-wheeler after eighteen-wheeler nose to the sky, as if launching the trucks toward heaven. Truckload after truckload of grain slid into a pit and augured off into the grain elevator, assayed, weighed, value computed. The printer in the office behind the lounge clacked out checks. Trucks drove in full and fifteen minutes later drove out empty, heading back for more.

Yuri called this "objectively good"; they were expensive trucks (much bigger and newer than Soviet trucks, he said), manned by expensive drivers (the wage scale amazed him), and both investments got well used. In the USSR, I'd seen shabby, open trucks waiting in lines for days while rain soaked the loads and drivers sold off sacks of grain on the side. This riverbank scene—barges and tugs, the tilting truck pad, the lacey catwalks and twenty-story storage towers—would have enraptured any ten-year-old, Soviet or American, but Yuri just poked about the farm magazines on the coffee table, chin down, disconsolate. Then, he saw worse news yet.

He pointed excitedly at a small newsprint catalogue. The Aldon Company of Waukegan, Illinois, would supply customers with railroad sidings.

"Anyone at all?"

"Sure—anyone solvent," the elevator manager said.

"With any item in the catalogue?"

"Any item."

Line drawings showed many styles of track, switches, ties, spikes, bumpers, signal lights.

"You could buy a real siding—not just parts?"

"No problem."

Fax in your order, the back page urged, *REQUEST TWENTY-FOUR HOUR DELIVERY*!

"One day telephone, next day come?"

"Yes, why not?"

Shaking the magazine as if he were a prosecuting attorney and it, the murder weapon, he shouted: "Getting access to these materials at home would take many meetings, many years. Then they would be bad materials. I see now it will take us a long time, a difficult time to catch up."

Yuri brought himself to watch the trucks tip and dump, tip and dump, for quite a while. Soviet coordination between industries—for example, assembling a siding, barges, elevators, trucks, computers, farmers, and funds, all under jurisdiction of different ministries—was characterized by preposterous arrhythmias, nonresponses, corruption. Only rare highest-priority defense projects and a few grand single-purpose campaigns did well, when one general or minister used dictatorial heft to muscle through the crazy structures. Normal commercial activity never came together effectively.

On Soviet collective farms, many directors tried, in fact tried hard, to grow crops in spite of missing infrastructure and unmotivated workers. We had witnessed, on our reciprocal journey, demoralized activity in hundreds of fields and barns across the faltering Soviet empire. Pushed to fulfill five-year plans, bureaucrats hovered over each farm like stacked thunderheads, threatening punishments and loss of Party membership. Many officials could say no, some could solve a few of the problems they'd helped create, but none could make the gears of the unwieldy system mesh.

Western-style, unrestricted, freely-spendable money, not government commands, had lured all necessary parties to the Mississippi riverbank, eager and able to grow, store, and ship grain enough for several nations. Soviet administrative authority had sent rockets from the drawing board to the moon. But no authority could plan solutions to the million daily problems on 50,000 state and collective farms strewn across eleven time zones, each a bureaucratic dukedom careening without reference to value. Modern farms were far harder to make than space rockets.

Railway stations remained in ceaseless rush hour. On a midsummer midnight in 1989, travelers jammed the Kursk Station almost shoulder to shoulder. The station connects Moscow and the south—the tastiest, most sinful direction out of town, the direction of bread and wine, of Ukrainian grain fields and the Georgian cornucopia spilling out tea and grapes and apricots and cognac. It was the summer following my American journey with Chernichenko and our reciprocal trip across Russia.

A friend and I pushed past a family hugging a tearful, boyish soldier. Teenagers huddled in the center of the wide, dingy waiting room, their teacher circling like a sheepdog who smelled wolf. Three wiry Tajik men squatted silently by battered cartons, eyes glazed, innocent of the pandemonium. Lines of tired travelers streamed across the floor toward a kiosk selling bread and another selling *Pravda*. In stations like this, from Leningrad to Vladivostok, big overhead notice boards posted all arrivals and departures in Moscow Central Time, and people added or subtracted time zones on their fingers—a metaphor of centralized management. Moscow ran the railway, and everything else, in its own good time, and damn the public.

Our train creaked slowly out of the station on schedule, headed for Poltava, in central Ukraine. Yuri had helped me arrange this trip, too, although he'd been elected a People's Deputy and had to stay in Moscow. I opened the corridor window and stuck my head out. A whistle sounded and the crowd on the platform, like the cast of a musical after a show, saw us off with big, slow, stiff-armed waves.

The train clacked and swayed out of Kursk Station. Western experts called the railways as outmoded as the rest of Soviet infrastructure. But the trains I took ran well more often than, say, Soviet phones worked. For that matter, they ran better than Amtrak, which Western experts also call outmoded. When it came to trains, the Soviet Union's nearly universal inefficiency relented. They'd long been a top priority in an empire that stretched across 10,000 kilometers. Intercity trains bound Europe to Korea across a vastness of bad roads and awful weather. Our train pulled mostly hard-class cars, musty and sociable and cheap; they'd piled up with peasants, a few of whom lugged piglets and chickens. A dormitory car and several cars of four-berth compartments led the train, the berths probably booked up weeks in advance. Our "SV" soft-class car rode in the middle of the train, behind a dining car of sorts and beyond the reach of most Soviet citizens.

Influential friends had performed a feat that would get tougher even a year later and that couldn't happen at all after 1991, when Communist authority withered following the attempted coup. Our friends had booked a private train compartment for two foreigners at the last minute. Every booking made for us doubtlessly displaced someone— probably someone also considered official, but vouched for by an organization with lesser clout. The Soviet Union ran by reenacting, millions of times a day, a mythic battle: You need meat? Your factory needs steel? A train seat? At the moment of every allocation decision on every level, clout-wielders on one side duked it out with access-deniers on the other. A travel clerk at my influential official host's research institute, "a Jew, waiting to emigrate," my host had said, knew special phone numbers that had reached the right railway bosses, who had bumped persons whose travel benefited the State less than ours.

On a previous excursion, northward, I'd ended up sharing a four-berth compartment with two Latvian schoolgirls, having probably evicted their parents. A slight, wide-eyed student nurse had chatted with her sister in shy near-whispers and giggled stiffly whenever we looked over. They'd turned in early. After midnight, I'd climbed up past the tiny nurse, who'd snorted like a horse.

This time, we'd gotten the cushy two-berth compartment. I traveled with another Mark, who was born in Odessa, and had a doctorate from the Soviet Academy of Sciences. He'd emigrated fourteen years before to Boston, did research at Harvard, and was giddy because he was riding toward his native Ukraine for the first time in years. At seven in the morning the train would reach Poltava. Someone named Tanya would meet us, "on behalf of the Academy of Sciences," their Moscow representative had told us.

Travel by foreigners still needed official approval and a hefty sponsoring organization. Some cities and some routes remained "closed." We were "the American Delegation," and we were never on our own. The Academy of Sciences still had a Tanya or two to greet and track foreigners and their contacts in every opened region. With Tanya would be one "Vitaly, an agricultural executive." We were institutional objects, and would be passed along from the Academy of Sciences' kind supervision to that of Gorbachev's new super-ministry of agriculture, Gosagroprom. "Vitaly knows farm chairmen. He will discuss what Ukrainian farms you will see," our Moscow sponsor had said. For whom did he work? Who'd requisitioned and paid for his excursion with us? The nation's business worked in spite of the official economy and laws, and because of personal contacts. "Arrangements were made," our host had said, smiling genially, his reach so obviously mysterious and vast.

Mark toasted the prospect of this Tanya with French brandy we'd brought. The cotton window curtains in our little cabin had been cross-stitched with an edging of hammers and sickles and ornamental silhouettes of a famous Poltava battle monument, and Mark recognized it at once from his boyhood. I felt sure I'd all too soon encounter the real thing—it was the nature of Foreign Delegations to view monuments, a liability of official travel, the only travel there was. The curtain trim matched the orange of the velvet seats.

The Soviet Union indulged in hierarchic pageantry. Some intercity routes had their own assigned color schemes, applied variously on its crack "trademark" trains and its rank-and-file trains. The fanciest coaches featured finer decor—our embroidered curtains hung above tablecloths in coordinated colors, and senior staff wore uniforms with matching detail. Trademark trains had priority at sidings. Passengers would likely be the heaviest-weight bureaucrats. Ordinary coaches had plainer curtains, no tablecloths, and junior crews, and passengers might be plodding pen-pushers. Dormitory cars would be full of workers and peasants without clout and lowly clerks far out of favor at the office. It seemed like protocol of Catherine the Great's reign, not of a classless society in the making.

Officially, even directors of enterprises and movie stars made just a few times the pay of factory workers. Indeed, fame alone bought little privilege, in contrast to what it bought in market economies. Nobility of service to the state—or what passed for service—was the only quality that did add privilege. War heroes and workers who had been awarded the right badges got it. They cut to the front of lines, flashing their pass-

books, and shopped in better-supplied stores. And by the same logic, senior bureaucrats got it, too, in their capacities as self-sacrificing admin-
istrators of the revolutionary will of the people. The small perks of
privilege seemed to matter, far more than the pile carpets and corner offices that accompanied Western rank. A Soviet perk was always access
to something necessary—a nice rib roast, a thousand tons of steel to
keep a factory running, train seats to where you had to go. But it was
often access to something the lowliest American burger flipper or ware-
house clerk could obtain back home, as needed.

Soviet society, officially thrusting toward classlessness even in its final years, actually embodied the strictest, most elaborated taxonomy of
privilege I've encountered anywhere. The ins and outs of British protocol are weak tea by comparison—although they also had mattered
mightily back when aristocracy was the only legitimate source of distinction. Sports, the arts, scholarship, and business all lend distinction to
able Englishfolk now, and the right to do well at things has moved beyond the reach of government. In Soviet Russia, every arena of accomplishment was controlled and manipulated by government, right up
until the Communist Party's fall.

I found it comfortable but awkward to be a guest of this ruling
clique I didn't much care for, and to have a bit of their influence by
proxy. We didn't have much choice about traveling in style. In John
Steinbeck's *Russian Journal*, written in 1948, I'd recognized the same
sheltered travel into rural provinces: "Being the guests of Voks, we
walked through the public waiting-room and into a side room where
there was a dining table, some couches, and comfortable chairs. And
there, under the stern eye of a painted Stalin, we drank strong tea until
our plane was called." I was isolated from normal Soviet life. But it was
an isolation shared with the Soviet *nomenklatura*, the ruling elite, my
fellow travelers in the soft-class train car to Poltava.

It was hard to discern privilege in the faces of the big men in suits
lounging stiff-legged in the carpeted corridor. An Uzbek family of six
had levered themselves and a dozen crates and suitcases into the tiny
chamber next to us; three kids with gleaming black eyes and ringlets
clambered over all surfaces from floor to luggage rack. Several wives,
cowled in muslin, watched the mayhem placidly. In the cabin on our
other side two stolid engineers sat immersed in two newspapers and a
shared bottle of vodka.

It was an old car; our cabin had been repaneled in wood-grain
vinyl. At the end of the corridor, a samovar glowed comfortingly in a
special niche. Coals may well have been burning in its cast-iron firebox
since czarist times. Half an hour out of the station our porter had first

appeared, a burly woman in her fifties with a face as red as the bright samovar fire. She spoke rapidly, one pointing finger and one word for each of us: *"Chai?"* Point. *Da.* *"Chai?"* Point. *Da.* She returned with tea in beautiful glasses, dime-thin to take on boiling water without cracking. She set them inside ornate tin holders that protected our fingers from the hot glass, a comfort in a place with little comfort. She did even better. With each cup of tea, she delivered four wrapped sugar lumps as big as fingers. It was a summer of severe rationing. The stores rarely had sugar, even for those presenting coupons. But the officials who ran soft class had access to sugar. We drank the tea straight up. In the corridor later, I saw that everyone's pockets bulged with sugar fingers. The car rattled into the next day.

I recalled that my grandmother had told a Russian sugar-shortage tale. She'd been born on the Polish-Russian border and as a toddler had come by steamer to America. "My family was so poor we'd hang a lump of sugar over the table on a string," she'd said. "We'd look at it as we sipped. That made the tea taste sweet, and the sugar lasted all winter."

I told the story to Mark. "It works, too," I said. "I've tried it."

"In Boston, it works," he answered. "In this country, nothing works."

Mark sized up the tea lady. "Such people have business buying things in Moscow to sell in Poltava and vice versa. That's how the country gets by in spite of itself. Such trade has long been their capitalism."

On the train to Latvia once, a porter had asked if I'd like supper brought. I'd worked all day without food—when one moved between organizations during mealtime in the USSR, one starved, because food was served in workplace cafeterias. Restaurants took hours and battles with waiters. The train porter had delivered imitation airline food that was an abomination. I was ravenous, but couldn't manage the mucusoid *kutlyeta*, nor the beans glued with rancid fat. I ate the bread and watched jealously as Latvians, who'd carried food aboard, gnawed hard sausage and big chunks of black bread.

On this train, too, sausage scent intertwined with scents of vodka, sweat, tobacco, smoke from the samovar, and drift from the W.C.—this was the consistent perfume of Soviet railroading. We broke out our own bread and sausage; I'd wised up. I placed a portable shortwave radio in the compartment window and tuned in BBC World Service— government jamming of their radio signals had stopped only a year before. Mark produced the French brandy. We listened to a program about dahlia gardening in Yorkshire, then to anecdotes of a Shakespearean troupe playing to full houses of Pakistani elementary school students in Liverpool, who were thereby bettered. In the dim compartment, I pictured thousands of ears cocked to this relic of Empire Britain.

I wondered what Uzbek schoolkids honing classroom English made of dahlias and Shakespeare for the new masses. Up the dial, Voice of America programming reflected demographic studies of audience. A calm woman read, at half-speed, in e-nun-cee-ay-ted English, an amiable tale about children on vacation. This was the once-banned firewater of Western propaganda. It went down as smoothly as an airline movie.

In our fancy train car, even in the midst of perestroikan turmoil, we privileged travelers lay down to sleep on clean white sheets. I dozed as we crept out of conquering Russia and into the submerged Ukraine. The train hooted and clanked. All night, sunk in fitful naps, I gazed up through the glassy surface of wakefulness. In the sudden stillness of some small station, I squinted out past the embroidered curtains at bleary peasant couples hovering over cloth bundles and rope-bound valises. We clacked onward, and then it was dawn and on a far platform yet another scraggily line awaited the opening of a tiny kiosk that might sell a shipment of something rare.

Across the USSR, people awaited access to anything, because whatever might come—a seldom-found food, pants a few sizes too big or small—would be tradable for something else. In every town, citizens somehow knew when to arise in the middle of the night and line up. Rumor motivated shoppers far more than advertising did back home. I dropped back to sleep. The clatter wove into my dreams, into thumping, imperious pounding.

The tea lady leaned into my face, hollering. She'd put on a baggy white smock, also trimmed in the train's orange theme colors, I blearily noticed. This morning she was cleanup lady with a harsh voice, not tea lady with sugar. She was all business. Her new outfit brought out new aspects of her official personality. She knew her duties, and like all Soviet workers, she also knew her rights. When we hit Poltava, she had as much right to be off the train as any citizen (this was the same philosophy that granted restaurant workers the right to close for lunch at lunchtime). Two hours before arrival was the time for her to collect bedsheets and roll up mattresses. She thumped on mine with the broad red heel of her hand, right by my one open eye. I got the idea, and scowled.

I soon discovered that in the morning she also stepped up her execution of the duty of locking washrooms before the train entered stations—she'd interpreted this mandate broadly and simply kept them locked. She'd cleaned in there and turned the key. My pantomime of desperation did not interest her. Mercifully, the porter in the next car ran a slacker principality.

Cleanup lady, her pillows counted and mattresses rerolled, watched from the platform with hands on hips as we all debarked. She wore civvies now—a baggy brown dress and a bandanna around her hair, so that only her proprietary posture distinguished her from a hundred other babushkas on the platform. True to plan, a smiling woman in her mid-forties emerged from the hubbub of melodious Ukranian greetings, grabbed my hand, and shook it, asking, "American?" I nodded.

"Tanya," this Tanya said, welcoming the new American delegation on behalf of the Poltava Section of the Academy of Sciences. She pointed to a slight, balding man limping toward us from far up the platform, squinting into bright sunlight. She introduced Vitaly Karpovich Chuiko, our new keeper, the gentleman from Gosagroprom, and dean of the local agricultural college.

Vitaly Karpovich proffered a crisp, clipped bow and inspected his new charges. It was obvious right away that he was a personage, no mere tour guide. Nearing sixty, he had a bit of fair hair remaining, framing tired blue eyes. A brown rumpled suit hung from his thin shoulders. His brow was permanently knit. He carried himself with martial stiffness and gestured in economical, miniaturized, curt flourishes. His smile came slowly. He had a way of issuing it, first holding back, then relenting. It ended up warm when it finally arrived, which threw off the assumptions I'd been developing about his demeanor. A considerable smile.

Gosagroprom gazed at Academy of Sciences, then they bowed and then shook hands. *Exeunt* this Tanya, and her institution. We had been signed over from one bureaucratic dominion to another, soft-class prisoners in transit.

We were in the grain belt of the land of scarcity; amber waves of wheat surrounded us. For the next week I was fattened like a goose, force-fed official banquets at every stop. I had come to report on the food problem, but within days my belt only clipped on its outermost notch, and then I had to punch a new notch. The feasts were relentless and good— the white bacon fat squares with garlic, the thick borschts (sometimes with kidney, usually with liver), and buttery kasha, the sharp brown bread and plate of soft butter. The plate of boiled eggs. The plate of pickles. The plate of fresh tomatoes, scallions, and dill. The sausage loaf, the stewed chicken, the stewed beef. I'd waddle off breathing heavily like one of Gogol's officials and inspect fields and the local store. And there, another surprise feast awaited, banquet tables set in some unlikely back room, serving women peeking out from the kitchen, smiling shyly at the American Delegation. We visited Gogol's Mirgorod, in fact, where the mud-mired intersection he'd described a hundred and fifty years earlier was maintained as a tourist site.

The fields I inspected, even on the show farms Dean Vitaly allowed us to see on this early *glasnost* trip, were always so-so, never groomed cleanly or pouring out grain like those fields in Kansas or Texas, or across a few borders, in Germany or Denmark. Even the best collectives farmed carelessly. In between lush areas, workers left poor spots with stunted, pale stands, streaks of rough ground the harrows had missed, stands of weeds, stands plowed too shallowly, stands where the seeder had clogged and no one had bothered to fix things. Lesser grains or sugarbeets grew where corn made sense. Soy production was a rare novelty. Broken-down combine hulks and rusted-out manure spreaders strewed the most fertile ground in the Soviet Union. Leaking oil smeared the tractors that still ran. Workers in little crews dabbed at jobs that machines or chemicals and tenfold fewer workers accomplished back in the fields around the Missouri grain elevator. Midwestern farmers who visited Soviet farms always came back shaking their heads.

Building materials were in such scarce supply that collective farm chairmen manipulated them to accumulate barter power. A few charismatic chairmen with influential friends had successfully wrested exemptions allowing them to run their own sawmills and brick kilns. Those chairmen could wheel and deal for anything they needed; farms with their own barter goods could triumph in the shadow economy. They subverted ministry power. In 1989 such secondary on-farm enterprises had just become legal—but there were still many officials standing in the way. Ministries had gone right on guarding monopoly prerogatives of manufacture and distribution as long as they were able; they could still impede farms struggling to fulfill the five-year plan.

We sensed that the alliances and local politics of such wheeling and dealing were intricate. Farm chairmen told us unabashedly about multi-staged shadow economy barters for coal, cement, and iron girders. A chairman might arrange with a combine monopoly bureaucrat to move his farm up on the order list in return for bricks, boards, labor, meat, vegetable oil, cheese. The factory would find clients for these things in other trades. The farmer would take delivery of the combine and pass it along to another farm in return for still other goods. Officials with access to trucks became powerful middlemen.

Perestroika policies indeed had increased enterprise heads' autonomy from planners. Most bosses had little real business experience to guide them through these new conditions. Local Party officials knew more, and, as usual, still took the lead. Webs of direct dealings were widening, though. Miners on strike, a TV news report said, wanted fifteen percent of the coal they dug so their organization could barter for itself. Rural cronies were patching together gnarled, restrictive little zones where their joint entrepreneurship locked out others—

capitalism at its worst. These were enduring missteps, shaping the
twisting path toward market economics. Long after the fall of the Communist Party, such alliances hung together, resisting the logic of individual opportunity.

Local bosses with the power of pashas could occasionally will into
being their small utopian daydreams. One organized a stable of show
horses and trained Olympic riders. Another made a project of combing
warehouses all over for basic hardware. He had opened a store as big as
a school cafeteria and stocked it with rarities—nails and screws, hammers
and sickles, kitchen pumps, hay knives, rubber mallets, and crosscut
saws—equipment that helped peasants live comfortably; this chairman
tended his flock. The store looked old-fashioned and everyday to me,
but any Soviet citizen chancing upon such hard-to-find wonders would
know at once that the boss had heavyweight contacts.

Our keeper, a technocrat to the core, scoffed at the chairman's troubling to ease "his" peasants' backward lives with backward solutions.
He browsed through books at the back of the store, then presented us
with Gorbachev's reformist speeches, in Russian. In another few years,
Vitaly Karpovich would be a modern patriot still, but he'd be pushing
his gospel of progress in a separated Ukrainian nation, with its own
chiefs and generals, and the world's third largest nuclear arsenal.

As we toured the Ukraine, an odd, red-haired high school English
teacher from Lokhvitsa, Yuri Alexandrovich Plakhtienko, kept popping
up, probably locally assigned both to eavesdrop and be helpful. After a
long day of inspecting sunflower production, I staggered back to "Motel
Poltava"—which was actually just another big, clumsy hotel with dili-
gent corridor ladies. He stood out front on the piazza and offered his
services with wonderfully British manners, grinning, bowing, shyly
muttering—"Well, I say good man," and, "Well, of course, now I have
just forgotten the word, of course." He'd never before been allowed this
close to a native English speaker, he said breathlessly.

I bowed and smiled back, then went on in, feeling rare, and beat. The
fattest mosquitoes in the universe had just grown up in Poltava, and
the Soviets hadn't bothered manufacturing screens. Yet it was far too hot
at night to close the windows. I turned to the BBC World Service again
for solace. They were broadcasting interviews with unhappy peasants in
Nicaragua.

A year earlier, on my previous trip, the Marlboro debacle had taken
place in this same Motel Poltava. Marlboros were the *baksheesh* of *perestroika*-era small favors. A pack got the laundry done in Kiev, and another bought an hour's taxi ride across Moscow. Parched after a long

day, my translator then, a huge ex-soccer star named Pavel Pavlovich, had been determined to get us beer.

"No beer—" the waiter had cut him off abruptly. Pavel had pointed to beer aplenty an arm's length away on the next table, then had ceremoniously handed back the menu, with a pack of Marlboros ostentatiously folded inside. "Beer," he'd said. The waiter had smiled and bowed, softened his gestures, lingered solicitously discussing our order. He had come back half an hour later—and said, "No beer." He hadn't returned the Marlboros. Pavel was new to capitalism and had just learned not to pay in advance.

I recognized the same waiter as we entered the Motel Poltava restaurant again. An angry-faced old man in a heavy brown suit with a tangle of medals on the lapel rushed at me, grabbing my shirt and shouting something. I spoke English as hard as I could and the old guy's buddies stepped between us. He squinted and melted away, looking bewildered.

The waiter smiled without recognition and kindly placed the foreign guests at a table right in front of the loud, bad band's big speakers. Poltava's hip, glamorously togged teens danced—quaintly to my eyes, but with glee—to newly permitted Western rock and to familiar Ukrainian stomps. An indignant woman rushed from the dance floor and thumbed me out of her seat. We shared their table. Her escort was an East German engineer, heading home from a thrifty Azov Sea holiday. She was a nurse. "If the Berlin Wall would be removed, I'm not sure many people would stay in East Germany," he said. "I certainly wouldn't." Five months later, Germans had demolished the wall. I dabbed thin beef gruel with half-American "state standard" bread. We drank beer, for which no Marlboros had been needed, toasting international friendship.

In the morning, the red-haired English teacher had reappeared on the hotel piazza. The Soviet Delegation, he was honored and pleased to let me know, was present to fulfill the scheduled mission of showing the American Delegation the significant regional museum in the provincial town of Lokhvitsa, if I pleased.

It was clunky, local, small, and revealing, a great museum, a shrine of sorts to place and state. The first room featured dioramas full of hairy trees and varnished rocks, and multicolored charts and nature-lore placards by glassed-in stuffed muskrats and porcupines, and a hare as big as a knapsack. Rows of rock cores. Explanations that started out, "Millions of years ago, there was an ocean here . . ." Rows of mammoth teeth. A tableau of bird eggs ordered by size. "There are 8,000 kinds of birds known on our planet. There are 350 kinds in our Ukraine. There are 150 in the Lokhvitsa District. The biggest, the domestic goose, the smallest, *reones*. Our district is rich in gas and oil . . ."

The next room added people to the natural inventory, exhibiting relics of civilization from 14,000 years ago. A town has been around since the year 1000. "There were many enemies then. Most awesome was the Tatar, who destroyed all places." There were mallet heads with handle-holes, and daggers. "Here are the weapons of our enemies." "Here are the weapons of our defenders, the Russians." The exhibit has a political tilt. Cossacks "came to help fight," and stayed. "Here is a specimen of the peasant from the seventeenth to the nineteenth centuries." "Here is an early-twentieth-century peasant."

And the next room showed off artifacts of the revolution of 1905. "In Lokhvitsa, on the fourteenth of December, peaceful demonstrators were shot, including the local poet Teslenko." "Here is the highest decoration." And, "Here is a proverb: 'If you move slowly, you'll travel farther.' "

The biggest room portrayed the victory of Communism. The red-haired English teacher presented the room, bowing modestly with arm outstretched. Banners, weapons, and smiling photographs of bedraggled heroes of the Revolution jammed the glass cases. I'd mentioned nothing about ethnicity, but the curator said to me, "We have the documents of Esther Pipshitz, Jewish Communist Party official. We had a lot of Jews—most later exterminated by the Germans. The country was in horrible shape. The Party taught people to write." Party artifacts went up to the beginning of the Second World War.

I asked about the collectivization of farming—wasn't that pre-war era the time of forced marches here, and confiscation of hundreds of thousands of families' winter food, and arbitrary executions? Many farmworkers had told me awful stories about their missing grandparents—stories their parents had whispered and cut off half-recited. Most rural families had been scarred by that great national trauma but couldn't even talk about it. Now articles revealed that perhaps twenty million citizens had been killed during the collectivization drive—not by Nazis but by Communists, and was this part of history accessible to museum goers now that such subjects had surfaced?

The director and some anonymous gray-suited gentlemen and the English teacher conferred. "We have a few items," the director said. "With the new openness, we talk about doing something more, but not yet. We have in this case the newspaper *Atheist*, a Kiev paper from 1930. This article says that in Bichovska, people decided to organize a collective farm. Here's another interesting clipping—it unfortunately represents the mood then: Local nuns who wanted to sabotage collectivization started rumors that if you join a collective farm you'll sit on a hot frying pan in hell, so

peasants refused to join. Here's another article—opportunists help ku-
laks and church activists 'assisting the forces who want to wreck collectivization of the peoples' agriculture.' That's all we have." I asked if
schoolkids could possibly catch the actual meaning of those clippings. "No
one ever mentioned them," the director said.

The next room vigorously memorialized another twenty million
victims—those killed in World War II. That carnage was not secret.
Flags and guns and helmets, battle maps with pins, bashed-up ammo
crates, and photos of the Soviet Mothers of Poltava filled every nook.

Their sentiment stirred by this last room, the Soviet Delegation
swept us into vans, while Yuri the English teacher shouted, "Come up,
come up!" Where to? "To famous memorial on Germans' Poltava battle platz." I recalled the memorial on the train curtains.

We solemnly crossed a wide lawn. The place teemed with ten-year-olds,
who were shouted into groups by their teachers. The groups stood before
a colossal statue and stared at an eternal flame flickering next to a gigantic
polished stone platform. A loudspeaker blasted marches. The monument's director ran out with chugging gait and pumped my hand. She
was a chubby woman with severe, pugilistic gestures but a soothing voice.
Above the sound of her greetings another soothing voice boomed a
recorded spiel, a looming, surrounding amplification, the Mother of the
Motherland herself weaving a tale of passion, patriotism, and sacrifice.

"General Mikhail Petrovich Kirponis," said the recorded voice, "re-
created in this statue eight meters high and weighing thirty tons, was
surrounded by German troops right here. His brilliance allowed us to
hold out for three days and three nights. The general showed enormous
courage, then died of a gunshot." ("Perhaps," Mark whispered to me,
"by his own hand when capture was near.")

The official narrative went on: "His troops, pinned by enemy fire,
couldn't remove the body, so they buried it." For a moment I imagined
these secret grave diggers who knew they, too, might soon die, and then
I caught myself. I had felt something close to reverence for a moment—
what the site was designed to induce. "See?" Mark said. "On the statue—
the general's name ends the Ukrainian way, spelled *I-S*, not the Russian
way, *O-S?*"

Although several hundred thousand soldiers died, a handful of the
general's grave diggers did survive, told the tale, and in 1947, the Soviet
Army located the body, "miraculously preserved." They carried it to Kiev.
Experts studied it. A decade later they reburied it in this park. "In appreciation of the sacrifice of the heroes," the booming Mother-voice said, "So-

viet citizens insisted on contributing half a million rubles for the statue."
Memorials were the only well-tended sites in the nation. The lawn got
mowed here and nowhere else. The loudspeakers that intoned this
durable tale of devotion and duty were of full timbre, distortion-free in
spite of the volume, and the message. The Soviets memorialized well.

Facing the general, a wedding party lined up in close formation. They
stood behind a big, shiny-faced, smiling bride and a tiny groom in a large
blue suit. Their parents beamed at them. They looked happy and confused. They awaited something. In the atheistic USSR, wedding parties
linked up with the power and glory of patriotic sacrifice at formerly sacra-
mental moments. And because the general had died protecting Kiev, the
Ukrainian wedding party's devotion felt authentic. They'd brought pride
intact to the ceremony before the big, granite, dual-purpose general.

The red-haired high school teacher urgently pulled me aside. He
wanted to "conspire" with me, he whispered. I could barely understand
him even when he spoke up. "Weell you bless me beeg thing speciaol
friends if pleece, kind sirrr?" The bride's parents are his friends. Yesterday, he said he would ask the American—could I possibly? I'd been on
the road for a month in rumpled jeans. He signaled my consent to the
wedding party with jubilant waves, as if directing a plane in for a landing.

The bride's mother ran up and shoved a wreath into my arms—
plaited red gladioli—and the high school teacher motioned that I was to
lay it on the polished altar, at the feet of the gigantic general, on behalf
of the bride and groom, then speak to them. "My speciaol friends," he
repeated, nodding, shrugging, pointing across to the bride and groom,
who stood as still as cake decorations.

The eternal flame flickered. Martial music blared. The sun glared
down. I paced slowly forward, in step with the music, composing my
face into solemn blankness, the wreath in my outstretched hands. I
stood a respectful moment, thinking about the great terrors of battle
and the lesser terrors of marriage. Neither was reflected in the groom's
eager grin.

I confabulated a short speech. I issued more international blessings
for world peace, and followed on with observations to the effect that mar-
riages are threads in the cloth of a strong nation. It was, of course, received in silence. The high school teacher shouted at the crowd for several
minutes, translating far more than I'd pronounced. Everyone clapped
and smiled at me then, nodding agreement repeatedly. Finally he handed
me a wilting bouquet and pushed me toward the bride, who stood rigidly.
I handed her the flowers, bent and kissed her cheek, inhaling her sweaty
scent. The bride and groom finally glanced up, smiling at each other, just

plain happy. Ceremonial oration flowed in full torrent as we drove off into the slow summer sunset. Normal lives played out here, too.

The van driver, barreling past trucks and walkers, made my own life flash in review several times. Soviet drivers reflected national history; anyone behind the wheel was an aristocrat among peasants. The lot of common folk was, as ever.

A year before I'd been in a black Volga taking a carful of reform-minded academics home from a picnic at Yuri Chernichenko's dacha. The chauffeur must have been doing forty miles an hour on a dirt lane among the dachas of the Moscow gentry. We'd struck a boy on a bike. He'd been pedaling carefully along the verge of the narrow road. The car had snagged his handlebar and flung up the rear tire. He'd flown sideways past the window, grazed the back fender, and landed belly down in a ditch. The driver had touched the brakes, slowing, turning his head and glancing as the boy eased up onto his elbows, then onto one knee. The father was running across the road behind us. The driver had stepped on the gas and left.

My fellow passengers, reputedly the most forward-thinking reformers of 1988, had laughed at my dismay. As the car sped many kilometers from the scene, they'd chided me: "The boy will be all right. You know he got up. His father is with him. Our driver would have such trouble if he had stopped. It simply wasn't our driver's fault. You saw how the boy drove the bicycle into the road suddenly."

Wouldn't the authorities track down the driver and question him? "No. Chances are that seeing the sort of car this is, they will hesitate to report it, because it would mean confronting someone unknown, who probably has considerable power. Better to let it go."

On the Poltava road, our van finally hung up behind two manure spreaders, and we drove on tamely at walking speed for minute after minute. The road twisted. Traffic streamed toward us. There was virtually no national highway system. Intercity roads were usually two, sometimes three lanes, and bumper to bumper. The vast USSR had a fifth as many miles of road as America. This was the skimpy infrastructure.

The bad road bisected fields of sunflowers as big as skillets, all cocked at the same angle. Two boys and a tethered cow lay flat on a grassy strip by the road. One boy read. The other stared up through the mountain ash trees quavering over him, into the sky. The cow chewed grass.

We crawled into town behind another farm wagon, our driver chain-smoking black tobacco. The Poltava District Party Agricultural Chief, Deputy Chief, and finally Dean Vitaly also lit up. The hot van grew foggy. Soviet health wisdom included the idea that one should never sit in a breeze, no matter what. I opened the sliding rear window. Vitaly reached back and slammed it. The driver pointed to the old women selling tomatoes from their tiny private plots by the roadside. He wanted some for his wife. Vitaly yelled for him to drive on.

Motel Poltava felt like home. The dining room band blasted its horrid music, but the waiter still had beer. I went upstairs early. The BBC held forth on the porcelain collection on view in the Victoria and Albert Museum, where it could give great pleasure to all.

On our third day with Vitaly, we drove several hours to Kirov Collective Farm and shook hands with its chairman, Saviely Golovko. He was friendly—would I please call him Saviely. He'd been chairman for twenty years—he was one of those who'd gotten himself firmly enough into position to farm somewhat autonomously. He was full of numbers. That year he'd fattened 4,000 beef cows, and his 1,000 dairy cows yielded 8,000 pounds each—fully half the U.S. average, and very good for the USSR. He'd fattened 2,500 pigs, tended 1,400 chickens, and ran a special breeding farm, "stocked with 300 Czech and GDR goats. We have sold 2,000 already. We have 8,500 applications from people wishing to buy our goats for breeding. In Kiev market, we just sold to a private individual a he- and she-goat pair for 540 rubles. Goat rearing is mainly the task of private individuals. Old folks sell them at 10 kilos, for 100 rubles." Saviely's farm had 832 "members who work productively," not counting families. The workers' average age was thirty-three—far younger than the national average, which showed Saviely's agile management.

Saviely had taken advantage of the scarcity of urban housing. His skill, long tenure, and political heft had indeed brought him building materials. He'd constructed nice houses and "the younger generation" had come from cities to occupy them. "We have 185 houses. A peculiar attraction of our farm is we say, 'Here is an apartment key. You needn't wait.' It's for recruiting. I still need people."

We drove about, looking at pretty good fields and good houses, at a fifty-patient hospital and an apothecary, and toured the old age home— a converted schoolhouse, very dark, but spotless. Two tiny ladies lay moaning in beds in the big, wax-smelling building. "We have four doctors: I give doctors good houses," said Saviely. "We have a forty-four-person brigade that just builds. This is my priority. Until two years ago, it violated state rules for me to pay cash for building materials—I had to win permission to obtain them through the right bureaucratic procedures."

The farm had pussyfooted along the margin of the law in order to do well. Now building houses without permission from higher up was legal. And the chairman had the right friends. He had an extravagant belly laugh that no doubt canceled debts for him. He was flamboyant. An audacious version of the mandatory Lenin picture hung behind his desk—not the glowering state-approved portrait, but one expressing the new slogan, "Socialism with a human face." It was modern, a bright vermilion brush-textured background behind a Rouault-like sketch of The Leader's face, bold and quizzical, outlined in rough black and twice life size. Saviely worked while dwarfed by his nation's father. The painting was trendy, but still reverential.

Saviely was taking care, in the waning days of state subsidies, to stock up. Until recently, new machinery had been delivered yearly, whether or not he wanted it, according to a quota schedule. But now it had to be requested and partially paid for by the farm. "I have three new Don 1500 combines because I jumped and got them for 14,000 rubles, with the state covering the difference—they now cost 50,000 rubles. The Don harvests wet grain better than earlier models. But it's heavy and its big wheels rip the topsoil. I'd like to choose among combines, and negotiate price. However, it's the only one made. In paradise I could do that!"

We washed up for supper, then drove in a small caravan of farm jeeps to a freshly spruced-up guest house by a pond. It smelled of paint and sawed wood. The outhouse was brand new. "We would like, in the future," said Saviely proudly, "to entertain parties of hunters and other Europeans who wish to stay here. That's why we built this facility." This translated into a common transition-time Soviet sentiment: "We need hard currency."

Saviely was a salesman, and he would succeed in any regime. For the evening, he was joined by the District Party Agricultural Chief, a dapper, dark, tall gentleman, who said only the right thing, although he somehow persisted in appearing like a sophisticate among rubes. Saviely was earthy—no sense that he came from the stuck-up side of the tracks. He admitted real problems right and left. I liked him. The District Chief said with a straight face, "There are three pillars to this farm: Discipline, Confidence, and Mutual Understanding." The conversation flowed around him. He was a rock in a stream that was heading elsewhere.

Where it was heading was toward drunken ruination. I had successfully resisted the glum toasts of Vitaly Karpovitch, and those of a dozen hosts in Moscow. But in a moment Saviely made me feel compelled, and ambitious about partying. He toasted my mother. I have a fine mother who is warm, witty, and a natural storyteller, I said, and took just a small sip. Saviely was short and roly-poly, and touched my shoulder imploringly. Looking with dog eyes, he said, "Ah, you insult your mother? Okay, then let us drink to my mother's memory, and I will be hurt if you do not drink bottoms-up!"

He was so innocent and sincere, I tipped my glass straight upside down. And then I did the same on behalf of his nation, my nation, and, yes, for international friendship, then went back and made up for the slight to my mother. We saluted his farm, my book, his wife, my family. Soon, I loved him, and he loved me, and I slurred out a lucid observation, "I see why you are the manager of a large and successful farm."

Saviely wanted to trade jokes. The translator on this outing was as cross-eyed as I was, but tried anyhow: "There is an international drinking competition, American, Frenchman, and Russian. There is a small glass, a regular glass, a bottle, and a bucket of vodka. The American starts; he gulps the small glass and a bit of the regular glass, and can't go on. The Frenchman has the small glass, the regular glass, and almost reaches for the bottle, but he's all disconnected and out of touch. Then the Russian starts with the bucket. He has the bottle, the glass, and even manages the little glass. You know how they figure out who is the winner? There's an old Ukrainian expression: 'Only your soul knows your full capacity . . .'"

They all roared. I'd understood every word said, but I didn't get it. "OK, here's another joke. The emperor wanted to kill an eagle. He believed that a duck was an eagle, see . . ." The evening trundled on.

I found myself outside. Peepers shouted from the grassy pond. I navigated around the pond with the District Party Agricultural Chief, who somehow must have communicated his desire to stroll with me, and we pledged eternal goodwill, I think, with me yelling English and him nodding agreeably and yelling Ukrainian, each of us understanding a few words, and both of us making many curlicued gestures that looped off into the air, starting right from the heart. I can remember the stark white evening sun, and the heavy smell of new hay in the field behind the pond, and of the freshly painted guest house. He kept uttering the same phrase as we walked back inside. We had it translated: "I don't change my message from year to year," he'd been telling me. "Shake."

I spent the next morning wandering around Saviely's farm very gently, for fear of jostling my headache. I viewed crops and animals and combines in good repair and combines under repair. There was a modest lunch, and when I refused to consume more than the tiniest sip of the vodka they poured, Saviely merely laughed and didn't press.

After lunch, we went to see the school. There was whispering between Saviely and two or three somber gentlemen of the farm, who kept approaching to check on something or another. We walked into a big room at the end of a school corridor.

The room crashed into song, into brash, rich chords. Eight Ukrainians stood in brocaded and embroidered national dress, and their singing was thrilling. The ingratiating Saviely had cultivated a traditional singing group to entertain at state occasions. There was a lead alto—a muscular blonde milkmaid with a throaty voice, who belted out modal melodies while standing on the balls of her feet. She came to me and pulled me out on the dance floor; the band started up a polka, while the officials of nether Ukraine observed.

I was suddenly blessed with sure feet. We whirled around and around and threw in a few fancy kicks and stomps, and everyone applauded, including separate demonstrations of fingertip clapping by the District Party Agricultural Chief and the mayor, a blocky woman in her forties who clapped, hands not quite meeting. Eventually, we stopped. The absurd English teacher—who had by this point confided in me sorrowfully that he couldn't speak English very well—attempted to translate the whirling songs.

> *Something is in the stalls*
> *Rye was in the stalls*
> *Everything has disappeared.*
> *It was barley. Where is it?*
> *There was fat. Where is the fat?*
> *You gave it to your relatives . . .*
> *You! No, you! You! No, you!*

and,

> *I was at the market.*
> *I saw a boy*
> *He was not near the fish soup.*
> *He did not kiss me.*
> *He paid no attention . . .*

My dear partner, the blessed alto, ran up as the crowd broke up. "Who are you?" she asked. "Why are we taken from work and told to sing for you? You must be very important for this!"

I told her I was not important and could not understand it myself.

Saviely soon explained it. "You will tell of this group in America. Someone will want to hear them over there." The quest for hard currency
was just getting started.

The blessed alto walked off with us, looking furtively behind her.
"I have never had this chance before," she whispered. "I have relatives.
In Saskatchewan. Can you tell them I want to know them, to come to
them?" We asked where they were, but she could not really say.

Tracy Kidder

Gabriel Amadeus Cooney

Tracy Kidder served ten years as a staff writer at *The Atlantic*, doing profiles, analytical articles, and scientific pieces. One day, his editor, Richard Todd, suggested he get in touch with one of Todd's college acquaintances who was the head of a computer design team at Data General in Boston. Kidder found the project worth more than an article. He spent months watching day and night as the team built a new computer in their basement offices. The resulting book, *The Soul of a New Machine*, won the Pulitzer Prize in 1982 for nonfiction.

Since then, Kidder's books have focused on people creating things. In 1985 he published *House*. In it, he watched a carpentry crew building a house, a mundane activity but one full of skill and financial risk. In 1989 *Among*

369

Schoolchildren chronicled a year in the life of a fifth-grade teacher and her class in Holyoke, Massachusetts, a district with a mixed ethnic population and a depressed economy. Kidder says that writing magazine articles produced a smattering of portraits of characters representing various categories or types. Now, writing books, he can concentrate on sustained narrative. "You end up with the same people you started with, and you've gone somewhere with them," he said.

"Memory" is drawn from his 1993 book *Old Friends*. He spent a year of steady research in all the shifts at Linda Manor, a nursing home in Massachusetts, and returned frequently for several more months. He wanted to figure out the institution and the staff, and to identify characters that interested him the most. In the end, he threw away hundreds of pages of polished material on costs, the management of institutions, and the general issues of aging, and instead wrote about the people he met. His main characters are Lou Freed, a ninety-one-year-old who is nearly blind and has angina, and Joe Torchio, a seventy-two-year-old stroke victim suffering from arthritis and diabetes. They are strangers thrown together as roommates.

"I set out with a general issue—old age—and found myself in a particular nursing home and facing a particular group of people," Kidder said. "At that point all the issues of aging ceased to interest me much. They're not interesting except when they're in a context of real people. I wanted to look at aging from the inside. I wanted to get close to what really matters—what it's like to be old."

Memory

There's clover in the grass outside. From Meadowview windows the surrounding bits of field are likely-looking pasture for a horse. Perhaps it is the grass that stirs Cliff's memory and brings him out of his room down on Meadowview. Cliff is lean and gnarled. He wears a baseball cap with a legend above its brim that reads, "We Are All In This Alone." He wears a cardigan sweater and has draped a down vest over the front rung of his walker. Cliff is ninety-three, partially deaf, and very unsteady on his feet, and he usually keeps to his room. The two nurses on duty and Meadowview's lone male aide look up, surprised, as Cliff comes slowly down the hall and stops near the nurses' station. They ask him where he's going. Cliff says that he is looking for his horses.

The male aide stands beside Cliff and shouts his questions while the two nurses bustle here and there, listening in.

"Cliff," shouts the male aide, "you used to deliver the mail up in the hill towns, didn't ya?"

"Yup," says Cliff.

"How'd you do it? With horses?"

"The first four years," Cliff says. "Then they started clearin' the roads, and I could go by car. I had a Reo Speedwagon." Cliff leans on his walker and peers down the long corridor as he talks. He says that in the wintertime he used to take the front wheels off his Reo and replace them with skis. "I made some money the first few years I had the Reo, but I spent it. And, shit, I haven't made any since."

"What'd you spend it on, Cliff?" shouts the aide.

"Liquor," Cliff says. "There were thirteen places between Pittsfield and Adams where you could get something to drink."

"You didn't drink on the job, did ya?"

"Sure!" exclaims Cliff, still peering down the corridor.

One of the nurses, passing by, lets out a hoot.

"Cliff," shouts the male aide, "were there any women on your route?"

"Oh, sure. A lot of 'em," Cliff says. "All accommodatin', too. Up through there."

The two nurses, heading in different directions, both hear this. Both make simultaneous, mock cries of distress—"Oh!"—and move on, laughing.

"How old are you, Cliff?" asks the aide.

"Ninety-three, I guess. I was born in '98."

"Where were you born? Plainfield?"

"No, Plainfield," Cliff says. "Well . . ."

"Well, what do you say we head back to your room," says the aide.

"You think I better head back?"

But only minutes later Cliff reappears, with his down vest still draped over his walker. "Hi," says a nurse. "Where you goin'?"

"I don't know," Cliff says. "Goin' down there where I live."

"Got a hot date?" asks the nurse.

Cliff, halted on his walker, once again peers down the long corridor toward Sunrise. People all the way down there look small, like figures seen through the wrong end of a telescope. Cliff is breathing heavily from his walk of thirty feet. "No," he replies. "I got some hosses down there. That's one thing that irritates me. Been there about two days."

Cliff moves on, grunting, and stops after a few steps. A female aide comes up to him and asks, "Where you goin', Cliff?"

"I got some hosses way down at the other end," he says. "Ain't seen 'em for three days, want to see how they are." Poking his chin forward, he peers hard down the long corridor. "Well, Jesus Christ, I'm on the right way to go down to the other place, ain't I?"

"You live down there," says the aide, pointing in the other direction.

"I just came from down there," says Cliff. "Christ, I came down through there. My room ain't down that way."

"Yes, it is."

"How the hell *can* it be?"

The aide hurries on. To himself Cliff mutters, "My God, I don't know if they're right. Prob'ly are." He looks around him. "Oh, I see where the hell I come out."

A nurse emerging from another resident's room stops beside Cliff. She tells him he looks tired. Doesn't he think he should go back to his room? Cliff guesses that he should. The horses will have to take care of themselves for another day. They'll be all right, he figures. The nurse stops to watch as Cliff makes his slow, painful-looking way back toward his room, and as she watches, she smiles and says, "Some people are very happily confused."

"How old are you?" the consulting psychiatrist asks the woman, who lies propped against her pillows in her bed on Meadowview. The curtains are drawn. It might be any time of year.

"Eighty-two," the woman says.

"What year were you born?"

"You're trying to check up on me," she says. She smiles, not warmly but brightly.

The psychiatrist laughs in a friendly way.

"I was born in 1907," she says.

"I hate to tell you. You're eighty-three."

"Well," she retorts without so much as a pause, "I give myself the benefit of the extra year."

Do her breathing problems frighten her?

"I don't think I'd go so far as to say *fear*, young man."

He asks her the date. She offers one. He tells her, gently, that she is a month off. She says, "Don't fool me. Don't ask me what year it is or I'll throw you out."

"I was just about to ask you that," the psychiatrist says, smiling.

But before he can, she asks him, "And where are *you* from, sir?" She traps him in a long digression.

Finally, the psychiatrist finds a way back. "I've always been very interested in someone who's had an intellectual life, and what happens as we get older. Do you think your memory's—"

"I don't think my memory's as sharp," she snaps. "I think I started losing some of that back when I was sixteen. The things I've forgotten are things I don't mind forgetting."

He'd like to give her a simple memory test. Would she be willing to take it?

She looks thoughtful. "I'm being an awfully good sport to say yes, I will."

He gives her three words—feather, car, bell. He asks her to repeat them. She does so. He says he'll ask her for those three words again in about a minute. She says she'd prefer to repeat them now.

"I want to distract you first."

"I know. But I don't want to be distracted."

"But it's part of the test." Quickly, he asks her to do some subtraction in her head—7 from 100, then 7 from the remainder, and so on.

She falters after 86, and in a moment the psychiatrist asks, "Now do you remember those three things?"

"No," she says.

"A feather," he says.

"Oh, the *things*," she says. She falls silent for a moment, and when she speaks again, her voice sounds small and plaintive. "A feather and a broom?"

He names the three items.

She looks pensive, then suddenly declares, "I wouldn't have remembered those in a hundred years. I think a smart person such as I am would forget them right away, because you said you were not going to ask me to repeat them." She looks quite regal, her head framed against white pillows, a lofty-looking smile on her face.

"Well, I thought I said I would," says the psychiatrist.

"I think you tricked me," she says.

"I don't like to trick people," he answers. He might be her pupil, in spite of his gray hair. He looks down at his feet. "I apologize."

"I accept your apology."

The warm weather, the long green afternoons, beckon Martha out more often now. She walks steadily along, a determined look on her face, her pocketbook dangling from her arm, through the lobby, out the front doors, and down the drive toward Route 9. A nurse runs after her.

Martha imagines that she is walking home to get supper for her husband. Martha was a nurse, a big nurse in charge of surgery and pediatrics in a hospital. From time to time, she issues orders to the Meadowview nursing staff, sweetly but firmly, often cogently. She'll come upon a fellow resident in need of "toileting," as it is called, and she'll tell the charge nurse to get on that job immediately. Once, a resident's grandson skinned his knee while visiting, and Martha bandaged it herself. She told a fellow resident's granddaughter that she would give her some doll clothes, and, a full week later, Martha, who could not have named the date or this place, made good on her promise to the child. Once every week or so, when one of the staff has coaxed her back from the brink of the highway, she will surface completely in this world of impoverished present time. Eyes wide, her voice choked with sobs, she'll say to one of the staff, speaking of her husband, "He's dead, isn't he." She'll weep over her husband for an hour or two. By dinner she will return to a time when her husband is alive. Whenever she remembers her husband's death, it is as if for the first time. Alzheimer's— that's what the doctors think she has—has fastened Martha to a wheel.

About once a week it brings her back to mourning. She has intermittent but never-ending grief.

Martha is escorted inward, and Ted sits alone in the lobby, his cane between his legs, looking through bay windows at the afternoon, like so many afternoons that he recalls and yet so strangely empty. "Just waiting for some company that isn't gonna come," says Ted. "She's comin' down. I can't remember when. I can't remember anything anymore."

Ted's wife died here last summer. During parties and events like bingo Ted often stands outside the activity room, looking as if he'd like to enter, but he doesn't. "That's the way I like it," he has said. "I just want to sit by myself and think about my wife. I do like pushing somebody down to a meal in a wheelchair. Physically I feel fine. Well, I thank God for that. But there's nothing else I can do."

In old age, memory often fades in the absence of apparent disease, through a process for which science has no real explanation but does have a name: benign senescent forgetfulness. A basic principle of neurology, promulgated in the nineteenth century, holds that failures in memory tend to proceed inversely with time. As memory fades, the past comes nearer. No doubt there's a biological cause, but the psychological result has a logic of its own. In old age, many people seem to remember best what has mattered most to them, and often it is work. Ted sits alone here in the lobby recalling his days on the railroad. He was a telegrapher, manning the key in switching towers in the remotest sections of the Berkshires, all alone in his high perch except for the occasional hoboes who would come by and ask for a place to sleep. Ted would accommodate the hoboes. They were, after all, just workingmen down on their luck. Ted can still see those towers in his mind, and though he often can't remember if any of his family has promised to visit on a given day, he can name all of the stations he worked at. "I can tell you every station, from the East Deerfield station to the Rotterdam station. Thank God I've got a good memory," he says. "I can still remember every letter of the Morse code today." Now and then, while sitting here in the lobby, or upstairs in his electric recliner, Ted drops his right hand to his thigh and taps out his thoughts in Morse code on his trousers.

"Dad? How's Earl Duncan doing?" Ruth asked Lou upstairs in the room.

"Well, I went down to see him the other day, and he was doing fine. Then I went down yesterday and the nurse said he wasn't feeling well, so I didn't go in."

"Oh," said Ruth.

Joe changed the subject. The subject was the weight that Joe couldn't lose, in spite of diet Jell-O and long rides on the bike.

Lou, from his seat by the window, said, "The best exercise, Joe, is—"

Joe sat up and said, "Pushing yourself away from the table. Jesus Christ, my grandfather said that."

Lou made a pantomime of shrinking back in his chair and swallowing his last words. Then he smiled and said, "I'm quoting your grandfather."

"And his grandfather told *him!*"

Lou's thoughts were already elsewhere. He had heard that three oranges cost a dollar.

"Jesus Christ! Three oranges for a dollar?" said Joe.

"I can't believe what Dave was telling me about coffee," said Lou. "Three dollars a pound." He shook his head.

"Well," said Joe, "we don't know what real life is. We're in a nursing home."

The price of things was one of Lou and Joe's continuing subjects. They agreed—vehemently sometimes, as if they were arguing—that the price of things nowadays proved they were superannuated. In the real world a pound of coffee cost almost as much as Lou had once earned in a week. There was no point in trying to keep track of such a crazy world. In agreement with Joe on that point, Lou got his cane and headed downstairs for Current Events. "See ya late-ah, Joe."

In the activity room every Friday, for about half an hour, the activities aide Rita read aloud articles from the regional newspapers. The turnout was usually thin. It would have been thinner if the Forest View staff hadn't routinely rounded up four or five demented residents and sent them down to hear the news. This was a way for the staff to get some respite, and was perhaps a silent protest against the general lack of activities designed for Linda Manor's demented. Zita, the gray-haired woman who paced the halls and tried to pluck flowers from the carpet, had already fallen asleep in her chair. The former innercity school-teacher was trying to read a newspaper upside down. The tiny Fleur, the woman who was always wanting to call her mother on the phone, asked the room in general, "We havin' a party or somethin'?" A couple of able-minded women were there. They were regulars. Lou and Joe's neighbor Hazel asked the aide to read *all* of the local obituaries. "The Irish comics," Hazel called them. Being Irish herself, she was entitled. She smiled sadly, hearing a couple of familiar names. To outlive one's contemporaries is, after all, a species of accomplishment. Lou was the only man there, as usual, and once the obituaries were read and the demented residents had fallen into attentive but puzzled-looking silences, he and the aide carried on, the aide reading the news and Lou offering commentary. "Here's an article about another beaching of whales on the Cape," said the aide, Rita.

"I think it's pollution that's causing it," Lou said.

"Bringing them in," Rita agreed.

Lou said, in a slightly higher voice, "What I don't understand—they claim the whales have to stay wet—why the fire department doesn't hook up its pumps."

"I like to read a few *good* things," Elgie put in.

"That's why I say we should write our own newspaper," said Rita.

But Lou was not afraid of bad news.

"They're expecting a big fight in Moscow today," said Rita.

"Maybe they'll bring the czar back," said Lou.

"Ooooh," said Rita. "Richmond, California. It says there's a rash of—"

Lou interrupted. He'd already heard this news. "Legionnaires'. It's in an area where they failed to clean their air-conditioning filters. That's what happened when they discovered so-called Legionnaires' disease at the Bellevue-Stratford in Philadelphia. They didn't clean the filters as often as they should."

"Isn't that something," said Rita.

"The problem is," said Lou severely, "they don't do the maintenance."

"Oh, here's something! A bicycle for eight."

"*That's* what this country needs," said Lou.

"Here's a bit of slightly good news. 'The Persian Gulf War should not cost the United States any money.' "

"So far the other countries haven't come across with their share," said Lou, wearing a dark look.

"I think they will," said Rita.

"I don't know," said Lou. "I think they're gonna hem and haw on it, that's for sure."

Rita read some figures. One country was going to give $12 million, another $11.5 *billion*.

"Promises, promises," intoned Lou.

Joe liked these hours and half hours when Lou went to activities. Over this last year he had discovered—it seemed like for the first time in his life—a capacity for calmness. Lou might have been astonished to hear that, but Lou hadn't known him before. The other night, for instance, Joe had called his wife and gotten no answer. At such times he used to fill up with worry. He would call his son to ask where the hell his mother was. But the other night he waited and called his wife back later, and sure enough, everything was all right. She'd just been out to dinner at the neighbors'. In his newfound calmness, Joe could see himself more clearly.

He remembered how as a young man he'd imagined himself like the movie actor Leslie Howard, suave, urbane, insouciant. Joe guffawed at that old fantasy, remembering himself back then, jealous, combative, always anxious. He was different now, both inside and outside. Somewhat more on the outside, he thought. "I still have things inside me."

Lou would return soon. Today being Friday, there'd be scrod for lunch, and before lunch Lou would probably tell his scrod joke, one of Lou's two or three off-color jokes. Lou would probably say again, "You know the story about the proper Bostonian lady. She said, 'I'm going to Boston to get scrod.' "

Joe wouldn't mind hearing the joke again. "He's seventy, eighty, ninety, ninety-one, for Chrissake. He can *tell* his joke. Good God."

But when Lou came back to the room, he had something else on his mind, obviously. He gave Joe his usual summary of Current Events, and then, shifting in his chair, lifting a hand, index finger extended, Lou said, "Changing the subject a little. Talking about tools . . ."

Joe grinned. He sat up in his bed and, still grinning, said toward Lou, "I wasn't aware we were talking about tools."

"I was up last night trying to figure this out," Lou went on. "Millers Falls. They made tools somewhere around here. Are they still in business?" Lou didn't wait for an answer. He lifted an index finger again. "The first tool I ever bought myself was a hand drill. I was working in a shop that made electrical fixtures. I had to drill small holes. And I paid three dollars and fifty cents for that drill, and three dollars and fifty cents was my wages for the week, and that tool is still in good working order. I gave it to my grandson. It has the Millers Falls label on the handle."

Still grinning, Joe sat up again and said toward Lou, "Changing the subject a little."

"A hundred and ninety degrees." Lou smiled. "Go ahead, Joe."

"I don't have anything to say." Joe lay back and let his laughter out. Then, the trace of a smile on his face, Joe lay listening to Lou reminisce.

Lou said he knew where all of his old tools had gone, and it was true. Joe had overheard Lou on the phone on Saturday mornings asking his grandson about the well-being of that old hand drill. Afterward, Lou had told Joe that the drill was still "in perfect working order." Over on the table beside him was Lou's album of photos of knick-knacks and furniture he had made. Lou had shown the pictures to Joe, and often Joe had lain here watching and listening while Lou, who could no longer see those photos himself, showed them to various visitors and staff. Joe had listened many times this past year as memory summoned Lou back to his workshops. Knowing where his old tools were and having pictures of things he'd made with them kept that part of his life real. Sitting there by the window, Lou would reconstruct the furniture, telling how he'd used this and that tool, now in his son's workshop, to make that grandfather clock, now in the album and in a granddaughter's living room. And lying on his bed, Joe listened.

That first tool, the seventy-eight-year-old Millers Falls hand drill, was like the fertilized egg of Lou's memory. It seemed to carry all the information Lou needed to reconstitute his long life. The drill took him back: Lou finishing up eighth grade on a Thursday in 1914 and skipping the graduation ceremony in order to start his first full-time job. Turning over his $3.50 paycheck to his mother, who somehow managed always to put food on the table for a large family. His father's delivery service that ended in failure, like all his other ventures, in this case when his horse went lame. The restaurant and boarding house in South Philadelphia, Lou's father's voice calling to his mother in the kitchen, speaking about a man who had ordered beef stew, which cost a nickel, "Take the beef out, the bum's only got three cents." Shutting his eyes tight, Lou described Philadelphia, in whole and in parts, and repopulated it, with that Irish cop with a voice like Joe's and that hawker down in the Tenderloin.

That old hand drill took Lou forward from boyhood, through his long succession of jobs, helping to wire up factories and shipyards. With that drill and a can of shoe polish, for covering up scratches in baseboards, Lou once again brought the first electricity to a number of houses in Philadelphia.

Joe could imagine the hollow feeling of unemployment that lay upon Lou these days. It lay upon Joe, too, sometimes. Probably it was that feeling that took Lou back once again to the time, in his late fifties, when after thirty-five years of running the pen factory in Burlington, the company went bankrupt and Lou was left with neither pension nor job, and at every interview he could see that his gray hair was being studied, and he waited to hear the interviewer say, "We'll get back to you." But that was all right, Lou would say. He and Jennie always lived frugally, and Jennie never complained. "She was never demanding." Lou got a job finally, working with industrial machinery again. "I invented a few things for them, too." Then he was sixty, moving to California, where their son Harold, who was an engineer, found Lou a job in the model shop at Lockheed. There Lou, who'd started out in the early days of electricity, made pieces of models of rockets and space stations. Then Lou was being forced to retire at the age of sixty-eight, and was enlisting as the maintenance man for the apartment complex where he and his wife lived, fixing locks and windows and appliances until he was seventy-five. Then he was in his workshop, building furniture.

Joe listened to Lou inventing things as a boy, working on designs for a perpetual motion machine, for a bobbinless sewing machine. When remembering the hand drill led to remembering the job for which he had bought it and that job led to his next jobs, which he sometimes skipped over, and he came finally to the fountain pen factory, then Lou was rising again at 4:30 in the morning, reriding the trolley through the quiet streets down to the ferry terminal, to cross the Delaware. He crossed it every day except Sundays for thirty-five years, wondering, when there was ice in the river, about the strength of the ferryboat's hull. He boarded the train on the other side. He remembered all the stops. Joe could hear the conductor calling them out. Lou also remembered the names of the factories that lined the tracks of his daily commute through that part of New Jersey. Once in a while he'd pick up some information from other commuters bound for other factories. He made it a point to visit the factories of his factory's suppliers. Lou was amazing, Joe thought. He still knew everything there was to know about how fountain pens were made, about the invention of ballpoints, about the fabrication of carbon paper. He had watched tinkers make their little dams of clay to catch excess solder, and then throw out the ruined clay, which was why, of course, tinkers' dams had become synonyms for worthlessness.

The first times he heard Lou repeating himself, nearly a year ago now, Joe had decided to say nothing about it because Lou seemed like a nice guy, and he was old, really old. Joe felt differently now. He liked to hear Lou repeat his stories. He actually liked to hear them again.

There was something beautiful about Lou in the act of storytelling, opening up his storehouse of memories and bringing them back to life. He summoned up his memories with what seemed like the force of necessity. Telling his stories, he sat quite still in his chair but his hands became animated, and if he was interrupted midcourse, by a visit from an aide or a nurse, he would stop. He might even chat with the intruder, but his fingers would stroke the arms of his chair or drum lightly upon them, and when the intruder departed, he would pick up his story just where he'd left off.

Joe recalled the old story about two prisoners locked up together so long that they no longer tell each other their jokes. One simply says, "Thirty-six," and the other at once begins laughing hysterically. Maybe he and Lou resembled those prisoners, two old pensioners who had run out of new things to say to each other. It was true that local news was scant. Around here, what qualified as a new story usually had to do with someone's new ailment. Lou's stories were more entertaining than most contemporary local ones. Heard only twice, Lou's memories could seem monotonous. Heard many times, they were like old friends. They were comforting. They lent stability to Joe's life in this room, and there was little enough of that around here, in many rooms in this building. Lou's memories seemed like an immortal part of him. They existed right now forever. Lou's memories contained such a density of life that in their presence death seemed impossible.

Here in the room, he was often at the business of keeping his wife alive. The fact that some of his memories about her were painful was part of the point. Joe understood this. His voice turning high and reedy, Lou would say, "I have a mental picture of my wife on the day she had her first stroke, which I can't eradicate from my mind. And which I don't *want* to eradicate from my mind!" As he said those last words, Lou's gentle countenance would turn stony, as if he meant to warn Joe against telling him to put such thoughts away. In a softer voice, Lou would describe that mental picture again. Though he couldn't smell anything in the present, in his mind he smelled the meal Jennie had been cooking—Canadian smelts. "Ahhh, beauty-ful." He heard the thud from the kitchen again, and he saw Jennie lying on the floor by the stove, and also, lying on the floor beside her—this detail had weight and was never omitted from Lou's telling—her wire-rim eyeglasses with the temple pieces bent.

Jennie didn't seem to be breathing. Lou had never been trained in artificial respiration, but he had read about it. He knelt down and breathed into Jennie's mouth, and she revived. Lou didn't always tell that part of the story, and when he did, he seemed to think it incidental. Joe did not agree. "How old were you?"

"It was a couple years ago," Lou answered.

He'd have been in his eighties when he did that. Good God.

Lou also worked on his memory now, Joe realized. That is, Lou maintained and improved his bank of memories. One of the nurses had brought in a collection of clocks. Nearly every time he and Joe passed them in the display case in the central corridor downstairs, Lou would stop and peer in and wonder aloud what had happened to that clock of his mother's that used to rest on the mantels of their many homes. "I've got to remember to ask my sister next time she calls." Next Saturday on the phone, Joe would overhear Lou asking his sister. Lou's mother used to tell him that when he was a baby, before the family moved to Philadelphia, Lou witnessed the return of Admiral Dewey's fleet from the Philippines. His mother said she carried him down to the New York City waterfront and stood among the crowd, holding him in her arms. Lou had carted this memory of a memory around for the better part of a century, but it was only recently, here at Linda Manor, that he had set out to verify the story. He asked his son-in-law to look up the date. Lou was born on May 2, 1899, and Admiral Dewey returned from Manila on October 3 of that year. These facts had become a necessary addendum to Lou's telling of the story. "The dates checked out," Joe would hear Lou say.

Lying on his back, listening to Lou today, Joe had watched himself scissor the fingers of his good hand, and had kept silent. Now Lou had left off. He'd left off too soon to suit Joe. Watching himself scissor his fingers, Joe said, "Hey, Lou, who was the relative you were visiting in New York and you got the cot and she was still talking?"

Lou smiled. "Oh, that was my sister-in-law, who called up a friend to borrow a cot."

Joe laughed.

"What are you laughing about? I haven't told the story yet," said Lou.

Joe backed off at once. "I just think it's funny, that's all."

Lou went on: "Harry and I walked a few blocks to the friend's house, said hello, got the cot, brought it back, and she was still on the phone talking to the person we borrowed the cot from."

"*That's* funny," said Joe.

"The story I like," said Lou, "my sister-in-law's sister was being courted, and her father came down in his robe and said to the young man, 'You expect to see my daughter again?' 'Yes.' 'Well, how you gonna see her again if you don't go home first?' "

Lou was on a roll now, once again. "In Philadelphia, shortly after I was married, my brother had a Ford. There was no regular shift in those days."

"Well, they hadda crank it up first," Joe said.

"That's not the main part of the story."

Joe, looking at the ceiling, made an exaggerated closure of his lips.

Lou went on: "And they didn't have signals at the crossings. The cops stood in intersections with signs. Philadelphia from Broad and Fairmount, going west on Fairmount was a real wide street." Lou drew a map with his hands. "And at Twenty-second and Fairmount there was a big prison. Eastern Penitentiary. Just before you come to Twenty-second there's a big steel gate." Lou shifted in his chair. "Anyhow, this Sunday morning my brother called me up. He said, 'There isn't much traffic, I'll take you out and teach you how to drive.' Out on Broad and Fairmount, he puts me in the driver's side. I couldn't see any traffic. I was tense as hell. We were riding along pretty good."

Joe chuckled at what was coming.

"Anyhow," Lou said, "we got out to Twenty-second. I don't know what happened. I drive up on the pavement, and where do we do that but right beside that prison gate. Fortunately we didn't hit it, and my brother says, 'Let's get the hell out of here before someone sees us.' And that's how I didn't learn to drive. That's my one and only time behind the wheel of a car."

"Wait a minute," Joe said. "You had another thing happen to you once. You drove a thing through a plate glass window."

"Out in California," Lou said. "A big department store. They had small hand trucks and . . ."

Lou went on for a while. Then he returned to the present. "Hey, Joe, incidentally, what's the definition of 'hospice'?"

Joe shook his head. Lou was amazing. Sometimes Lou would get to thinking about his wife and say, "I think I've seen about everything God meant me to see." And then, often moments later, he'd raise his index finger and say, "Incidentally, Joe . . ." He'd want to know if Joe knew what this term they kept using on the radio, "Dolby sound," meant. If humanity continued to extract such vast amounts of minerals, oil, and water from the earth, would the globe collapse? Did chickens raised in incubators lose their nesting instinct? Could hail be used as ice cubes if it was tainted with acid rain? Could you eat salmon after they'd spawned? If vultures ate tainted meat, why didn't they get sick? "Sitting here, I think of some of the damnedest things," Lou said once. He didn't have to tell Joe that. Lou would sit in his chair, his brow knitted, his lips pursed, like a student at an arithmetic problem, and Joe would know that pretty soon a question would be asked. What was chicory? Someone had said a wild duck had been seen on the grounds outside. What did a wild duck look like? What was the origin of the expression "freeze the balls off a brass monkey"? Did anyone ever try filling a football with helium? If someone down on the first floor and someone up on Forest View each simultaneously pushed the button to summon the same elevator, what would happen? Where did the expression "sow your wild oats" come from? What kind of wood were George Washington's teeth made from? They'd been discussing that one for three months.

When Joe didn't know the answer, which was often, Lou would hold the question until Ruth came in. The other day Lou asked Ruth, "I wonder what lesbians actually do?" Then, with sudden force, Lou said to his sixty-five-year-old daughter, "But don't *you* tell me."

Ruth told Joe that it had gotten to the point where her friend the reference librarian wouldn't even say hello to her. The librarian would see Ruth coming and say, "All right, what does your father want to know now?" The man was almost ninety-two years old and he asked more questions than any child Joe had known. Joe used to think seventy-two was old. Well, it still was, as far as Joe was concerned. Life was mysterious. Maybe ninety-one was, in its way, younger.

What was the definition of "hospice"? Lou had asked a moment ago.

Joe looked thoughtful. "I don't know," he said finally.

Then, suddenly, Joe sat up. "Here. I'll go get the, uh, medical thing. They got a, a . . . Oh, what the hell."

Joe's steel brace clattered on the floor. He was putting on his orthopedic shoes.

"Where ya goin'?" Lou asked.

"Well, I'm gonna find out what 'hospice' means. They got a, uh, medical dictionary."

Lou rolled his shoulders and settled back in his chair, his eyes shut, like an old cat in the sun.

Joe headed out toward the nurses' station. He limped along on his cane down the carpeted hallway, then stopped for a moment to rest and catch his breath. "Lou's always thinking of these things. It's good. It keeps him active."

Joe started on again, limping toward the nurses' station and the medical dictionary. "Keeps *me* active."

Jane Kramer

In his article "Notes on the Balinese Cockfight," the cultural anthropologist Clifford Geertz wrote:

> The culture of a people is an ensemble of texts, themselves ensembles, which the anthropologist strains to read over the shoulders of those to whom they properly belong. There are enormous difficulties in such an enterprise, methodological pitfalls to make a Freudian quake, and some moral perplexities as well. . . . [O]ne can start anywhere in a culture's repertoire of forms and end up anywhere else. One can stay . . . within a single, more or less bounded form, and circle steadily within it. One can move between forms in search of broader unities or inform-

ing contrasts. One can even compare forms from different cultures to define their character in reciprocal relief. But whatever the level at which one operates, and however intricately, the guiding principle is the same: societies, like lives, contain their own interpretations. One has only to learn how to gain access to them.

Jane Kramer writes about Fernande Pelletier, a French farmer who pursues her traditional occupation in changing times. The arrival of the European Common Market has collapsed centuries-old economic barriers and French farmers have felt the effects strongly. Kramer's strategy echoes Geertz's summary of tactics. She reads a French agricultural family's culture "over the shoulder" of her subject, spirals outward to link in French agriculture and the European Community, then returns to the illusory stability of Fernande Pelletier's changing life.

Jane Kramer's skill in gaining access to other cultures gives her writing an erudition that has been admired by anthropologists, social historians, and general readers. Her longest reach may have been *The Last Cowboy* (1977), in which she overcame the reluctance of a cowboy to reveal his life to a woman writer from New York.

As for "Fernande Pelletier," Kramer said, "I came to write it because, ever since *The Last Cowboy*, I've been fascinated—almost obsessed—with notions of the land, of the way particular people are attached to particular soil they call their own, of notions of 'home,' of agriculture." Parisian friends introduced her to Fernande Pelletier, and they became friends. Lately Pelletier has grown asparagus, but it hasn't paid the bills. Along with that backbreaking labor, she has started taking in tourists for a week or two at a time to give them a farm experience. "I think there must be a lot of embarrassment in the arrangements," Kramer said, "the embarrassment of a proud woman having to turn her home into a Disneyland or theme park of *la France profonde*."

Kramer has been writing for *The New Yorker* since 1964. Her "Letter from Europe" features in the magazine since 1978 have been collected in *Europeans* (1988). Her other books include *Off Washington Square* (1963), *Allen Ginsberg in America* (1969), *Honor to the Bride* (1971), and *Unsettling Europe* (1980). In 1981, she won the American Book Award for nonfiction. She lives in Paris and New York.

Fernande Pelletier

The trip south from Paris to the Pelletier farm takes just a few hours now that a little Air Limousin De Havilland Twin Otter meets the Paris plane at Limoges. From Limoges, you can fly to the town of Brive-la-Gaillarde in ten or eleven minutes, and after that it is an easy, pretty drive down the Vézère River into the Périgord, past the village I will call Sainte-Lucie and the hamlet of Sainte-Lucie-le-Pont and, finally, up the steep dirt road that ends at the Pelletiers' Périgord farmhouse. Fernande Pelletier talks sometimes about "flying to Paris for the day," and then she howls with laughter until the dogs come running in to investigate and Fernande herself has to sit down with a glass of water, to recover. The idea of flying to Paris for the day is Mme Pelletier's idea of something so preposterous, so improbable, that laughing about it is a way of laughing at life, or at herself, if she is disappointed or confused or is feeling helpless because someone in the Common Market has traded, say, a butter-and-milk quota for a beet-sugar quota and the world has intruded again on the hundred acres of France that her family has farmed for centuries. Before the Common Market, there used to be only what she regarded as natural intrusions on the Pelletier farm— wars or plagues or phylloxera.

Fernande Pelletier was in Paris for a day in 1964. She and her husband, Georges, drove here with their son, who was four and slow in talking and had an appointment with a famous Paris doctor. They left the farm at three in the morning, arrived at noon, found the hospital, saw the famous doctor (who said that he didn't know why the boy was slow), and headed home without another stop. It was not that Paris intimidated the Pelletiers or put them off. The Pelletiers had a book of photographs of Paris. They knew Paris from their book and from the evening news and from the pictures in *Le Pèlerin*, the Catholic weekly that Fernande's mother gets in the mail on Fridays. It was simply that they never thought to stay in Paris and look around—just as they never think to look around Brive, say, or Périgueux after a weekly market or around Sainte-Lucie after a sheep sale. The Paris of doctors' appointments and all the other business of daily life is not the Paris that Fernande Pelletier means when she talks about "flying to Paris for the day."

Seven years ago, I met an old sherry vintner in Jerez who talked about flying to New York for the day. It amused him to imagine getting on a Concorde in the morning, enjoying a glass of his best sherry at the Knickerbocker Club, and heading home in time for a good night's sleep in the carved-oak bed where his father and grandfather and great-grandfather had slept before him. He must have been about ninety then, because he described skating on the Neckar with his friend Alfonso XIII when they were both at boarding school in Heidelberg at the turn of the century. He remembered the long fall trips from Jerez to Heidelberg. He went in his father's coach, north through most of Europe, and while he couldn't say—not at the age of ninety—exactly how many weeks he was in the coach each fall, he did not find anything odd about the trips he made and the time they took. He liked the time of traveling. He found it consistent (his word) with the occasion.

It may be that only the middle class is really comfortable about starting a day at home and, with not much more than a case of jet lag to show for it, ending up on another continent in a couple of hours. There are still people in Europe who are profoundly *located*, and they are mainly peasants like Fernande Pelletier and old aristocrats like the vintner in Jerez. Their little jokes about flying to Paris for the day or taking the Concorde to New York for a glass of sherry at the Knickerbocker Club are really the same story—a way of reminding themselves that the world beyond their land and their attachments may control their fortunes but that it has nothing at all to do with who they are or with the rhythm and etiquette of an appropriate life.

The first time I visited the Pelletiers, I took the train. Fernande was curious about the trip, because she had taken a long train trip herself in the summer of 1955, when she and Georges got married and went to the Pyrenees for a week and stopped in Lourdes for the blessing of the Virgin. Fernande never took another holiday. She thinks that there is one allotted holiday in a peasant's life, and that is a honeymoon spent in pursuit of blessings. Sometimes she can hear a train passing above Sainte-Lucie-le-Pont in the morning, but she rarely sees it now that she has sold the sheep that used to graze in pastures with a view of the railroad tracks. In the old days, she would take her sheep and her dogs and a copy of the racing news out to one of those far pastures of the farm, and she would watch for the train and think about her weekly bet and about her honeymoon and the *pension* at Lourdes where she discovered how disappointing love was compared with Mass in the grotto or the sight of a ton of corn filling the family's orange metal crib after a good harvest. The farm was still her father's then. His name was Olivier Tricart, and he was a blunt, intelligent man (*"C'est quelqu'un,"* people who knew him always said), a man of dignity and authority, and a proud farmer. *"Nous, les paysans,"* he would begin when the other Sainte-Lucie farmers came to him for advice. Today in Sainte-Lucie, the farmers call themselves *cultivateurs* and refer to their farms not as farms but as *exploitations agricoles*, and it is mainly the young farmers—who go off to agricultural school in places like Périgueux, or even Limoges, and meet boys and girls from the city and talk about coming home as "returning to the land"—who use the word "peasant." They say *"nous, les paysans"* the way Parisians on my street say *"nous, les intellectuels."* There are two or three young farmers starting out now in Sainte-Lucie-le-Pont. They come to consult Fernande, just as their fathers used to consult M. Tricart, and when they talk excitedly about "ecology" and "natural farming" it amuses Fernande, because she knows they are really talking about the kind of farming everybody has to do these days to stay alive. She worries about her son, Maurice, who is twenty-five now and has so little of the excitement, the sense of starting an adventure, that those other young farmers have. She thinks that the life of a farmer starting out should be full of feeling and excitement, because it has to supply the memories to sustain him later on.

Fernande likes to remember the day that she and Georges took over the farm from her father. It was the fall of 1972, and M. Tricart had decided to celebrate his seventy-fifth birthday by retiring. Not that he was stopping work—he was stopping to enjoy a long last word against the government. At his birthday dinner, he signed over his entire property to Fernande—it cost him a gift tax of about three thousand francs, or, at the time, about six hundred dollars—and announced that he had saved the Pelletiers the price of at least twenty acres in inheritance taxes. Fernande concluded that she had twenty acres coming to her. She took out a loan at the Crédit Agricole in Sainte-Lucie and bought the land at a good price from her neighbor and admirer Pierre Lagorce, an old farmer who had had his eye on Fernande since she was a rosy girl with a flock of sheep and he was an ardent husband with a complaining wife. It happened that Fernande had something of her father's authority. She tried it out on Georges, who was a sweet-tempered, diffident sort of person, much happier when he was out somewhere on his tractor than when he was in the barnyard giving orders to someone else. She paid the bills, ordered the feed and the fertilizer, kept the books, bid on the sheep they bought at auction, and bargained with the three hard men from the farmers' union who ran the marketing cooperative. People with business on the farm would pay their respects to Georges, off by himself in a tobacco shed or a cornfield, and then they would head for the farmhouse and M. Tricart and his daughter. Fernande was nearly forty-two when she took over the farm. She was getting stout, but her cheeks were still rosy and her hair was as red and curly as it was when Lagorce first saw her, sitting on a rock with her dogs at her feet and her sheep all around her, studying the weekly racing form. She won nine thousand francs in the pari-mutuels that year, and bought a Deux Chevaux with some of the money. She drives it today; it is a kind of talisman. When she puts on her old duffel coat and a pair of mud boots and gets behind the wheel of that Deux Chevaux and goes bumping up the road with her bottle-red hair poking out of a plaid kerchief, she looks the way she must have looked the year she got her farm, and her horse came in, and she had a shy husband for nighttimes and a lusty old lover for the afternoons.

There is something young about Fernande at fifty-four, an awkward optimism that makes her touching. This year, she is feeding ducks for foie gras. Last year, it was geese as well. The year before, she had 120 veal calves in one barn, and was feeding them corn from her own hand. She is raising tobacco, too—not just the dark tobacco her father planted years ago on three acres up the hill from the farmhouse, where the soil is particularly fine, but light tobacco, which is not a Common Market surplus crop and brings a high price at auction. She is thinking about pressing oil from any walnuts which she doesn't sell. She used to make sunflower oil, but, with the price she gets now, it is not worth her time to go on with it, and, besides, she wants to see what walnut oil will bring if she puts it in little tin jars marked *"Fabrication Artisanale"* and sells it to a co-op for fancy-food stores. She is also thinking of saving walnut *brou*—the dark, fibrous casing around walnut shells that stains farmers' hands brown at harvest time—and selling it in Belgium, where it is bottled as "winter tanning lotion" and put on the cosmetic counters of expensive department stores. There are three acres of walnut trees on the farm, and it is getting hard for Fernande to compete with California walnuts, which come from huge farms and are artificially dried in only forty-eight hours; her walnuts are better, but she dries them naturally, and that takes three straight weeks of decent weather.

Still, the price of walnuts does not upset Fernande the way the price of lamb does. She has always thought of herself as a sheep farmer, despite her three acres of tobacco and her three acres of walnuts, not to mention her twenty-four acres of corn, her twelve acres of wheat, her twelve acres of barley, her sunflowers, her kitchen garden, her fruit trees, her six cows, her two pigs, her geese and chickens and the eighteen hundred ducks that pass through her barns each year to help keep France in foie gras and pâté. She is not a woman who regrets, she likes to say, but in spite of herself she regrets that there are no more sheep grazing out by the Vézère, and no lambs suckling in the pasture behind the barn. She gave up sheep in 1983. By then, she had 360 ewes and their lambs, and she was using a couple of prefab hangars to feed another fifteen hundred baby lambs, to be sold as Roquefort spring lamb when they got to eighty-five or ninety pounds. That spring, her ewes suddenly started dropping, and after the blood tests were in an inspector from town confirmed what Fernande herself suspected, once she was seeing two or three aborted lambs every time she left the house—and that was brucellosis. There was no insurance—Fernande was saving money in 1983—and no way for her to claim damages from the man who had sold the infected sheep to her. In the end, she got 225 francs from the state for every ewe she slaughtered—it was called a *prime d'abattage*— and 300 francs for each of the few that were still healthy and could be sold. It was not much money. No one wanted her lambs after that, and for a while, she says, she was close to ruin. She blamed herself. She blamed stray sheep crossing the Pyrenees from Spain and breeder sheep imported from Australia, because sheep that were not French were, to her mind, diseased to begin with and survived only to spread their diseases around. She blamed the Communists, because people said that rich Communist farmers here were buying weak, sickly sheep from Eastern Europe in order to give their friends a chance to earn some hard currency. By now, she doesn't blame the brucellosis. She says that brucellosis was merely the *coup de grâce* to her career as a sheep farmer, since there was no way to make a living from sheep anyway once the English had started selling their Commonwealth lamb in France at a lower price than she or most other small French farmers could afford to ask. It does not console her that there was also no way for a small English farmer to match the low price of all the good French fruit at an English supermarket.

Fernande Pelletier keeps going, and keeps her farm going, and in her way—with or without her sheep—is prosperous. The neighbors say she has a *"grosse exploitation."* To them, she is a rich woman. She has that "extreme love of the soil" which Tocqueville wrote about—that "illuminating attachment" of a French peasant to his land which is probably the most profound attachment of the civilization. When a farmer like Fernande—when anybody French—talks about France, that person is talking literally, talking about soil and trees and vines. The idea of La France, which is held so fervently here and mocked so insistently abroad, is drawn from that experience of the countryside. Strangers are astonished at this. They decide that the French are primitive under their immense sophistication, but what they describe as primitive to their friends at home is really an identification of soul and place of great ethnographic purity. Every Frenchman has his *pays*, his corner of the provinces, his ancestral soil, even if that soil belongs to somebody else by now or is confined to the flowerpots of a family farmhouse that has been restored by bickering cousins for country Christmases and August holidays. Fernande would not know what to make of the abandoned countryside in southern Italy or Spain or Portugal. The idea of a French family abandoning its corner of France is as strange, as unnatural, to her as the idea of a ewe abandoning her lamb or a mother her child. She considers the land of France a trust and the peasants who tend it the custodians of that trust.

In a way, they are. It has been three hundred years since the nobility began to leave the countryside, keeping their châteaus for hunts and holidays, and gradually selling off their fields to pay the potlatch cost of court life in Paris and Versailles. By the Revolution, most of the local *châtelains* in France were people who could not afford to move to town, and half the farmland was peasant freeholds. The family across the valley from the Pelletiers can trace their births and their bans and their funerals in village records back to 1300. Their farm was surveyed in the 1700s and the deed to it entered at the *mairie* seven generations ago. Georges Pelletier's family goes back that far in *its* village, over on the south side of the Vézère. And Pierre Lagorce, who spent seventeen days in school in 1920 and only learned to sign his name in 1969, when he took out a loan for his daughter's dowry, was once the owner of 150 acres and a dilapidated château with twenty-five rooms. His daughter did well with her dowry. She married a plumber and lives in a house in town and, according to Fernande, puts on terrible airs and pretends that the family was a noble family once—the de la Gorce family, she says— and suffered some mysterious calamity. The truth is that M. Lagorce bought his château a few days after the war, and the only family that suffered a calamity was the one that sold it to him for a few hundred dollars. Lagorce talks a lot about working, but he is at his best at the Pelletiers' kitchen table with a glass of wine in his hand and a discourse to deliver. Working itself never agreed with him. He was not happy as a *châtelain*. He lived in an old farmhouse on his land, out of sight of the château and the walls that needed pointing and the roof that needed tiling. He let the trees and the fields go. Eventually, he sold the place to a young vicomte from Paris who was a passionate farmer, and he went to work for the vicomte as part of the bargain—an arrangement that consisted of Lagorce "supervising" and the young vicomte and his vicomtesse getting up with the sun to build walls and dig up rocks and plant flowers while their supervisor slept.

Fernande's family worked for the château once. It was before the Revolution, and the Tricart family was what the French call *en métayage*, which means that they were sharecroppers, turning over half their harvest to the château according to the terms of yearly contracts that they could never extend and never anticipate. After the Revolution, they began to rent the land they farmed. They were *fermiers* then—tenant farmers, with a proper lease in the *notaire*'s safe, and the knowledge that they would never have to ruin another Christmas wondering whether their *châtelain* was going to throw them out on December 31. They started to buy their land, acre by acre, the year Fernande got married. Her father wanted the land for her. He wanted to settle it on her, the way he would have settled a chest of sheets and tablecloths on an ordinary daughter. That land has been the romance of her life—not the affable husband who runs errands for her on his tractor, or the garrulous old lover who has overstayed his welcome by a quarter of a century, or the son who, at twenty-five, is often as slow as he was at four, when his mother took him to the Paris doctor and asked if he was going to talk.

Fernande and Georges had an understanding. They never talked about it, but it was agreed that when they married Georges would turn over whatever land he inherited to his brothers and sisters, so that Fernande and her land could stay together. Or, rather, it was accepted that Fernande's attachment was stronger. Certainly she would never have sold her farm, the way Lagorce sold his to the vicomte. As it is, she is reluctant even to share it with Maurice—or with her daughter, Mercedes, who is married and lives in Tulle and has a family of her own. Other farmers in Sainte-Lucie-le-Pont are overjoyed if their sons stay home, the way Maurice did. They do everything to please them. They are paterfamilias at the table, but on the farm they cede their authority. Lately, in Saint-Lucie, they are signing contracts with their sons so that father and son become a kind of family cooperative—a GAEC, or *groupement agricole d'exploitation en commun*—and are partners, dividing the family's property and its profits along with the work there is to do. Fernande does not approve of this sort of arrangement. Perhaps she does not trust anybody else to love the farm as she does. Or perhaps she does not expect the farm to outlast her optimism for it, now that the Pelletiers have had to give up their sheep for ducks and some of their dark tobacco for light tobacco and their sunflower oil for walnut oil, and the man at the Crédit Agricole in Sainte-Lucie—he was sent to the village after losing a couple of million francs through bad loans in one of the big-city branches—says to concentrate on crops that haven't made the EEC agenda, and the man down the street at the state agricultural office says no, it is more important to concentrate on the quality of the crops they already have, and their deputy says that small farmers are the future of the Common Market, and their mayor tells them that farms like theirs will be obsolete by the end of the century.

Twenty-five years ago, there were two and a half million farmers in France. De Gaulle was President. He was provincial and puritanical and profoundly Catholic. He had, Fernande says, "farmers' values," and he believed that those values were France's power. He held them insistently, while the rest of Europe was abandoning the countryside for the city, the farm for the factory, the reality of property for the illusions of paper capital; and because of this France entered the Common Market shrewdly, at great agricultural advantage, "sacrificing" the industrial advantages to Germany. The Minister of Agriculture then was Edgard Pisani, and most people who know anything about French farming consider Pisani the best Agriculture Minister the country ever had. In his way, he was a visionary. His particular vision was the ideal French farm—an *exploitation familiale* that could be farmed to its potential by the members of one family working together and that could support that family completely. He talked about *la tâche primordiale*— the primordial task of farming—and at the same time about an entirely new relation between the French farmer and his land, and between the collectivity of French farmers and what he called "the space of the nation." Pisani's rhetoric was thick, but, simply put, what he wanted was to see each ideal French farm join with the other ideal French farms in its neighborhood, creating chains of cooperatives and collectives, and linking the farmland of France by region and husbandry and local culture. He resigned from the government in 1968, and broke with de Gaulle in 1969 and joined the Socialists, but by the time he did, French family agriculture had been eased into the century and spared the kind of brutal modernization that was turning farmers in most of Europe into a disaffected proletariat. Oddly, the prototype for Pisani's ideal French farm was the ideal English farm—eighty or a hundred acres of intensively cultivated land, which compensated for its small (by England's colonial standards) size through the extravagant attention of its farmers. French farmers had a fine tradition of *main d'œuvre* themselves, and Pisani's genius was to encourage it in ways that never undermined the technology that was really changing their lives. The fact that they could think of France as a breadbasket, and not a container truck or a carton for square tomatoes, was a measure of the extent to which de Gaulle and his minister had reassured them that the France they knew, the old France—*la France profonde*—was the real source of their prosperity, and that the changes that frightened them were changes only on the surface of their lives.

When France made its arrangements with the Common Market, in 1962, the country was as close to being self-sufficient in food as any place in Europe except, maybe, Sweden, which was not a member. French farmers were in the business of feeding France, the way they had always been. They were not really in the business of exporting food, and certainly none of them dreamed that in twenty-three years there would be a million tons of surplus butter sitting in Common Market freezers and another million tons of powdered milk in Common Market silos. They thought of "export" in terms of the Brie and the Roquefort and the château wines and the first-press olive oils they sold to fancy stores in London and New York. Most of the grains and the milk and butter they produced—the survival foods—stayed in France. What the French call *concurrence*—the dropping or balancing of trade and tariff barriers to create a competitive common market, in which, say, a French string bean could cost in Hamburg what it cost in Paris—began in 1962, when they sold cereal grains in Germany for what would have been the market price at home. In 1968, French milk became Community milk. Meat was put *en concurrence* during the sixties and seventies (although the *concurrence* was adjusted according to what sort of meat it was), and was followed, in the last few years, by wine and fruit (with more complicated adjustments and readjustments). For a while, French farmers were thriving. They were expanding their farms and in some cases doubling their crops—and they were making money doing it, because everyone else in Europe was buying. They were joining storage collectives and marketing cooperatives, and—the Pelletiers do this—were getting together with other farmers to invest in expensive harvesters and corn chutes and tractors that they could never have bought alone.

People like the Pelletiers discovered credit in the early days of the Common Market. Maître Prot, the *notaire* in Sainte-Lucie, says that most of the local farmers had never used a check before 1962. They kept a big wallet full of franc notes, and when they went out they attached it, for safety, to a chain on their vest, and did their business and paid their bills that way. But once the Crédit Agricole opened a branch in Sainte-Lucie they joined and started writing checks, and then they started borrowing money to pay for what they bought with those checks. Fernande herself had a checking account and two loans paid up before she had electricity on the farm, or even running water. She may have decided that borrowing money was less shameful, in the end, than no lights and no toilet and a yard that looked like the *basse cour* of a set for some medieval movie. By the time she went to the bank for money for Pierre Lagorce's twenty acres, the Crédit Agricole had six hundred clients in Sainte-Lucie, and those clients were also buying new land and, with it, new machines, and they were farming efficiently enough to let a few of their children leave home—the way Fernande let Mercedes leave for Tulle and marry an arms-factory worker. All told, since 1960 a million French peasants have left the land they farmed or their parents farmed. (During those twenty-five years, the agricultural yield in France has nearly doubled.) One reason they left was that they had somewhere to go. There was a labor shortage here in the 1960s and 1970s. Factories were recruiting—first the million new French workers and then a few million immigrant workers—because back on the farm the workers' parents were buying machines and wiring the house and starting to buy the gadgets these factories produced. The honeymoon between agriculture and industry—with farmers making more money with less manpower and using it to buy the sorts of things they had never thought about until their children moved to towns like Tulle and Lille and Clermont-Ferrand and started making them—was a little like France's honeymoon with Germany when France was the only breadbasket in the EEC and Germany was the machine shop. In twenty years, both honeymoons were over. The idea of "Europe" had been moving only as long as no one suffered from it, or thought he suffered. "Europe" itself ended up in the kind of family fight where everyone divides the pots and pans and the flatware and tries never to meet again except at funerals.

The fact is that people like the Pelletiers think of themselves as French farmers, not European farmers. When English lamb (which often means New Zealand or Australian lamb) or Italian wine arrives in Sainte-Lucie selling for less money than the Pelletiers' lamb or their neighbors' wine, they say that France is threatened, not that "Europe" is served. The agreements that have been signed in Brussels since 1962 by politicians determined to promote the interests of France, say, or Germany or England while defending the rhetoric of "Europe" have got so complicated by now, so elaborate, that it is much easier to add to them than to explain them, let alone make them work. Every formula for fair subsidies or quotas seems to create a new set of inequities to replace the ones it was supposed to remove (one Community bureaucrat called the EEC Gödel's proof), and every national gesture seems to offend "Europe" as much as Europe's gestures offend its members. Of course, the commitment to a European community grew out of the Second World

War—out of a common experience of demented nationalism and the impulse, after that experience, to soften borders and create connections. People in Europe knew that any real economic recovery would have to be shared. Jean Monnet could speak convincingly of "European unity," because they never expected to be undone by nationalism again, especially the fairly respectable kind of nationalism that seems to be the common experience now. The charter of the EEC is clear—any European state that meets Community criteria involving democratic elections, civil and economic freedom, and human rights is eligible for membership—and so is the assumption of the men who signed it that belonging to "Europe" is the best way to keep on meeting those criteria. When Greece gets rid of its colonels, or when the Generalissimo dies in Spain, the EEC is under a kind of contractual obligation to let that country in. The country applies, and its application is welcomed with a lot of speeches and a lot of tight smiles—and then the members get together and argue for years about how to protect themselves against their would-be partner. Everybody knows vaguely that the EEC is a good thing. Presumably, Spain and Portugal, which are trying to join now, know, too. But it is hard for people in the Community to explain exactly why it is such a good thing when they spend so much of their time trying to get around it.

The arrangements and rearrangements and exceptions and exemptions and subsidies that have made lamb chops coming from England a better buy in Sainte-Lucie than Fernande Pelletier's lamb chops are coded and stored in the Common Market computer, and perhaps a few people in Brussels understand them. They are beyond Fernande. She has asked about them in Sainte-Lucie. She asked the manager at the Crédit Agricole; he is a little odd, because of his disgrace, and he looked cross and peered at Fernande in case she was a spy from the *caisse* in Paris posing as Mme Pelletier and trying to catch him out in another bad loan, and finally he said, "Madame, it is illusory to expect that international agriculture is going to adapt itself to your small enterprise." He told her to accept the fact that, with a hilly piece of property like hers, and only a couple of acres of really "serious" soil, she would never be able to compete with an English sheep farmer, let alone with any of the thousands of big one-crop farms in France. He said he had seventy-four sorts of loans, with seventy-four different sets of terms, at his disposal, and that he was certain they could find a nice one—although he did acknowledge that the rules about lending money were a little stricter under Mitterrand than they had been under Giscard, who rarely paid attention. Polyculture was the answer, he said. This year, people at his branch of

the bank were thinking in terms of three specialities per farm: one vegetable crop, one pasture animal, and one *exploitation hors sol*—which literally means "off the ground," and which in Fernande's case means
plants or animals that do not use land, like hydroponic tomatoes or veal
fattened in a feed pen. The manager told Fernande to "spread her risk"
(*"Diversifiez vos investissements, Madame"*) and accept the realities of the
market, and choose crops that the Pelletier family could raise on a hundred acres but that a robot on a thousand acres could not.

Fernande thought about what the bank manager had said. That
night, she talked it over with Georges and with Pierre Lagorce, who
had started eating at the Pelletiers' when his wife died and now that he
was "retired" was around all day, offering advice (which was often good
advice) and keeping Fernande company, so that Georges could disappear on his tractor and do the farming. Lagorce had been gossiping
about some new neighbors in Sainte-Lucie-le-Pont—two Dutch couples who shared a house and, apparently, their affections. It was a scandal of great interest to Lagorce and to the Pelletiers, who believed that
rich city people usually bought country houses in order to be depraved
in private. Fernande does not talk about her own household arrangements, although she certainly considers it much more respectable to be
eating with Georges *and* Pierre Lagorce than it would be to be eating
with Lagorce alone. In a way, the Pelletiers have come to regard Lagorce
as if he were an old relative with nowhere else to go—an embarrassment, maybe, but, in the end, their charge. Lagorce regards himself as
indispensable. When Fernande complained that they were already as
"polycultural" as they could get, considering that they had grown or
raised or fed just about every plant or animal the area could support,
Lagorce said that polyculture was not their problem anyway—their
problem was that they were not *hors sol*. And then Maurice spoke up,
and said that *he* had heard about *hors sol* at some point during his year
as an apprentice on a "scientific farm." Usually, nobody pays much attention to Maurice except his wife, Clémentine, and *she* always tries to
pay attention—if they are at supper, say, or in bed, and she isn't busy
doing anything important. Clémentine is the daughter of dirt farmers
from the next village, and (it is acknowledged) she is not a beauty. She
never expected to find a husband, let alone a husband who was tall and
handsome in a blank, cheerful sort of way, and the heir to a hundred
acres. Three years ago, she married Maurice in the church in Sainte-
Lucie-le-Pont where Fernande had married Georges in 1955, and like
Fernande, she spent a brief honeymoon at Lourdes—after which she was
put to work on the farm, feeding the ducks in the barn and washing up
after meals and doing the laundry and keeping the family accounts in

Fernande's big green ledger, and doing all the other things that are expected of a daughter-in-law without a dowry. She was paying attention when Maurice said that, to his mind, force-feeding eighteen hundred ducks for foie gras in a small barn was farming *hors sol*. She even blushed, because the word "mind" sounded so intelligent. But Pierre Lagorce disagreed. He said that feeding ducks in a barn was not, in itself, *hors sol*, and the next afternoon he called everybody into the barn to demonstrate what a real *"exploitation hors sol"* was. He fastened one of the duck coops to a rope. Then he threw the rope over a rafter. And while everybody watched and Clémentine made careful notes in the ledger, he hoisted the coop a few feet off the ground—*"Voilà, hors sol,"* he said—and left it there and tipped his blue beret and waited for congratulations.

Once or twice a year, Fernande invites her neighbors Odette and Paul Martignac to a big Sunday lunch. The Martignacs are what people in Paris would call *petits hobereaux*—little provincial nobles. They live in a château down by the Vézère, and possess a title on Odette's side and a Gaullist officer on Paul's, and are a couple with *"un peu de race,"* as Fernande puts it. They always drive to the farm in a 1967 Peugeot, but they like to look as if they had been out hunting and had just dismounted—in hacking jackets and jeans and leather riding boots. The Pelletiers, for their part, dress for the occasion. Georges puts on his Sunday suit, and Fernande puts on the outfit she copied from a picture in *Le Pèlerin* six years ago—a yellow-and-green plaid kilt and a dark-green blouse to go with it. As soon as she says hello, she covers her outfit up with her old nylon housecoat and starts stirring and beating and basting in the kitchen, and never thinks to remove the housecoat until the Martignacs are gone.

The Martignacs are important farmers for Sainte-Lucie-le-Pont. They have corn and wheat, and thirty acres just in walnut trees—that means a harvest of thirty tons a year to dispose of—and Paul Martignac has even been to California to look at some of the astonishing walnut farms where the trees are tended by machines and the nuts are dried in forty-eight hours. The nuts taste terrible, he says, but by now they sell as well as the Martignacs' nuts, because nobody else seems to care about the difference. Someone in California told Martignac about the Diamond Nut Company, which produces eighty thousand more tons of walnuts in a year than all the farms in France put together, and he has been depressed about this ever since he came home to Sainte-Lucie-le-Pont. He worries about his farm, and about the family furniture and the family portraits on his walls. There are robbers around Sainte-

Lucie—*brocanteurs* who arrive at night in trucks and make off with your antiques to sell at flea markets to important Paris dealers—but Martignac says that, given the nut competition from California, he will never be able to afford alarms for his château and will have to depend on his aging cocker spaniel, Irène, to defend his treasures. Thinking about his pictures and his Louis XV candlesticks and his set of twenty-four dining-room chairs that may or may not have put in time at Fontainebleau makes him nervous when he is out at the Pelletiers', say, having Sunday lunch, but he always accepts their invitation and is always easy with them and talks a lot and exchanges local gossip and enjoys Fernande's cooking. He and Odette, who is a handsome woman with long black hair in a bun and her mother's emeralds pinned to her hacking jacket, do not acknowledge Pierre Lagorce at the Pelletiers' table. Martignac consults with Georges about the weather and the crops and the criminals in Mitterrand's government, and Odette Martignac talks to Fernande about food, and the women exchange recipes, and then everybody compares the Martignacs' strawberry wine with the Pelletiers' walnut wine and gets a little drunk and barely notices that Pierre Lagorce has started talking, too. Sunday lunch at the Pelletiers' runs from noon till three or four in the afternoon when there is company. It begins with fresh foie gras and Fernande's foie-gras pâté, and then, if it is the mushroom season, there is a gratin of *cèpes* and maybe a mushroom tart, too, and afterward one of Fernande's fat ducks or a corn-fed chicken from the yard, and cheese, of course, and the glazed apple turnover from her grandmother's recipe book (which is often charred now that Fernande is teaching Clémentine to make it) and an ice-cream bombe with two flavors in the middle. There is wine from the *cave*, and, after dessert, cognac and Armagnac and coffee and, always, a plate of ordinary chocolates that Fernande drives all the way to Brive to buy at the confectioner's, and, being the only part of the meal she pays for, are what she assumes has made it special.

Fernande likes having company. Eight years ago, she added a big new room to the farmhouse to be her company room, and fixed it up until, to her mind, it was just like the living room the young vicomtesse from Paris had put together when she bought Lagorce's château. Fernande had helped the vicomtesse with that room—she had unpacked the plates and the pictures and the walnut side tables and had fitted together the stone fireplace that the vicomtesse had found, in pieces, at a convent auction—and once they had got the room in order and Fernande was used to everything in it being so old she decided to admire the room as much as she admired the vicomtesse. Actually, Fernande would have preferred a modern room for herself, something easy to wipe down, but not long afterward—it was a year when her sheep were selling well—she asked Georges and Pierre Lagorce to strip the beams and the tiles from two old barns on the farm, and went out looking for a stone fireplace of her own and a brass chandelier for the ceiling. Her room looked a little bare, though, so she improved on the vicomtesse's salon. She bought smoked glass for the windows, so that everything outside was blurry and romantic, and you couldn't see the old machines and the tractor in the barnyard. She ordered fringed lampshades from a farm-wife catalogue, and velvet armchairs the color of tarragon mustard, and a couple of brand-new "Oriental" rugs that were much more cheerful than the vicomtesse's faded carpets, and after Maurice got married she added seven rubber plants that Georges' sister had sent as a wedding present, tied with pink-and-white taffeta bows and trailing ribbons on the floor.

Fernande thinks the room is perfect now, but she never uses it if the family is alone. When the telephone in the room rings, she stands to answer it and talk; she is not really comfortable in her velvet chairs—the way she would not be comfortable in one of the twenty-four chairs in the Martignacs' dining room. Odette Martignac has never invited the Pelletiers for a Sunday lunch at her house, and if she did Fernande would feel awkward and embarrassed and would never invite the Martignacs to the farm again. The rules in Sainte-Lucie-le-Pont are severe, though probably less so to the people who follow them than to the people who try to write them down, and according to those rules a *châtelain*—Fernande considers the Martignacs *châtelains*—can visit a peasant in the peasant's house and sit comfortably at his table but the peasant can never sit down at the *châtelain*'s table without doing a curious kind of damage to their relations. There is a common culture in France, and Fernande can open a family album begun in 1847 and read her great-grandmother's notes for scalloping a sheet or making a chestnut mousse or the fine menu for her mother's confirmation, in 1913, but what is shared is not class but appreciation. Appreciation and discretion and delicacy and assurance. Fernande's mother has a great deal of delicacy. She is eighty years old, and beautiful, and her face, framed by the black scarf and the collar of the long black cardigan she put on when M. Tricart died, is delicate, and so are the flutter of her hands and her laugh, like a chirp, whenever something funny or outrageous is happening in the house—whenever, say, Pierre Lagorce starts talking. Sometimes she says she wishes she had "gone" with M. Tricart, but there is nothing morbid about her. She feels not so much out of place as out of her proper time in the house she used to manage. When she is thinking about M. Tricart, she will disappear into the *cave* and dust the dining-room furniture that was part of her dowry—and that Fernande uses now for storing preserves and drying apples. There is a table of blackened oak, and there are two massive sideboards with little doors and balconies and pillars all over them which Mme Tricart calls her Henri II sideboards, because that was how the man in the furniture store described them in 1926, when she and *her* mother went shopping for something that nobody in Sainte-Lucie-le-Pont was apt to have. She has never understood why Odette Martignac looked so disappointed after she climbed down into the *cave* to see the sideboards for herself. Mme Tricart comes from Limoges and is the only one in the family who has ever—if the word applies—travelled. Once a year, when she was a bride, she used to leave Sainte-Lucie-le-Pont for Limoges to see her father, who was a carter and carried barrels of wine from the great Bordeaux châteaus to the Limoges merchants. Now she never travels. She rarely goes out of the house at all. She stays in the kitchen, cooking or knitting or looking at the pictures in *Le Pèlerin* or daydreaming. When there is company, and the Pelletiers are eating in their big new room, she will join them as long as she can sit at the place nearest the kitchen door, and the only thing she insists on anymore is that the television set stay in the kitchen, so she can watch *Dallas* and *Dynasty* from her old chair at the foot of the kitchen table. Her only excursions now are her annual visits to the *notaire*, Maître Prot, who is nearly eighty, too. She admires Maître Prot for his clarity. She still talks about the day her husband bought his first tractor and Maître Prot came out to the farm himself and explained so beautifully what "depreciating one's tractor" meant: he told Olivier Tricart to think of the tractor as if it were the oxen that used to pull his plow and lived for twenty years and lost a little of their value every year as they got older.

Last fall, Maître Prot sat behind his big Empire desk in Sainte-Lucie and received Fernande and her mother and talked with tears in his eyes about *"vous braves paysans."* Maître Prot was born in Sainte-Lucie, and he could see what happened to his old friends when an agricultural adviser arrived from Toulouse or Limoges or one of the other big towns and told them to raise beef, and, on his next visit, to forget beef and grow tobacco, and then, when tobacco prices fell, to switch to grazing sheep—that is, until cheap lamb started coming in from England and he had to come back and explain that there had been a *petite erreur*, and that he should have said walnuts or snails or foie gras. Maître Prot was the mayor of Sainte-Lucie-le-Pont for a long time. It was during his last year as the *mairie* that the local chapter of the big farmers' union, the Fédération Nationale des Syndicats d'Exploitants Agricoles, joined a roadblock against trucks carrying foreign meat through the Périgord.

That was also the year some Sainte-Lucie farmers tried to do what the farmers down in Cahors had done to protest against the foreign meat—drive their sheep to the prefecture and open the door and let the animals in. Maître Prot did not know what to advise Fernande then, and he did not know what to advise her in December, when she and her mother came for their yearly visit and Fernande announced, suddenly, how much she missed her sheep and said she was unhappy in a barn feeding ducks, even with a daughter-in-law to do it for her. He told Fernande that she could buy new sheep and feed them well and still lose so much money because of the *concurrence* that she would have to sell them—and then discover in a year or two that French lamb was in demand again. Right now, the government was paying farmers about fifteen hundred francs for every milk cow they slaughtered, and Maître Prot wondered what was going to happen when people needed milk again and raising cows was profitable and those farmers who had worried about a surplus in 1984 had slaughtered all the cows they had.

There is no doubt that Fernande and the other farmers in Sainte-Lucie-le-Pont could plan better and work better and get the kind of quality in their meat and produce which may be their one hope against the dizzying competition from abroad. Fernande knows this, but she also knows that life was much simpler for a farmer when Maître Prot and her father were young men. The smart young farmers today are trained to plan better and work better, and even so—unless their farms are enormous—they eventually have to forget about raising cows or sheep or planting their own wheat, and turn their barns into feed hotels for strangers' animals on their way from their mothers' milk to the slaughterhouse. That kind of work is shaming to a real farmer, and in the end it is not much more secure than keeping a pasture full of Charolais cows and a bull in the barn and raising their own calves. They borrow to begin with. They buy too much feed or too many machines or take on too many animals. Like their parents, they end up fattening veal or lambs on ninety-day contracts or stuffing ducks or geese with corn for foie gras or incubating snails, and then discovering that it is the wrong market for veal or baby lambs or ducks or snails. They are left with rusty machines and three loan payments a year to make to the Crédit Agricole so that no one will come to claim those machines or the cars and television sets and electric stoves that were bought so proudly on expectations of a good life.

This year, Fernande is paying the interest on two bank loans. She is paying what amounts to seven hundred dollars in taxes to Sainte-Lucie-le-Pont and a land tax of four hundred dollars to the village of Sainte-Lucie, which is a cantonal seat with eight incorporated hamlets like

Sainte-Lucie-le-Pont, and a population of twelve hundred, and she is paying a house tax and a tax to a town forty miles away to which Sainte-Lucie is attached for obscure bureaucratic purposes, and another two thousand dollars for social security and health insurance. She could pay less if she itemized her taxes. Clémentine—who is happiest when she can sit on one of the velvet chairs in the company room with Fernande's ledger in her lap, adding and subtracting and in general savoring the numbers that belong to Maurice's family—wants to prepare a proper tax form for her mother-in-law, with columns and calculations, but Fernande wants to sign the simplest standard form the state provides and have done with it. She is like her father in this; she wants the last word when she is doing business with the government. She knows that someone in Paris is bound to check her taxes if Clémentine complicates them—and deprive her of the great pleasure of cheating on her declaration.

Lately, Fernande has been thinking a lot about the way she ended up at home on her father's farm—by now a kind of father to the family, too. She loves the highland of the Périgord, with its dips and its rises and the patches of landscape that catch her storybook memories and make her wait for the knights of some imaginary gentle time to pitch their pointed tents and start their games while their ladies wave pretty scarves and sigh. She loves the riverbanks and the old steel bridge in Sainte-Lucie-le-Pont, and even the weather that is always turning. Sometimes she feels the appropriateness of her life on the land, and then when she talks about it she is blunt and eloquent and sentimental—and I think of Millet, who painted peasants like her and talked about how planting wheat and sowing potatoes was noble. There are other times when Fernande shrugs and says that there was nothing for her to do but farm. She was a schoolgirl during the war, and was sent off with the other village girls to a convent in the hills while their mothers stayed home with the animals and their fathers either were taken prisoner of war or were put to work in factories or disappeared into the Resistance. There were nights when she heard German soldiers on the road and German guns in the distance, and once she and her friends at the convent saw a group of farmers run out of the woods and dynamite a bridge along the Germans' route. She remembers the nuns telling them that Germans had stopped at Oradour-sur-Glane, up in the Haute-Vienne, and shut the women and children in a church and killed them all, and how after that, whenever there were steps on the road at night, they hid in the cold *caves* of the convent, too terrified of the rats to cry. She was fifteen when she came home to Sainte-Lucie-le-Pont, and, she likes to say, she was *"très, très collet monté"*—very straitlaced and prudish. For a while, the only times she saw her neighbors were Sunday mornings, when the family walked the three miles down from the farm to the village church. Then her grandmother died, and she was in mourning for a year, and then her grandfather died, and she was in mourning for another year, and finally another grandfather died, and one of her uncles, too—which meant that Fernande Tricart wore black and stayed at home until she was nearly twenty-five and met Georges Pelletier at a neighbor's wedding. He was the first young man in the house since the family had put away its mourning bands, and Fernande wondered when there would be another—and told her father to settle the marriage contract. She wanted to have a wedding with bridesmaids and a trainbearer and a hundred farmers dancing, like the one the neighbor had. When the wedding was over, and she had been to Lourdes and collected her blessing, she settled down to her old duties on the farm and took her orders from her father until he died and she started giving the orders herself. It may be that she has kept her hair red all these years—even though the sun on the dye turns it orange and gives it strange metallic splotches—in order to keep her future open. When this year's Agriculture Ministry adviser came to the farm and told her that the Israelis were now exporting foie gras to France—cheap foie gras, which could ruin the market for Fernande's foie gras—Fernande just smiled at him and offered him a glass of her walnut wine and said that she was not going to be discouraged or confused, the way she was sometimes when she turned on the evening news and heard about its costing France more money to give away food surpluses to people starving in Ethiopia than to let the surpluses rot at home. She told him she knew all about how French farmers should cut their harvests and reduce their costs. She had read (she thinks it was in *La France Agricole*) that less than 15 percent of the farmers in France study anything at all, let alone farming, after high school, but she did not know why studying was so important when the ducks that Pierre Lagorce had lifted *hors sol* were doing just as well as the ducks that Maurice, with his year on a scientific farm, was raising on the barn floor.

France right now accounts for about a third of Europe's food, and in Fernande's part of France wealth *is* food, not killing your cows or cutting back your harvest. Fernande believes that she is rich when her granaries are full and her animals are having babies. Her sense of who she is is something she can measure directly against the corn in her cribs and the dry tobacco plants hanging in her sheds. She would never vote for a Socialist, but the fact is that the only Agriculture Minister she has approved of since Edgard Pisani was Mitterrand's first Minister of Agriculture, Édith Cresson, because Mme Cresson stood up to the union that was protecting the interests of the big farmers, and spoke for the farmers like Fernande, and for *their* land and the dignity of *their* commitment. Édith Cresson was not a realist. The average French farm is about sixty acres; by the end of the century, it will be ninety or a hundred, and, as the people at the Ministry here in Paris say, "the farm pyramid will turn over—" by which they mean that there will be bigger farms and fewer farmers, and that those farmers will be specializing in the kinds of experiments they learned about in agricultural schools. They will know how to produce a pig like the pigs in China, which have five more piglets in a litter than French pigs do, or hybrid corn like the corn in America. There will be discipline in French farming then. Competition will be harsh, and a farm will survive on its cost-plus figures, not on the courage of its farmers.

John McPhee

In 1937 Pare Lorentz made a black and white film for the Farm Security Administration called *The River*. Beginning with melting icicles dripping on clear-cut ground in Minnesota and running ever southward, the film followed the Mississippi River. By the time the river reached New Orleans, viewers understood how it floods, how poverty festered in the greatest river valley in the world, and how government operations could change things.

John McPhee follows a similar small-to-large structure. At the beginning, "Atchafalaya"—the opening chapter of his book *The Control of Nature* (1989)— focuses on one government control structure. Eventually, the piece fans out to give a sweeping feel for the river itself.

McPhee said he first heard about the Old River Control Structure while canoeing with his daughter, Sarah, in the Atchafalaya Swamp (pronounced *At-CHAF-a-laya*). She had taken a course on Walker Percy with Robert Coles at Harvard and had talked her father into a tour of Percy country during spring break. The deal included a short canoe trip, during which they heard about the Control Structure, fifty miles away, holding back the mighty river from its shortest route to the sea. "It was so symbolic," McPhee said. "That's where *The Control of Nature* started."

McPhee's early books were profiles. The profile was invented and named at *The New Yorker*, and had been developed by A. J. Liebling, Joseph Mitchell, Alva Johnston, and other writers. But the broader canvases that McPhee likes to paint had few progenitors. McPhee writes carefully and with a creative flair that makes him a writer's writer.

His topics have ranged from Bill Bradley's career as a basketball player at Princeton University (*A Sense of Where You Are* [1965]) to the geology of North America (*Basin and Range* [1981], *In Suspect Terrain* [1983], *Rising from the Plains* [1986], and *Assembling California* [1992]). He has written about *The Pine Barrens* (1968) of New Jersey, builders of both birch bark canoes (*The Survival of the Bark Canoe* [1975]) and nuclear bombs (*The Curve of Binding Energy* [1974]), homesteaders in Alaska (*Coming Into the Country* [1977]), the captain of a merchant marine ship (*Looking for a Ship* [1990]), the Swiss army (*La Place de la Concorde Suisse* [1984]), a game warden in Maine named John McPhee (*Table of Contents* [1985]), a brand inspector in Nevada ("Irons in the Fire" [1993]), and a collector of modern art from the Soviet Union (*The Ransom of Russian Art* [1994]). In all, McPhee has written twenty-three books.

"Someone comes up and says, 'My favorite book of yours is *Oranges*,'" McPhee said. "Later, someone else will say, 'My favorite book is *The Curve of Binding Energy*,' or *Rising from the Plains*. I've had this nifty experience over time. I never know what's coming next, and I love that.

"The point is, you go out and get the materials. You get rid of the materials you don't want, keeping the good materials in your view, and *you make the best possible thing you can out of that*. I went through the same experience with every one. I really do not have choices among them at all."

Atchafalaya

Three hundred miles up the Mississippi River from its mouth—many parishes above New Orleans and well north of Baton Rouge—a navigation lock in the Mississippi's right bank allows ships to drop out of the river. In evident defiance of nature, they descend as much as thirty-three feet, then go off to the west or south. This, to say the least, bespeaks a rare relationship between a river and adjacent terrain—any river, anywhere, let alone the third-ranking river on earth. The adjacent terrain is Cajun country, in a geographical sense the apex of the French Acadian world, which forms a triangle in southern Louisiana, with its base the Gulf Coast from the mouth of the Mississippi almost to Texas, its two sides converging up here near the lock—and including neither New Orleans nor Baton Rouge. The people of the local parishes (Pointe Coupee Parish, Avoyelles Parish) would call this the apex of Cajun country in every possible sense—no one more emphatically than the lockmaster, on whose face one day I noticed a spreading astonishment as he watched me remove from my pocket a red bandanna.

"You are a coonass with that red handkerchief," he said.

A coonass being a Cajun, I threw him an appreciative smile. I told him that I always have a bandanna in my pocket, wherever I happen to be—in New York as in Maine or Louisiana, not to mention New Jersey (my home)—and sometimes the color is blue. He said, "Blue is the sign of a Yankee. But that red handkerchief—with that, you are pure coonass." The lockmaster wore a white hard hat above his creased and deeply tanned face, his full but not overloaded frame. The nameplate on his desk said RABALAIS.

The navigation lock is not a formal place. When I first met Rabalais, six months before, he was sitting with his staff at 10 A.M. eating homemade bread, macaroni and cheese, and a mound of rice that was concealed beneath what he called "smoked old-chicken gravy." He said, "Get yourself a plate of that." As I went somewhat heavily for the old chicken, Rabalais said to the others, "He's pure coonass. I knew it."

If I was pure coonass, I would like to know what that made Rabalais—Norris F. Rabalais, born and raised on a farm near Simmesport, in Avoyelles Parish, Louisiana. When Rabalais was a child, there was no navigation lock to lower ships from the Mississippi. The water just poured out—boats with it—and flowed on into a distributary waterscape known as Atchafalaya. In each decade since about 1860, the Atchafalaya River had drawn off more water from the Mississippi than it had in the decade before. By the late nineteen-forties, when Rabalais was in his teens, the volume approached one-third. As the Atchafalaya widened and deepened, eroding headward, offering the Mississippi an increasingly attractive alternative, it was preparing for nothing less than an absolute capture: before long, it would take all of the Mississippi, and itself become the master stream. Rabalais said, "They used to teach us in high school that one day there was going to be structures up here to control the flow of that water, but I never dreamed I was going to be on one. Somebody way back yonder—which is dead and gone now—visualized it. We had some pretty sharp teachers."

The Mississippi River, with its sand and silt, has created most of Louisiana, and it could not have done so by remaining in one channel. If it had, southern Louisiana would be a long narrow peninsula reaching into the Gulf of Mexico. Southern Louisiana exists in its present form because the Mississippi River has jumped here and there within an arc about two hundred miles wide, like a pianist playing with one hand—frequently and radically changing course, surging over the left or the right bank to go off in utterly new directions. Always it is the river's purpose to get to the Gulf by the shortest and steepest gradient. As the mouth advances southward and the river lengthens, the gradient declines, the current slows, and sediment builds up the bed. Eventually, it builds up so much that the river spills to one side. Major shifts of that nature have tended to occur roughly once a millennium. The Mississippi's main channel of three thousand years ago is now the quiet water of Bayou Teche, which mimics the shape of the Mississippi. Along Bayou Teche, on the high ground of ancient natural levees, are Jeanerette, Breaux Bridge, Broussard, Olivier—arcuate strings of Cajun towns. Eight hundred years before the birth of Christ, the channel was captured from the east. It shifted abruptly and flowed in that direction for about a thousand years. In the second century A.D., it was captured again, and taken south, by the now unprepossessing Bayou Lafourche, which, by the year 1000, was losing its hegemony to the river's present course, through the region that would be known as Plaquemines. By the nineteen-fifties, the Mississippi River had advanced so far past New Orleans and out into the Gulf that it was about to shift again, and its offspring Atchafalaya was ready to receive it. By the route of the Atchafalaya, the distance across the delta plain was a hundred and forty-five miles—well under half the length of the route of the master stream.

For the Mississippi to make such a change was completely natural, but in the interval since the last shift Europeans had settled beside the river, a nation had developed, and the nation could not afford nature. The consequences of the Atchafalaya's conquest of the Mississippi would include but not be limited to the demise of Baton Rouge and the virtual destruction of New Orleans. With its fresh water gone, its harbor a silt bar, its economy disconnected from inland commerce, New Orleans would turn into New Gomorrah. Moreover, there were so many big industries between the two cities that at night they made the river glow like a worm. As a result of settlement patterns, this reach of the Mississippi had long been known as "the German coast," and now, with B. F. Goodrich, E. I. du Pont, Union Carbide, Reynolds Metals, Shell, Mobil, Texaco, Exxon, Monsanto, Uniroyal, Georgia-Pacific, Hydro-carbon Industries, Vulcan Materials, Nalco Chemical, Freeport Chemical, Dow Chemical, Allied Chemical, Stauffer Chemical, Hooker Chemicals, Rubicon Chemicals, American Petrofina—with an infrastructural concentration equalled in few other places—it was often called "the American Ruhr." The industries were there because of the river. They had come for its navigational convenience and its fresh water. They would not, and could not, linger beside a tidal creek. For nature to take its course was simply unthinkable. The Sixth World War would do less damage to southern Louisiana. Nature, in this place, had become an enemy of the state.

Rabalais works for the U.S. Army Corps of Engineers. Some years ago, the Corps made a film that showed the navigation lock and a complex of associated structures built in an effort to prevent the capture of the Mississippi. The narrator said, "This nation has a large and powerful adversary. Our opponent could cause the United States to lose nearly all her seaborne commerce, to lose her standing as first among trading nations. . . . We are fighting Mother Nature. . . . It's a battle we have to fight day by day, year by year; the health of our economy depends on victory."

Rabalais was in on the action from the beginning, working as a construction inspector. Here by the site of the navigation lock was where the battle had begun. An old meander bend of the Mississippi was the conduit through which water had been escaping into the Atchafalaya. Complicating the scene, the old meander bend had also served as the mouth of the Red River. Coming in from the northwest, from Texas via Shreveport, the Red River had been a tributary of the Mississippi for a couple of thousand years—until the nineteen-forties, when the

Atchafalaya captured it and drew it away. The capture of the Red increased the Atchafalaya's power as it cut down the country beside the Mississippi. On a map, these entangling watercourses had come to look like the letter "H." The Mississippi was the right-hand side. The Atchafalaya and the captured Red were the left-hand side. The crosspiece, scarcely seven miles long, was the former meander bend, which the people of the parish had long since named Old River. Sometimes enough water would pour out of the Mississippi and through Old River to quintuple the falls at Niagara. It was at Old River that the United States was going to lose its status among the world's trading nations. It was at Old River that New Orleans would be lost, Baton Rouge would be lost. At Old River, we would lose the American Ruhr. The Army's name for its operation there was Old River Control.

Rabalais gestured across the lock toward what seemed to be a pair of placid lakes separated by a trapezoidal earth dam a hundred feet high. It weighed five million tons, and it had stopped Old River. It had cut Old River in two. The severed ends were sitting there filling up with weeds. Where the Atchafalaya had entrapped the Mississippi, bigmouth bass were now in charge. The navigation lock had been dug beside this monument. The big dam, like the lock, was fitted into the mainline levee of the Mississippi. In Rabalais's pickup, we drove on the top of the dam, and drifted as well through Old River country. On this day, he said, the water on the Mississippi side was eighteen feet above sea level, while the water on the Atchafalaya side was five feet above sea level. Cattle were grazing on the slopes of the levees, and white horses with white colts, in deep-green grass. Behind the levees, the fields were flat and reached to rows of distant trees. Very early in the morning, a low fog had covered the fields. The sun, just above the horizon, was large and ruddy in the mist, rising slowly, like a hot-air balloon. This was a countryside of corn and soybeans, of grain-fed-catfish ponds, of feed stores and Kingdom Halls in crossroad towns. There were small neat cemeteries with ranks of white sarcophagi raised a foot or two aboveground, notwithstanding the protection of the levees. There were tarpapered cabins on concrete pylons, and low brick houses under planted pines. Pickups under the pines. If this was a form of battlefield, it was not unlike a great many battlefields—landscapes so quiet they belie their story. Most battlefields, though, are places where something happened once. Here it would happen indefinitely.

We went out to the Mississippi. Still indistinct in mist, it looked like a piece of the sea. Rabalais said, "That's a wide booger, right there." In the spring high water of vintage years—1927, 1937, 1973—more than two million cubic feet of water had gone by this place in every second.

Sixty-five kilotons per second. By the mouth of the inflow channel leading to the lock were rock jetties, articulated concrete mattress revetments, and other heavy defenses. Rabalais observed that this particular
site was no more vulnerable than almost any other point in this reach of
river that ran so close to the Atchafalaya plain. There were countless
places where a breakout might occur: "It has a tendency to go through
just anywheres you can call for."

Why, then, had the Mississippi not jumped the bank and long since
diverted to the Atchafalaya?

"Because they're watching it close," said Rabalais. "It's under close
surveillance."

After the Corps dammed Old River, in 1963, the engineers could not
just walk away, like roofers who had fixed a leak. In the early planning
stages, they had considered doing that, but there were certain effects
they could not overlook. The Atchafalaya, after all, was a distributary
of the Mississippi—the major one, and, as it happened, the only one
worth mentioning that the Corps had not already plugged. In time of
thundering flood, the Atchafalaya was useful as a safety valve, to relieve
a good deal of pressure and help keep New Orleans from ending up in
Yucatán. The Atchafalaya was also the source of the water in the
swamps and bayous of the Cajun world. It was the water supply of
small cities and countless towns. Its upper reaches were surrounded by
farms. The Corps was not in a political or moral position to kill the
Atchafalaya. It had to feed it water. By the principles of nature, the
more the Atchafalaya was given, the more it would want to take, because it was the steeper stream. The more it was given, the deeper it
would make its bed. The difference in level between the Atchafalaya
and the Mississippi would continue to increase, magnifying the conditions for capture. The Corps would have to deal with that. The Corps
would have to build something that could give the Atchafalaya a portion of the Mississippi and at the same time prevent it from taking all.
In effect, the Corps would have to build a Fort Laramie: a place where
the natives could buy flour and firearms but where the gates could be
closed if they attacked.

Ten miles upriver from the navigation lock, where the collective
sediments were thought to be more firm, they dug into a piece of dry
ground and built what appeared for a time to be an incongruous, water-
less bridge. Five hundred and sixty-six feet long, it stood parallel to the
Mississippi and about a thousand yards back from the water. Between
its abutments were ten piers, framing eleven gates that could be lifted or
dropped, opened or shut, like windows. To this structure, and through

it, there soon came a new Old River—an excavated channel leading in from the Mississippi and out seven miles to the Red-Atchafalaya. The Corps was not intending to accommodate nature. Its engineers were intending to control it in space and arrest it in time. In 1950, shortly before the project began, the Atchafalaya was taking thirty per cent of the water that came down from the north to Old River. This water was known as the latitude flow, and it consisted of a little in the Red, a lot in the Mississippi. The United States Congress, in its deliberations, decided that "the distribution of flow and sediment in the Mississippi and Atchafalaya Rivers is now in desirable proportions and should be so maintained." The Corps was thereby ordered to preserve 1950. In perpetuity, at Old River, thirty per cent of the latitude flow was to pass to the Atchafalaya.

The device that resembled a ten-pier bridge was technically a sill, or weir, and it was put on line in 1963, in an orchestrated sequence of events that flourished the art of civil engineering. The old Old River was closed. The new Old River was opened. The water, as it crossed the sill from the Mississippi's level to the Atchafalaya's, tore to white shreds in the deafening turbulence of a great new falls, from lip to basin the construction of the Corps. More or less simultaneously, the navigation lock opened its chamber. Now everything had changed and nothing had changed. Boats could still drop away from the river. The ratio of waters continued as before—this for the American Ruhr, that for the ecosystems of the Cajun swamps. Withal, there was a change of command, as the Army replaced nature.

In time, people would come to suggest that there was about these enterprises an element of hauteur. A professor of law at Tulane University, for example, would assign it third place in the annals of arrogance. His name was Oliver Houck. "The greatest arrogance was the stealing of the sun," he said. "The second-greatest arrogance is running rivers backward. The third-greatest arrogance is trying to hold the Mississippi in place. The ancient channels of the river go almost to Texas. Human beings have tried to restrict the river to one course—that's where the arrogance began." The Corps listens closely to things like that and files them in its archives. Houck had a point. Bold it was indeed to dig a fresh conduit in the very ground where one river had prepared to trap another, bolder yet to build a structure there meant to be in charge of what might happen.

Some people went further than Houck, and said that they thought the structure would fail. In 1980, for example, a study published by the Water Resources Research Institute, at Louisiana State University, described Old River as "the scene of a direct confrontation between the

United States Government and the Mississippi River," and—all constructions of the Corps notwithstanding—awarded the victory to the Mississippi River. "Just when this will occur cannot be predicted," the report concluded. "It could happen next year, during the next decade, or sometime in the next thirty or forty years. But the final outcome is simply a matter of time and it is only prudent to prepare for it."

The Corps thought differently, saying, "We can't let that happen. We are charged by Congress not to let that happen." Its promotional film referred to Old River Control as "a good soldier." Old River Control was, moreover, "the keystone of the comprehensive flood-protection project for the lower Mississippi Valley," and nothing was going to remove the keystone. People arriving at New Orleans District Headquarters, U.S. Army Corps of Engineers, were confronted at the door by a muralled collage of maps and pictures and bold letters unequivocally declaring, "The Old River Control Structures, located about two hundred miles above New Orleans on the Mississippi River, prevent the Mississippi from changing course by controlling flows diverted into the Atchafalaya Basin."

No one's opinions were based on more intimate knowledge than those of LeRoy Dugas, Rabalais's upstream counterpart—the manager of the apparatus that controlled the flow at Old River. Like Rabalais, he was Acadian and of the country. Dugie—as he is universally called—had worked at Old River Control since 1963, when the water started flowing. In years to follow, colonels and generals would seek his counsel. "Those professors at L.S.U. say that whatever we do we're going to lose the system," he remarked one day at Old River, and, after a pause, added, "Maybe they're right." His voice had the sound of water over rock. In pitch, it was lower than a helicon tuba. Better to hear him indoors, in his operations office, away from the structure's competing thunders. "Maybe they're right," he repeated. "We feel that we can hold the river. We're going to try. Whenever you try to control nature, you've got one strike against you."

Dugie's face, weathered and deeply tanned, was saved from looking weary by the alertness and the humor in his eyes. He wore a large, lettered belt buckle that said TO HELP CONTROL THE MISSISSIPPI. "I was originally born in Morganza," he told me. "Thirty miles down the road. I have lived in Pointe Coupee Parish all my life. Once, I even closed my domicile and went to work in Texas for the Corps—but you always come back." (Rabalais also—as he puts it—"left out of here one time," but not for long.) All through Dugie's youth, of course, the Mississippi had spilled out freely to feed the Atchafalaya. He took the vagaries of the waters for granted, not to mention the supremacy of their force in flood. He was a naval gunner on Liberty ships in the South Pacific during the Second World War, and within a year or two of his return was astonished to hear that the Corps of Engineers was planning to restrain Old River. "They were going to try to control the flow," he said. "I thought they had lost their marbles."

Outside, on the roadway that crosses the five-hundred-and-sixty-six-foot structure, one could readily understand where the marbles might have gone. Even at this time of modest normal flow, we looked down into a rage of water. It was running at about twelve miles an hour—significantly faster than the Yukon after breakup—and it was pounding into the so-called stilling basin on the downstream side, the least still place you would ever see. The No. 10 rapids of the Grand Canyon, which cannot be run without risk of life, resemble the Old River stilling basin, but the rapids of the canyon are a fifth as wide. The Susitna River is sometimes more like it—melted glacier ice from the Alaska Range. Huge trucks full of hardwood logs kept coming from the north to cross the structure, on their way to a chipping mill at Simmesport. One could scarcely hear them as they went by.

There was a high sill next to this one—a separate weir, two-thirds of a mile long and set two feet above the local flood stage, its purpose being to help regulate the flow of extremely high waters. The low sill, as the one we stood on was frequently called, was the prime valve at Old River, and dealt with the water every day. The fate of the project had depended on the low sill, and it was what people meant when, as they often did, they simply said "the structure." The structure and the high sill—like the navigation lock downstream—were fitted into the Mississippi's mainline levee. Beyond the sound of the water, the broad low country around these structures was quiet and truly still. Here and again in the fields, pump jacks bobbed for oil. In the river batture—the silt-swept no man's land between waterline and levee—lone egrets sat in trees, waiting for the next cow.

Dugie remarked that he would soon retire, that he felt old and worn down from fighting the river.

I said to him, "All you need is a good flood."

And he said, "Oh, no. Don't talk like that, man. You talk vulgar."

It was odd to look out toward the main-stem Mississippi, scarcely half a mile away, and see its contents spilling sideways, like cornmeal pouring from a hole in a burlap bag. Dugie said that so much water coming out of the Mississippi created a powerful and deceptive draw, something like a vacuum, that could suck in boats of any size. He had seen some big ones up against the structure. In the mid-sixties, a man alone had come down from Wisconsin in a small double-ended vessel with curling ends and tumblehome—a craft that would not have been unfamiliar to the Algonquians, who named the Mississippi. Dugie called this boat "a pirogue." Whatever it was, the man had paddled it all the way from Wisconsin, intent on reaching New Orleans. When he had nearly conquered the Mississippi, however, he was captured by the Atchafalaya. Old River caught him, pulled him off the Mississippi, and shot him through the structure. "He was in shock, but he lived," Dugie said. "We put him in the hospital in Natchez."

After a moment, I said, "This is an exciting place."

And Dugie said, "You've heard of Murphy—'What can happen will happen'? This is where Murphy lives."

A towboat coming up the Atchafalaya may be running from Corpus Christi to Vicksburg with a cargo of gasoline, or from Houston to St. Paul with ethylene glycol. Occasionally, Rabalais sees a sailboat, more rarely a canoe. One time, a cottonwood-log dugout with a high Viking bow went past Old River. A ship carrying Leif Eriksson himself, however, would be less likely to arrest the undivided attention of the lockmaster than a certain red-trimmed cream-hulled vessel called Mississippi, bearing Major General Thomas Sands.

Each year, in late summer or early fall, the Mississippi comes down its eponymous river and noses into the lock. This is the Low-Water Inspection Trip, when the General makes a journey from St. Louis and into the Atchafalaya, stopping along the way at river towns, picking up visitors, listening to complaints. In external configuration, the Mississippi is a regular towboat—two hundred and seventeen feet long, fifty feet wide, its horsepower approaching four thousand. The term "towboat" is a misnomer, for the river towboats all push their assembled barges and are therefore designed with broad flat bows. Their unpleasant profiles seem precarious, as if they were the rear halves of ships that have been cut in two. The Mississippi triumphs over these disadvantages. Intended as a carrier of influenceable people, it makes up in luxury what it suffers in form. Only its red trim is martial. Its over-all bright cream suggests globules that have risen to the top. Its broad flat front is a wall of picture windows, of riverine panoramas, faced with cream-colored couches among coffee tables and standing lamps. A river towboat will push as many as fifty barges at one time. What this boat pushes is the program of the Corps.

The Mississippi, on its fall trip, is the site of on-board hearings at Cape Girardeau, Memphis, Vicksburg, and, ultimately, Morgan City. Customarily, it arrives at Old River early in the morning. Before the boat goes through the lock, people with names like Broussard, Brignac,

Begnaud, Blanchard, Juneau, Gautreau, Caillouet, and Smith get on—people from the Atchafalaya Basin Levee Board, the East Jefferson Levee Board, the Pontchartrain Levee Board, the Louisiana Office of Public Works, the United States Fish and Wildlife Service, the Teche-Vermilion Fresh Water District. Oliver Houck, the Tulane professor, gets on, and nine people—seven civilians and two colonels—from the New Orleans District of the Corps of Engineers. "This is the ultimate in communications," says the enthusiastic General Sands as he greets his colleagues and guests. The gates close behind the Mississippi. The mooring bitts inside the lock wail like coyotes as the water and the boat go down.

The pilothouse of the Mississippi is a wide handsome room directly above the lounge and similarly fronted with a wall of windows. It has map-and-chart tables, consoles of electronic equipment, redundant radars. The pilots stand front and center, as trim and trig as pilots of the air—John Dugger, from Collierville, Tennessee (the ship's home port is Memphis), and Jorge Cano, a local "contact pilot," who is here to help the regular pilots sense the shoals of the Atchafalaya. Among the mutating profiles of the river, their work is complicated. Mark Twain wrote of river pilots, "Two things seemed pretty apparent to me. One was, that in order to be a pilot a man had got to learn more than any one man ought to be allowed to know; and the other was, that he must learn it all over again in a different way every twenty-four hours. . . . Your true pilot cares nothing about anything on earth but the river, and his pride in his occupation surpasses the pride of kings." Cano, for his part, is somewhat less flattering on the subject of Twain. He says it baffles him that Twain has "such a big reputation for someone who spent so little time on the river." Today, the Atchafalaya waters are twelve feet lower than the Mississippi's. Cano says that the difference is often as much as twenty. Now the gates slowly open, revealing the outflow channel that leads into old Old River and soon to the Atchafalaya.

The Mississippi River Commission, which is part civilian and part military, with General Sands as president, is required by statute to make these trips—to inspect the flood-control and navigation systems from Illinois to the Gulf, and to hold the hearings. Accordingly, there are two major generals and one brigadier aboard, several colonels, various majors—in all, a military concentration that is actually untypical of the U.S. Army Corps of Engineers. The Corps consists essentially of civilians, with a veneer of military people at and near the top. For example, Sands has with him his chief executive assistant, his chief engineer, his chief planner, his chief of operations, and his chief of programming. All these chiefs are civilians. Sands is commander of the Corps' Lower Mississippi Valley Division, of which the New Orleans

District, which includes Old River, is a part. The New Orleans District, U.S. Army Corps of Engineers, consists of something like ten Army officers and fourteen hundred civilians.

Just why the Army should be involved at all with levee systems, navigation locks, rock jetties, concrete revetments, and the austere realities of deltaic geomorphology is a question that attracts no obvious answer. The Corps is here because it is here. Its presence is an expression not of contemporary military strategy but of pure evolutionary tradition, its depth of origin about a century and three-quarters. The Corps is here specifically to safeguard the nation against any repetition of the War of 1812. When that unusual year was in its thirty-sixth month, the British Army landed on the Gulf Coast and marched against New Orleans. The war had been promoted, not to say provoked, by territorially aggressive American Midwesterners who were known around the country as hawks. It had so far produced some invigorating American moments ("We have met the enemy and they are ours"), including significant naval victories by ships like the Hornet and the Wasp. By and large, though, the triumphs had been British. The British had repelled numerous assaults on Canada. They had established a base in Maine. In Washington, they had burned the Capitol and the White House, and with their rutilant rockets and air-burst ballistics they tried to destroy Baltimore. New Orleans was not unaware of these events, and very much dreaded invasion. When it came, militarily untrained American backwoods sharpshooters, standing behind things like cotton bales, picked off two thousand soldiers of the King while losing seventy-one of their own. Nonetheless, the city's fear of invasion long outlasted the war.

Despite the Treaty of Ghent, there was a widespread assumption that the British would attack again and, if so, would surely attack where they had attacked before. One did not have to go to the War College to learn that lightning enjoys a second chance. Fortifications were therefore required in the environs of New Orleans. That this was an assignment for the Army Corps of Engineers was obvious in more than a military sense. There was—and for another decade would be—only one school of engineering in America. This was the United States Military Academy, at West Point, New York. The academy had been founded in 1802. The beginnings of the Army Corps of Engineers actually date to the American Revolution. General Washington, finding among his aroused colonists few engineers worthy of the word, hired engineers from Louis XVI, and the first Corps was for the most part French.

The Army engineers chose half a dozen sites near New Orleans and, setting a pattern, signed up a civilian contractor to build the fortifications. Congress also instructed the Army to survey the Mississippi and its tributaries with an eye to assuring and improving inland navigation. Thus the Corps spread northward from its military fortifications into civil works along the rivers. In the eighteen-forties and fifties, many of these projects were advanced under the supervision of Pierre Gustave Toutant Beauregard, West Point '38, a native of St. Bernard Parish, and ranking military engineer in the district. Late in 1860, Beauregard was named superintendent of the United States Military Academy. He served five days, resigned to become a Confederate general, and opened the Civil War by directing the bombardment of Fort Sumter.

So much for why there are military officers on the towboat Mississippi inspecting the flood controls of Louisiana's delta plain. Thomas Sands—with his two stars, his warm smile, his intuitive sense of people, and his knowledge of hydrology—is Pierre Gustave Toutant Beauregard's apostolic successor. Sands is trim, athletic, and, in appearance, youthful. Only in his Vietnam ribbons does he show the effects of his assignments as a combat engineer. One of his thumbs is larger and less straight than the other, but that is nothing more than an orthopedic reference to the rigors of plebe lacrosse—West Point '58. He grew up near Nashville, and has an advanced degree in hydrology from Texas A. & M. and a law degree he earned at night while working in the Pentagon. As a colonel, he spent three years in charge of the New Orleans District. As a brigadier general, he was commander of the Corps' North Atlantic Division, covering military and civil works from Maine to Virginia. Now, from his division headquarters, in Vicksburg, he is in charge of the Mississippi Valley from Missouri to the Gulf. On a wall of his private office is a board of green slate. One day when I was interviewing him there, he spent much of the time making and erasing chalk diagrams. "Man against nature. That's what life's all about," he said as he sketched the concatenating forces at Old River and the controls the Corps had applied. He used only the middle third of the slate. The rest had been preempted. The words "BE INNOVATIVE, BE RESPONSIVE, AND OPERATE WITH A TOUCH OF CLASS" were chalked across the bottom. "Old River is a true representation of a confrontation with nature," he went on. "Folks recognized that Mother Nature, being what she is— having changed course many times—would do it again. Today, Mother Nature is working within a constrained environment in the lower Mississippi. Old River is the key element. Every facet of law below there relates to what goes on in this little out-of-the-way point that most folks have never heard about." Chalked across the upper third of the slate were the words "DO WHAT'S RIGHT, AND BE PREPARED TO FIGHT AS INFANTRY WHEN REQUIRED!!!"

Now, aboard the towboat Mississippi, the General is saying, "In terms of hydrology, what we've done here at Old River is stop time. We have, in effect, stopped time in terms of the distribution of flows. Man is directing the maturing process of the Atchafalaya and the lower Mississippi." There is nothing formal about these remarks. The General says that this journey downriver is meant to be "a floating convention." Listening to him is not a requirement. From the pilothouse to the fantail, people wander where they please, stopping here and again to converse in small groups.

Two floatplanes appear above the trees, descend, flare, and land side by side behind the Mississippi. The towboat reduces power, and the airplanes taxi into its wake. They carry four passengers from Morgan City—latecomers to the floating convention. They climb aboard, and the airplanes fly away. These four, making such effort to advance their special interests, are four among two million nine hundred thousand people whose livelihoods, safety, health, and quality of life are directly influenced by the Corps' controls at Old River. In years gone by, when there were no control structures, naturally there were no complaints. The water went where it pleased. People took it as it came. The delta was in a state of nature. But now that Old River is valved and metered there are two million nine hundred thousand potential complainers, very few of whom are reluctant to present a grievance to the Corps. When farmers want less water, for example, fishermen want more, and they all complain to the Corps. In General Sands' words, "We're always walkin' around with, by and large, the black hat on. There's no place in the U.S. where there are so many competing interests relating to one water resource."

Aboard the Mississippi, this is the primary theme. Oliver Houck, professor of ecoprudence, is heard to mutter, "What the Corps does with the water decides everything." And General Sands cheerfully remarks that every time he makes one of these trips he gets "beaten on the head and shoulders." He continues, "In most water-resources stories, you can identify two sides. Here there are many more. The crawfisherman and the shrimper come up within five minutes asking for opposite things. The crawfishermen say, 'Put more water in, the water is low.' Shrimpers don't want more water. They are benefitted by low water. Navigation interests say, 'The water is too low, don't take more away or you'll have to dredge.' Municipal interests say, 'Keep the water high or you'll increase saltwater intrusion.' In the high-water season, everybody is interested in less water. As the water starts dropping, upstream farmers say, 'Get the water off of us quicker.' But folks downstream don't want it quicker. As water levels go up, we divert some fresh water into marshes, because the marshes need it for the nutrients and the sedimentation, but oyster fishermen complain. They all complain except the ones who have seed-oyster beds, which are destroyed by excessive salinity. The variety of competing influences is phenomenal."

In southern Louisiana, the bed of the Mississippi River is so far below sea level that a flow of at least a hundred and twenty thousand cubic feet per second is needed to hold back salt water and keep it below New Orleans, which drinks the river. Along the ragged edges of the Gulf, whole ecosystems depend on the relationship of fresh to salt water, which is in large part controlled by the Corps. Shrimp people want water to be brackish, waterfowl people want it fresh—a situation that causes National Marine Fisheries to do battle with United States Fish and Wildlife while both simultaneously attack the Corps. The industrial interests of the American Ruhr beseech the Corps to maintain their supply of fresh water. Agricultural pumping stations demand more fresh water for their rice but nervily ask the Corps to keep the sediment. Morgan City needs water to get oil boats and barges to rigs offshore, but if Morgan City gets too much water it's the end of Morgan City. Port authorities present special needs, and the owners of grain elevators, and the owners of coal elevators, barge interests, flood-control districts, levee boards. As General Sands says, finishing the list, "A guy who wants to put a new dock in has to come to us." People suspect the Corps of favoring other people. In addition to all the things the Corps actually does and does not do, there are infinite actions it is imagined to do, infinite actions it is imagined not to do, and infinite actions it is imagined to be capable of doing, because the Corps has been conceded the almighty role of God.

The towboat enters the Atchafalaya at an unprepossessing T in a jungle of phreatophytic trees. Atchafalaya. The "a"s are broad, the word rhymes with "jambalaya," and the accents are on the second and fourth syllables. Among navigable rivers, the Atchafalaya is widely described as one of the most treacherous in the world, but it just lies there quiet and smooth. It lies there like a big alligator in a low slough, with time on its side, waiting—waiting to outwait the Corps of Engineers—and hunkering down ever lower in its bed and presenting a sort of maw to the Mississippi, into which the river could fall. In the pilothouse, standing behind Jorge Cano and John Dugger as they swing the ship to port and head south, I find myself remembering an exchange between Cano and Rabalais a couple of days ago, when Cano was speculating about the Atchafalaya's chances of capturing the Mississippi someday despite all efforts to prevent it from doing so. "Mother Nature is patient," he said. "Mother Nature has more time than we do."

Rabalais said, "She has nothing but time."

Frederic Chatry happens to be in the pilothouse, too, as does Fred Bayley. Both are civilians: Chatry, chief engineer of the New Orleans District; Bayley, chief engineer of the Lower Mississippi Valley Division. Chatry is short and slender, a courtly and formal man, his uniform a bow tie. He is saying that before the control structures were built water used to flow in either direction through Old River. It would flow into the Mississippi if the Red happened to be higher. This was known as a reversal, and the last reversal occurred in 1945. The enlarging Atchafalaya was by then so powerful in its draw that it took all of the Red and kept it. "The more water the Atchafalaya takes, the bigger it gets; the bigger it gets, the more water it takes. The only thing that interrupts it is Old River Control. If we had not interrupted it, the main river would now be the Atchafalaya, below this point. If you left it to its own devices, the end result had to be that it would become the master stream. If that were to happen, below Old River the Mississippi reach would be unstable. Silt would fill it in. The Corps could not cope with it. Old River to Baton Rouge would fill in. River traffic from the north would stop. Everything would go to pot in the delta. We couldn't cope. It would be plugged."

I ask to what extent they ever contemplate that the structures at Old River might fail.

Bayley is quick to answer—Fred Bayley, a handsome sandy-haired man in a regimental tie and a cool tan suit, with the contemplative manner of an academic and none of the defenses of a challenged engineer. "Anything can fail," he says. "In most of our projects, we try to train natural effects instead of taking them head on. I never approach anything we do with the idea that it can't fail. That is sticking your head in the sand."

We are making twelve knots on a two-and-a-half-knot current under bright sun and cottony bits of cloud—flying along between the Atchafalaya levees, between the river-batture trees. We are running down the reach above Simmesport, but only a distant bridge attests to that fact. From the river you cannot see the country. From the country you cannot see the river. I once looked down at this country from the air, in a light plane, and although it is called a floodway—this segment of it the West Atchafalaya Floodway—it is full of agriculture, in plowed geometries of brown, green, and tan. The Atchafalaya from above looks like the Connecticut winding past New Hampshire floodplain farms. If you look up, you do not see Mt. Washington. You see artificial ponds, now and again, as far as the horizon—square ponds, dotted with the cages of crawfish. You see dark-green pastureland, rail fences, cows with short fat shadows.

The unexpected happens—unthinkable, unfortunate, but not un-

imaginable. At first with a modest lurch, and then with a more pronounced lurch, and then with a profound structural shudder, the Mississippi is captured by the Atchafalaya. The mid-American flagship of
the U.S. Army Corps of Engineers has run aground.

After going on line, in 1963, the control structures at Old River had to
wait ten years to prove what they could do. The nineteen-fifties and
nineteen-sixties were secure in the Mississippi Valley. In human terms,
a generation passed with no disastrous floods. The Mississippi River
and Tributaries Project—the Corps' total repertory of defenses from
Cairo, Illinois, southward—seemed to have met its design purpose: to
confine and conduct the run of the river, to see it safely into the Gulf.
The Corps looked upon this accomplishment with understandable
pride and, without intended diminution of respect for its enemy, issued
a statement of victory: "We harnessed it, straightened it, regularized it,
shackled it."

   Then, in the fall of 1972, the winter of 1973, river stages were
higher than normal, reducing the system's tolerance for what might
come in spring. In the upper valley, snows were unusually heavy. In the
South came a season of exceptional rains. During the uneventful era
that was about to end, the Mississippi's main channel, in its relative
lethargy, had given up a lot of volume to accumulations of sediment.
High water, therefore, would flow that much higher. As the spring
runoff came down the tributaries, collected, and approached, computers gave warning that the mainline levees were not sufficient to contain
it. Eight hundred miles of frantically filled sandbags were added to the
levees. Bulldozers added potato ridges—barriers of uncompacted dirt.
While this was going on, more rain was falling. In the southern part of
the valley, twenty inches fell in a day and a half.

   At Old River Control on an ordinary day, when the stilling basin
sounds like Victoria Falls but otherwise the country is calm and dry—
when sandy spaces and stands of trees fill up the view between the
structure and the Mississippi—an almost academic effort is required to
visualize a slab of water six stories high, spread to the ends of perspective. That is how it was in 1973. During the sustained spring high water—week after week after week—the gathered drainage of Middle
America came to Old River in units exceeding two million cubic feet a
second. Twenty-five per cent of that left the Mississippi channel and
went to the Atchafalaya. In aerial view, trees and fields were no longer
visible, and the gated stronghold of the Corps seemed vulnerable in the
extreme—a narrow causeway, a thin fragile line across a brown sea.

   The Corps had built Old River Control to control just about as

much as was passing through it. In mid-March, when the volume began
to approach that amount, curiosity got the best of Raphael G. Kazmann, author of a book called "Modern Hydrology" and professor of
civil engineering at Louisiana State University. Kazmann got into his
car, crossed the Mississippi on the high bridge at Baton Rouge, and
made his way north to Old River. He parked, got out, and began to
walk the structure. An extremely low percentage of its five hundred
and sixty-six feet eradicated his curiosity. "That whole miserable structure was vibrating," he recalled years later, adding that he had felt as if
he were standing on a platform at a small rural train station when "a
fully loaded freight goes through." Kazmann opted not to wait for the
caboose. "I thought, This thing weighs two hundred thousand tons.
When two hundred thousand tons vibrates like this, this is no place for
R. G. Kazmann. I got into my car, turned around, and got the hell out
of there. I was just a professor—and, thank God, not responsible."

Kazmann says that the Tennessee River and the Missouri River
were "the two main culprits" in the 1973 flood. In one high water and
another, the big contributors vary around the watershed. An ultimate
deluge might possibly involve them all. After Kazmann went home
from Old River that time in 1973, he did his potamology indoors for a
while, assembling daily figures. In some of the numbers he felt severe
vibrations. In his words, "I watched the Ohio like a hawk, because if
that had come up, I thought, Katie, bar the door!"

The water was plenty high as it was, and continuously raged
through the structure. Nowhere in the Mississippi Valley were veloci-
ties greater than in this one place, where the waters made their hydraulic jump, plunging over what Kazmann describes as "concrete
falls" into the regime of the Atchafalaya. The structure and its stilling
basin had been configured to dissipate energy—but not nearly so much
energy. The excess force was attacking the environment of the structure. A large eddy had formed. Unbeknownst to anyone, its swirling
power was excavating sediments by the inflow apron of the structure.
Even larger holes had formed under the apron itself. Unfortunately, the
main force of the Mississippi was crashing against the south side of the
inflow channel, producing unplanned turbulence. The control structure
had been set up near the outside of a bend of the river, and closer to the
Mississippi than many engineers thought wise.

On the outflow side—where the water fell to the level of the
Atchafalaya—a hole had developed that was larger and deeper than a
football stadium, and with much the same shape. It was hidden, of
course, far beneath the chop of wild water. The Corps had long since
been compelled to leave all eleven gates wide open, in order to reduce to

the greatest extent possible the force that was shaking the structure, and so there was no alternative to aggravating the effects on the bed of the channel. In addition to the structure's weight, what was holding it in place was a millipede of stilts—steel H-beams that reached down at various angles, as pilings, ninety feet through sands and silts, through clayey peats and organic mucks. There never was a question of anchoring such a fortress in rock. The shallowest rock was seven thousand feet straight down. In three places below the structure, sheet steel went into the substrate like fins; but the integrity of the structure depended essentially on the H-beams, and vehicular traffic continued to cross it en route to San Luis Rey.

Then, as now, LeRoy Dugas was the person whose hand controlled Old River Control—a thought that makes him smile. "We couldn't afford to close any of the gates," he remarked to me one day at Old River. "Too much water was passing through the structure. Water picked up riprap off the bottom in front, and rammed it through to the tail bed." The riprap included derrick stones, and each stone weighed seven tons. On the level of the road deck, the vibrations increased. The operator of a moving crane let the crane move without him and waited for it at the end of the structure. Dugie continued, "You could get on the structure with your automobile and open the door and it would close the door." The crisis recalled the magnitude of "the '27 high water," when Dugie was a baby. Up the valley somewhere, during the '27 high water, was a railroad bridge with a train sitting on it loaded with coal. The train had been put there because its weight might help keep the bridge in place, but the bridge, vibrating in the floodwater, produced so much friction that the coal in the gondolas caught fire. Soon the bridge, the train, and the glowing coal fell into the water.

One April evening in 1973—at the height of the flood—a fisherman walked onto the structure. There is, after all, order in the universe, and some things take precedence over impending disasters. On the inflow side, facing the Mississippi, the structure was bracketed by a pair of guide walls that reached out like curving arms to bring in the water. Close by the guide wall at the south end was the swirling eddy, which by now had become a whirlpool. There was other motion as well—or so it seemed. The fisherman went to find Dugas, in his command post at the north end of the structure, and told him the guide wall had moved. Dugie told the fisherman he was seeing things. The fisherman nodded affirmatively.

When Dugie himself went to look at the guide wall, he looked at it for the last time. "It was slipping into the river, into the inflow channel." Slowly it dipped, sank, broke. Its foundations were gone. There was nothing below it but water. Professor Kazmann likes to say that this was when the Corps became "scared green." Whatever the engineers may have felt, as soon as the water began to recede they set about learning the dimensions of the damage. The structure was obviously undermined, but how much so, and where? What was solid, what was not? What was directly below the gates and the roadway? With a diamond drill, in a central position, they bored the first of many holes in the structure. When they had penetrated to basal levels, they lowered a television camera into the hole. They saw fish.

This was scarcely the first time that an attempt to control the Mississippi had failed. Old River, 1973, was merely the most emblematic place and moment where, in the course of three centuries, failure had occurred. From the beginnings of settlement, failure was the par expectation with respect to the river—a fact generally masked by the powerful fabric of ambition that impelled people to build towns and cities where almost any camper would be loath to pitch a tent.

If you travel by canoe through the river swamps of Louisiana, you may very well grow uneasy as the sun is going down. You look around for a site—a place to sleep, a place to cook. There is no terra firma. Nothing is solider than duckweed, resting on the water like green burlap. Quietly, you slide through the forest, breaking out now and again into acreages of open lake. You study the dusk for some dark cap of uncovered ground. Seeing one at last, you occupy it, limited though it may be. Your tent site may be smaller than your tent, but in this amphibious milieu you have found yourself terrain. You have established yourself in much the same manner that the French established New Orleans. So what does it matter if your leg spends the night in the water?

The water is from the state of New York, the state of Montana, the province of Alberta, and everywhere below that frame. Far above Old River are places where the floodplain is more than a hundred miles wide. Spaniards in the sixteenth century came upon it at the wrong time, saw an ocean moving south, and may have been discouraged. Where the delta began, at Old River, the water spread out even more—through a palimpsest of bayous and distributary streams in forested paludal basins—but this did not dissuade the French. For military and commercial purposes, they wanted a city in such country. They laid it out in 1718, only months before a great flood. Even as New Orleans was rising, its foundations filled with water. The message in the landscape could not have been more clear: like the aboriginal people, you could fish and forage and move on, but you could not build there—you could not create a city, or even a cluster of modest steadings—without declaring war on nature. You did not have to be Dutch to understand this, or French to ignore it. The people of southern Louisiana have often been compared unfavorably with farmers of the pre-Aswan Nile, who lived on high ground, farmed low ground, and permitted floods to come and go according to the rhythms of nature. There were differences in Louisiana, though. There was no high ground worth mentioning, and planters had to live on their plantations. The waters of the Nile were warm; the Mississippi brought cold northern floods that sometimes stood for months, defeating agriculture for the year. If people were to farm successfully in the rich loams of the natural levees—or anywhere nearby—they could not allow the Mississippi to continue in its natural state. Herbert Kassner, the division's public-relations director, once remarked to me, "This river used to meander all over its floodplain. People would move their tepees, and that was that. You can't move Vicksburg."

When rivers go over their banks, the spreading water immediately slows up, dropping the heavier sediments. The finer the silt, the farther it is scattered, but so much falls close to the river that natural levees rise through time. The first houses of New Orleans were built on the natural levees, overlooking the river. In the face of disaster, there was no better place to go. If there was to be a New Orleans, the levees themselves would have to be raised, and the owners of the houses were ordered to do the raising. This law (1724) was about as effective as the ordinances that compel homeowners and shopkeepers in the North to shovel snow off their sidewalks. Odd as it seems now, those early levees were only three feet high, and they were rife with imperfections. To the extent that they were effective at all, they owed a great deal to the country across the river, where there were no artificial levees, and waters that went over the bank flowed to the horizon. In 1727, the French colonial governor declared the New Orleans levee complete, adding that within a year it would be extended a number of miles up and down the river, making the community floodproof. The governor's name was Perrier. If words could stop water, Perrier had found them—initiating a durable genre.

In 1735, New Orleans went under—and again in 1785. The intervals—like those between earthquakes in San Francisco—were generally long enough to allow the people to build up a false sense of security. In response to the major floods, they extended and raised the levees. A levee appeared across the river from New Orleans, and by 1812 the west bank was leveed to the vicinity of Old River, a couple of hundred miles upstream. At that time, the east bank was leveed as far as Baton Rouge. Neither of the levees was continuous. Both protected plantation land. Where the country remained as the Choctaws had known it, floodwaters poured to the side, reducing the threat elsewhere. Land was not cheap—forty acres cost three thousand dollars—but so great was the demand for riverfront plantations that by 1828 the levees in southern Louisiana were continuous, the river artificially confined. Just in case the levees should fail, some plantation houses—among their fields of sugarcane, their long bright rows of oranges—were built on Indian burial mounds. In 1828, Bayou Manchac was closed. In the whole of the Mississippi's delta plain, Bayou Manchac happened to have been the only distributary that went east. It was dammed at the source. Its discharge would no longer ease the pressures of the master stream.

By this time, Henry Shreve had appeared on the scene—in various ways to change it forever. He was the consummate riverman: boatman, pilot, entrepreneur, empirical naval architect. He is noted as the creator of the flat-hulled layer-cake stern-wheel Mississippi steamboat, its shallow draft the result of moving the machinery up from below to occupy its own deck. The Mississippi steamboat was not invented, however. It evolved. And Shreve's contribution was less in its configuration than its power. A steamboat built and piloted by Henry Shreve travelled north against the current as far as Louisville. He demonstrated that commerce could go both ways. Navigation was inconvenienced, though, by hazards in the river—the worst of which were huge trees that had drifted south over the years and become stuck in various ways. One kind was rigid in the riverbed and stood up like a spear. It was called a planter. Another, known as a sawyer, sawed up and down with the vagaries of the current, and was likely to rise suddenly in the path of a boat and destroy it. In the Yukon River, such logs—eternally bowing—are known as preachers. In the Mississippi, whatever the arrested logs were called individually, they were all "snags," and after the Army engineers had made Shreve, a civilian, their Superintendent of Western River Improvements he went around like a dentist yanking snags. The multi-hulled snag boats were devices of his invention. In the Red River, he undertook to disassemble a "raft"—uprooted trees by the tens of thousands that were stopping navigation for a hundred and sixty miles. Shreve cleared eighty miles in one year. Meanwhile, at 31 degrees north latitude (about half-way between Vicksburg and Baton Rouge) he made a bold move on the Mississippi. In the sinusoidal path of the river, any meander tended to grow until its loop was so large it would cut itself off. At 31 degrees north latitude was a west-bending loop that was eighteen miles around and had so nearly doubled back upon itself that Shreve decided to help it out. He adapted one of his snag boats as a dredge, and after two weeks of digging across the narrow neck he had a good swift current flowing. The Mississippi quickly took over. The width of Shreve's new channel doubled in two days. A few days more and it had become the main channel of the river.

The great loop at 31 degrees north happened to be where the Red-Atchafalaya conjoined the Mississippi, like a pair of parentheses back to back. Steamboats had had difficulty there in the colliding waters. Shreve's purpose in cutting off the loop was to give the boats a smoother shorter way to go, and, as an incidental, to speed up the Mississippi, lowering, however slightly, its crests in flood. One effect of the cutoff was to increase the flow of water out of the Mississippi and into the Atchafalaya, advancing the date of ultimate capture. Where the flow departed from the Mississippi now, it followed an arm of the cutoff me-ander. This short body of water soon became known as Old River. In less than a fortnight, it had been removed as a segment of the main-stem Mississippi and restyled as a form of surgical drain.

In city and country, riverfront owners became sensitive about the fact that the levees they were obliged to build were protecting not only their properties but also the properties behind them. Levee districts were established—administered by levee boards—to spread the cost. The more the levees confined the river, the more destructive it became when they failed. A place where water broke through was known as a crevasse—a source of terror no less effective than a bursting dam—and the big ones were memorialized, like other great disasters, in a series of proper names: the Macarty Crevasse (1816), the Sauvé Crevasse (1849). Levee inspectors were given power to call out male slaves—aged fifteen to sixty—whose owners lived within seven miles of trouble. With the approach of mid-century, the levees were averaging six feet—twice their original height—and calculations indicated that the flow line would rise. Most levee districts were not populous enough to cover the multi-plying costs, so the United States Congress, in 1850, wrote the Swamp and Overflow Land Act. It is possible that no friend of Peter had ever been so generous in handing over his money to Paul. The federal gov-ernment deeded millions of acres of swampland to states along the river, and the states sold the acreage to pay for the levees. The Swamp Act gave eight and a half million acres of river swamps and marshes to Louisiana alone. Other states, in aggregate, got twenty million more. Since time immemorial, these river swamps had been the natural reser-voirs where floodwaters were taken in and held, and gradually released as the flood went down. Where there was timber (including virgin cy-press), the swampland was sold for seventy-five cents an acre, twelve and a half cents where there were no trees. The new owners were for the most part absentee. An absentee was a Yankee. The new owners drained much of the swampland, turned it into farmland, and demanded the protection of new and larger levees. At this point, Congress might have asked itself which was the act and which was the swamp.

River stages, in their wide variations, became generally higher through time, as the water was presented with fewer outlets. People began to wonder if the levees could ever be high enough and strong enough to make the river safe. Possibly a system of dams and reservoirs in the tributaries of the upper valley could hold water back and release it in the drier months, and possibly a system of spillways and floodways could be fashioned in the lower valley to distribute water when big floods arrived. Beginning in the eighteen-fifties, these notions were the subject of virulent debate among civilian and military engineers. Four major floods in ten years and thirty-two disastrous crevasses in a single spring were not enough to suggest to the Corps that levees alone might never be equal to the job. The Corps, as things stood, was not yet in charge. District by district, state by state, the levee system was still a patchwork effort. There was no high command in the fight against the water. In one of the Corps' official histories, the situation is expressed in this rather preoccupied sentence: "By 1860, it had become increasingly obvious that a successful war over such an immense battleground could be waged only by a consolidated army under one authority." While the Civil War came and went, the posture of the river did not change. Vicksburg fell but did not move. In the floods of 1862, 1866, and 1867, levees failed. Catastrophes notwithstanding, Bayou Plaque-mine—a major distributary of the Mississippi and a natural escape for large percentages of spring high water—was closed in 1868, its junction with the Mississippi sealed by an earthen dam. Even at normal stages, the Mississippi was beginning to stand up like a large vein on the back of a hand. The river of the eighteen-seventies ran higher than it ever had before.

In 1879, Congress at last created the Mississippi River Commission, which included civilians but granted hegemony to the Corps. The president of the commission would always be an Army engineer, and all decisions were subject to veto by the commandant of the Corps. Imperiously, Congress ordered the commission to "prevent destructive floods," and left it to the Corps to say how. The Corps remained committed to the argument that tributary dams and reservoirs and downstream spillways would create more problems than they would solve. "Hold by levees" was the way to do the job.

The national importance of the commission is perhaps illuminated by the fact that one of its first civilian members was Benjamin Harrison. Another was James B. Eads, probably the most brilliant engineer who has ever addressed his attention to the Mississippi River. As a young man, he had walked around on its bottom under a device of his own invention that he called a submarine. As a naval architect in the Civil War, he had designed the first American ironclads. Later, at St. Louis, he had built the first permanent bridge across the main stem of the river south of the Missouri. More recently, in defiance of the cumulative wisdom of nearly everyone in his profession, he had solved a primal question in anadromous navigation: how to get into the river. The mouth was defended by a mud-lump blockade—impenetrable masses of sediment dumped by the river as it reached the still waters of the Gulf. Dredging was hopeless. What would make a channel deep enough for ships? The government wouldn't finance him, so Eads bet his own considerable fortune on an elegant idea: he built parallel jetties in the river's mouth. They pinched the currents. The accelerated water dug out and maintained a navigable channel.

To the Corps' belief that a river confined by levees would similarly look after itself the success of the jetties gave considerable reinforcement. And Eads added words that spoke louder than his actions. "If the profession of an engineer were not based upon exact science," he said, "I might tremble for the result, in view of the immensity of the interests dependent on my success. But every atom that moves onward in the river, from the moment it leaves its home among the crystal springs or mountain snows, throughout the fifteen hundred leagues of its devious pathway, until it is finally lost in the vast waters of the Gulf, is controlled by laws as fixed and certain as those which direct the majestic march of the heavenly spheres. Every phenomenon and apparent eccentricity of the river—its scouring and depositing action, its caving banks, the formation of the bars at its mouth, the effect of the waves and tides of the sea upon its currents and deposits—is controlled by law as immutable as the Creator, and the engineer need only to be insured that he does not ignore the existence of any of these laws, to feel positively certain of the results he aims at."

When the commission was created, Mark Twain was forty-three. A book he happened to be working on was "Life on the Mississippi." Through a character called Uncle Mumford, he remarked that "four years at West Point, and plenty of books and schooling, will learn a man a good deal, I reckon, but it won't learn him the river." Twain also wrote, "One who knows the Mississippi will promptly aver—not aloud but to himself—that ten thousand River Commissions, with the mines of the world at their back, cannot tame that lawless stream, cannot curb it or confine it, cannot say to it, 'Go here,' or 'Go there,' and make it obey; cannot save a shore which it has sentenced; cannot bar its path with an obstruction which it will not tear down, dance over, and laugh at. But a discreet man will not put these things into spoken words; for the West Point engineers have not their superiors anywhere; they know all that can be known of their abstruse science; and so, since they conceive that they can fetter and handcuff that river and boss him, it is but wisdom for the unscientific man to keep still, lie low, and wait till they do it. Captain Eads, with his jetties, has done a work at the mouth of the Mississippi which seemed clearly impossible; so we do not feel full confidence now to prophesy against like impossibilities. Otherwise one would pipe out and say the Commission might as well bully the comets in their courses and undertake to make them behave, as try to bully the Mississippi into right and reasonable conduct."

In 1882 came the most destructive flood of the nineteenth century. After breaking the levees in two hundred and eighty-four crevasses, the water spread out as much as seventy miles. In the fertile lands on the two sides of Old River, plantations were deeply submerged, and livestock survived in flatboats. A floating journalist who reported these scenes in the March 29 New Orleans *Times-Democrat* said, "The current running down the Atchafalaya was very swift, the Mississippi showing a predilection in that direction, which needs only to be seen to enforce the opinion of that river's desperate endeavors to find a short way to the Gulf." The capture of the Mississippi, in other words, was already obvious enough to be noticed by a journalist. Seventy-eight years earlier—just after the Louisiana Purchase—the Army officer who went to take possession of the new country observed the Atchafalaya "completely obstructed by logs and other material" and said in his report, "Were it not for these obstructions, the probability is that the Mississippi would soon find a much nearer way to the Gulf than at present, particularly as it manifests a constant inclination to vary its course." The head of the Atchafalaya was plugged with logs for thirty miles. The raft was so compact that El Camino Real, the Spanish trail coming in from Texas, crossed the Atchafalaya near its head, and cattle being driven toward the Mississippi walked across the logs. The logjam was Old River Control Structure No. 0. Gradually, it was disassembled, freeing the Atchafalaya to lower its plain. Snag boats worked on it, and an attempt was made to clear it with fire. The flood of 1863 apparently broke it open, and at once the Atchafalaya began to widen and deepen, increasing its draw on the Mississippi. Shreve's clearing of the Red River had also increased the flow of the Atchafalaya. The interventional skill of human engineers, which would be called upon in the twentieth century to stop the great shift at Old River, did much in the nineteenth to hurry it up.

For forty-eight years, the Mississippi River Commission and the

Corps of Engineers adhered strictly to the "hold by levees" policy—levees, and levees only. It was important that no water be allowed to escape the river, because its full power would be most effective in scouring the bed, deepening the channel, increasing velocity, lowering stages, and preventing destructive floods. This was the hydraulic and hydrological philosophy not only of the U.S. Army Corps of Engineers but also of the great seventeenth-century savant Domenico Guglielmini, whose insights, ultimately, were to prove so ineffective in the valley of the Po. In 1885, one of General Sands' predecessors said, "The commission is distinctly committed to the idea of closing all outlets. . . . It has consistently opposed the fallacy known as the 'Outlet System.' "

Slaves with wheelbarrows started the levees. Immigrants with wheelbarrows replaced the slaves. Mule-drawn scrapers replaced the wheelbarrows, but not until the twentieth century. Fifteen hundred miles of earthen walls—roughly six, then nine, then twelve feet high, and a hundred feet from side to side—were built by men with shovels. They wove huge mats of willow poles and laid them down in cutbanks as revetments. When floods came, they went out to defend their defenses, and, in the words of a Corps publication, the effort was comparable to "the rigors of the battlefield." Nature was not always the only enemy. Anywhere along the river, people were safer if the levee failed across the way. If you lived on the east side, you might not be sad if water flooded west. You were also safer if the levee broke on your own side downstream. Armed patrols went up and down the levees. They watched for sand boils—signs of seepage that could open a crevasse from within. And they watched for private commandos, landing in the dark with dynamite.

Bayou Lafourche, a major distributary, was dammed in 1904. In something like twenty years, the increased confinement of the river had elevated floodwaters in Memphis by an average of about eight feet. The Corps remained loyal to the teachings of Guglielmini, and pronouncements were still forthcoming that the river was at last under control and destructive floods would not occur again. Declarations of that sort had been made in the quiet times before the great floods of 1884, 1890, 1891, 1897, 1898, and 1903, and they would be made again before 1912, 1913, 1922, and 1927.

The '27 high water tore the valley apart. On both sides of the river, levees crevassed from Cairo to the Gulf, and in the same thousand miles the flood destroyed every bridge. It killed hundreds of people, thousands of animals. Overbank, it covered twenty-six thousand square miles. It stayed on the land as much as three months. New Orleans was saved by blowing up a levee downstream. Yet the total volume of the

1927 high water was nowhere near a record. It was not a hundred-year flood. It was a form of explosion, achieved by the confining levees.

The levees of the nineteen-twenties were about six times as high as their earliest predecessors, but really no more effective. In a sense, they had been an empirical experiment—in aggregate, fifteen hundred miles of trial and error. They could be—and they would be—raised even higher. But in 1927 the results of the experiment at last came clear. The levees were helping to aggravate the problem they were meant to solve. With walls alone, one could only build an absurdly elevated aqueduct. Resistance times the resistance distance amplified the force of nature. Every phenomenon and apparent eccentricity of the river might be subject to laws as fixed and certain as those which direct the majestic march of the heavenly spheres, but, if so, the laws were inexactly understood. The Corps had attacked Antaeus without quite knowing who he was.

Congress appropriated three hundred million dollars to find out. This was more money in one bill—the hopefully titled Flood Control Act (1928)—than had been spent on Mississippi levees in all of colonial and American history. These were the start-up funds for the Mississippi River and Tributaries Project, the coordinated defenses that would still be incomplete in the nineteen-eighties and would ultimately cost about seven billion dollars. The project would raise levees and build new ones, pave cutbanks, sever loops to align the current, and hold back large volumes of water with substantial dams in tributary streams. Dredges known as dustpans would take up sediment by the millions of tons. Stone dikes would appear in strategic places, forcing the water to go around them, preventing the channel from spreading out. Most significantly, though, the project would acknowledge the superiority of the force with which it was meant to deal. It would give back to the river some measure of the freedom lost as the delta's distributaries one by one were sealed. It would go into the levees in certain places and build gates that could be opened in times of extraordinary flood. The water coming out of such spillways would enter new systems of levees guiding it down floodways to the Gulf. But how many spillways? How many floodways? How many tributary dams? Calculating maximum storms, frequency of storms, maximum snowmelts, sustained saturation of the upper valley, coincident storms in scattered parts of the watershed, the Corps reached for the figure that would float Noah. The round number was three million—that is, three million cubic feet per second coming past Old River. This was twenty-five per cent above the 1927 high. The expanded control system, with its variety of devices, would have to be designed to process that. Various names were given to this blue-moon superflow, this concatenation of recorded moments written in the future unknown. It was called the Design Flood. Alternatively, it was called the Project Flood.

Bonnet Carre was the first spillway—completed in 1931, roughly thirty miles upriver from New Orleans. The water was meant to spill into Lake Pontchartrain and go on into the Gulf, dispersing eight and a half per cent of the Project Flood. Bonnet Carre (locally pronounced "Bonny Carey") would replace dynamite in the defense of New Orleans. When the great crest of 1937 came down the river—setting an all-time record at Natchez—enough of the new improvements were in place to see it through in relative safety, with the final and supreme test presented at Bonnet Carre, where the gates were opened for the first time. At the high point, more than two hundred thousand feet per second were diverted into Lake Pontchartrain, and the flow that went on by New Orleans left the city low and dry.

For the Corps of Engineers, not to mention the people of the southern parishes, the triumph of 1937 brought fresh courage, renewed confidence—a sense once again that the river could be controlled. Major General Harley B. Ferguson, the division commander, became a regional military hero. It was he who had advocated the project's many cutoffs, all made in the decade since 1927, which shortened the river by more than a hundred miles, reducing the amount of friction working against the water. The more distance, the more friction. Friction slows the river and raises its level. The mainline levees were rebuilt, extended, reinforced—and their height was almost doubled, reaching thirty feet. There was now a Great Wall of China running up each side of the river, with the difference that while the levees were each about as long as the Great Wall they were in many places higher and in cross-section ten times as large. Work continued on the floodways. There was one in Missouri that let water out of the river and put it back into the river a few miles downstream. But the principal conduit of release—without which Bonnet Carre would be about as useful as a bailing can—was the route of the Atchafalaya. Since the lower part of it was the largest river swamp in North America, it was, by nature, ready for the storage of water. The Corps built guide levees about seventeen miles apart to shape the discharge toward Atchafalaya Bay, incidentally establishing a framework for the swamp. In the northern Atchafalaya, near Old River, they built a three-chambered system of floodways involving so many intersecting levees that the country soon resembled a cranberry farm developed on an epic scale. The West Atchafalaya Floodway had so many people in it, and so many soybeans, that its levees were to be breached only by explosives in extreme emergency—maybe once in a hundred years. The Morganza Floodway, completed in the nineteen-fifties, contained farmlands but no permanent buildings. A couple of towns and the odd refinery were surrounded by levees in the form of rings. But the plane geometry of the floodways was primarily intended to take the water from the Mississippi and get it to the swamp.

The flood-control design of 1928 had left Old River open—the only distributary of the Mississippi to continue in its natural state. The Army was aware of the threat from the Atchafalaya. Colonel Charles Potter, president of the Mississippi River Commission, told Congress in 1928 that the Mississippi was "just itching to go that way." In the new master plan, however, nothing resulted from his testimony. The Corps, in making its flow diagrams, planned that the Atchafalaya would take nearly half the Mississippi during the Design Flood. It was not in the design that the Atchafalaya take it all.

The Atchafalaya, continuing to grow, had become, by volume of discharge, one of the three or four largest rivers in the United States. Compared with the Mississippi, it had a three-to-one advantage in slope. Around 1950, geologists predicted that by 1975 the shift would be unstoppable. The Mississippi River and Tributaries Project would be in large part invalidated, the entire levee system of southern Louisiana would have to be rebuilt, communities like Morgan City in the Atchafalaya Basin would be a good deal less preserved than Pompeii, and the new mouth of the Mississippi would be a hundred and twenty miles from the old. Old River Control was authorized in 1954.

The levees were raised again. What had been adequate in 1937 was problematical in the nineteen-fifties. New grades were set. New dollars were spent to meet the grades. So often compared with the Great Wall of China, the levees had more in common with the Maginot Line. Taken together, they were a retroactive redoubt, more than adequate to wage a bygone war but below the requirements of the war to come. The levee grades of the nineteen-fifties would prove inadequate in the nineteen-seventies. Every shopping center, every drainage improvement, every square foot of new pavement in nearly half the United States was accelerating runoff toward Louisiana. Streams were being channelized to drain swamps. Meanders were cut off to speed up flow. The valley's natural storage capacities were everywhere reduced. As contributing factors grew, the river delivered more flood for less rain. The precipitation that produced the great flood of 1973 was only about twenty per cent above normal. Yet the crest at St. Louis was the highest ever recorded there. The flood proved that control of the Mississippi was as much a hope for the future as control of the Mississippi had ever been. The 1973 high water did not come close to being a Project Flood. It merely came close to wiping out the project.

While the control structure at Old River was shaking, more than a third of the Mississippi was going down the Atchafalaya. If the structure had toppled, the flow would have risen to seventy per cent. It was enough to scare not only a Louisiana State University professor but the division commander himself. At the time, this was Major General Charles Noble. He walked the bridge, looked down into the exploding water, and later wrote these words: "The south training wall on the Mississippi River side of the structure failed very early in the flood, causing violent eddy patterns and extreme turbulence. The toppled training wall monoliths worsened the situation. The integrity of the structure at this point was greatly in doubt. It was frightening to stand above the gate bays and experience the punishing vibrations caused by the violently turbulent, massive flood waters."

If the General had known what was below him, he might have sounded retreat. The Old River Control Structure—this two-hundred-thousand-ton keystone of the comprehensive flood-protection project for the lower Mississippi Valley—was teetering on steel pilings above extensive cavities full of water. The gates of the Morganza Floodway, thirty miles downstream, had never been opened. The soybean farmers of Morganza were begging the Corps not to open them now. The Corps thought it over for a few days while the Old River Control Structure, absorbing shock of the sort that could bring down a skyscraper, continued to shake. Relieving some of the pressure, the Corps opened Morganza.

The damage at Old River was increased but not initiated by the 1973 flood. The invasive scouring of the channel bed and the undermining of the control structure may actually have begun in 1963, as soon as the structure opened. In years that followed, loose barges now and again slammed against the gates, stuck there for months, blocked the flow, enhanced the hydraulic jump, and no doubt contributed to the scouring. Scour holes formed on both sides of the control structure, and expanded steadily. If they had met in 1973, they might have brought the structure down.

After the waters quieted and the concrete had been penetrated by exploratory diamond drills, Old River Control at once became, and has since remained, the civil-works project of highest national priority for the U.S. Army Corps of Engineers. Through the surface of Louisiana 15, the road that traverses the structure, more holes were drilled, with diameters the size of dinner plates, and grout was inserted in the cavities below, like fillings in a row of molars. The grout was cement and bentonite. The drilling and filling went on for months. There was no alternative to leaving gates open and giving up control. Stress on the structure was lowest with the gates open. Turbulence in the channel was commensurately higher. The greater turbulence allowed the water on the Atchafalaya side to dig deeper and increase its advantage over the Mississippi side. As the Corps has reported, "The percentage of Mississippi River flow being diverted through the structure in the absence of control was steadily increasing." That could not be helped.

After three and a half years, control was to some extent restored, but the extent was limited. In the words of the Corps, "The partial foundation undermining which occurred in 1973 inflicted permanent damage to the foundation of the low sill control structure. Emergency foundation repair, in the form of rock riprap and cement grout, was performed to safeguard the structure from a potential total failure. The foundation under approximately fifty per cent of the structure was drastically and irrevocably changed." The structure had been built to function with a maximum difference of thirty-seven feet between the Mississippi and Atchafalaya sides. That maximum now had to be lowered to twenty-two feet—a diminution that brought forth the humor in the phrase "Old River Control." Robert Fairless, a New Orleans District engineer who has long been a part of the Old River story, once told me that "things were touch and go for some months in 1973" and the situation was precarious still. "At a head greater than twenty-two feet, there's danger of losing the whole thing," he said. "If loose barges were to be pulled into the front of the structure where they would block the flow, the head would build up, and there'd be nothing we could do about it."

A sign appeared on one of the three remaining wing walls:

FISHING AND SHAD DIPPING
OFF THIS WING WALL
IS PROHIBITED

A survey boat, Navy-gray and very powerful and much resembling PT-109, began to make runs toward the sill upstream through the roiling brown rapids. Year after year this has continued. The survey boat drives itself to a standstill in the whaleback waves a few yards shy of the structure. Two men in life vests, who stand on the swaying deck in spray that curls like smoke, let go a fifty-pound ball that drops on a cable from a big stainless reel. The ball sinks to the bottom. The crewmen note the depth. They are not looking for mark twain. For example, in 1974 they found three holes so deep that it took a hundred and eighty-five thousand tons of rock to fill them in.

The 1973 flood shook the control structure a whole lot more than it shook the confidence of the Corps. When a legislative committee seemed worried, a Corps general reassured them, saying, "The Corps of Engineers can make the Mississippi River go anywhere the Corps directs it to go." On display in division headquarters in Vicksburg is a large aerial photograph of a school bus moving along a dry road beside a levee while a Galilee on the other side laps at the levee crown. This picture alone is a triumph for the Corps. Herbert Kassner, the public-relations director and a master of his craft, says of the picture, "Of course, I tell people the school bus may have been loaded with workers going to fix a break in the levee, but it looks good." And of course, after 1973, the flow lines were recomputed and the levees had to be raised. When the river would pool against the stratosphere was only a question of time.

The Washington Post, in an editorial in November of 1980, called attention to the Corps' efforts to prevent the great shift at Old River, and concluded with this paragraph:

> Who will win as this slow-motion confrontation between humankind and nature goes on? No one really knows. But after watching Mt. St. Helens and listening to the guesses about its performance, if we had to bet, we would bet on the river.

The Corps had already seen that bet, and was about to bump it, too. Even before the muds were dry from the 1973 flood, Corps engineers had begun building a model of Old River at their Waterways Experiment Station, in Vicksburg. The model was to cover an acre and a half. A model of that size was modest for the Corps. Not far away, it had a fifteen-acre model of the Mississippi drainage, where water flowing in from the dendritic tips could get itself together and attack Louisiana. The scale was one human stride to the mile. In the time it took to say "one Mississippi," if fourteen gallons went past Arkansas City that was a Project Flood. Something like eight and a half gallons was "a high-water event." "It's the ultimate sandbox—these guys have made a profession of the sandbox," Tulane's Oliver Houck has said, with concealed admiration. "They've put the whole river in a sandbox." The Old River model not only helped with repairs, it also showed a need for supplementary fortification. Since the first control structure was irreparably damaged, a second one, nearby, with its own inflow channel from the Mississippi, should establish full control at Old River and take pressure off the original structure in times of high stress.

To refine the engineering of the auxiliary structure, several additional models, with movable beds, were built on a distorted scale. Making the vertical scale larger than the horizontal was believed to eliminate surface-tension problems in simulating the turbulence of a real river. The channel beds were covered with crushed coal—which has half the specific gravity of sand—or with walnut shells, which were thought to be better replicas of channel-protecting rock but had an unfortunate tendency to decay, releasing gas bubbles. In one model, the stilling basin below the new structure was filled with driveway-size limestone gravel, each piece meant to represent a derrick stone six feet thick. After enough water had churned through these models to satisfy the designers, ground was broken at Old River, about a third of a mile from the crippled sill, for the Old River Control Auxiliary Structure, the most advanced weapon ever developed to prevent the capture of a river—a handsome gift to the American Ruhr, worth three hundred million dollars. In Vicksburg, Robert Fletcher—a sturdily built, footballish sort of engineer, who had explained to me about the nutshells, the coal, and the gravel—said of the new structure, "I hope it works."

The Old River Control Auxiliary Structure is a rank of seven towers, each buff with a white crown. They are vertical on the upstream side, and they slope toward the Atchafalaya. Therefore, they resemble flying buttresses facing the Mississippi. The towers are separated by six arciform gates, convex to the Mississippi, and hinged in trunnion blocks secured with steel to carom the force of the river into the core of the structure. Lifted by cables, these tainter gates, as they are called, are about as light and graceful as anything could be that has a composite weight of twenty-six hundred tons. Each of them is sixty-two feet wide. They are the strongest the Corps has ever designed and built. A work of engineering such as a Maillart bridge or a bridge by Christian Menn can outdo some other works of art, because it is not only a gift to the imagination but also structural in the matrix of the world. The auxiliary structure at Old River contains too many working components to be classed with such a bridge, but in grandeur and in profile it would not shame a pharaoh.

The original Old River Control project, going on line in 1963, cost eighty-six million dollars. The works of repair and supplement have extended the full cost of the battle to five hundred million. The disproportion in these figures does, of course, reflect inflation, but to a much greater extent it reflects the price of lessons learned. It reflects the fact that no one is stretching words who says that in 1973 the control structure failed. The new one is not only bigger and better and more costly; also, no doubt, there are redundancies in its engineering in memory of '73.

In 1983 came the third-greatest flood of the twentieth century—a narrow but decisive victory for the Corps. The Old River Control Auxiliary Structure was nothing much by then but a foundation that had recently been poured in dry ground. The grout in the old structure kept Old River stuck together. Across the Mississippi, a few miles downstream, the water rose to a threatening level at Louisiana's maximum-security prison. The prison was protected not only by the mainline levee but also by a ring levee of its own. Nonetheless, as things appeared, for a while the water was going to pour into the prison. The state would have to move the prisoners, taking them in buses out into the road system, risking Lord knows what. The state went on its knees before the Corps: Do something. The Corps evaluated the situation and decided to bet the rehabilitation of the control structure against the rehabilitation of the prisoners. By letting more water through the control structure, the Corps caused the water at the prison to go down.

Viewed from five or six thousand feet in the air, the structures at Old River inspire less confidence than they do up close. They seem temporary, fragile, vastly outmatched by the natural world—a lesion in the side of the Mississippi butterflied with surgical tape. Under construction nearby is a large hydropower plant that will take advantage of the head between the two rivers and, among other things, light the city of Vidalia. The channel cut to serve it raises to three the number of artificial outlets opened locally in the side of the Mississippi River, making Old River a complex of canals and artificial islands, and giving it the appearance of a marina. The Corps is officially confident that all this will stay in place, and supports its claim with a good deal more than walnuts. The amount of limestone that has been imported from Kentucky is enough to confuse a geologist. As Fred Chatry once said, "The Corps of Engineers is convinced that the Mississippi River can be convinced to remain where it is."

I once asked Fred Smith, a geologist who works for the Corps at New Orleans District Headquarters, if he thought Old River Control would eventually be overwhelmed. He said, "Capture doesn't have to happen at the control structures. It could happen somewhere else. The river is close to it a little to the north. That whole area is suspect. The Mississippi wants to go west. Nineteen-seventy-three was a forty-year flood. The big one lies out there somewhere—when the structures can't release all the floodwaters and the levee is going to have to give way. That is when the river's going to jump its banks and try to break through."

Geologists in general have declared the capture inevitable, but, of course, they would. They know that in 1852 the Yellow River shifted its course away from the Yellow Sea, establishing a new mouth four hundred miles from the old. They know the stories of catastrophic shifts by the Mekong, the Indus, the Po, the Volga, the Tigris and the Euphrates.

The Rosetta branch of the Nile was the main stem of the river three thousand years ago.

Raphael Kazmann, the hydrologic engineer, who is now emeritus at Louisiana State, sat me down in his study in Baton Rouge, instructed me to turn on a tape recorder, and, with reference to Old River Control, said, "I have no fight with the Corps of Engineers. I may be a critic, but I'm not mad at anybody. It's a good design. Don't get me wrong. These guys are the best. If it doesn't work for them, nobody can do it."

A tape recorder was not a necessity for gathering the impression that nobody could do it. "More and more energy is being dissipated there," Kazmann said. "Floods are more frequent. There will be a bigger and bigger differential head as time goes on. It almost went out in '73. Sooner or later, it will be undermined or bypassed—give way. I have a lot of respect for Mother . . . for this alluvial river of ours. I don't want to be around here when it happens."

The Corps would say he won't be.

"Nobody knows where the hundred-year flood is," Kazmann continued. "Perspective should be a minimum of a hundred years. This is an extremely complicated river system altered by works of man. A fifty-year prediction is not reliable. The data have lost their pristine character. It's a mixture of hydrologic events and human events. Floods across the century are getting higher, low stages lower. The Corps of Engineers—they're scared as hell. They don't know what's going to happen. This is planned chaos. The more planning they do, the more chaotic it is. Nobody knows exactly where it's going to end."

The towboat Mississippi has hit the point of a sandbar. The depth finder shows thirty-eight feet—indicating that there are five fathoms of water between the bottom of the hull and the bed of the river. The depth finder is on the port side of the ship, however, and the sandbar to starboard, only a few feet down. Thus the towboat has come to its convulsive stop, breaking the stride of two major generals and bringing state officials and levee boards out to the rail. General Sands, the division commander, has a look on his face which suggests that Hopkins has just scored on Army but Army will win the game. There is some running around, some eye-bulging, some breaths drawn shallower even than the sandbar—but not here in the pilothouse. John Dugger, the pilot, and Jorge Cano, the local contact pilot, reveal on their faces not the least touch of dismay, or even surprise, whatever they may feel. They behave as if it were absolutely routine to be aiming downstream in midcurrent at zero knots. In a sense, that is true, for this is not some minor navigational challenge, like shooting rapids in an aircraft carrier. This is the Atchafalaya River.

A poker player might get out of an analogous situation by reaching toward a sleeve. A basketball player would reverse pivot—shielding the ball, whirling the body in a complete circle to leave the defender flat as a sandbar. John Dugger seems to be both. He has cut the engines, and now—looking interested, and nothing else—he lets the current take the stern and swing it wide. The big boat spins, reverse pivots, comes off the bar, and leaves it behind.

Conversations resume—in the lounge, on the outer decks, in the pilothouse—and inevitably many of them touch on the subject of controls at Old River. General Sands is saying, "Between 1950 and 1973, there was intensification of land use in the lower Mississippi—a whole generation grew up thinking you could grow soybeans here and never get wet. Since '73, Mother Nature has been trying to catch up. There have been seven high-water events since 1973. Now the auxiliary structure gives these folks all the assurance they need that Old River can continue to operate."

I ask if anyone agrees that the Atchafalaya could capture the Mississippi near the control structures and not through them.

General Sands replies, "I don't know that I'm personally smart enough to answer that, but I'd say no."

Lieutenant Colonel Ed Willis asks C. J. Nettles, chief of operations for the New Orleans District, if he thinks the auxiliary structure will do the job.

Nettles says, "The jury is out on that one," and adds that he is not as confident about it as others are.

At Old River a couple of days ago, near the new structure, Nettles and LeRoy Dugas were looking over a scene full of cargo barges, labor barges, crawling bulldozers, hundreds of yards of articulated concrete mattress revetments recently sunk into place, and millions of tons of new limestone riprap. Nettles asked Dugie how long he thought the new armor would last.

Dugie said, "Two high waters."

General Sands advances a question: "Had man not settled in southern Louisiana, what would it be like today? Under nature's scenario, what would it be like?" And, not waiting for an answer, he supplies one himself: "If only nature were here, people—except for some hunters and fishermen—couldn't exist here."

Under nature's scenario, with many distributaries spreading the floodwaters left and right across the big deltaic plain, virtually the whole region would be covered—with fresh sediments as well as water.

In an average year, some two hundred million tons of sediment are in transport in the river. This is where the foreland Rockies go, the western Appalachians. Southern Louisiana is a very large lump of mountain butter, eight miles thick where it rests upon the continental shelf, half that under New Orleans, a mile and a third at Old River. It is the nature of unconsolidated sediments to compact, condense, and crustally sink. So the whole deltaic plain, a superhimalaya upside down, is to varying extents subsiding, as it has been for thousands of years. Until about 1900, the river and its distributaries were able to compensate for the subsidence with the amounts of fresh sediment they spread in flood. Across the centuries, distribution was uneven, as channels shifted and land would sink in one place and fill in somewhere else, but over all the land-building process was net positive. It was abetted by decaying vegetation, which went into the flooded silts and made soil. Vegetation cannot decay unless it grows first, and it grew in large part on nutrients supplied by floodwaters.

"In the seventeenth century, the Mississippi was very porous along its banks, and water left it in many places," Fred Chatry reminds us. "Only at low water was it completely confined. Now, in two thousand miles, the first place where water naturally escapes the Mississippi is at Bayou Baptiste Collette—sixty miles below New Orleans."

What was a net gain before 1900 has by now been a net loss for nearly a hundred years, and the Louisiana we have known—from Old River and the Acadian world to Bayou Baptiste Collette—is sinking. Sediments are being kept within the mainline levees and shot into the Gulf at the rate of three hundred and fifty-six thousand tons a day— shot over the shelf like peas through a peashooter, and lost to the abyssal plain. As waters rise ever higher between levees, the ground behind the levees subsides, with the result that the Mississippi delta plain has become an exaggerated Venice, two hundred miles wide—its rivers, it bayous, its artificial canals a trelliswork of water among subsiding lands.

The medians of interstates are water. St. Bernard Parish, which includes suburbs of New Orleans and is larger than the state of Delaware, is two per cent terra firma, eighteen per cent wetland, and eighty per cent water. A ring levee may surround a whole parish. A ring levee may surround fifty-five square miles of soybeans. Every square foot within a ring levee forces water upward somewhere else.

An Alexander Calder might revel in these motions—interdependent, interconnected, related to the flow at Old River. Calder would have understood Old River Control: the place where the work is attached to the ceiling, and below which everything—New Orleans, Morgan City, the river swamp of the Atchafalaya—dangles and swings.

Something like half of New Orleans is now below sea level—as much as fifteen feet. New Orleans, surrounded by levees, is emplaced between Lake Pontchartrain and the Mississippi like a broad shallow bowl. Nowhere is New Orleans higher than the river's natural bank. Underprivileged people live in the lower elevations, and always have. The rich—by the river—occupy the highest ground. In New Orleans, income and elevation can be correlated on a literally sliding scale: the Garden District on the highest level, Stanley Kowalski in the swamp. The Garden District and its environs are locally known as uptown.

Torrential rains fall on New Orleans—enough to cause flash floods inside the municipal walls. The water has nowhere to go. Left on its own, it would form a lake, rising inexorably from one level of the economy to the next. So it has to be pumped out. Every drop of rain that falls on New Orleans evaporates or is pumped out. Its removal lowers the water table and accelerates the city's subsidence. Where marshes have been drained to create tracts for new housing, ground will shrink, too. People buy landfill to keep up with the Joneses. In the words of Bob Fairless, of the New Orleans District engineers, "It's almost an annual spring ritual to get a load of dirt and fill in the low spots on your lawn." A child jumping up and down on such a lawn can cause the earth to move under another child, on the far side of the lawn.

Many houses are built on slabs that firmly rest on pilings. As the turf around a house gradually subsides, the slab seems to rise. Where the driveway was once flush with the floor of the carport, a bump appears. The front walk sags like a hammock. The sidewalk sags. The bump up to the carport, growing, becomes high enough to knock the front wheels out of alignment. Sakrete appears, like putty beside a windowpane, to ease the bump. The property sinks another foot. The house stays where it is, on its slab and pilings. A ramp is built to get the car into the carport. The ramp rises three feet. But the yard, before long, has subsided four. The carport becomes a porch, with hanging plants and steep wooden steps. A carport that is not firmly anchored may dangle from the side of a house like a third of a drop-leaf table. Under the house, daylight appears. You can see under the slab and out the other side. More landfill or more concrete is packed around the edges to hide the ugly scene. A gas main, broken by the settling earth, leaks below the slab. The sealed cavity fills with gas. The house blows sky high.

"The people cannot have wells, and so they take rainwater," Mark Twain observed in the eighteen-eighties. "Neither can they conveniently have cellars or graves, the town being built upon 'made' ground; so they do without both, and few of the living complain, and none of the others." The others may not complain, but they sometimes leave. New

Orleans is not a place for interment. In all its major cemeteries, the clients lie aboveground. In the intramural flash floods, coffins go out of their crypts and take off down the street.

The water in New Orleans' natural aquifer is modest in amount and even less appealing than the water in the river. The city consumes the effluent of nearly half of America, and, more immediately, of the American Ruhr. None of these matters withstanding, in 1984 New Orleans took first place in the annual Drinking Water Taste Test Challenge of the American Water Works Association.

The river goes through New Orleans like an elevated highway. Jackson Square, in the French Quarter, is on high ground with respect to the rest of New Orleans, but even from the benches of Jackson Square one looks up across the levee at the hulls of passing ships. Their keels are higher than the Astro Turf in the Superdome, and if somehow the ships could turn and move at river level into the city and into the stadium they would hover above the playing field like blimps.

In the early nineteen-eighties, the U.S. Army Corps of Engineers built a new large district headquarters in New Orleans. It is a tetragon, several stories high, with expanses of sheet glass, and it is right beside the river. Its foundation was dug in the mainline levee. That, to a fare-thee-well, is putting your money where your mouth is.

Among the five hundred miles of levee deficiencies now calling for attention along the Mississippi River, the most serious happen to be in New Orleans. Among other factors, the freeboard—the amount of levee that reaches above flood levels—has to be higher in New Orleans to combat the waves of ships. Elsewhere, the deficiencies are averaging between one and two feet with respect to the computed high-water flow line, which goes on rising as runoffs continue to speed up and waters are increasingly confined. Not only is the water higher. The levees tend to sink as well. They press down on the mucks beneath them and squirt materials out to the sides. Their crowns have to be built up. "You put five feet on and three feet sink," a Corps engineer remarked to me one day. This is especially true of the levees that frame the Atchafalaya swamp, so the Corps has given up trying to fight the subsidence there with earth movers alone, and has built concrete floodwalls along the tops of the levees, causing the largest river swamp in North America to appear to be the world's largest prison. It keeps in not only water, of course, but silt. Gradually, the swamp elevations are building up. The people of Acadiana say that the swamp would be the safest place in which to seek refuge in a major flood, because the swamp is higher than the land outside the levees.

As sediments slide down the continental slope and the river is prevented from building a proper lobe—as the delta plain subsides and is not replenished—erosion eats into the coastal marshes, and quantities of Louisiana steadily disappear. The net loss is over fifty square miles a year. In the middle of the nineteenth century, a fort was built about a thousand feet from a saltwater bay east of New Orleans. The fort is now collapsing into the bay. In a hundred years, Louisiana as a whole has decreased by a million acres. Plaquemines Parish is coming to pieces like old rotten cloth. A hundred years hence, there will in all likelihood be no Plaquemines Parish, no Terrebonne Parish. Such losses are being accelerated by access canals to the sites of oil and gas wells. After the canals are dredged, their width increases on its own, and they erode the region from the inside. A typical three-hundred-foot oil-and-gas canal will be six hundred feet wide in five years. There are in Louisiana ten thousand miles of canals. In the nineteen-fifties, after Louisiana had been made nervous by the St. Lawrence Seaway, the Corps of Engineers built the Mississippi River–Gulf Outlet, a shipping canal that saves forty miles by traversing marsh country straight from New Orleans to the Gulf. The canal is known as Mr. Go, and shipping has largely ignored it. Mr. Go, having eroded laterally for twenty-five years, is as much as three times its original width. It has devastated twenty-four thousand acres of wetlands, replacing them with open water. A mile of marsh will reduce a coastal-storm-surge wave by about one inch. Where fifty miles of marsh are gone, fifty inches of additional water will inevitably surge. The Corps has been obliged to deal with this fact by completing the ring of levees around New Orleans, thus creating New Avignon, a walled medieval city accessed by an interstate that jumps over the walls.

"The coast is sinking out of sight," Oliver Houck has said. "We've reversed Mother Nature." Hurricanes greatly advance the coastal erosion process, tearing up landscape made weak by the confinement of the river. The threat of destruction from the south is even greater than the threat from the north.

I went to see Sherwood Gagliano one day—an independent coastal geologist and regional planner who lives in Baton Rouge. "We must recognize that natural processes cannot be restored," he told me. "We can't put it back the way it was. The best we can do is try to get it back in balance, try to treat early symptoms. It's like treating cancer. You get in early, you may do something." Gagliano has urged that water be diverted to compensate for the nutrient starvation and sediment deprivation caused by the levees. In other words, open holes in the riverbank and allow water and sediment to build small deltas into disappearing parishes. "If we don't do these things, we're going to end up with a skeletal framework with levees around it—a set of peninsulas to the Gulf," he said. "We will lose virtually all of our wetlands. The cost of maintaining protected areas will be very high. There will be no buffer between them and the coast."

Professor Kazmann, of L.S.U., seemed less hopeful. He said, "Attempts to save the coast are pretty much spitting in the ocean."

The Corps is not about to give up the battle, or so much as imagine impending defeat. "Deltas wax and wane," remarks Fred Chatry, in the pilothouse of the Mississippi. "You have to be continuously adjusting the system in consonance with changes that occur." Southern Louisiana may be a house of cards, but, as General Sands suggested, virtually no one would be living in it were it not for the Corps. There is no going back, as Gagliano says—not without going away. And there will be no retreat without a struggle. The Army engineers did not pick this fight. When it started, they were still in France. The guide levees, ring levees, spillways, and floodways that dangle and swing from Old River are here because people, against odds, willed them to be here. Or, as the historian Albert Cowdrey expresses it in the introduction to "Land's End," the Corps' official narrative of its efforts in southern Louisiana, "Society required artifice to survive in a region where nature might reasonably have asked a few more eons to finish a work of creation that was incomplete."

The towboat Mississippi is more than halfway down the Atchafalaya now—beyond the leveed farmland of the upper basin and into the storied swamp. The willows on the two sides of the river, however, continue to be so dense that they block from sight what lies behind them, and all we can see is the unobstructed waterway running on and on, half a mile wide, in filtered sunlight and the shadows of clouds. A southwest breeze has put waves on the water. Broad on the starboard bow, it more than quells the humidity and the heat. Nevertheless, as one might expect, most of the people remain indoors, in the chilled atmosphere of the pilothouse, the coat-and-tie comfort of the lounge. A deck of cards appears, and a game of bouré develops, in showboat motif, among various civilian millionaires—Ed Kyle, of the Morgan City Harbor & Terminal District, dealing off the top to the Pontchartrain Levee Board, the Lafourche Basin Levee Board, the Teche-Vermilion Fresh Water District. Oliver Houck—the law professor, former general counsel of the National Wildlife Federation whose lone presence signals the continuing existence of the environmental movement—naturally stays outdoors. He has established an eyrie on an upper deck, to windward. Tall and loosely structured, Houck could be a middle-aged high jumper, still in shape to clear six feet. His face in repose is melancholy—made so, perhaps,

by the world as his mind would have it in comparison with the world as he
sees it. What he is seeing at the moment—in the center of the greatest
river swamp in North America, which he and his battalions worked fifteen years to "save"—is a walled-off monotony of sky and water.

General Sands joins him, and they talk easily and informally, as two
people will who have faced each other across great quantities of time and
paper. Sands remarks again that on inspection trips such as this one he
has become used to being "beaten on the head and shoulders" by almost
everyone he encounters, not just the odd ecologue attired in alienation.

Houck addresses himself to the head, the shoulders, and the chest,
saying that he has deep reservations about Sands' uniform: all those
brass trinkets and serried stars, the castle keeps, the stratified ribbons.
He says that Sands' habiliments constitute a form of intimidation, especially in a region of the country that has not lost its respect for the military presence. Sands' habiliments are not appropriate in a civilian
milieu. "You are Army—an untypical American entity to be performing a political role like this," Houck says to him, beating on. He tells
Sands that he reminds him of "a politician on the stump, going around
stroking his constituency." He calls him "a political water czar."

Sands implicitly reminds Houck that if it were not for the U.S.
Army Corps of Engineers there wouldn't be any stump, the constituency would be somewhere else, and Houck's neighborhood would
be nine feet under water. He says, "Under nature's scenario, think what
it would be like."

The water czar, I feel a duty to insert, is not the very model of a major
general. If he were to chew nails, he would break his teeth. I am not at-
tempting to suggest that he lacks the presence of a general, or the mien, or
the bearing. Yet he is, withal, somewhat less martial than most English
teachers. Effusive and friendly in a folk-and-country way, courteous, ac-
commodating, he is of the sort whose upward mobility would be swift in
a service industry. Make no mistake, he is a general. "Shall we just go to
the Four Seasons? A nice little place to have lunch," he said one day in
Vicksburg, and we drove to a large building in the center of town, where
his car was left directly in front of the main entrance, beside a bright-
yellow curb under various belligerent signs forbidding parking. It stayed
there for an hour while he had his crab gumbo.

We approach, on the right, a gap in the Atchafalaya's bank, where
the willows open to reveal a plexus of bayous. Houck has been complaining that the old Cajun swamp life of the Atchafalaya Basin is gone
now, and has been for many years, as a result of the volumes of water
concentrated in the floodway and of rules forbidding people to live
inside the levees. "This single piece of plumbing," he says of the

Atchafalaya, "is the last great river-overflow swamp in the world and *also* the biggest floodway in the world—all to protect Baton Rouge and New Orleans." We now come abreast of the gap on the right, and it ends the tedium of the reach upriver. It is a broad window into stands of cypress, their wide fluted bases attached to their reflections in still, dark water. "How I love them," says Houck, who is a conservationist of the sunset school, with legal skills adjunct to the force of his emotion. Pointing into the beauty of the bayous, he informs General Sands, "That's what it's all about."

The General takes in the scene without comment. In silence, we look at the water-standing trees and into narrow passages that disappear among them. They draw me into thoughts of my own. I first went in there in 1980—that is, into the Atchafalaya swamp, away from its floodway levees, and miles from the river. There were four of us, in canoes. The guide was Charles Fryling, a professor of landscape architecture at Louisiana State University, who, among the environmentalists of the eighteenth state, plays Romulus to Oliver Houck's Remus. Fryling is a tall man with a broad forehead, whose hair falls straight to his eyes without the slightest suggestion that comb or brush has ever been invited to intrude upon nature. In 1973, when he moved into his house, on the periphery of Baton Rouge, it sat on a smooth green lawn, in a neighborhood of ranch contemporaries, each on a smooth green lawn. Fryling's yard is now a rough green forest, its sweet gums, grapevines, pepper vines, rattan vines, hackberries, passionflowers, and climbing ferns a showcase of natural succession. In Fryling's words, "It beats the hell out of mowing the lawn." The trees are thirty feet high.

Fryling speaks in a slow country roll that could win him a job in movies. He would be Li'l Abner, or Candide at Fort Dix—the soldier who appears slow in basic training and dies on an intelligence mission twenty-five miles behind enemy lines. He is a graduate of the illustrious forestry school of the State University of New York (Syracuse), his advanced degree is from Harvard, and—to continue the escalation—he knows how to get from here to there in the swamp. This is a remarkable feat in seven hundred thousand acres that change so much and so often that they are largely unmappable. Fryling understands the minor bayous. Sometimes they run one way, sometimes the other. The water contains sediment or is clear. "See. The water is clearer. It's coming toward us. It's coming down from Bayou Pigeon. We'll get through."

If you ask him what something is, he knows. It's green hawthorn. It's deciduous holly. It's water privet. It's water elm. It's a water moccasin—there on the branch of that water oak. The moccasin doesn't move. A moccasin never backs off. Dragonflies land on the gunwales.

In the Atchafalaya, dragonflies are known as snake doctors. Leaving the open bayou, the canoes turn into the forest and slide among the trunks of cypress under feathery arrowhead crowns. "Young cypress need a couple of years on dry land to get started, but we send so much water through the Atchafalaya that young trees can't get going. So existing cypress are not—as trees are generally thought to be—a renewable resource. We have to protect them in order to have them."

To be in the Atchafalaya is to float among trees under silently flying blue herons, to see the pileated woodpecker, to hope to see an ivorybill, to hear the prothonotary warbler. The barred owl has a speaking voice as guttural as a dog's. It seems to be growling, "Who cooks for you? Who cooks for y'all?" The barred owl—staring from a branch straight down into the canoes—appears to be a parrot in camouflage. In the language of the Longtown Choctaw, "Hacha Falaia" meant "Long River." (The words are reversed in translation.) Since my first travels with Fryling, those rippling syllables have symbolized for me the bilateral extensions of the phrase "control of nature." Atchafalaya. The word will now come to mind more or less in echo of any struggle against natural forces—heroic or venal, rash or well advised—when human beings conscript themselves to fight against the earth, to take what is not given, to rout the destroying enemy, to surround the base of Mt. Olympus demanding and expecting the surrender of the gods. The Atchafalaya— this most apparently natural of natural worlds, this swamp of the anhinga, swamp of the nocturnal bear—lies between walls, like a zoo. It is utterly dependent on the U.S. Army Corps of Engineers, whose decisions at Old River can cut it dry or fill it with water and silt. Fryling gave me a green-and-white sticker that said "ATCHAFALAYA." I put it in a window of my car. It has been there for many years, causing drivers on the New Jersey Turnpike to veer in close and crowd my lane while staring at a word that signifies collision.

In the Atchafalaya more recently, we came upon a sport fisherman in a skiff called Mon Ark. "There's all kind of land out there now," he said. He meant not only that the wet parts were low but also that the dry parts were growing. In the Atchafalaya, the land comes and goes, but it comes more than it goes. As the overflow swamp of the only remaining distributary in the delta—the only place other than the mouth of the Mississippi where silt can go—the Atchafalaya is silting in. From a light plane at five hundred feet, this is particularly evident as the reflection of the sun races through trees and shoots forth light from the water. The reflection disappears when it crosses the accumulating land. If land accretes from the shore of a lake or bayou, the new ground belongs to the shore's owner. If it accretes as an island, it belongs to the state—a situation of which Gilbert would be sure to inform Sullivan. Some fifty thousand acres are caught in this tug-of-war. Wet and dry, three-quarters of the Atchafalaya swampland is privately owned. Nearly all the owners are interested less in the swamp than in what may lie beneath it. The conservationists, the Corps, landowners, and recreational interests have worked out a compromise by which all parties putatively get what they want: floodway, fishway, oil field, Eden. From five hundred feet up, the world below is green swamp everywhere, far as the eye can see. The fact is, though, that the eye can't see very far. The biggest river swamp in North America, between its demarcating levees, is seventeen miles wide and sixty miles long. It is about half of what it was when it began at the Mississippi River and went all the way to Bayou Teche.

The old life of the basin is not entirely gone. It is true that people don't collect moss anymore to use in stuffing furniture, true that the great virgin cypresses are away. Their flared stumps remain, like cabins standing in the water. From the beginning of the nineteenth century, Cajuns made their lives and livings in the swamp. Their grocery stores were afloat, and moved among them, camp to camp. It is true all that has vanished, and the Cajuns live outside the levees, but they and others—operating for the most part alone or in pairs—go into the swamp and take twenty-five million dollars' worth of protein out of the water in any given year. The fish alone can average a thousand pounds an acre, and that, according to Fryling, is "more fish than in any other natural water system in the United States"—two and a half times as productive as the Everglades. The fish are not in the conversation, however, when compared with the crawfish.

I know a crawfisherman named Mike Bourque, who lives in Catahoula. I remember as if it were today running his lines with him. "Watch your hands. Don't put 'em on the side of the boat. 'Cause smash 'em," he said as we went out of Bayou Gravenburg and headed into the trees. His boat was not a canoe, and the object on the stern was no paddle. It was a fifty-horse Mariner, enough for lift-off if the boat had wings. Bourque's brother-in-law was with us. In French, Bourque told him that he was affecting the balance and to shift his position in the boat. Then, addressing me in English, he said, "Watch yourself, I got to jump that log." Ahead of us, half hidden in water hyacinths, was an impressive floating log, with a solid diameter of about two feet. The boat smashed against it, thrust up and over it, with a piercing aluminum screech. The boat was about seventeen feet long. The brother-in-law, Dave Soileau, called it a bateau. Bourque called it a skiff. "French and English—we mix it up," he said. Ordinarily, he works alone, and talks a good deal to himself. "When I talk to myself, I talk in French. When I meet other fishermen, ninety per cent of the time we speak French." If he doesn't know them, he knows where they live, because each town has its accent.

Like everyone else, he calls the hyacinths lilies—water lilies. This densely growing plant—a waterborne kudzu, an exotic from the Orient—has come to plague Southern waterways and spread over marshes like nuclear winter closing many forms of life. That is not the case, however, in the Atchafalaya, where the lilies are good for the crawfish. The young feed on stuff that clings to the roots. On heavy stems, the water hyacinths grow three to four feet high, so a lot of power is needed to get through them. "You'll never see a fisherman with less than a fifty-horse motor."

Bourque moved the skiff from tree to tree as if he were on snowshoes in a sugarbush emptying buckets of sap. The crawfish cages were chicken-wire pillows with openings at one end. Bourque pulled them out of the water on cords that were tied to the trees, and poured the crawfish into a device that looked something like a roasting pan and was hinged to the side of the boat. He calls it the trough. Open at the inner end, it forms a kind of ramp down which the crawfish crawl until they drop into a bucket. Dead bait fish, dead crawfish, and other detritus remain in the trough, and thus the living creatures winnow themselves from what is thrown away. Snakes are thrown away. Some of the used bait fish have less remaining flesh than skeletons lifted by waiters who work in white gloves. The larger crawfish weigh a quarter of a pound and are nine inches long, with claw spans greater than that. When the bucket is full, the crawfish in their motions seem to simmer at the top. *"C'est bon. C'est bon. Où est le sac?"* said Bourque, and Soileau handed him a plastic-burlap sack. Containing forty pounds each, the sacks began to pile up. The crawfish lay quiet. When a sack was moved, or even touched, though, the commotion inside sounded like heavy rain.

The boat climbed another log. The engine cavitated. We broke through brush like an elephant. Bourque had been following what he called the driftwood line, where a small change in depth had caused driftwood to linger. To him the swamp topography was as distinctive and varied as the neighborhoods of a city would be to someone else—these subworlds of the Atchafalaya, out past Bayou Gravenburg, on toward the Red Eye Swamp. "This line used to go in back there, but I moved them out in front," he said in a place that seemed much too redundant to have a back or a front. Colored ribbons, which he called flags, helped to distinguish the fishermen's trees, but he could run his lines without them, covering his four hundred cages. He did about sixty an hour. Soileau, using a grain scoop, shovelled dead alewives and compressed pellets of Acadiana

Choice Crawfish Bait into each emptied cage, and Bourque returned it to the water. Bourque told Soileau, who is a biologist with the United States Fish and Wildlife Service, to quit the government and come work for him. Soileau said, "For ten dollars a day?"

Bourque said, "Good future. No benefits."

We were in a coulee, which is like a slough but deeper and with slushier muds at the bottom. A cage came up with seventy crawfish, all dead. The cage had been too low in the muck, where the creatures died in an anoxic slurry. They stirred it up themselves. The cage should just lightly touch the bottom, with the closed end slightly raised.

Bourque next pulled up an empty cage. "Somebody helped me out," he remarked, and added that he had occasionally met a thief in the act of raiding one of his cages.

Soileau said, "There's only one thing to do. Go straight to him, board his vessel, and start slugging. There have been no deaths."

Theft was rising in direct proportion to unemployment. Oil companies owned that part of the swamp. Fishermen have, in fact, been arrested for trespass. Fryling's wife, Doris Falkenheiner, defends them in court. Meanwhile, so many fishermen work the watery forest that there is a plastic ribbon on almost every tree. The fishermen say they have to bring their own trees.

We hit another log. We ran between a cypress and its knees. "We're getting up on the ridge," Bourque said, referring to a subtle, invisible feature of the bottom of the swamp. Out of a cage came a white crawfish, a male. (The male has longer arms.) Crawfish are red, white, or blue. The white ones like the sand of the ridge. Blue ones are rare. Bourque sees fewer than twenty a year. Now he was reaching down into the water for a cage that had been separated from its string by another fisherman's motor.

"*Touchez la?*" asked Soileau.

Bourque answered, "Yes." Then he said, "*Ah, bon,*" as he retrieved the cage.

"Are y'all hungry?" Bourque asked.

"I live hungry," said Soileau.

Bourque turned off the motor and we stopped for lunch: ham sandwiches, Royal Crown, Mr. Porker fried cured pork skins. It was seven-thirty in the morning.

We got up around three-thirty and were driving down the levee by four o'clock—in Bourque's pickup, with the skiff behind. Soileau made the comment that the levees were like cancer, because they had to keep growing while they sank into the swamp. After twenty-five miles, we went down a ramp to a boat landing, where forty-one pickups had arrived before us. Roughly five thousand people take crawfish from the swamp, annually trapping twenty-three million pounds.

Now, at lunchtime, as the early-morning sun began to penetrate the trees, we were looking out on one lovely scene, with tupelo and cypress rising from the water, and pollen on the water like pale-green silk. "The best months are Epp Rill and May," Bourque said. "The water might rise in October sometimes. I'll come and try." He was wearing mirrored sunglasses, a soft cap with a buttoned visor, white rubber boots, and yellow rubber overalls slashed at the crotch. Of middle height, blond and fine-featured, he had sandy hair around his ears and a large curl in back, like a breaking wave. His lowsill mustache looked French. He went to St. Martinville High School, as did Soileau, who married the youngest of Bourque's six sisters. In large script below the windows of a drugstore in St. Martinville, a sign says, *Sidney Dupois Pharmacien— Au Service de la Santé de Votre Famille.* The Teche *News*, published down the street, has a regular column headlined "PENSE DONC!!" and contains marriage and death notices about people with names like Boudreau, Tesreau, Landreaux, Passeau, Bordagaray, Lajoie, Fournier, Angelle, and Guidry. Bourque was the youngest in his family and the only sibling male. He explains that Cajuns keep going until they get a male, and this was where the Bourques stopped.

Soileau passed the pork skins. Bourque chewed them crunchily. "Crawfish are *écrevisses* in French," he said. "We call them crawfish."

I mentioned that *écrevisses* are cherished by chefs in France.

Soileau said, "I hear you get only three or four."

Bourque had a recipe of which the nouveaux cuisiniers may not have heard. "Sauté onions in butter, then put in fat out of the head for ten or fifteen minutes, then put meat in for a few minutes more," he said. "Salt. Cayenne pepper. Onion tops. What makes the étouffée is the fat. Some people put a little roux in there. You can stretch it like that." Crawfish étouffée: the Cajun quenelle de brochet. The meat is ground, but not to the end of texture. On Easter Sunday morning in Catahoula, the Bourques have a crawfish ball. At least, I thought that's what they were saying until I saw what they did. They boiled a hundred pounds of crawfish. They ate a crimson mountain of condensed lobsters.

Now we were running in Bayou Eugene, which Soileau and Bourque lyrically pronounced in three syllables—"by yooz yen." We came upon a beaver on a floating log. This was not the animal that founded a nation, the alert and agile slapper of the boreal lakes. This was a Louisiana beaver—huge, half asleep, prone like a walrus, a mound of cinnamon fur with nothing much to do but eat. There was no need to dam a thing here. The Corps of Engineers would see to that.

The beaver topples trees just to eat the bark. There is no mandate to practice conservation when you are what is being conserved. "A willow branch eaten by a beaver is just as smooth as if it had been sanded," Soileau remarked. "There's nothing prettier than a willow branch eaten by a beaver." Nutria live in the swamp as well. Bourque said that he sees only four or five alligators a year. A friend of his lost a finger to a cottonmouth. "He was walking through thick lilies, very high lilies, to make a road for his pirogue. The snake bit his finger through a glove." Among the crowns of the cypress, a heron flapped by. Bourque called it a *gros bec*. Soileau called it a yellow-crowned night heron. Bourque said, "The *gros bec* is here for the same purpose we are: to get crawfish." A mulberry-blue crawfish came into the boat from a cage that was deep in the Red Eye Swamp.

Farther down the trap line, Bourque said, "Crawfish is something hard to understand. When it's muddier, they're hungrier. The water's not muddy enough out here." There was a time when that sort of thing was a fact of nature. Now, of course, he blamed the Corps. "I'd like more water," he continued. "A lot of times, they've got much more in the Mississippi than they can use. They say they give us thirty per cent. We don't know if that's true."

I told him I had seen a tally sheet at Old River Control, and it said that 31.1 per cent had gone down the Atchafalaya the day before.

"I'd like to see that paper when the river starts dropping," Bourque responded. "I don't see that we get thirty per cent except when there is plenty of water. If they close the locks, it start dropping fast."

I mentioned the towboat Mississippi and its low-water Atchafalaya inspection trip, and asked if he had ever gone aboard to complain.

"I never heard of that until you mentioned it right now," he said. "They know we want more water. They don't have to ask."

I remembered Rabalais saying, "After they built the structure and started stabilizing this water and so on, the main complaint was the people from the Atchafalaya Basin—all your crawfish fishermen, and so on. They claimed they wasn't getting enough water, but over the years they've learned to live with it, and they catch as many crawfish, I would say, now as they did then."

And Peck Oubre, the lock mechanic, asking Rabalais, "Before they put in Old River Lock and the control structure, what was the people talking about when the water used to rise and come through here? Were they complaining about it?"

"No," said Rabalais. "They wouldn't complain, because there wasn't nothing you could do."

Bourque said that farmers who raise crawfish in artificial ponds—a

fairly new and rapidly expanding industry—were influencing the
Corps to keep the water low in the Atchafalaya in order to squeeze out
swamp fishermen like him, whose forebears were swamp fishermen. It
is possible that the charge he was making was based on pure suspicion,
but now that the structures were emplaced at Old River—and the
Corps had assumed charge of the latitude flow—suspicion was one
more force they had to try to control.

As we were heading back toward the landing, Bourque remarked,
surprisingly, "It's good we have the levees. Before the levees, the crawfish, they was spread all over."

For bait, for gasoline, and so forth, the cost of the day's run was
seventy-five dollars. At the boat landing, Bourque sold the crawfish for
three hundred and sixty. The buyer was Michael Williams, a youth
from New Iberia with a mane of Etruscan hair. He identified himself as
a poet, and said, "For poems there's not a market anymore. The days of
the Romantic poets is gone. That's like in the past." So he also writes
country-and-western lyrics. He recited one that began, "Oh, it's hard to
write a love song/If you've never been in love." He had a pit bull named
Demon with him. Demon went into the water and snapped at waves.
He tried to bite motorboat waves.

I emerge from my remembrances standing at the rail, bewitched by the
impenetrable vegetation. No part of those scenes that lie behind it can be
felt or sensed from the decks of the Mississippi as the towboat moves on
between the curtains of willow and straight down the middle of the bifur-
cated swamp. The others continue to talk, argue. The point is made that
if the Mississippi River were to shift into the Atchafalaya the entire basin
would fill with sediment and become a bottomland hardwood forest.
"When nature shifts, man shifts," Oliver Houck says. The petrochemical
industries would move to the basin, too, rebuilding themselves on Bayou
Eugene, extruding plastics in the Red Eye Swamp. There are people
in Morgan City who envision another Ruhr Valley up the Atchafalaya.
Morgan City would be the new New Orleans.

The new New Orleans—seventeen miles from the Gulf—is not far
ahead of us now. The landscape is changing to coastal marsh. Going below, I make a circumspect visit to the card game in the lounge. The
Pontchartrain Levee Board draws three, Teche-Vermilion needs two.
Ed Kyle, of Morgan City, whose pockets are familiar with United States
currency bearing portraits that most people in their lifetimes never see
and do not even know exist, throws one dollar into the pot. In the center
of the table, the greenbacks reach flood stage.

Now, through the picture windows at the front of the lounge, our destination is in view: Morgan City, the Cajun Carcassonne—a very small town behind a very high wall. A railroad bridge and two highway bridges leap the Atchafalaya and seem to touch gingerly on the two sides, as if they were landing on lily pads. Flood stage in Morgan City is four feet above sea level. A dirt levee protected the town until 1937. It was succeeded by concrete walls six and then eight feet high. As floods grew—and the Atchafalaya became the only distributary of the Mississippi—sandbags and wooden baffles were piled up in haste on top of the eight-foot walls. Since it is the Corps' intention that fifty per cent of a Design Flood go down the Atchafalaya, and since Morgan City is on a small island of no relief situated directly in the path of the planned deluge, the Corps has built the present wall twenty-two feet high. It is of such regal and formidable demeanor that it attracts tourists. It is a wall that imagines water—a sheet of water at least twenty feet thick between Morgan City and the horizon. The seawall, as it is known, rises to the skirts of palms that stand in rows behind it. From the approaching towboat we can see a steeple, a flagpole, a water tower, but not the town's low avenues or deeply shaded streets. Damocles would not have been so lonely had he lived in Morgan City. In a proportion inverse to the seawall's great size, the seawall betokens a vulnerability the like of which is hard to find so far from a volcano.

Water approaches Morgan City from every side. The Atchafalaya River and its surrounding floodway come down from the north and pass the western edge of town. The seawall is a part of the floodway's eastern guide levee. When there are heavy local rains, as there were at the time of the great flood of 1973, water that is kept out of the floodway by the seventy-five miles of the eastern guide levee—water that used to go into the swamp and the river when the basin was under the control of nature—pools against the levee, caroms in the direction of the Gulf, and assaults Morgan City from the back side. The levee ends on Avoca Island, five or six miles south. The Atchafalaya floodwaters are sometimes so high that they go around the end of the levee and come back against Morgan City. Hurricanes also bring floods from that direction, surging from the Gulf like tidal waves.

Professor Kazmann, of L.S.U., said, "You can't sell Morgan City short, or I would." To end its days, Morgan City does not require a Design Flood. The Design Flood, at Morgan City, is a million and a half cubic feet per second. LeRoy Dugas, of Old River, once explained to me, "The Old River Control Structures can pass seven hundred and fifty thousand cubic feet per second and the Morganza Spillway six hundred. In that situation, if both of them are wide open, we've got Morgan City gasping for air." The people of Morgan City are not easily frightened.

They would tell Professor Kazmann to get back into his college and Dugie to shut a few gates. Mayor Cedric LaFleur says, "I feel safe. I feel secure. We're not going to wash away." If there is a slightly hollow sound as he speaks, it is because Morgan City is sort of like a large tumbler glued to the bottom of an aquarium. The Corps, of course, built Morgan City's great rampart, and graced it with bas-reliefs of shrimp boats and oil rigs—consecutive emblems of Morgan City booms. Everyone is grateful for the wall. Morgan City—in its unusual setting—is dependent on the Corps of Engineers in the way that a space platform would depend on Mission Control. The fate of Morgan City is written at Old River. Anything that happens there is relevant to the town.

As the towboat passes under the second bridge and turns toward a berth below the seawall, I ask General Sands what sort of complaint he most frequently receives when he comes here. He says, "The Corps of Engineers isn't doing enough to protect Morgan City from disaster."

The hearing is at nine the next morning, aboard the Mississippi in the thoroughly transformed lounge. Where Teche-Vermilion was taking pots, the scene is now set for the court-martial of Billy Mitchell. In front of various standing flags, the three generals and two civilian members of the Mississippi River Commission sit at a large formal table, with General Sands in the central position. A colonel is master of ceremonies, and three other colonels are in the front row. This seems an unlikely place for Clifton Aucoin to present his petitions, but now he stands before them—a man in bluejeans and an open shirt, whose remarks suggest that he has spent a good many days of his life up to his hips in water. "My name is Clifton Aucoin," he testifies. "Very few people pronounce it right, so don't feel bad about it." He tells the commission that he once kept a boat tied to the knob of his front door. "As far as us people in the back floodwater area, we feel neglected," he continues. "As far as we can tell, nothing has been fixed. Atchafalaya water just comes around Bayou Chene, it comes right on us backwater people. . . . We feel that it's just another major flood that's waiting to hit us if nothing is done about it." As a hunter, he further complains of dying trees, of disappearing browse and cover—changes no longer ascribable to nature but now quite obviously conceded to be under the control of the Corps.

The commissioners hear Cedric LaFleur, a trimly built man with curly hair and dark, quick eyes. LaFleur says it is "a dire relief" to have the seawall completed, and suggests that the Corps stop studying the Avoca Island levee and extend it several miles south—to prevent the floods of the Atchafalaya from going around the levee's tip and coming back upon the town. Terrebonne Parish, east of the proposed extension,

has complained to the Corps that an extended levee would deprive Terrebonne marshes of sediment, thereby destroying the marshes. The survival of one parish is in conflict with the survival of another, and each is
appealing to the Corps.

They hear Mark Denham, of St. Mary Parish: "We appreciate y'all
coming down. We really consider having the Corps as a presence in our
area a tremendous asset to our area as far as protection of floodwaters
and as far as economic development also."

They hear Jesse Fontenot, Curtis Patterson, Gerald Dyson—
chambers of commerce, levee boards, the government of the state. And,
as they inevitably do in Morgan City, they hear Doc Brownell. He
comes forward slowly, slightly stoop-shouldered, septuagenarian. This
man once entered prize-fights. There is a trace of smile on his face. He,
too, thanks the commission. "It's always a pleasure to see you people
come down here. It gives us a little encouragement." And then, in effect, he tells the Corps to get its act mobilized and extend the levee. For
thirty-two and a half years, Doc Brownell was the mayor of Morgan
City. LaFleur has been described as his clone. In 1973, when the water
went around the end of the levee and came back up Bayou Chene,
Brownell, without authority, sank a fifteen-hundred-ton barge in the
bayou. The barge acted as a dam and held off the water long enough for
the people to build up their defenses and save the city. "The nightmare
of '73 is still with us," Brownell reminds the commission. "We live in a
state of apprehension; we live on the whims of the weather of over
forty-two per cent of the United States. . . . We live with it twenty-four
hours a day." He praises the beauty of the new seawall but points out
that to the people of Morgan City its extraordinary height is an unambiguous message from the Corps. "We can expect that much more water.
It makes us very apprehensive. We have got to extend our defenses."

Brownell, who went into medicine because the lumber business was
dying, became a sort of bayou Schweitzer, delivering babies far out in
the swamps, doing surgery in an un-air-conditioned operating room for
twelve and fourteen hours a day. Among his closest companions was an
alligator called Old Bull, who lived with the Brownell family for thirty-
five years. Old Bull died in 1982 and is now in a glass-sided mahogany-
framed case—in effect, a see-in coffin—looking almost alive among
simulated hyacinths, iris, and moss in Brownell's parlor. Tip to tip, Old
Bull is ten and a half feet long. There is a brass footrail next to Old Bull
and a padded bar above him, with beer tap, soda siphon, and a generous
stock of bottles. Brownell took Charlie Fryling and me there one spring
day to admire Old Bull and to show us, with the help of pictures, the
predicament of Morgan City. What struck me most of all as he talked

was his evident and inherent conviction that a community can have a right to exist—to rise, expand, and prosper—in the middle of one of the most theatrically inundated floodplains in the world. To be sure, the natural floodplain is also an artificial floodway—concentrated and shaped—and, accordingly, its high waters are all the more severe. In Morgan City, it has become impossible to separate the works of people from the periodic acts of God. "We have a lot of restaurants now and various types of establishments in places vulnerable to the water," Brownell said. "We got to develop on the floodplain. It's the only place we got to develop. We still have got to look for places for people to live. Now, you can see from this map that we're right in the middle of this floodway. It's like a funnel with a spout, and we're at the end of that spout. We're in the concentration part of it. We have our homes, our families, our whole future in the floodway. We've got to live with these problems—and to me it ought to be some type of priority for the people who live under these conditions twelve months out of the year should be given some type of preference as to what our future is. It's the nation's problem, and we are only the victims here of a lot of things that does happen here that are imposed upon us. We lost the big live oaks in the park because of the long-standing floodwater. A flood doesn't last for weeks here, as it does in some of those northern places. Our floods last for months. The more ring levees are built to the north, the more water Morgan City gets. In whatever way the people upriver protect themselves, they send more water to Morgan City. If people dig canals to get water off their land, it goes to Morgan City. When you're drowning, you don't need more water."

Tarzan of the Apes once leaped about among the live oaks in the park. The first Tarzan movie was filmed in Morgan City. The Atchafalaya swamp was Tarzan's jungle. Black extras in costumes pretended they were Africans.

Not far from Old Bull, the head of another alligator was in use as a lamp—its mouth open, a light bulb in the back of its throat. Stuffed owls and hawks were hanging on the walls, and Canada geese were flying through the air. There were the heads of deer, of black bears from the Atchafalaya swamp. Brownell said his father had killed six bears shortly before he died. There was a stuffed tarpon head as large as the head of a horse. The tarpon was caught in the Atchafalaya River near Morgan City before the river, increasing in volume and power, pushed back the salt water. Islands now stand where the river was a hundred feet deep. As the Atchafalaya has grown, more and more sediments have, of course, come with it, stopping where they reach still water. This is the one place in Louisiana, other than the mouth of the Mississippi, where new coastal land is forming. Large areas of what was once Atchafalaya Bay have become dry flats. The soil broke the surface as the flood receded in 1973. Whole islands appeared at once. The bay was choked. Brownell says the river built a dam there. A geologist would call it a delta.

Charles Morgan, a shipper in New Orleans in the eighteen-fifties and sixties, was so irritated by New Orleans' taxes, New Orleans' dockage fees, and New Orleans' waterfront clutter that he moved his operation to the Atchafalaya and developed a competing city. It seems unlikely that he was aware that the Mississippi River meant to follow him. Morgan City thrived on shipping, on oysters. When the big cypresses were felled in the Atchafalaya swamp, Morgan City became the center of the cypress industry in the United States: numerous sawmills, hundreds of schooners in the port. Brownell's great-grandfather owned a sawmill. In the nineteen-thirties, Captain Ted Anderson, a Florida-based fisherman, was blown off course by a storm, and put in at Morgan City. In the hold of his boat were shrimp of a size unfamiliar in Morgan City—big ones, like croissants, from far offshore. They were considered repulsive, and at first no one wanted them, but these jumbos of the deep Gulf soon gave Morgan City the foremost shrimp fleet in the world. As the Atchafalaya River pushed back the salt water, it pushed out of the marshes the nurseries of shrimp. Caught in the westbound littoral drift, the shrimp went to Texas, where much of the business is now. The growth of cypresses was too slow to keep up with the lumber industry, so the lumber industry collapsed. The next boom was in oil. The big offshore towers come out of the marshlands surrounding Morgan City. They are built on their sides and dominate the horizon like skeletons of trapezoidal blimps. Of the twelve hundred and sixty-three permanent platforms now standing in the Gulf on the continental shelf, eighty-eight per cent are off Louisiana.

In other words, the people of Morgan City are accustomed to taking nature as it comes. Cindy Thibodaux, the town archivist—a robust young poet with cerulean eyes and a fervent manner of speaking—said to me one day, "When you're fishing in the bayou, you're out in nature with the oil industry all around you." She has written a poem about the oil industry and nature from an alligator's perspective.

In the presence of the tribunes on the towboat, as the Pontchartrain Levee District recites its needs and the State of Louisiana its concerns— as the discussion touches upon the varied supplications of the whole deltaic plain, and on the growth of the extremities of the great levee system not only below Morgan City but down the Mississippi from Bohemia to Baptiste Collette—my mind cannot help drifting back to Old River, where every part of this story in a sense had its beginnings and could also have its end. Near the mouths of the intake channels of Old River Control, the Corps maintains another towboat, smaller than the Mississippi but no less powerful—a vessel on duty twenty-four hours a day and not equipped with white couches, wall-to-wall windows, or venetian blinds—the name of which is Kent.

Kent is a picket boat. It defends Old River Control. With its squared bow and severed aspect, it appears to be a piece of wharf that loosened like a tooth and came out on the river. Kent's job is to catch, hold, and assist any vessel in trouble. If barges break loose upstream and there is insufficient time to tie them up, Kent is supposed to divert them. Technically, it is a twin-screw steel motor tug, eighty-five feet long, with two nine-hundred-horse diesels that can start at the touch of buttons. (Compressed air makes that possible.) It cost two million dollars and differs from most river towboats only in its uncommon electronics—the state and variety of its radar, the applications of its multiple computers. In addition to the onboard radar, two radar beams sweep the river from the bank at stations four miles apart, and anything that reflects from these beams appears on a screen in Kent. If a tow rig is moving at the speed of the current, an alarm goes off, for the coincidental speed suggests that the rig is without power. Kent can tell this eight miles away.

Fifteen miles up the river, in April of 1964, twenty barges full of ore were tied to the bank and left there unattended. Eight of them broke free. There was no picket boat then. As a functioning valve, the control structure at Old River was nine months old. As the ore-laden barges drifted near, they were drawn away from the Mississippi, sucked into the structure by the power of the Atchafalaya. One of them plunged through the gates and sank on the lower side. Three sank in front of the gates and effectively closed the structure. A standard barge is a hundred and ninety-five feet long. Water piled up. Weeks went by. Much of the time, the difference in water level between the Mississippi and Atchafalaya sides was thirty-five feet, a critical number that resulted in damage and "threatened the integrity of the structure"—the Corps' way of saying that it might have been wiped out.

Today, it is illegal to tie anything to either bank of the Mississippi within twenty upstream miles of the structures at Old River. Every approaching vessel has to radio Kent and, as Dugas puts it, "say what he is, who he is, and if he has a red-flag product." And for ignorant river pilots and all uninitiated craft there's a very large sign high up the bank of the river—its first three words in red:

WARNING
DANGEROUS DRAW
1 MILE—WEST BANK
OLD RIVER CONTROL STRUCTURE
U.S. ARMY
CORPS OF ENGINEERS
NEW ORLEANS DISTRICT

Spring high water often knocks the sign away.

It would be difficult to overestimate the power of the draw, deriving, as it does, from the Atchafalaya, by now, in point of discharge, one of the twenty to thirty strongest rivers in the world. The Coast Guard once tried to set five warning buoys in the west side of the Mississippi, but could not keep them in place, because the suction was so fierce. This threat to navigation could be called an American Maelstrom—a modern Charybdis, a Corryvreckan—were it not so very much greater in destructive force. In Dugie's words, "Any rig on the right side of the river is in trouble."

An empty barge and three barges loaded with quarry stones were sucked into the low sill in 1965. Two loaded barges went through the structure and sank on the Atchafalaya side. The other sank against the gates without causing apparent damage, but it must have contributed to the turbulences that even then were undermining the structure. After the great flood of 1973 and the considerable debilitation it disclosed, there was the constant danger that if several loose barges were to block the flow and the difference in water levels were to build to catastrophic proportions nothing could be done about it. One barge spent a flood against the gates in 1974, but the structure survived.

People in Simmesport often refer to Old River Control as "the second locks." John Hughes, the supervisor of Kent and one of its operators, does his best to correct them. "That's not a lock, that's a control structure," he says. And a Simmesport person says, "Well, we was born and raised here, and we call it the second locks." To judge by the amount of traffic erroneously attracted to the control structure, they have a point. A boat comes down the river, takes a right, and heads for Old River Control, thinking that it is Old River Navigation Lock. Usually, the boat is small—a cabin cruiser, or something of the sort—but the mistake has been made by a fifteen-barge tow. Its skipper called in on the radio to the navigation lock, announcing his arrival. The people at the lock replied that they didn't see him. He said, "I'm right here looking at you, I'm coming in." The mistake was corrected just in time.

In 1982, thirty-nine barges broke loose thirteen miles upstream at four in the morning. The whole rig just came apart. Dugie recalls, "He was in a bend of the river. He couldn't maneuver the river. He hit the bank." The picket boat went after the barges. Five other skippers, joining their units together, detached four towboats that came to help. "They could see the picket boat had a lot of problems, trying to catch thirty-nine barges by hisself," Dugie says. At 6 A.M., right at the entrance to the intake channel of Old River Control, the last barge was caught. Not even one hit the gates. Two of the thirty-nine were red-flag barges, loaded with petroleum. Later that year, a fifteen-barge rig heading north in the dark swung too close to Old River Control, was drawn off course, and—its engines overmatched by the force of the water—crashed in the sand on the north side of the intake-channel mouth. In 1983, at midnight, a towboat with three jumbo barges lost power at Black Hawk Point, two miles above the structure. The picket boat caught it before it reached the channel.

The operator on that occasion was Gerald Gillis, whose broad full face and long jet-black hair lend him the look of an Elizabethan page after twenty-five years in Morgan City. He is one of eight men who work Kent—two on a shift. One day, he took me out on the beat with him, running up the river. He said the speed of the Mississippi current ranges from about three knots in low water to six in spring and eight in flood. A rig coming downstream on this September day would be averaging about eight knots. To conserve fuel, the big thirty-five-barge tows like to crawl along just barely ahead of the speed of the river, and that confuses Kent, because the tows could be dead in the water. An example was descending toward us now, called Gale C, shoving thirty-five barges of grain and coal, and much alive in the river, as Gillis learned from his transceiver. While the huge rig was passing by us—really an itinerant island, eight thousand horsepower and a quarter of a mile long, with its barges in seven ranks of five—he said the rough rule of thumb for fuelling such an enterprise on journeys upstream is one gallon per horsepower per day.

Gillis turned on the depth finder. We had come up the Mississippi's east side, and now he swung crosscurrent, heading for the cutbank of the west-convexing bend just above the structures of Old River. As we traversed the Mississippi, the depth, which was being sketched by a stylus on graph paper, dropped steadily and kept on dropping the closer we came to the bank. We were only a few swimming strokes from shore when the depth reached a hundred feet. It was notable that the riverbed was fifty feet below sea level more than three hundred miles from the mouth of the river, but what particularly astounded me was the very great depth so close to the west bank. It showed the excavating force of a tremendous river. The foundations of skyscrapers are rarely that deep. And this was the bend where the water swung off and into Old River Control—a bend armored with concrete where the Mississippi might break free and go to the Atchafalaya. Kent was so close to the bank that it had no room to turn. Gillis backed away.

Twenty years before, a barge that broke loose and was crumpled after sinking at the structure was hauled up the intake channel and left by the edge of the river. The barge had not moved since then, but the Mississippi's bank—consumed by the scouring currents—had eroded to the west. The barge now lay five hundred feet out in the Mississippi.

General Sands, reflecting on these matters, once said, "The Old River Control Structure was put in the wrong place. It was designed to a dollar figure."

And Fred Bayley, his chief engineer, added, "That is correct. It was done during the Eisenhower Administration."

The Corps once attempted to barricade the intake channel with a string of barges anchored in the river. Drift—as the big logs are called that unremittingly come down the river—amassed against the anchoring cables until enough had gathered to heave high and start breaking the cables. As if drift were not enough of a problem, ice has been known to appear as well. It may come only once in twenty years, but ice it is, in Louisiana.

The water attacking Old River Control is of course continuous, working, in different ways, from both sides. In 1986, one of the low-sill structure's eleven gates was seriously damaged by the ever-pounding river. Another gate lost its guiding rail. When I asked Fred Smith, the district geologist, if he thought it inevitable that the Mississippi would succeed in swinging its channel west, he said, "Personally, I think it might. Yes. That's not the Corps' position, though. We'll try to keep it where it is, for economic reasons. If the right circumstances are all put together (huge rainfall, a large snowmelt), there's a very definite possibility that the river would divert—go down through the Atchafalaya Basin. So far, we have been able to alleviate those problems."

Significant thanks to Kent.

A skiff rides on Kent's stern. A part of the skiff's permanent equipment is a fifteen-foot bamboo pole. Kent is alert to everything that moves in the river, including catfish.

About the Editors

NORMAN SIMS is a professor of journalism at the University of Massachusetts in Amherst. He teaches classes in newswriting, the history of journalism, freedom of the press, and literary journalism. He was the editor of an earlier anthology, *The Literary Journalists* (1984), and of a collection of scholarly articles, *Literary Journalism in the Twentieth Century* (1990).

MARK KRAMER teaches graduate seminars in literary journalism at Boston University, where he is writer-in-residence, professor of journalism, and adjunct professor of American studies. He was writer-in-residence at Smith College from 1980 to 1990. His books include *Mother Walter & The Pig Tragedy* (1972); *Three Farms: Making Milk, Meat, and Money from the American Soil* (1980); and *Invasive Procedures: A Year in the World of Two Surgeons* (1983). His book about Russian farmers and bureaucrats during and since *perestroika* is *Travels with a Hungry Bear*.

Comments on this anthology may be e-mailed to Norman Sims at sims@journ.umass.edu or to Mark Kramer at litj@bu.edu.